THE COMPLETE GOODIES

Robert Ross

B.T.Batsford • London

Acknowledgements

First and foremost to the Goodies themselves. The peerless Tim Brooke-Taylor who has supported this pet project of mine for several years and was always more than happy to chat about life, *The Goodies* and everything, sincere thanks. The equally peerless Graeme Garden for info-packed emails, delicious bemusement and total support. The equally, equally, peerless Bill Oddie who filled my childhood with nutty songs, wacky visuals and a bit of cool ranting. His reflective and frank memories have proved invaluable. Thanks also to Tim, Graeme and Bill for exclusive use of their photograph archives. To my commissioning editor Jeremy Theobald for proving, once and for all, that less is more. My great Uni pal, Graham Hill, aka Old Gray Bags, who, despite having to suffer the torture of editing *The Goodies* (I'm telling Tim, Graeme and Bill!) for UK Arena still remains one of the best of the bunch – oh, and thanks for the copy of you know what! Cheers pal. My dad, Peter Ross, who has proved his usual totally invaluable self in research, correction and encouragement. Alan Coles, who seems determined to get a name check in every book I write: thanks for the *Radio Times* gift matey. Peter Tatchell and Matthew K Sharp for compiling the hugely informative *Goodies' Fact File* for *Laugh* magazine and an extra special big thanks to Peter for videos, information and unflagging encouragement. Andrew Pixley for exhaustive Goodies research and kind words. Brett Allender for his pioneering paper *The Goodies Episode Summaries* and, almost last but by no means least, Alison Bean of The Goodies Rule OK internet site, for all her help, support and devotion to the cause. She's one in a million. Finally, to my darling Cheryl… for not really remembering but laughing anyway.

Text © Robert Ross 2000

A catalogue record for this book is available from the British Library.

ISBN 0 7134 8575 2

Printed in Spain

Volume © B T Batsford 2000

First published in 2000 by
B T Batsford
9 Blenheim Court
Brewery Road
London N7 9NT

A member of the Chrysalis Group plc

Contents

Foreword
by The Goodies

Tim Brooke-Taylor, Graeme Garden and Bill Oddie

Robert Ross first swum into my ken when he asked me to be patron of a comedy magazine I had admired – *Cor!* It wasn't the most beautifully produced magazine but it was obviously put together by someone who cared about comedy, all types of comedy. And what was so great was that he didn't come with all sorts of preconceptions. If it made him laugh that was all that mattered. He liked new stand-ups, Carry Ons, Monty Python and above all *The Goodies*. Excellent chap.

There was one slight worry. He knew too much. Was he following us? Were we bugged? Or even worse, was he a comedy anorak who just amassed facts for the sake of it, but had no actual sense of humour? It was therefore with some trepidation that I agreed to be interviewed by him at the Theatre Royal, Windsor where I was doing pantomime. And what a shock. No anorak by any means. Instead a good-looking, sparky, young fellah who quite clearly loved comedy. It is true that the interview didn't appear in print for a year, but no one's perfect!

The Goodies hasn't really been shown in the UK properly since the early Eighties (although there have been recent noises from the BBC which might put this right), so when he contacted me to say he was doing a Goodies book I metaphorically patted him on the head and murmured something along the lines of 'in your dreams mate'. But he's done it and it's frightening. He has uncovered things that I had forgotten, things that were probably best forgotten. There's no hiding now. And I'd no idea that Bill and Graeme were doing so many things behind my back. But what is so flattering is that he chose to do it at all and saved me many hours rummaging around in the attic.

Anyway, I hope the reader is as interested as I am. It's all here except my inside leg measurement. And for the second edition, Robert, you might as well know it's 29 inches.

This work contains more information about *The Goodies* than anyone should need, want, or be allowed access to. If we had realised someone was researching our lives and careers in such detail, we would have demanded police protection.

Publish and I shall sue.

PS It's a pack of lies anyway. Tim's inside leg is 29 and a half inches. I should know, I worked with it for 10 (wasted) years.

PPS Who's Graeme?

Introduction

For over a decade Tim Brooke-Taylor, Graeme Garden and Bill Oddie created the most imaginative, inventive and consistently hilarious television comedy around. Conquering the small screen, becoming groovy teenage pop icons and best-selling comic authors, the Goodies were a Seventies force to be reckoned with. Arguably the most potent of all comic cult successes, *The Goodies* seems unfairly stuck in a vintage time warp of flared trousers, Spangles and glam rock, while the heritage of over 70 programmes plays as fresh and vibrant as classic Buster Keaton. Within the pages of this book, I, a self-confessed, ever-faithful follower of *The Goodies'* genius since childhood, will lay bare the entire story of three writer–performers who injected rejuvenating life into post-war Britcom. Treading the familiar path of Monty Python, the Goodies, after their 1982 disbanding, have since found renewed success as sitcom giant, off-the-wall medic and professional birder. But their individual and, more importantly, collective contribution to comedy history has largely gone uncelebrated. Familiar favourites on Australian television, the British audiences have been terrestrial *Goodies*-free for decades. Half-hearted reunions and nostalgia slots have been humiliatingly brief. Cult telly folk proclaiming the trio as the greatest of comedy teams make little headway. But practically everybody you mention *The Goodies* to becomes misty-eyed, excited and amazed as to why the programmes have seemingly been tossed into television's waste bin. Things are about to change...

For the very first time, we can delve deeply into the fascinating, enigmatic and just plain side-splittingly funny world of *The Goodies*. Through the following pages, each and every contribution of the three Goodies, together and apart, will be credited, reviewed and discussed. Again, as with the *Monty Python Encyclopedia*, the easiest and most effective system was to present the entire thing in strict alphabetical order. Thus, between motoring magazines and pantomimes and compact disc collections and game shows, there's a wealth of writing, performing, presenting and voiceover credits as well as, of course, a very, very hefty chapter dedicated to the letter 'G'.

All the BBC classics, their ill-fated, albeit really rather grand, ITV season, hit recordings, books, near-miss projects, guest-starring appearances, fringe *Goodie* episodes and low-key reunions are included, alongside solo credits (*Me & My Girl*, *Body Matters*, *The Bubblegum Brigade*), early successes (*At Last the 1948 Show*, *Twice a Fortnight*, *Doctor in the House*) and contemporary cult classics (*I'm Sorry I Haven't a Clue*, *If I Ruled the World*, *Shooting Stars*).

In his *Radio Times* 'My Choice' interview (15–21 February 1997), Bill Oddie was quoted as hoping that 'it would be nice if they repeated the best ones!' Several years later, the fragmenting, cable channel-shunning British public are still holding their breath but with their 30th and mine just around the corner, surely it's time to resurrect those legendary 'inbetweenies' and praise them. Happy birthday lads, thanks for all this and, don't forget, it's never too late to be as free as a bird...

This book is my affectionate tribute to the most endearing and heroic comedy collective of their generation. So prepare to sit astride your trandem, take a long overdue trip back to Cricklewood, get your black puddings out, do the *Funky Gibbon* and chase that dreaded kitten Twinkle. It's the ultimate salute to a comic force to treasure... *The Goodies*.

Prologue:

In 1970, the 'Fab Four' may have finally called it a day but it was a glorious 12 months that was balanced with the formation of the 'Tremendous Three'. The lads of Walruses and Strawberry Fields gave way to the purveyors of Funky Gibbons and Cricklewood. In November 1970, Tim Brooke-Taylor, Graeme Garden and Bill Oddie opened up for business, promising to do anything, anywhere and for anyone. Over the next 12 years, with a belated and ill-fated channel switch along the way, the lads did exactly that.

Few comedy collectives can literally get the heart pumping with excitable and affectionate anticipation. The Goodies are, arguably, the all-time passion kick-starter. It's the combination of nostalgic memories, happy times guaranteed, class performers having a ball and the community spirit of like-minded dedicated viewers continually in the debt of this trio of comic ground-breakers. While an earlier generation can blissfully remember being 17 when *Sgt Pepper* was released, we can equally bask in the light of being seven when *Dodonuts* was first broadcast. The images are a blur of childhood memories, half-remembered comic situations and a clutch of unforgettably catchy songs on *Top of the Pops*. *The Goodies* conjures up a gallery of classic moments forever locked into our collective consciousness: tomato sauce dispensers dishing out a messy death, countless Rolf Harrises running across the country, three Stone Age figures jumping down a slope. During university's halcyon days, one's eagerness to recapture those innocent times fuelled months of bar-locked inactivity, drinking, chatting and analysing those long-gone classics. Revelling in repeated listening of Goodies albums on the Student Union's dodgy tape deck, re-living favourite shows over countless bottles of ultra-cheap cider and joyfully recalling a shared childhood in which the Goodies could be forever relied

on to win the day, dig the groove and puff the weed. Student heroes if ever there were any. Who needed Ernesto 'Che' Guevara with Bill Oddie about?

The Goodies revelled in a unique mixture of the satirical clout of Peter Cook, the timeless visual style of Buster Keaton and the musical cool of Marc Bolan. Springing from the combined loins of Frank Muir and Denis Norden, the Crazy Gang, Chuck Jones, Abbott and Costello, Tommy Handley, Max Miller, the Marx Brothers, the Goons, Olsen and Johnson, Tex Avery, Will Hay and Robert Dhery, the Goodies took from the past and sculptured for the future. Indeed, in a 1973 *Radio Times* interview Tim Brooke-Taylor commented that, 'ideally, *The Goodies* will be great in 70 years time.' Almost halfway towards that impressive goal, the promise still holds good. Injecting traditional clowning elements, bucket-loads of the corniest, groan-worthiest gags and an almost equally healthy dollop of biting, social and political comment, *The Goodies* may have been beloved and admired as family and, even, shock, horror, scream, children's favourites, but their Trojan horse antics ushered in more touchy, feely debate than a bushel of Malcolm Muggeridges.

As with a half of those other innovative BBC boys, the *Monty Python* crew, the early, make or break days for the Goodies were spent at Cambridge University. Tim Brooke-Taylor, Bill Oddie and Graeme Garden were all contemporary, or just about contemporary, students with Graham Chapman, John Cleese and Eric Idle. During the long and winding road from university education to ultimate comedy stardom in 1969, it's stunning how many times the two pioneering factions cross and mould. The inspirational spectre of *The Goon Show* loomed large as a past masterpiece that shaped Fifties comedy. Whereas the surreal genius of Spike Milligan would directly fashion the Python vision, the

Goodies, via *I'm Sorry I'll Read That Again*, would follow the style of the early-departing Goon, Michael Bentine, having one foot dipped in madness while firmly planting the other in traditional music hall. In the wake of the grand daddy of them all, Peter Cook, Cambridge was the catalyst and the Footlights the crucible.

The fledgling 1962 Cambridge revue *Double Take* saw writing and performing teamwork from Brooke-Taylor, Chapman and Cleese, with musical contributions from Oddie. With the following year's effort, *A Clump of Plinths*, Oddie had joined the lads on stage for some primitive semi-satire, ancient gags and flamboyant mugging. After various transmogrifications, this delicious piece of nonsense would be knocked into the classic stage revue *Cambridge Circus* which would wow hip London with its streetwise student cool. If hardly *Beyond the Fringe*, it proved the perfect springboard for its astounding cast. The next 10 years of Britcom were safe in the hands of these guys. Meanwhile, the 1964 Cambridge Footlights effort, *Stuff That Dreams Are Made Of* boasted Graeme Garden and Eric Idle finding their feet. But it was destined to be a mere footnote in the Footlights. *Cambridge Circus*, however, had enjoyed a successful tour of New Zealand, an off-Broadway run and one-off BBC radio enactment. Garden and Idle had already been drafted in for written and performing contributions by this stage, with a string of pilot shows and the launch of Series One of radio's *I'm Sorry I'll Read That Again*, lighting the blue touch paper. Both Chapman and Idle made limited contributions to this, while Cleese and the entire collection of future Goodies ran with the initial plan to create *The Goon Show* for the Sixties. Delighting in a seemingly never-ending string of corny gags, the team succeeded in creating a weird, bizarre universe with its own rules of timing, content and normality. Eventually, Oddie and Garden were totally instrumental in the script-writing, twisting and turning logic through obvious one-liners, surrealism and sheer comic determination. Running well into *The Goodies* history, *I'm Sorry I'll Read That Again* acted as the ultimate, on-air gathering of the show's diverse comic elements.

That was only part of the story. On stage and television, Cambridge buddies Brooke-Taylor and Oddie had been clutched under the umbrella of talent employed by David Frost, contributing to *That Was The Week That Was*, *The Frost Report* and, ultimately, the ground-breaking sketch series for ATV, *At Last the 1948 Show*. While Oddie's writing and performing skills were included, it was Brooke-Taylor, alongside Graham Chapman, John Cleese and Marty Feldman, who was the star of the piece. While Chapman and Cleese soldiered on towards Python, Brooke-Taylor and Feldman joined forces for the latter's own BBC series, *It's Marty*. Meanwhile, Oddie was content with writing and performing for *Twice a Fortnight* with Graeme Garden, which fully explored the speeded-up, quick-cut, Dutch-angle filming techniques that would infiltrate *The Goodies*. This skill with innovative camera tricks and the wealth of *I'm Sorry I'll Read That Again* puns was the mixture the team were after. This was further embraced with Brooke-Taylor's pet project, *Broaden Your Mind – an Encyclopaedia of the Air*. A Brooke-Taylor and Garden-heavy programme, its surrealist assortment of tongue-in-cheek lectures, bizarre sketches and Marx Brother-movie passion proved hugely popular. For the first series, pre-Python writing skill was employed, along with Bill Oddie's musical interjections which, by the second series in 1969, were even more prominent. And, at the same time, Oddie and Garden had undertaken to write the vast majority of LWT's *Doctor in the House* episodes. Wallowing in cast ensemble playing, knockabout student humour and telling touches of social comment, the entire premise had been masterminded by the opening edition – penned by Graham Chapman and John Cleese. Although Oddie and Garden would continue to write for the spin-off successes, *Doctor at Large* and *Doctor in Charge*, it was writing and performing for the BBC where their hearts were happiest.

Broaden Your Mind was the final piece in the jigsaw puzzle. Popular certainly, but once *Monty Python's Flying Circus* had reared its world-beating head in October 1969, there seemed little point in trying to find the next great thing in sketch comedy. Six other people had just done that, so the seed was sown to recreate the shared, Cambridge, off-the-wall wackiness and stick it within a traditional, safe, situation comedy format. Clearly, the three writer–performers needed a fresher, more structured form to channel their unique brand of comedy through. As Tim Brooke-Taylor remembers,

Broaden Your Mind was always 'a cover to hatch this idea for a series which became *The Goodies*.' An idea was indeed hatched that cast the three leads as surreal caricatures of their own personalities. The landed gentry, patriotic coward. The working class, anarchist labourer. The bespectacled, scientific, modernistic boffin. Little England was perfectly captured, personified and mocked within the three-way team. Living and working together, up for hire for any strange assignment going and happy to do anything, anytime, the Goodies succeeded in creating an ever-changing, time-zone hopping format which remains, essentially, the same throughout.

Fundamentally, the Goodies latched on to the madcap, musically interspersed antics of The Monkees. As those four Anglo-American nutters were, in essence, The Beatles meet the Three Stooges, it was more than an apt blueprint for Brooke-Taylor, Garden and Oddie. Indeed, although with The Monkees, the music was the main thing and the comedy secondary, it wasn't simply bog-standard, mimed song interludes that enhanced the series. Tellingly, visual gags and speeded-up pratfalls would be complemented with a musical number background as well. Not only that, but the legendary Hanna-Barbara cartoon series *Scooby Doo... Where Are You?* (I'm talking the class, post-Sinatra's *Strangers in the Night*, pre-tiny irritant Scrappy Doo) mixed animated cloning of *X File*-inspiring horror and sequences of visual comedy moments with Scooby and Shaggy, accompanied by hip, groovy late Sixties West Coast pop music. With these very American influences firmly in place, the final British signal towards *The Goodies* came from, arguably, the most influential British artiste and writer of the century – John Lennon. His poem, *Deaf Ted, Danoota (and me)* featured in his first published collection, *In His Own Write*, included the immortal line, 'We fight the baddy baddies'. Not only that, but when the piece was dramatised for *Not Only... But Also...* with Dudley Moore, Norman Rossington and Lennon himself, the trio rode through the countryside on bikes. The trandem and *The Goodies* was merely a step away.

Michael Miles, Head of Light Entertainment for the BBC, had dozens of office-based situation comedy ideas landing on his desk at a rate of knots. Indeed, the basic notion had sort of been milked by Norman Hudis'

Carry On Regardless in 1961. However, Miles had been a huge admirer of *Broaden Your Mind* and, indeed, had been instrumental in securing the aborted third series. As such, he trusted the judgment and skill of Brooke-Taylor, Garden and Oddie. Barry Took, champion for both the Pythons and Goodies, agreed and the trio were allowed to plan ahead for their new project. Negotiations for a new programme starring the trio began on 5 June 1970 and by 14 July they were contracted for a run of seven episodes. Well, at least, seven episodes of something!

The concept was in place but a catchy name was needed and the trio gathered for a name-launching brain-storming session. One of the hottest favourites for a long time was a charming little thing by the name of Super Chaps Three. Planned as a parody of all those Gerry Anderson puppet shows for ATV like *Thunderbirds* and *Captain Scarlet*, it was Bill Oddie who finally woke up in a cold sweat with the perfect handle – *The Goodies*. It sounded like a pop group which was, of course, his none-to-serious ambition. It sounded like all those cult action caper television shows like *The Avengers* and *The Champions*. And it sounded heroic – albeit a tad wet for all of them to live with for the next 30 years. Wet it may have sounded but wet it certainly wasn't. On 31 July, the team officially signed off on the title. *The Goodies* – 'as opposed to the Baddies' as the *Radio Times* pointed out on their first appearance – was the ultimate comic vehicle, defending BritCom against the scum of humanity.

As opposed to Monty Python's ferment denial of guest star appearances and television convention, the Goodies wallowed in an almost Morecambe and Wise-like reliance on famous names dropping in as various clients and villains. Despite a post-*Dambusters* and pre-*Inspector Wexford* George Baker, Series One's guests were gleaned from that indispensable collection of character players like Richard Caudicott and Paul Whitsun-Jones, but the Goodies had their sights aimed at bigger names than that. However, the BBC weren't that keen to help. Lists of performers wanted for new series were delivered to the casting bod by the team and systematically ignored. Finding out that the artist's agents were not even being approached, the Goodies took on the job themselves and discovered the vast majority of wish-list actors were happy to play ball.

Importantly, these great and good performers were always kept within the realms of Goodie comedy, never mocked but often gloriously cast against type fully to milk their long, distinguished baggage in entertainment. As with Python, newsreaders, presenters and commentators were an obsession – Eddie Waring, Kenneth Wolstenholme, Patrick Moore, Richard Baker and the like were favourite walk-on players – but, apart from John Cleese's legendary rant in *The Goodies and the Beanstalk*, the trio never brought in contemporary or the hero-worshipped cool dudes of the pre- and post-Oxbridge comic invasion. Spike Milligan, Peter Cook and Marty Feldman would have been obvious inclusions but, instead, the guests were selected from the traditional pool of variety and drama. Some of the finest actors ever to walk into a television studio – Harry H Corbett, Patrick Troughton and Carry On stars, Joan Sims, Bernard Bresslaw and Jack Douglas, innovative comic originals – Stanley Baxter, ex-satire and now comfy sitcom favourite – Roy Kinnear. All were drafted into the Goodies' universe

and eagerly hammed it up like AE Matthews in *The Goon Show: The Evils of Bushy Spon*. Graeme Garden remembers them all as 'a delight. I think our favourite was Henry McGee but all these great actors were perfectly happy to send up their own images.'

For 12 years, *The Goodies* reigned supreme on British television, just about combating the invasion of Ben Elton and alternative comedy, with a mixture of right-on, politically geared comedy, more of the same visual wizardry and interesting, reflective guest players like Mel Smith and David Rappaport. With their Spangles-like titles, outlandish fashions, tongue-in-cheek Britishness and facial hair to embarrass Slade, *The Goodies* may be very much a part of the decade – The Seventies – that they multimedia-conquered. But far, far more importantly than that, alone and, most potently of all, as a full-on, three-pack team, the Goodies were responsible for some of the most powerful, impressive and unforgettable television ever created. World-beaters to this day and a vital part of the fabric of British comedy history, the Goodies remain the coolest.

AA MEMBERS' MAGAZINE

Issue One of the 1999 journal for the UK's biggest motorists' organisation gave 'comedian, ornithologist and ex-Goodie' Bill Oddie the opportunity to grab his copy of the *AA Book of Britain's Countryside* and stroll through his favourite beauty spots in the Isles of Scilly, North Norfolk, Teesdale and Shetland for his two-page article *Best of British*.

ADAM'S FAMILY TREE

An enjoyable children's drama series that took elements from *Dr Who*, cross-fertilised them with the ethos of *Jamie and the Magic Torch* and chucked in a huge dollop of tongue-in-cheek humour before delivery. The hero of the piece, a charming 12-year-old lad played by Anthony Lewis, gets himself out of minor league scraps thanks to a back catalogue of eccentric historical ancestors he can magic up via a natty CD-Rom. Simply by pushing 'Return' on his computer and thanks to some mind-blowing tricks with the time-loop continuum – where's Jon Pertwee when you need him! – his problems are sort of solved and the adventure begins. Bill Oddie guest-starred in the fifth episode as a flamboyant painter enlisted to help trap Stan the Gorilla.

Adam ANTHONY LEWIS Jane SAMIA GHADIE Salvador Griffiths BILL ODDIE. Written by Brian Walsh and Neil Armstrong. Producer Richard Callahan. Executive Producer Patrick Titley. Monday 3 February 1997, YTV.

THE AGE NEWSPAPER

Bill Oddie was interviewed for the publication in 1993 for the piece, *An Oddie But Goodies*.

ALADDIN

The perfect way to kick start your mince pie abuse or to relax you after Hogmanay excess, this neat little panto production headlined that glorious Goodie, Tim Brooke-Taylor, as that glorious baddie, Abanazar, and presented my first opportunity not only to see live but also meet a childhood comic hero of the highest order. The production may have left a lot to be desired and, as with every other 1997 Christmas bash worth its salt, we were not spared Tellytubbies and Spice Girl gags, but several of the cast gave

rich performances, not least of which, was one Christopher Beeny hamming it up like a good 'un while basking in *Upstairs, Downstairs* cache. Jenny Tomasin, also late of that Seventies dramatic gem, was less than impressive, fluffing her way through with nervous delivery and worried expressions, while *'Allo, 'Allo* heavy Hilary Minister failed to cope with some of the most groan-worthy, unhip hip rhyming dialogue it has ever been my misfortune to witness. However, all was saved by Brooke-Taylor's perfectly judged doer of evil things and thinker of evil thoughts, bounding on to the stage to set the scene and effortlessly walking away with every scene he forced his way into. Hard work it may have been – Tim could be heard to mutter 'It's far easier being a Goodie!' as he finally fell down the trap-door – but the performer deliciously send up the panto structure in mock partnership with Beeny and brilliantly attacked the gratingly cheerful but infectiously caricatured work of Rod Hull. It was a real whiz bang of a family entertainment. One can almost forgive the truly teeth-grating Emu song if only for Tim's spirited, airborne, retained ad lib 'Eat your heart out Richard Branson' and for some leggy, upbeat and gleeful business from Challenge TV babe Carryl Varley.

Thursday 11 December 1997–Saturday 17 January 1998. Theatre Royal, Windsor.

ALL-STAR COMEDY CARNIVAL

ITV's answer to the BBC's *Christmas Night with the Stars*, showcased the greatest stand-up, sitcom and sketch successes of the year. The 1969 edition naturally included a small festive glimpse into *Doctor in the House*. Barry Evans, Geoffrey Davies, Robin Nedwell and George Layton reprised their roles in the Graeme Garden and Bill Oddie scripted vignette. Other highlights included *On the Buses*, Bernard Cribbins, *Please Sir!* and Sid James in *Two in Clover*.

Director Mark Stuart. Producer Humphrey Barclay. Thursday 25 December 1969, ITV.

ALL THINGS BRIGHT AND BEAUTIFUL

The very first Goodies single from the very first Goodies album, *The Goodies Sing Songs From The Goodies* is a glorious bit of vinyl projecting Bill Oddie (after *I'm Sorry I'll Read That Again* discs) as a rocking force to be reckoned with. A heavy beat rendition of *All Things Bright and Beautiful*, the stirring track kicks off with the provocative, '1, 2, 1, 2, 3, 4' and a burst of heavenly choir juxtaposed with rock guitar gusto. Imagine the hymn you know and love put through a Jimi Hendrix crash course and you'll get the idea. Oddie's 'Ooh so beautiful!' interjections give real clout to the piece, the drum backing literally pounds along and there's even a Tom Jones-fashioned scream in there somewhere as well. Tim and Graeme, assigned to almost inaudible backing vocals, happily step aside to allow Oddie centre stage with a rocking piece of work. *Winter Sportsman*, on the other hand and other side, is fully in comic Goodies mode. Originally performed by Oddie in the Series Two episode *Winter Olympics*, Brooke-Taylor grabs the mike for the recorded release, camping it up with macho athleticism. The tinkerly bells intro and an endearing chorus of girlie groupies sets the scene for this classic 'barrel of fun and a barrel of snow!' while the jazz interlude creates an effective musical contrast.

All Things Bright and Beautiful traditional arrangement by Bill Oddie, Miki Antony and Andrew Jackman. Winter Sportsman written by Bill Oddie. F 13449 Decca 1974.

THE ALMOST TOTALLY COMPLETE I'M SORRY I HAVEN'T A CLUE

An hilarious collection of the best jokes to emerge from BBC radio's glorious tongue-in-cheek panel game *I'm Sorry I Haven't a Clue.*

Written by Tim Brooke-Taylor, Barry Cryer, Graeme Garden and Humphrey Lyttleton. Orion Media 1999.

ANIMAL HOUSE

While the BBC had Rolf Harris and Channel 4 had Wendy Turner, television's poor relation recruited Bill Oddie to look into the wonderful world of animals. Typically off the wall and comically weird, Oddie strolled through the splendours of Twycross Zoo spinning witty banter links for some very odd filmed features. With topics ranging from an elephant car wash, cat marriages in Bangkok, a bear dentist and Brighton nudists adopting painted zebra disguises, Oddie's deliciously cynical observations lifted an average small screen peep-hole into absurd goings on. A catchy theme – *The Baby Elephant Walk* – and an endless torrent of groan-worthy gags from our under-used host made the series worth catching.

Mondays, 6 July–24 August 1998, Channel 5.

ANIMAL ROADSHOW

Bill Oddie appeared with Sarah Kennedy on 8 September 1989 on BBC1.

ASK ASPEL

Fondly remembered children's request programme in which it seemed the legendary Michael Aspel could deliver dream-team television entertainment for the cost of a postage stamp. Importantly, it played a big part in establishing *The Goodies* with a younger audience. A double-edged sword in the long run, *Ask Aspel* led to many perceiving *The Goodies* as nothing more than a kid's programme. However, regular *Ask Aspel* requests for, and screenings of, Series One material during November and December 1970, launched *The Goodies* into the family-based mainstream. Indeed, Brooke-Taylor, Garden and Oddie became such firm favourites with *Ask Aspel* viewers that they made an appearance on the show on 18 December 1970. As a direct result of requests to Aspel, the BBC decided to repeat *The Goodies* in an early Saturday evening BBC1 slot during the Summer of 1971. The Goodies returned to *Ask Aspel* for some Series Six promotion on 8 September 1976. A champion and a curse, Aspel played the smooth presenter, Michael Aspirin, in *Chubby Chumps* and achieved Goodie immortality by being memorably squashed by Kitten Kong.

ASK ODDIE

Although part of Children's ITV, this Bill Oddie investigative environmental programme was pretty hard hitting. The *Radio Times* plugged the show with an article *Just Ask Oddie* (2–8 March 1991) and the first edition looked at whether animals should be kept in zoos and how the trend of Ninja Turtles affected real turtles and terrapins. Other Series One programmes tackled the rain forests, cosmetic testing, blood sport and the effect of the Gulf War on the environment. The heavy issues dealt with by the Green Team were balanced with appearances from Captain Ozone. Series Two welcomed in Billie the Pig to help with nature questions and Bill looked at the future of zoos.

Series One: Fridays, 8 March–17 May 1991. Series Two: Thursdays, 29 August–10 October 1991, ITV.

ASSAULTED NUTS

In between regular situation comedy exposure on *Me & My Girl*, Tim Brooke-Taylor wandered into this hit and very much miss sketch series with old *Hello Cheeky* cohort Barry Cryer. Very much an ensemble piece, Tim was recruited as the token 'Python' player. As such he was continually used as an ironic icon for the show. Rip-offs were obvious and unashamed, such as the book shop sketch where Tim desperately tries to buy a copy of *Sparkling Cyanide* by Agatha Christie from assistant Daniel Peacock. Finally, Tim goes through humiliating, anarchic Python-esque business by removing his overcoat and revealing French knickers and suspenders underneath. So embarrassed by the scene, Tim insisted on a closed set in order to limit the number of people he would look stupid in front of. A sketch with a bit more class saw Tim put on the cool, clipped persona of Trevor Howard for a *Brief Encounter* parody while he was a fabulous Dirk Bogarde in the corny *Deaf in Venice* quickie – the film parodies on *Casablanca*, *Gone with the Wind* and *Pyscho* proved fruitful and apt in light of Channel 4's vintage programming. Tim was a hassled vicar, a nervous guy asking for contraceptives, a holiday-maker told of plane hijacks as part of the package, an ancient duffer playing the game show *Sudden Death*, a befuddled old lawyer, a distressed businessman complaining of continually faulty purchases and even a client of The Total Insurance for Rather Unlikely Accidents Company. Python anybody? And that was the point, this really was low-grade Python 15 years late. It was as though *Not the Nine O'Clock News* had never happened. There was even a pet shop sketch featuring Tim's cocky assistant desperately trying to sell a squid to a punter requiring a puppy. Tongue-in-cheek all this may have been but the in-jokes, send-ups (including a neat Benny Hill interlude) and complete embrace of the Python stream of consciousness just seemed clumsy. The traditional *It's Marty* trick of the cast addressing the audience at the close was employed with further comic nods to *The Goodies* – with camp mock adverts and Tim's briefly seen Union flag jacket. Even the funniest sketches – Tim's inept, 500-year-old Father Christmas, a frantic publisher concerned with the dictionaries' obsession with rude words and phrases, a casual reminiscence about reincarnation memories as gladiators, a stunning monologue on the problem of accountancy addition – were mildly re-treading the terrain of *At Last the 1948 Show*. Perhaps the programme's most inventive moments came when the cast chipped in with the 'round the telly viewers' comments on the sketches. Tim, a scruffy Peter Cook type, added to the fun, with hilarious diatribes on what Mick Jagger keeps down his trousers, loving

TIM BROOKE TAYLOR, ONE OF THE STARS OF ASSAULTED NUTS

glances at his preserved 'private parts' in an aspirin bottle and heated debate about the realism of *Alien*. Regular writers Andrew Marshall and David Renwick had been favourites of Brooke-Taylor during *The Burkiss Way* days and he would work with Renwick again on *One Foot in the Grave*. More to the point, they had been tuning their wacky, offend everybody, quick-fire style on Kenny Everett's television shows and in many ways *Assaulted Nuts* was a half-hearted attempt at doing an Everett series without Everett. Cryer was an Everett-friendly talent as was writer, producer and director Ray Cameron, while outstanding (in every way) support, came from Cleo Rocos, as usual restricted to stunning, cleavage-heaving cameos. Thanks to its strong American cast – including the man who starts all the problems in *Jurassic Park*, Wayne Knight – the series was syndicated in the USA and found safe haven on Channel 4 but proved unsuccessful. Despite this, a second series was commissioned – although Tim Brooke-Taylor opted out and was replaced by Emma Thompson. Timbo clips were later featured on Graham Kennedy's *World of Comedy*. In its way, *Assaulted Nuts* broke sketch comedy barriers: breast nudity was frequent, while references were made to sadism and lesbians, but the whole thing played like twee, sniggering sixth-formers doing a Python show. Sketches would merge into one without any sign of clever invention, characters would criticise their performances, players would grin into camera, question the quality of a sketch and allow recurring figures to build up through the series, but, despite all this, it wasn't going to be *The Fast Show*. The break-neck speed and total, repeated self-mockery was lacking. Still, if only for Tim's catalogue of comic vignettes and the much welcome sight of Cleo Rocos stripping down to her undies, these shows are well worth searching out.

TIM BROOKE-TAYLOR, RAY CAMERON, BARRY CRYER, ELAINE HAUSMAN, WAYNE KNIGHT, GAIL MATTHIUS, DANIEL PEACOCK, CLEO ROCOS, MARCELLE ROSENBLATT, BILL SADLER. Written by Ray Cameron, Barry Cryer, Andrew Marshall, Terry Ravenscroft, David Renwick and Peter Vincent with Glen Bruce, Ian Davidson, Kim Fuller, Brian Leveson, Hazen Macintyre, Ken Meredith, Paul Minet, Vicky Pile, Jim Pullen, Tim Rivett, Cathy Shambley, Bob Sinfield, Andrew Solomons and Dick Vosburgh. Produced and directed by Ray Cameron. Thursdays, January 17–February 28 1985, Channel 4.

ASTERIX AND THE BIG FIGHT

An animated version of the classic cartoon strip, this film, and several other feature-length adventures made during 1996, were blessed with the outrageously French vocal talents of Bill Oddie as the cowardly, cunning Viking warrior.

ASTRONAUTS

An era awash with the *Star Wars* trilogy, *Star Trek* making it count on the big screen and the impending departure of Tom Baker from the TARDIS, was perfect for a bit of fun-poking at the entire science fiction genre. Alas, this wasn't *Red Dwarf*. Written by Graeme Garden and Bill Oddie during the break between BBC *Goodies* in 1980 and ITV *Goodies* in 1981, the original idea was to extend the comic tension found in such *Goodies* classics as *The End* and *Earthanasia* and create a Pinter-esque claustrophobic situation. Writing restrictions made the scripts tight and self-contained, there was no room for an easy laugh or any excuse to 'bring in the funny plumber when things got dull!' The seven episodes delighted in the comic misadventures of Britain's first space mission aboard the 'sky lab' Piglet, but the

decidedly *Red Dwarf*-styled idea – one posh chap and one North Country bloke bickering in outer space – failed to gel. However, what the programme lacked in major star names was effortlessly counterbalanced by joyous scripts, plenty of fun with Bimbo the dog and angst-ridden support performances from Bruce Boa as a former astronaut restricted to dishing out comments from his ground-based mission control position. Great swathes of comedy came from the jargon – the Sky lab being Piglet, mission control was dubbed 'Pooh' – and attacks of homelessness, space and toilet difficulties. There was a fine line in anarchic and archaic humour from Christopher Goodwin's ex-RAF chappie who couldn't deal with people on any level and, a typical Oddie strand concerning biological experimentation with cages of victimised insects and white mice. Help for incompetent colleagues and on-board sexual tension came from Carmen Du Sautoy.

Did You Know? Graeme and Bill were interviewed for the TV Times (24–30 October 1981) revealing secrets of the forthcoming space series as well as comments from rehearsing the new series of The Goodies for ITV. Adaptation rights for Astronauts were picked up by the American company Elmar Productions, who got a commission for a pilot episode from CBS. Changing the name to The Astronauts, the three principals were played by Granville Van Dusen, Brianne Leary and Bruce Davison while M*A*S*H's McLean Stevenson stole the plaudits as the mission control grouch. The show was screened on 11 August 1982 but no series was developed. Bill Oddie allocates blame for the show's British demise firmly at the feet of ITV. Bill considers the evening time-slot a mistake, while the corporation insisted on a female, love interest figure and filming in front of a live audience. For the writers, this doomed the show from the outset.

Commander Malcolm Mattocks CHRISTOPHER GOODWIN Technical Officer David Ackroyd BARRIE RUTTER Dr Gention Foster CARMEN DU SAUTOY Beadle BRUCE BOA. Written by Graeme Garden and Bill Oddie. Script editors Dick Clement and Ian Le Frenais. Produced by Tony Charles and Douglas Argent. Executive Producer Allan McKeown. Director Douglas Argent. Mondays, October 26–December 7 1981, ITV.

AT LAST THE 1948 SHOW

One of the most important television programmes in the development of post-war comedy, it is packed with dozens of sketches still fresh and vibrant. Moreover, from its loins the immediate successes of *Monty Python's Flying Circus* and *It's Marty* sprang. The four principal players, Tim Brooke-Taylor, Graham Chapman, John Cleese and Marty Feldman, were under the umbrella of talent steered by David Frost and the programme

JOHN CLEESE GOES INTO FACE-PULLING OVERDRIVE FOR THE SPY SKETCH WITH A BEMUSED AND CONFUSED TIM BROOKE-TAYLOR LOOKING ON DURING *AT LAST THE 1948 SHOW*

developed from merged plans to headline Brooke-Taylor and Cleese in their own small screen series. The two old Cambridge boys thought a joint effort would be a better idea, Chapman was enlisted thanks to Cleese's recommendation, and Feldman – for the last decade known only for script-writing in the business – was a controversial casting suggestion from both. Frost and Rediffusion were uncertain about Feldman's bulbous eyes – the feature that would make his mark and fortune – but Brooke-Taylor and Cleese won the argument as well as retaining editorial control over the programmes. The two future Pythons were busy writing the film *The Rise and Rise of Michael Rimmer* for David Frost in a villa in Ibiza when Mr and Mrs Marty Feldman, Tim Brooke-Taylor and David Frost – primarily checking that the duo were actually slaving over a hot typewriter – arrived to discuss the new project.

SERIES ONE

As the focal points within the group, Brooke-Taylor and Cleese had some clout as to the direction this new show took. Desperate to move away from the strait-jacketed satire and less dangerous slapstick of *The Frost Report*, the team allowed a sense of a stream of consciousness to evolve within the series. Written by the four major players, usually in familiar Cleese/Chapman and Brooke-Taylor/Feldman partnerships, ideas for the show would be dreamt up and considered during a Sunday morning footie kickabout in Hyde Park. Brooke-Taylor, Chapman and Cleese were sharing a flat together at the time and thus the scripts reflected shared memories, shared experiences and shared friendships. Feldman, although just over five years older than the others, was the experienced comedy elder statesman of the group with

15

credits ranging from *The Army Game* to *Round the Horne*. Indeed, his partnership with Barry Took alternated with Tim time for *1948* material. Interviewed by the *TV Times* (1–7 April 1967), the *1948* quartet effortlessly spouted required off-the-wall banter but, perhaps, unknowingly, revealed continued inspiration from *I'm Sorry I'll Read That Again*, patriotic basking in recent World Cup victory, an attempt to play the commercial, laddish game, while hiding homosexuality, and paying tribute to the self-publicising group guru, respectively, 'The underlying theme of the series will be ferrets', Tim, '…and football', Marty, '…and females', Graham, 'not to mention Frost', John. The first series of six was given a late-night slot just before the Summer of Love.

EPISODE ONE
Tim Brooke-Taylor, John Cleese, Graham Chapman, Marty Feldman and a cast of thousands, one or two of whom will be appearing this week, back on your screens for the first time. A Doctor's consultation with skinny-legged man, Witch sketch, One-Man Wrestling, Secret Service Chief, Treasure Trove, Vox Pop.

EPISODE TWO
A shared holiday for the Four Sydney Lotterbys, Lucky Gypsy and the *Cambridge Circus* show-stopper Judge Not.

EPISODE THREE
Another *Cambridge Circus* throw-back with patients being replaced by visitors for the use of. Bed-ridden guest star Bill Oddie contrasts the nose-tapping, nurse-fancying robotic antics of a mechanical Tim Brooke-Taylor. An appeal on behalf of sleep starvation sufferers. Mice Laugh Softly, Charlotte, Brooke-Taylor's sheepish interviewer chats to Farmer Chapman as his sheep-dog devours the flock at the Sheepdog Trials, Book Shop and Job Description.

EPISODE FOUR
Stolen News, Grublian Holidays, Memory Training, One-Man Battalion, Ministerial Break-Down, the Engine Driver and the all-time corpsing dragged-up classic, Undercover Policeman, has sophisticated Chapman blowing his cover with a puffed pipe, Cleese biting his lip, Feldman going all cockney as he waxes lyrical on his 'English rose complexion' and Brooke-Taylor just about keeping control as he screams 'Gentlemen!' in a desperate bid to stop them breaking up.

EPISODE FIVE
Cleese oversees the school kid quiz Top of the Form with Brooke-Taylor hamming it up as a bright pupil. Gentleman Farmer, the Wonderful World of Ants (famously written by all four team members late one night) and Malaya, with Jo Kendall recreating the original Cleese/Oddie scripted John and Mary sketch from *Cambridge Circus*.

EPISODE SIX
Surreal genius as the four, bowler-hatted nightschool businessmen blankly take it in turns mournfully to mutter 'I am a chartered accountant!' before Feldman tosses insanity to the four winds with his wide-eyed rant 'I am a gorilla!' Headmaster, Siege in the Frock, Choral Repetition, the silent tension of Chinese Restaurant, Bee-keeping and a glorious end of term reprise of John Cleese's Ferret Song.

SERIES TWO
A major success for the ITV network, the team reconvened later in the year for a second and final series of seven programmes. Reflecting on their bulging post-bag the team revealed that the most asked question had been 'Why *At Last the 1948 Show*?' In answer to thousands of requests from one or two people, it was bluffed away in a surprisingly unmocking and uncomic response. The fact was that it was a 'non-title' which could cover a multitude of sketches, styles and situations. In reality there was more to it than that. Brooke-Taylor and Cleese, fresh from BBC television restrictions and refinements but about to plunge head-long back in with the sharks, were already amazed at the slow rituals and frantic mind-searching rampant in British broadcasting. It tickled them to create the illusion that some stuffy executive on the top floor had only just cleared a programme for screening 19 years after it was made.

EPISODE ONE
The team have written and are now seen together in the 1949 edition of this show with their special guest The Incredible Milton Oysterhiatus and his fire-eating penguins and sketches, Spiv Doctor, Reptile Keeper, a Nutty Thief in the Library, Come Dancing, Joke Shop.

EPISODE TWO
Presenting for your special entertainment, The Amazing Astragones, diving into a swamp from a height of 1000 feet. Shirt Shop, Cleese's ranting quiz host terrorises, humiliates and abuses aged female contestant Brooke-Taylor on The Nosmo Claphanger Show, Clothes Off!,

ROYAL AIR FORCE STIFF UPPER LIPS AT THE READY WITH TIM BROOKE-TAYLOR, JOHN CLEESE AND GRAHAM CHAPMAN IN *AT LAST THE 1948 SHOW*

Insurance for an Accident-Prone Man and thuggish supporters of the beautiful game are reinvented as ballet-obsessed nutters.

EPISODE THREE

We welcome the sensational Gertrude Sparefarthings, four hands in harmony, while the lads present the Pessimistic Customer, Meek Bouncer, Men's Club, Neurotic Scientist, the four Sydney Lotterbys crave the test score and deaf and blind punters and assistants fall over themselves in the Shop for the Sight and Sound Impaired.

EPISODE FOUR

Introducing Carl Cress-Spindle in The Globe of Death. A heated discussion on pornography, Door-to-Door Undertaker, Uncooperative Burglars, the arts programme Topic discusses freedom of speech, an unclear announcement and a whistle stop Studio Tour leaves you breathless.

EPISODE FIVE

You are invited to crave your support for Grenville Sneersmarme and his musical finger-bowls while being entertained or otherwise by the Reluctant Choir. Cleese's devilish psychiatrist twists the knife of nervous tension in Brooke-Taylor's bothered, bewildered and timid patient – a performance helped by Feldman stamping on Cleese's foot in order to give Tim the desired, full-on, rant character to react to. A cleaner's insight into the Secret Service, a reprimanded footballer and a disastrous architectural model with a mind of its own lets the side down with some deadly misbehaviour.

EPISODE SIX

Sydney Lotterby returns, Chartered Accountants Dance, Dangers of Dentistry and the sublime beyond words, Four Yorkshiremen: 'Luxury!'

EPISODE SEVEN

Current Affairs on Television, Railway Carriage, Pet Shop and a climatic full cast performance of Cleese's *I'm Sorry I'll Read That Again* anthem, *The Rhubarb Tart Song*. *Did You Know?* Aimi McDonald's dizzy blonde links forced the embarrassed Brooke-Taylor and Cleese to check out night clubs for wannabe dancers, nervously audition a string of glam girls and basically write clichéd show-girl dialogue. While the Cambridge boys struggled, Feldman built a shrewd intelligence behind the bimbo, created the 'Make Miss Aimi MacDonald a Rich Lady Appeal' and planned to develop a cloned chorus line all speaking the linking material in unison. One extra girl was added each successive episode, although the subtlety of the joke was lost on certain regional areas that broadcast the series out of order. Other regions opted out of transmission completely. In a knowing piece in the TV Times, Tim Brooke-Taylor was described as an unmarried 26-year-old, a day-dreaming coward and the sort of bloke plagued by nightmares, screaming attacks and a fear of mice. Bless him... With high ratings already clocked up, the four were interviewed by the TV Times once more (15–21 April 1967) under the legend, 'Here We Are – AT LAST!' The feature mainly took the form of a manic piece of prose written by the team celebrating and plugging their new book, *The Amazing Adventures of Captain Gladys Stoatpamphlet and her Intrepid Spaniel Stig, Among the Giant Pygmies of Corsica, Volume III*. Their shared ambition in life was to be a clue in the TV Times crossword!

Written and performed by TIM BROOKE-TAYLOR, GRAHAM CHAPMAN, JOHN CLEESE, MARTY FELDMAN with AIMI MacDONALD and BARRY CRYER, FRANCIS DEAN, ERIC IDLE, JO KENDALL, MARY MAUDE, JACQUELINE ROCHELLE, CHRISTINE RODGERS and DICK VOSBURGH. Additional material by Chris Stuart-Clark and Bill Oddie . Design John Clarke. Editors Tim Brooke-Taylor and John Cleese. Music Director Bob Leaper. Executive Producer David Frost. Director Ian Fordyce. **Series One:** Thursdays, 6 April–11 May 1967. **Series Two:** Tuesdays, 26 September–7 November 1967, ITV.

AT LAST THE 1948 SHOW: the record

Quick to capitalise on the show's success, Pye records released an album compilation, *At Last the 1948 Show*, gathering together the best moments from Series One. *The Ferret Song* was a newly recorded version and, billed as just John Cleese and the 1948 Show Choir, released on a single (Pye 7N17336) alongside a re-recorded rendition of *The Rhubarb Tart Song*. Both tracks (complete with a *1948* cast photo) appeared on the 1996 compilation *A Pye in the Face*.

Book Shop, Sheepdog Trials, Where Were You?, The Wonderful World of the Ant, Gentleman Farmer, Witch, Top of the Torm, Someone Has Stolen the News, One-man Battalion, Doctor and Man with Skinny Legs, Ministerial Breakdown, Job Description, Engine Driver, The Four Sydney Lotterbys, Bee-keeping, The Ferret Song, Vox Pop. NPL 18198 Pye 1967.

After 1948

Apart from being one of the happiest professional assignments for any of the four team members, *At Last the 1948 Show* also included some of the finest writing of Brooke-Taylor, Chapman, Cleese and Feldman. It was thus doubly distressing for the quartet when it was discovered David Frost's own company, Paradine Productions, had wiped almost the entire collection of original tapes from the series. Only Episodes Four and Six from Series One and Series Two Episode Three survive intact. In the late Eighties, five 'best of' compilations made for Swedish transmission were discovered and one of these was presented as an ultra-rare treat on the first *TV Heaven*, 1967, hosted by Frank Muir on Channel 4, Saturday 8 February 1992. Nothing survives from the first programme but retained Series One sketches are Four Sydney Lotterbys, Visitors for the Use of, Sleep Starvation, Mice Laugh Softly, Charlotte and Top of the Form. The remnants of Series Two are Spiv Doctor, Reptile Keeper, Thief in Library, Nosmo Clanger Game Show, Thuggish Ballet Supporters, Uncooperative Burglars, Topic, Programme Announcement, Studio Tour, Reluctant Choir, Psychiatrist, Secret Service Cleaner, Chartered Accountants Dance and Railway Carriage. Off-screen home audio recordings of all 13 episodes also survive as an invaluable archive of a ground-breaking comedy classic while the 1968 special *How to Irritate People* saw Brooke-Taylor, Chapman and Cleese recapture the spirit and several old scripts from the series. However, the quality and rarity of the sketches made them perfect for plundering away from the David Frost stable. Tim Brooke-Taylor was involved when *At Last* moments were recreated for *Marty Amok* and *The Secret Policeman's Other Ball*. Marty Feldman latched on to the Door-to-Door Undertaker, performing it with James Villiers in *Marty Back Together Again* and even taking it to the tuxedoed refinement of *The Dean Martin Show* in America. The Two Ronnies were given Grublian Holidays, Spiv Doctor, the Psychiatrist and Choral Repetition for their third series in 1973. Grublian was featured on the first BBC record for the programme, *The Two Ronnies* (REB 138 M) released in 1976. But the most prolific reinterpretators of old *At Last* classics were Monty

THE FIVE PRINCIPALS SEND UP VARIETY FOR *AT LAST...* PUBLICITY

JANET ELLIS, THE REFORMED GOODIES AND A TOTALLY CONVINCING MASKED HERO PROMOTE *BANANAMAN* ON *BLUE PETER*

Python. Chapman's One-Man Wrestling became a staple of the stage shows, Sight and Sound Impaired Shop cropped up in the second German show and Book Shop enjoyed another resurrection for Python's *Contractual Obligation Album*. Most familiar of all, of course, was the glorious, dinner-jacketed, droning ramblings of Joshua, Obadiah, Ezekiel and Josiah, universally known as the Four Yorkshiremen. Such a major and celebrated element of live charitable and commercial Python performances that many believed it an original of the team. John Cleese, Terry Jones, Michael Palin and Rowan Atkinson performed it for *The Secret Policeman's Ball*, the recording of which (ILPS 9601) credits the writer as *At Last the 1948 Show*, while *Monty Python Live at the Hollywood Bowl* saw Graham Chapman, Eric Idle, Terry Jones and Michael Palin

perform the sketch. Tim Brooke-Taylor and Marty Feldman are thanked accordingly in the closing credits of the 1982 feature film of the shows. Later video, cassette and compact disc compilations have featured Four Yorkshiremen on *Panama Comedy Greats* (Andy Beven/LSB Ltd ARP 001, 1986), Clothes Off! on *The Dead Parrot's Society* (Springtime/Rhino R2 71049), the Python trio and Atkinson Yorkshiremen on *Best of the Balls* (Laughing Stock LAF CD 15) and *The Mermaid Frolics* version of Book Shop with John Cleese and Connie Booth in *The Secret Policeman's Private Parts*. At *Last the 1948 Show* sketches have been published in *No More Curried Eggs for Me*, *Son of Curried Eggs*, *The Golden Skits of Wing-Commander Muriel Volestrangler FRHS & Bar* and *The Utterly, Utterly Amusing and Pretty Damn Definitive Comic Relief Sketch Book*.

B

BABBLE

Another one of that seemingly endless selection of celebrity-based game shows partaking in a cheerful and, hopefully, witty, war of words. Here, *DrWho* assistant and *Blue Peter* dude Peter Purves served as chairman. At least this particular edition was an interesting Goodies get together with Tim Brooke-Taylor joined by *Winter Olympics* guest star Peter Jones and HRH Sheila Steafel.

Producer Gill Stribling-Wright. Director Terry Kinane. Saturday 24 August 1985, Channel 4.

BACK ON THE BOX

A special, one-off celebrity contest in which Gary Wilmot revealed vintage footage of major show business stars in early roles. Among those trying to guess who was who and what was what was Tim Brooke-Taylor alongside Spike Milligan and Barry Cryer.

Producer Richard Lewis. Director Annette Martin. Sunday 5 February 1989, BBC1.

BACK TO SQUARE ONE

Chris Searle tried his best to keep things together during this comic-edged and tongue-in-cheek examination of current English phrases for the discerning Radio 2 listener. Bill Oddie twice joined in the fun.

Producer Paul Z Jackson. Tuesday 10 May and 7 June 1988, Radio 2.

BANANAMAN

'This is 29 Acacia Road, and this is Eric the schoolboy who leads an exciting double life, for when Eric eats a banana, an amazing transformation occurs – Eric is Bananaman, ever alert for the call to action!' So opened each thrilling episode of *Bananaman*, the most potent introduction since *Mission: Impossible*. For many die-hard fans, myself included, it's the greatest post-*Goodies* experience available. Although still officially a recognised team, the ITV series was just a year away and a repeat season was even fresher in the memory, *Bananaman* captured the trio on ITV re-bound and presented the Goodies for the last time in almost five years, before *Comic Relief* brought them briefly back together again in 1988. More importantly, this outstanding cartoon series, developed from DC Comics tongue-in-cheek answer to Marvel's world of Superheroes, literally wallowed in painful puns. Running like a four-minute condensation of an *I'm Sorry I'll Read That Again* programme, visual slapstick, custard pies, awful word-play and the corniest gag was tossed into the mix, the overall feel is of three mates having a ball. Graeme is perfectly cast in the central role, playing his action hero with the strength of 20 men as a slow-witted buffoon. Tim, resurrecting his patriotic Goodies glory days delivery for the narration, also brought life to the cheeky young, banana-chomping Eric, while Bill, after years of devotion to bird-watching, finally gets to play a feathered friend as the wise-cracking Crow often at the side of thick Bananaman to pinpoint mistakes, advise or simply relish yet another deadening joke, notably the 'whale of a time' pun opposite Graeme's Scots gull in *Fog of Fear*. The supporting cast was spread evenly between the three, with Oddie notable as the very Oirish Police Chief O'Reilly and the handyman Mr Grindley. Perhaps the best characters were the villains and there were plenty of them: the evil Captain Cream who dreams of smothering everyone with stale cream buns, Tim's West Country Apple man cloned in *Double Trouble* ('We're rotten to the core') and the Peter Lorre-style Dr Doom. The smooth-as-silk slimeball, King Zorg, leader of the dreaded Nerks (usually voiced by a monosyllabic Bill) and Colonel Blight, the Moriarty to Bananaman's Holmes, blessed with all the embittered menace Graeme could muster. Jill Shilling helped out for the glam girls, particularly the stunning Newscaster and love of Bananaman's life, Fiona.

Did You Know? As well as starring in his own Monster Fun comic strip, Bananaman was featured on a set of Barrett's sweet cigarette collector's cards. Producer Trevor Bond and director Terry Ward had previously made, comedy great, Arthur Lowe, a children's hero with the Mr Men. In association with Saturday Superstore the Radio Times (22–28 October 1983), promoted the first series with the Bananaman Family Holiday Competition – eight questions about bananas stood between contestants and a fortnight in Jamaica.

Episodes: Bananaman Meets Dr Gloom, The Big Breakout, Ice Station Zero, Alien Planet, The Kidnap Caper, Bananakid, Destination Danger, Wall of Death, Jaws of Steel, Auntie's Back in Town, Tunnel of Terror, Final Orbit, House on Hangman's Hill, Mystery of the Old Mine, Disaster at Devil's Cove, The Pirate TV Station, Cavern of the Lost, The Last Banana, Lost Tribe of the Tapiocas, Trouble at the Mill, The Web of Evil, The Mummy's Curse, The Night Patrol, Fog of Fear, A Tank Full of Trouble, Double Trouble, Intergalactic Olympics, Night of the Nerks, The Snowman Cometh, The Pirate TV Station, The Battle of the Bridge, Harbour of Lost Ships, Visibility Zero, Battle of the Century, The Perils of Ping Pong, The Great Air Race, Clown Capers, Banana Junction, The Crown Jewel Caper, Operational Total, Memory Lane. Producers Trevor Bond and Terry Ward. Director Terry Ward. Monday 3 October 1983 to Wednesday 15 June 1988, BBC1.

HUMPHREY BARCLAY

Born on 24 March 1941, Barclay had theatrical glamour in the family, his cousin was *Salad Days* composer Julian Slade. As part of the Cambridge Footlights, he worked with Tim Brooke-Taylor and Bill Oddie, directing the hugely successful revue *Cambridge Circus*. Performance credits were limited but Barclay did appear during the West End run before trying for a position at the BBC. Like Brooke-Taylor, he failed to get his application for general traineeship accepted but thanks to the initial transfer of *Cambridge Circus* to BBC Radio he found a production assignment almost immediately. Teamed with the far more experienced producer Ted Taylor, the first show was practically straight revue from stage to air, although Barclay's producing credit during the opening four series of *I'm Sorry I'll Read That Again* saw the team writing effort whittled down to just Graeme Garden and Bill Oddie's surreally scripted view of the world. By 1969, Barclay was Head of Comedy at LWT, producing *Doctor in the House* and the subsequent spin-off *Doctor* series with Garden and Oddie contributing 39 half-hour episodes. In the early Nineties, Barclay and Garden reunited for another burst of television medical comedy, *Surgical Spirit*.

BARNABY

Enchanting animated tales of a bumbling, overly-friendly sheepdog, featuring the voices of Tim Brooke-Taylor as the star of the show and Harry Enfield as a rat.

Episodes: Barney Gets Into Music, Barney's Hungry Day, Barney's Treasure Hunt, Barney's Forgotten Birthday, Barney Nabs a Crook, Barney's TV Spot, Barney's Big Spring Clean, Barney the TV Director, Barney's Winter Holiday, Barney Goes to the Seaside, Barney on TV, Barney Gets a Visitor, Barney Gets Into Mischief, Barney's TV Act.
From Wednesday 8 February 1989, BBC1.

BBC-3

The very last hurrah for the golden satire boom that had kicked in with *That Was The Week That Was*, developed into *Not So Much a Programme More a Way of Life* and made stars of the Oxbridge generation of comedians and writers. Instead of David Frost, genteel Robert Robertson was in the chair, presenting the familiar mix of topical sketches, topical film interludes, topical serious discussion and topical songs provided by Lynda Baron. Leonard Rossiter made an early mark, John Bird cut

deep with his Harold Wilson interludes, Alan Bennett (finding his feet post-*Beyond the Fringe*) presented his legendary monologue on Virginia Woolf, and Kenneth Tynan broke the ultimate television taboo by uttering the 'F' word on the edition screened 13 November 1965. Bill Oddie was employed as occasional actor but, in the main, performed original songs, often from the *I'm Sorry I'll Read That Again* collection. Featured in the opening edition, broadcast on 2 October 1965, Oddie was prominent in much of the first batch but, despite returning for New Year's Day 1966, was seldom used in subsequent 1966 editions, replaced, in the main, by *Not So Much* player Michael Crawford. The plug was pulled on 16 April 1966 and much of the footage was destroyed by the BBC.

ROBERT ROBERTSON, ALAN BENNETT, LYNDA BARON, DAVID BATTLEY, JOHN BIRD, ELEANOR BRON, PATRICK CAMPBELL, MICHAEL CRAWFORD, ROY DOTRICE, JOHN FORTUNE, MALCOLM MUGGERIDGE, DENIS NORDEN, BILL ODDIE, HARVEY ORKIN, LEONARD ROSSITER, NORMAN ST JOHN STEVAS. Written by Christopher Booker, Caryl Brahms, Peter Dobereiner, David Frost, Herbert Kretzmer, Peter Lewis, John Mortimer, David Nathan, Bill Oddie, Peter Shaffer, David Turner, Steven Vinaver, Dick Vosburgh and Keith Waterhouse. Producer Ned Sherrin. Directed by Ned Sherrin and Darrol Blake. Saturdays, 2 October 1965–16 April 1966, BBC1.

THE BERT NEWTON SHOW

On 7 October 1993, Bill Oddie was interviewed on the serious topic of conservation for this down-under chat show during his birding trip to Australia.

BEST FOOTLIGHTS FORWARD

A radio documentary examining the legendary success of the Cambridge Footlights. Graeme Garden was the perfect, witty host for the show, while the glories of Peter Cook, John Cleese, Stephen Fry, Hugh Laurie and Emma Thompson were recaptured through archive material. Douglas Adams, Clive Anderson, John Bird, Eleanor Bron, Rory McGrath and Bill Oddie were interviewed for the show.

Tuesday 5 August 1998, Radio 2.

THE BEST MEDICINE: GRAEME GARDEN'S BOOK OF MEDICAL HUMOUR

A collection of comic medical anecdotes compiled and illustrated by Dr Graeme Garden. All profits went to charity and the celebrities who contributed hospital quips and memories included Ronnie Barker, Paul Daniels, Paul Eddington, Frankie Howerd, Derek Nimmo, Julie Walters, Kenneth Williams and Mike Yarwood.

Robson Books 1984.

BEST OF... THE GOODIES

A greatest hits round-up of the Bradley's Goodies recordings compiled for only the Australian market. A standard release apart from an alternative version of *Sick Man Blues*.

The Funky Gibbon, Black Pudding Bertha, Charles Aznovoice, The Inbetweenies, Sick Man Blues, Good Ol' Country Music, Panic, Father Christmas Do Not Touch Me, The Goodies Theme. M7 MLX-150.

BILL ODDIE

Not the man but the radio show. During a Radio 2 break for Derek Jameson, Bill Oddie stepped into the slot. The *Radio Times* asked, 'What's a Goodie like him doing in a place like this?'

Thursday 20, Monday 24, Monday 31 August, Tuesday 1–Friday 4 September 1987, Radio 2.

BILL ODDIE – BIRD-WATCHER

A *Nature Watch* special edition with roving reporter Julian Pettifer tracing the progress of the complete and perfect British bird-watcher – one WE Oddie Esq., of course. Bill discusses the origins of his obsession, recalling catching the bird bug as a youngster, revisiting old haunts from his youth and explaining why his fascination continues to grow. Indeed, this was the beginning of a whole new career for the ex-Goodie, as our foremost broadcaster and writer on the subject.

Did You Know? Bill was interviewed for the article Birds About Town by James Gilheany and Malcolm Penny, published in the TV Times, 27 July–2 August 1985.

Director/Producer Geoff Raison. Tuesday 30 July 1985, ITV.

BILL ODDIE'S BIRDING MAP OF BRITAIN AND IRELAND

A beginners' field guide from Britain's best-loved birder. A *Saga Magazine* interview, 'The Birdman of Hampstead', plugged the publication.

Written by Bill Oddie and David Tipling. New Holland Publishers 1999.

BILL ODDIE'S BIRDS OF BRITAIN AND IRELAND

A definitive, blow-by-blow guide to the nations' bird population with witty and informative commentary from the birding Goodie and some 1000 illustrations for easy identification.

Written by Bill Oddie and Dave Daly. New Holland Publishers 1998. The same publishers released *Bill Oddie's Birds of Britain* in February 2000.

BILL ODDIE'S GONE BIRDING

The thrilling and fascinating story of Bill's early bird-watching life, relating tales of discovered bad eggs, water bailiffs, interesting schoolgirls, disgruntled farmers, puffins and those birds he just couldn't identify.

Methuen 1983.

BILL ODDIE'S GRIPPING YARNS

Bill's selection of outlandish and amusing birding tales.

A&C Black 2000.

BILL ODDIE'S LITTLE BLACK BIRD BOOK

Condensing a lifelong love into one handy published companion, this is Bill's funniest and most invaluable birding book. A massive elongation of the How to be a Bird-watcher section from *The Goodies File* (which is the only place to start), Bill's aggressive, besotted enthusiastic passion radiates from every page and there's more than enough fun to be had even for the most vehement anti-watcher. Distancing himself from other celeb supporters (Billy Fury, Robert Dougal, Eric Morecambe and most of the Royal family), Bill Oddie reveals himself as the genuine article, happy to suffer for his passion. The book kicks off with some tongue-in-cheek praise about the author and Bill Oddie's qualifications, detailing the first sign of interest (keeping a newly discovered egg in May 1947) through to initial birding holidays, being side-tracked by 'doing silly radio and television programmes and making idiotic records' and on to continuing his search abroad through the Seventies. Cherish the youthful pics from Fair Isle and the bogged down Bill in India, 1979. The author's forward sets the scene before Chapter One, Why Watch Birds? – What Makes a Bird-watcher Tick? which tackles the bleeding obvious right away. A little background information, characteristics of your typical bird person, a convincing contrast with stamp-collectors and train-spotters, and an all important run through of the lists birders keep, gets the juices flowing. Chapter Two, What Am I? What Are You? splits the atom to define the serious ornithologist, the comic Baden Powell boy scout implication of the bird-spotter, the joker's dream: bird-fancier (aren't we all mate…), the overused, uncool bird-watcher and the preferred, 'ruggedness' of birder. The obsessed, do anything to tick that bird, band of twitchers are also dealt with as are any harm that can come to a young fellow or environmental location and the rules of the game: no dead or zoo escapees allowed… so cross them out! Chapter Three, Equipment and Clothing, gallops through the essentials from binoculars and a super-hip telescope to the dreaded anorak. There's also a useful identification chart for spotting spotters. By his own, *I'm Sorry I'll Read That Again* wallowing admission ('Oh what a give away!') Bill falls into the 'immature male', foul-mouthed league! Chapter Four, Identification, unfolds the joy of actually working out what a bird is and explaining that, as a rule, that black bird is almost always a starling regardless of your elaborate description. Chapter Five, Covering the Cock-up, is a straight to the point guide to getting over birding disbelievers via both the two-bird theory – where in the great scheme of things they saw the common bird, you saw the rare one – or the rather less convincing pitch that your sighting looked a bit funny… pull the

BILL ODDIE IN DRAG – HARDLY A NEW FROCK!

other one. Chapter Six, Brightening Up a Dull Day, continues Bill's unhealthy obsession with Richards' Pipit to illustrate a way to get the 'rarities' buzz from common sightings, while Chapter Seven, Bird Books, wittingly sifts through what's on offer and continually plugs the 'must have' field guides. Chapter Eight, Bird Noises, examines the thrill of a trill and promotes the safety in numbers system for true identification while mocking the 'old wives tale' bird signals akin to human speech; after all, have you ever heard anybody say 'A little bit of bread and nooo cheese', well, there you are then. Chapter Nine is the fairly self-explanatory Where to Look for Birds – hint, it's not by putting your head in a gas oven… although… Chapter 10, Listening to the Layman, sets out ways of disquieting the birding novice. That really rare bird in their garden is a Jay and not a Sinai Rosefinch, honestly, although it could be a roller! Chapter 11, Specialised Pursuits, relates fun and games bird-watching at sea, with Chapter 12 proving a helpful way of dealing with the pub bore/pub clown. Mind you, Bill's already endearingly jokey style takes a turn towards *Goodies* anarchic with his parody of the RSPB's *Bird* magazine and Chapter 13's collection of jolly birding shanties. Resurrect *The Music Man*'s multi-trombones as 76 Greenshanks, pay homage to George Formby with When I'm Watching Warbles or even get all Mel Blanc-like with I Tawt I Taw A Spotted Crake. Great fun. In the mid-Eighties the book went out of print and instantly became a hotly sought after collector's item among birders. Almost a decade later, it was reissued, with a surreally confusing white cover, in its original form apart from an updated recommended reading list and a 'new introductory bit' hilariously debating to amend the text, reflecting on the last 15 years and happily taking the easier, more sensible option of leaving the thing as it was. *The British Birds Magazine* dubbed it 'the funniest book on bird-watching I have ever read' and you'll get no argument from me.

Eyre Methuen 1980. Reprinted Robson Books 1995.

BILL'S NEW FROCK

Bill Oddie starred in this radio dramatisation of Anne Fine's best selling story as the poor unfortunate who wakes up one morning to find he has turned into a girl!

Wednesday 20 March 1991, Radio 5.

THE BILLY BUNTER STORIES

'I say you fellows… Billy Bunter's back!' A glorious descent against political correctness, this 1993 radio series of six Billy Bunter tales rejoiced in cries of 'fattie', wallowed in racial stereotypes (with choice Indian and American creations from Graeme) and upper class twits, widened the class system gaps, promoted bullying and celebrated caning in educational establishments. But more to the point, these richly comic recreations of Frank Richards's bygone age reunited Tim Brooke-Taylor, Graeme Garden and Bill Oddie for its sterling cast. As with the *Bananaman* shorts, each ex-Goodie played several supporting roles throughout the run although Tim, delightfully turned on the charm regularly as the Terry-Thomas-style Bob Cherry ('Hello, hello, hello'), while Graeme cruised through the final two instalments as the infamous reform tutor, Mr Quelch. As for the fat owl of Greyfriars, the tuck-pinching, wheeze-pulling, much-kicked, conceited young ass, William George Bunter, there was only one man for the job, Bill Oddie, of course. Tittering at others misfortune, strolling through the stories with listlessness, grabbing tarts, cakes and doughnuts at every corner, promoting laziness as the only way to live and wailing 'Yaroo!' with each new crisis, it was a part Bill was born for. Initially, one waits for Tim's narrator to crack dreadful puns or twist one of the character's comments into a joke but this isn't *I'm Sorry I'll Read That Again* or, indeed, a resurrection of the *I'm Sorry* team's Bunter presentation from Series Seven. The performances may sound identical but this is played with comic respect for the written pieces and positively glows with charm.

BUNTER THE HERO

Our fat friend is misdirected by his fellow pupils and sold a duff coconut by Graeme's canny gypsy, Joseph. Untypically, the forever-hungry schoolboy rescues the gypsy's young daughter from the railway lines, grabs three fat nuts for his reward (still no jokey comments!) and has his bravery totally disbelieved by his chums – 'Beasts!' A wonderful opening episode adapted from *Bunter, the Hero* reaching a Goodie-esque peak with Tim's earnest narrative celebration of Bunter's 'genuine British pluck' as *Land of Hope and Glory* soars in the background. Glorious stuff.

BILLY BUNTER AFLOAT

The fat owl stumbles on a letter confirming boat hire, grabs it himself and secures *The Nautalas* for a jolly day out on the river. Suddenly flavour of the month with his pals, things turn sour when the rightful punter, Mr Coker, tackles the boat-keeper and the famous five plus Billy are on the threat of a good beating. Typically, the boys turn on the fat one, rescue Coker from a watery fate and enjoy the boat in comfort. Bill's his usual outstanding self as Bunter but it's as the cranky boat-keeper, suppressing laughter opposite Graeme's repeated, angst-ridden Coker, that he really steals the show.

BILLY BUNTER ON TRIAL

The classic story of Bunter's relentless search for tasty tuck leads him to mock legal condemnation from his peers. The whole thing, of course, is corrupt, with Tim's sleepy judge hanging around through the pomp just waiting to deliver his guilty sentence. Graeme's Northern prosecuting counsel has the easiest time of it – the boy is guilty of food stuffing 24 hours a day – but Tim, 30 years since his Cambridge law education, bravely tackles the boy's defence with relish. He is found guilty, naturally, and kicked for his trouble, but Tim's towering, impassioned performance bristles with confidence.

BUNTER IN BRAZIL

The lads are off into darkest Brazil and Bunter's dragged along for the ride. Complaining from the outset, causing problems and demanding rests all the time, Bunter is his expected dead weight self. Even more so, in fact, when he feigns a sprained ankle, screams his medical inaccuracies at the fellows and demands to be carried for the rest of the way. A sudden brush with a less than friendly native soon cures the scurrying scoundrel and his lies are dealt with in the only civilised way – a jolly good kicking!

BUNTER'S NIGHT OUT

Illegal trespassing on private land gets the boys pulses racing, although it's Bunter who comes face to face with the keeper, falls foul of his toothy terrier, Tiger, and nervously gulps back his fear as an eerie trek through the country turns obvious owl noises into potential ghosts. Taken from *Billy Bunter and the Blue Mauritius*, Bill's performance is rich with comic invention during this classic solo spot and reaches a pinnacle in confused discussion with Tim's addled old gentry who continually fails to grasp the boy's name before dismissing it as stupid anyway. Bunter's bungled and unaware interaction during a burglary sort of gets him out of grief but Graeme's Quelch makes a stunning first appearance, whispering disdain, while the semi-brave tale is emblazoned with Billy falsehoods for a suitably mocked retelling to his school pals.

CHUNKLEY'S STORES

A classic to finish on, Bunter hatches his most brilliant wheeze ever, impersonating the dreaded Quelch on the telephone and succeeding in ordering copious amounts of tuck. A stunning bit of confused business with the store's switchboard system leaves Bill's starving fat boy even more wheezed out than usual, but eventually the deed is done and the food is awaited. However, things don't run smoothly when Graeme's tyrannical teacher turns up and discovers the collection of sweetmeat consumables. In a delightful bit of character work, Tim's narrator explains that the rant man's taste for confectionery has failed him and Graeme can semi-share in a comic deconstruction of Bill's aged tutor. The guard is down for just a second though and soon the fat boy is running from the cane-wielding fury of his master. Curtain – commission the second series... oh go on. Beasts!

Written by Frank Richards. Produced by Melanie Miller. Tuesdays, 13 July–17 August 1993, Radio 2.

BIRD IN THE NEST

In his bird-watching element, Bill Oddie presented a Bank Holiday live broadcast covering five different nesting sites across Britain. In discussion with RSPB representative Peter Holden and surrounded by a bank of television monitors contained within the BBC Birdmobile, Bill commented on progress in the Blue Tit garden, Kestrel nest, the ill-fated Kingfisher retreat, his beloved robins happily protected in an outside loo and the swallows, safe within a farmyard setting. A family of wagtails secured in the tool box of a working, active tractor, proved an added bonus at the swallow location and promoted a Bob Marley's *Don't Worry 'Bout a Thing* backed montage of other bizarre nests suggested by viewers for the update programme screened three weeks later.

BILL ODDIE with PETER HOLDEN and SIMON KING. Producer Hilary Jeffkins. Director Roy Chapman. BBC 1994.

BILL ODDIE'S LONELY VIGIL

HAVE TELESCOPE WILL TRAVEL... A STUNNING SHOT OF BILL ODDIE AT HIS HAPPIEST

BIRD IN THE NEST: the book

The book of the series written by Bill Oddie.

Robson Books 1995. Parkway Publications, paperback, 1996.

BIRD WEEK

In the days when Tony Soper was television's Mr Bird Man, Bill Oddie was reduced to a one-off appearance in this five-day celebration of 40 years of bird-watching. With such treats as the great Birdtable Mastermind, a crow lighting a match and a tit outwitting humans, Bill's brief interlude came live from Slimbridge on the fourth programme in the run.

TONY SOPER, NICK DAVIES, BILL ODDIE. Producer Robin Hellier. Director Alastair Fothergill. Thursday 13 November 1986, BBC1.

BIRDING IN KENT

A guide to the best the county can offer written by Don Taylor and Bill Oddie.

Pica Press 1996.

BIRDING WITH BILL ODDIE

What Michael Palin had became to world travel, Bill Oddie was to ornithology. Combining hilarious writing and presentation skills with an unflagging, zestful passion for his subject, this series provided the perfect scope for the complete bird-watching compendium.

SERIES ONE

1: Bill visits a reserve at Minsmere, Suffolk. **2:** A search for osprey, golden eagle and the rare slavanian grebe in the Scottish highlands. **3:** August Bank Holiday at Rutland and the British Bird-watching Fair exposes Bill's talent for bird art, a bit of fun with a tree sparrow and a manic Bird Race. **4:** A look at the magic of migration from the Farne Islands and a brief encounter with an Arctic tern. **5:** Canada geese on the Island of Islay in Scotland and a trip to Brent Reservoir. **6:** It's a case of from bald eagle to Donald Duck on the family holiday in

Florida, with birding at the JFK Space Centre, delight in a burrowing owl and vultures over the Magic Kingdom!

SERIES TWO

1: The Shetlands, Bill's favourite haunt, allows close-up access to curlews, golden plovers and an awe-inspiring moment with a puffin. **2:** Farmland fun with a family of house martins, a deconstruction of Wordworth's Ode to a Skylark and a charming sighting of the Little Owl. **3:** Dorset and the New Forest with cygnets and a trip to the RSPB reserve. **4:** Bill's beginnings with a return to his childhood location, Birmingham's Bartley Reservoir. **5:** Choice birding in London. **6:** A journey to Trinidad in the West Indies finds Bill on the trail of the common bare-eyed thrush, large and small-billed terns, and the ultra-rare oil bird.

SERIES THREE

Featured Bill in Majorca, Wales, Poland, the Netherlands, America and Israel. The interview circuit allowed Bill time to have another moan about no Goodie repeat on Ian Payne's live Radio 5 show.

Did you know? A popular and Bill-active website allowed viewers to go on-line and have their birding questions answered by Oddie. To tie in with the programme, Bill Oddie contributed an article, 'I Was a Juvenile Egg Robber', for the June 1998 issue of BBC Wildlife Magazine. The second series was greeted with the full Radio Times advertising campaign, with Gareth Huw Davies conducting Oddie interviews for 'Where You Can Watch the Birdie' and Bill's 'My Kind of Day' showing the great man surrounded by his Mickey Mouse-packed kitchen and a Simpsons Chess Set.

Produced and directed by Stephen Moss. **Series One:** Wednesdays, 21 February–28 March 1997. **Series Two:** Fridays, 11 May–8 June 1998. **Series Three:** Fridays, 18 February–31 March 2000, BBC2.

BIRDING WITH BILL ODDIE: A PRACTICAL GUIDE TO BIRD-WATCHING

Written by Bill Oddie and Stephen Moss. BBC Books, paperback, 1997.

BIRDS OF EILAT

An Israeli bird-watching television documentary by Bill Oddie.

BIRD-WATCHING WITH BILL ODDIE: THE BIRD-WATCHER'S HANDBOOK

Getting slightly more serious about his subject, although still tinged with the comic touch that sweetens the informative pill, this book goes over similar ground to *Bill Oddie's Little Black Bird Book* with an additional spotters field guide section. A witty foreword from Bill is followed with a chapter on essential equipment – binoculars, telescope, notebook, pencil and clothes, naturally – as well as a charming illustration of a Blue Tit looking at himself in a book and muttering 'Do I really look like that?' Throughout the book there are copious photographs of Bill enjoying his hobby, although it's all the feathered friends in Identifying Birds with tips on everything from Pipits to birds of prey that forms the project's heart. Making the Most of Your Time celebrates 24-hour bird races in aid of wildlife charities and details the best places for watching in town, woodlands, reservoirs and the like. Making Mistakes gently mocks the notion of identification via computer while endorsing the gut reaction – the essence or 'jizz' of a bird. The bulk of the book, The Birds, is an honest, incomplete gallop through the most seen British species, with a half-time break and classification between bigger and small birds. These 65 pages are very reassuringly uncomplicated and user friendly. To Twitch or Not To Twitch again covers these obsessive watchers, Birdwatching in the Rest of Europe and Beyond tackles Bill's out of Britain experiences and A Final Thought positively drips with devotion to the subject. Things are rounded off with a useful recommended reading guide and societies worth joining.

Macmillan Press Limited 1988. Reprinted by Papermac 1989.

BLACK CINDERELLA II GOES EAST

Or Confessions of a Glass Slipper Tryer Onner – the show that will do for pantomime what Mozart did for fluid mechanics. With seasonal panto fever balanced with minority considerations, big screen sequel convention and knowing Biggles reference, the *I'm Sorry I'll Read That Again* team unofficially reunited for this hour-long Christmas knees-up. Importantly, the gang were joined by respected elder statesmen of the comedy airwaves, Richard Murdoch, and loose canon, funniest man of the century, Peter Cook, as the glorious evil Prince Disgusting. Tim Brooke-Taylor, Graeme Garden and Bill Oddie delighted in the campy, bitchy roles of the three Ugly Sisters. Rob Buckman turned on the

Ecky Thump!

mock charm as Prince Charming, Jo Kendall ripped through her Wicked Stepmother, Liberal MP John Pardoe sent himself up as the Fairy Land Liberal Prime Minister and John Cleese minced through his politically correct role as Fairy Godperson. The *Radio Times* included the writer's explanation of the Cambridge connection, 'the fact that every one involved in this show is an ex-member of Cambridge Footlights is completely coincidental and has nothing to do with any form of nepotism or old boy network at all, whatsoever, honestly.'

With RICHARD BAKER, CHRIS BEETLES, DAVID HATCH and MAGGIE HENDERSON. Script by Rory McGrath and Clive Anderson. Produced by Douglas Adams. Monday 25 December 1978, Radio 2.

BLACK PUDDING BERTHA (THE QUEEN OF NORTHERN SOUL)

The mystic ethos of black puddings and Northern chip pans had already featured heavily in the Series Five classic, *Kung Fu Kapers*, before this sublime Oddie-written number crept into the Top 20 and struck a long-standing nerve with the Goodies follower. Second only in popularity to the *Funky Gibbon*, *Black Pudding Bertha* is a raucous romp, incorporating the essence of brass band melody with the hip energy of disco fever. Presenting an Anglicised version of The Beach Boys hit *California Girls* — with Southern chicks failing to match their Northern counterparts —

Oddie pre-empts the good-natured sexism of the much-debated Queen song, *Fat Bottomed Girls*, with his cheery imagery of greasy lips and shaking bums. Besides that, it's also very funny, with really groovy keyboard backing, a stunning bass guitar riff and ''E, By gum'' chanting spinning into infinity. Far less potent and certainly less celebrated, the B-side song, *Panic*, is, nevertheless, an undervalued Oddie classic, featuring inventive, challenging lyrics and a delicious sense of relaxed, anti-patriotic satire. With half-hearted cries of 'England' in the angst-ridden style of frustrated sports fans, the fundamental reality of strikes, bleak crisis and poverty is at the heart of this deceptively optimistic piece. Endorsing the great British skill of panicking in the face of adversity, this cheerfully chugging salute to the national psyche is lead by Bill's upbeat vocals and the very British acceptance that everything is getting worse. Graeme, presenting his best BBC newscaster tones to highlight historical events where panic was paramount, allows Bill the laugh – notably the unquestioned but unconvinced chorus of 'Panic!?!' when the love match between Anthony and Cleopatra is mentioned – and there's a stunning musical shift to include a brief snatch of the *National Anthem* fully to drive the grit in the Brits' situation home.

Did You Know? The single entered the charts on 21 June 1975 and stayed for seven weeks. Its highest chart position was number 19.
BRAD 7517 Bradley's Records 1975.

BLANKETY BLANK

During the classic days of Terry Wogan and his stick microphone, Tim Brooke-Taylor joined in the innuendo-laden fun of this celebratory panel game on Tuesday 22 May 1984. When the Irish charmer gave way to the cynical gruff of Les Dawson, Bill Oddie threw caution to the wind and played the game on Friday 21 October 1988.

BLOWING OFF

The only single released from the album *Nothing To Do with Us*, this is a wonderfully tasteless Oddie-scribed Goodies effort. For the first time on a Goodies A-side, lead vocals are handed over to Graeme Garden, wallowing in his frequent country and western singer guise and pouring his wind-breaking heart out to the nation. It's a three-minute musical tribute to the spirit of *Le Petomaine* with relentless sound effects from Billy Kristian. Guaranteed to offend your Auntie – surely a huge vote in its favour – Graeme relishes the lyrics, farting his way to the top of the New Orleans scene, joyfully repeating the 'It's a gas' hook chorus and graphically celebrating his difficult birth with the unforgettable line – 'what goes in ain't nothing to what comes out!' Shocker! Bill Oddie comes back to the fore for the classic B-side, *Elizabeth Rules – UK!* An angst-ridden love letter to the Queen, it moodily starts with Beatles-esque atmosphere akin to the opening chords of *Lucy in the Sky with Diamonds* while the lyrical quality of the piece further suggests McCartney's *Back in the USSR* and, most notably, *Her Majesty,* the final track on the final Beatles album. The song is also heavily influenced by 10cc's *I'm Not in Love*, even down to Charlie Dore's regal response begging the lovesick Oddie to 'try not to cry!' Besotted with spending a penny and licking stamps to see his lady love's smiling face this is an epic track of forbidden passion. Venomously attacking the 'old man' drinking, swearing and standing around the place with his hands behind his back, Bill creates a mini-patriotic masterpiece.
WIP 6360 Island December 1976.

BLUE PETER

The Goodies made four appearances on the perennial BBC children's magazine programme. They performed *Stuff That Gibbon* on the 7 April 1975, *Make a Daft Noise for Christmas* on 17 November 1975 and *M.I.C.K.E.Y. M.O.U.S.E.* on 11 May 1978. They returned in 1983 to promote *Bananaman*.

THE FINAL APPEARANCE OF THE GOODIES ON *BLUE PETER*, CHATTING TO PRESENTERS SIMON GROOM AND JANET ELLIS ABOUT THE CARTOON ANTICS OF *BANANAMAN*

BODY MATTERS

A magical mystery tour of our own flesh and blood. While Terry Jones made history anarchic, Graeme Garden put his medical training to good entertaining use for this BBC series designed to instruct on basic facts via silly games, gigantic working models of human bits 'n' pieces and an 'audience of intrepid volunteers'. Happy to throw himself into the madness of presenting, Graeme was lifted up by bearded monster Geoff Capes and perched like a parrot on his huge biceps. He was even hung upside-down to illustrate how the eyes play tricks – filmed the right way up, looking normal and highlighting the reverse point of view by pouring out a glass of champagne… upwards. Clever stuff all round.

Did You Know? *The first episode of Series One was accompanied with a Radio Times article, 'You Should See the Doctor', with Graeme Garden contrasting his serious colleagues with a wacky pair of comic glasses, while the third series was heralded by another Radio Times piece (25–31 July 1987), with Graeme explaining, 'We presenters are made of stern stuff… it says so in our contracts'. Series Four, in 1988, was initially promoted with a brief article in the 31 July–4 August issue.*

Series One: More Than Meets the Eye, How To Do It Standing Up, Breathing Spaces, Skin Talk, On Your Knees, Mind Over Matter, Family Fortunes. Thursdays, 25 July–12 September 1985, BBC1. **Series Two:** What A Mouthful!, Speakeasy, You're Got A Nerve!, Hair Today, Gone Tomorrow, Muscling In, Forget Me Not, Male Mothers, A Cure For Infertility?, Gut Feelings. Thursdays, 31 July–18 September 1986, BBC1. **Series Three:** Bloody Matters, Ouch!, Ear We Go!, As Time Goes By, Wake Up To Sleep, Hands Up, Body Electric, Dem Bones, Dem Bones… Thursdays, 30 June–17 September 1987, BBC1. **Special:** Cancer – To mark Europe Against Cancer Week, Thursday 5 May 1988, BBC1. **Series Four:** Water, The Beat Goes On, Radiation – Fact and Fiction, Against All Odds, The Fats of Life, What's Your Poison?, Body Heat. Thursdays, 4 August–15 September 1989, BBC1. Presented by Dr GRAEME GARDEN, Dr ALAN MARYON, Dr GILLIAN RICE. Studio director Stuart McDonald. Series editor David Filkin. Programme Associate John Junkin.

BOUNCE

A vastly under-rated Bill Oddie song which failed to reach the Top 40 after a successful string of five hit singles for the Goodies. The last single release from Bradley's records, it was a case of back-tracking to past glories for continued pop fame, with the number having originally featured in the Series Two episode *Charity Bounce*. This is a full-blooded version of the number, kicking off with Tim – in definitive military rant mode – patriotically geeing up the masses with his enthused 'Come along everybody, let's bounce for Britain!' A George Harrison-style guitar riff keeps the thing moving along impressively, while Graeme enjoys himself with Nazi-like efficiency, spitting out bouncing orders with fiendish glee. A smooth French verse, a further very bizarre Welsh outburst and Tim's frightfully posh, politically geared 'No, bounce to the right!' muttering, all hit the right comedy buttons but it's Bill's really rather fab, screeched 'bounce all night!' invitation for rock 'n' roll excess that sets this one apart. A wailed country interlude, concluding spiralling violins and a delicious slag off of other musical styles (The Twist and the Quick, Quick, Slow) sets things up rather nicely for *Good Ole Country Music* which generously hands the lead vocals over to Graeme. He delivers a total hatchet job on country music with a priceless performance of mournful, blinkered obsession to songs of heartache and pain. With aversion to everything from the Beatles to Bing Crosby's crooning, a stunning jaunty piano and slide guitar backing adds power to the delivery, culminating lines with off-beat coyote howling. The 'sing me the harmony!' instruction following the instrumental interlude gives vent to Bill Oddie's rousing backing, turning on the cowboy hick attitude with true passion.

BRAD 7612 Bradley's Records May 1976.

BREAKAWAY

A Radio 4 holiday programme, produced by Sara Jay Hall and presented by Bill Oddie on Saturday mornings from 10 October 1992 to 27 February 1993.

BROADEN YOUR MIND: AN ENCYCLOPAEDIA OF THE AIR

The final rung on the ladder before Brooke-Taylor, Garden and Oddie forever became linked as the Goodies, this important comedy sketch show was the brainchild of Tim. Inspired by the galaxy of weekly publications building up to a complete set of encyclopaedias on certain subjects, this was the stick and paste together television alternative, presenting a series of semi-linked comic lectures, spoofed educational programmes and comically relevant songs.

SERIES ONE

Primarily scripted by Tim Brooke-Taylor and Graeme Garden, reheated moments from past glories (*Cambridge Circus* and *I'm Sorry I'll Read That Again*) and supporting performers Bill Oddie and Jo Kendall, provided a backdrop of familiarity. The spirit of *Round the Horne* was delivered via Took and Feldman's viewer competitions, while the new age of comic tradition was well covered with on-screen and writing contributions from all the

British, immediate pre-Python brigade. However, the major hit of the series was Graeme and Tim's beloved old buffers, Teddy and Freddy, whose joyous, aged eccentricity staggered through long-winded explanations of a wide variety of topics. Sort of like David Baddiel and Rob Newman's history experts from *The Mary Whitehouse Experience*, with the malice removed, they gave the show an endearing quality. With each staggering off the point, comic misunderstanding building on comic misunderstanding and Tim helpfully providing the odd, and often very odd, sound effect to the scene, these were fondly performed, spirallingly written comedy gems. The essence of Teddy and Freddy was, later, lovingly recreated for the tail-end of *The Goodies* masterpiece, *The End*. Interestingly enough, the series also firmly rooted Tim and Graeme in their familiar stereotypes adopted for *The Goodies* a few short years on. Tim, refined and sophisticated but prone to panic attacks, would introduce the topics for comic discussion and nervously relate viewer's opinions on the programme, while Graeme as often as not, referred to his new-fangled computer for assistance. At one stage, the machine took over the entire show when the lads inadvertently vanished.

EPISODE ONE

Art: abstract paintings and how to understand them. History: the Magna Carta as interpreted by Teddy and Freddy. Music: a visual representation of Oddie's *I'm Sorry I'll Read That Again* opera, *El Budgerigar*. Law: pre-empting Episode Three of the first *Goodies* series, a discussion and filmed interlude on the fact that British policeman have a bad image but they only desire to help and be loved. Hospitality: the social technique in dealing with unwanted house guests without uncalled for embarrassment, and finally, the Quiz in the shape of a bizarre IQ Test.

EPISODE TWO

Tim Brooke-Taylor reveals the true and praise-laden, made-up viewer's opinion on the first *Broaden Your Mind* programme. Nature: a John Cleese and Graham Chapman reworking of the *At Last the 1948 Show* ant sketch in terms of birds who get their food by dropping rocks on tins of fruit. Modern languages: a stuffy business meeting is hijacked by an aggressive translator. Music: those old codgers, Teddy and Freddy attempt to sing their own composition – a cool, licking modern jazz number. Nature: Man Valley, a wordless Terry Jones and Michael

TIM BROOKE-TAYLOR GETS THE BIRD!

Palin piece twisting the Walt Disney wildlife films and presenting a similarly styled look at human activity. History: Uncle Hugh, played with eccentric panache by Graeme Garden, explains the fascinating story of how James Watt invented the steam engine to wide-eyed, naïve and inquisitive youngster, Tim (Brooke-Taylor). Science: the future of television… today with the world's first fully automatic, robotic screen personality. Quiz: the Python-esque 'Can you identify these objects?'

EPISODE THREE

The unveiling of the lad's machine for reversing time. Law: the British crime wave and how to avoid getting involved. Sociology: the eternal problem of how gentlemen recognise each other. Science: nuclear physics as ditheringly explained by Teddy and Freddy. Economics: a mock documentary film investigating the factory where British businessmen are produced. History: a much welcome resurrection for the Brooke-Taylor/Stuart-Clark *Cambridge Circus* classic, Swap-A-Jest, in which Shakespearean banter is delivered as a music hall turn. Religion: an obsessed and spiritually guided vicar adopts commercial angst and bullying tactics to increase attendance at his church services. Quiz: true or false? John is having a bath!

EPISODE FOUR

History: problems facing the Royal Air Force. Sociology: Britain's eating revolution. History: the all-time classic Teddy and Freddy sketch when attempts at relating information on Egyptology are abandoned in favour of even harder attempts at relating a joke, 'What's the difference between an egg, a carpet and a bit of crumpet?' 'You can beat an egg, you can beat a carpet but you can't beat a bit of crumpet!' Crime: an illegal Swedish 'art' movie is dubbed into refined, censored, English. Art: the sneak preview of Bill Oddie's new musical, *The Sound of Monks*, adapted from *I'm Sorry I'll Read That Again*'s merging of Julie Andrews hits, *Mary Poppins* and *The Sound of Music*, and featuring the hit song *Antibellamlaudidartaarmomutatorum*. Quiz: Arthur sets off from London in search of adventure.

EPISODE FIVE

Viewer's letters regarding *Broaden Your Mind*. Art: young Tim listens as kindly Uncle Hugh explains why great paintings are often full of nude people. Science: the historic first telephone call to America and the talking clock. Nature: a pleasant walk in the countryside with Teddy and Freddy. Agriculture: the story of how eggs get from the chicken to your breakfast table. Music: confused folk singers stumble through some numbers. Sociology: military convention at the altar with Permission to Wed and school day problems with the Quiz, George has two apples, David only has one…

EPISODE SIX

Literature: in the wake of DH Lawrence and the *Lady Chatterley's Lover* trial, a pornographic discussion on whether dirty books should be considered great literature. Folklore: Teddy and Freddy out-scare each other relating a chilling ghost story. Economics: how heavy taxing affects English currency (a spy-plane is encouraged to defect to East Germany for financial reasons). History: it's the scrap heap for 1930. Sociology: what happens when newly married couples meet old loves and, lastly, the Quiz: there are 10 mistakes in this picture, can you spot them?

TIM BROOKE-TAYLOR, GRAEME GARDEN, JO KENDALL, NICK McARDLE and BILL ODDIE (Episode Four only), GRAHAM CHAPMAN, TERRY JONES, MICHAEL PALIN. Written by Tim Brooke-Taylor and Graeme Garden. Additional material by Bob Block, Simon Brett, Graham Chapman, John Cleese, Derek Collyer, Barry Cryer, George Evans, Marty Feldman, Eric Idle, Terry Jones, Jo Kendall, John Law, David McKellar, Bill Oddie, Michael Palin, Chris Stuart-Clark, Barry Took. Producer Sydney Lotterby. Directed and edited by Jim Franklin. Mondays, 28 October–2 December 1968, BBC2.

SERIES TWO

While a crowd-pleaser, the most popular elements of the first series were moving away from dangerous comedy into cosy family entertainment. Both Tim Brooke-Taylor and Graeme Garden happily admit to having a great time scripting the shows and eagerly wandering through realms of Teddy and Freddy's gentle sparring. Their personalities and writing styles were too similar to cause creative clashes and thus fully stimulating, society-questioning comic rants were restricted. To this end, Barry Took approached the harder-edged Bill Oddie to jump fully aboard for this second series. Instructed to 'come in and be unpleasant!' he appeared in all seven editions, although his scripted contributions were mostly reworked pieces from *I'm Sorry I'll Read That Again*. However, his influence and the desire from the top for a more cynical streak was reflected in the new material penned by Brooke-Taylor and Garden. Their cherished Teddy and Freddy characters were restricted to just one appearance, while their aged bewilderment was usurped by a fresh regular slot, 'The Buffies'. This took the form of three old buffers (Brooke-Taylor, Garden and *It's Marty*'s Roland MacLeod) in an exclusive gentleman's club, taking the Four Yorkshiremen's view on the young and condemning everything à la Harry Enfield's old gits. The programme also highlighted darkly manic contributions from Graeme Garden's evil Germanic scientist, Dr Findish from the Institute of Applied Science and Not Germ Warfare, celebrating the endless roots to death and destruction with rich glee. On the other hand, Brooke-Taylor presented his whining old crone, Babs Lamour, a sort of extension of his *At Last the 1948 Show* and *It's Marty* old ladies, who would natter away on a certain subject and pepper it with compliment-seeking self-denial, 'I'm 93! I fought in the war you know, and I lost!' Another frequent spot pointed fully in the direction of *The Goodies*. Nerve-wracked Tim and logical Graeme were stuck on a giant rostrum with no visible means of support and no visible means of getting down. Tim's perennial scream of 'How do we get down?' would be greeted by Graeme's brilliant suggestion, which invariably ended in total failure. And, apart from Oddie's continual injection of class comic songs, the old theme was jazzed up for a groovy new image.

A FRESH-FACED BILL ODDIE ENJOYS PERFORMING AN ENERGETIC NUMBER DURING THE BROADWAY RUN OF *CAMBRIDGE CIRCUS*

EPISODE ONE

'How do we get down?' Jump! Archaeology: a guide to reading hieroglyphics and the skilled dating of historical artefacts by the use of torture, a performance and post-show discussion of The Grand Old Duke of York, the Evolution and search for the real Camelot. Craft: that dotty old nut Babs Lamour demonstrates the art of making things yourself. Geography: an Australian tourist travelogue made in Britain to keep the budget down, Mr Bill Oddie performs his police-geared radio hit, *My Identikit Gal*. Science: Dr Findish discusses the power of heat and reveals his controversial theory on defending England by using giant kettles and toasters, the future for plastic clothing, what happens if computers are treated like human employees and how cars react to the music being played on their radios. Quiz: how well do you know your kitchen?

EPISODE TWO

An outlandish, show business, commercially geared, overly hyped opening to the show. Music: a Palm Court Orchestra is brutally savaged by the surrounding greenery, Tubby the Tuba parody, rare silent footage of the world's greatest pianist and dedicated football supporters rehearsing their supportive chants. A mockery of Ken Russell's elaborate composer biopics with Ken Bussel's cinematic treatment of the life of Yaputcha Leftleggin, the creative genius behind almost every classic commercial jingle. 'How do we get down?' Staircase No. 1. Oddie breathes new life into his *I'm Sorry I'll Read That Again* rendition of *On Ilkla Moor Baht'at*. Meteorology: Teddy and Freddy make their only appearance for this series, predicting the weather with seaweed, a barometer, a barograph and pinecones, we are treated to a long-term weather forecast for the year 2050 and discoveries for controlling the weather are revealed, the secret life of a couple living in a weather house and the closing Quiz on medicine.

EPISODE THREE

'How do we get down?' Staircase No. 2. Money: is it safe in a bank? The history of money, a taxi driver and passenger change places, a commentary on inheritances, how foreign exchange rates can affect British television programmes sold abroad. Angling: the salmon, Bill performs his old radio classic *We Love Jimmy Young.* Sociology: the British Aristocracy (breeding aristocrats), the Buffies on Entertainment and the Atkins Family Quiz.

EPISODE FOUR

'How do we get down?' Staircase No. 3. Architecture: the anti-historic practice of replacing old buildings, cut-price builders, homes designed to fit the occupants, the cruel landlord, Irish builders and other class stereotypes. Physical education: innocent housewives following exercise tuition on the radio are subconsciously forced to commit burglaries. Another family favourite from *I'm Sorry I'll Read That Again*, *Here Comes the One-Man Band*. Agriculture: the insane mumblings of the incomprehensible rural farmer, Dr Findish delights in displaying powerful poisons for your garden and the latest in pest control, the nuclear scarecrow, we take a look inside the Night Club especially constructed for farmers and the secret pleasures of the muck spreader dance. Science: invisible mending, Quiz for men digging a ditch.

EPISODE FIVE

'How do we get down? Snake-charm a rope! Art: the human form as inspiration for great artistic works, the

Renaissance and deep psychological analysis of abstract paintings. Heritage: Britain's alternative Royal family and a portrait of Her Gracious Majesty, Ex-Queen Gladys of Stretton, the soon-to-be Goodies perform *Baby Samba*, five years before recording it properly from the original *I'm Sorry I'll Read That Again*. Medicine: the male pill, early intelligence development in very young children, the highs and lows of the common cold, Dr Findish lectures on the disease Turgonitis and a nervous and embarrassed visitor to the doctor's coyly insists 'My friend has a problem…' Quiz: Metrics and decimalization.

EPISODE SIX

'How do we get down?' Dive into a bucket of water. The Supernatural: horoscopes, prophets, spiritualism and presenting the psychic poet, Babs Lamour. Safety: highlights the multiplicity of hidden dangers in the home. Entertainment: a behind-the-scenes look at the latest British animation feature film, Snow Pinocchio and the Seven Bambis and the Tramp, being filmed with real people to keep the budget low, including the golden oldie song, *Let's Laugh*. The Army: the decline and decline of the British Army, a mad Commander who doesn't understand the meaning of the word fear, military teaching recruits artistic skills and the Buffies reminiscing about the tough days of war. Complaints focusing on real people playing the parts of animals in the latest British film and an addressing of the balance when animals are cast in the roles of people for The Hound of Music, including the legendary, oft-repeated dog rendition of *Anything You Can Do I Can Do Better*.

EPISODE SEVEN

A special edition reviewing the first 69 years of the 20th Century. The turn of the new century and the death of Queen Victoria, Babs Lamour's memories of the suffragette movement, the hectic days of the roaring Twenties, the arrival of talking pictures, a stagy recreation of the Thirties' stage farce tradition, the first BBC television pictures from 1939 and Neville Chamberlain's paper tearing trick after talks with Herr Hitler – a gag later adapted by John Cleese for *Peter Cook and Company* in 1980. The Second World War edition of *It's a Knockout* inspiration *Guerre Sans Frontiers*. A television programme teaches French, Dr Findish presents a brief (and typically gruesome) history of electricity and, finally, bang up-to-date comment on the decade's permissive society and a look at the new musical smash hit, Knees, Britain's less controversial answer to the naked love-in of *Hair*.

Did You Know? *Although one of the BBC's flagship comedy programmes and one of immense importance in the development of television through the Seventies, the BBC archive retains no master-prints of any of Broaden Your Mind's 13 episodes. Remnants have survived, including the Jones/Palin visual snips rescued thanks to the archivist tenacity of Terry Jones, and the singing dogs from Series Two, Episode Six which later, of course, appeared to even greater success, in The Goodies: Kitten Kong. A brief extract from Series Two, Episode two was included in the 30-minute compilation special, BBC2's Company of Comedy (transmitted 26 December 1969) in which host John Cleese celebrated the best in BBC2 comedy for the year. Amateur off-air audio recordings of all 13 programmes are also in existence.*

TIM BROOKE-TAYLOR, GRAEME GARDEN, JO KENDALL, BILL ODDIE, ROLAND MacLEOD, NICK McARDLE. Written by Tim Brooke-Taylor and Graeme Garden. Additional material by Bill Oddie and Roland MacLeod. Producer Sydney Lotterby. Directed and edited by Jim Franklin. Mondays, 17 November–29 December 1969, BBC2.

Broader and broader...

The BBC were very pleased with the results of *Broaden Your Mind* Series Two and happily considered commissioning a third series for broadcast towards the end of 1970. Tim Brooke-Taylor, Graeme Garden and Bill Oddie were less than interested in the idea. With Chapman, Cleese, Idle, Jones and Palin having left after Series One and founded *Monty Python's Flying Circus* in October 1969, the trio felt there was little point in trying to battle it out in the sketch show format. A decision was made to move away from the form completely and try to construct some sort of surreal situation comedy in which the three recognised characterisations could interact and evolve. Close ties with *Broaden Your Mind* were planned for the new hybrid and a very serious working title idea for the show was *Narrow Your Mind*. This was eventually dropped and the programme finally began life in November 1970, as *The Goodies*.

BRING ME THE HEAD OF LIGHT ENTERTAINMENT

A comedy game show devised by comedian Lee Hurst for the fledgling and floundering Channel 5. A bizarre mix of *Have I Got News For You*, topical one-liners and the surreally silly parlour games of *I'm Sorry I Haven't a Clue*, two episodes wallowed in the comic assurance of panellists Tim Brooke-Taylor and Graeme Garden on 22 February and 29 March 1998.

BRITISH SCREEN AWARDS

The Goodies was nominated as Best Light Entertainment Programme in March 1976.

TIM BROOKE-TAYLOR

Actor, scriptwriter, doctor of law, teacher, director, Union flag waistcoat wearer, editor, author, Goodie and comic genius, Timothy Julian Brooke-Taylor was born on 17 July 1940. Illustrious experience in sport was the family's claim to fame, with his mother an international lacrosse player and Cheltenham School sports mistress, while his maternal grandfather, Parson Pawson, had played centre forward for England in the 1890s. Despite a passion for cricket, golf and football, a lifelong supporter of Derby County (he is the club's Honorary Vice-President), show business was Tim's first love. A fan of film comedy from Buster Keaton to Abbott and Costello's various brushes with Universal's monsters and radio comedy from Tony Hancock, Frank Muir, Denis Norden, Sam Costa and Richard Murdoch, Tim was star struck by visits to local pantomimes. Legends like Norman Evans as the Dame fuelled his theatrical interest, while local performer Patrick Cargill instilled a sense of innovative humour with panto principal boys played on skates. The young Tim was naturally funny. Indeed, he told the *Radio Times* that at the age of 12, he was invited to a girl's party simply 'because her mother insisted I made her laugh.' However, Tim had no real acting experience to talk of until he attended Winchester College. The end of term revue presented him with the chance to make his fellow pupils laugh and the show's great success lead a future-thinking teacher to write in his report, 'No doubt if his A-levels fail, Tim could become a film star, or, as he would probably prefer to be, an old-time music-hall comedian.' Tim's brother had been in the Cambridge Footlights during the era of Jonathan Miller. When Tim was asked what else he would be doing apart from working during his interview for a grant from the Derbyshire Education Committee, the Footlights was the obvious and instant choice. Coming from a family of legal folk (his father was a lawyer), Tim decided to study law but during his first year, 1960–61, he read Economics and Politics to avoid the dreaded horrors of Roman Law. At Pembroke College, Tim spent much of his time hanging out with

Bill Oddie and fellow law student, John Cleese, playing the Beatles' *Twist and Shout* to cheer themselves up. Tim remembers Cleese as the college swot, 'he used to go to all the lectures! But we were good friends, we would revise together. He generously lent me his lecture notes and, of course, in exam situations, B for Brooke-Taylor and C for Cleese were sat near each other. One of the points he had anticipated came up as the very first question so I was able to turn round and signal, 'Thank you very much John!' He, I and Graham Chapman would spend a lot of time together.' Tim's first brush with acting was less productive. He auditioned for a part in the straight production of Sheridan's *The Rivals*. As Tim explains, 'I think there were 31 parts and 32 people auditioned. I failed to get a part!' Mind you, it was comedy that really appealed and he found a niche in the Pembroke Players Smoking Concerts, the domain of Peter Cook for a full three years. During Tim's time much of the material was written by Geoffrey Paxton as well as song contributions from Bill Oddie. In 1962, Tim auditioned new boy Eric Idle for the Footlights and accepted him. The following year, Tim's last, he was voted President of the Footlights for 1963. During his final year, Tim rounded up the Footlighters for the revue, *A Clump of Plinths*, assigned director Humphrey Barclay and delighted in the gloriously sick humour of actual legal cases, put to the best of use in Cleese's elongated piece, Judge Not. During the initial popularity of *Cambridge Circus* on stage and radio, Tim failed to land a position on a BBC General Traineeship and worked at an advertising agency before rebounding with a job as a researcher for ATV. This was quickly curtailed, with performances of *Cambridge Circus* in New Zealand and America. Radio's development of the revue, *I'm Sorry I'll Read That Again*, kept Tim busy until 1973 by which time he had pioneered ground-breaking television sketch shows, *At Last the 1948 Show* and *Broaden Your Mind*, made a minor mark in films (*The Statue*, *Willy Wonka and the Chocolate Factory*) and became a major small screen star with *The Goodies* from 1970. Radio panel games (*I'm Sorry I Haven't a Clue*), television guest spots (*Jokers Wild*), books (*Rule Britannia*) and a successful pop star career filled in time during the 12-year run of *The Goodies*. Stage farces, summer seasons with old heroes like Richard Murdoch, panto, corporate videos (for Insercourt Law Courts and

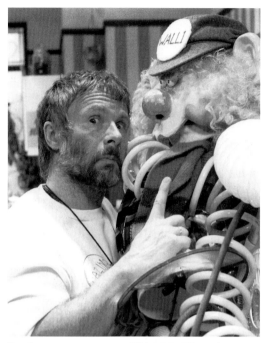

BILL ODDIE WITH HIS OFFICE PAL W.A.L.L.I. – WILLIAM'S ABSOLUTELY LUDICROUS LOOKING INVENTION – IN *THE BUBBLEGUM BRIGADE*

1998, Tim started the raft race for the Marlowe Rugby Club and has even been sucked into internet activity, taking part in a *Goodies*-geared interview on the BBC website, Beeb Oi Chat, on 14 July 1998. He has listed his favourite things as roast lamb and onion sauce, travelling with skis and Buster Keaton. His favourite films are *M. Hulot's Holiday* and *Raiders of the Lost Ark*. A *Radio Times* feature, 'My TV Dinner' (12–18 July 1997) detailed Tim's choice, Gunge: a mixture of pasta, chicken, cheese and spices. Favourite *Goodies* songs are *Wild Thing*, *Cricklewood* and *Cactus in My Y-Fronts*, while his least favourite is *Custard*. Tim has been married to Christine for over 30 years and has two sons, Ben and Edward. A Goodie forever and one of the funniest blokes around.

THE BUBBLEGUM BRIGADE

Co-writer and ex-Goodie star Bill Oddie, played William, another do-gooder here as the adult leader of a bumbling gang of children whose aim was to help people anytime, anywhere. Familiar or what! Actually, the motto was 'Broken hearts mended while you wait' but good intentions always ended in comic misunderstanding. The scripts from Mr and Mrs Oddie were charming enough and Bill was always worth catching, but only one series of six was produced. The central cast remained the same from the *Dramarama* pilot apart from Flora Fenton who played Jinx.

Devised and executive produced by Peter Murphy. Producer Pennant Roberts. Directors Pennant Roberts and Alistair Clark. Tuesdays, 2 May–6 June 1989, HTV.

THE BURKISS WAY

Less inspired and popular than *I'm Sorry I'll Read That Again*, this first success for writers David Renwick and Andrew Marshall was the show's natural successor during the era of television dominance. From Series Two, Jo Kendall gave the show a familiar ring and no sacred cow was left unslaughtered. Tim Brooke-Taylor eagerly accepted a one-episode guest-starring role as the Lady Constance clone, Dame Cecily.

Series Four, Episode Seven: Lesson 40 – Avoid Like the Plague the Burkiss Way. JO KENDALL, CHRIS EMMETT, FRED HARRIS, NIGEL REES, Guest star TIM BROOKE-TAYLOR. Script by Andrew Marshall and David Renwick. Features: The Masque of the Red Death, Houdini and The French Revolution.

Michael Barratt's Jobs for Kids programme), quizzes (*3-2-1*), endorsement of quizzes (revealing his dream prezzie for the *TV Times' The Price Is Right* tie-in, 29 November–5 December 1985), presenting (*Cartoon Alphabet*, *Spin-Offs*) and a profitable wallow in situation comedies (*Me & My Girl*, *You Must Be the Husband*, *One Foot in the Grave*) followed. Tim was appointed Rector of St Andrews University in Scotland and served in the post from 1980 until 1983 and was made a honorary doctor of law of the University in 1983. He has published his thoughts on accountancy, animal care, the food industry, hotels and catering, the law and the media. Eager to support the local community, one of his most bizarre stunts even made it to BBC television thanks to an episode of *Pie in the Sky* (*This Other Eden*, broadcast 12 May 1996) which featured a copy of the *Barstock and Middleton Advertiser* and its headline *Goodie Tim Has a Tree-Mendous Time*. On Saturday 1 August

C

CABBAGES AND KING

Another one of those cheap television parlour games entirely saved by the legendary talents dragged in. This ITV series basked in such greats as Peter Cook and Kenneth Williams, while, for one night only, it welcomed Graeme Garden into the fun contest of half truths, quips and witty banter on 15 July 1979.

CALL MY BLUFF

Probably the greatest of those cheap television parlour games, Tim Brooke-Taylor happily stepped into the fray for a few appearances during the golden days on 23 and 30 January and 16 and 23 April 1984, 26 March and 2 April, 19 and 26 November 1987. However, the days of Robert Robertson, Frank Muir and Graeme Garden's painfully accurate parodies on *The Goodies* were long gone when the series returned in 1998 as a mid-morning time filler with Bob Holness in the chair, a female captain (Sandi Toksvig) shock, horror, and guest panellist Graeme Garden humbly playing his role as dial-a-wit for the spot the bluffs from the true definition antics. Tim returned on 15 September 1997 and, finally, in September 1999, an early afternoon, unheralded, semi-Goodies reunion, when both Tim Brooke-Taylor and Graeme Garden played the game.

CAMBRIDGE CIRCUS

The major break into show business for all three Goodies and, indeed, a couple of Pythons, can be traced back to some point in the long and varied life-span of this classic Footlights revue. Its origins lie in the 1963 production *A Clump of Plinths* which enjoyed minor editing and a title change to *Cambridge Circus* before opening as a Michael White presentation at the New Arts Theatre, Cambridge on 10 July 1963. The show proved so popular that the scheduled three-week run was quickly extended to five, closing to packed houses on 14 August 1963. Following in the hallowed footsteps of Peter Cook and the *Beyond the Fringe* invasion, Tim Brooke-Taylor, John Cleese and the team of merry funsters deliberately steered away from

satirical material and delighted in presenting a slightly old-fashioned, music hall joke-dominated, evening of comedy. Material like Swap-A-Jest and Patients For the Use Of would have lengthy afterlife in various cast projects but, by common consent, the revue's highlight came with the John Cleese scripted legal vignette, Judge Not, with the towering writer as prosecuting council, Chris Stuart-Clark on defence, David Hatch as the judge and Tony Buffery as Arnold Fitch. However, it was the two pre-Goodies that continually stole the limelight. Bill Oddie played the roles of an usher and Sidney Bottle. An address to a seemingly empty dock would get a huge laugh when it was revealed Bottle was, in fact, already present. Instant laughter on his first appearance prompted Oddie to milk the sequence for more and more laughs, initially making his meagre presence felt by a creeping hand slowly emerging from behind the stand. On tour, the scene would get even more eccentric with a mysterious third hand appearing

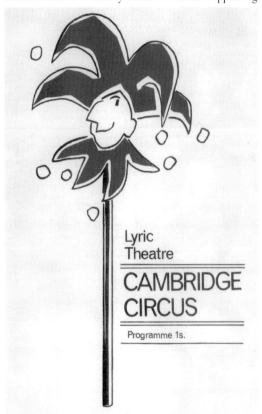

Lyric
Theatre

**CAMBRIDGE
CIRCUS**

Programme 1s.

FRONT COVER OF THE *CAMBRIDGE CIRCUS* PROGRAMME

TIM BROOKE-TAYLOR PERFORMING PATIENTS FOR THE USE OF WITH A WORRIED-LOOKING BILL ODDIE

'masterly parody of Jean Martin's 'Lucky' in the original French production of *Waiting For Godot*.' A transfer to the West End was inevitable in the face of such praise and the gang decamped to the Lyric for a three-month run from 16 August to 9 November 1963. However, even by this early stage, the cast was beginning to disperse with Tony Buffery opting out before the show started its 100-plus performances at the Lyric. Graham Chapman gratefully stepped into his shoes. By the close, Chris Stuart-Clark had left to be replaced on stage by director Humphrey Barclay. It was with this cast that the BBC recorded a half-hour edited highlights version of the show.

Written by Humphrey Barclay, Tim Brooke-Taylor, John Cleese, Bill Oddie and Chris Stuart-Clark. Design Stephen Mullin. Costumes Judy Birdwood. Music by Hugh MacDonald and Bill Oddie. Lighting Tim Fell. Director Humphrey Barclay.

Cambridge on vinyl

A highly collectable *Cambridge Circus* album featuring the original cast in classic moments from the revue.

Green Line Bus, Patients For the Use Of, Boring Sexy Song, Great Moments in British Theatre (How Green Was My Buttonhole?), Pride and Joy, BBCBC, Sing Sing, Boring Straight Song, Swap-A-Jest, Those Were the Days, O.H.M.S., Judge Not. PMC 1208 Parlophone 1963. Re-issued PCS 3046 Odeon 1965.

Cambridge on radio

For the BBC's grand presentation of *Cambridge Circus* on radio, Humphrey Barclay was employed as producer to capture the full flavour of the Lyric production, while established radio producer Ted Taylor was also assigned to keep the thing on the straight and narrow. As such, the mix resulted in a very straight rendition of the revue's highlights without the comic heart that made it great in the first place. Audiences, both of the November recording and the December broadcast, were bemused rather than fully amused. The rather stilted performance featured the opening number, *Feel Like Taking in a Show?*, Cleese's archaic broadcast, BBCBC, Sing Sing, the affectionate parody of performance tradition with Great Moments in the British Theatre, Those Were the Days, Oddie letting rip with *Jazz Song*, Brooke-Taylor's much cherished Swap-A-Jest, the less than impartial Football Results, the Cleese/Oddie scripted John and Mary in Malaya, O.H.M.S. and the classic court room battle, Judge Not.

HUMPHREY BARCLAY, TIM BROOKE-TAYLOR, GRAHAM CHAPMAN, DAVID HATCH, JO KENDALL and BILL ODDIE. Music performed by Burt Rhodes and his Quintet. Produced by Humphrey Barclay and Ted Taylor. Monday 30 December 1963, BBC Home Service.

from somewhere and, ultimately, a fourth hand which was black! Tim Brooke-Taylor also eagerly exaggerated his performance for comic effect, relishing the wise-cracking, fast-talking role of defendant Percy Molar – company director and music hall comedian eagerly trying to crack the 'Jamaica?' 'No, she went of her own accord' gag before being silenced. However, it was as the shuffling, aged usher that Tim scored his biggest hit. What began life as a fairly hasty walk-on, walk-off part, merely to present a bidet as evidence, eventually became a one act play in itself. The walk became more and more staggered and time-consuming, he would often forget to leave the item on purpose and stagger back for another attempt, while literally stopping the show with enthused audience reaction. The radio review programme *The Critics* singled out Brooke-Taylor's ancient comic turn as the show's masterpiece, rather grandly and optimistically celebrating this

TIM BROOKE-TAYLOR, JOHN CLEESE, GRAHAM CHAPMAN, BILL ODDIE, JEAN HART, JO KENDALL, DAVID HATCH AND JONATHAN LYNN PACKING THEIR TRUNK FOR THE CAMBRIDGE TOUR OF NEW ZEALAND

Cambridge abroad

With all the cast members having recorded three further try out broadcasts for the BBC – now under the title *I'm Sorry I'll Read That Again* – Humphrey Barclay rounded the cast up for a six-week tour of New Zealand from May to June 1964. Billed as 'Masters of Mirth' thanks to their University pedigree, the team met with enthused crowds, uncertain locals (many wondered where the elephants in this so-called circus were!) and the chance to record four more radio programmes presenting various edited highlights of the revue for the New Zealand market. These were dubbed with parody secondary titles – *The Cardinal Richelieu Show* (a throwback to when the old boy was credited for writing some of the original material), *The Peter Titheradge Show* (BBC producer later to work on *I'm Sorry I'll Read That Again*) and even *The Mrs Muir Show* (after the squad's delightfully dotty landlady). Distinguished theatrical impresario Sol Hurok, renowned for his presentations of ballet and opera, booked the *Cambridge Circus* revue for Broadway. Playing for just 23 performances at the Plymouth Theatre, New York from Saturday 6 to Wednesday 24 October, the show was beset with

CUSTARD PIES AT THE READY – A STUNNING, VINTAGE SHOT OF THE PRE-GOODIE GOODIES

artistic problems. Sure-fire crowd pleasers, like Brooke-Taylor's flamboyant Dame Edith Evans impersonation during the Oscar Wilde sketch, were dropped, more visual material from Chapman and Cleese was adopted, while new cast member, 1965 Cambridge graduate Jonathan Lynn, was recruited into the team. New material was supplied by Lynn's colleague Eric Idle, who sent over a Beatles Hallelujah chorus which Brooke-Taylor enhanced with an idea to play the head-shaking lads as choir boys. Moreover, the Oxford infiltration took hold with the inclusion of the Terry Jones/Michael Palin masterclass in physical comedy technique, Humour Without Tears. Performed here by Tim Brooke-Taylor, Bill Oddie and Jonathan Lynn in its purest, most pathetically realistic and painful sense, it captured the heart of the piece like never before or since. The reviews were brilliant and Bill Oddie found himself singled out, 'I would actually get the best notices purely because I was doing the music as well – the critics recognised the concept of songs and praised me accordingly! So I got rave reviews in America and London. Tim was probably next and John

Cleese was nowhere. We always thought John was the funny one, which just shows that writer–performers know far more than critics do… or indeed audiences. It was obvious that John was the genius. I just jumped around and sang a bit!' As the show was closing, respected journalist Walter Kerr published an article in the *New York Times* putting these new British guys on a par with Chaplin. Appearances on *The Ed Sullivan Show* and at the JFK Library in Connecticut, preceded a run off-Broadway at Greenwich Village, 'Square East', 15 West 4th Street, until February 1965 when an entirely American cast took over. Brooke-Taylor, present as overseer and spectator for initial auditions and rehearsals, was distressed to see the director insist on exact copying of the original cast's performance and thus removing the needed spontaneity and confidence in the material. By October, the cast were largely back in England and set for the first official series of *I'm Sorry I'll Read That Again*. George Seddon, who commented that *Cambridge Circus* would 'start nothing' had got it completely wrong. The radio cult that sprang from the Cambridge ashes lasted until 1973.

PLYMOUTH THEATRE, OFF BROADWAY

CARTOON ALPHABET: AN A–Z OF ANIMATED COMEDY

Before Tony Robinson had a fair crack at highlighting the artistic importance of classic cartoons, the young viewer had to settle for Rolf Harris and his wacky drawing style or the campy brilliance of Derek Griffiths's performance in *Film Fun*. The Chuck Jones era *Tom and Jerry* shorts and the occasional Thirties *Bugs Bunny* was great but when it came to class presentation, the main man with the main plan was Tim Brooke-Taylor. A dedicated cartoon fan, Tim's pioneering Channel Four series balanced enthusiasm with a mission to unearth primitive gems. Displaying all the skill and charm of your all-time favourite schoolteacher, Tim would effortlessly throw himself into the corny world of slapstick and groan-worthy gags, tossing in comments like 'Now we go to L – if you'll pardon the expression!' with perfect timing. Jiving to the opening song – *Felix Keeps on Walking* – and basking in his persona as beloved Goodie with memories of playing the back end of a panto horse opposite black-hearted villain Bill Oddie, these gentle, alphabetic lectures were a joy. My eternal thanks are

owed for first viewings as a transfixed 11-year-old to cartoon milestones like Windsor McKay's awe-inspiring 1914 masterpiece *Gertie the Dinosaur* and UPA's 1951 minimalism Oscar-winner *Gerald McBoing Boing*, not to mention David Hand's British Animaland series, *KoKo the Clown* and the gloriously primitive *Little Nemo*. Alongside all the old favourites, a light-hearted attempt at setting animation in place as a historically important form of cinematic art praised master craftsmen like Walter Lantz, Chuck Jones, Max Flesicher and the peerless Tex Avery, while revealing new technology in colouring (shock, horror) old cartoons and unveiling never before seen treasures from Yugoslavia. A vitally important and under-rated re-evaluation of cartoon heritage.

Written and produced by Richard Evans. Directed by Don Clayton. 1982, Channel 4.

A British, Swedish, Finnish, Norwegian co-production shot on location during the summer of 1971, this bizarre musical comedy thriller headlined the unique teaming of Cliff Richard and Tim Brooke-Taylor. Stretching believability to breaking point, the story featured Cliff and Timbo dragging their show through Scandinavia. The seed of the plot is sown at a hectic railway station with Tim in comic disguise and Cliff mistakenly picking up the wrong suitcase. Typically, for an international chase adventure, the suitcase contains ill-gotten gains from a couple of bank robbers. This, naturally, spurs a manic, comic, musical and thrilling trek through Sweden, Norway and Finland. They just don't make 'em like that any more.

With OLIVIA NEWTON-JOHN, MATTI RANIN, PEKKA LAIHO. Written by Eric Davidson. Producer Michael Hurll. Saturday 2 September 1972, BBC1.

CASTLE CLUES: EXPLORING THE TOWER OF LONDON

Goodie get togethers were fairly rare occurrences in the late Eighties and you certainly didn't expect to see them in history education programmes but that's exactly what this Royal Armouries introductory guide to the Tower of London embraced with its inspired choice of presenters in Graeme Garden and Bill Oddie. Structured to work as a visual study pack before a school's visit to the Tower, the 900 years of history in the place was split into three handy chunks and discussed in terms of an historic detective story. Questions would be posed by our hosts and while some would be answered, others would be down to you, the viewer, on your visit. *The Conqueror's Tower* relates William the Conqueror, 1066 and all that, with Bill peppering his commentary with witty remarks and Graeme counterbalancing with serious restraint, even when discussing the toilet facilities! Part Two, *Fortress and Palace*, moves on to life in the Middle Ages, a look at the King's private rooms and a brilliant demonstration of the castle's protection against arrow attack, played out by Graeme and Bill like kids in the oldest playground in the land. The final section, *Treasure and Traitors*, moves through King Henry VIII's time at the castle, hints at the place's history of wild animals and prisoners, allows Bill to indulge in his bird passion via the ravens and even gives the 8–12 target audience a chance to giggle over their enclosed study notes as the Bloody Tower is mentioned.

Researched, produced and directed by Colin Still. 1987.

CAT'S WHISKERS

A Radio 4 magazine programme hosted by Julie First and Adrian Moorhouse. Tale-telling Bill Oddie was enlisted to read *A Job Well Done* by Roy Apps.

Producer Mary Kalemkerlan. Sunday 19 February 1989, Radio 4.

CELEBRITY COUNTDOWN

Unsurprisingly, a special celebrity edition of the perennially popular Channel 4 word and number game. Sixties satire survivors Alan Coren and Graeme Garden battled it out with the one third of the Goodies losing the match with 29 points to 35. Still, the fun was in the inter-contest ramblings with medical and Cambridge memories, tongue-in-cheek and incorrect mutters about *Black Pudding Bertha* selling only two copies in Wakefield – it was only one – and sixth sense pleas for a 'U' in his choice of consonants coming good for an inspired 'What a Funky Gibbon he is!' comment from Richard Whitely.

Producers Mark Nyman and Michael Wylie. Director Brenda Wilson. 1998, Channel 4.

CELEBRITY SQUARES

Ritual humiliation for nine notable stars of stage, screen and radio on ITV as Bob Monkhouse quipped merrily, bantered with bumbling contestants and interacted with the celebrities for possible assistance with the answers. Bill Oddie appeared on the 18 January 1976 edition, followed a few weeks later by fellow Goodie, Tim Brooke-Taylor, on 2 February. Several years later, Graeme Garden completed the trilogy with appearances on 17 March, 16 June and 23 June 1979. Tim returned for four more attempts on 31 March, 7 April, 2 June and 14 June 1979.

CHARLIE'S CLIMBING TREE

A 12-part ITV children's cartoon series narrated by Graeme Garden from 9 February 1979.

CHART SUCCESS

Despite the fact that two singles from the album *The Goodies Sing Songs From The Goodies* failed to dent the Top 40, Bill Oddie, Graeme Garden and Tim Brooke-Taylor would go on to become the most popular and successful comedy rock group in history. In just one year, between December 1974 and December 1975, the Goodies enjoyed pop stardom, *Top of the Pops* applause, frantic groupie attention and five – yes five – hit singles. *The Inbetweenies* and *Funky Gibbon* cracked the Top 10 with follow-up discs *Black Pudding Bertha*, *Nappy Love* and *Make a Daft Noise for Christmas* hitting numbers 19, 21 and 20, respectively. It was a hectic, heady, power to the people 12 months and in 1976 *The Goodies* were listed as the sixth best-selling group in the country. Moreover, WE Oddie was the fifth most successful songwriter – all the hits, save *Wild Thing*, were Bill compositions. However, in a flash, the glory days were over, the television series was rested and a venture into Disney whimsy with a single release of *M.I.C.K.E.Y. M.O.U.S.E.* left Britain's pop teeny boppers colder than last year's turkey. Still, with an amazing 38 weeks in the British charts, two weeks longer than the 1967 singles from The Beatles, *The Goodies* left a rollicking musical legacy to be proud of.

Did You Know? The glorious musical achievements of the Goodies were catalogued in the April 1999 edition of Record Collector (issue 236). The article, 'Fifty Odd Years of British Comedy,' by Martin O'Gorman and Tim Jones, devoted a section to the Goods. Current prices for Goodies singles (£2.50) and Goodies albums (£5) were also included. During the Seventies, Goodies singles were promoted with a badge.

CHILD'S PLAY

Kids say the funniest things and this ITV panel game set out to prove it. Tim Brooke-Taylor was suitably embarrassed on his single appearance on 7 October 1984.

CHILDREN IN NEED

Bill Oddie joined in the annual BBC1 fun and games to raise money for charity on Friday 22 November 1991. Basking in his fame as a wildlife presenter on *Ask Oddie*, Bill featured in the David Bellamy 'Talk to the Animals' section with *Animal Magic* hero Johnny Morris and *The Really Wild Show* team. The *Radio Times* (16–22 November 1991) featured the nature line-up, with Bill in stunning, angst-ridden Safari gear pose.

CHILDREN'S ROYAL VARIETY PERFORMANCE

A magical musical mystery adventure held in the presence of Her Royal Highness Princess Margaret in aid of the NSPCC. The themed show followed the antics of Indiana's younger brother, Bill Jones, during a quest to recover a rare ruby stolen from the depths of the British Museum. The star-studded cast included an appearance from Bill Oddie.

Monday 3 May 1993, BBC1.

CHRISTMAS NIGHT WITH THE STARS

The final nail in a beloved Christmas television tradition, this was the very last wholly original *Christmas Night with the Stars* which had been the seasonal highlight a decade earlier. Tim Brooke-Taylor, Graeme Garden and Bill Oddie, riding high in the

popularity stakes, were drafted in to write and perform a classic filmed interlude: *The Goodie's Travelling Instant Five-Minute Christmas*. In its brief running time, the vignette tackled a mountain of visual gags with Christmas choral service problems, exploding Christmas puds, a manic attack from a swarm of Christmas Tree fairies, Bill's tubby Santa getting stuck down the chimney and that legendary moment as Tim's groovy singer is smothered by a giant bell. Other BBC favourites drafted in for the evening included the cast of *Dad's Army*, *The Liver Birds*, *The Two Ronnies* and Mike Yarwood.

Did You Know? The format was briefly resurrected for Fry and Laurie Host A Christmas Night with the Stars (Tuesday 25 December 1994, BBC2) which featured new material alongside clips from past editions, including a condensed version of the 1972 Goodies piece in a montage featuring traditional yule tides from Benny Hill, Jimmy Edwards and Dick Emery.

With DENISE DISTEL, PAUL ELLISON. Produced and directed by Jim Franklin. Monday 25 December 1972, BBC1.

CILLA

Tim Brooke-Taylor and Graeme Garden, alongside Graham Chapman, backed up this hit Sixties series for that beloved Liver Bird, Cilla Black. The Cambridge three injected manic comic interludes in between the pop song belting and special guests.

THE CLARION AND GLOBE

Named after the Goodies-run newspaper in *Cunning Stunts*, this is the Internet and postal newsletter for the Australian-based Goodies Rule OK Fan Club, attracting over 850 members in 11 countries. President Alison Bean (who contributed a non-Goodies tribute to the trio, 'Other Projects', to the *BritComedy Digest*) created this haven for Goodie-philes, and both Tim Brooke-Taylor and Graeme Garden became firm supporters of the group. It was the ultimate reflection of the importance of *The Goodies* to Australian culture. In the Nineties, the trio seemed to be national heroes. *Rip 11 Up's* 'What's Hot What Not' segment in issue 42 (20–26 March 1997) declared that *The Goodies* was hot… and what was not: not knowing who the Goodies are! Lisa McCure, star of the television series *Blue Heelers* cited the series as one of her favourites in the *Sunday Age TV Guide*. Gabby Milgate, appearing on the topical comedy quiz *Good News Week* (10 October 1997) discussed the merits of Wales and admitted she only knew about the country through *The Goodies: Wacky Wales*. Fellow player Colin Lane got a huge round of applause when he said, 'Everything that was in *The Goodies* was true!' One overawed gentleman even voted *The Goodies* as sexiest men over 50! The popular Oz tennis duo, Mark Woodforde and Todd Woodbridge are often cheered from the crowd with a chorus of 'Woody, Woody Yum Yum!' Students seem obsessed with the facial hair of Graeme Garden and Bill Oddie. But it is, perhaps, the musical revolution that has taken the Goodies to heart. The group Spiderbait recorded a cover version of *Run* in 1992 and opened their debut album, *Shasahvaglava*, with the track. Augogo records released the tune on an EP together with two live versions of the Oddie classic. The three members of the band even produced a video for the release, recreating such classic *Goodies* moments as Tim's Winston Churchill from *War Babies*, Bill's sherbet-sucking, Tim's Queen impersonation, the ball and chain antics from *Goodies in the Nick* and Tim's bellybutton angst. A very short-lived group called Kitten Kong kept the Goodie tribute sound ticking along while Melbourne-based band, Plastic Spacemen, named themselves after the advert product featured in *Radio Goodies* and peppered their first compact disc, *Exhibit A*, with actual soundbites from the shows – including the spacemen advert that gave the group its name. Feverdream, yet another Oz rock outfit with Goodie aspirations, featured the Oddie/Garden *Radio Goodies* banter, 'I've just done a jingle!' 'There's a good boy!', Graeme's 'sleepy bo bos' chat from *Snooze*, and the *Walk in the Black Forest* intro/outro on their brilliant, slowed-down version of *The Goodies Theme* on the 1995 album *Moniker*. The internet club remains at the cutting edge of *Goodies* fandom and on 13 January 1999, Tim Brooke-Taylor plugged the group and took 20 questions on 3AW Melbourne Radio from the comfort of a Gloucester phone-line. *The Goodies* renaissance is coming!

THE CLIVE JAMES SHOW

The Aussie guru's ITV chat show welcomed Graeme Garden to take a suitably comic look at world events in the newspapers on Sunday 3 and 22 March 1998. With typical irony, Graeme chatted about such subjects as a new 'unsinkable' ship, eccentrics for the lost city of Atlantic and an obscene religious icon.

CLOUD NINE

Graeme Garden starred in this stage production at the Royal Court Theatre, London.

CLUE

A Graeme Garden appearance on Radio 4 in 1996.

A CLUMP OF PLINTHS

The crowning glory of Tim Brooke-Taylor's Cambridge Footlights experience. As President for 1963, he assigned director Humphrey Barclay and oversaw the revue's development with John Cleese. Allegedly, the initial title for the piece was to have been *You Can't Call a Show 'Cornflakes'* which was quickly usurped by *A Clump of Plinths*, using the favourite words of Brooke-Taylor and Cleese, although few people were happy with it and insisted the ballot to find a name had been fixed. As it was, it inspired the limited Cambridge budget to provide a wonderfully economic, minimalist set, comprising of several large boxes which could be opened or rearranged as a sketch or number dictated. Of the 34 items featured in the revue many became oft repeated classics. One of Brooke-Taylor's personal favourites, Swap-a-Jest, saw him exchange Elizabethan banter in the style of a music hall routine with Chris Stuart-Clark. It Can't End Like This was a rare scripting collaboration between Bill Oddie and John 'Otto' Cleese, creating a Somerset Maugham parody which launched those stuffy *I'm Sorry I'll Read That Again* characters John and Mary. Oddie contributed his usual musical inspiration with three old gentlemen pondering the route map in the style of a negro spiritual for *Green Line Bus*. Due to its Cambridge success, *A Clump of Plinths* bypassed the Edinburgh festival and, thanks to Michael White, the company secured equity cards and the offer of a West End slot. Before that, the team played a one-week engagement at the Robin Hood theatre, Averham, near Newark, and a further week at the York Festival. By the time a five-week run at the New Arts Theatre had started on 10 July 1963, the production's name had been changed to *Cambridge Circus*.

TIM BROOKE-TAYLOR, JOHN CLEESE, DAVID HATCH, JO KENDALL, BILL ODDIE and CHRIS STUART-CLARK. Written by Tim Brooke-Taylor, John Cleese, David Hatch, Jo Kendall, Bill Oddie, Peter Pagnamenta and Chris Stuart-Clark. Additional material by Cardinal Richelieu. Director Humphrey Barclay.

THE COLE PORTER REVUE

Bill Oddie contributed written material and made appearances in this 1966 West End show. 'I was in it – I didn't write it, Cole Porter did!' *Bill Oddie.*

A COLLECTION OF GOODIES

A selection of 'new' *Goodies* sketches including the aged glams Pan's Grannies, babysitting problems and the lengthy gymnasium sequence featuring the famous runaway, bucking bronco, vaulting horse later adopted for *The Goodies* opening credits. Perhaps the most famous moment features Tim, clad in a tracksuit, pulling on a rope and finding himself smothered by a giant bell. Still in the gym, Graeme carelessly drops a medicine ball onto poor old Tim for another visual favourite. The rarity of this collection, originally featured during the team's regular appearances on *Engelbert and the Young Generation*, between January and April 1972, left many followers clueless as to where these sequences came from. Duncan Wood, Head of BBC Comedy, initiated this collection when he wrote to the Goodies on 25 February 1972 suggesting a 'special compilation programme', selecting five of the specially filmed *Goodie* interludes (Gymnasium, Plum Pudding, Pan's Grannies, Good Deed Day and Street Entertainers), for an instant special. Four minutes of new, linking footage was required and, following their contractual signing for 1972, the Goodies were recruited for a single day's work on 26 April. As a result of its cheap and cheerful, cut and paste construction, the programme is alternatively known as the *Special Tax Edition*.

Produced and directed by Jim Franklin. Sunday 24 September 1972, BBC2.

COLLECTOR'S LOT

A good-humoured Channel 4 celebration of collections and obsessions which wouldn't always find time on *The Antiques Road Show*. Bill Oddie, one-time guest celebrity discussing his vast Mickey Mouse collection, stepped into the temporary presenting shoes left vacant by the rather wooden Sue Cook in 1997. Making his first appearance atop a mountain with 'Hello, and welcome to *Collector's Lot*. I'm Bill Oddie doing an impression of Sue Cook!', his enthusiasm and general interest in all things collectable made him a likeable,

ideal host but before the nation could fully wake up to the fact that a comedy legend was in the chair, Cook was back and Bill was history.

COMEDY BOOKCASE

Bill Oddie was recruited to read from some of his favourite comic literature for this show; firstly from Tom Sharpe's South African satire *Riotous Assembly* and then a selection from Billy Bunter, which pointed the way towards the Goodies getting back together for a radio series based on the stories.

Wednesday 13 and 20 January 1993, Radio 2.

COMIC RELIEF 1988

I well recall the excitement hearing the rumour that for the 1988 *Comic Relief* television extravaganza (at this stage a bi-annual comic fest and still in its infancy), those glorious Goodies were going to reform for tonight and one night only, for charity. It was akin to the sensation when, in 1985, Live Aid's best kept secret was the top billing appearance of Paul McCartney, George Harrison and Ringo Starr on stage together for the first time since 1966. Sadly, as with the promised three-quarters Beatles bash (when Macca simply strolled on stage to muddle through *Let It Be*), this 1988 get together of the decade was also slightly disappointing. Although, mind you, all three did at least turn up and do the business, albeit the entire gig lasted just under 90 seconds. Just under three and a half hours into the mammoth comedy fest, the Goodies were back together again. Tim in casual jumper, Bill sporting one of *Miami Vice*'s cool Eighties suits and Graeme proudly clad in a Union flag waistcoat, were set to total send-up mode from the outset. Chucked into the quick-fire, filmed interlude sketch collections that were dotted throughout the evening (a sort of elongated *Three of a Kind* format cunningly entitled *73 of a Kind*) as opposed to the live, loud, proud and dangerous to know, television centre reunion we were all hoping for, their appearance consisted of the disgruntled reading out of their letters of invitation. Typically, Graeme's name is spelt wrong! Tim, having introduced his fellow Goods, explains that the *Comic Relief* producers are 'very, very, very young'. Indeed, they would have to be for the joke to work. It was fewer than five years since the Goodies had made their last television series and this eager, comical placing of themselves in the annals of comedy

47

history seems a tad premature. But eager they are, for Tim starts to read the letter: 'In preparing our star-studded bill of wit, humour, fun and frolic it has been suggested that we include something by *The Goodies*... to provide a bit of contrast!' Bill takes up the baton, 'We are very much aware that people remember *The Goodies* with the same nostalgic affection that they remember ration books, hoo-la hoops, and Wolverhampton Wanders', before Graeme drives the knife fully into Timbo's side with, 'We are also aware, of course, that today one of you is a doctor, one of you is a bird-watcher and one of you has left the entertainment business entirely!' Distressed at the heartless dismissal of *Me & My Girl* and *You Must Be the Husband*, Tim mouths 'Bastards!' before Graeme concludes, 'We've been told you also had a hit record called The Funky... Gilbert and we thought you might like to recreate that.' Bill, suitably miffed at the misunderstood disparages cast on his music, reads on through gritted teeth, 'So we got it out of the archives and played it and then we thought perhaps you wouldn't like to recreate it after all, but don't worry it's for charity so it doesn't have to be very good!' With crestfallen, angry attitude, the lads screw up their letters before wonderfully throwing themselves into the old, hand-clapping gibbon dance routine. However, as the sweet refrain of 'Do, do, do the funky...' get the heart pumping faster, the screen fades to black and the Beeb have no more. It's a funny joke and the team are peerlessly good together but there's a sense of two-fingered payback from the BBC. Besides, the watching millions wanted and needed more but, having said that, there's something undeniably magical about seeing the three back together again — short but poignant. Tim returned for another *73 of a Kind* appearance discussing cricket, cricket commentators nicknames, cake and thoughts of birds invading the pitch during a Test Match with Brian Johnston, David Gower and Gary Linnekar in the wee small hours of the morning while Bill, live from Telecom Tower, sat with Kim Wilde, Claire Rayner and Mike Smith, discussing his parrot-like, multicoloured Barry Manilow false nose and proclaiming a 'war of the noses' before covering the corny gag with... 'it doesn't matter, it's for charity.' An hour through the evening, this single Goodie appearance promised the major BBC Centre studio reunion which wasn't to be...

Friday 5 February 1988, BBC1.

COMMERCIALS

A Ritz biscuit campaign from the late Eighties memorably reunited a couple of bird hide-encased Goodies, Bill Oddie and Tim Brooke-Taylor, with Bill in familiar birding mode and Tim's crunching frightening the feathered focal point away. In the early Nineties, Bill Oddie found himself as the voice for Cadbury's Magic Stars chocolates before squeaky Joe Pasquale landed the assignment. Luckily, Bill bounced back with voiceover plugging Sugar Puffs in 1997. In December 1999, Bill voiced British Gas and British Beef campaigns, while Graeme advertised Sainsbury's, and was joined by Tim on the radio commercials.

THE COMPLETE AND UTTER HISTORY OF ALMOST EVERYTHING

Tim Brooke-Taylor played Lord Sandwich in this BBC Millennium comedy fest on Sunday 2 January 2000.

THE CONCH QUIZ

OK, so a radio panel game named after a shell may not exactly set the world alight, but this harmless gallop through a friendly battle of natural history wits and wisdoms was fun nevertheless. Besides, not only did such burning issues as whether kangaroos can swim or why Ancient Britons were so fond of cabbages get addressed, but celebrated Goodie and birder, Bill Oddie, popped in for a couple of appearances as well.

Producer John Harrison. Monday, 9 December 1985 and 6 January 1986, Radio 2.

PETER COOK

Along with Spike Milligan, the sorely missed Peter Cook was the architect for modern comedy. An influence on all three Goodies, Cook would join forces with them several times for high-profile charity concerts (*A Poke in the Eye* and *An Evening at Court*), television reminiscences (*Footlights: 100 Years of Comedy*) and super substitute in the *I'm Sorry I'll Read That Again* unofficial Christmas reunion radio show *Black Cinderella II Goes East*. The Goodie with the closest connection with the sublime Cook was Tim Brooke-Taylor. Tim's brother had been at Cambridge at the same time as Peter Cook and Tim himself was part of Pembroke College where Cook had been such a major force. There was a real sense of Pembroke spirit and Cook was still a powerful set of Footlight footsteps to follow.

Beyond the Fringe, more than *The Goon Show*, totally transfixed the young Brooke-Taylor. He recalls the celebrated West End run, 'I bought 10 tickets for the opening night and 10 tickets for the last night. I couldn't sell them all for the first night but I could have charged 20 times the amount for the last night – it was such a breakthrough and it was Peter Cook specifically. I remember hitting my head on the seat in front of me because I was laughing so much. It was just so clever.' After *Not Only… But Also*, Cook lost some of his clout, while reassuringly keeping his place on comedy's top table. He remains a vital part of any discussion on British comedy pioneers and his achingly sustained comic observations and comments could reduce crowds of professionals and students to exhausted jelly. It was a shared passion for golf which ultimately brought Tim out of the fan's shadow and into Cook's inner sanctum of friends, but even then, as Tim remembers, 'he still made me laugh more than anybody else. He changed a generation!' Cook's death on 9 January 1995 at the age of 57 cut short an enriched and enriching career.

COR!

British comedy subscription magazine founded in tribute to Bernard Bresslaw on 11 June 1993 by editor and writer Robert Ross. The honorary members include Tim Brooke-Taylor, as well as Goodies guest stars, John Cleese, Jack Douglas, Liz Fraser, Peter Jones, Norman Mitchell and the late Jon Pertwee. Issue 14, published in December 1998, was a special dedicated to *The Goodies* and featured the Tim Brooke-Taylor interview – *True Brit!*

COR!!

Cracking children's comic and subconscious influence on the title for the above, which brought the glories of *The Goodies* to the printed page for the first time. During 1973, a double-page comic strip was dedicated to the wacky trio's antics. Although no artist or writer was ever credited, the strip was exclusively copyrighted to Tim Brooke-Taylor, Graeme Garden and Bill Oddie. The weekly strips were authorised and approved by the Goodies and, to this day, Tim Brooke-Taylor proudly displays an original *Cor!* strip in his study. Even more interestingly, 1973 classics such as *For Those in Peril on the Sea* and *Camelot* saw Bill forsake his

BILL ODDIE PLUGGING TIGER BREAD WITH A LITTLE HELP FROM HIS FURRY FRIENDS

usual reading matter, *The Beano*, in favour of *Cor!!* 'The Aerial Display', a story featured in the 1973 *Cor! Annual* and 'The Treasure Hunt' from the comic issued on 18 August 1973, are preserved for inspection on the Goodies Rule OK Internet site.

THE CRACK-A-JOKE BOOK

A compilation of jokes sent in by children and published to raise money for Oxfam. Tim Brooke-Taylor wrote the introduction.

Written by Kenneth Mahood and Gerry Downe. Puffin 1978.

CRACKERJACK

In 1974, the annual children's television treat of the *Crackerjack* pantomime was enlivened even further by a guest appearance from the Goodies. Happy to camp it up in the traditional children's television seasonal treat as a favour to Michael Aspel, the Goodies led the studio audience in a sing-a-long of their pop hit, *The Inbetweenies*, and *ET*-like, pedalled the trandem into outer space in this production of *Aladdin*.

Did You Know? The show was recorded just over two weeks before Michael Aspel staggered back into the official Goodies ring to film his appearance in the Series Five episode, Chubby Chumps.

MICHAEL ASPEL, JACQUELINE CLARK, DANA, PETER GLAZE, TIM BROOKE-TAYLOR, GRAEME GARDEN, BILL ODDIE, BARRIE GOSNEY, DEREK GRIFFITHS, DERYCK GUYLER, DON MACLEAN, PAN'S PEOPLE, ED STEWART, RICHARD WATTIS. Tuesday 24 December 1974, BBC1.

STUDIO SHOT OF THE OFFICE IN CRICKLEWOOD

CRICKLEWOOD

'Life isn't Hollywood, it's Cricklewood' *Eric Morecambe*
In the Seventies there were two ways of writing to the Goodies. The most direct and boring way was care of BBC TV Centre, Wood Lane, London. The alternative was The Goodies, No Fixed Abode, Cricklewood. Amazingly, both would reach them eventually… even the BBC address! The London borough became the adopted home for the trio, referenced in the shows, books and album covers. Indeed, the place was immortalised twice in song with the outstandingly Beatles-esque *Cricklewood*, and the rather less outstanding but still rather fine *Cricklewood Shakedown*. Akin to the Beatles' shared life in *Help!*, an urban myth was created which implied the three were constantly together in some Cricklewood office, à la the Wombles down their warren or the Clangers under their dustbin lid. For over a decade it was a charming untruth we believed wholeheartedly. In reality, Cricklewood was chosen as *The Goodies* base simply because both Tim Brooke-Taylor and Graeme Garden were living there in 1969–70. Bill Oddie wasn't too far away in frightfully posh, Hampstead.

CRIMINAL RECORD

A Rick Wakeman disc featuring Bill Oddie's vocals on the track, *The Breathalyser*.

CULT TV

Essential but quickly defunct (after just 11 editions) glossy magazine devoted to the best in classic television. Despite failing to pinpoint exactly what constituted cult television – at one glance it seems to include almost anything on the small screen – its heart was certainly in the right place. Besides, any publication that resurrects the delights of *Bod*, *The Prisoner*, *3-2-1* and *Jason King* can't be all bad. Edited by Karne Levell, April 1998's Issue Nine, or Season 2 Episode 4 as they insisted on calling it, featured a seven-page retrospective of *The Goodies*, Nick Setchfield's 'Goodfellas'. The affectionate prose and a stunning interview with the lads unearthed nothing new but there were some priceless reunion snaps.

Did You Know? *An earlier issue of Cult TV (Season 1, Episode 4) featured 'Five ne'er to be forgotten moments' from The Goodies.*

THE CULTURE VULTURES

An extremely short-lived situation comedy starring Leslie Phillips in familiar raffish mood as the senior lecturer in Anthropology at the University of Hampshire. His love of gambling, leisure and the opposite sex made this perfect fare for the Carry On and *Doctor* film cad. The 'Hello!' charm combined with a casual attitude to work caused the expected problematic clashes with authority which provided much of the comedy. A tail-ender sense of swinging Sixties permissiveness gives the show an added historic value and three of the five episodes remain interesting to this volume, boasting scripts written by Colin Mares and Tim Brooke-Taylor.

Did You Know? *During filming, Leslie Phillips was taken ill with an internal haemorrhage and, despite, returning to the set, remained unwell throughout. Accordingly, the schedule was cut short and, thus, only five episodes were completed.*

Dr Michael Cunningham LESLIE PHILLIPS Dr Ian Meredith JONATHAN CECIL Professor George Hobbes PETER SALLIS Vivienne SALLY FAULKNER. Written by Colin Mares and Tim Brooke-Taylor. Producer Graeme Muir. Fridays, 24 April–22 May 1970, BBC1.

DAVID FROST'S THAT WAS THE WEEK THAT WAS

In February 1965, well over a year since *That Was The Week That Was* had been lifted from the BBC, cast members Willie Rushton and Al Mancini travelled to America with the first Mrs Bill Oddie, Jean Hart, to star in this extended satire tour. They joined forces with Tim Brooke-Taylor and Bill Oddie who were in the US anyway, having just completed their off-Broadway season of *Cambridge Circus*. As such, this stage show used vast quantities of old *TW3* and, naturally, several leftovers from the Cambridge revue. It was a tour of extremes, from the atmosphere of intimate revue with audiences of 300 to rock stadium-sized crowds of 6000. Canada, the West Coast and the South were on the schedule, with Anglo terminology cut to a minimum and touchy references to Governor Wallace removed. The only problem was that many punters were distressed when David Frost, highlighted as the star of the show judging by the title, didn't actually appear. Frost made only infrequent guest-starring appearances during the tour.

DAYTIME UK

Lunchtime chat show from the BBC hosted with wry charm by Judi Spiers. Tim Brooke-Taylor made an appearance in 1991 discussing the first *Goodies* episode and his new stage venture *The Philanthropist*. Fellow guest Barry Cryer joined Tim in a quick round of Mornington Crescent.

DEADPAN

An ill-fated but influential comedy review magazine which, although mainly concerned with the alternative scene, found room for such great comic dinosaurs as Frankie Howerd. The Goodies reunited for an interview.

DEALING WITH DANIELS

A sort of radio card game with magician Paul Daniels acting as the smooth-talking casino croupier, trying to out fox his celebrity guests. Tim Brooke-Taylor recorded a batch of four editions of this quirky bit of radio fun.

Produced by Richard Edis. Tuesdays, 1–22 April 1986, Radio 2.

DENNIS THE MENACE

An animated series of adventures featuring the legendary anti-hero from the *Beano*. Made for the British cable station TCC 24 Seven, the famous voices employed included Willie Rushton and his *I'm Sorry I Haven't a Clue* cohort Tim Brooke-Taylor.

DES RES

An interior decorating poke around a famous house programme for the Australian's Foxtel Lifestyle channel, Bill Oddie, his wife, Laura Beaumont, and their daughter, Rosie, were featured in a five-minute gallop through their Hampstead abode. The eccentric tastes of parents, cartoon-obsession and the legendary jungle master bedroom – complete with plastic giraffes and rubber snakes – were featured.

THE DETECTIVES

After years of plugging his obsession with bird-watching, Bill Oddie was finally invited back to some rare comic acting for the BBC – playing, of all things, a bird-watcher! *The Detectives* had sprung from golf buddies Jasper Carrott and Robert Powell camping through brief interludes on Carrott's stand-up/sketch series *Canned Carrott*. This enjoyably silly elongated sitcom went from prattling pratfalls to bizarre banter before it was finally pulled from the air. *Twitchers*, the last episode from Series Two welcomed a brain-addled support from the twitching Goodie, overacting with wide-eyed passion, he was stunningly introduced by presenting a fascinating birding slide show. Lecturing on the plight of the Red Kite and establishing the bird's sacred nesting hide out on The Isle of Wight, the scene is set for our hapless heroes to guard a quartet of ultra-rare eggs from dreaded, heartless egg collectors. Panicking with comic grandeur on the sidelines, Oddie's bemused eccentric is an effective contrast to the bumbling duo's catalogue of comic bird references, country community insults and bickering stakeout discussions. Clad in typical green anorak, revelling in his usual enthusiasm for the subject while embracing a reassuringly hyped-up sense of conservation, Oddie is a joy throughout, stumbling through the incompetence of Carrott and Powell with quiet, restrained dignity. He is even allowed an injection of mystery and red herring sinisterness opposite Roach's burly rural copper.

It's great to have Oddie back where he belongs, combining his comic skills with his naturalist passions — even though Powell's Brummie lad twice dubs him the suitably fine-feathered friend geared insult of a 'bearded tit'. Charming!

Bob Louis JASPER CARROTT Dave Briggs ROBERT POWELL Professor Rose BILL ODDIE Barman ROGER WALKER PC Drake PAT ROACH Bumpkin GEORGE MALPAS. Written by Steve Knight and Mike Whitehill. Producer Ed Bye. Director Steve Knight. Monday 16 January 1995, BBC1.

DICK WHITTINGTON

Tim Brooke-Taylor's first bash at the pantomime dame performed for the 1981–82 season at the Shaw Theatre was followed at the same venue by Bill Oddie who played the cook in 1989–90.

DID YOU SEE...?

Ludovic Kennedy's intelligent, populist guide for what you had missed on the box. A witty Graeme Garden joined the panel to discuss *Hospital Ward*, *Architecture at the Crossroads* and *Boon*.

Producer Charles Miller. Friday 21 February 1986, BBC2.

DISTINCTLY ODDIE

Before the Goodies became a pop-winning combination, Bill Oddie tried his solo artiste luck with this classic collection of comic numbers lifted and adapted from his huge back catalogue of *I'm Sorry I'll Read That Again* originals. Playing with the conventions of recording from the very outset, the vinyl crackles like a frying pan full of bacon before cheeky young Bill breaks in and mutters, 'Hey, I'd take it back, it's scratched!' before sound quality is improved and the jazz-orientated diminutive lament, *I'm Small*, is presented. Wonderfully tongue-in-cheek and self-mocking, Oddie sets himself in comic context with a reference to Charlie Drake, and delights in typical puns ranging from desire to be a minister to teeny-age memories. The number was memorably plundered for the Series Five *Goodies* classic *South Africa*. *Home Outward Bound* from Series Four, drew inspiration from the second track, *Square Bashing Dance*, with Bill's loud-mouthed regimental sergeant major barking out 'It's a kid's life in the British Army!' and drilling his boys in square dance beat: 'Polish your boots and cut your hair!' *Old Boutique* is a gloriously tongue in cheek, jaunty cockney jamboree, taking the essence of Carnaby Street Sixties cool from The Kinks classic *Dedicated Follower of Fashion* and giving it a traditional knees-up, pearly King, slant. *The Lawman* was later restructured for the Anglified demystification of *Bunfight at the OK Tea Rooms* with a bit of *Goodies in the Nick* tossed in for good measure. The haunting tale of Somerset's finest, PC Herbert Pled, joyfully relies on tried and tested mocking of thick-eared Colonel Blimpish obsession with the English way of things. Add dollops of comic pathos and you have an Oddie classic. *A Man's Best Friend* is a fairly standard comic burst of country and western in celebration of the ever-faithful dog, while the delicious *Rhubarb Tart Blues* — a musical homage to something which, according to the album's sleeve notes, is Oddie's least favourite food — hits the perfect pitch of mocked religious evangelist and Fanny Craddock-besotted believers. The song was entirely resurrected and reworked for *The New Goodies LP* track *Custard Pie* complete with eternal happiness promises and 'Mama's little baby' chanting. Finally, on side one, *The Wind* is a dramatic excuse for the lowest common denominator laugh — a loud burp at the close which Oddie embarrassingly apologies for, blaming the producer for editorial control and reassuring the listening public that it won't happen again on the other side. Happen again it does, of course, immediately the needle hits the grooves and Bill is once more overcome with shame, insisting it's only on this copy and pleading with you to buy another! Very clever sales tactics... *Recorded Live* is an interesting homage to King of the Lounge singers, Frank Sinatra, with Bill gamely wading through *One for My Baby* while the café clientele chatter, joke, order food loudly, drunkenly bicker and generally cause enough noise completely to ruin the recording, much to the timid, non-effective distress of the sound engineer. *Take It Off* is a two-tier music hall-style bit of business right out of the realms of Gus Elen. A couple of unrelated comic tales of a toothless codger and a stripper putting on weight forms the hook for some outlandish, free-wheeling seaside postcard jauntiness, while the sedate rendition of *Ferrets of Old England* taps into Noel Coward satire, *I'm Sorry I'll Read That Again* legend and brilliant broadcasting commentary with 40,000 of the creatures working at the BBC! *I'm Sorry's BLIMPTH* is repeated with the more intriguing title *L.O.V.E.?* as a crooned, cool swing arrangement mercilessly mocking all those naff lyrics spelling out heart-felt emotions in song. His 'still not right!' comment at the close is charmingly coy. *Beethoven's Fifth* is grooved up with a sweet and hot

Twenties jazz feel with the same 'something for the kid's to like' attitude as the Peter Sellers Trumpet Volunteer, but the album's major highpoint comes with *Stop It I Like It*. Antics with a relentless lover put to an infectious relentless Herb Alpert-inspired beat, it's a real masterpiece. *Family Favourites* slows things down a tad with an old-fashioned radio request programme filtering signals of love on the airwaves to various servicemen's best girls in the world. Bill delivers the classic amalgam of Forties tear-jerkers with last waltzes, white cliffs of Dover and nun's choruses all tossed into the emotional melting pot. *When You Come to the End* really speaks for itself – the last song with an Elvis-sized souring vocal suddenly cut to crackles and the needle whacking into the thing that sticks through the middle of the record. A brilliant piece of work which successfully detached the musical genius at the core of *I'm Sorry I'll Read That Again* to allow singer–songwriter Bill Oddie to bask in deserved glory.

Side One: I'm Small, Square Bashing Dance, Old Boutique, The Lawman, A Man's Best Friend, Rhubarb Tart Blues, The Wind (Oddie/Lee). **Side Two:** Recorded Live – includes One For My Baby and One More For the Road (Arlen/Mercer), Take It Off, Ferrets of Old England, L.O.V.E.?, Beethoven's Fifth (Beethoven, arranged by Oddie), Stop It I Like It, Family Favourites, When You Come To the End. All songs written by Bill Oddie except where indicated. Songs published by Tudor Music (Side 1, track 1/Side 2, tracks 3, 5, 8), Noel Gay Music (Side 1, tracks 2–7/Side 2, tracks 2, 4, 6, 7) and EH Morris (Side 2, track 1). Arrangements by Nicky Welsh. Producer Richard Hill. Sleeve design Paragon Publicity. 582 007 Polydor 1967.

DO GO ON

A spoof chat show for Radio 4, four episodes were broadcast from September 1997 and regularly featured Graeme Garden. As part of Late Night On 4, a new series of this mock live radio discussion programme showcased Griff Rhys Jones as inapt chairman Ainsley Elliot. In the opening edition, *Health*, Dr Graeme Garden guest-starred as charming Brussels Medical Commission member Professor Wim Van Dyke, cheerfully counteracting claims about closing down fish shops in West Hartlepool and remembering leaving a valued lap-top behind in a post-operation patient. The hasty, seemingly half-off-the-cuff and half-cut comic banter was relentlessly charming without stimulating the senses, but Garden was energetically enthused and Griff, in a near-permanent state of unease, proved the perfect comic sounding board. Luckily, Graeme Garden returned as a panel member for the rest of the series.

Series One: Fridays, 5–26 September 1997. **Series Two:** Thursdays, 1 April–6 May 1999. A new batch was recorded in April 2000. Written by the cast, with Nick Canner and Paul B Davies. Producer Paul B Davies. Radio 4.

DOCTOR AT LARGE

The first spin-off series from ITV's hugely popular medical situation comedy *Doctor in the House* saw our hapless hero Dr Mike Upton, played by Barry Evans, enter the big wide world of medical practice. Encountering familiar faces throughout (Geoffrey Davies, George Layton, Ernest Clark), eight episodes (3–7, 10, 12 and 13) were written by Graeme Garden and Bill Oddie. The first six broadcasts (affecting three of the Garden/Oddie scripts) were filmed and screened in black and white owing to a technician's strike.

YOU MAKE ME FEEL SO YOUNG

Finally escaping the confines of St Swithins, Evans and Layton land posts at Arthur Lowe's run down London practice. Madeline Smith, as the Major's tasty daughter, is a plus point but none of the old surgery regulars take to the fresh-faced arrival and it's down to Lowe's cunning trickery to expose the medical skill of the new boy.

DOCTOR DISH

Evans goes from rejection to adoration, when his bumbling sex lessons for the local girl's school rocket him to pin-up heart-throb. A suitably jealous Layton is the cocky charmer, doing anything for a giggle and spicing things up by sending passionately signed photos to his pal's besotted fans. Barbara Mitchell, guest star in *The Goodies: Superstar* plays the lusting schoolmistress.

MODERNISING MAJOR

Plans to modernise the surgery are helped by the arrival of Geoffrey Davies and the departure of Arthur Lowe. Bucket loads of pathos and layers of corny gags (Layton's 'Dear! Dear!' when a couple of antlers drop off) make for a classic episode.

CONGRATULATIONS – IT'S A TOAD

Layton's latest hair-brained, money-making scheme provides a pregnancy test via toads, but a newspaper ad placed by Layton attracts the prying eyes of a Scottish troublemaker. Played with relish by Fulton MacKay, the battle of wits against cheerful Lowe and nervous Layton is priceless. The toad vocals are provided by David Jason!

CHANGE YOUR PARTNERS

Romantic by-play as Madeline Smith irritates Evans, Davies plays for Smith and Evans gets jealous. Fairly average fare for the close of the Arthur Lowe story line, the writers liven things up with a bizarre 'comic strip' rant involving the love triangle.

UPTON SELLS OUT

Barry Evans grabs a cosy little job in a Harley Street clinic, learns charm from Davies and is ritually humiliated by Layton's 'poor' interruption of the posh private medicine brigade. Fabia Drake as the Grand medic who also looks after the less fortunate and Ivor Dean as Jarvis the bemused butler add to the fun.

WHERE THERE'S A WILL

An elderly patient dies soon after Evans treats him for the first time and the will leaves the entire fortune to his doctor. Typical black farce and money-grabbing relatives are contrasted with a stunning Bergman meets Hammer dream sequence with swirling mist and Evans done up as Death!

STUDENTS AT HEART

A return to *Doctor in the House* basics with a student riot ushering in the George Layton versus Richard O'Sullivan bickering which would inform the up-and-coming *Doctor in Charge*. With rugby, booze and destruction, it's hilarious in a relentless sort of way but it's easy beer money for Bill and Graeme as well!

Directed by David Askey and Bill Turner. Sundays, 14 March–11 April, 2 May, 16 and 23 May 1971, ITV.

DOCTOR AT THE TOP

Over a decade since doctors Robin Nedwell and Geoffrey Davies had hung up their white coats, they made a high-profile return to the small screen with this short-lived reprise for BBC1. Davies was now the respected Head of Surgery at St Swithins and Nedwell a general practitioner. Bill Oddie wrote Episodes Four, Six and Seven, while the remaining five were penned by George Layton who also returned as Paul Collier for the first time since *Doctor in Charge* in 1973. Ernest Clark made brief appearances as Sir Geoffrey Loftus and Chloe Annett was a welcome addition to the cast as Rebecca Stuart-Clark.

THE KINDEST CUT

Nedwell and Layton both face the thought of a vasectomy, but will they both be brave enough to go through with it and, more to the point, will they admit it if they aren't?

IT'S ALRIGHT I'M A DOCTOR

The smooth dude Layton finds national fame as a television doctor and has his ego stroked by a mountain of fan mail from young, attractive females.

WARING GOES PRIVATE?

Nedwell calls Layton a yuppie. But is it just jealously?

Producer Susan Belbin. Director Sue Longstaff. Thursdays 14 and 28 March, 4 April 1991, BBC1.

DOCTOR IN CHARGE

SERIES ONE

With Barry Evans having thrown in his stethoscope at the end of *Doctor at Large*, this third helping of *Doctor* shows welcomed back Robin Nedwell as the central figure of St Swithins. Geoffrey Davies, George Layton and Ernest Clark were also reassuringly in place. Episodes Four to Six, Eight, 14, 15, 17, 21 and 24 were scripted by Graeme Garden and Bill Oddie.

THE BLACK & WHITE MEDICAL SHOW

Racial tension on the ward with Scots bigot Jimmy Logan and mystic medical man Marne Maitland. Nedwell collapses into paperwork boredom and there's a magic moment concerning the new jargon… 'It's Hindi… Hindespicable!'

HONEY LAMB

Nedwell, the eternal comic loser, ends the episode tucked between his parents (Mollie Sugden and Victor Platt), but two American penthouse pets and the fight to win back his British babe give this an air of French farce. Layton and Davies give stunning, two-faced, support.

DOCTORS' LIB

With fond memories of American pay, Nedwell is fed up with his overworked and underpaid job at home. Davies and Layton back his complaints but send one tabloid rant to the British Medical Association!

CLIMBING THE LADDER

The Freemasons are explored and mocked with self-ingratiating Davies desperate to become a member and falling for the Layton/Nedwell prank using every black magic icon in the book! Davies tries to get his own back by flaunting his Big Summer Orgy and Nedwell gets to do his posh voice and silly Welsh man for maximum laughs.

HONEYMOON SPECIAL

Richard O'Sullivan has finally got hitched to the clinging Helen Fraser and the lads see them off with pranks – sticking the groom's leg in plaster for starters! There's physical comedy, bed-hopping misunderstanding and a seedy cameo from 1963 chart player Christopher Stanford.

THE LONG, LONG NIGHT

Richard O'Sullivan is stuck with cheerful cockney patient, John Blythe, in an atmospheric, claustrophobia and Pinter-esque farce, while Nedwell's energetic bluster keeps the confined situation buzzing.

ON THE BRINK

The usually full of testosterone and full of beans Layton is moping around the hospital like the proverbial wet weekend. So when he's spotted hanging off scaffolding everyone is on suicide alert with Nedwell mixing calm and bellowed angst, while Davies dallies with cheerful words of encouragement.

THE TAMING OF THE WOLF

Nedwell is eagerly awaiting the new crop of student nurses and is smitten with Debbie Watling. Soon it's all holding hands and Cliff Richard concerts but Nedwell is dumped for being dull and O'Sullivan tries his luck!

THE BIG MATCH

O'Sullivan clashes with Nedwell over Common Room funds: it's a table tennis table versus a colour television. Sport wins out and a hotly contested, hilarious match is played.

Directed by Alan Wallis (Episodes 4–6, 8, 24), David Askey (Episodes 14, 15, 17) and Bill Turner (Episode 21). Sundays 30 April–14 May, 28 May, 9, 16 and 30 July, 27 August and 17 September 1972, ITV.

DOCTOR IN THE HOUSE

If the books could become hugely popular feature films then why not a hugely successful television series? So was the reckoning of Thames comedy boss Frank Muir and producer Humphrey Barclay. Dr Graeme Garden and Bill Oddie wrote Episodes Two to Seven, 10, 11 and 12 of Series One and all of Series Two. Graeme recalls that 'the pilot was written by John Cleese and Dr Graham Chapman. However, they were at the same time developing Python and decided they couldn't write both series at once. Bill and I had been writing for *I'm Sorry I'll Read That Again* and John called me to ask if we would be interested in taking on the bulk of the writing for the Doctor series. I said yes, and off we went. Humphrey Barclay was pleased to have medical writers, me and Graham, on board and we did use our own experiences or apocryphal tales we'd heard at Medical School which were quite different from the stories in Richard Gordon's wonderful books, simply because everyone already knew the gags about 'What's the bleeding time?' and 'Big breaths'.

SERIES ONE

SETTLING IN

Rugby, booze and sex are to the fore as the lads settle in. The skeleton's called Adam – 'he certainly hasn't got 'em now!' and Barry Evans impresses his mates by chatting up Julia Foster.

IT'S ALL GO...

A distraught Barry Evans faces anatomy dissecting, while Robin Nedwell defuses the situation with comedy, as a few pints of the potent Appleyard Cider send the fledgling medics into paradise.

PEACE AND QUIET

Evans is in student accommodation but the noise is too much so it's a search for another room. After several sexual advances he settles on Renee Houston's pad. The problem is that his fellow students are sharing and sexy Yutte Stengaard wanders round the place in next to nothing. That's a problem!

THE STUDENTS ARE REVOLTING

Indeed they are! Evans is mistaken for a student demonstrator in the papers but the lads defuse a right-on sit-in and Ernest Clark injects his authoritative ideals into the plot.

RALLYING ROUND...

A sort of *Genevieve* homage with Angela Scoular and Bridget Armstrong (guest star in *The Goodies: The Lost Tribe*) involved in a vintage car rally and pregnancy antics.

IF IN DOUBT – CUT IT OUT!

Evans is hit by appendix pain and Davies, Layton and Martin Shaw seem more concerned with beer, cards and women.

THE ROCKY MOUNTAIN SPOTTED FEVER CASINO

The lads, struck by gambling fever, attract some dodgy attention – including Bernard Bresslaw's burly hard-man – before learning their lesson.

KEEP IT CLEAN!

The Entertainment Committee gather to plan the annual Summer Show for the patients and camp ballet from Barry Justice and religion singing from Mike Grady replaces rousing drinking songs at rehearsal. But culture is replaced with smut by the final performance.

ALL FOR LOVE...

Evans falls in love and studies go out the window but a little untruth about being pregnant finally puts him back on course and the girl (Lynn Dalby) goes off with that utter Welsh cad, Martin Shaw.

Directed by David Askey (Episode 2), Maurice Murphy (Episodes 3–7) and Bill Turner (Episodes 10–12). 25 July–23 August, 13–26 September 1969, ITV.

SERIES TWO

IT'S ALL IN THE LITTLE BLUE BOOK

Barry Evans and the gang are back and Arthur English is straight in with cut price bargains, while Nedwell and Davies muck about as usual.

WHAT SEEMS TO BE THE TROUBLE?

Harry Shacklock infuriates Nedwell, David Jason's aged Yugoslavian nut bemuses Evans and *Dad's Army* legend James Beck steals the show as the ward's sex-mad patient.

TAKE OFF YOUR CLOTHES... AND HIDE

Norman Mitchell presents the strippers – Jan Rossini and *Carry On* cutie Sally Douglas – but the medical skills of the laddish students are required when the lovely Rita (Rossini) faints.

NICE BODYWORK – LOVELY FINISH

A black comedy classic with the lads buying a hearse – complete with dead body in the back!

LOOK INTO MY EYES

Evans is wrapped up in the spooky lectures of Peter Bayliss while Nedwell sends up the hypnotic business.

PUT YOUR HAND ON THAT

Evans faces the reality of being a doctor and Nedwell helps him overcome fear by faking an accident.

THE ROYAL VISIT

The Prince and Princess are due to be greeted by a speech from Evans but Jonathan Lynn's anti-establishment chappie ruins the day.

IF YOU CAN HELP SOMEBODY... DON'T!

A whining old lady and her daughter sap the energy of the ever gullible Evans but a drunken Nedwell, Layton and Lynn liven things up.

HOT OFF THE PRESS

The college mag is brightened up with controversial glam girls and Evans is the new man in charge while Nedwell is killing himself at Richard Gordon's original novel – 'big breaths!' and all.

A STITCH IN TIME

Nedwell and Evans are on night duty and have to treat criminal Dudley Sutton and a drunken Ernest Clark.

MAY THE BEST MAN...

Jonathan Lynn finds his lady love (Susan George) flirting with Evans and a romantic battle results.

DOCTOR ON THE BOX

A telly crew expose life at St Swithins and the final, on-screen report, is hosted by none other than co-writer and real-life doctor, Graeme Garden as a straight-laced and probing chairman. It's a fairly nondescript role but hugely important.

FINALS

The hapless medics face their final exams, Evans misses his, due to emergency treatment of a heart attack victim, and, after a pathos-ridden interlude, he passes – along with everybody else!

Directed by David Askey. Saturdays 10 April–3 July 1970, ITV.

DOCTOR WHO

Small screen science-fiction that delighted each new generation from William Hartnell's white-haired time-traveller in 1963 to Paul McGann's stylish dude in 1996. Two of the leading actors enjoyed headlining guest turns in *The Goodies* – Who Number Two, Patrick Troughton, in *The Baddies*, and his successor, Jon Pertwee, in *Wacky Wales*. The fifth doctor, Peter Davidson, had a bit part in *Pollution*. A trivia fiend's gem: Tim Brooke-Taylor's Goodie throne was the same one used in the 1978 Tom Baker Who tale *The Androids of Tara*. *The Goodies*, within context, also made use of *Doctor Who's* iconic images, featuring a brief orbital glimpse of the TARDIS in *Invasion of the Moon Creatures*, a hasty word from a Dalek in *U-Friend or UFO?* and an anti-K9 rant in *Robot*. The continued cult success of the series into the Nineties returned the references to *The Goodies* with the trio making a thinly disguised appearance in the *Land of Fiction*-based *New Adventures of Dr Who* Steve Lyon novel *Conundrum*. An even more interesting publication from the Virgin range, Paul Cornell's 1994 Who effort, *No Future*, featured a lengthy cameo appearance from the team. Set in an alternative England of 1976, the meddling monk and pesky Vardans are causing all sorts of problems for the good doctor and his fiction-based companion, Bernice. The author captured the mannerisms of the Goods with Bill joining the terrorists, ranting and raving and being shot for his trouble, Graeme turning on the boffin cool and Tim getting patriotically fired up and idolising the leader of the alien invasion threatening the planet. For those keen to read *The Goodies*-related passages, it's in Chapter Nine, pages 118–120.

DOES THE TEAM THINK?

A short-lived television version of the hugely popular radio panel game where members of the general public, aided by a celebrity guest, fire questions at the star line-up. The answers were hopefully hilarious and with the game's deviser, Jimmy Edwards, Beryl Reid, Willie Rushton and Frankie Howerd constantly involved it was always worth catching. Although critic Philip Purser rather unkindly commented, 'Does The Team Think? – of itself, highly!' Poor old chairman Tim Brooke-Taylor gamely battled against the onslaught of quips and tomfoolery with a bemused shake of the head.

Producer Robert Reed. Wednesdays, 14 January–11 March 1982, ITV.

DON'T JUST LIE THERE, SAY SOMETHING!

Tim Brooke-Taylor starred in two productions of this classic Michael Pertwee political farce alongside *Round the Horne* mince machine, Hugh Paddick.

DOUBLE TAKE

The fairly unremarkable 1962 Cambridge Footlights revue, *Double Take* did, nevertheless, boast contributions from two future *Goodies* and two-sixths of Monty Python. Robert Atkins, the current president of the Footlights, was less than chuffed when Trevor Nunn bagged almost all the budget for his lavish production of *Much Ado About Nothing*. This left Tim Brooke-Taylor, John Cleese and the boys to do their stuff against an uninspiring set consisting mainly of wrought iron. Mind you, the scripted material was what really counted and despite collecting together an uneasy mixture of anti-satire tomfoolery and tongue-in-cheek old-fashioned music hall mugging, gems like *Don't Touch the Duke* and *MeekWeek* would later resurface on *I'm Sorry I'll Read That Again*. Although not appearing in the revue, Bill Oddie contributed a musical number inspired by news that Adam Faith had had an audience with the Archbishop of Canterbury. This would subsequently appear in *That Was The Week That Was*. Cleese's *Statistics* would also be purloined by David Frost's satire classic while, again under the Frost regime, Brooke-Taylor, Chapman and Cleese would recreate the karate sketch for *At Last the 1948 Show*. Despite excellent reaction at the Edinburgh

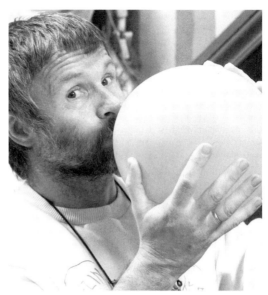

WELL BLOW ME! DO-GOODER BILL ODDIE PLAYS THE CHIEF BUBBLE IN THE ORGANISATION

festival, some items were best forgotten, notably the dreaded caveman sketch. Later, Goodies and Pythons would share chilled, toe-curling memories of wandering on stage, clad in furs, staggering through a shuffling dance and embarrassingly diving into the song, 'We're a most important caveman!' – Gulp!

ROBERT ATKINS, HUMPHREY BARCLAY, TIM BROOKE-TAYLOR, NIGEL BROWN, GRAHAM CHAPMAN, JOHN CLEESE, ALAN GEORGE, TONY HENDRA, MIRIAM MARGOLYES. Written by Robert Atkins, Humphrey Barclay, Tim Brooke-Taylor, Graham Chapman, John Cleese and Bill Oddie. Director Trevor Nunn.

DRAMARAMA: THE BUBBLEGUM BRIGADE

A one-off children's adventure written by Bill Oddie and Laura Beaumont for junior television's equivalent of *Comedy Playhouse*. Starring Bill as a charming bloke who rounds up a gang of kids to help the local community it led to a six-part series in 1989.

William BILL ODDIE Alph IAN KIRKBY Bunny MICHELLE MOORE Fuddle JAMES HYDEN Jinx LAURA SHEPHERD-ROBINSON Auntie Doodah VERONICA CLIFFORD Tommy Hammer STEVE STEEN The Bully LEE MacDONALD Little boy DALIAS CLEMANTS. Devised and produced by Peter Murphy. Director Roger Cheveley. Monday 15 August 1988, HTV.

E

EARTH AWAKES!

The world's first environmental pantomime written by Graeme Garden and staged in 1987 with an inspiring cast including Judi Dench, Peggy Ashcroft and John Cleese.

THE ED SULLIVAN SHOW

Towards the end of 1964, Tim Brooke-Taylor, Bill Oddie and the other Cambridge cronies, followed in the footsteps of Elvis, the Stones and the Beatles by performing two *Cambridge Circus* sketches on the legendary Ed Sullivan Show.

ENGELBERT AND THE YOUNG GENERATION

Somewhat bizarrely, the Goodies contributed a brief comic interlude to all 13 of Engelbert Humperdink's variety shows. Produced by the BBC in association with the West Germany station ZDF, it rather uneasily showcased treasurable mini-bursts of trio greatness alongside the bellowed pop songs and guest stars. Each week Engelbert would visit the Cricklewood office with a problem or suggestion ranging from music festival requirements to a cure for his insomnia and the Goodies would do their mini contribution. The first three of these linking contributions were recorded before *Charity Bounce* in the BBC's Studio TC8 on 10 December 1971, while another five were shot during January 1972's session for *The Baddies*. With contracts dated 17 January 1972, further *Goodies* filming took place in early February. No studio linking footage of *The Goodies* was used in Episodes Seven, Eight, Nine, 10 or 13. Several inserts were simply extracts from official episodes such as *Snooze* and *Kitten Kong*, although, far more interestingly, some shows welcomed the trio into the studio and presented a unique, specially filmed interlude. Only one of the programmes, Episode Eight, survives.

Ironically, it is one of the five which didn't feature studio banter between Engelbert and the Goodies. Indeed, *The Goodies* footage retained (*The Gym*) is one of the inserts luckily retained in the later compilation *A Collection of Goodies*, along with the extracts from Episodes Seven, 10, 11 and 13. Thus, *Country Codes* and *Body Guards* are missing *Goodies* links from these programmes.

1: Pets. The Goodies are on the look out for a wealthy nutter and find Engelbert, who asks them to walk his pets and ushers in the speeded-up Dumb Animals park antics from Kitten Kong. **2:** Pop Festival. Engelberts want an open air gig and the boys present the festival clip from The Music Lovers. **3:** Keep Fit. The Goodies are amazed at the star's physical condition and exercise on the busy Engelbert's behalf thanks to the Superman section from The Commonwealth Games. **4:** Post Office. Engelbert wants the Goods to deliver some letters and Graeme reveals his latest brain-wave via the pirate postal service scene from Radio Goodies. **5:** Sleepwalking. Engelbert can't sleep but Graeme's handiwork – playing Humperdinck's recording of The Last Waltz – merely sends Bill off on a sleepwalking trek, as featured in Snooze. **6:** Factory Farm. The Goods are asked to run Engelbert's farm to relax on but he's busy for the next thirty seven years and allows The Goodies to help – the results come from the episode previously known as Farm Fresh Food. **7:** Good Deed Day – Babies. Engelbert answers viewer's letters – including 'Why are The Goodies called The Goodies?' – and having explained how the lads feel about the enquiry, shows a clip of The Goodies living up to their new, taking care of nappy rashes and bottle feeding – the interlude features the Give Police A Chance song Love. **8:** Gymnasium. Engelbert introduces an interlude showing The Goodies move so fast via a clip of Goodies Gym mayhem. **9:** The Country Code. Engelbert apologises for the boys' absence and previews their Government educational short. **10:** Street Entertainers. Engelbert highlights the lads performing in the West End – well performing There's No Business Like Show Business in the streets of the West End at least! **11:** The Plum Pudding. Engelbert hasn't honoured his Goodies bill – forcing Graeme to wash Tom Jones' miner's helmet – and a ravenous Bill pinches his pud for a hasty chomp to the tune of Catch Me If You Can. **12:** Bodyguards. The Goodies take their duties lightly, play darts with Engelbert's picture as the board and prove their protective value to the star by looking after an image of him! Features the Oddie song One More Chance. **13:** Pan's Grannies. The Mothers of Tim, Graeme and Bill write into Engelbert asking him to show footage of the Old Generation – he does! Producer Stewart Morris. Sundays, 9 January–2 April 1972, BBC1.

EQUAL PARTNERS

A Comedy Playhouse pilot written by John Lloyd and Graeme Garden which failed to get a situation comedy series commission.

Nicky NICKY HENSON Pauline ANGELA SCOULAR. Producer Graeme Muir. Thursday 29 April 1971, BBC1.

ESTHER

Tim Brooke-Taylor plugged the play *The Philanthropist* in this 1991 television interview with Esther Rantzan.

AN EVENING AT COURT

In their first stage appearance together since the 1976 Amnesty concert *A Poke in the Eye with a Sharp Stick*, the Goodies reunited for this charity revue organised by Adrian Slade. The old boys ruled, with David Frost turning on the charm and greatness being touched with John Cleese and Peter Cook strolling through *Inalienable Rights*.

With ROWAN ATKINSON, ELEANOR BRON, DAWN FRENCH, JENNIFER SAUNDERS and JULIAN SLADE. Director Humphrey Barclay. Friday 21 January 1983, Theatre Royal, London.

FAIR GAME

A bizarre, one-off quiz game show for BBC children's television which failed to get a series commission. Capturing all the fun of the fairground, presenter Bill Oddie added a dash of slapstick pleasure as he punished incorrect answers and failed contestants with insults and playful attacks. Nick Wilton had a less than tight hold on the reigns as he asked the questions and the entire show was governed by huge celebrity judge Geoff Capes. In this pilot edition, Samantha Fox was on hand to spice things up a bit, as pairs of players from London, Manchester, Norwich and Nottingham fought it out for two cash prizes for themselves or a worthy charity on the good turn wheel of fortune.

Director Simon Betts. Sunday 17 November 1985, BBC1.

THE FAME GAME

Somewhere between Hughie Green and Jonathan Ross, Tim Brooke-Taylor hosted this pioneering live television talent show with Stan Boardman. Broadcast from Granada's Manchester studio, thousands of wannabe contestants had been whittled down to those lucky few ranging from bog standard comics, singers and dancers to such bizarre performers as the manic man whose act consisted of talking to a pedal bin. Great television!

Producer Trish Kinane. Director Patricia Pearson. Saturdays, 19 January–30 March 1985, ITV.

FAST FORWARD

Australian Channel 7 television chat show programme with squeaky voiced irritant Pixie-Ann Wheatly interviewing Bill Oddie during his 1993 promotional trip for the Royal Australasian Ornthological Union. Bill, slightly miffed and tense, reacts with dumbfounded disinterest to her 'do birds watch English comics?' line of enquiry.

FATHER CHRISTMAS DO NOT TOUCH ME

The third Goodies single and the first to make the British charts, this was perfect fare for the comic Christmas market. However, the song most played and performed was the totally groovy B-side, *The Inbetweenies*, a classic comment on the fickle nature of pop stardom. Kicking off with a wonderfully weeping guitar solo and a rowdy, chanting choir akin to John Lennon's *Give Peace a Chance*, this is Oddie the wannabe rock star pricking the bubble of pomposity. Fully aware that he and his colleagues were thirty-something in an industry dedicated to the teenager, the pleading edge to this great recording is heart-warming indeed. Mind you, most of the other Seventies' pop icons were in the same age bracket as the Goodies, and their records weren't supposed to be funny – 'we can compete with the rest as long as you give us a rest!' There's a real sense of Fifties' rock 'n' roll in the song's structure and, indeed, Oddie's teenage years were influenced by the new wave of Fifties' sounds from the States. The relentless saxophone backing on *The Inbetweenies* conjures up the audio montage of a dozen Little Richard numbers and the do-wop chorus is perfectly juxtaposed with the disco beat feel of the Seventies. A classic generation gap-filling rant – sort of like *Your Mother Should Know* from the Beatles with added giggles – you will irresistibly be forced to get your air guitar out for the spiralling 'To old to be a teenage idol…' conclusion. Although far from a novelty Christmas recording, *The Inbetweenies* single was released during the funny farm, funny season, 'pop goes berserk' festive season – a fact reflected in the bizarre Side One track, *Father Christmas Do Not Touch Me*. A mini Goodies Christmas special – with characters for all three to play – this is a totally off-kilter sing-a-long number obviously constructed after Oddie had consumed one or two sherries. A bawdy rugby song in format, Bill delivers the lead narrative lyrics with Tim's tasty little girl awaiting her gift-wrapped surprise. Howling cockney Graeme as a 'most immoral Santa' is sex-obsessed, attracted to the bigger, glam girls on his round and, while filling stockings, fills his boots for Christmas. Embracing the musical signifier and sound effects for the time of year (the effective intro injects reindeers galloping and jingle bells jingling), the seemingly never-ending repeated chorus of the title – with a word dropped each time on a surreal twist on *The 12 Days of Christmas* – takes this beyond insanity, but it's good for a Christmas Eve after the pubs shut. Mind you, Bing Crosby's *White Christmas* sold more copies!

Did You Know? The single entered the charts on 7 December 1974 and stayed for nine weeks. Its highest chart position was Number 7.

Father Christmas Do No Touch Me (traditional arrangement Bill Oddie), The Inbetweenies. Written by Bill Oddie. Producer Miki Antony. BRAD 7421 Bradley's Records November 1974.

<small>BILL ODDIE WANTS YOU!</small>

FAVOURITE WALKS: A BIRD WALK WITH BILL ODDIE

In this second edition in a series of six BBC programme showcases for the British Tourist Board, Bill Oddie took the viewer on a bird-watching ramble across Fair Isle on the look-out for rare migrants.

Producer Mike Weatherley. Monday 24 June 1989, BBC2.

FAX!

Bill Oddie was the chief presenter for this BBC Television series which tried to settle major debates, discussions, trivia obsessions, friendly rivalries, 'family disputes, pub arguments or shop-floor squabbles'. Here to save the world, Bill made a likeable, frantic, energetic host with Wendy Leavesley and 'Mr Trivia' Billy Butler, in support. Kick-starting in 1986, a 14-programme series was broadcast every Tuesday and Friday over a seven-week run. Bubblegum telly with an edge, a second series of 16 programmes was broadcast in 1987 when Miss Leavesley was usurped by the charming Debbie Rix and Bill's major goal seemed to be to unearth the Fax Grand Master of Trivia from the viewing general public. Series Three in 1988 saw the 16-part format pretty much unchanged and featured *The Goodies'* guest-star Wayne Sleep in two programmes.

Did You Know? In the Radio Times (15–21 November 1986),
Bill and the gang were featured in an article, 'Fax Is Back',
promoting the new series and requesting further queries to solve.
Readers were invited to 'post your poser' to Bill.

Series One: Tuesdays and Fridays, 7 January–7 March 1986. **Series Two:** Tuesdays and Fridays, 6 January–27 February 1987. **Series Three:** Sundays, 3 January–24 April 1988. Producer Alan Walsh. BBC1.

MARTY FELDMAN

Celebrated scriptwriter of *The Army Game*, *Bootsie and Snudge*, *Educating Archie* and *Round the Horne*, Marty Feldman was born in 1933. After an ill-fated initial stab as a variety turn – as the middle part of Maurice, Marty and Mitch – Feldman discovered life as a scribe more profitable. He was made chief writer of *The Frost Report*, bringing him into contact with Cambridge's finest, Bill Oddie and Tim Brooke-Taylor, for the first time. David Frost's showcase for John Cleese, Tim Brooke-Taylor and Graham Chapman, *At Last the 1948 Show*, cast Marty as the eccentric fourth man, leading to popularity as a comic performer. Tim Brooke-Taylor had largely written with Feldman for the *1948* shows and often watched recordings of the classic BBC radio cult *Round the Horne* which Marty wrote with Barry Took. Having secured a close working relationship, Brooke-Taylor and Feldman joined forces again for Marty's starring television vehicle, *It's Marty* between 1968 and 1969. The two were reunited for *Marty Amock* and the Royal Command Performance in 1970, after which Feldman was tempted away to Hollywood blockbusters with Mel Brooks and Gene Wilder. Brooke-Taylor recalls an insecure, introspective personality, 'I always got on really well with him but when I was 28 and he was 33 he said a very illustrative thing, 'When you get to my age you'll understand what I mean!' It was as though he had some sort of foreboding that he would die young. I suppose he did get rather spoilt towards the end but, thankfully, I didn't see much of that. All I saw was a brilliant writer and performer.' Frank Muir dubbed Feldman, 'the ideal second banana' and indeed, many consider his best work as an ensemble player in *At Last the 1948 Show*. Once he had found the major, international success he searched for, he suddenly seemed to realise it wasn't worth the effort. After too much Hollywood excess and doom-laden attempts to write, direct and star in his own film adventure with *The Last Remake of Beau Geste*, Feldman happily wandered aboard Graham Chapman's pirate romp *Yellowbeard*. Fun in the sun with old pals John Cleese, Eric Idle, Spike Milligan and Peter Cook formed his life's coda, dying with impeccable comic timing on the last day of filming, 2 December 1982. Fittingly, he is buried in Forest Lawns, California, close to his comic idol Buster Keaton. An evening's retrospective of Marty Feldman on Tuesday 23 March 1993 formed part of the National Film Theatre's Funny Men season with Tim Brooke-Taylor joining him in a selection of clips from *At Last the 1948 Show* and *It's Marty*.

THE FERRET SONG/THE RHUBARB TART SONG

A single release for a couple of songs from *At Last the 1948 Show*. John Cleese and the 1948 Choir are credited and that definitely is Graham Chapman and Tim Brooke-Taylor on the chorus; 'I remember being annoyed that Marty hadn't turned up!'

Written by John Cleese. 7N 17336 Pye 1967.

FESTIVAL

A God slot travelogue programme with an emphasis on music festival. This short-lived but enjoyable show was hosted by Bill Oddie and despite its religious slant, set its stall out from the outset – a celebration of music, with Christians, minority faiths and even people with no faith at all a target for Bill's questioning skills. The *Radio Times* (7–13 July 1990), however, favoured the religious slant and interviewed Oddie under the banner *In All Goodie Faith*. The opening episode of the six-part series took Bill to Bredon Village Fair on the edge of the Cotswolds. Chatting to the village community Bill discovered the delights of country community. Subsequently, shows travelled to Clydebank near Glasgow (looking at how the town has re-built itself since the war with the help of local heroes, Wet, Wet, Wet), Glastonbury (the favourite of self-confessed 'ageing hippie' Bill with plenty of midsummer solstice spiritualism and cool sounds from the Hothouse Flowers and Ladysmith Black Mambazo), Leeds (with a trip to the first multicultural festival, a Hindi community centre and the City Arts Gallery, while a 96-year-old resident recalled the joy of community), Stratford-upon-Avon (taking a look at the three-week festival and why a town rich with Elizabethan tradition selected a Nordic theme) and Cheltenham's International Festival of Music (with a bit of Mozart in the elegant Pump Room, song poet Johnny Coppin and a peek behind the Regency facades to reveal a vibrant community).

Producers Simon Hammond, Stuart Miller, Christopher Mann, Noel Vincent and Diana Reid. Sundays, 1 July–5 August 1990, BBC1.

FIVE FEET TWO

A single release by Spencers Washboard Kings of the classic standard number. Playing like a cross between Spike Jones and the Temperance Seven, Bill Oddie provided the vocals on this obscure but hugely enjoyable 1966 disc. His comic, angst-ridden plea of 'Anybody!' near the close is a highpoint. Bill's first wife, Jean Hart, joined the Kings for the B-side track, *If You Knew Susie*.

Five Feet Two written by Henderson, Lewis and Young. LCR 1001 Rayrik Records 1966.

FIVE HUNDRED MILE WALKIES: ONE MAN AND A DOG VERSUS THE SOUTH-WEST PENINSULAR PATH

An engaging romp documenting Mark Wallington's solo walk with only his faithful dog, Boogie, for company. Mr Cool Nature himself, Bill Oddie, read the original book for this entertaining tape version.

Random House Audiobooks 1996.

FOLLOW THAT BIRD

An engaging one-man showcase for Bill Oddie, birder extraordinaire, discussing his lifelong passion from childhood memories to earnest searches through Papua, New Guinea. An informal and informative chat and slide show, Bill supped a beer as he chatted, brought in a friendly, cuddly puffin and even injected a John Cleesian silly walk. An All Electric Theatre Production, Bill performed the piece at the New Vic Theatre, Newcastle-Under-Lyme, on 8 July 1999. Having delivered the piece over 50 times across the country, this particular performance was covered by Scott Hamilton for the North Staffordshire paper the *Sentinel*. The article, *Talk About Bill's Past? Not Such A Goodie Idea* was typically underwhelming.

FOLLOW THAT BIRD!: AROUND THE WORLD WITH A PASSIONATE BIRD-WATCHER

Bill Oddie's record of world travel in search of birds.

Robson Books 1994. Parkwest Publications, paperback, 1997.

FOOD FIGHT

Channel Five's answer to the nation's obsession with food-based telly programmes, this combined tasty tips with a game-show format owing more than a nod to *Endurance UK*. Among the celebrities suffering the fate of guessing what certain, unspeakable, items of food were, was our very own Bill Oddie on 8 April 1998.

FOOTLIGHTS '64

In the wake of *Beyond the Fringe* and *Cambridge Circus*, anything coming hot from the Footlights was big news to television. This edited highlights ATV presentation of the 1964 hit *Stuff That Dreams Are Made Of* featured scripted and on-screen performance material from Graeme Garden.

JOHN CAMERON, GRAEME GARDEN, DAVID GOODERSON, SUSAN HANSON, ERIC IDLE, MIRIAM MARGOLYES. Director Albert Locke. Sunday 27 September 1964, ITV.

FOOTLIGHTS: 100 YEARS OF COMEDY

In celebration of the 100th anniversary of the founding of Cambridge Footlights, the greatest stars to emerge from the movement got together to reminiscence on 4 June 1983, BBC1. All the Goodies were rounded up, alongside two other major greats, Peter Cook and John Cleese.

40 YEARS OF TV STARS – THEN AND NOW

As part of the Australian celebrations of Sydney's Channel 9's landmark birthday, presenter Don Lane introduced this major, two-hour retrospective on 20 September 1996. Bill Oddie, representing the eternal Oz favourite *The Goodies*, was interviewed. Bill explained the writing structure for the shows, discussed his contemporary bird-watching career and delighted in classic clips from *Kung Fu Kapers* and *Clown Virus*.

FROM THE GRAVEYARD – 10 TALES OF TERROR

On a cold winter's evening, there's nothing better than curling up by a roaring fire and listening to a ripping good ghost story. This choice selection of chillers may not be a rival to *The Signalman* by Charles Dickens but it certainly hits the spot and with an impressive collection of story tellers like this, who's complaining? What with a Dr Who (Colin Baker), *Carry On Screaming!*'s velvet-voiced vamp (Fenella Fielding), Mr Wombles (Bernard Cribbins) and a Goodie, this is heaven for your tape deck. Bill Oddie is given one of the longest and certainly creepiest tales, Robert Eastland's *The Ogre of the Scraggs*, deceptively geared towards children in his narrative style. In fact, although told from a kid's point of view and steeped in cunning touches that may suggest everything's

BILL ODDIE LOOKS LESS THAN HAPPY ABOUT BEING THE LATEST, AND OLDEST, PUPIL AT THE JOLLY THEATRE SCHOOL IN *FROM THE TOP*

just a huge joke, Oddie's rasping delivery breathes life into the lonely mining community locations, the cocky manner of our central anti-hero and the devilish, centuries old mystery of the stark wasteland.

Telstar Talking Books 1995.

FROM THE TOP

Before *The Bubblegum Brigade*, Bill Oddie and Laura Beaumont tried their hand at children's comedy drama with this teenage antidote to *Fame*. Bill starred as the 43-year old bank manager William Worthington whose career mid-life crisis leads to an enthused fulfilling of theatrical ambition. Enrolling in the Jolly Theatre School, Bill adopts the garish purple uniform, reverts to childlike behaviour in the playground and eagerly helps put on shows. The first series, directed and produced by Monkee drummer, Mickey Dolenz, ended on a successful high — with Bill starring as Dorothy in a production of *The Wizard of Oz* and a guest appearance from Pearl Hackney as his mum, Hattie.

Did You Know? The series is, allegedly, based on the career of Buster Merryfield who took early retirement from his bank manager position at the age of 57 and took up acting — becoming a comedy star as Uncle Albert in Only Fools and Horses.

William Worthington BILL ODDIE Annie Jolly MOYRA FRASER Dolly Jolly MAGGIE RENNIE Leslie Finsbury GAVIN FORWARD Janis Kopowitz CATHERINE HOLMAN Wayne Laine MICHAEL QUILL Joyce Torrington-Hawksby ERICA SHEWARD Mr Spadley STAN HOLT Hemphrey Kulumbebwe SCOTT SHERRIN Polly Jolly JOIESE WALLER Molly Jolly PAMELA MANSON Solly Jolly JOHN BURGESS. Written by Bill Oddie and Laura Beaumont. **Series One:** Directed and produced by Mickey Dolenz. Mondays, 23 September–28 October 1985, ITV. **Series Two:** Director Tony Ferris. Producers Paul Harrison and Peter Murphy. Mondays, 10 November–14 December 1986, ITV.

A ROSE BETWEEN TWO THORNS — BILL ODDIE LOOKS UNEASY IN THE COMPANY OF MAGGIE RENNIE AND MOYRA FRASER IN *FROM THE TOP*

FROM THE TOP: the book

From the Top, a novelisation of the first series, the complete story of the hilarious ITV programme.

Written by Bill Oddie and Laura Beaumont. Illustrations by Laura Beaumont. Methuen Children's Books Ltd/Magnet, 1985.

DAVID FROST

If Peter Cook was the heart of the satire boom, then David Frost was the head. The architectural brains behind the movement, picking out the perfect talent, cracking the whip and keeping the entire ethos together. Born in 1940, his healthy obsession with the sublime Cook led to a longing to perform comedy. Failing that, he would surround himself with the greatest post-graduate writers in the country and do the entire thing by proxy. He used old and fresh material from Cambridge whiz-kids Tim Brooke-Taylor and Bill Oddie for the 1963 topical benchmark *That Was The Week That Was*. In the main, restricted to brief written contributions, Oddie did make several fleeting appearances, before the three were, occasionally, reunited on stage during the American stage tour of *David Frost's That Was The Week That Was*. Brooke-Taylor, along with Cleese, became a key figure in Frost's pool of talent and the 1967 ATV sketch series *At Last the 1948 Show* was designed to launch both into the big time. It did just that but the stars eagerly escaped the restrictive net of Frost control and for a full decade mercilessly mocked him in their independent successes, *Monty Python's Flying Circus*, *I'm Sorry I'll Read That Again* and *The Goodies*. In 1983, their paths crossed twice more, for the centenary television salute to Cambridge theatre (*Footlights*) and the charity concert, *An Evening at Court*.

THE FROST PROGRAMME

Commercial television lured David Frost away for this ill-fated clone of *The Frost Report* complete with retained on-screen ranting from John Cleese and new faces, Michael Palin and Tim Brooke-Taylor in support.

THE FROST REPORT

Moving the satirical goalposts to incorporate more comedy sketch material, David Frost rounded up his usual collection of comedy greats for his live and personal onslaught on a given topic. The full variety package with songs, routines and monologues, the wealth of writing talent kept the show's finger on the pulse. Bill Oddie and Tim Brooke-Taylor, often working with Eric Idle, were on the scribing staff. Backrooms boys Jim Franklin and Ray Millichope later worked on *The Goodies*.

Series One: Thursdays, 10 March–9 June 1966. **Series Two:** Thursdays, 6 April–29 June 1967. Producer James Gilbert. BBC1.

THE FROST REPORT ON BRITAIN

Re-recorded album highlights from Series One of *The Frost Report* with written contributions by Tim Brooke-Taylor and Bill Oddie.

DAVID FROST, JOHN CLEESE, JEAN HART. Produced by James Gilbert. PMC 7005, Parlophone 1966. Re-issued as *Report on Britain* MRS 5084 EMI 1966

THE FULL MOTTY

A star-studded television tribute to the beloved footie pundit, John Motson. Derby County fan and ex-Goodie, Tim Brooke-Taylor, could be spotted in the audience.

FULL SWING

If darts could make a great game show and snooker pack them in on a Saturday night then why not golf? Well, why not indeed, but this half-hearted 1996 attempt failed and lasted just the one BBC1 series. Jimmy Tarbuck weakly wise-cracked his way through the presentation but at least the opening episode was blessed with cheery pleasantness from that 'fine actor, super comedian and keen golfer', Tim Brooke-Taylor. Partnered with Linzi, a charming, dizzy blonde bombshell contestant, Tim strolled through the contest. Three for the Tee presented a computerised virtual reality of the 18th hole at the Belfrey. Making a head-start with a cracking drive resting 28 yards from the pin, Tim whizzed round the hazard rabbits on a mock green thanks to correct general knowledge answers and finally completed all the putts for a thrilled-to-bits babe and £1000 for his chosen charity Sport Aiding Medical Research for Kids (SPARKS), an organisation of which Tim is the Vice-President.

THE FUNKY GIBBON

The ultimate groove to emerge from the astounding pop career of the Goodies – as much a part of the Seventies' scene as Marc Bolan, Sweet and Bowie's Ziggy Stardust trip. With their garish tank tops, coloured flares and self-deprecating coolness, the Goodies paraded the song on *Top of the Pops* and various other youth culture outlets, creating the arm-swinging, loose-limped dance craze and rocketing the single into the Number Four position.

Oddie's song-writing and the group's gibbon obsession – their previous single, *Stuff That Gibbon* failing to chart – had stemmed from radio's *I'm Sorry I'll Read That Again*. The perennial cult music classic, the team performed it for the televised rock gig *The Goodies – Almost Live* during the show's sixth series, featured it as part of their contribution to the pioneering Amnesty International show, *A Poke in the Eye with a Sharp Stick* and even sent it up for their *Comic Relief* reunion in 1988. Indeed, so important has *Funky Gibbon* become to Goodies folklore, that it is possible to forget how damn well brilliantly the song stands up today. From that spine tingling 'Come on, it's gibbon time!' intro from Bill, it's a perfect free-wheelin' bit of Edward Lear meets Lewis Carrol via David Frost class nonsense which doggedly refuses to budge from the subconscious. With contemporary sci-fi name checks for *Planet of the Apes*, an upbeat dance tempo, Graeme's booming 'Funky Gibbon' repeats, a cornucopia of gibbering oohs and even brief, Chubby Checker-influenced instructions on how to get with the beat – reaching a pinnacle with Tim's effete 'drop one arm like a bent baboon!' – this is way beyond criticism. Instant pleasure. And not only that, but the B-side is easily the equal to the gibbon ditty. The truly earth-shattering *Sick Man Blues* also found its way on to the Goodies play list for television and Amnesty. A very short number (one minute 47 seconds), this is almost the perfect Goodies hit with a real sense of energetic gusto, class-mocking mournful lyrics and a peerlessly rasping lead vocal from Bill. Quite arguably their finest recording, all three happily throw themselves into the venture with angst-ridden back-biting, the pumping, blues piano gets so under the skin it hurts and Oddie structures some delicious grotesque imagery all in a style Howlin' Wolf would celebrate. Graeme's 'better out than in, man!' is wonderfully down beat, the echo-heavy blue suede shoes interlude is perfect Elvis 1955 and Bill's suppressed giggles over full-blown recollections of vomiting on 'the baby's chair' is probably my all-time favourite Goodies vinyl moment. Sheer poetry.

Did You Know? *Funky Gibbon's rhythm track was inspired by the fusion experiments of Miles Davis and fragmented-licks pioneered by Sly and the Family Stone. Obviously failing to grasp this notion, the drummer was replaced by Bill himself, producing the required tempo by whacking a closed piano lid with a rolled-up newspaper. Throughout the 1975 season, Oddie's lyrics were featured scribbled on the Goodies office walls and a running commentary on the record's chart position was tallied on the area just by Graeme's computer. Trying this number across the globe, Oddie, Brooke-Taylor and Garden heard several attempts to perform Funky Gibbon. One motley Italian group, instead of following the all important 'Ooh ooh ooh – put them all together and what have you got?' with the multitrack collection of gibbish oohs, simple uttered the one, disconnected and misunderstanding 'Ooh!' It lost a lot in the translation! The song even found its way into mainstream commercial television comedy with a 1977 edition of The Benny Hill Show launching a new dance crash – the Flash – and promoting the notion with the lyric, 'You can keep the Funky Gibbon…' While The Beatles issued the upbeat version of Revolution as a companion piece to The White Album which featured the false start acoustic track, their natural comic followers also played fair with the record-buying fans, presenting a slightly different version of Funky Gibbon on the album – The New Goodies LP – Bill Oddie interjects at the close instead of Garden's single release 'scarlet gibbons' version – the Bunch of Blue Gibbons mix is still cherished by fans. The Goodies Greatest album included yet another variation, with no tongue-in-cheek false ending at all but simply a standard pop fade out. There really is room for a Funky Gibbon three-track CD single mega mix re-release! Oddie later confessed that Sick Man Blues was written in reaction to Tim Brooke-Taylor's singing abilities! Released in February 1975, the single entered the charts on 15 March 1975 and stayed for 10 weeks. Its highest chart position was Number 4.*

Written by Bill Oddie. Arranger Tom Parker with interference from Bill Oddie. Producer Miki Antony. BRAD 7504 Bradley's Records February 1975.

FUNNY BUSINESS

Enjoyable and informative late-night ITV comedy review show which cast its eye over everything from the *Carry On* to *The Fast Show*. Despite its liking for weird camera angles and unexpected, arty cuts into black and white photography – very disconcerting after a heavy evening down the pub – it was essential viewing for comedy buffs. Bill Oddie made an appearance in 1997 promoting the release of *The Goodies* compilation CD *Yum Yum! The Very Best of The Goodies* and despite slightly wacky host, Iain Coyle, interviewing with respect and affection, there was the expected, self-mocking, ex-Goodie and defending himself style to the piece. Tongue-in-cheek shame at this past comic life coming back to haunt him just as a new career as a second division David Attenborough television naturalist had taken off, covered clear pride in the glorious achievements of the Seventies' singer–songwriter.

Written and presented by IAIN COYLE. Produced and directed by Jim Reid.

WELL, IT'S GRAEME GARDEN, OF COURSE!

FUNNY HE NEVER MARRIED

Two Marty Feldman sketches from the BBC's first series of *It's Marty*, released as a record in tandem with the album *Marty*. Tim Brooke-Taylor features on both tracks. *Funny He Never Married* is a very subtle bitchy sketch with Marty and Tim's quiet old queens chatting about a like-minded associate who has just died. Pondering why he remained single throughout his life while commenting on his love of boy scouts, sailors and dressing up in woman's clothes, the two continually find semi-reasonable explanations for their funny friend's habits. Put those rubber-tipped claws away! *Travel Agency* captures Tim's dragged-up aged rant monster opposite Marty's aged rant bumbler. Classic

7N 17643 Pye 1969.

G

THE GALTON & SIMPSON COMEDY: THE SUIT

The opening programme in a season of one-off, self-contained half hours from the finest writing team in comedy history. Leslie Phillips starred as his usual suave self with Bill Oddie supporting as the chirpy chappie, Jimmy.

Howard Butler LESLIE PHILLIPS Penny Butler JENNIE LINDEN Jimmy BILL ODDIE Burglar FRANK JARVIS Wife JAN HOLDEN. Produced and directed by David Askey. Saturday 19 April 1969, ITV.

GRAEME GARDEN

'For the sake of the comedy we had to give me a fatal flaw in my plans, but I know how they could really have worked!' *Graeme Garden*

Actor, scriptwriter, doctor, director, eccentric scientist, wit, author, Goodie and comic genius, David Graeme Garden was born in Aberdeen on 18 February 1943. The family moved to Preston, Lancashire in 1947 and he studied at Repton school until 1961. A skill for physical comedy was spotted early on and Graeme told the *Radio Times* in February 1975 that 'When I was nine, I was ever so good at falling over. I used to be invited to perform before the assembled company.' It was a talent that *The Goodies* used fully, notably during the *Death in Bognor* interlude for *Movies*. Having taken part in several pieces of drama at school, the young Graeme's major interest lay in Art. A keen artist and cartoonist, he read medicine at Emmanuel College, Cambridge from 1961, experimenting with acting with CULES – the Cambridge University Light Entertainment Society – whose members frequently crossed over with the chaps from the Footlights. During his first year, Graeme toured the West Country with CULES, performing free shows at hospitals, prisons and orphanages. His second year saw him join the Footlights proper, auditioning with a single sketch act and being accepted immediately. The following year he was on the committee for the 1963 revue, *A Clump of Plinths*, contributing some material but failing to get a part on stage. In 1964 Graeme became President of the Footlights, immediately following Tim Brooke-Taylor's tenure. That year's revue, *Stuff What Dreams Are Made Of*, featured many of his sketches and saw him make his major performing

debut. Eric Idle, who also appeared in the revue, took over the Footlights presidency in 1965 and, although Garden had left the previous year, his influence was still felt via written contributions to the revue *My Girl Herbert*. By this stage, Graeme had joined the cast of *Cambridge Circus* and starred in *I'm Sorry I'll Read That Again* on radio. Having finished his medical studies at Cambridge – he earned the right to have BA, MB and BChir (Cantab), after his name – Graeme spent time at King's College Hospital, London, passed his final exams in 1967 and just needed a year of hospital experience before he could begin in a practice. Sharing a flat with old Cambridge pal, Eric Idle, Garden was advised by agent Roger Hancock that he couldn't be in two minds over a career in entertainment. It was medicine or show business. The decision was made for him when Hancock received an urgent phone call from another Cambridge chum Tony Palmer, desperate to direct Garden in *Twice a Fortnight*. Headlining the television series with Bill Oddie, this led to productive work with Tim Brooke-Taylor for *Broaden Your Mind* and the ultimate combination of the three in *The Goodies*. As well as performing, Garden and Oddie were writing the bulk of *The Goodies* and *I'm Sorry I'll Read That Again*, as well as episodes of LWT's *Doctor in the House*, *Doctor at Large*, *Doctor in Charge* and later the science-fiction comedy *Astronauts*. As with Monty Python's Graham Chapman, Graeme's medical skills were often called on during location work on *The Goodies*, notably during Series Three filming on Jersey, when Bill Oddie sustained an injury to his left thumb after a bit of business with a stretchable pig tail went wrong! After Goodies' stardom, Garden reverted to medicine with television presenting (*Body Matters*), advertising (notably providing a series of witty voiceovers for computer companies), writing (*The Best Medicine*, *Surgical Spirit*) and radio (*What's the Bleeding Time?*). Garden has written a novel, *The Seventh Man*, been a long-serving panellist on radio's *I'm Sorry I Haven't a Clue* and acted in *Yes, Minister* and *My Summer With Des* as well as appearing at the Phoenix and National Theatres. He directed the award-winning *Diumide K* for Illustra films. and commercials for a company in America. He presented Radio 4's *Stuff and Nonsense* on Saturday 1 April 2000. Married in 1968 and extending his family with a daughter, Sally, Graeme re-married and had two sons, John and Tom. Graeme wished that Margaret Rutherford could have played him in the film of his life story just so people could say 'it's nothing like him' and be

To Robert Best wishes from Tim Brooke Taylor PTO.

GIDEON IS SORRY THAT HE CANNOT SIGN HIS AUTOGRAPH BUT HE
FINDS IT VERY DIFFICULT HOLDING A PEN IN HIS WEBBED FEET

right! He listed his hobbies in 1972 as 'painting, drawing, reading, fishing, reading about fishing, playing the guitar and banjo, apologising for playing the guitar and banjo, trying not to travel in cars and being a Goodie.' For many of us, he always will be.

THE GARDEN PARTY

BBC1 magazine programme that featured famous father and daughter, Bill Oddie and Kate Hardie on Thursday 21 July 1988, strolling round the Glasgow Garden Festival and discussing their Relative Values with Mavis Nicholson.

THE GARDENING QUIZ

This Radio 4 show gave you the chance to test your gardening knowledge. Guest Bill Oddie tried out his green fingers with question master Dr Stefan Buczacki on Friday 9 June 1989.

THE GHOST TRAIN

Arnold Ridley's glorious old stage farce was brought to life by Jack Buchanan and Arthur Askey, reworked for Will Hay and Frankie Howerd and finally resurrected on stage for Bill Oddie at the Lyric Hammersmith in 1992. Taking the comic weight of the ghostly classic on his shoulders, it remained an interesting theatrical experience due to the supporting cast including Oddie's actress daughter, Kate Hardie.

GIDEON

One of the great children's cartoon series, it may not have the nostalgic clout of *The Clangers* or *Mr Benn* but these imported French shorts were an important part of my formative years. Based on the famous stories by Benjamin Rabier, the original French cartoons employed six actors for vocal characterisation. In the British translation, Tim Brooke-Taylor supplied character voices for the entire cast of farmyard creatures. He made an endearing hero out of the naïve yellow duckling, while creating a glorious galaxy of friends and foe to put Gideon through the hoop, with Winston the circus dog, Cornelia the tortoise, Stalker the poacher and flying rabbits creating a bizarre universe. The actor estimates that he had to do some 57 voices for the shows, finally getting stuck on the right sound for a Mother Fish!

Producer Steve Haynes. Thursday 5 April 1979–Friday 8 January 1982. Gideon Finds a Friend, Gideon and the Circus Dog, Gideon Finds a Job for Winston, Gideon and the Frightened Rabbits, Gideon Looks for a Proper Home, Gideon Meets a New Neighbour, Gideon Helps Snap Again, Gideon Rescues Lupin, Gideon and the Soup Maker, Gideon and the Secret Passage, Gideon Traps the Hawk, Gideon Frees his Friends, Gideon Muzzles Slinker, Gideon and the Sausage String, Gideon Puts Slinker in a Barrel.

GIVE US A CLUE

Long-running camp ITV charade game in which celebs cavorted about doing the 'it's a book', 'it's a film', 'it's a nuclear submarine' mimes. Bill Oddie suffered for his art on 20 March 1979, Graeme Garden had a bash on 27 September 1983, Tim joined in on Boxing Day 1983, while Bill returned for more of the same on 2 July 1985.

GIVE US A CONCH!

A sort of natural history quiz take on the above parlour game. Birding favourite Bill Oddie added to the riotous evening of quips and queries. The grand prize was the highly valuable glittering conch shell. The show was later renamed *The Conch Show*, and Bill, once again, took part.

Producer Melinda Barker. Wednesday 15 and 21 February 1984, Radio 4.

THE GLORIA HUNNIFORD SHOW

I can honestly say that I never imagined Gloria Hunniford could say something to turn my knees to jelly. The impossible happened one classic afternoon in August 1994 when she proudly muttered those immortal words 'they're back!' It was, of course, The Goodies, loud and proud in the studio plugging the couple of 'at long last' video releases from the BBC. Yes my friends, there before your very ears were Tim Brooke-Taylor, Graeme Garden and Bill Oddie chatting with affection, candour and good humour. And not only that, but Gloria bless her, seemed interested and knowledgeable and, more to the point, allowed them to talk – for about 20 minutes! Shock, horror – and this was the BBC you know! Projects before and after the golden decade of trandem travel formed part of the discussion but the main point was Goodie conversation and, although little or nothing new was revealed for the die hard fan, this was a perfect reunion interview. Much irony was made of the belated video releases, Tim's measured failure to understand the Beeb's policy was offered up first before Graeme cracked wise and Bill simply turned on the natural angst concerning hatred of satellites, the 'delusion of quality' multichannels bring and the fact that this stopped him enjoying cable *Goodies* repeats. More to the point, a disgruntled comment that the Goodie name prompts potential audiences to 'watch another Python video' was probably most telling. Royal support, chart success and the vital importance of Bill's music within the framework of the show, was interestedly tackled, as was the seriousness of the issues the team wanted to address. As Bill recalled, a list was usually compiled which resembled themes for planned *Panarama* specials rather than comedy starting points and the listening nation nodded in agreement. Spine-tingling tracks peppered this airwave treat, with *The Goodies Theme* introducing the lads, *The Funky Gibbon* jumping in at the halfway mark and *A Man's Best Friend Is His Duck* culminating the interview. As per usual, Tim and Bill held court for most of the time, with Graeme's terribly witty interruptions puncturing their dialogues perfectly. There's a warm atmosphere, intelligent questioning, relaxed answers and a vibrant

(sadly short-lived) sensation that The Goodies were on their way back – Tim is full of optimistic talk about terrestrial repeats, Christmas specials and a new series and Bill asserts that 'it's a waste that we don't!' For a few glorious weeks I really believed it. As such this was the ultimate get together. A pity then that, broadcast at the time it was, the vast majority of those who would have relished a chance to hear it, missed it. Still, for me it was a true magical radio experience – *Television's Greatest Hits* please copy!

Did You Know? *The following broadcast featured Tim Brooke-Taylor's selection of three discs, selected immediately after The Goodies interview. He choose, obviously, We Three by the Ink Spots, Mad Dogs and Englishmen for Noel Coward's 'wonderful lyrics' and Carly Simon's Nobody Does It Better because it was about him!*

GOLDEN HOUR OF COMEDY

A compilation of *The Frost Report*, *The World of Beachcomber*, *It's Marty* and *Round the Horne* featuring Tim Brooke-Taylor in Feldman skits Funny He Never Married, Travel Agency and Father and Son.

RONNIE BARKER, JOHN CLEESE, RONNIE CORBETT, MARTY FELDMAN, DAVID FROST, KENNETH HORNE, SPIKE MILLIGAN, KENNETH WILLIAMS with TIM BROOKE-TAYLOR. GH 530 Golden Hour.

THE GOLDEN ROSE

On 10 May 1975, The Goodies presented a lively and hilarious half-hour documentary concerning the up-coming Montreaux Light Entertainment Festival of 1975, illustrated with clips from entries across Europe and their own representation for the BBC, the Series Five classic, *Movies*, which won the team their second Silver Rose.

GOOD MORNING BRITAIN

A short-lived and oft-rearranged extension of ITV's weekday breakfast show for Saturday morning fun. Hosted by Michael and Mary Parkinson, the format was hardly going to impress youngsters but the recruitment of Bill Oddie – fresh from youth audience cool on *The Saturday Banana* – was heading in the right direction. Typically, Bill was cast as the friendly, accessible face of naturalism pursuits, discussing the delights of Mother Nature, strolling through country lanes and doing the odd spot of bird-watching in picturesque English gardens. His short *Wild Weekend* interludes, starting with a 10-minute chunk from

7.50am on 19 March 1983, were ultimately swallowed up in the vague umbrella package of *The Weekend Starts Here* before producers finally realised on 28 May that nature rambles weren't uppermost in teenagers' plans for their two-day break from school.

GOOD MORNING WITH ANNE AND NICK

ITV's fest for the late brekkie audience saw a quite remarkable 1994 Goodies' reunion for the hedgehog charity, St Tiggywinkles at Aylesbury. Bill Oddie, the clear spokesman for the item, roped in Tim Brooke-Taylor and Graeme Garden for an unheralded and uncelebrated on screen reunion which lasted less than a minute. Tim just about got a mention for the British Telecom phonecard which was supporting the Back to Action appeal to raise £350,000 for a new therapy unit, while Graeme did nothing but stop some poor hedgehog toppling out of his enclosure. Still, despite the lack of interest from Anne Diamond and Nick Owen, this was magic television. Besides that, there was Peter Davison, Colin Baker and Sylvester McCoy in an equally rare Eighties' *Dr Who* gathering – cool or what!

THE GOODIES

'Buster Keaton meets Tom and Jerry' *Bill Oddie*
Did the BBC really present the finest comedy series ever and still not realise it? Well, it's possible. Read on… and discuss! With the exception of the specials, episodes were never titled on screen or, indeed, in the *Radio Times*, thus the titles provided are gleaned from various sources. Episodes in Series Three to Eight correspond with the BBC Television Enterprises listing for overseas sales and these tally with titles featured on original clapper boards on the master video tapes. Likewise, Episodes One, Three, Four, Five, Seven and 11 of Series Two are, by common consent, accepted via video and clapper board evidence, while the ITV Series Nine, identifies Episodes One to Four in the same way. The last two episodes from Series Nine, the remaining shows from Series Two and the entire Series One have been officially agreed on by the writers, Tim Brooke-Taylor, Graeme Garden and Bill Oddie, especially for this book, presenting the official collection for the very first time.

SERIES ONE

With the full backing of Michael Mills and the Goodie triumvirate ready and willing to do anything, anytime, filming for the first series began at the BBC Ealing Film Studios on 14 September 1970. A television legend was born. The writing for this series set the norm for the entire run. Initially, all three Goodies would have a brainstorming meeting to come up with fresh ideas and suggestions for the forthcoming episodes. Tim Brooke-Taylor's 'with' writing credit acknowledged his contributions of dialogue snatches and visual routines, although his major strength was in determining what worked and what didn't work in the finished scripts. Less precious than either of the major writers, Tim could objectively sense what was right for the team as a whole. Graeme Garden and Bill Oddie would, as often as not, split the entire episode down the middle and write half each. Other times, one would create the visual interludes, while the other worked on the dialogue-heavy office sequences. The only time the trio really worked together as a full-on, American-style sitcom writing committee was for Episode Seven of this opening series, *Radio Goodies*. Following the outbreak of Python and, more importantly, an intensive period writing *Doctor in the House*, Garden and Oddie favoured the use of anarchic sketch comedy but within the more disciplined format of a situation comedy. In other words, a concentrated half hour of silliness. For the three stars, the show was very much a hands-on experience. The writers would sit in on the BBC planning and budget meetings, contribute to editing and sound effects sessions, construct the scripts around the cost of special effects, haggling over certain requirements and making sure each trick was funny enough to justify the price. Problems within the scripts were addressed from the outset and if a stunt was written, the writers would attempt to solve filming difficulties before the major, round table BBC meeting. Graeme's drawing expertise would be used with set designs and costume sketches, while Bill would scribble story boards and other suggestions for the relevant department to improve. Also, it was normal for the Goodies themselves to do all their own stunts – with the exception of intricate business on horseback or, naturally, falls from high buildings. Dummies were employed for these shots! The Goodies hit the floor running with all the basic, familiar character traits fairly well established from the outset. Tim was the patriot, Graeme the boffin and Bill the anarchist. Of course, Bill's weight and facial hair arrangements would fluctuate, Tim's British pride would became even more vehement and Graeme would gradually get more and more insane. It should also be noted that the first series saw Graeme adopting a normal pair of glasses before he finally settled on the full Buddy Holly, thick-rimmed set which we all know and love. Off duty he favoured contact lenses.

Starring and written by Tim Brooke-Taylor, Graeme Garden and Bill Oddie. Film cameraman John Tiley with John McGlashan (Episode 5) and Max Samett (Episode 7). Film editor Alan Lygo. Visual effects Ron Oates. Costume Betty Aldiss. Make-up Rhian Davies. Lighting Derek Slee. Sound Laurence Taylor. Music by Bill Oddie and Michael Gibbs. Design by Roger Murray-Leach (Episodes 1, 3, 4, 6 & 7) and Janet Budden (Episodes 2, 4 & 5). Film direction by Jim Franklin. Produced by John Howard Davies.

THE TOWER OF LONDON

A milestone in television history, this first-ever episode of *The Goodies* sets the scene perfectly. Full of visual business and clever verbal banter, the three-tier class system of the team is mapped out from the very outset, while this so-called 'children's programme' cuts the radical cards straight away with drug references, bare breasts and a regal scandal right at the heart of the narrative. New shows seldom started like this! Indeed, as Tim, boyish charm and patriotic energy in full bloom, first wanders into the office which will be home for over a decade, he delightfully enthuses, 'Oh! It's fantastic!' It certainly is fantastic. With the huge amount of dosh left from Tim's look-a-like Auntie, the scientific genius that is Graeme Garden has designed a self-contained, all working, all powerful office for the Seventies' businessman about town. In actual fact, all the food, toilet facilities and sleeping arrangements are fairly unimpressive colour separation overlay effects and the huge computer looks like it fell off the back of a very old lorry indeed, but 30 years ago this was state of the art stuff and the trio are suitably mesmerised by the place. Naturally, unsubtle digs at other artistes are not long coming in this opening episode and Garden's Rent-A-View picture window displaying scenes (thanks to colour separation overlay again) and emotive musak from London, Paris and finally Sydney, fouls up the ear drums by dishing up a burst of Rolf Harris delivering *Tie Me Kangaroo Down Sport*. But be warned, a Rolf plague would soon take over Britain – but that's another story! The lads may have a place to do their doings but what their exact doings are nobody knows. If there's something to blame on someone it's always best to pick on Tim and pick on Tim they do, resulting in his sheer desperation in explanation, 'We are the Goodies… and we do good to people!' Bill is less than

impressed ('How wet!') and his wide blanket of advertising reflects his lack of organisational awareness. Tim is pleased *The Times* has been approached, less pleased about the smutty mag and as for *The Beano* and *Rubber News* (which clearly amuses the audience almost as much as Bill himself), well anything could result from that. And that's it – it's the Goodies, anything, anywhere and if Graeme's bemused 'that's a bit vague isn't it!' reaction to the ad's wording is disconcerting as well as totally hilarious, then the lack of a telephone makes business fairly unbusinesslike. In an idea that was hastily dropped, the elderly, wordless (and thus, cheaper) lady who lives in the flat below them acts as a secretary. She can't speak and she certainly can't spell – the first note is addressed to the Giddies – but Bill soldiers on and Tim, reacting to their first assignment like a mother holding her first baby, is a picture of contented happiness. It certainly is a great feeling being needed and that's a cue for a Bill Oddie song if ever I heard one! The ever-catchy, oft-repeated (thankfully) refrains of *Needed* enhance the lads preparation for this initial position, based at the Tower of London. Indeed, the song even ushers in the first appearance of the legendary mode of transport – the three-seater trandem – cunningly wheeled out from behind a parked car à la Keaton. This really is television magic in the making, complete with swift customising of the bike (Goodies flag and a flashing siren on Tim's head) before clumsy, falling-off slapstick and a speedy journey to The Tower. Bill's safety precautions seem a little underfunded – pumping up a cuddly guard dog with the sign 'It Bites' as a deterrent – but it's quickly into the spooky corridors of regal history and a sudden change in music from jaunty to mood. The already jittering Goods, what with first day nerves and weird, unfamiliar surroundings, are further freaked out by a staring eye at the keyhole. Bill, all Goodies t-shirt and mop-haired bravado is less than discreet – 'Hey, there's an eye!' But in the end, it's simply kindly, dusky old George Baker – somewhere between *The Dambusters* and *Inspector Wexford* – in a kindly, dusky old office cum kitchen cum torture chamber. The visuals bear out the converted and converted again style of the room, with a refrigerating iron maiden, a pit and the pendulum-like chopper for slicing the corn beef and thumb screws that double as garlic crushers. However, the business is serious and it's time the Goodies got down to serious business: the beefeaters have no beef. Bereft of beef they struggle through on the poorly,

EARLY *GOODIES* PUBLICITY WITH THE LADS SHAMELESSLY PLUGGING *GOODIES* T-SHIRTS

corned variety, dwindling down to midget-sized versions of their former selves. It's a crime to watch, the stout yeomans are anything but, the ill-omened ravens have been consumed in desperation and even the madly barking guard dog has wolfed the Sunday joint. Not surprisingly, Baker cracks up – both mentally in terms of the script and laughingly in terms of filming it. Back at base camp, Bill's sucking on his hallucinogenic lemon sherbet (bless!) and Tim's illogically getting all logical. The culprits are either bulls (saving their bacon, as it were) or poultry farmers (in a cunning bid to convert the famous beefeaters into the less than imposing chicken eaters). Graeme is outraged but, much to Tim's smug pleasure, the worshipped computer – fat on a quickly inserted beef sandwich – bears out the blonde one's theory. But still, Bill's too gone, man, and far out, to bother. On a late Sixties' trip to the stars, Bill's having a ball, screaming 'I don't believe that!' with so much

energetic pleasure that you slam your eyes shut to join him. Luckily, Graeme's computer brain scan thingy makes life a lot easier and after a brief glimpse of Bill's topless sunbathing babe and a short-lived journey into Jimmy Saville's world of *Top of the Pops*, a cryptic, beefeater mystery-solving message comes fresh from Bill's addled brain. Tim and Graeme hilariously milk every gag and misunderstood comic guess out of the mad hieroglyphs, but it's a gloriously politically incorrect exchange ('Old lady with a big mouth!' 'My mother-in-law!') which shoots the comedy into orbit. But any bloke with half an ear and a head full of yellow powder can see it spells out 'Crown Jewels' so it's into the quick change compartment, time for beefeater disguises and off, with deadly pike in hand, all for the good of England. Typically. Tim's royalist bent quickly fades with fear but soon it's all for one and one for all on their three-seater, riding without due care and attention, wasting a group of pedestrians and getting to The Tower just in time for the tearful, Last Post farewell for the totally vanishing beefeaters. A touching, poignant sight indeed. But meanwhile, here on BBC2, the unexpected – a commercial break. Comedy versions of commercials had been paraded on the Beeb by everybody from Benny Hill to the Monty Python boys, but the Goodies were the first literally to cut their shows into two halves and insert a semi-realistic set of ads in the gap. This first offering sees Graeme (charmingly sans glasses) demonstrating the very practical Goodies tea set – complete with repeated jingle – and Tim, camping it up like a good 'un with the very tasty, 'grey, grey, grey, grey', willingly stripping Maria O'Brien, trying out the 'right to the dirt of the wash', Fairy Puff powder. Part Two kicks in with the lads whistling their own theme tune, while constructing a fool-proof burglar alarm around the crown jewels. Beautifully British, the 'Please Do Not Steal' sign and Graeme's polite recorded message, gives way to mock policemen, noise aplenty, dangling skeleton and a lit cannon. But still a clichéd, stripped sweater, swag bag carrying criminal wanders into the protected zone. But this is no ordinary crook my friends – oh no, he's a burglar by royal appointment. Young Prince Charles is shockingly in the picture as Mr Big – ears, horses and polo point totally in his direction – but Tim's not a happy bunny. Tellingly he blames the student pranks learnt at their shared seat of education, Cambridge, before Oddie's *Catch Me If You Can* ushers in a torrent of visual gags. It's basically polo conventions for warfare, with skittle-style defeat of the Goodies, fresh fruit for ammunition and 'on me head' footballing antics with pawnbrokers balls. An endearing bit of tourist photo snapping stops play for a few seconds and Tim spins for England when his pike gets lodged in a tree trunk, but the chase ends in failure and, worse still, concrete proof that the crowned horseman is indeed, who they think he is. Tim can do nothing but turn on the Stan Laurel tears and Bill, injecting a 'Flipping heck!', can do nothing but join him. Knowing they 'really blew it' Bill sees the end of the Goodies coming nigh before things have hardly begun. Tim, meanwhile, is eagerly making plans to see some friends – in Canada! But wait, Gertan Klaubar, looking like Brian Blessed's brother, strolls in as Black Rod and offers a Royal message – the Queen, financially embarrassed what with flogging Balmoral to the Burtons, had in fact, pawned the jewels, replaced them with fake ones and sent off her

eldest to replace them again with the real thing. The Goodies had broken up hush, hush royal action but, in the first of many tantalising sniffs of OBEs, the team are reassured that 'we shall see ya right!' – don't hold your breath fellows! But hey, more importantly than that, the Goodies are still very much in business. Join in the trio's jubilation, puff your chest with pride and strap in for a series that took comedy into uncharted seas.

Did You Know? *This first series kicks off with opening credits featuring moments from the opening show, (the hooded polo action), Oddie's exploding sleep walker (from Snooze) and Garden's lawnmower tumble (Cecily) as well as footage of the lads doing A Hard Day's Night, slow motion leaps and singing the oh-so-catchy title song. Check out how the song is extended here, allowing a few more lines to be heard as the camera pans across the empty Goodies office. For its evening programming the Australian Broadcasting Commission made two cuts, removing the naked woman featured during Oddie's sherbet vision and the entire limp-wristed Fairy Puff advert. Location filming and the visual bits of business were, obviously, caught on film, while the studio office-based material would be performed at the BBC in front of a live audience. Thus, the laughter is for real folks… as if you doubted that! For Goodie completists and television trivia obsessives, this episode reveals the telephone number for the Goodies office. So, if you want anything, anywhere, simply call Cricklewood 0831234…*

GEORGE BAKER, MAX LATIMER, GERTAN KLAUBER, MARIA O'BRIEN as The Fairy Puff Girl. Episode One, recorded Thursday 8 October, broadcast Sunday 8 November 1970, 10.10–10.40pm, BBC2.

SNOOZE

Another day, another dollar and another assignment for those fledgling Goodies, grabbing the commercial bull by the horns and tackling the power-mad, greed is good, corruptible world of product promotion. However, there's calm before the storm and Graeme's ultra-comfortable waking-up arrangements are as calm as calm can be. As the Goodies sleep, Graeme's mechanical hand gently taps him out of slumber and as that fails, a sudden, shock tactic of fast descending medicine ball does the job instantly. For Garden it's the only unnerving moment in the entire morning procedure – his tea is piping hot in his hot water bottle and with a host of inventions worthy of Caractacus Potts himself, his breakfast, morning paper and dressing for the day are made simplicity itself. It's the first appearance of the legendary all-in-one suit of clothes, while the interactive painting, which provides a spoon for his egg and a napkin to wipe his mouth, is a visual delight. Tim, meanwhile, is literally pulled out of bed in his valiant but fruitless attempt to grab the speeding paper. But as

Graeme says, this is the 'magic of science, dear boy!' and the glories of sleep are key to a happy, healthy lifestyle. Mind you, Bill doesn't seem to be in tune with the ideal, slumped in his pit and too frightened to close his eyes for fear of the sleepwalking that is the bane of his existence. Timbo, hyped up and squawking with panic as a client approaches, highlights his far from relaxed persona. Things are soon forgotten, however, with the arrival of Roddy Maude-Roxby as the fast-talking, insanely active businessman Rupert Wincheater. Played like Ian Carmichael's Boultings satire simpleton, Stanley Windrush on speed, Maude-Roxby charges into the Goodies' domain brandishing his less than successful bedtime drink Venom and muttering on about being far too busy to make an appointment. Tim happily goes with the flow but Bill, bolshy, arrogant and willing to have a poke, tells him to 'get out!' in no uncertain terms. But the motor-mouth isn't listening, talking nine to the dozen, embracing every obvious suggestion and half sent up comment as the greatest theory of all time. Eventually he talks money (although it's only a tenner to the Goods and fifty million to him), but, still the lads need work and he's the only bloke around. In a flurry of 'cheers', 'fine's and 'okay's he's gone, leaving the trio pondering on an apt name for this wonder kip nip. In the second dig in the space of just two programmes, Bill has another go at Rolf Harris, suggesting his name as an ideal replacement because he always sends him to sleep. Eyebrows are raised in bemusement at Graeme's Sleepy Bobos baby talk but everybody agrees on Snooze as the ultimate knockout name for this knockout formula. Dodgy ad posters, even more dodgy slogans (Sn 'you know' ooze) and a commercial jingle from Bill (complete with over-flamboyant Bing Crosby-fashioned bo-de-bo introduction and a hilarious, wild-eyed, 'I've got rhythm man' bit of syncopation from Tim) form part of the overall campaign. But nut Graeme, as per usual, isn't satisfied. Ever the searching brained scientist, the boffin we know and love comes up with the all conquering new improved Snooze. The old mixture with added 'POW!' factor. There's only one person nuts enough and sleep conscious enough to be Gray's human guinea pig and that's little Bill – forced to consume the liquid and peg out almost immediately. It's not long before the entire board of directors at Snooze are out for the count and Bill, still driving 'em home, slumbers for three days before the dreaded sleepwalking takes hold and that guy is out of

here. With Bill gone walkies and Graeme slaving over a hot bunsen burner in search of an antidote, it's left to valiant Tim to track down their loose comrade. The three-seater is out of the question, of course, so interestingly, Tim takes the never-seen-again transport alternative – The Goodies van. Mind you, the tax date, marked October 1970, was overdue by the time the show was aired so probably a couple of charlies from the following episode impounded it. Anyway, it successfully keeps tabs on Bill as the wonderful, spine-tingling chords of *Show Me the Way* accompany the visual humour of minefield strolling and double decker bus manoeuvres. A slower, more mellow, Bill solo version as compared to the later rendition released on the record, *The Goodies Sing Songs From The Goodies* , Bill staggers through life, avoiding disaster with Harold Lloyd-like agility, partaking in a bit of handball park play and working on Harpo Marx-style autopilot for some beach babe pursuing. The mock ads are both, unsurprisingly, for Snooze – with Oddie's Scots miss voiceover complete with a clever juxtaposition of the show's narrative as sleepwalking Bill wanders through, and Garden's disgruntled, angst-ridden attempt to put his overenergetic dog down with the sleep-inducing muck – before it's back to Tim, a welcome burst of *Needed* and doggedly unstoppable Bill who, like Felix the cat, keeps on walking. By now, of course, Graeme's perfected the antidote, had a quick swig of Snooze and collapsed with sleep before completing the test. So with a repeat of those haunting slide guitar passages from *Show Me the Way*, suddenly there are two sleepwalking Goodies parading round the place. With prop and people juggling, Tim finally gets his mates back to the office, feeds them the anti-Snooze and almost gets things back to normal. But, my friends, this is the Goodies and nothing's normal for too long. Bill gets one of the biggest laughs of the show by crawling straight back to bed again and Graeme gets Wincheater's sleepy answer phone. The Snooze marketing has been so successful that the entire country has latched on and dropped off thanks to it – even Graeme's watch has gone to sleep… that's powerful stuff – and the Goodies' beloved face of BBC news, Corbett Woodall makes his series debut in go slow mood. Tim reassuringly goes into expected panic overload but Graeme has the solution – to infiltrate the nation's water supply with the antidote. It's all a bit sudden and tenuous, certainly Bill's well-timed sneeze carries less water than the barrel and the climatic newsflash played out at 100 miles an hour – with sporting records aplenty, Enoch Powell in full rant and Woodall's Tarzan chest-bashing exit – is funny in a rather obvious way. It is slightly back-tracking to *Broaden Your Mind* technique. Maude-Roxby's anguished fume is beautifully played and his manic-obsessed twitching trigger happy finger builds to a classic close – the Goodies consuming the speed formula, waiting for Roddy's starting pistol action and racing off at high speed. It's far from a classic and the team are still, naturally, caught up with the structured, business venture aspect of the office. Flights of bizarre fancy were soon to come but not quite yet.

RODDY MAUDE-ROXBY, CORBETT WOODALL. Episode Two, recorded Thursday 29 October, broadcast Sunday 15 November 1970, 10.30–11pm, BBC2.

GIVE POLICE A CHANCE

One of the great Series One efforts, simply because it's so on the edge. Police corruption is at the epicentre of the plot and in a television age when Jack Warner's *Dixon of Dock Green* still reigned supreme, the shared, assumed knowledge that law-enforcing brutality, suspicious reaction to 'certain substances' and overzealous siege situations for the least little things (Tim's mum is held hostage while a missing pair of gloves is hastily located), were very radical indeed. Hard to image that this came before television drama offered up *The Sweeney* and almost 30 years before Ben Elton's *The Thin Blue Line* softened the comic edges again. And even harder to believe that *The Goodies* would soon be given the back-handed label as a show for children. All fares well initially in the Goodies office – Tim struggles to read the *Radio Times* with a magnifying glass, Bill lazes about with a high-brow broadsheet and Graeme idly looks out on a rain torn scene before flicking a switch on the Rent-A-View and transforming the image to a sun-drenched desert island, complete with Hawaiian guitar musak. Tim objects semi-ferociously but much, much worse is to come. Paul Whitsun-Jones as Police Commissioner Butcher (played like Frances L Sullivan with a touch of the Norman Mitchells) bursts into the happy scene with Sergeant Roland MacLeod at his side. It's a police raid with every Goodies utterance repeated sarcastically, pulled apart or used in evidence against them. This mini dictator wants to get the police a good name, to walk away from their tarnished image as uniformed muggers and be liked by the great British public. Still, even for the Goods it ain't gonna be easy. When Graeme grasps the notion, Whitsun-Jones instructs his lackey to 'Kill 'im!'

and Bill ends up on the receiving end of a severe roughing up – his arm flopping in the breeze like a wind sock with no wind. But Tim is still naïvely fixed in that coy Fifties' world of the good old British bobby. After all, this is England and the boys in blue are simply in high spirits – bless 'em. An impartial recce is called for and Bill, never one to skirt round the edges of indiscretion, goes for it in cropped hair, bovver boot style. The trio are looking for trouble but they don't have to look very far – poor old Tim almost has a heart attack begging to find out the time from a policeman, while parking restrictions and hastily painted yellow lines trap the lads into parking fines. A road sign hell blocks the Goods in, and an Oddie strip search removes all items of dangerous clothing before the helpless chap is arrested for indecent exposure. These cruel, hated, blue bottles are clearly a lost cause – even Garden's foolproof computer is fooled – but Bill's drugged-up hippie, visions up the answer, after yet another *Top of the Pops* interlude and an opening fire across the bows of that 'poof' Tony Blackburn. Tim's advertising campaign – the game Identikit with sub-Gumby coppers muddling through criminal stereotypes and the bargain ('for only a few coppers' – groan!), second-hand Coppe Shoppe, featuring the deliciously cutting 'gets rid of fuzz in no time' razor quip – falls on deaf ears, but Oddie's dropped-out ideal of love and peace man seems to hit the mark. Whitsun-Jones is distressed at the thought of laughing policemen but Bill's winning ways, all 'don't hit me baby' comments and cheerful grins, captures the essence of the times. In one of the most sustained and effective musical interludes in the entire *Goodies* run, the three lads take on policemen mantles and ride out in flower power attitude. With the spirit of The Beatles' *Summer of Love* and even more recent biking memories of Dennis Hopper on the razzle in *Easy Rider*, the Goodies set off with dark shades, dope-puffing and flower-tossing hip. Oddie's song, *Love Love*, complete with Beatles-esque harmonies and the overpowering sense of love will conquer all, is reflected on the do good to anyone re-evaluation of the police force – speed limits are altered from 30 miles per hour to 80, Tim's helmet helpfully has an in-built cuckoo clock for instant time checks, zebra crossings are produced at the drop of a helmet and Graeme's rabbit magic trick enchants the free to play anywhere children. But, of course, as in life, good turns can turn sour, and comfort to the homeless (including Garden kindly reading them a bedtime story), grooving in the park and, ultimately, nude bathing, brings the down fall of the cool cops. The police are enraged, the down 'n' outs complain of noise pollution and even the Hell's Angels reject ideas for a free Hyde Park concert (in a satirical touch aimed at the apocalyptic, decade-climaxing, Rolling Stones gig). Self-punishment on behalf of Whitsun-Jones does no good (besides this mad masochistic soon begins to enjoy it), so it's undercover work for him, posing as a buxom blonde and a spot of shameless entrapment of those three uniformed love groovers. On trial, with Whitsun-Jones in the dock, his son and 11 fellow policemen forming the jury, paid witnesses and every bit of legal stuff stacked against them, the future looks decidedly bleak for our boys. There's certainly something funny going on here but Tim, adopting blonde wig and taking on their own defence, pulls out the emotive stops, pleads their case, gets helpful mood music from Graeme's saxophone accompaniment and even plunders the same 'quality of mercy' Shakespearean back up used by Tony Hancock in *Hancock's Half Hour: Twelve Angry Men*. The boy does good, the cops break down into tears and everybody gets together in a panto sing-a-long of *Give Police a Chance*. John Lennon probably wasn't consulted, he certainly wouldn't have sued for this tongue-in-cheek encapsulation of the unity of mankind in full flow at the time. The Beatles had split asunder, Vietnam still raged and a new decade was already sinking into depression after the bright optimism of the Sixties, but Lennon and the Goodies together bring laughter-capped hope for a generation.

Did You Know? *The Australian Broadcasting Commission edited out the sequence featuring a completely naked Bill Oddie cavorting in the park pond.*

Special guest PAUL WHITSUN-JONES, ROLAND MacLEOD, JIM COLLIER, ALEXANDER BRIDGE, BARTLETT MULLINS, KATYA WYETH. Episode Three, recorded Thursday 22 October, broadcast Sunday 22 November 1970, 10.40–11.10pm, BBC2.

CAUGHT IN THE ACT

The ultimate Goodies rarity. The original broadcast print was long-thought ditched from the BBC archives and, although a black and white film recording does now exist, it has, so far, never been repeated on terrestrial or cable television. Indeed, the episode hasn't been screened anywhere since 1975. In terms of plot narrative, the episode again offers our three heroes a challenging assignment. With a major brush with the British government, scandal and corruption on a Profumo-like scale is threatened when sexually compromising photographs of politicians are unearthed. It is the Minister for Trade and Domestic Affairs (oh yeah!) who employs the boys to get these pics safely back under wraps, but during the investigation, the full horrific story is revealed. The Playgirl Club, catering for all manner of weird and wonderful perversions, satisfies many of its clientele with the male alternative to Bunnie Girls – the Wolves. Gulp! A couple of mouth-watering guest stars – Mollie Sugden, pre-*Are You Being Served?* as the minister, and Liz Fraser, whose roll-call of comic co-stars includes Benny Hill, Sid James, Peter Sellers and Tony Hancock, as the club manager – make this an even more tantalising missing *Goodies'* link. Bill Oddie kindly tries to fill in some gaps, 'I've got a vision – which isn't pleasing me one bit – of Graeme done up as a male bunny and he had this enormous lock over the serious parts down there with this big phallic key sticking out. The idea was that the woman could pay to unlock the secret. It doesn't bear thinking about really… no wonder the BBC won't let it escape!' The Holy Grail of Goodie comedy is pretty disappointing. With OAP GPO chaps fixing the phone and Tim's blow-up bimbo secretary, the familiar pattern of guest artiste up-staging the boys comes into play with Mollie Sugden's distraught Minister. Banging on about budgies and cat food, Tim's female persona finally gets the truth – she's being blackmailed over compromising pictures from the Playgirl Club. Bill's on a three-week sherbet trip and Graeme is done up as a Wolf – a sort of male bunnie girl! The ads plug first aid treatment and sliced butter but it's soon back in the club and an arrest at the hands of Liz Fraser's seductive policewoman – the Mae West-style owner of the club in disguise. Tim's female alter ego is corrupted, Tim is redeemed, the lads semi-save the day and Mollie goes berserk. It's a delight that this episode has finally been tracked down but it's a lost gem with a lot of flaws… be gentle with it!

MOLLIE SUGDEN, LIZ FRASER, QUEENIE WATTS, PAULINE DEVANEY, ERICKA CROWNE, BERT SIMMS, ERNEST JENKINS. Episode Four, recorded Thursday 15 October, broadcast Sunday 29 November 1970, 10–10.30pm, BBC2.

THE GREENIES

After four very diverse and taxing assignments, the Goodies are preparing for a well-deserved holiday. Merrily chanting along with *Oh! I Do Like To Be Beside the Seaside* and packing their contrasting suitcases, it's all joy and light until conservationist Oddie shoots down all their British Isle destination suggestions on the basis of his detailed, radioactive activity map of England. In the grip of military clout, government apathy and nuclear power station fever, almost everywhere is covered with oil, blown to bits or saddled with the threat of a missing atom bomb. Still, the little Cornish haven of Penrudden Cove seems inviting enough and with the reassuring mistreatment of worker Bill as the luggage-carrying lackey, the trio hitch on their cycle clips and head off – even though, early man overboard victim Oddie, runs all the way. Their arrival is less than inviting with the picturesque resort looking like something out of *Village of the Damned* and the welcoming committee (George Benson's shotgun-firing Rev Rose) being less than welcoming. It's all a mistake, of course, and once recognising the baby-faced Timbo – last seen in the village at the age of four – it's delicious cream teas and sympathy all round. The kindly old man of the cloth, now forced to single-handedly keep the village going (including everything from dentist to police force, as well as the less than reverend service of the Saucy Midwife massage and sauna), explains the mysterious disappearance of his fellow inhabitants. Continually peppering his speech with biblical quotations and emphasising his gentle lisp for sinister effect, Benson relates his eerie tale of military infiltration and sudden abduction. The spooky hill seems to be the focal point. Although gloriously sent up via the poor chap, 'old Jed Treviddick' who returned a raving, mindless idiot – as Tim muses 'I remember old Jed Treviddick – he always was a raving, mindless idiot' – the seed for a political cover up is set. Suitably enough, in this year that not only saw *The Goodies* established but Jon Pertwee become a TimeLord, there's an essence of third *Doctor Who* about this military-slanted episode. The secretive military power taking over a seemingly sleepy little village, corruption in high places and even a Nicholas Courtney-style Brigadier in the shape of Richard Caldicot. Bringing all his authoritative clout from long-serving duty in *The Navy Lark* (note Timothy Carlton's laid-back notion to blame the Navy if things go wrong), Caldicot injects his pompous, crusading patter with tons of 'cracking good show!' exclamations and, more importantly, exposes the double standard of progress when certain areas of the cove are left untouched because he lives there. Cutting comedy. There's also a telling moment when, among tons of human fatalities at a New Forest military exercise, the only complaints received concerned the death of a brace of ponies – typical, animal-loving British attitude. Bill's all powerful, visionary lemon sherbet sucking, and a bit of Graeme jiggery pokery, allows the

viewer and the Goodies easy access to this top secret briefing. It's an upper crust madhouse, where Harrods can soft land on Aldershot, *King Lear* can reduce an audience to emotional wrecks via tear gas testing and Caernarfon Castle is destined to be the world's biggest hole in the ground, military might can carry on regardless and the humble man in the street sees his destiny sinisterly fashioned. With Bill's vision overheating and Graeme, reduced to tipping a jug of water over him to cool things down, it's clear that everything lies at the feet of the Goodies and Rev Rose. It's the peace-loving vicar who holds the key to success. Having already relished his most spine-tingling moment (when Tim explains Bill's trip as revealing the 'true nature of reality', and allows the Rev to savour 'I rather thought that was my job!'), here Benson can muff dialogue, semi-ad lib and still wring maximum clout out of Oddie's convincing use of biblical learning. The wordless conversion from peaceful dissenter to man of action is breath-taking. With Bill's pseudo Bob Dylan protest song blasting in the background, Benson quietly takes on the military might to allow the Goodies the chance to break into the establishment – but that's not before the customary commercial break, here resurrecting Fairy Puff washing powder from show one in the shape of Bill's Molly Weir modelled Scot. The speeded film, sitcom dialogue and energetic sales pitch are all a cover for the hasty waste-a-weir Westminster submachine gun, while Tim's voiceover builds up BBC2 News as the sexiest, most kicking, happening programme around. With suitable big time movie trailer delivery in place, it's quickly back to *The Goodies* and a nervous poke round the heart of the military action. Throwaway gags (a sign reads Germ Warfare – closed owing to ill health) and lavatorial humour, leads the unsuspecting viewer down a primrose path to grim reality. In an uncaring world where even a Goodie (Graeme's nasty mad scientist tendency showing through) can laugh at animal experiments, porn is the literature of the day (capturing the imagination of Tim and Bill to such an extent that Graeme's hammed and repeated 'Ahh! Here we are!' revelation falls on deaf ears and captivated eyes) and a children's playground is wiped off the face of the map by army play things. The boffin makes minor alterations and back at the vicarage Benson pleases himself with a rather good, made-up, pearl of wisdom. A speedy construction of the military camp, now the old kid's playground thanks to good old Graeme, is half of the plan, while a stripper allows our lads to take over an official experts vehicle from London and complete the ruse. Employing a 'dashed clever' clipped accent, Garden juxtaposes play with destruction as his lads – a wonderfully barking squaddie Oddie and Tim hitting grenades for six in the most dangerous game of cricket – test the equipment and drop the ultimate bombshell… that Caldicot and his men are to be used as equalising political pawns and being sold to the black South Africans. With one final controversial comment, the Goodies see off the army bods and recruit the new military force – a truck load of kids. Class stuff… and Tim's bullied and girl bullying time on the swing is just an added bonus of pure pleasure. As Oddie's song goes, 'Hey, Hey, the revolution's here!'.

GEORGE BENSON, RICHARD CALDICOT, TIMOTHY CARLTON, PAULINE DEVANEY. Episode Five, recorded Thursday 12 November, broadcast Sunday 6 December 1970, 10.50–11.20pm, BBC2.

CECILY

On face value, this is both the least effective and potent episode from Series One. It's the Goodies having a bash at the horror genre – Bob Hope, Will Hay, Arthur Askey and the *Carry On* team had done it so why not them? Reference points for *Psycho*, *The Old Dark House*, *The Cat and the Canary*, *Jane Eyre* and every other creepy tale with something mysterious locked in a secret room, are tossed into the usual mix of cowardice and sight gags, but despite a very enjoyable second half, there's a sense of end of term desperation in much of the show. Indeed, the programme kicks off with the trio searching through the newspaper columns in search of employment with Bill even unearthing the Goodies own ad and suggesting a call to them may be in order. Tim's prickly, fussy refusal to do home-help work and shocked reaction to Graeme's interest in sharing a boat with some swinging dolly birds pretty much narrows the choice down to nothing but he's as keen as any of them, and readily agrees to take the first job that's phoned through. Naturally, that first job is as a home help – imagine the three writer–performers sat round discussing suitable projects for this first series, a rejection of standard domestic fare and a sudden U-turn of acceptance out of time-filling requirements. Besides, Graeme's cool phone manner is hilarious, repeating everything the caller says for audience clarification, while any excuse for Tim's vowel strangling, Edith Evans-like female grotesque from *I'm Sorry I'll Read That Again* is a worthy one. The excuse here is that a female nanny is essential and Tim's flamboyant, shockingly flirty femme

fatale is a show highlight, greeted with bemused, outraged glances from his fellow Goods and capped with a disgruntled 'I'm not doing it!' once the receiver is down and the pretence over. Of course, he is doing it, for these are the Goodies, ready to do anything, anywhere, even slip into sub-standard *Upstairs, Downstairs* territory and face the prospect of weird owners clearing off for the day, a huge, rambling country estate and a sweet but deadly young lady by the name of Cecily. Ann Way is her usual furtive bag of nervous energy (seen at its peak in *Fawlty Towers: The Gourmet Night*), while Robert Bernal embellishes every elongated utterance, manic stare and raised eyebrow with an absent-minded air. Wonderfully sinister and just a tiny bit odd, the trio are left in charge of the house with a lengthy list of things to do and firm instructions of the time table for the couple's niece, Cecily. Tim (as the loveable nanny requesting Bill to blow on his wig suffocated hair once the disguise is off), Bill (as the carefree chef planning a simple meal of beans on toast before facing the requirements of egg and cheese savoury pie) and Graeme (as the gardener in charge of a plot of land more like the plains of Serengeti) take on the manic duties with bucket-loads of slapstick, visuals and bizarre touches. There's plenty of fun to be had, but the ideas are overstretched and the most effective redeeming feature is Bill's endearing and familiar *Needed* song chivvying along the action. Snoggers, giraffes, zebras and Zulus inhabit Garden's garden, he pumps up cucumbers and hammers weeds to death, adopts a flower pot and does an impromptu Tommy Cooper impression and literally gets egg on his face from Bill's experimental cooking habits. There's obvious madness with the lawn mower, frozen short crust pastry and a murderous attack from a killer vine as Tim battles for his life, and leaves us to rejoice in the fact that Alan Freeman faced similar angst in *Torture Garden* and Tom Baker would later whip the green stuff's arse in *Doctor Who: The Seeds of Doom*. Some wonderfully twisted bits of business – Tim goes for a doughy Burton with a rolling pin, stone rabbits popping up all over like rabbits and a surreal hand grabbing freshly planted flowers down to an earthy fate. The mock ads (for a Supermatic Camera and a Razz two for one swap offer) and Bill's twice-repeated record turntable idea tends to drag a bit, despite a nice piece of small screen referencing with the potter's wheel interlude. However, once the black clad little darling, Cecily, breaks into the scene things really start hotting up. Tim makes a sinister journey to her bedroom to wake her up but the endearing horsy wallpaper and nervously screaming waif presents a pleasant picture of youthful innocence. However, truth is she's like the nasty flip side of Roald Dahl's Matilda, cursed with mystical powers, a tad nutty and blessed with a charm that gets the lads on her side. Hilariously, Timbo, so full of fear on the initial meeting, starts talking in his normal voice before suddenly lapsing into the throttled female vocals, but his nannying duties are made less than straightforward with the booby-trapped garden and playful antics of his ward. Tim is full of mock bravery and macho-powered boastfulness about being Super Nanny but the hazards of coming out to play – leopard wrestling à la Tarzan, skeletons in every cupboard/hedge, hidden mires, head-bobbing vultures and that legendary kite-assisted dive into the lake which memorably adorned later title sequences – all tend to put him a bit ill at ease. Cecily's tale of dead nannies, fortune-hunting relatives, bequeathed monies and locked cellars, mishmash elements of everything from *Arsenic and Old Lace* to *Psycho* and, indeed, Hitchcock's classic 1960 chiller is enhanced with a Norman Bates' mum look-a-like and direct homage to Hitch's skin-jumping intro for the mummified mummy. Every horror cliché in the book is thrown in, to the dank, creepy, creaking doors, stagger through the spooky house and just to wrap the thing up, there's even a kitchen sink in there as well. It calls for major action so, over a whispered, candle-lit discussion, the lads – out of duty and total, blind fear – vow to stay awake all night and play the appropriate card game of Happy Families. In a sequence that emulates old-fashioned penny arcade machines, the trio play on as eye-flashing portraits, growling wolves, a giant spider, a severed head, whacko hands, ghosties, ghoulies and all sorts of toe-curlingly scary things pop out for a breath of fresh air. A peak of chilling hilarity is reached with Graeme and Tim's scream fest as they meet in the spooky corridors and the cheeky, hand-wringing, thumbs up play of the clock-inhabiting spook latches all this enjoyable nonsense to the 'he's behind you!' pleasure of pantomime. But, typically of this sort of thing, it's not the mad uncle and aunt at the heart of this but the sweet young girl the team are desperately trying to protect. Hastily making their excuses and even, shock, horror, running away without pay, the poor misinformed Goodies send Cecily off packing with a hankie bundle and

a kiss goodbye. An explosive climax (Cecily bombs both the summer house and the house itself) is the only way to go and a Benny Hill-style speed scarper romp in ragged clothes is the closing game. It's a patchy little show but there are bits that get right up there among my all time favourite series moments.

Did You Know? *The Australian Broadcasting Commission edited out the Supermatic Camera advert featuring Tim as cool dude Bob Murphy photographing a young lady and revealing the image as a nude.*

ANN WAY, ROBERT BERNAL, JILL RIDDICK, LENA ELLIS. Episode Six, recorded Thursday 5 November, broadcast Sunday 13 December 1970, 10–10.30pm, BBC2.

RADIO GOODIES

With Radio One having fired its warning shot across the bough of celebrated pirate stations like Radio Caroline, the enforced hip and groovy cats at the BBC smugly rubbed their hands and celebrated victory. But just as the threat was vanishing into popular culture history, those glorious Goodies eagerly resurrected the tradition for their bash at the grass roots of disorganised communications. Indeed, if Tony Blackburn could do it, then Tim, Bill and Graeme were damn sure they could do it as well. Bill feverishly works on a catchy jingle, Tim throws himself into his high-pitched 'Ya!' and close harmony accompaniment, while Graeme grouchily dismisses such rubbish as totally unimportant in light of his highly skilled work on the transmitter design. However, Bill, the obsessed, dedicated composer, won't take no for an answer and wants Graeme's all important closing, 'Boom!' delivered with full feeling. It becomes a running gag throughout the show and even the establishing link line, 'Where's your boom?!?', basking in obvious, childish humour, is a winner from the outset. Surprisingly law-abiding, the lads actually write off for government permission before embarking on a pirate venture and the three-month wait for second class mail, a deliberately unhelpful postman and the sarcastic attitude of the Post Master General, instils a secondary parallel notion which fires Garden's imagination – that of a pirate postal service. The other lads are not convinced – it's radio notoriety, fortune and, above all, teenage groupies, they want, but a dual-action compromise is adopted with Garden's cunning wooden row boat disguising the intricate, underwater submarine operation of the business. Never one for false modesty, Graeme proudly admits he can do anything, sets the team up past the five-mile legal limit off the Essex coast and dubs their new headquarters The Good Ship Saucy Gibbon. With

Needed, as per usual, burrowing into our collective subconscious, the lads journey down to the coast and inspect Garden's really rather impressive state of the art work place – sort of *Doctor Who: The Space Pirates* meets *Star Trek*, complete with dodgy sliding doors and Captain Kirk-style high chairs. It's pretty cool but Tim and Bill are far more interested in breaking onto the airwaves with a Tiny Tim tulip rendition quickly castigated by Graeme's anti-youth culture put downs. His stern 'children, children!' lecturing tones are clearly a premonition of the self-opinionated leader he is destined to become. Mind you, he need not worry about his fellow Goods being hailed as groovy babe magnets for the only up-to-date sound in the library is *A Walk in the Black Forest* and the disgruntled disc jockeys are fated to run the disc into the ground – making the repeated gag funnier with each repeated reference. A masterpiece. Graeme's postal baby is firing on all cylinders, he eagerly uses the radio airwaves to send out the message to the great British population and his latest invention – the all-in-one letter stamp – sends him into fits of delighted, self-congratulatory ecstasy 'I'm working well tonight!'… much to the bemused reaction of Tim and Bill. Still, the notion seems to work and to the tune of one of Oddie's all-time great songs, the deliciously Beatles-esque *Postman!*, Tim and Bill are set to hard labour. Staggering round the place in Goodie post boxes, sprinting through the streets with speedy delivery, injecting Robin Hood-style bow and arrow letter-forwarding, they even hurl pigeons (with insufficient weight ratio) into the realms of parcel post. Graeme comes up with the better idea of employing kangaroos for that – using the pouches you see – but by this stage he's completely lost it and the system has gone totally barking (with first class service coming on a silver plate… check out Tim's miffed, overheated head scratching… and overly familiar singing telegrams). The ad break sees Brenda Cowling promoting the Goodies Plastic Spacemen cereal with a free cornflake in every pack, and a slim Tim in drag plugging a bizarre weight-reducing technique. But happily, it's soon back to Tim spinning… yes, you've guessed it, *A Walk in the Black Forest*. Graeme's gone totally nuts, with megalomaniac ideals of an outer five-mile limit bus service, as the letters continue to pour in. Tim's had enough and braving the consequences, he announces the close of the Goodies post office, followed by a bit of black

forest walking – a radio message that at least an unaccredited Gilly Flower hears, as well as an outraged Graeme Garden. The calm, final relaxation is short lived, however, for mad Graeme is on the prowl, now totally sucked into his own power-crazed universe, donning an imposing black uniform, sinister eye patch, Nazi ideals and one hell of an attitude problem. His determined dream to create a new, better world in which he is the undisputed leader builds into a towering semi-comic performance of impressive depth. Perhaps Graeme's finest Goodies achievement, he deserves at least an Oscar, a couple of OBEs and a stuffed gibbon for his pains, if only for that golden, captivating radio rant rounded off with the unexpected Black forest record – priceless. He wants a pirate state, achieved by towing the entire UK outside of the five-mile limit even if he has to do it single-handedly. Crazed like never before, his two old chums can simply stand on the beach, offer a cup of tea, scream 'You're a megalomaniac!' and watch his pathetic, obsessed figure stress himself out to oblivion. Sinking without remorse, Graeme suddenly sees the light and reforms, facing his outrageous behaviour with shame. Although he has one final surge of non-common sense for a pet project – a pirate Church of England – he joins his cohorts in feet in bowls of hot water mode, before his previous UK relocating idea is readily taken up out of his hands and the Goodies office merrily floats adrift past the Statue of Liberty. Arguably the pick of Series One and certainly the first episode to take full, albeit, tentative steps away from the office business and into a surreal world to delight a generation.

Did You Know? *During the Australian clean-up campaign of 1976, when Goodies episodes were made safe for family viewing, this episode saw Bill and Tim's sex mad giggling over young female groupies removed. Also Bill's powerful bursting of Tim's British heroics speech concerning Graeme's demise, with 'No he bloody won't!', was broadcast with the 'bloody' silenced out. Indeed, that print still surfaces with alarming regularity today! In Sydney, Australia, a radio show entitled A Walk in the Black Forest, aired on Wednesday mornings from 1–6am on 2BRR (88.5 FM). The coastal scenes were shot on location in Bognor. Clearly this episode pointed towards the future, classic days of the Goodies. Instead of a high-profile guest actor coming in as a sort of guest villain, akin to the Sixties television series Batman, the great shows saw one of the Goodies go totally insane and dictate the other two rally round to sort out the problem.*

BRENDA COWLING, LIONEL WHEELER. Episode Seven, recorded Thursday 19 November, broadcast Sunday 20 December 1970, 10–10.30pm, BBC2.

SERIES TWO

Although unquestionably patchy, the first series was an unqualified success. Audience figures peaked at a loyal three million viewers and, more importantly than that, the big wigs at the BBC seemed over the moon with the programme. Producer John Howard Davies considered the most successful editions were those that steered furthest away from satire, selecting *The Tower of London*, *Snooze*, and particularly, *Radio Goodies*, as the highlight shows. Robin Scott, the Controller of BBC2 no less, was even more gushing. After only the first three editions had been broadcast, he sent Davies a memo on 27 November 1970 congratulating him on a 'delightful series'. Such high-level support resulted in the team being offered a second series and, on 9 December 1970, the Goodies signed a contract to write and star in 13 more episodes, helpfully dubbed 'The Goodies II' by the BBC. Despite the fact that all these episodes would form part of the mammoth-length Series Two, the shooting schedules were split into two blocks. Work began on the first chunk on the 31 May and location filming would take the trio to Walpole Park and Ealing, with Episodes One to Seven all planned, written and filmed during May, June, July and August. The BBC kept plugging the show with a Saturday evening repeat season of Series One from 5 July–23 August 1971 and filming on the remaining six shows for Series Two began on 30 September and took in location shoots at Folkestone and North Harefield. These latter editions occupied October, November and December 1971, often being recorded a few weeks before broadcast. The device of Bill's sherbet-sucking visions was dropped after extensive use in Series One. Oddie himself wanted the scenes retained and firmly believed that if it had been American television, such a familiar and liked part of the show would have been kept as a Goodie signifier. But the BBC wanted it out.

Starring and written by Tim Brooke-Taylor, Graeme Garden and Bill Oddie. Film cameramen Stewart A Farnell (Episodes 1–7, 10–13) and Phil Meheux (Episodes 8 & 9). Film editor Stephen Ray (Episodes 1–7) and Ron Pope (Episodes 8–13). Visual effects Ron Oates. Graphics Oliver Elmes. Costume Betty Aldiss. Make-up Rhian Davies. Lighting Derek Slee (Episodes 1, 2 & 4), John Dixon (Episodes 3, 5 & 6) and John Green (Episodes 8–13). Sound Laurence Taylor (Episodes 1–7), Michael McCarthy (Episodes 8–12) and Peter Rose and Neil Sadwick (Episode 13). Music by Bill Oddie and Michael Gibbs. Design by Roger Murray-Leach (Episodes 1, 4, 5, 9, 11 & 13), Kenneth Sharp (Episodes 2, 3 & 6), Roger Liminton (Episode 8), John Stout (Episode 9), Peter Kindred (Episode 10) and David Jones (Episode 12). Film direction by Jim Franklin. Produced by John Howard Davies.

SCOTLAND

An absolutely cracking episode to kick start this all important second series. The plot is simple: a beside-himself zoo keeper must find a monster to fill a new enclosure. The physical visual comedy is lengthy: a huge chunk set in and around the waters of Loch Ness in search of the mysterious

ON YER BIKE FOR A *GOODIES* PROMOTION!

Scottish beastie. The supporting cast straight from the top drawer: the mighty Bernard Bresslaw and the sustained genius of Stanley Baxter. It's poor old Bernie who's set with the monster problem at London Zoo. Having been discovered by the pedalling Goodies feebly trying to throw himself off a bridge from a very small step ladder, much silent play acting (note Tim's overtly pronounced hand gestures), leads to a Bill Oddie rescue and sanctuary in the lad's office. Wet, ashamed and mournful, Bresslaw is reluctant to let his emotions pour out but, Oddie – unable to swim but canny nevertheless – piles on the ritual humiliation of the gentle giant and provokes a stunned 'Now hang on!' The bubble of embarrassment bursts and Oddie's little trick is a success. As a result the full ghastly tale unfolds. In answer to Lord Snowdon's great white elephant – the new bird aviary – the dear old Lord has tried to top his success with a Monster House, set for Royal endorsement. The Goodies indulge in much mockery of the newly erected addition to the zoo before taking the idea one step forward with Bresslaw's half-hearted attempts at disguising four elephants to play the monstrous creature. Of course, it's all doomed to fail and the emotionally charged chap simply breaks down into renewed self-pity. Tim, on the other hand, has an idea hatching – one mention of Her Majesty and he's off to his patriotic record player and into a stirring speech of British pluck. Besides, there's always the chance of an OBE in the deal and that's enough for his juices to start flowing. So blinkered by thoughts of regal distinction and so uneducated in monstrous matters (despite an O-level in biology), he immediately happens on the thought of checking out pet shops for any prehistoric stock they may have. He even dismisses Graeme's rant about the non-existence of monsters – after all Tim has just seen an old film, The Lost World, with loads of them in starring roles. In one of the greatest lines of the show, Graeme's well-balanced reaction that they died out thousands of years ago is greeted with Tim's bemused pondering 'That was an old film!' As it happens, as a result of all this, Graeme stumbles on the Loch Ness Monster notion and suddenly it's chocks away and och aye the noo into kilt country. Splendidly decked out in all the tartan gear, the Goodies encounter suitably altered road signs and markings ('Hoots') before resting in the terrorised Scottish countryside. Every Scottish cliché is ripped apart in an affectionate interlude of bizarre genius – Bill offers milk to a few sporrans and

sees them breed like rabbits, Graeme bags the local vermin (a few wild haggis) for supper, while Tim is attacked by a deadly giant bagpipe spider. Terrified, his fate is to dance the Highland Fling and then die, but Gray Bags is at hand with a well-timed shot and scare tactic. A wonderfully inventive vignette that will leave you gasping, the show wisely takes a breather for a Goodies commercial break – Tim's nervous beans boy plugging Cornflakes by mistake and Graeme's voiceover promoting telephone calls to your friend when there's no one in. On returning to the wild and wacky world of The Goodies, January has almost gone in a flurry of preparation and a well-timed visit to the Scottish Tourist Board is the way forward. Desperate to disguise their Englishness – to totally no avail – the trio ham up all the jargon and complete the hilarious display with a perfectly timed rendition of Sir Harry Launder's Roamin' in the Gloamin'. The man in charge is none too impressed – a brilliantly canny, money-mad Scot played with relish by the sublime Stanley Baxter. In a Goodies guest turn to equal Harry H Corbett, Patrick Troughton, Jon Pertwee and Alfie Bass, Baxter goes gloriously into full speed Scottish ham. Deliciously bemused by the lad's equally overblown Scots performance, Baxter happily explains the monster-catching ritual – flogging The Observer's Book of Monsters, fishing permits, special cameras for fuzzy, out of focus pictures, an array of diving gear and even some scare tactics – basically a board with 'Boo!' on one side and, shock, horror, a picture of Andy Stewart on the other! Cynical, greedy and wonderfully mean, Baxter – helped by dimmed lights from the crew – sets the frightening scene for Nessie's appearance. Delivering his long and winding monologue concerning the night he saw the creature, tension is injected into the moment. A quite stunning bit of comic acting, it's soon off to the Loch with the boys, a biting 'best of English luck!' from Baxter and into the extended visual interlude backed by Oddie's It Got Away number. A telescope with a Nessie silhouette stuck on the lens isn't fooling Graeme and besides he's got far too much to worry about keeping upright with his heavy deep sea diving helmet on – check out the huge outer spectacles on his under water headgear. Tim, meanwhile, goes for the subtle English gent approach – fishing from the bank and using tasty morsels (cake and champers) as bait. Eventually, all three are submerged under the loch – with Tim holding his umbrella aloft and keeping his mouth firmly shut. It's a mini commercial tourist trap beneath the surface and Baxter – clad in his own diving suit – eagerly boasts of flogging genuine monster eggs for, you've guessed it, a fiver each. Just when everybody thinks it's a hoax, the monster – a gloriously tatty looking thing from the Ed Wood school of creature props – appears and famously bites poor old Graeme's helmet off! Subsequently, that landmark image was used in the opening credit sequence but, unscathed and discovery mission almost completed, the lads haul the humped beastie back to London. The sight forces a memorable mistake in a hump back bridge road-sign painter and the lads struggle to stop the basketed creature from making a speedy exit in a ladies convenience, but all is safe and well back at the office. Bresslaw is overcome with emotion, although his pleasure is very short lived once talk turns to mating Nessie with a Russian species – the one and only Stanley Baxter (bringing these two great comedy talents together for an instant), doesn't relish that at all and hastily reveals himself within the monster skin. It's all a con trick by the miserable Scot but the Goodies, never one to let a client down completely, help the defeated zookeeper in his suicide attempt. Full circle to the opening sequence – the bridge, the step ladder and *Needed* playing in the background – Bresslaw's over the side before Graeme faces a *Jurassic Park*-like egg hatching and desperate thoughts of finally filling that vacant cage in Regent's Park. A compact and tightly written episode, the screamed 'Come back!' to Bresslaw is very effective.

Did You Know? The theme tune remains the same from Series One, although several of the opening credit sequences are altered. New additions include the post box ambush and Graeme's watery mugging (Radio Goodies), Tim's cuckoo clock helmet and instant zebra crossing from Give Police a Chance and Graeme's manic weed killing (Cecily).

STANLEY BAXTER, BERNARD BRESSLAW, LYNN HOWARD. Episode One, recorded Friday 2 July, broadcast Friday 1 October 1971, 9.25–9.55pm, BBC2.

THE COMMONWEALTH GAMES

Another day in the Goodies office with Bill and Graeme enjoying a semi-quiet game of chess, while Tim relaxes in front of the telly intensely watching the test match. To undermine his Englishness, the sainted game of cricket is lampooned as the ultimate in boredom and even Timbo's enthralled statistics – 'that's the first time a cover point has moved in a Test Match since 1937!' – does little to protect the game's image. There is, however, a patriotic monologue based round the glorious game, with Tim, centre stage, proudly setting cricket in contrast to

Britain's commonwealth clout and effortless training of a host of foreigner Johnnies. To the refrain of Land of Hope and Glory Tim proudly celebrates the British game as the ultimate divider between us and them – 'the greasy wops, frogs, krauts and dagoes…' The chess, meanwhile, has well and truly collapsed with Graeme's computer assisting his master and Bill's lyrically helpful, sing song warning 'you're Queen's in danger!', resulting in an Oddie sledge hammer attack and the manic curtailing of the game. Besides, with Tim in full regal flow, Bill's far more interested in a bit of political argument and Communist rights movement banter. With upper class, well-played, gentleman versus a little red under the bed, a high-brow discussion about the link between sport and politics soon descends into childish bickering – 'Infinity plus three!' 'You can't have that!' – but a correspondence from the Minister of Sports make the lads feel really needed. That timeless song carries them through some rearranged and riderless antics with the trandem before finally arriving at the House of Commons. In a bleak, Orwellian decayed state, the minister's office is situated within the workings of Big Ben with austerity the name of the game. Reginald Marsh, in a twilight zone before finding comic fame as Terry Scott's boss in *Terry and June*, relishes the 'jolly good', misinformed, dithering and furiously British characterisation, relating his ideal that good politics are always enacted out on the playing fields of international gatherings. It's the Commonwealth Games whittled down to just the August Bank Holiday Islands and us – amazingly, in a fit of pique to attract any competition at all, old boy Marsh has offered up the entire Commonwealth as the prize… much to Tim's shocked bemusement. Thus, so precious and important is the stake that mere athletes are not considered suitable enough. Instead, our representation will be a group of aged MPs all fit for nothing else but dropping. Besides, every man jack of 'em fails to pass the sex test as administered by Marsh's sexy secretary, Miss Foster, played with delicious style by Valerie Stanton. Having caught the eye in hot pants dishing out cotton wool in Marsh's office – Big Ben's noisy and all that you know – she reappears in even skimpier wear and reveals discreetly, in front of some rather sheepish but secretly quite chuffed with themselves Goodies – that the old lads may have muffed it but these three certainly haven't! If not just for sex then certainly for England and for money, the Goods happily become the British

Commonwealth Team and throw themselves into training. Weight-lifting and chest-expanding antics stand parallel with Richard Lester's field-based frolics for the Beatles and there's a cool, upbeat song, *Superman*, to keep things ticking along. Tim trapped in a muscle-building spring lingers in the memory but it's the massage Garden inflicts on Oddie that really stands out. The hilarious rubbery leg abuse was later incorporated into the opening credits and even picked up on by Peter Sellers when he guested on *The Muppet Show*. Training completed, the team are shipped off by helicopter to receive the usual island welcome of rifle fire, ritual abuse and fresh fruit attack. Sort of *Carry On Up the Khyber* meets Python's pointed stick! During the journey, we have been treated to a couple of ads – Tim's boyish, mis-timed *My Favourite Dream* poem to baked beans and Garden's frustrated, unsuccessful experiment for cleaning messy shirts with Square Deal Surge – but for the disgruntled and unpopular sporting Goodies it's quickly into their lowly wooden hut headquarters, boasting the legend Whitey Go Home on the outside. Charming! More to the point, the August Bank Holiday folk have a huge five-star hotel. Inside British HQ sits Reggie Marsh, gleefully celebrating the impossible aspects of the games (they are held on the top of a 7500m mountain which no Englishman has conquered), unveiling the altitude-busting heavyweight shoes specially made for the mountain top competition and, if anything, projecting a manic sense of total patriotism even in excess of our beloved Tim's. Indeed, following Marsh's greatest line ('There's very little air… in fact, there isn't any!'), Tim breaks down into tears. Sobbingly enquiring about how they are going to breath, the boss man deliciously barks back, 'You're British!' That seems to answer the question. Restricted by unnecessary boffin-powered invention, the Goods are fighting a losing battle from the outset and with a suitable Oddie song, *Far Away*, sort of mixing Noel Coward irony with a flavour of *Those Magnificent Men in Their Flying Machines*, the sporting disaster begins. It's failure all the way and although the frizzy-haired opponents are the most base kind of stereotypes, it's the high-principled Brits who are the real fools. Shooting themselves in the foot initially and bravely battling through shameless foul play – the shot put explodes, the sand pit implodes, Bill's heavy boots prove unhelpful in the boxing ring and the water jump is infested with fake-looking crocodiles – the Brits tumble to failure. The Brits are beaten 185 points to a half point, and to rub

salt in the wound, the August Bank Holiday Islands have done it with just one athlete and his seven-year-old son! The wordless, slow burn facial expressions of Marsh speak a thousand words and even the glorious, strained, real-time, slow motion running replay sees the lads beaten fair and square. The Commonwealth is lost, the national anthem is amended and the Union flag droops in shame. Back at Cricklewood, Tim is beside himself – his favourite position. With one final patriotic speech about the end of Britain's Empire he aims to kill himself with a hand gun before, cowardly, deciding to shoot Graeme and Bill instead. This carnage and end of the Goodies partnership is halted by Marsh's reappearance. Under the new King, the Commonwealth is happily back together again for the next games – all except Britain. A dreadful sporting record, compounded by the Goods, dictates that we are banned!

Did You Know? This episode was wiped from the BBC archives and only resurfaced years later in a copy held in Australia. Unfortunately, the tape only survived in black and white. Furthermore, thanks to a 1976 Australian Broadcasting Commission decision to screen The Goodies in a late afternoon children cum family viewing slot, several episodes had dubious words and sequences cut. These remnants are believed to be preserved in the National Film Archive in Canberra. However, broadcast versions of The Commonwealth Games saw some risqué sex test banter with Miss Foster hit the cutting room floor and, sadly, this edited version was the only retained print. Still – black and white… bits missing… this is still far better than a gap in The Goodies catalogue.

REGINALD MARSH, VALERIE STANTON. Episode Two, recorded Friday 9 July, broadcast Friday 8 October 1971, 9.25–9.55pm, BBC2.

POLLUTION

Perhaps the most unsung and thought-provoking of early Goodies' attempts to put the world to rights via comedy. England is drenched in pollution, and things – including the atmosphere outside – are looking very black indeed. The newspaper shouts out headlines of destruction and Graeme's pet parrot looks decidedly worse for wear. But, this being England, that most English of English gentlemen – Tim Brooke-Taylor – has far more important things on his mind… the test match. Gray Bags orders him to take precautions when putting his arm outside to check for rain. The designated time for bare flesh exposure is a mere 1.57 seconds and that's all Timbo needs to get a handful of black goo. The match will certainly be played on a sticky wicket! Bill, in the meantime, has been out in the stuff, infesting the office with smog and killing Polly the parrot simply by breathing on him – check the Python reference and wonder where the 'polly-gone' gag went. Woodall's coughing newscaster makes the news official, the entire nation is bogged down with muck and Graeme's computer predicts the world will end on Monday. Tim is frantic, after all the test match isn't due to end until Tuesday. Worried enough to phone the Government complaints department, Tim is greeted with a recorded message finally giving the lads a lead to the Ministry of Pollution down in Eastbourne. Thoughts of a charming time down by the seaside and Oddie's moodily up-lifting song, *Day in the Country*, counter balances the wasteland that the three pedal through. Gas mask wearing holiday-makers, brave swimmers covered in industrial waste, radioactive Highland cattle and acid rain so powerful poor Tim's umbrella is instantly melted, paint a blacker than black picture of the British way of life. All disastrous routes seem to lead to the mysterious Ministry of Pollution and minister Ronnie Stevens. A bowler-hatted bod masquerading as a pest control officer in a destructive attack on an old bloke's marrow, he mercilessly flogs the diminished and distraught chappie a fresh, smaller one from his own stock. Cunning and corrupt work is afoot and the Goodies, with high moralistic standing never before or, indeed, again, seen to such an extent, vow to find out the truth. The *North by Northwest* pesticide plane attack isn't played for laughs at all and, although the climatic moment – a flying sheep falls dead from the air (bizarre and a further nod to Python, Series One, Episode One) – is comic, the image of the team standing in a deserted field with flocks of dead birds falling around them is a chilling one indeed. There's no humour within the visual structure or dialogue exchange – just stark polluted reality and the sense that something must be done. Stevens is remorseless and proud of his plan – welcoming in our three spying heroes unaware of their wristwatch cameras, hat-concealed recording device and fake hand, microphone cover. The nose pegs – useful to avoid pollution – also double as voice distorters, changing Bill's cheerful rough tones and his colleagues voices of normality into whining, Hooray Henries right out of the Ministry. Stevens has an evil plan of creating a continual night of polluted sky for non-stop work. No fresh air, uncontaminated countryside and enjoyment of any kind can get in the way of maximum productivity. Thus, pollution is being manufactured by the government just to be tempered by a special government work force. The potential 'Department for putting

BILL ODDIE IN VINTAGE GOODIES MODE

everything right' is set to create the problem, solve it, keep creating it and make the guv look cool. Bill's song, *Change Don't Change*, is as ironic as *Dr Strangelove*'s use of *We'll Meet Again*. Tim's rant is frank and forthright and even Bill is uneasy at the use of such language but this ideal of effluence means affluence has to stop. In the meantime, beanz meanz effluence in the Goodies commercial break with Tim's blonde 'What I like' schoolboy threatened with Graeme's boxing glove on a stick if he responds incorrectly and the trio present a quite stunning freeze frame transition from pure pleasure to legs in the air dying as the Rolo-like chocy, 'Dodo', works its strange, staccato sensation. A mini vignette of visual comic genius. Meanwhile, Tim's angrily phones the Prime Minister. His bottle may leave him at the crucial moment and his pathetic diatribe cuts no ice at all but the three musketeers seed has been sown – the Goodies are on the ball and stand tall as the men for the clean-up job. Sore noses (from those pesky pegs), regal mockery (from Bill and Graeme), thoughts of contacting the ultimate authority figure (David Frost) and Britain's economic future based on filth notwithstanding, nothing can stand in the way of the team's naturalistic plan for the country. Aloft in their hot air balloon powered tricycle and equipped with huge sacks of Graeme's grass growing, rain purifying mixture, the team prepare for action stations. But sharp shooting Ronnie Stevens is no mug and, à la Dennis Price in *Kind Hearts and Coronets*, punctures their ambitions and signals an energetic abandon bike situation. Gray and Bill cause some airborne mayhem with seat changing while Tim remains reassuringly Tim with a frantic scream of 'We're all gonna die!' Graeme's first choice for lightening the load is Bill Oddie but the toff and the working man soon rally against the scientist and ditch his precious formula – all into the same rain cloud. Back at base, Gray Bags is not best pleased, eagerly tracking the cloud's progress via shipping forecast broadcasts before the tension gets to breaking point, the winds die down and the furry blob of white is stalled right over London. Instant green belt district is the result with Buck House, Trafalgar Square and other notable landmarks adopting a fetching exterior of healthy grass. The stuff grows everywhere – policemen adopt lawn mowers instead of cars and barbers use sickles on overgrown heads of green. The Goods seem very happy with their organic new look. Salon camp seeps into their banter with Bill decorating his barnet with a scarecrow, Graeme effeminately puffing up his garden gnome adorned image and Tim girlishly enquiring if his 'Keep Off The Grass' sign is straight. Every one seems over the moon including, rather disconcertingly, the evil Mr Stevens. With money tied up in lawn mowers and the perfect, overgrown clump of grass right next to London, he has stoked the nation's coffers thanks to the Goodies handiwork and discovered the ideal site for a new airport – cue plane right overhead and the team's slump into unwitting commercial assistance.

RONNIE STEVENS, CORBET WOODALL, PETER DAVIDSON, ERIC KENT, GORDON HANN.
Episode Three, recorded Friday 23 July, broadcast Friday 15 October 1971, 10.10–10.40pm, BBC2.

THE LOST TRIBE

Ooh! It's cold, my word it's cold, it's so cold in fact that our three heroes are sharing the same scarf for warmth. Tim, overboard as usual, has an expression of total frozen discomfort, his hands are tightly over his ears and a teapot – still in its cosy – is his only protection from a frost-bitten head. Bill makes light of the conditions – his comic chattering teeth come out and munch up Tim's rock solid biscuit for him – while Graeme seems in the dog house. His nuclear reactor hasn't really successfully replaced the office's central heating system. Still, his very British computer comes to the rescue, dishing out a nice cup of tea, even though the stuff is frozen and Tim is reduced to licking it like an ice lolly. Distressed at the business going down the tubes thanks to an abundance of charitable assignments, the three are united in their determination to avoid any further jobs with no pay attached. It's an ambition that lasts about three seconds before leggy, busty upper class beauty Bridget Armstrong topples in with a heart-wrenching, financially embarrassed tale of her Professor father going missing up the Orinoco. It's the start of a much-maligned Goodies' episode. Indeed, by common consent, even among the group themselves, this is often cited as the worst example of Goodies excess and comic desperation. So why do I love it so much? For me, and famous fan Lenny Henry, it's one of the team's funniest and most potent half hours. Certainly, it would get in my top 10 shows. OK, the humour is stretched a bit thin occasionally and the basic punch line of a lost tribe repeating 'Boom, Boom!' after every corny gag isn't exactly earth shattering in its brilliance. But it works perfectly. There's a real sense of Milligan grandeur about the narrative – following the Professor's diary through darkest Kent in search of this tribe of cannibals. The playing by the Goodies is sincere, Bill's song *Such a Long Way To Go* is stunning, Sir Arthur Conan Doyle's flare for adventure is injected into the spirit of the piece without full mockery and, arguably best of all, there's a belated but well worth while waiting for, guest turn from the one and only Roy Kinnear. As the great joke white hunter's daughter explains, he's been missing since 1951 and in her naïve, ask no questions English way, she believed her late mother's story that Papa was hard at work in the potting shed for all those years. It was only when he failed to show at his wife's funeral that alarm bells started ringing. The Goodies, of course, are totally hooked by this stage, blindly agreeing to do anything for the merest sign of affection from their dewy-eyed, well-proportioned client. Besides, as Graeme points out, the South American climate is very, very hot at this time of year. Just the tonic for three very, very cold Goodies. After some banter about women always spraining their ankle on such expeditions, it's agreed to leave the sexy piece behind. The tropical costume cabinet sees her wrapped in nothing but a towel and despite the tempting thought of taking her with them, a cheery, nice and warm song and dance routine from Tim and Graeme soon puts carnal thoughts out the window. All except in the case of Bill Oddie of course. But soon, the daughter is really fed up and the trio are deep into the Prof's diary, recreating every step and fall – including over their own parked bike. Graeme's earnest narration is suitably underplayed, adding a sense of historical adventure novel to the visual gagging but cold reality is always breaking through. The girl turns up unannounced and unwanted on a red double decker bus and some tense tent banter ensues. Graeme's illogical canvas television set is soon discarded despite perfect picture quality, while the weakness of the Goodies' flesh is sorely tested by nubile female legs gingerly tiptoeing over them. It's a scene lifted almost word for word from Garden and Oddie's *Doctor in the House* episode *Peace and Quiet*, but played in broader comic style for added effectiveness. Desperately trying to think of her as just 'one of the boys' in the same hapless fashion of Tony Curtis and Jack Lemmon in *Some Like It Hot*, sex is too hard a spectre to ignore for long. Relish the sequence as all three Goodies simultaneously emerge from the covers as the lady walks past. Graeme's 'One of the boys just went through!' is fooling nobody! Luckily, the lads have a commercial break – Tim's beanz boy getting a face full of the stuff from Graeme's disgruntled interviewer – to cool their ardour. Onwards into the uncharted undergrowth of Kent, Tim faces a killer feral sheep and receives grateful thanks from his lusty female admirer, the boys have an ill-fated, *Carry On Up the Jungle*-style bit of tomfoolery with the Tarzan-like sheep vine swinging and the distant, foreboding sound of drums signals they quest is almost over. The diary entry comes to a close just outside Sevenoaks and – with the exception of the odd native artefact in shop windows – it all looks pretty civilised. Syncopated drummer Roy Kinnear explains all about it in a brilliantly laid-back, matter of fact fashion. The fact is that he isn't a real Professor at all – no, he's Professor Knutt, the educated comedian. If nothing else, a glorious excuse for young Hazel Knutt's reticence about completely revealing the entire truth. Having exhausted his home-grown audience and run out of jokes to make the nation laugh, Roy has trekked to the far flung back waters of Sevenoaks to entertain the naïve and easier-pleased natives of the lost

Orinoco tribe. The corniest – and let's face it, pretty hilarious – gags (firewater/petrol *et al.*) get their impulsive 'Boom, Boom!' chant going. The need for white man's magic to save the lads from cannibalistic climax results in a bit of cliché abuse (Hazel's sprained ankle is feigned) and television cookery technique (Graeme sans glasses, goes all Galloping Gourmet Graeme Kerr in his preparation of clear soup without human meat). Besides, the natives, Roy and his stunning daughter, seem more interested in boy scout songs than lunch and the trio edge away quietly. Their fate is to get totally lost and stuck in the middle of the Atlantic, eventually find the land in darkness and pitch up tent in the Himalayas – even colder than they were before – but the show remains one of the most treasurable in *The Goodies* cannon.

Did You Know? *During a decidedly unresponsive studio recording session, the Goodies were fully aware that the audience were less than impressed with the show. Frankly, they were dying on their feet but, together with an equally aware and professionally uplifting pep talk from Roy Kinnear, the three dragged themselves through the ordeal. Filming for this episode started on Monday 31 May 1971 and kicked off work on the all-important second series. Location work was filmed at Walpole Park.*

ROY KINNEAR, BRIDGET ARMSTRONG, OLU JACOBS. Episode Four, recorded Friday 16 July, broadcast Friday 22 October 1971, 10.10–10.40pm, BBC2.

THE MUSIC LOVERS

Unsurprisingly one of Bill Oddie's favourite episodes for it is so musically heavy and varied. An absolutely stonking show, the support villains (Henry McGee and Norman Mitchell) were so popular that a return was arranged for *For Those in Peril on the Sea* and the sing-a-long interludes could have made up an entire Goodies' concept album of their own. Ironically, none of the songs was subsequently released. The scene is set with our heroes listening to a dodgy string quartet in the park – Tim is dressed in dickie bow and dinner jacket, Graeme looks like Giles' Grandma on a day trip to Brighton and hip groover Bill is totally unimpressed by the live sounds, preferring a jangling radio set. However, all three's interest is suddenly aroused when the performing musicians are mysteriously grabbed away by black clad Mafia-type chappies. Graeme's evening has been ruined and Tim is just plain bemused. The television is full of the missing musicians and Corbet Woodall is snowed under, but at least there's some good news to report – Rolf Harris is among the folk on the 'lost in action' list. There are relentless Rolfie gags throughout and

Cilla Black doesn't fare much better – her high notes just set Bill's teeth on edge too much. Everybody from Kenneth McKeller's Scottish highland songs to the Royal Albert Hall concert has been silenced and instead all live venues are pumping out recorded, disco music. Graeme, a music lover with discretion, isn't taking that lying down. As a united, albeit uncertain, force, the Goodies vow to become famous musicians and use themselves as bait to trap the hooded mastermind behind the crime. There's a very brief, wonderful jam session with Oddie hamming it up, Jerry Lee Lewis-style, on the piano – his less than subtle tuning skills make all the notes sound identical, while Tim and Graeme's accordion duet turns into an over-stretched mess. Graeme's endearing display of his string section à la Russian dolls is greeted with warm applause from the studio audience. Their recording contract could possibly have emerged from this mockery of the industry. Once the lads are at ease, it's time for some real cool music. Graeme goes all classical while retaining his individual sense of the contemporary thanks to computer-generated backing, Tim gets the girls in (a couple of mini-skirted tartan lasses for Glee Club singers) and Bill fulfils his rock dream with flamboyant electric guitar plucking. It may be a dreadful piece of miming from Bill's spirited rocker but the team's super cool, heavily charged rendition of *Land of Hope and Glory* remains one of the greatest series moments ever. Going for it big time, wailing the Bill Oddie wail and balancing the comic input from Tim and Graeme, this is what makes *The Goodies* so brilliant. Although the glam girls are taken in, Norman Mitchell's shaded heavy, Gerald, barks 'You ain't good enough!' and refuses to steal the lads. Never blokes to give in, it's the Philharmonic Glee Club Rock 'n' Roll Band Festival plan which is trawled out next. A composite of the three's musical tastes, Woodstock and the Isle of Wight are as nothing to the Goods on Hackney Marshes... Backed by a stunning, 1967 Beatles-style number from Bill, Gray Bags moodily unpacks the deck-chairs – facing away from the stage – and the boys eagerly throw themselves into every musical style – from Acker Bilk jazz to Mozart String quartet. The tambourine-slapping coloured trio became universally familiar from a subsequent set of opening credits and the idea of musical instruments as cooking equipment – Graeme's blue grass guitar chip cutter and Bill's fish fryer drum – works well. Ultimately, Tim is even bathing in a drum as the flower power joy of the event begins to wear thin with no audience and, more importantly, no hooded thieves. A dejected team is mysteriously whisked away as the ads break things up with Tim's wannabe millionaire beanz boy decrying the product as usual and Graeme's voiceover, headache commercial mocking commentary promoting Baldy Cleanse Ink Remover as the perfect solution to getting rid of 'Tension', 'Stress' and 'Pain' from your exposed bonce! Meanwhile, the lads find themselves at the secret country hide-out of Mr Big and signal a grand entrance from vampiric Henry McGee bashing out *I Do Like to be Beside the Seaside* on his huge organ. In a cross between Dr Phibes and Professor Moriarty, he reveals himself as the Music Master, failed record producer turned mad man (having to plug unsellables like The Julie Andrews Album of Rugby Songs and the blank disc, The Best of Rolf Harris). In a priceless exchange, Tim tries to find out more information. He's very devious, 'I have a little trick up my sleeve that sometimes works... Who are you?' McGee doesn't quite fall for it, but he does reveal his name (MJ Coggleton) and part of his *Bananaman* pre-empting, address (17 Acacia Villa), so it's not a bad bluff. But the fiend has no time for such games. He has kidnapped every recording star in the world so he can corner the music market. He has orchestras, he has Cilla, he has Englebert ('Please release me, let me go!'), he has Rolf Harris, he's even got the ultimate coup – he's got the Beatles back together again amidst very private legal wrangling. It's one of the best gags in the show as the studio door is opened to admit no music but heated argument and a tossed out guitar! Anyway, punctuating all exclamations and shock revelations with dramatic organ music, McGee mercilessly admits to doing everything for the money and forces our heroes to record a hit record in just one hour. Norman Mitchell's numb-skulled binding and gagging of the trio rather restricts them musically but with an extra, final chance, Bill calls for a square dance rhythm, shames his musically backward colleagues and fires the imagination of keyboard wizard McGee. Forcing the gullible quartet of heavies to jump out of windows, walk into walls and, ultimately, thanks to a lullaby interlude, fall asleep, via the power of music, the Goodies make their escape. In a brilliant visual set piece, the Halle Orchestra lends a hand employing violins and bows as bows and arrows. A trombone reinvents itself as a canon and the glories of classical music (a stirring rendition of Beethoven's Fifth) heightens an 'orchestrated' battle. McGee is defeated and the world of music sighs a relief – Oddie, on the other hand, is far too busy dramatically singing *Edelweiss* in the bath to accompaniment from the Northern Dance Orchestra. But one last musical fire-cracker has yet to go off – Cilla Black, left locked up in McGee's domain, has come for vengeance. And folks, it is her actual voice tracking down the Goods, muttering 'I'm gonna punish ya!', singing that bristling high note which brings the office to its knees and wailing into the closing credit theme.

HENRY McGEE, CORBET WOODALL, NORMAN MITCHELL, CILLA BLACK, KEN HALLIWELL, WALTER HENRY, PATRICK MILNER, MARIA O'BRIEN, KATRA WYETH. Episode Five, recorded Friday 30 July, broadcast Friday 29 October 1971, 10.10–10.40pm, BBC2.

CULTURE FOR THE MASSES

Hot on the heels of their masterly look at musical heritage, the Goodies delivered a less satisfactory romp through national art treasures. Tim's on his usual patriotic trip, for Sotheby's has turned into a cockney market place with initially refined Tommy Godfrey lapsing into his beloved turn as the poor man's Sid James and flogging masterpieces to a coach-load of super rich Americans. Bill, never that impressed with anything not connected to electric guitars or birds, expresses little interest in all this cut price art stuff. To him £50,000 can purchase a lifetime's subscription to *Playboy* magazine and any establishment in Soho can deliver a more convincing nude that the oversized canvas variety from Renoir. He may not know much about art but he knows what he likes – and he likes *The Monarch of the Glen*. Still, a mate is a mate and when the yanks invade (with 10-gallon hats and cigar chomping loudness), the Goodies need to unite for the common course, the crown, British heritage and, primarily, to keep Tim from breaking down completely. After all these are foreign Johnnies and valuable art is leaving the country, so with Graeme's mood saxophone playing, Bill's fumbled, ad-libbed, corpsed bit of banter with the Union flag and Tim's stalled, gagging for it, rant on the future of the land, the big British guns are out. Treasure Tim's shocked, 'But they're not art lovers, they're Americans!' It's OK when Julie Andrews and, particularly, David Frost, are lifted by the Yanks but art is something else – even if it is painted by the Spaniard Velasquez. When his impassioned performance fails, Tim goes completely mad and outbids the overseas art jerks with an amount of money so big it wouldn't fit in this book. The bloke in the poofy tie gets the lot of his dreams, British trust and a downpayment of 13p secures the upside-down piece of guff and a small piece of Englishness is preserved forever... at least that's the idea. Tim's chuffed with himself but the bowler-hatted

TIM BROOKE-TAYLOR AS MONA LISA AS SEEN IN *CULTURE FOR THE MASSES*

figure of authority – a quite sublime piece of effete contrariness from Julian Orchard – isn't overly bothered one way or the other. A typical Brit, he's happy to accept anything for nothing but when the lovingly framed Bill comes as part of the package, the gilt radically drops off the ginger bread. Graeme and Bill's fanfares may be charming but as examples of the British people, this latest rescued art treasure isn't worth putting one's own hand in one's own pocket. The only solution is enforced, thrice daily visits to art galleries, charging folk £25 a throw and £40 if you're an OAP. It's flabbergasting and Tim is the first to show his gast getting flabbered. Art must be kept free for the nation at all costs and there's only one person to figure this out – the cleverest man in the known universe, Graeme Garden. Tim's wonderfully unaware telephone call to the National Gallery reveals their insurance premium and the fact that the place is closed for its annual Spring clean. Graeme's brilliantly overplayed, thrice 'Ah!' nose-tapping bit of business is perfectly repeated down the line to the very people who should be kept in the dark and Tim's delighted expression is heart-warming. Besides Bill's song *Philistine*, can always raise a smile. The travelling cleaning business employs an expected slap-dash technique, with grand masters beaten like carpets, statues receiving lathered hair washes (later incorporated into the titles), Graeme's Mona Lisa teeth cleaning and vanity towel wrapping around male stone figures. A quick clean and cunning criminal operation sees the Goods scarper with the art, leaving Tim's prized upside-down portrait the last remaining asset for the Gallery. Orchard's flamboyant unveiling, to just our three heroes, reveals a dreadful copy of the original and the unattractive safe containing the prized masterpiece. Value, security and apathy join forces to produce an art gallery with absolutely no visitors. The only option is closure and a hasty advert break to give Tim time to think – two glam girls testing no Cathay lather and over-Cathay lather soap allows Bill just a bit of juicy narration before we rejoin the action and Tim's energetic, corrupt petition lobbying. Orchard's already reacting as the post box gobbles up his written protest, but red tape, déjà vu script, time-loops and some delicious mugging from the team, produce a seemingly endless confusion of money, insurances and missing art. The long and short of it all is the Goodies are challenged to make art galleries fun and with their National archive and dream convention pinching of fairgrounds, fun it is going to be. Leonardo da Vinci cartoons play like low-grade Felix the Cat, a shooting gallery targets a rocking *Whistler's Mother*, you can pin the ear on Van Gogh, knock the arms off Venus and have a bash at the Henry Moore Crazy Golf Course. Genius at work (check out Bill's *Laughing Chevalier* interlude) indeed, but Orchard's no fool and the Goodies are sacked, their idea nicked and poor old Tim left wandering with his own, disenchanted thoughts. Patriotic certainly but no sucker, Tim's bagged the Yanks and, although the Foghorn Leghorn-style big mouth isn't really impressed with anything, there's always Graeme's endless supply of *Monarch of the Glen*... the frantic sale continues through into the closing credits.

JULIAN ORCHARD, TOMMY GODFREY, RAY MARLOWE. Episode Six, recorded Friday 6 August, broadcast Friday 5 November 1971, 10.15–10.45pm, BBC2.

KITTEN KONG

'I can't stand watching Kitten Kong because that's the one everyone keeps banging on about. I don't say it doesn't make me chuckle though!' *Graeme Garden*

Amazing this, perhaps the most famous *Goodies* episode of all, was actually wiped by the BBC video library in the late Seventies. Alongside *Dr Who*, Hancock, Alf Garnett and The Beatles on *Juke Box Jury*, it was unceremoniously chucked in the BBC furnace. It is believed that a black and white print may be held but this has never been confirmed. However, thankfully, the magic, as well as added visual humour and guest star (Michael Aspel), is retained in the widely available Montreaux edition, first screened on 9 April 1972.

Did You Know? Location work for this lost classic was filmed on the streets of Ealing in June 1971. As Bill Oddie recalls, one of the show's most celebrated sequences was actually written for another comedian. 'I'm happy to say that Ronnie Barker turned down the piece of material where Tim takes the kitten – basically a bit of fluff on a stick – for a walk. I wrote the bulk of that as a three-minute bit for Ronnie several years before and he dismissed it completely. I think there was too much running around for his liking! But I thought, it will be useful later and, sure enough, I put it into Kitten Kong and it worked great. Nothing was wasted!'

CORBET WOODALL. Episode Seven, recorded Friday 13 August, broadcast Friday 12 November 1971, 10.15–10.45pm, BBC2.

WICKED WALTZING

Ballroom dancing may have made a man of Paul McCartney but it simply makes chums out of the Goodies. Tim's culture vulture personality is totally enchanted by the delights of *Come Dancing* live from the Cricklewood Morsonic Baths. Bill's expression speaks volumes and before long he voices his rigid boredom, while Graeme sums up the nation's apathy with a disgruntled 'what a load of old rubbish!' The lads are not happy, but Tim's airy fairy pleasure in the clean and pleasurable world of florid dresses and quick steps is in for a rude awakening. Underlying hints at drug tests and foul play, are like water off Tim's duck-like back, but his illusions are destined for complete shattering – there's only one woman to keep his rock solid faith totally rock solid and that's the powder puff of a dancing queen, June Whitfield as Penelope Fay. There's evil work afoot on the dance floor and Whitfield's stout trio of dancers are hopelessly wounded – it's down to the Goodies to don dinner jackets and take the floor for the cause. In the show's greatest moment, Tim and Bill struggle to learn the art of dance via a flamboyant record hosted by Lionel Blair – it's hardly subtle comedy but Bill's dismissive 'camp old fruit!' line is a classic. The rest of the show drags out the fairly thin plot-line of two rival ballroom gurus battling it out via Thirties gangster conventions. Whitfield, sweet and innocent at the beginning, faces cigar-chomping, unwise-cracking, trilby-sporting ruffian, Delia Capone, played with intense brilliance by Joan Sims. A larger than life villain for the distinguished character actress to sink her teeth into, Sims storms through the madness. Mixing Al Capone grimaces with Mae West acid, she departs with a spat out 'Suckers!' Sims treats the entire thing with deserved contempt, threatening 'You might have a little accident' as she pours a drink over Bill's trousers. Meanwhile, Graeme, living up to his eccentric scientific genius label, has invented a very eccentric radio-controlled dance suit which makes any old twit a gliding vision to behold – or so it is hoped… Posing as *Come Dancing* bank clerks and automatically reacting to the unison bimbo chanting of their hair stylist, frilled-up partners, the battle lines are drawn. An ad break sees Tim whine his way through a very close shave with a Wilkinson, sorry, Wilmington, sword razor and Graeme ham it up as Clement Freud's dog food orator. Dogginosh is the stuff to give 'em or, at the very least, the stuff to give telly folk who promote the product. Anyway, Graeme, stupidly and proudly, reveals his hidden, magical dancing suit technique, the control box is in enemy hands and the bow-tied Goodies go berserk on the floor to the tune of *Baby Face*. Jiving independently, breaking through the wall, encountering coppers and boogying with pillar boxes is all on the madcap, silent comedy cards, before banter over money and the true identity of Whitfield is revealed as gangster's moll 'Peaches' Stiletto. A duel to the death is the only option and our heroes, clad in female dancing attire for the purpose, milk every ounce of mist-strewn, guns at dawn, convention from the sequence. Mixing in bucket-loads of boxing technique further to add to the tooth and nail angle on serene dancing, Tim voices the over-the-top barker, punches are beautifully choreographed and victory is theirs. Still, Tim's hero has to face a frozen chicken for his battle weary eye as opposed to the traditional steak. Worse, a new trend has swept through his beloved world of dancing – the show ends with two hardened wrestlers prancing around in tutus. Arguably one of the weakest Goodies efforts, this still packs more laughs than your average comedy half hour.

Did You Know? Maybe not a classic but thankfully saved from complete destruction, the original BBC tape for this Series Two episode was junked during the great Seventies cull of the organisation's back catalogue. Thankfully, an export, slightly edited, black and white back-up copy was retained and discovered in Australia. It is this copy which plugs the gap in The Goodies collection and was screened on UK Gold through the early Nineties. For the true Goodie fan, ultra rare extracts of colour Wicked Waltzing footage appear during the opening credits of other Series Two episodes. The manic out of control dance through the street and a brief pillar box waltz moment are featured.

JOAN SIMS, JUNE WHITFIELD, ROLAND MacLEOD, WILLIAM JENNER, THE FRANK AND PEGGY SPENCER PENGE FORMATION TEAM, WENDY HILLHOUSE, LINDA HUTCHKIN, BEBE ROBSON. Episode Eight, recorded Friday 12 November, broadcast Friday 19 November 1971, 10.15–10.45pm, BBC2.

FARM FRESH FOOD

The horrors of artificially created, chemically enhanced food is an ideal one for the Goodies' attention and has contemporary clout with Frankenstein food and Mad Cow Disease. There are similar sorts of comic threads running through *Kitten Kong*, but this tasty episode goes right for the modern farming jugular. Bill is slaving away in the kitchen as the two well-bushed chaps, Tim and Graeme, stagger in expecting copious amounts of grub. As per usual, Garden's wait is made much more comfortable thanks to wacky invention, he is hastily eased via huge, comfy slippers and a huge, comfy newspaper. Tim, poor lad, has to suffer in discomfort as health-food freak Bill dishes out the brown food-like substances on offer – even the milk is brown. The edible, brown ink on brown paper Natural Health Cookbook rules his dietary heart. Unlike those poor days of *Beanstalk* hardship to come, the minuscule food portions (this time round a solitary sultana) are all part of the healthy living kick. But, flesh is weak and hungry flesh even weaker, once the seaweed offers up a nasty nip from a disturbed crab and the main course turns out to be flower pots full of worm-infested soil, the lads throw down their spoons and revolt. Graeme and Tim head off for the traditional Ye Olde Shepherd's Cottage Restaurant and Bill, suddenly a might peckish himself, is downing morals and letting his stomach rule. Food glorious food here we come but is the food glorious? Graeme's suspicions are roused with a cursory glance at the menu but Bill's table-banging ruffian simply wants a mound of anything that's handy. This is no ordinary restaurant: fresh food is frowned on and coloured, preserved and generally mucked about with grub is positively celebrated. Frank Thornton's silky waiter, looking down his nose with complete contempt for the trio and skilfully pouring a tin of pea soup à la vintage wine for a more than satisfied customer, grits his teeth and battles through these uncouth underlings with a desire for natural farm produce. Everything comes from either a tin, off a very large, almost meatless bone or from a packet, and chemists rather than chefs seem to be in charge of the nation's taste buds. Thornton seems to delight in the fullest detail of animal slaughter and repackaging, explaining every force feeding and grilling action. He powerfully captures the entire clout of the episode with his energetic selling of eggs with the added bonus of that 'subtle absence of flavour!' Besides, he also has the opportunity to milk maximum pained amazement from the 'Your sweet!' 'Thank you very much!' banter with Brooke-Taylor. This is not a time for towing the horrible food line, this is a time for the Goodies to act. Besides, Bill is starving hungry. So it's off to Tim's Uncle Tom, a kindly old farmer chappie who's guaranteed to welcome them in. Welcome them in he does but Uncle, perfectly sketched by John Le Mesurier, is the sort of chemically geared farmer who supplied the dreaded Shepherd's Cottage establishment with their wares. Jim Franklin, like Humphrey Barclay (*Doctor at Large: Mr Moon*) and Alan JW Bell (*Ripping Yarns: Roger of the Raj*) after him, skilfully isolates that rare touch of bizarre, but kindly, dash of eccentricity which lies at the heart of Le Mesurier's beloved *Dad's Army* figure Sergeant Wilson. Throughout he's his usual, charming self, but there's a darker edge hinted at, whether it be suppressed shock at the Goods traditional yokel dress, high-tech glee in his push-button farming chores, mistimed surreal ramblings about experimental cows without wasteful appendages like heads, or full embracing of glorious corny gags like the battery chickens and those who feed straight off the mains. Standing as one of the most prized, important and relished guest stars, the lads seem at times in awe at having him around and there's total pleasure in playing opposite someone who throws the comedy ball back with such force. With some of their best visual moments – the salvaged attacked cow which collapses after producing pre-wrapped butter, the legendary, title-resurrected herding of a flock of duck pies – balanced with a guest star in full throttle, this episode is a *Goodies* classic. Bill is still earnestly looking for fresh food but Le Mesurier merely compounds the hunger without helping by parodying non-appetising appetisers like, gained via strains, square eggs and a creepy boneless chicken. By-passing the script and muttering away to himself Le Mesurier dishes out a long list of odd jobs for the boys to handle as the show fades into a commercial break. This plugs GLO scalp anti-dandruff shampoo which does the trick via total hair loss, and presents Andrea

Lawrence's typically saucy, coy barmaid flirting with Tim's camp as a row of pink tents, beer customer. However, back at Uncle Tom's weird farm, Graeme has conjured up a nutrient-testing machine with lips like Mick Jagger, to ascertain the goodness contained in this new fangled meat. As with *The Tower of London*, prime stuff is sacrificed to the mechanical slaughter and the results are clear – the new product just does not cut the mustard. But, by now, Bill's frantic with hunger, tapping into desert island cliché and pondering a bite of Graeme before swallowing his pride and tucking into a chemically reared chicken. His careless 'have a chicken!' business with Tim is hilarious but there's no escaping the fact that actually swallowing the stuff could seriously damage your health. It's horrible, but Graeme, offered jobs as waiters in the restaurant from hell, sees a chance to infiltrate the enemy and cause a major blow for real food. Explaining the oh so British trait of never complaining about anything, a bit of hasty wire switching rearranges the animal's eating habits and creates new variations on the old semi-edible rubbish. To the strains of Oddie's funky *Down on the Farm*, our three familiar waiters let rip in the food parlour, serving everything from exploding eggs to flying sausages before the place closes and a slap-up meal back at Uncle Tom's is called for. Even Tim quickly lets his nervousness vanish and eagerly offers his services in slaughtering a happy chicken, but John's a changed man and the cheerful Esmerelda and his other creatures are now his very emotional life's blood. With an actor of his calibre, the moving, creaky piano accompaniment for his tearful, soul searching, childhood reminiscences on the days when he wanted to be a zoo keeper – which could have nose dived into schmaltz – remains a wonderful, emotive piece of work. Delightfully played with the exact mix of crest fallen pathos and dithering bemusement, he flashes up a bit of trick photography chicken dance akin to Franklin's *Broaden Your Mind / Kitten Kong* singing dogs, before the lads, now 10 days without grub, really crack up. Still, what was good for the chicken is now just as good for the Goodies and Le Mesurier's mechanised feeding system seems the ideal place for nasty, uncaring humans to be fulfilled while experiencing life from the battery hen's point of view. The lads even delivery a trio of mega-sized eggs! It's hardly a fair fate for the three pioneers of healthy, free-range farming, but food is food!

JOHN Le MESURIER, FRANK THORNTON, ANDREA LAWRENCE, REG TURNER. Episode Nine, recorded Friday 19 November, broadcast Friday 10 December 1971, 10.10–10.40pm, BBC2.

WOMEN'S LIB

Over a decade before comedy became alternative and correctness became political, the Goodies were sowing the seeds for right-on awareness and respect for women in the humour arena. While Sid James and the gang were still gearing up for a full-on anti-rant against feminism in *Carry On Girls*, our trio of lads were embracing the movement. Thus, it's amazing that this important and very funny episode is more or less ignored by students of small screen comedy and, more importantly, all but forgotten about by many fans. More shocking is its offering as an example of *The Goodies* being sexist – another one to file alongside the alleged racism of *South Africa* and *Alternative Roots*. Even more amazing in terms of Goodies' mythology, it's the bearded sex god Bill Oddie who blows the male chauvinist pig whistle on his colleagues and decries mistreatment of females as merely sex objects. Is this the bird-obsessed chap we know and love? It doesn't really matter much anyway, for in the format of this episode, Bill's militant, hipness proves the starting point for perfect comedy confrontation. Graeme's dug up some right little blonde cracker, giggling, turning on the stupid bimbo charm and filling a green blouse tighter than a very tight thing. Tim is mildly impressed as well, dishing out overplayed 'Cor!' reactions and happily throwing himself into the second-hand car dealer banter concerning the stunning Debbie's assets. Bill may enter on (an albeit unsuspecting) innuendo – 'Did you make her?' – but his distant naïvety and dumbfoundedness is endearing. The poor lad is convinced it's a robot knocked up – and probably knocked off – by boffin Garden... but noooo! She talks, walks, swings her hips and flirts like a good 'un and Tim loves it. But Bill's not standing for this – he's immediately on the phone, adopting a high-pitched, sister of mercy tone, and setting the feared women's liberation movement on the case. Gaye Brown's hyperactive, mistimed and ferociously intense campaigner is suitably scary but she is not painted as some unattractive do-gooder. The Goodies' script is crafted stuff, comically geared towards highlighting man's weaknesses and the abuse of women. Bill's sexy beard is admired (that's really going for complete equality) and the bimbo is condemned from both sides of the fence. But once the liberating, early Seventies' all-praise Germaine Greer, act of bra-abandonment is completed, Debbie is a new, switched-on woman with attitude. It's that simple, but more than an instant demonstration is needed to turn Garden and

Brooke-Taylor away from cheap sexual innuendo and a wanton groping fest. A taste of their own medicine is dished out by Brown's upper class, Victorian-valued father. Secured with jobs as butler (Graeme) and downstairs' maid (Timbo as Timbellina), the lads journey to the glorious, rolling homestead of Allan Cuthbertson. Class doesn't come into the equation here, it's your sex that makes all the difference. Before long Garden's lowly butler is on first name terms, supping sherry, looking forward to a comfy night's sleep in the second bedroom and enjoying a jolly chat about horses. Tim, on the other hand, adopting his legendary Lady Constance vocals from *I'm Sorry I'll Read That Again*, is slapped about and discussed in terms of good horse-breeding stock. She must address Cuthbertson as Master and readily accept her position as mistress and maid – a bit of slap and tickle is, after all, all these fillies understand! Garden takes to the relaxed male lifestyle with relish and Oddie's haunting number, *A Woman's Work Is Never Done*, perfectly balances the slapstick farce of Tim's heavy work load. Washing, hedge-cutting, hanging out the clothes, serving the drinks and often most of the above at once, Tim is worked to a frazzle. Graeme beats him with a cricket bat, whips him like a stagecoach horse as he travels on a tea trolley (an image subsequently familiar from the opening credits) and boozely rejoices in a less than seductive semi-striptease (again used in the title sequence). The ad break presents the most sustained and effective of all the Goodies' commercials. Just one, Honest Holidays, plugs the resort, with an uncertain Graeme telling us how it is, blocking Miss Glam's sun and camera angles, tentatively rejoicing in truthful comments concerning airport nightmares and revealing the agony of unfinished hotels via Brooke-Taylor's casual voiceover narration and Bill's drunken, on-screen, work-shy construction chappie. Pure class. It's like *Carry On Abroad* for those with short attention spans and Graeme's nervous, pregnant pause while waiting for the filmed interlude to cover his embarrassment is a subtle touch of genius. Part two still sees Tim's maid being treated like a horse (Graeme force feeds him oats from a horse bag), while Cuthbertson's daughter brings home the shocker of all shockers – her new unkempt boyfriend, Bill Oddie. Much sexist banter and weight throwing ensues but Bill gets the last laugh with a camp sigh and a minced wander away. As the 'men' plan a night of drink and dirty songs, Bill takes on his role-reversal relationship with pleasure. It's he who is being

BILL ODDIE IN VINTAGE *GOODIES* MODE

motion filming, moody music and a huge dollop of visual comedy Bill, Graeme and their respective loves, stroll, skip and prance through woodlands in Barbara Cartland style. There's the legendary hand-in-hand skipping with Graeme and databank, some childish antics in the playground and, best of all, Bill's television convention twisting moment as the soft focus image is cheekily wiped into clarity. But even a delightful burst of *Some Enchanted Evening* and the sweet memory of Bill's *Got To Make You Mine* can't save the organisation now – the lads are in love and Tim's been shown the door. Like soldiers returning from war and Beatles letting it be, the Goodies are splitting up… over women – well a woman and a female computer who sounds like Fenella Fielding! It seems like Tim is going to get himself to a nunnery, for his pals are planning the double wedding of the decade – with Gray's beloved arriving in a Southern Electronics Transport Company van. Impending happiness is halted by Tim's long-haired, hippie chick protests – it's really Lady Constance in disguise, valiantly claiming her soap box, ranting about equality, condemning marriage (nothing but 'washing meals and cooking babies!') and gamefully arousing Bill's inner thoughts on the subject. Hosing off the make-up from the assembled females, making Bill crack up with laughter and, finally, getting through to Graeme's love-sick scientist, Tim saves the day, gets a marriage proposal from Cuthbertson and is snapped for the local rag in full Jack Lemmon mode. Perfect for a comedy show with its finger on sexist content, the lads pedal off earnestly chased by disappointed women. Speeded up in true Benny Hill-style, it's the ultimate, farcical conclusion.

Did You Know? Bill's sharing, caring persona here may contrast with his usual Goodies fun beast but his sexist conflict with Tim Brooke-Taylor reflects a Cambridge moment from their shared past. Tim was among those who voted against allowing women into the Footlights, much to Bill's disgust. An opinion that 'girls wouldn't be any good' was widespread but Brooke-Taylor defended himself – believing these were true theatrical people who would give and justify the Footlighters via legitimate expression and, more crucially, cramp the lads style. 'Brits are, as a rule, hopeless at letting their hair down for silliness in front of girls…'

ALLAN CUTHBERTSON, GAYE BROWN, ELAINE BRILLIE, MAXINE CASSON, ZIBBA MAYS, TINA REEVES. Episode 10, recorded Friday 26 November, broadcast Friday 17 December 1971, 10.15–10.45pm, BBC2.

GENDER EDUCATION

wined and dined, tempted with chocs and flowers and laden with booze for a tipsy snog with the dominant female. Tim, meanwhile, has lived this *Some Like It Hot* fantasy for too long and really believes he's a woman – at least he understands the plight fully, rues his treatment of sexy pieces in the past and vows to stop girls being looked on like second-class citizens. He's proud damn it – no longer will Tom Cat Tim lure young girls and Big Fat Nellie of Cockfosters to his den. Graeme can't help playing out the scene like the Bill Oddie of old – nervously wondering if Tim's gone the full hog and had the operation, frantically trying to stop his blonde totty for the night from storming off and, ultimately, heeding Timbo's wise words about minds being more important than bodies, and succumbing to the girlish charms of his beloved computer. A cosy, romantic meal for two is just the beginning. With slow-

The ultimate two-finger salute to *The Goodies'* most vocal and prized critic, Mary Whitehouse, this stonking half hour investigates the use of titillation in small screen entertainment, highlights the truth behind the, still raging, argument that television effects an audience towards copying dramatic acts from the screen and pinpoints blind corruption behind a beloved BBC, which leads to the celebrated destruction of television centre. After the previous episode's lapse in Bill's sexist personality, the bearded one is back, loud and proud, joyfully reliving choice moments from the film *Torrid Nudes of Grope City*. Tim and Graeme, meanwhile, have been enjoying a serene evening of gramophone records. But even the dignified delight of *Come into the Garden, Maude* is the subject of intense scrutiny by the Keep Filth Off Television Campaign. Creeping about with heavy foliage disguise and protruding periscope even for Twenties' recordings, takes the cause a step too far. Although her philosophy dictates that the only good television is no television at all, total smut can manifest itself in any art form. Bringing this corrupt, super-sensitive and chilling Mary Whitehouse parody to life is the glorious Beryl Reid, strutting round the place in prissy glasses and tweed suit as the crusading Desiree Carthouse – subtle stuff lads... Tim's terrified and her misconceived belief that the Goodies are goody goody is helpfully reinforced by the patriotic one. Bill's flamboyant diatribe on the 'Phooahh!' factor of the local picture house's main feature doesn't help the cause at all (check out Tim's frantic birds equal feathered variety explanations and Bill's 'I should say!' enthusiasm when the film's dubbed a wildlife picture), but where there are money, fame and steady employment at stake the three always become one. Shocked at suggestions that the Beeb are producing an 'S, E... embarrassed crossed sign in the air' education film for schoolchildren, Reid hires our heroes to make an alternative, clean production from a script specially written by herself. The magnum opus, How to Make Babies by Doing Dirty Things, is a masterpiece of inventive deconstruction of school instruction film-making, allowing Tim's token 'man' character to stand around hopefully and Graeme's languid, slightly uneasy, narrator to tell it exactly how it isn't. Given a completely free hand (ooh err!), with Reid busy monitoring sexy close-ups of Robert Dougal's lips (ooh err! again), the lads catch the spirit of those coy, shifty education movies forced down our throats at school. Garden's upbeat, detailed look at the differences between men and those other things, boils down to us lads being better at football – glorious!

Backed by restrained music and clad in white cloth bags – without the cool, symbolic awareness of John and Yoko – Tim and his prospective mate have their really naughty bits pinpointed vaguely with a stick, woo with suitably bagged flowers and boxes of chocs, and, ultimately, hold hands on a wrapped bed, indulge in a bit of censored business and produce a wrapped babe in arms. Even the bees and birds are clad in innocence-retaining bags! But, amazingly, the film is not to Miss Carthouse's liking. Even before the titles have vanished she storms into an outraged rant. The use of the word 'gender' is just one short step from the other three-lettered term and it's not acceptable. Akin with every other television production she complains about and gets banned, she's taking a stand against this one without even seeing it – satire you see folks. Suddenly 'these so-called Goodies' are branded public enemies numbers one, two and three, their controversial film is greeted with acidic attack from education, religious and parliamentary authority, while that noted stuffed shirt Sir Reginald Wheel-Barrow is all set for some live television dismissal of this offensive motion picture. But all's fair in love, war and sex education film-making, with the Goods tempting the bewhiskered half-wit away from House of Commons playtime with an ever increasing array of tempting lollipops. Very soon, that dear old queen Richard Wattis is resplendent in pink suit and camp old fruit mood with his telly exposure of smut for the masses – of course, our trio of hard done-by chaps are masquerading as the opinionated MP bigot, synchronising speeches, crossing legs in unison (until Tim fouls up the pattern and hastily apologises) and sharing the same, huge handlebar moustache. Having praised the film, decried all those who considered it '...a bit off!', and even relished a bit of class innuendo ('Would you show it to young girls?' 'Pardon!?!'), the game is up, Wattis notices something not quite right and eagerly celebrates their cleverness at dancing between the raindrops of controversial attitude. The BBC, it seems, merely puts out certain sexy programmes to keep Miss Carthouse, Miss Whitehouse and all the other no-good do-gooders away from the real juicy stuff – violence... It's hardly British but Bill doesn't care – he's a violence junkie and just to prove it he goes into strangle mode on poor old Graeme. Tim as a plain Jane office worker glams up for a chewing gum ad but Bill's television regime has no room for such fluff. Edited highlights of the football now keep ball action to a minimum and concentrate on the punch-ups, while the news is plugged as the ultimate gore fest. Bill, of course, has sold out for success and television power. He has a cigar long enough to put Lew Grade's to shame and plans to rip the lid off the small screen – who needs digital with ideas like converting epilogues with exploding vicars and the ultimate children meets blood splatter version of Cinderella. Tim and Graeme need help and there's only one person for the job – the formerly loathed and hated Beryl Reid. Tim contradicts the patriotic freedom he loves with unconsidered comments that the British public shouldn't get what they want on telly. Uncharacteristically, he gets heavy – his spelt-out angst C.O.W. attack causes a momentarily fainting shock and cries for police and of rape before Reid comes to her senses. It's just in the nick, for an on-location visit to Bill's ambitious new production is on the cards. Besides, it's an excuse to dig out Oddie's classic *Needed* song from Series One. Years before Jim Davidson toned it down, Bill's Sinderella is a real delicious sex-obsessed, bloodbath of excess with black leather-clad whip girls, machinegun-toting Buttons and the leading lady smoking a fag – shock, horror. Bill, the sainted God of television, lords over his people with dictator's clout, almost killing old Beryl Reid with a well-timed 'Knickers!' and gleefully indulging himself and his sickened but intrigued audience, to a sneak preview of his murderous pantomime. Again, years before Chunky the killer doll from the *Child's Play* movies was blamed for violent acts in reality, Bill's passion for destruction brings on a funny turn, he reacts with intense energy to the images he has just seen and literally goes ape against his film crew. Massacring BBC employees, extras and glam girls alike, while supported by his own haunting, chilling composition, *Berserk*, Bill gets deep and dirty with his inner most violent emotions. The Buster Keaton bit of business with the collapsing house is the tamest moment here, among machinegun madness, screaming nightmare and total small screen destruction. The feeling comes and goes but a second attack brings on Guy Fawkes-like desire to destroy his own House of Lords – the sainted BBC Television Centre. Security job's worths on the door prevent Tim and Graeme's valiant attempts to quash the lit fuse and the sudden disappearance of the building is greeted with huge rounds of applause from the studio audience – perversely celebrating the destruction of the place they themselves are currently sitting in… Anyway, with the Beeb down the tube and the dismissed ITV network pumping out nothing but nice programmes, Reid can rest quietly. Like a left-over from *A Clockwork Orange* Bill sits with white-washed glasses to avoid watching corrupting material. Graeme's half-hearted attempts at home entertaining (banjo plucking and Rolf Harris impersonations) don't exactly hit the spot and the aged old campaigning fusspot is bored with nothing left to blame. But Bill, always a Goodie happy to please, points out the only activity left – a bit of the other. With screamed anger and renewed devotion to the cleansing cause, Reid's off on another one while the lads dig out three stunners, set the scene for a bit of expected horizontal athletics before twisting the small screen smut convention and settling into a cosy game of chess – cue credits.

Did You Know? *Far from being in Mary Whitehouse's bad books at this stage, The Goodies was considered a shining light of 'nice' television comedy. Indeed, the three were shocked and embarrassed to receive a telegram from Whitehouse on the conclusion of the broadcasting of Series One, expressing her pleasure at the production of such a good, clean programme. This episode was an unsubtle attempt to buck the nice trend and it worked! Even 10 years later, when Tim donned that carrot-motif pair of underpants for Saturday Night Grease, Whitehouse was still complaining.*

BERYL REID, RICHARD WATTIS, ALEX MACINTOSH, JOHN LAWRENCE, JIM COLLIER, VALERIE STANTON, TONY WEST. Episode 11, recorded Friday 3 December, broadcast Friday 31 December 1971, 9.35–10.05pm, BBC2.

CHARITY BOUNCE

Like a rubber ball the Goodies are bouncing right back to your heart and delivering one of the hottest contenders for the worse ever episode of all time. Despite a few lovely moments along the way, three comedy greats bouncing around in toothpaste suits is about as funny as three other people bouncing around in toothpaste suits. The bouncing thang is complimented by Oddie's upbeat *Spacehopper* song, so at least the toes are tapping. But great swathes of money-grabbing panic from tight-fisted boss Freddie Jones eats into the fun, while Jonathan Cecil's Public Relations creep Arthur Minion camps and 'yes man's' his way through the action. Everything starts promisingly enough, with the Goods standing on the corner watching all the old girls walk by. Desperately trying to collect money in their charity tins, the *Needed* theme adds to the opening sequence, with Bill's earnest 'get off!' as he's beaten about the head. Before long, charity leads the lads to desperate attempts, blocking the street, halting a posh Rolls Royce and unleashing a none too convincing Timbo into the main man's vehicle. The boss man of Freddie Jones seems slightly unaware of the pleasure of giving concept. Suggesting the need for a fund-raising notion, Jones invites the boys back to his factory when an idea strikes. Even Gray Bags struggles for anything original, but go the Goods do and end up in the bizarre, Roald Dahl-style universe of Sparkipegs Toothpaste. False, whiter than white smiles greet the boys from every avenue and the office of Jones – complete with teeth design desk and teeth booby-trapped safe – is right out of *Batman* villainy. A masterpiece of interior design the script, sadly, is rather lacking. Apart from Graeme's heartfelt, unpenetrating pathos dripping speech and a classic drinking suggestion to Timbo, the whole sequence descends into a muddled, one-sided plan to use the good-natured lads to further toothpaste publicity via a sponsored walk between London and Brighton. Signing blank contracts, leaving themselves open to last minute alterations and gamely surviving the inane, blonde bimbo grin of secretary Miss Simpkins (Gilly McIvor), the boys leave sort of happy with the plan. Ten quid a mile can't be bad, but Jones hasn't finished yet. With a load of other charitable folk joining the original trio, the walk is changed to a sponsored bounce – much to the delight of the bouncing expert Goodies. And that's about it really. Off they bounce, round the world, turning down desperate offers from Jones to stop, avoiding the pursuit of Cecil, getting the world – from Germany to India – bouncing, injecting a brief, unofficial Rolf Harris cameo in Oz and setting up the gags for 1975's misunderstood classic, *South Africa*, with a black and white key segregated piano and a 'Keep White' road sign. Freddie Jones has some good moments. When he believes the lads are lost at sea the tight swine opens up the champers but only offers tea, with no sugar, to his two faithful employees. His constant panic at the ever-growing amount of money he owes is barn-stormingly overplayed, but class Goodies material is solely needed. The commercial break is quite fun – with Tim's aged, old hag promoting Soft Olive Toilet Soap and the xenophobic cool of the oriental Yellow Pages – but after the whistle stop world tour, it's back to the office and collection time. Jones is suicidal (he now owes £1,200,000), but the upward sales figure for the worldwide toothpaste market momentarily pleases him (pound signs charmingly light up in his glasses), while the ultimate realisation that the Goodies chosen charity – The Grieving Grannies Fund – is one of his tax dodges, and thus, the money rightfully belongs to him, really sets him

up for the day… The lads meanwhile, toss themselves out of the window and bounce up and down for eternity – well three times at least, before the closing credits cap this one for better or worse.

Did You Know? *It may not be the best, but the bounce your way to happiness ideal was subconsciously taken up by the Natural Law Party some 20 years later. Its promised government policies included bouncing across rooms for inner peace – George Harrison gave the movement a brief endorsement… Cool. Bill Oddie explains about the show: 'We were often standing around like stooges allowing the guest villain to get all the best lines. That's why we later changed the format to allow one of us to go power mad. Usually it was either me or Graeme. Tim seemed to retain his own type of sanity most of the time. His madness was to be even more normal or even more patriotic! Freddie Jones was very good in the show but we had no idea what he was going to do next. We really didn't know what he was talking about most of the time! He couldn't remember the lines and he covered it up with this wide-eyed bluster. It was almost impossible to perform. But that really is us in those toothpaste tubes. It may seem that anybody can dress up as a toothpaste tube and bounce on a space hopper but they can't. There are special skills and you have to do it in a funny way! It was probably the most uncomfortable, physically, of all the shows. To keep those tubes upright you had to have a harness over your shoulders and a metal plate went on top of your head. If you got out of sync during the bounce it would hurt like hell. This thing would crash down giving you an instant lobotomy. Thank God it was filmed like a silent movie because the noise of us going along was a constant stream of – 'Oh Christ… Oh Shit… Oh Bugger!' It was hilarious.'*

FREDDIE JONES, JONATHAN CECIL, GILLY McIVOR. Episode 12, recorded Friday 10 December 1971, broadcast Friday 7 January 1972, 10.15–10.45pm, BBC2.

THE BADDIES

A stunning return to form for the lads thanks to a lip-smacking guest star turn from one of the greatest of all television actors and the oppressive atmosphere of intense panic which is breathtakingly contrasted with the expected glories of slapstick comedy. The Goodies being the Goodies are running the nicest person in the world competition and they've put themselves as favourite for victory… well, after all, as Bill points out they are the Goodies. Besides, the money will be handy and the reputation for good business even handier. A self-plugging phone call from David Frost sails right in at odds of 2 million/1 but the lads have no time for such Sixties' grudge matches. They get on their bike, grab the flowers and try and spread further sweetness for last minute vote catching. The *Needed* tune is intact but the public support has hit rock bottom. Boos, clouts and fruit 'n' veg pelting greet their every turn while the trandem is pinched – much to Timbo's sobbing distress. Even the police have turned against them with a cameo from John Junkin turning on the childish name-calling. He's only following instructions – a poster warns against the very ungood Goodies and face-pulling is all part of the police policy, but an urgent phone call detailing yet more nastiness from the trio causes mental blockage. Eventually, the real lads convince the numbskull copper that it can't possibly be them causing trouble because they are there. The other lot are in the street outside, stealing milk from babes, pinching cigars and frightening old ladies. And they look just like the Goodies… shock, horror, grasp! The Goodies android dummies are spookily effective. Yes, I know, it's the boys playing them as well, but Tim, in particular, gives a brilliantly eerie performance of cold, detached evil. Blessed with Oddie's *Bad, Bad Lot* song and some heavy guitar intro, the terrible threesome storm through Cricklewood with relish. And it's not just the Goodies… Tony Blackburn, Liberace, Lord Longford, Moira Anderson (opening a sex boutique!), nuns, bishops and all the other nice people are going round doing thoroughly un-nice things – even resorting to saying 'knickers' to Vera Lynn! Scouts are mucking road-crossing old ladies about, religious bods are giving away the pill, lollipopmen are hoarding up children for Uncle Jollies meat pies and Sally Ann leaders are stripping. Things are not quite as they should be and a certain nice person competition candidate, Dr Petal, has to be at the bottom of it. Patrick Troughton storms into view! With the spooky house conventions dripping from the walls, Bill's brave nonsense slowly vanishes and the sudden, scary appearance of the Frankenstein monster-like Goodies clawing for their inspirations, sets up a powerful pseudo-Hammer universe for Troughton to sweep into. It's a brief moment but that first appearance, with dark, slicked hair, flowing cloak, sinister grimace and perched vulture, Apprecia, is a masterpiece. The advert break cuts the sequence short, with a brief, throwaway telephone conversation between a sweet old dear and her relatives in Canada. Sending up the joy of far away chat, the call is reversed and the pained reaction says it all but no one really cares. He turns on the Dracula charm with his mad scientist iconography, chilling laughter and mega-evil plan to seize the nicest person award for himself. Troughton – as the gloriously named Dr

Wolfgang Aldophous Rat-Phink Von Petal – pleads his case for goodness recognition due to his helping the Nazis and his invaluable work on the H-Bomb. Bitterly complaining that 'nobody loves me', he even admits that his pet vulture only sticks around because she gets him in his will! Troughton is powerful, sick and hilarious. Bill's song may beg for *One More Chance* but things look decidedly bleak. The Goods, bound together by rope, readily support his manic ranting. But flattery will get you nowhere and a combined alligator–acid bath death is established. In a glorious ad lib, Troughton struggles with the fuse – 'When it lights…' – while the Dick Barton theme sees him on his way. The Goodies plan their escape, sending up their very own codes and conventions, with part two ending and immediately beginning part three with the Goodies free. Part three merges into part four, using the familiar Goodies' font and brilliantly captures the break-neck, derring-do of radio adventure serials. Having knobbled the entire opposition (the Bishop of Manchester's hobbies are cited as whipping choirboys and blue movie stardom aspirations), Troughton awaits his nice person crown from host 'Michael Aspirin' but, just in the nick, the bomb explodes, the Goods are catapulted across town and justice is just about done. The mock Goodies are convincing nobody, Troughton's insane slip of the tongue sees him defeated and, with a typically screamed, 'Curses!' he's gone… but not for long. Tim may be proudly wearing the nice crown but Pat's not finished yet. He whips it away, puts it on and immediately declares himself nice with frantic gusto. Tim can do nothing and, in the final chilling scene, robotic Graeme and robotic Bill go for the throat. A masterpiece.

Did You Know? This episode has been unscreened since 1975.

PATRICK TROUGHTON, JOHN JUNKIN, PETER REEVES, FELIX BOWNESS, MAY WARDEN, LOLA MORICE. Episode 13, recorded Friday 17 December 1971, broadcast Friday 14 January 1972, 10.15–10.45pm, BBC2.

KITTEN KONG: MONTREAUX '72 EDITION

'50% more Twinkle footage!' *Tim Brooke-Taylor*

Alongside the almighty *Beanstalk* episode, this is what epitomised *The Goodies* for an entire generation. Indeed, in terms of praise heaped on the series by television's great and good, this is the ultimate classic for them. Initially broadcast as part of Series Two, the episode was completely refurbished and re-recorded to represent the BBC in the 1972 Montreaux festival. When the winners were announced at the end of May, *Kitten Kong* came in at second place, picking up the coveted Silver Rose. As part of the rules of the competition, the actual show submitted had to be screened in its country of origin within six months of the festival judgment. For the international market, there is slightly more of a shift to visual comic expression than before and, for some reason definitely unfathomable to your average European viewer, the guest star squashing of poor Michael Aspel was an additional bonus in this Montreaux edition. But the heart and soul remains intact and it's this version that has been repeated, released on video, plundered for choice clips and lifted to the pinnacle of Goodies' expression. Ironically, the rip-off Fifties' atomic mutation monster movie, when the delightful kitten Twinkle outgrows her welcome, only forms a small part of the show but the destructive push on the (then) Post Office Tower and head popping through St Paul's Cathedral scenes have become such an indelible set of images, that the rest of the animal-based comedy is largely forgotten. It all starts with Chef Bill conjuring up a connoisseur's delight with roast chicken (slightly underdone and still clucking), roast potatoes and button mushrooms. A bit of wine tasting during preparation does not go amiss but no sooner has Bill settled down to presenting his meal than those chess hooligans Graeme and Tim burst onto the scene. Embracing football fan terminology with their raucous hand-clapping chants of 'Gerbosky!' and detailed obsessions concerning cunning moves, the lads play up to male stereotypes and demand food after sporting pleasure. But Bill hasn't got time for these starving layabouts. He's a Goodie and he's doing anything, anytime – in this case looking after a rather temperamental guinea pig with a slap-up bean feast. The illogical situation is, naturally, water off a duck's back to the others and soon after Tim's attempted chomp of the defenceless creature, he's getting all pompous about the fact that Bunter, the furry one, isn't using his mini knife and fork. Mind you, with a clean plate in the guinea pig's cage, Graeme can see a money-making scheme in its primitive stages. He eagerly voices his impressed reaction – of course, Tim, always a little bit slow on the uptake is rather more miffed at the food reversal... the lads are now reduced to chewing on rather unpleasant soggy lettuce leaves and potato peelings. Once desert is unveiled Tim's classic and outraged exclamation 'Ruddy Hell!' launches a typically bitchy diatribe between Posh Good and Scary Good. With housewife complaints about the money being brought into the house and oft-repeated threats of 'going back to Mother', Bill adopts his hurt, arms

folded pose. Tim's synchronised back turning and arm folding is a great comic banter, echoing a well-delivered 'And you keep out of this!', as Gray Bags tries to inject a bit of sanity to the proceedings. A semi-corpsed 'Ooh!' brings the bickering couple out of their camp mode and Tim, finally grasping the business sense in this animal lark, thinks up a good idea light bulb and begins work on the new venture. Special effects – who needs them? – just a hastily scribbled thought bubble, three comic pros and Oddie's endearingly relentless ditty *Needed*. Out and about on the trandem, with a large wicker basket dragged in tow, Tim gets down to it, requesting the Cricklewood population to bring out their loony animals and stick them in the unpractical, communal receptacle. Bill's lumbered with a huge, unhelpful dog, while Tim struggles manfully with a massive snake straight out of the props department of Ed Wood. But back at home, Dr Garden has things nicely under control. He adopts a protective glove before attempting to reveal a camera shy, child-loving mongoose, injects a wonderful bit of visual business with an overtly affectionate bush baby, lavishes loving care on a paranoid vampire bat and complains bitterly about the two noisy dogs relegated to the back yard. One of the all time great *Goodies* moments, the team's visual flair and sense of comic awareness where animals are concerned fuses brilliantly to present the repeated and backward played images of the dog's lip synced to a rendition of Sammy Cahn's *Anything You Can Do I Can Do Better* from *Calamity Jane*. Despite a return to the ever-attentive bush baby gag from Garden (unceremoniously wiping his nose with the creature before tossing it away), it's Tim's baby talk delight to the tiny, 23-year-old kitten, Twinkle, that really starts the magic kicking in. Exercise is the name of the game and, accompanied by yet another, shamelessly commercially unrecorded, Oddie composition, *Dumb Animals (Everyone Needs a Friend)*, the Goodies throw themselves into slapstick walkies. Bill is, once again, stuck with that lazy lump of hound, huffishly lifting his ear in rhythm to the bearded ones energetic push ups. Graeme has a more sedate task at hand, encouraging a spot of speedy sprinting from Colin the tortoise and, although there's less meat to the visual comedy, he succeeds in digging in with one of the best moments as he sheepishly gives the slow chap a helpful nudge with his foot. Smitten with the kitten, Tim takes on the small powerhouse and is dragged through the park at a million miles an hour, spun round a roundabout, sent flying down a slide and finally gets bashed by a tree. The customary end of part one sees a couple of so so comic ads with Graeme's injection of economy petrol into Tim's car merely proving the strength of Robinson's Paper which wrecks the full throttle vehicle, and Tim again, camping it up as a Seventies' fashion dude, chased by glam girls, puffing on his Butch Tobacco for men and revealing his gay tendencies with the burly henchman at his side. But it's back to basics, back to Oddie's *Dumb Animals* and back to that pesky tree, as the Goods desperately go for the common denominator and tempt down Twinkle with an extended saucer of milk. Sadly, Timbo's stuck up there but, as per usual, his fellow team members don't seem to be bothered. Bill pokes his ruler into the completely empty shell of the office tortoise. Garden certainly isn't bothered, for he's totally sewn up with his Twinkle experiment, preparing a bucket-load of grub for the ever-growing kitten and hardly noticing the distressed return of the prodigal Tim. Poor lad, he's a bit fretful as it is, but he's hardly prepared for the sight that meets his eyes – Twinkle, well on her way to Kong super status. There's a stunning juxtaposition of images as the cute cat with the devil in her eye breaks into the hyper, nightmarish, screaming face of Brooke-Taylor. A wonderfully structured night time discussion – with Tim too panicked to sleep, Bill adding a bit of light relief to the situation ('I'm not licking you!') and Graeme fussing round his pet project with a huge vitamin pill – soon breaks down to cold terror as Oddie's disastrous faux pas of letting the cat out of the office is let out of the bag. Yet another, bush baby gag is included from Garden's ashen mad scientist but Kitten Kong is on the prowl and there's every chance human flesh is on the menu. Graeme quickly gets into his famous, one-piece outside clothes, sticks his bed back into the wall and encourages his fellow cat chasers to rush through it. One of Jim Franklin's directorial masterpieces sets the comic tension with our trandem-seated trio of cowardly heroes, vainly searching for the kitten. As the camera pans upwards and away, a huge, black pussy footprint is slap bang besides them. The trail is hot, the juices are flowing and Oddie's thundering title song adds extra bite to the moment. Unearthly meows, screaming crowds and terrified dogs (including a helpfully pointing Lassie-a-like) lead the lads to the white monster casually chewing on a lamp-post. Wisely they don't stick around for a full-on confrontation. Instead, it's the good old BBC news reporter that fills in the mass destruction.

Goodies news personified, Corbet Woodall, links in the studio, while the man with the mic before he was the man with the big red book, Michael Aspel, sends his final outside comment from within the heat of battle. Famous landmarks are put to the sword and the future of the country is threatened, so with Graeme's anti-growth formula, a suitably oversized hypodermic needle, a Superhero-fashioned quick change cabinet and some rather fetching mouse costumes, the lads go in pursuit. Bill, seasoned with pepper, is offered up as the bait, but this mouse fit for slaughter can hardly register his chagrin, before panto cries of 'It's behind you!' are yelled at the television set. Homage rules as the Goods crash into a Tom and Jerry scenario – the coloured housekeeper jumps onto a stool, the mouse-eye view of a pair of frantic slippers and a scream of 'Thomas!' before the team do a Wile E Coyote pause, look into camera and painlessly fall between two high rise buildings. The major film source is acknowledged when Bill does his Fay Wray impression, trapped in the grasp of Kitten Kong. There's an endearing rub of the fur and a hasty injection of size-reducing stuff, resulting in Twinkle ending up as her old, tiny self in the middle of one of her giant footprints. Naturally, it's not all plain sailing for the Goodies as their needle bursts the hot air balloon and Concorde sails into view to whip them off into oblivion. However, in the spirit of cartoons, the trio are back safe and well in their office, paper wrapping cured pets for redistribution. But wait – shock, horror – Graeme's secret, size-increasing food is half eaten and the office is invaded by a load of mega mice. In a climax to make the hairs on the back of your neck tingle, Twinkle is swiftly brought out of retirement and cries of 'Feed the cat!' fill the air.

Did You Know? Filming for this new edition of Kitten Kong took place over a four-day period from 26 February 1972, with some extracts retained from the original Series Two version. The justly celebrated Anything You Can Do dog duet was, in fact, lifted directly from Series Two Episode Six of the 1968 Brooke-Taylor/Garden sketch show Broaden Your Mind. Film editor Jim Franklin, who worked on both shows, got the idea when his wife fed their pet dog a toffee and the poor thing struggled to free it from its teeth, forcing its head upwards and opening its mouth wide. It looked like it was singing, so with a massive budget of £500, Franklin filmed his dog and another, at five times normal speed, added freeze frames, film loops and repeated footage to gain the required result. He had delivered a similar piece for the Harold Wilson/George Brown dance in The Frost Report. The legendary dog piece of work became an oft-repeated favourite. The Kitten's destruction of the capital was *captured by model work, clever use of camera lenses and slow-motion photography. The Australian Broadcasting Commission edited a 'bloody' from the show's soundtrack. The classic mouse disguises which remain one of the great Goodie images, do, in fact, link across to the dreadful film Rentadick, ostensibly cobbled together by a stitched-up John Cleese and Graham Chapman. In the film's less than dramatic climax, Kenneth Cope and Richard Briers adopt mouse costumes but, if the David Frost pool of talent (Feldman, Barker, Corbett, Cleese) had been cast as originally intended, no doubt Tim Brooke-Taylor would have tasted the mouse life on the big screen as well. Talking about the absurdity of filming in February 1975, Graeme Garden commented, 'We might be in the middle of a perfectly rational, serious discussion and it will suddenly dawn on the three of us that we're actually standing in the middle of a field dressed as mice!' The end credits for this special edition of Kitten Kong features recap images from the show — the credits for the three prinicpals are accompanied by manic slapstick shots of them from the Dumb Animals segment. Jim Franklin is credited as film director, instead of his usual production credit (which was the BBC compromise of his job as both producer and director). Original Monty Python producer John Howard Davies was in the production chair. This was a cleaned-up version of the show after Michael Mills had expressed his sadness at the Goodies' swearing. The show was too 'nice' for that and for Mills bad language in the show was as bad as Bertie Wooster saying 'shit!' Thus, Tim's overplayed 'Ruddy hell!' here and not the original 'Bloody hell!' The Graeme Garden bat attack clip was featured on the telly request show Pick and Mix. The basket that Tim uses for animal collections is the very same one featured in the Brooke-Taylor/Feldman Vet Sketch from It's Marty. The Michael Aspel squashing clip was used for the BBC comedy panel game, Gag Tags, where Jonathan Ross chaired a mixture of Joker's Wild joke-telling and A Question of Sport for comedians trivia quiz. Bob Monkhouse and Frank Skinner captained the teams and a major Radio Times comedy family tree attaching the two comedians found time to mention The Goodies as a spin-off from At Last the 1948 Show and poor relations of Monty Python. This Montreux edition of Kitten Kong was selected by the BBC as the series representation for the corporation's massive retrospective season, TV50. Its broadcast at 6pm on Tuesday 4 November 1986 is the last time an episode of The Goodies has been screened on British terrestrial television to date.*

MICHAEL ASPEL, CORBET WOODALL, MILTON REID. Written by Graeme Garden and Bill Oddie with Tim Brooke-Taylor. Music by Bill Oddie and Michael Gibbs. Costume Betty Aldiss. Make-up Rhian Davies. Lighting John Green. Sound Laurence Taylor. Film cameramen Stewart A Farnell and Leonard Newson. Film editors Martyn Day and Stephen Ray. Visual effects Ron Oates. Design by Roger Murray-Leach and David Jones. Film direction by Jim Franklin. Produced by John Howard Davies. Recorded Saturday 18 March, broadcast Sunday 9 April 1972, 10.05–10.35pm, BBC2.

SERIES THREE

Having seen a copy of the original *Kitten Kong* before its broadcast, the trio's chief champion, Michael Mills, began expressing doubts about the series. With 'one 'bleeding',

THE CLASSIC POSE — WE ALL GOT A SIGNED COPY FROM OUR SEVENTIES FAN LETTERS TO THE TEAM

one 'bloody' and a number of 'God's' in it', the show seemed to be far from a family-aimed show. The major reason was that the show wasn't a family-aimed show. Well, to the main men at the BBC, it certainly was now, and so began a lengthy conflict between the Goodies and the corporation. The battle lines were drawn, with controlled smut and social comment counter-balanced with speeded playground antics and corny puns. The result, of course, was the classic Goodies episode. However, John Howard Davies didn't have to face the firing squad. Having completed work on Series Two and the Montreaux special, he handed the reigns over to Jim Franklin. Now doing both directing and producing jobs, the BBC hierarchy insisted that only one credit could be billed. Alan JW Bell displeased the Beeb by crediting himself with both during Eighties episodes of *Last of the Summer Wine* and eventually got round it by featuring a director credit at the start and a producer credit at the end. Despite the attitude of Mills, the BBC were still very much behind *The Goodies*. On 10 April 1972, the day after the Montreaux version of *Kitten Kong* aired, Head of BBC Comedy, Duncan Wood, requested a further 13 episodes to form 'a major part of our BBC output in 1973'. As with the second series these would be recorded in two separate batches, although this set of 13 titles would be broadcast as six in Series Three, six in Series Four and the 'adult' special *Superstar*. Contracts for the new shows were signed on 8 May 1972 and BBC1 had already begun to stoke *The Goodies'* fire with Saturday evening repeats of Series Two from 4 May with *Scotland* screened at 8pm. Filming for Series Three started on 2 October 1972, with location filming in King's Lynn, Slough and on Jersey.

Film cameraman Stewart A Farnell. Film editor Ron Pope. Visual effects John Horton. Costume Mary Woods. Make-up Rhian Davies (Episodes 1–4) and Penny Norton (Episodes 1, 5 & 6). Lighting John Dixon. Sound John Holmes. Music by Bill Oddie and Michael Gibbs. Design John Stout (Episodes 1, 3–6) and Geoffrey Patterson (Episodes 2, 4 & 6). Produced by Jim Franklin.

THE NEW OFFICE

The times were changing and after a couple of series and a reheated brush with an oversized kitten, The Goodies were back with accommodation problems. Work is completely curtailed for a major office redecoration programme and our heroes haplessly suffer outside the door in anticipation. A six-month schedule is one thing but the industrial noise – helpfully provided on a tape recorder for added atmosphere – is more than the soul can bear. Particularly if you are a delicate soul like Tim. Meanwhile, in an echo of the even more poverty-stricken times to come, Graeme is lovingly overcooking the team's joint lunch – a single bean! In a comment on the grand British workman, the office hasn't changed one bit during six months and Joe Melia, brilliantly capturing the work-shy, arrogant embodiment of the lazy labour forces, turns on his nasty attitude. It's time for downing the newspapers and taking up the teacups for a break from doing nothing. Even the most heartfelt, cowardly pleas from a whining Tim doesn't cut any ice with this hard-nosed construction cowboy – probably a reflection of Tim's imperialistic, upper class, 'I know how to treat workers' attitude, previously adopted. As a result, our trio are left with a ramshackle office, six

months wasted and nothing more than a disgruntled 'Get stuffed!' in their ears. So it's off to the hand-wringing world of corrupt estate agents. Playing up on the homeless stereotypes and, poignantly, injecting the emotion of *Cathy Come Home* into their comic universe, Tim is the perfect distraught mother, Bill the bearded, gurgling babe and, best of the lot, Graeme, embracing cockney sparrow mannerisms 'guv' all over the place to twist the sentimental knife. However, satire is satire and these sort of money-grabbing estate agent people don't care about human suffering. Especially when the man in black – laughing like a maniac and momentarily sporting Count Dracula fangs – is played by none other than Joe Melia again. There's a sense of Cleese-like grandeur about his protesting to claims that he isn't the same person as the builder, while the entire scene is enriched with a Dickensian decay. Indeed, there's more than a touch of the Ebenezer Scrooge about Melia's wonderfully flamboyant delivery, offering a dog kennel for £5000, double bluffing as a way of life, pinpointing the cost of living via a square foot of land sold to the Goods for some loose change – £100,000 – and ultimately running off with archetypal sexy brunette secretary, Julie Desmond. Never ones to be totally down and out, the ads promote free footballers with petrol and Tim's 'My Favourite Supper' Heinz meanz beanz goes through the motions, as the lads pick themselves up, dust themselves down and start all over again – building their very own, brand, spanking new, disused railway station for their office – note the Offices, Shops and Railway Premises Act hanging outside the office, required by law to be posted at every station in the land. Helped along by another Oddie musical winner, *That's My Home*, it serves as the perfect mood music for a classic onslaught of visuals, pratfalls and reheated slapstick routines. The spirit of Mack Sennett and the Marx Brothers was alive and well and living in Cricklewood in 1973 and this outstanding sequence affectionately tips its hat to Keaton, Langdon and, particularly, the Laurel and Hardy gem, *Busy Bodies*. This Goodies apartment reflects the occupants, with Tim's regal throne and Balmoral experience, Graeme's cool, up-to-the-minute computer and Bill's chill out, scruff bag corner with body-moulded sag bag, a Tony Blackburn punchbag and a very unbag-like pin up on a motorbike. Check out Tim's counter-action, with his poster of Her Majesty on a motorbike, and Graeme, an Albert Einstein sex babe on a motorbike. However, this perfect environment doesn't last long for no sooner has Bill condemned Tim's choice of an elephant's foot umbrella stand and the lads have hitched up their wagon to set up business, than their private hideaway is invaded by pin-striped, bowler-hatted businessmen waiting for the next train. Like a bizarre, time warp from Tony Hancock's *The Rebel*, the spectre of boring normality breaks through the barrier and the only escape is a speedy transportation to the middle of nowhere. Safe from the mundane existence of civilised life, the lads must face the heart-wrenching terror of huge, driverless, monstrous land diggers ripping apart our green and pleasant land with an air of aimless disdain. Just think *Dual* with laughs! Tim's flowing and patriotic chest-puffing monologue gives an air of *Henry V* destiny to the battle ahead and although, as usual, his commitment is muted by total cowardice at the crunch time, the stirring refrain of *Rule Britannia* and a roared 'Arm yourself my friends!' never fails to get the old juices flowing. With construction vehicles given life à la Ray Harryhausen's monster movies, the lads throw themselves into a pretty ineffective battle technique – Bill's conker is conquered, Graeme struggles with a bull-fighting approach and Tim, bless him, just panics... Eventually, it's music that charms the savage beasties, with an impromptu, pied piper Cha-Cha tempting these metal, gnashing dinos over a cliff to oblivion. The chuffed to bits, mutual handshake of success signals that the Goodies are back... loud and proud.

Did You Know? *The opener for the third series earned the Goodies their first appearance on the cover of the Radio Times (3–9 February 1973) bearing the legend 'Goody, Goody, Goody'. With a cracking colour shot featured Brooke-Taylor, Oddie and Garden peering out from inside a mechanical digger's scoop, a two-page article, 'In Pursuit of a Load of Goodies' saw Russell Miller chatting to the lads on location in Norfolk. The typically manic interview, with references to Bill's bird-watching and Graeme's fishing, produced a picture of three very contented Goodies and Tim, thoughtfully, pondered that 'ideally The Goodies will be great in 70 years time' while Bill remarked that 'basically we are trying to produce the funniest half hour anyone has ever seen'. The Australian Broadcasting Commission insisted that Joe Melia's uttering of 'Get stuffed!' be haphazardly overdubbed with 'Get lost!' As Tim settles in the new office, look out for him watering the Montreux Silver Rose the team had just won for Kitten Kong. The moment he covers it with gold paint is one to treasure.*

JOE MELIA, JULIE DESMOND. Episode One, recorded Thursday 30 November 1972, broadcast Sunday 4 February 1973, 8.15–8.45pm, BBC2.

HUNTING PINK

All is normal at Goodies Headquarters with Bill lazily bringing in the paper and Graeme cleaning his teeth via mad science, but Tim is even smarter and erect than ever, clad in full Buck House guard uniform, complete with a lush Busby hat. The lads naturally take the mickey and question his sexual motives but tunes are quickly changed when a world of money, elderly relatives and big country seats is alluded to. Yet another one of Tim's eccentric Uncles pops up and with Graeme and Bill clad in Hawaiian holiday gear (note Oddie's bit of Python iconography – the Gumpy knotted handkerchief), it's all off to the rolling estate of Great Uncle Butcher ('butcher than what!') and a crack at the old fool's dosh. Tally Ho Towers is the embodiment of landed gentry country squire living: horses everywhere and that includes an upstairs bedroom and a replacement for the cuckoo in the clock. Naturally, bolshy Bill continually undermines the aristocracy with working class attitude and laid-back disgust. His cheeky 'cheerio mate!' to Erik Chitty's disgruntled man servant, Basterville, is a telling poke at the upper crust vitals and his slap-happy treatment of the leggy crumpet waitresses is joyfully downmarket. Pretty boy sophisticate Tim can merely look on with helpless longing as his pals get down to off-camera sexual business, but things quickly change when Tim's aged Unc – looking uncannily like Tim with a grey fright wig on – staggers into view. Clad in riding gear, bow legged from a life in the saddle, falling backwards with aged arrogance and bellowing about nothing in a bigoted, condescending manner, Tim's wonderful grotesqueness captures the spirit of out of touch British insanity. Their split screen meeting belies the lack of technology of the day and the uneasy cut-away shots to Tim patiently waiting out of the main frame while his two chums and 'Uncle' natter are obviously primitive. Sporting plus fours and stupid voices, the two money-grabbing Goodies eagerly throw themselves into the flamboyant discussion about hunting, riding and lying, bursting into a gloriously manic rendition of Lee Marvin's *Wandering Star* before spiralling into a surreal shared train of thought rant about the nostalgic delights of being born in the saddle. The back-dating memories of Bill (about being able to ride before he was born) brings on a priceless uttered exclamation from Tim ('pack of lies!') and highlights the wonderfully timed rapport between the three. It sort of plays like a high-class variation of *The 1948 Show*'s exaggerated excess of the Four

Yorkshiremen, and Chitty's coconut accompaniment to simulate horse's hoofs pre-dates *Monty Python and the Holy Grail* by a year. It's the old buffer's money the lads want, so if that means stoking the irritating fellow's ego, walking the fox-hunting walk and talking the fox-hunting talk, then so be it. Lugging the senile chap in his bath chair, pushing him onto his trusted steer and standing idly by as the blood hots up, the horn is blown and the defenceless rabbit is blown to bits thanks to an allied tank gun, the mad Uncle expires from excitement and Timbo inherits the earth – or at least, his small corner which will be forever England. All this visual mayhem meanwhile is accompanied by arguably Oddie's most potent composition, *Ride My Pony* – a masterpiece of groovy sound hastily resurrected for the team's debut album. But now, at the halfway mark, the mildly satirical upper class name calling gives way to the hard-hitting bite – Graeme, and particularly Bill's vehement hatred of 'revolting' fox hunting. A laudable and impassioned campaign for the abolishment of blood sports, Bill finds the perfect brainless, 'follow the posh herd' mentality in the heartless, traditional, newly landed land owner cad of Tim Brooke-Taylor Esquire. However, needs must when the devil shoots you in the foot and two penniless Goodies gratefully seize the opportunity to became boot-licking, forelock-tugging domestics to the pompous servant beater. An overlong bit of business concerning an overlong dining room table – kippers are hooked by Tim's fishing net, eggs are bashed like tennis balls and coffee is pumped over Tim's ever getting wetter trousers – happily embraces two classic Goodies moments, the terrifically cheesy mounted head of Tim's Uncle still going on about the glories of blood only to be blown away once and for all by young Timbo's shotgun and Bill's frantic tabletop tricycle attack on the old ways of the ruling classes ending in a collapsed, pathetic heap. Tim, meanwhile, has bigger kippers to cure, marrying the impossibly pompous, long-winded, horsewoman of the year ('more horse than woman!') and deliciously revealing his ideals of wedded bliss knee deep in blood, entrails and other ghastly leftovers from a day on the happy hunting ground – 'We're gonna slaughter a rabbit, hang the giblets around her neck, paint her cheeks with blood and slap her round the kisser with its bladder!' Mind you, this young lady does seem to spend her entire life within a wardrobe – lifted from an unsung Pete 'n' Dud sketch from 1968's *Goodbye Again* – while Tim's hoped for transformation of his

abode into the world's biggest blood sports centre is a fairly low-key affair kicking off with a Glenn Miller-style swing band jam session. Still, Graeme is worried and, what's more, he's lost for words – desperately trying to communicate with a lacklustre Bill through a stunning Harpo Marx-like sequence of mime. The long and the short of it sees Tim mounting a pantomime horse, a cute white rabbit is pursued through the wilderness and our pioneering hunt saboteurs adopt floppy ear costumes to confuse the bloodlust fiends. Oddie's song, *Run!*, adds gusto to the chase, Tim's rearing up control of the trandem is a bit of primitive trick photography and there's even time for a Harvey Smith two-finger salute. It's capped by a totally incongruous red Indian round-up (pointing the way for Python's bizarre *Grail* conclusion). Aversion therapy is required and all Tim's bad, upper class habits are painfully chipped away. The moral, of course, is Bill – still protesting the cruel foulness of blood sports – finding his own irresistible, enjoyable bloodlust from whacking Tim into submission. The thrill of the kill even grabs the ultimate comic environmentalist. It's fun after all, and with Graeme's tally ho's and Bill's eager fox-hunting horn blowing, it's bloodlust business as usual – but at least it's not a white rabbit to the slaughter.

Did You Know? *The Australian Broadcasting Commission edited out the mention of 'big knockers' in reference to Tim's fiancée Lady Amanda. Its absence, as a hilarious pay-off for the girl's outlandish name – which includes notable railway stations, a celebrated football team and at least one Sixties' beat combo, was unforgivable. Early suggestions of Tim's homosexuality and a laugh about the word 'bum' were also cut.*

ERIK CHITTY. Episode Two, recorded Thursday 7 December 1972, broadcast Sunday 11 February 1973, 8.15–8.45pm, BBC2.

WINTER OLYMPICS

Every inch of newspaper column, from Bill's *Sun* to Tim's *Times*, seems packed with really bad news and Julie Ege. In a time when she really was everywhere, Julie is everywhere – name-checked via everybody from a familiar bikini-clad beauty to a less than familiar bearded sportsman. In a throwaway comment on the corrupt sponsorship of sport (with whisky, Mafia and drug-pushing franchises pulling out), the poor depleted British team for the Winter Olympics has bitten the dust. Basically, this is almost an exact remake of the Series One show, *The Commonwealth Games*, with wicked delight in Britain's sporting hopelessness (Graeme's half-hearted defence concerning one gold medal we picked up is quickly undermined by Bill's cheerful 'They made him put it back again!' comment) and Peter Jones brilliantly refilling the shoes of Reginald Marsh as the bizarre, bowler-hatted Minister of Sport. But this time, nobody is going to fool the Goodies. They're sick of taking on rotten jobs and getting hurt but Jones, if anything, even more surreally detached and barking mad than Marsh, effortlessly twists the bargaining knife and explains the fact that the lads will be representing their country. It doesn't matter that a principle is at stake. It doesn't even matter that they have already represented their country once before and made complete arses of themselves. Tim's on a patriotic trip, the National Anthem starts blaring, the flag waves with pride and the British spirit comes to the fore – and still, with hands outstretched, the Goodies will do anything, anywhere, as long as there's money in it. The deal is struck and Jones, staggering through the madness with an amazed sense of 'taking candy from babies' ease, lets rip with trusted untrustworthiness in the best political tradition. The venue is fixed for the snowy reaches of the North Pole, the training facilities are in place – following Bill's unionist rant about treating sportsmen right – and the place is so top secret that the lads are blind-folded before being send on their way. A cactus, allegedly a relief map – 'that's a relief!' – leads them to the coldest place in Britain (Bognor on a bank holiday) and the pitiful hut – again reminiscent of *The Commonwealth Games* episode – is set in the austerity ravaged world of Fifties' holiday camps. Full of hopeless inventions, almost killer pull down beds (Bill jumps out of the way as the prop falls slightly before cue and laughs at his near miss), a gallant, crestfallen Hall of Fame and equipment so archaic (from an orange box sleigh to crummy roller skates) that defeat stares them in the face from the beginning. But Tim is ultra-keen to get in the peak of fitness. Exercising furiously, much to the amusement of Bill, Tim dismisses mere technicalities like rubbish gear, with a confident, 'we're British!' and we can do it with anything attitude. The Dunkirk spirit is all very well but under normal circumstances it won't work in the North Pole with a load of grotty old tat. As ever, Graeme's not too far from a wild, madcap, hair-brained and successful scheme. Throwaway ads for baked beans (again) and Golden Dairy Margarine, cover the very brief travelling time from Bognor to the North Pole. Jones is already settled in the lap of semi-luxury that the North Pole Hilton can offer and Tim flogs a dead gag about using

a handy kettle for a map – it taps into the previous cactus visual and is later enforced when Jones palms off a teapot as a training manual but, seemingly, only one bloke in the audience gets the point and Tim hastily moves on. There's ice, ice everywhere but not a drop for Tim's drink – the fridge is on the blink – and Bill, ready for food as ever, screams for the varied menu consisting of variations on whale blubber, whale blubber, whale blubber and... whale blubber. Roast chicken surprise, of course, is whale blubber – all together now 'That's the surprise!' – and Walrus pie, fit for Desperate Dan and sporting a pair of huge tusks, is hardly the most mouth-watering of prospects. Bill eagerly embraces his two favourite obsessions, music and birds (the unfeathered kind in this case), with some hot, boogie woogie icicle jamming and a bit of short-lived chatting up of Helli Louise's yellow bikini-clad Eskimo Nell. Tim's all shy and nervy but a hasty water squirt from an American submarine cools Bill's ardour and Peter Jones, putting down morale, orders a bit of training despite the British being the 'very best losers in the world!' No training required I should imagine. The Goods obviously agree, for their visual bit of ice-bound tomfoolery is short-lived and uninventive but, at least, there's the pleasure of that classic song *Winter Sportsman*. Later hammed up by Tim's effete chappie for *The Goodies Sing Songs From The Goodies*, here we have the more funky Bill Oddie mix. A promised flash of bare flesh from Miss Louise soon drives away those frozen solid blues and Graeme's cunning plan is hatched – fundamentally to melt the snow, allow the Goods to walk... or at the very least, swim, through the competitions and strike a blow for British sport. He works out that a hot water bottle could melt the place in just 178,000 years! Of course, he's totally mad, but soon it's up, up and away in my beautiful balloon with trandem feature. Decked out in Biggles' flying goggles and leather jackets, Tim bags a huge butterfly – incongruously just flying pass – and Gray Bags attaches the heat-wave melting device thingamy-bob to the poor creature. Bill, registering his environmental complaint that this is cruelty to nature, soon throws himself into the cheerful rendition of *Zip-A-Dee-Doo-Da* as the sun has got his hat on and the snow begins to melt. Unprepared, the band and competing nations stroll through an ever-rising stretch of water but the Goodies (charmingly attired in Edwardian swimming costumes emblazoned with the Union flag) politely raise

GRAEME GARDEN, IN A RARE *GOODIES* ERA SHOT, ALMOST WITHOUT SPECS APPEAL

their straw boaters and glide along astride dolphin water toys. A joyous image of British comic strength, the games are ours – with those hopeless roller skates coming in handy with no ice. Tim's outer wetsuit tutu gets a bit damp while the manic skiing business hits the right spot and we sail into success. This time round the Brits, proving a bit of tampering with the elements can help, stand victorious – but at what cost? In the excitement, the ray lamp is forgotten, Bill's concern is still with the butterfly, but the scientist senses impending doom. In an age when polar ice cap melting and the ozone layer was unheard of, the lads have pre-empted the concern of rising sea levels and, while making a joke out of the situation, highlight the

potential disaster in cold realistic terms. Minister Jones is wet and wild outside the flooded window of the Cricklewood office and naïve old Tim merrily goes to let him in. But that closing, screamed 'No!' from the others carries an hilarious, weighty message indeed.

PETER JONES, HELLI LOUISE. Episode Three, recorded Thursday 14 December 1972, broadcast Sunday 18 February 1973, 8.15–8.45pm, BBC2.

THAT OLD BLACK MAGIC

One of my all time favourite Goodies' episodes weighs in like a priceless cross between *Carry On Screaming!* and *The Goon Show*. There's enough touchstones to Hammer horror mythology and classic comedy to sink the Titanic, Patricia Hayes throws herself into the gloriously ad-libbed, overplayed guest star slot like no other and, apart from all that, it sees the Goodie premiere of Oddie's earth-shattering musical interlude *Stuff That Gibbon*. The 'small, fat man with a beard' is doing his usual lazy thing – sucking sherbet and browsing through *Woman* magazine – but Tim is extremely worried. The lads that do anything anywhere haven't done anything, anywhere for two months. Anyway, life is just about getting so boring that it's almost down to joke telling, when the delightful Patricia Hayes, screaming with insane laughter, sporting one of Carmen Miranda's cast off hats and wearing more face glitter than Marc Bolan on New Year's Eve, staggers into the office looking for assistance. She's no loony, although you could have fooled almost anybody in the land, but her sad story (cue portable mood music) is winning enough to convince Timbo – but he's desperate for employment. Even money-hungry Bill is less than eager to tackle the assignment, particularly after this nutty Witch (dubbed Witch Hazel) reveals her obsession with furry animals. Besides, she's given our hairy Goodie some interesting looks and all his usual roughneck charm and off colour quips are tossed in (he considers Black Witch to have been in the coven too long! –the gag is cracked again later with a photograph of a naked Satanic dancer bearing the caption 'Bum in the Coven'), in the hope that she will be tossed out. All to no avail, for Graeme – fresh from hard labour flogging 'orrible, 'airy spiders' is just the man for the job. The Witch's earnest monologue of undead things, evil doings and the mysteries of the other side may have been used for a very cheap, very funny jibe at independent television, but she's in deadly earnest and Graeme is the only one with hidden, ghostly powers... or so she thinks. Tim, revealing a cunning streak willing to do anything for a bit of work, eagerly sets up a hoax for their client's benefit, adopts familiar tones during his crystal ball charade and openly encourages Bill's lacklustre bit of Tommy Cooper – complete with flowerpot head attire and grovelling delivery. The actual darkened room setting and spooky goings on are brilliantly played by the four. Semi-lifted from a similarly structured Marty Feldman sketch, the lads elongate the situation with variety tricks (Bill's 'correct – and the next item!' banter when the watch is produced), a healthy bash at pet targets (Tony Blackburn), knock knock puns so bad they're terrible and shameless scriptwriting to allow Graeme his repertoire of spot on impressions of Eamonn Andrews, Walter Gabriel and Eddie Waring during his spirit possession session. It is the collection of voices continually cropping up in *The Goodies* and, earlier, *I'm Sorry I'll Read That Again*, that brings on a warm reaction from the audience and a knowing smile from his co-stars, akin to Tony Hancock's continual delight in doing his legendary Charles Laughton, George Arliss and Robert Newton turns. Indeed, Patricia Hayes links the two, having spun her mystic nonsense opposite the lad 'imself in *Hancock's Half Hour* as Mrs Cavette, the 'lady that does' from hell. The Goodies are aware of the comic heritage, giving Hayes the chance to recreate her classic 'come again another day!' incantation from 1959's *Hancock's Half Hour: The Cold*. Cheerfully unaware of her magical powers, she chirpily wanders through the surreal Goodies universe, muttering to herself, injecting spontaneous chatter into the confused dialogue, gainfully relishing the most painful of gags and setting up the entire concluding Hammer black mass with Graeme cracking up with crazed, supernatural power. Hoping things will calm down in the interim, Tim, Bill and Pat clear off to savour the sweet delights of the local flick house's presentation of Dracula's Entrails, but on their return, the ironic, blood red sign proclaims the familiar do anything Goodies' claim and sinister voodoo needles puncture Tim's doll. Graeme's gone through some Dr Jeykll horror and the office looks like Bela Lugosi's bedroom. Playing to the salacious Sunday rags, Graeme's evil pursuits are splashed across the papers, the goody goody Goodies name is brought screaming into disrepute (he is photographed sporting a Goodie t-shirt) and, worse still, his creepy, undead domain is none other than Clapham Common. Like Dennis Wheatley on an acid trip, Graeme's hippie sorcerer is surrounded by scantily clad nymphets and baying worshipers watching dumbstruck as he weuads a giant axe over the sacrificial

offering – a frozen, plastic-wrapped chicken. In the camp tradition of early Seventies Hammer, Graeme hisses like Christopher Lee receiving his pay cheque and scarpers off into the night. Long shadows, swirling mists, moonlit trees and a sense of ill omen all conjure up the perfect atmosphere for Bill and Tim, our very fearful vampire hunters, to get all dolled up in white dress and blonde wig for the Veronica Carlson vampire fodder virgin bit. Although 'a bit ropey!' in the fanged one's eyes, everything seems to be going swimmingly with Graeme's flamboyant Al Jolson interlude and dodgy variety magic act (complete with leggy assistant Betty, obviously on leave from Wilson and Keppel). Bill mutters, 'I've seen Sooty do better!', this is nothing to the top of the bill – the summoning up of the devil in the shape of, yes you guessed it, David Frost. Well at least, a shadowy version of Frostie with vocal business from Tim Brooke-Taylor. Hayes employs a spot of white magic to conquer Graeme (she bashes him over the head with a mallet), and with the Hammer magic well and truly sucked dry, it's into madcap visual antics with a gibbon-possessed Graeme going off the rail. Oddie's *Stuff that Gibbon* (sans the classic 'Stuff It!' comments from the recording, here replaced by gibberish harmonising) and a resurrection of the gorilla nightmare from Edgar Allan Poe's *Murders in the Rue Morgue* add bite to Graeme's hilarious routine, reaching an almighty peak with an organ grinder interlude. A cured Garden faced with chicken Tim and that old dog Bill and struggling to make sense of Pat's ripped asunder Witchcraft book, may be an easy, unsatisfactory closure but any ending to this comedy would be far too soon.

Did You Know? *Those total spoilsports at the Australian Broadcasting Commission removed that classic gag book title 'A Bum in the Coven' as well as cutting out the underwear-clad campfire dancers, the lads' virgin disguise discussion and the utterance of 'I'm knackered!'*

PATRICIA HAYES. Episode Four, recorded Thursday 21 December 1972, broadcast Sunday 25 February 1973, 8.15–8.45pm, BBC2.

FOR THOSE IN PERIL ON THE SEA

Displaying all the realism of that car at the start of Hitchcock's *The Lady Vanishes*, Graeme begins to relate the historical saga of Vikings on the oceans blue of 620AD – but this dodgy-looking boat is a model in Graeme's bath and the truth is hastily revealed as Bill disturbs the water and heartlessly pulls the plug. He's hardly taking Gray Bags seriously, dive bombing his bath-time pleasure with giant loofers. Tim, of course, is more concerned about tracing his rubber duck but Graeme is in earnest and his exciting book sets the scene for an enjoyable Goodies romp – somewhere between the *Bedknobs and Broomsticks* cartoon and a satirical comment on environmental issues. Typically, their goal – the legendary lost island of Munga – has been dealt a severe blow on its only other rediscovery, when the French exploded an H-Bomb on it in 1965. But now the three must find it for England and Tim, patriotic rant at the ready, is prepared for the call to action. He's always frightened, of course, but a traditional Viking docked at Southampton and the Queen's half-hearted blessing – her answer service promises the children will be in attendance at the launch – sets the lads on their way. Thanks to their Superhero-style quick change cabinet the team adopt three different impressions of the nautical man – Tim done up like a dog's dinner as a campy, peak-capped sailor boy, Bill the picture of a black-bearded pirate rogue, complete with stuffed vulture on his shoulder, and Graeme the scientifically accurate embodiment of the lusty Viking. At the moment of sea-faring truth, 'Anne' grabs hold of the giant champers bottle, the little 'uns and the band go for a Burton skittles fashion while big-eared 'Charles' hits with a typically Goonish cry of anguish. Naturally, the boys are helpless within seconds, Bill's vulture is a mere shell of its former self, Tim's bombarded by Biggles-style flying fish and Graeme's brilliantly garbled gibberish attempt at finding calculations finally breaks down into embarrassed admittance that they're lost. Damn those scientists and damn those hell bent on destroying the natural beauty of the oceans. With their 'ancient mariner' mucking about sequence at an end, the Goodies can face the ultimate topic at the heart of the show – oil tankers billowing out waste. It's all down to money, but Henry McGee's tug does pick up the trio and deck them out in fetching naval uniforms. It's a glorious life on the ocean waves, with McGee sipping something wet and alcoholic, Norman Mitchell's knuckle-headed Gerald setting the scene for eight discs with his rendition of *Sleepy Lagoon* and a quartet of bikini-clad bimbos doing the business. McGee is a Greek oil millionaire going by the name of Stavros Monopolopolous, delighting in his track record of dead fish and memorably cutting short the corny bellbottom joke to test these three would-be sailors. The test? What else but diving head first into the collective consciousness of Morecambe and Wise's Christmas Show, putting them through a hasty, brilliantly performed hornpipe and straight into *There's Nothing Like a*

Dame from *South Pacific*. The Goods fail to find the breath for the climatic musical moment and, failures, McGee cheerfully mutters, 'That last note always sorts them out!' A stirring bit of comic footwork is hardly enough to save them from a villain of McGee's calibre and it's the clichéd walking of the plank for the intruders. Mind you, ads for The Best Poem I Know Heinz beanz and delicious, veggie-promoting animal burgers, not to mention a narrative sign-posted, hasty swim, finds the lads on the Lost (renamed Found) Island. A burst of Oddie's *Desert Island* song and a host of classic visuals make the trip more than worthwhile. A tearful Tim proudly waters his instant crop of Union flags, there's a nifty land-friendly shark gag and there's plenty of grub to be found – jellyfish – in various flavours – dot the beach and even the coconuts have udders, but all is not what it seems. The grass-skirted lovelies of the island are chucking freshly cut chips into the sea and the mysterious place begins to take on a shade of the Lost World. Conan Doyle is right – McGee's arch villain is none other the Music Master from *The Stolen Musicians* episode, also known as, Nasty Person, the Prince of Mischief and Master of Disguises, Sussex University, (the lads should have really clicked when Mitchell's familiar henchman was on the scene) and his Napoleon of Wickedness drags the show into pseudo-Holmesian territory. His plan is indeed evil, filling the seas with oil, dead fish and now chips for the biggest fish 'n' chip supper in history. Previous incarnations reveal him to have been Nixon, Enoch and… shock, horror, David Frost, and now the mad man of disguises is about to turn Munga into something approaching Blackpool's Golden Mile. Graeme, ever the wag, produces his James Bond poison gas pencil, tricks McGee into a cupboard, fools Mitchell that his boss is now disguised as the Goodies – clever eh – and gets off that island big time. A native rain dance kicks up a storm (with everything blowing away and a plastic duck doing a Disney Donald retreat) and our heroes finally drift back to Blightly with 'Anne' (voiced by Tim) still swinging for England. There's even a trio of Goodie friendly beach babes for afters. McGee, of course, gets the villain's comeuppance with a face full of fish and if it's hardly a classic Goodies' romp, there's still plenty to smile about.

Did You Know? *The 'Get knotted' comment on the Queen's answer phone message was wiped from the screened print by the Australian Broadcasting Commission.*

HENRY McGEE, NORMAN MITCHELL, THE FRED TOMLINSON SINGERS, Queen's telephone voice SHEILA STEFEL. Episode Five, recorded Thursday 4 January, broadcast Sunday 4 March 1973, 8.15–8.45pm, BBC2.

WAY OUTWARD BOUND

Bill and Graeme face another lazy breakfast but, different as always, Tim is full of the joys of spring, summer, winter and autumn. Old Gray Bags hasn't even got the energy to turn his beloved computer on but there's no room for slacking in Tim's keep fit regime, forcing the reluctant duo through a brief bit of physical jerking to the refrains of *Narcissus*. However, these chaps are no mugs and strenuous exercise soon turns into resumed sitting position before Tim is distracted, outraged and distracted once more by the postman delivering a circular. Not only is it round but it plays on the gramophone, instructing our heroes, in *Mission: Impossible* terms to round up all young children for the high profile Duke of Glasgow Award (get it!). Tim, still reeling from Graeme's glorious postal put down ('Dear Sir or Madam, Tim, it's for you!') sees it as his patriotic duty to hand pick Britain's finest kiddie winks for this prestigious scheme and, besides, at 25 quid a head, it more than appeals to his money-grabbing nature. Taking on the slickly, super-suspicious attitude of Robert Helpmann's dreaded child-catcher from *Chitty, Chitty, Bang, Bang* is probably not the avenue to take and the pseudo-pied piper pursuit of this juvenile gold mine is a huge disaster, but hey, these are the Goodies! When reputation and, more importantly, money are at stake anything can be done and anything certainly is. The three don children's clothes and volunteer for the Loch Jaw school themselves. Bill – in definitive, Dennis the Menace school terror outfit – is joined by Tim – kitted out in Little Lord Fauntleroy mood, complete with curly golden locks and huge teddy bear – while Graeme opts for the off-the-wall approach as a saucily naïve St Trinian's girl, Amazing Gracie. Together they face the rigours of character-building outdoors action. Unfortunately, the entire operation is organised with military clout and the games (rifle practice and H-Bomb dropping) hardly fit the criteria set out in the manual. Eyes rolling continuously, barking orders with manic relish and with unsubtle slips into army terminology, Bill Fraser brings a ton of comic baggage from his towering role of Snudge in *The Army Game* for this towering authoritarian Ex-Sergeant Major Ballcock. Making lascivious comments to Graeme's demure schoolgirl, running his youthful charges through the rigours of battle and mocking the OBE with an impassioned comment that those are given away but medals must be earned, Fraser is outstanding value. He invests much vintage power into, 'In this school we have no sex and no smoking – so if you could spare us a pack of fags and a dirty book, we'd be very grateful!' The lads are put through their paces over the assault course – with much humour coming from Graeme's pig-tails being used as a rope – while Oddie's song, *Run*, keeps the action cheerful. It's Joan Sims, as the warm-hearted Matron that seems the best chance for escape. Although initially sign posted towards *Carry On* innuendo – Fraser's 'get your particulars down' aside results in an inviting, knowing wink from Sims – her endearing rendition of the song *Other People's Babies* and affectionate regard for dear little Bill, sets her out as a real Florence Nightingale. The wooden bed exploits are hilariously played, with Sims making even the notion of wooden sheets sound inviting, but all this sweetness and light hides a much darker secret. The script is greatly blessed with an actress of the calibre of Sims, switching instantly from pseudo-Hattie Jacques to full-on Ghengis Khan, ranting and screaming her way through a plan to control the world via war-trained babies. Bill Fraser, it seems, is merely a pawn in the crazy woman's plot. Shocked at the thought that his military war games could actually hurt people, the roaring Sergeant Major crumbles as Sims ploughs on through her off-kilter dreams of conquering. Even Tim's sheepish revelation of their true identity, Bill's final request for Des O'Connor singing Morecambe and Wise's *Bring Me Sunshine* and Graeme's priceless bit of Goodies intertextuality about taking over the world – 'I've even tried it myself!' referring to Series Two's *Radio Goodies*, can't dent the evil ambitions of Sims. Dozens of crawling babies – a real infantry if ever there was one – attack the Goodies in a sort of dry run for the *Beanstalk* geese manoeuvres. Baby bottles are dropped from the skies, tin-hatted nappy-wearers fire from every angle and Oddie's song, *They're Taking Over*, adds an edge of pessimistic grandeur. The solution is quickly found – raiding the supply depot cow of its milk and getting the kids to sleep – and the slumbering war babies are hastily transferred to the Goodies office. Graeme's majestic speech of oppressed populations and peaceful understanding is translated into babyish gibberish by Tim, but the military efficiency seems totally in-bred – catching the power-crazed ruler syndrome, Tim flies off the tracks, overcome by his control of a tiny tot army, screams about knighthoods, OBEs, becoming King of the World and even taking over the *Radio Times* as he wraps himself in the Union flag and rants into the closing credits. Thankfully, Bill's desperate attempt to force milk into his system obviously did the trick in time for July's *Goodies'* special.

Did You Know? *The Australian Broadcasting Commission edited the phrase 'we're knackered' from the show's soundtrack.*

JOAN SIMS, BILL FRASER. Episode Six, recorded Thursday 11 January, broadcast Sunday 11 March 1973, 8.15–8.45pm, BBC2.

SPECIAL: SUPERSTAR

A reflection on the perceived blasphemy of *Jesus Christ Superstar*, an embrace of Rock Star as God mentality and the multifaceted, exposed sexualities of performance legends, dictated that, although this was originally planned as part of Series Three, the BBC insisted on giving it a later time slot. Thus, it was presented as a special edition of *The Goodies*. It's fairly tame today, although the constant suggestion of corrupt rock promotion, groupie sex and homosexual audiences were more than enough to make the time change justifiable in the early Seventies. However, within the context of the show, the Goodies are the moral crusaders. Tim is outraged at the constant stream of filth that Fluff's radio pop picking is pumping out. The Beeb are shameless and Bill rather enjoys it – even Julie Andrews is getting down and dirty for pop success. But material like Come On Baby, Drop Your… is too much for Tim's self-appointed clean-up campaigner. Buzzing out the rude swear words, dismissing the trend as disgraceful and even adopting a pair of Mary Whitehouse glasses, Tim is a man with a mission. Besides, leader of a pop group! It's Bill's dream, and with Tim busily writing a nice little song to perform, the sweep across porn pop is about to begin. Ozzie manager Isabel Chintz – a deliciously over-the-top turn from Barbara Mitchell – knows what the punters want and even struggles to force Mr Clean – even in 1973 – Cliff Richard, to take on nude wrestling to plug his music. Thus, she's none too impressed with the Goods – initially promoting themselves as the ever so nice Cherubs and eventually performing Tim's (in reality Graeme's) number, *The Sparrow Song*. Immediately knowing their own awfulness and immediately walking out, Mitchell is sure she can make something of them – by giving their song new words and a new tune. Bill, as cool dude Rock Bottom, has a voice and The Goodies has an ironic, 'so good sounding they must be bad' quality, and clearly the group has some kind of potential. So much so, that the oh-so-sincere and sweet Maxie Grease Show seems the perfect

television platform for the trio. The WI audience, the pitiful Granny-o-Meter and the need to make these dear crinklies weep buckets for instant stardom is all very Python-esque indeed. But Bill twists the knife, delivers a new, potent song to impress the aged ones and takes centre stage with his pals flanking him. *Mummy, I Don't Like My Meat* is a classic of pathos-wringing sentimentality and tasteless tastiness. As with the record (although this is a different recording, note the lack of Tim's pained enquiry, 'Why don't he sing Mummy?'), Tim is baby, and Graeme comes into his own as the shawl-clad mother figure giving Bill's rocking tear machine overpowering and class looks of amazed disdain. The audience effect is devastating and even if Tim and Graeme aren't chuffed, Bill's on his way to mega-stardom. Like a little schoolboy before the headmistress, poor old Oddie is putty in the hands of the manipulative Mitchell. Reacting with *Carry On*-like energy to obvious and perfectly played innuendoes ('I want to handle you!'), falling into the exploitative trap with careless abandon and facing his dream come true as images of fame cloud his vision with fairy chords and dazzling camera trickery. There's only one thing Tim and Graeme dislike more than corruption and that's corruption which makes money for somebody other than them. Like Groucho and Chico via Grade and Delfont (they even consider sticking Bill on *The Golden Shot*), Tim and Graeme emerge as the ever so slightly Jewish Brian and Roger with huge noses, huge cigars and huge distrust in the loophole-ridden (cue sight gag) contract proffered to Billy boy. But stardom is all conquering and Bill's back is turned on his old pals in favour of countless bimbos (well five actually), cigar puffing, laziness, notoriety, and chart busting without even releasing any singles. Seventies' pop is so fickle… Reinvented as Randy Pandy, Bill's groupie lifestyle makes him a national sex symbol in the tabloids despite Graeme's rather unkind but apt dismissal of the bearded one as 'hairy and horrible…' But nobody minds. This is the business we call show and if you say it and play it enough times, people will believe anything. But in this David Bowie becomes Ziggy Stardust and believes it era, Bill's instant image must be radically altered again for a cross-culture, cross-sexuality, 'nancy' audience. Embracing Lloyd Webber rocking and overturning the sacred BBC cow of *Top of the Pops*, Bill takes on the world as the camp Queen incarnate – St Augustine. All these elements were later reused for *The Making of the Goodies' Disaster Movie* book with mincing monks, soul sisters and the Pan's Nuns swanning around in the background. The studio audience is quite correctly depicted as girls with big knockers who must be over 16 years old but under 17. Transported to the Beeb in a truck and herded in like cattle, it's a delicious irony that the Goodies themselves would be playing along with the codes and conventions of the show within 18 months. The token pop stars with attitude, the lads happily did the gibbon dance, winked at the fans and played the game of music business. Here, Bill is the king pin and Tim and Graeme reduced to sticking Wembley's Twin Towers down their fronts and passing themselves off as girlie groupies. Bill's routine really is Marc Bolan gone insane and despite the fact that Tony Blackburn may die of embarrassment – as Graeme comments, 'as least some good will come of it…' – the lads still aren't happy. Taking a leaf out of Peter Cook's book – when his dead pan, morbid denial of attraction to female fans created a love-struck hysteria in the classic film *Bedazzled*, Bill's camp, sparkling, flared rendition of *I Don't Want Your Love* drives the screaming teens wild. John Peel's neat cameo as Jimmy Saville is a major bonus as the ethos of *Top of the Pops* is deliciously ripped asunder with a psychedelic striptease, Bill's ultimate entrustment to two hunky security guards and his cult status elevation to Super Poof… But that's old news before the ink dries, and Bill is hastily reinvented as 'Big Fat Nellie' (an old girlfriend of Tim's from *Women's Lib*) but it's clearly a case of not on yours as the star-struck rocker squeezes a bit more innuendo, wallows in his dream coming true and finally turns his back on the hollow mockery of teeny bopper adulation. His defeated, 'I don't care fellows', binds the Goodies back together with real emotion.

Did You Know? *Great swathes of material about St Augustine's homosexuality were cut by the Australian Broadcasting Commission. Guest star and frequent Goodies target, John Peel, was involved in the most sensational, invented, bit of gossip about the trio. Apparently, the pop singing comedians beat up disc jockey Peel at London's Marquee Club after he had given them a bad press review. Bill Oddie, having made a record for Peel's Dandelion label in 1970, seemed to have kept out of it, while Graeme Garden and Tim Brooke-Taylor, the worse for drink, were reported as attacking Peel. They only backed off when big Led Zeppelin dude Robert Plant told them to clear off in no uncertain terms. Peel, apparently, was bruised but more embarrassed than injured, facing ridicule for being attacked by the inventors of the Funky Gibbon. It was all lies… lies I tell you! The John Peel clip was featured in the documentary The Radio One Story celebrating the 30th anniversary of* the station with a BBC2-themed night on 20 September 1997. *Interestingly, it seems the press were out to make the Goodies appear to be troublemakers. In 1975 a story was published concerning a punch-up between Graeme Garden and wonderfully off-centre disc jockey Kenny Everett. This was later revealed as a well-managed publicity stunt. Following this slight departure from the norm, a further Goodies repeat season on BBC1 acted as a prelude to the premiere of Series Four.*

BARBARA MITCHELL, JULIAN CHAGRIN, JOHN PEEL, THE FRED TOMLINSON SINGERS. Vocal Backing WANITA FRANKLIN, RUBY JAMES. Written by Graeme Garden and Bill Oddie with Tim Brooke-Taylor. Music by Bill Oddie and Michael Gibbs. Costume Mary Woods. Make-up Penny Norton. Lighting John Dixon. Sound John Holmes. Film editor Ron Pope. Film cameraman Stewart A Farnell. Visual effects John Horton. Design John Stout. Produced by Jim Franklin. Recorded Thursday 18 January, broadcast Saturday 7 July 1973, 9.50–10.20pm, BBC2.

SERIES FOUR

Filming began on 12 March 1973, with location shots in Norfolk and Hastings.

Film cameraman Stewart A Farnell. Film editor Ron Pope. Visual effects John Horton. Costume Mary Woods and Rupert Jarvis (Episode 4). Make-up Penny Norton and Sandra Shepherd (Episode 4). Lighting Alan Horne and Peter Catlett (Episode 5). Sound John Holmes. Music by Bill Oddie and Michael Gibbs. Design John Stout with Geoffrey Patterson (Episodes 2, 4 & 6). Produced by Jim Franklin.

CAMELOT

Having finished off Series Three with a barn-storming guest turn from Bill Fraser, it was only natural to grab his old *Bootsie and Snudge* sparring partner, Alfie Bass, into the world of *The Goodies*. He was so good that he was hastily brought back for his legendary tiny giant in the Christmas *Beanstalk* special. *Camelot* kicks off with Bill and Graeme doing what comes naturally – not a lot – and Tim doing what comes naturally – energetically getting all patriotic and regal over nothing. Or at least, it appears to be nothing. The lads take the mickey relentlessly but Tim bravely soldiers on with his chatter about his Uncle King Arthur – or rather King, Arthur as it appears in the phone book. 'Mock if you like!' – and they do – but Tim grandly reads the scroll delivered from Camelot, 33 Acacia Road (almost re-used for Eric's address in *Bananaman*), Birmingham… sorry, Solihull, after all they are rather posh you know! After the florid introductory spiel it's all downmarket, newsy tit-bits about trips to the seaside and cheery 'nice one, Tim old son!' banter. An Englishman's castle is his home and the Goodies stagger up to the royal settlement for a spot of property protection. The town planners are after the land and with bowler-hatted bovver boys and a diminutive, apologetic but ruthless little dictator in Alfie Bass, dreaded thoughts of a three-lane highway to the Buck House Cement Factory smack bang through a Medieval utopia loom large. Even Timbo's heartfelt patriotic rant about national tragedies and irreplaceable heritage is radically cut short. His Uncle may be a raving loony but blue blood is thicker than water – besides the impressive homestead of the King and his Queen Doris looks fit for Richard Harris and, with a suitably Richard Dimbleby-style commentary from Graeme (note the huge applause from the *I'm Sorry I'll Read That Again* aware audience when Spot the dog is name-checked), the nobs are equipped with Gumby-style hanky headgear and coached off to the far away delights of Bognor Regis – the Goodies are left in charge. It's here where the real gold dust lies, with the trio going all ye olde England and milking the situation for every gag in the book. After a bemused few moments Graeme gets stuck in a rhyming couplet rut while Bill immediately lowers the tone with his corny coat of arms gag – it was old even when Olsen and Johnson scored with it in *Hellzapoppin'*. The frozen fish fingers – cod piece visual is perfectly sign-posted as well but, it's Tim who really lets rip. Ever since *Cambridge Circus* he seemed to have a longing to be a downgrade music hall comedian and for a glorious few minutes he becomes one. He's like an echo of Frankie Howerd from *Up the Chastity Belt* and crams a barrel-load of puns into the smallest possible time scale like the vintage days of *I'm Sorry I'll Read That Again*. Making his entrance with an energetic shake of the leg, Tim fires on all cylinders, injecting speeded Max Miller-style patter and tug of the forelock references to Frankie Howerd. There are disparaging comments aimed towards Des O'Connor, joyous disappointment as he repeats the 'already done it' coat of arms / cod piece gags of Bill's, a tap into the long tradition of xenophobic humour with a historical slant (delivering a Saxon joke) and going almost too far with his sucking pig banter. Graeme is appalled, Bill is speechless with corpsing pleasure and the final dancing duet for *Bring Me Sunshine* closes one of the greatest *Goodies'* moments. Not to be out done, Oddie delivers one of his greatest songs – the emotive, guitar-soaring *Taking You Back* – for a delicious visual representation of the castle's first day open to the public. The American tourists are glorious stereotypes and most of the dark ages comic touchstones are obvious (the groovy dancing bear, cock fighting with boxing gloves on), but it works perfectly and the surreal (a wild boar on wheels), the television ethics questioning (travelling Minstrels are the black and white variety) and repeated injustice (the witch hunt attracts a red-coated fox hunter) add extra weight to the comedy. The damsel in distress threatened by a dodgy-looking dragon ploy is all a nasty scheme to get the trio out and the horrible little Alfie Bass in – donned in armour and dealing in the fiendish torture of our hapless heroes. Cowardly Tim hangs about and thinks of England, Bill seems keen to get stretched out of his small stature and Graeme devours the pinching crab dropped in to torment him, but with threats to cut out tongues and ram red hot pokers where the sun don't shine biting the dust, Bass reverts to death by a thousand chuckles. With the ultimate captive audience he finds satisfaction in a bit of stand-up comedy, rattles through a couple of awful medieval titters and uses a cast-off Ken Dodd tickling stick to get Tim chortling uncontrollably. Of course, the fool can't break our lads and with a reprise of *Taking You Back*, some nutty jousting exploits (with the Black Knight brigade on horse back and the Goods on the trandem), Bill's legendary woody woodpecker in armour impersonation (later to crop up in the opening credits) and a final unveiling of ye secret weapon – a magnet – to save the day, it's game, set and ye match to the Goods. However, in the end, the very commercialism that the Goodies have fought against, is celebrated as the way of normality – with the returning King getting stuck into advertising his Castle's Bingo nights – and even if the idea of money-grabbing exploitation of historical sites is laid bare and raw, the Englishman's rightful home is still forever his rightful castle.

ALFIE BASS. Episode One, recorded Thursday 10 May, broadcast Saturday 1 December 1973, 8–8.30pm, BBC2.

INVASION OF THE MOON CREATURES

Returning to mission control, Bill and Tim are not happy – the bearded one is simply knackered, Posh Good just wants a nice cup of tea, while Graeme has futuristic things on his mind. Just over four years after Neil Armstrong made his gigantic step for mankind, the Goodies are all keyed up to further Britain's pitiful space programme – Bill even injects a ham-fisted and muffed version of Armstrong's earth-shattering comment. The entire thirst for knowledge and contemporary space hype is successfully countered by Graeme's mad scientist figure – tapping into the use of monkeys and dogs for space travel via his collection of white rabbits and twisting the plot with monstrous sci-fi overtones. Project Moon and inflated astrobunnies is one thing, but Tim's earnest devotion to the patriotically geared British Lunar mission gives the manic comedy a sense of insane destiny. Of course, his majestic determination quickly spirals into baby chatter with the adorable rabbit, Leonardo – before

Graeme dismisses sentimental attitude and hastily throws himself straight into a priceless bunnie, wunnie line. Garden's upbeat attempt to prove his rabbit a genius – by reciting reams of garbled rubbish (which almost confuses himself) and letting nature take its course – is beautifully countered by Bill's camped up Hughie Green impression. This singly unimpresses the rabbit and forces Bill to turn the creature round with a giggled 'come here!' before dropping into a delicious bit of corpsing. The usual bit of animal cruelty – so relished by Bill and seen here bashing bunnies with a tennis racquet as they shoot out of a space-simulating wind tunnel – sets up the dark alien revenge of the rest of this pseudo-sci fi adventure. Time may be a great healer but it also enables moon-based rabbits to breed, well, like rabbits, establishing a colony and planning to take over the world. With their fingers firmly on the pulse of popular television, this resolves itself into a comic comment on *Dr Who* and *Star Trek*. There's the almost obligatory appearance by Patrick Moore – chuntering on about folk changing into a buck-toothed rabbit person and playing with his carrot, there's Graeme Garden longing for help from telly's Mr Fix It, Jimmy Saville, there's a few insane comments from *Goodies'* regular Roland MacLeod as a sub-James Burke hosting a totally off-kilter space programme and there's even a wonderful poke at one of the show's favourite target (second only to David Frost), with a biting little dig at Monty Python. With Graeme panicking that it's 10.15pm, he hastily switches his telly on to be greeted by the ultra-familiar strains of Sousa's *The Liberty Bell*. Naturally, this shameless plug for a beleaguered Python is quickly scuppered by Dr Garden's realisation that he's missed Moira Anderson. With a disappointed flick of the off switch, Gilliam's animations bite the dust. But it's pure small screen science fact and big screen science fiction that really captures the imagination here. *Python* may have burst open the comic psyche in 1969 but the world's eyes were firmly skywards. The Goodies use legendary news archive footage of man's greatest adventure, send up the entire notion with Tim's cheeky admission of posting a couple of letters in the home-made British rocket and add a sense of Stanley Kubrick's lyrical understanding via a classical music interlude à la *2001: A Space Odyssey*. The brash hipness of American television's *Star Trek* is brought down to BBC poverty row with cheekily obvious incorporations of the infamous Captain's Log monologue (via a nervous Graeme Garden) and

there's even an effective 'boldly go' rant thanks to the Garden-voiced, power-crazed, moon-ruling, Big Bunny. Check out the rabbit gang gleefully joining in with the heavenly *Star Trek* chorus. The *Quatermass* legacy too, is far from forgotten, with the returning Bill bitten by the bunny bug and bursting out all over with fur and teeth and things. The concept of landing the crippled shuttle in Clapham Common is pure Goodies, but the structure, military might and scientific panic is *Quatermass Experiment*. Even the all-important moment of removing Bill's protective glove to reveal a furry appendage is directly parodying the harrowing performance of Richard Wordsworth in Val Guest's film version for Hammer. However, above and beyond everything else, this episode is gleefully having a go at the Beeb's flagship sci-fi product, *Dr Who*. Enjoying its 10th year and with Jon Pertwee having already met his two previous selves in celebration, the texture of this show is pure *Who*. The land-based threat, the invasion from unknown alien forces, the military intervention, the insane conspiracies and, above all, the wonderfully dodgy creatures, all add up to something approaching U.N.I.T's up-and-coming hassles with *The Planet of the Spiders* in 1974. Indeed, the old Time Lord's TARDIS even makes an unscheduled appearance just to add full the seal of approval. The sequence, with Tim and Bill strapped down with carrots in their ears, merely takes the whole *Who* ideal to its ridiculous extremes and the hilarious abduction by white rabbits – before the Pythons shocked a medieval nation with an equally unconvincing killer bunny – is sheer perfection. The entire notion of space travel is presented as a kitsch adventure playground with bits of info gleaned from *The Sky at Night* crossed with remnants of Buster Crabbe in *Flash Gordon* to present a wonderfully childlike world of *Dan Dare* and travel signs in space. The funniest scene, with Bill and Tim en route to the moon, is an essential item for any 'best of' compilation – hamming it up with determination, falling foul of the tea/food/weightlessness situation, without a care that Bing Crosby and Bob Hope had been there a decade earlier for *The Road to Hong Kong,* and ending every sentence with 'beep'. They soon forget to do it and Graeme's delivery seems to suggest he knows the idea is flogged to death, but it doesn't matter. It's obvious, corny and totally hilarious, especially when, wild-haired, terrified and finally in receipt of the disastrous facts, Tim and Bill exclaim with one voice 'What! Beep!' The heart-warming patriotic

STUNT DUMMIES FOR *THE GOODIES* TAKING A WELL-DESERVED REST DURING THE MAKING OF THE *BEANSTALK CHRISTMAS* SPECIAL. TIM BROOKE-TAYLOR COMMENTS, 'WHY DOES MY DUMMY HAVE TO BE LABELLED DUMMY!'

moment as Tim plants his Union flag, the shocked anti-Yank reaction to a sea of Stars and Stripes, Bill's goldfish-infested space helmet, slow-motion golf antics, moon dust hoovering and the hair-raising discovery of mad rabbits on the moon, all pale in the shadow of one of the great Goodies moments – as Tim and Bill soft shoe dance their way through By the Light of the Silvery Earth… Of course, back at home and after their rabbit brain washing, our chums are slightly worse for wear. Graeme gets himself momentarily arrested and the bunny duo are saying nothing – save 'Ahh! What's Up Doc!' (check out Tim's Mickey Mouse impression in an attempt to usurp Bugs Bunny from the screen). Shockingly, the country is at the mercy of carrot chompers. Indeed, in its underground, less-celebrated fashion, this is by far the most subversive and haunting – with Tim and Bill seizing the iconography of another Kubrick classic, A Clockwork Orange, and adding pronounced single ear make-up, bovver boots and bowler hats to their bizarre rabbit costumes. The ultimate realisation of the idea, with Her Majesty's Own Highland Ferrets coming to the rescue and Graeme's trickery resulting in cannibalistic consumption of rabbit pie, doesn't do the theme justice. The promise contained in that manic gaze into camera from Bill's obsessed nutter is rich indeed, and the brainless, semi-Nazi salutes give an added brutality to the whole show.

Did You Know? Admitting a great debt to classic cartoons, this episode features use of the portable hole during the climatic musical rabbit chase – a device pioneered in Warner's award winning 1952 short, The Whole Idea.

ROLAND MACLEOD, PATRICK MOORE. Episode Two, recorded Thursday 10 and 17 May, broadcast Saturday 8 December 1973, 8–8.30pm, BBC2.

HOSPITAL FOR HIRE

Bill is not a happy man, in fact, he's hopping mad. Thanks to the awful NHS not only has he waited three whole weeks to get his broken leg in plaster but when the deed was done, it was done to the wrong leg! Timbo, patriotic and eager to assist, immediately gets on the blower to the totally unhelpful, foul-mouthed Minister of Health. After a bit of cleaned-up translation, the crux of the matter is revealed – treatment is so slow and disorganised because selfish sick people are clogging up the system. The solution is simple: our helpful trio are instructed to become doctors and cure the sick. With a hasty retrieval from the toilet roll holder of the Radio Times (complete with medical application form), the lads are off on a magical medicine tour of free beer and as many nurses as they can pull. Graeme had had plenty of experience during his training and, with Bill in tow, penned enough episodes of Doctor in the House to sink an ambulance. The humour plays like a wacky version of the Barry Evans' antics with a decidedly Python-esque track and field event to prove medical skill. Backed, as always, by a classic Oddie song – Medical Man (I'm Gonna Be a Doctor) – judges look on as beer drinking bursts the belchometer and nurses do the hop, skip and jump thanks to a well-placed pinch on the bum. The end result is drunk, exhausted, collapsed Goodies qualified to practice medicine for the good of society. But the state of the hospitals is shocking, as old hand Tim shows the new bods round in stiff upper lip mode. Crippin Ward is packed with dirt-infested patients, Victorian decay and shameful experimental treatment – not only are the hypodermic needles tossed dart style but the bed ridden are forced to listen to Little Jimmy Osmond records! Far from satisfied, the Goods head off for a word or two in the Minister of Health's shell-like. In a series with lip-smacking guest stars at every turn, this episode presents arguably the finest of all – Harry H Corbett as a glorious Scottish eccentric, obsessed with medical matters, both feet firmly planted in hot water and a mad stare and white fright wig giving him a grotesque edge. Seeming to enjoy the scene hugely, Tim is clearly suppressing the giggles as Corbett rips through the script and bangs on about nasty little germs 'wiggling away!' Sneezing at every unsubtle reference to hay and momentarily popping under the table in a healthy bit of script by-passing, Corbett is his usual priceless self through a totally unforgettable sequence. Tapping into Tim's patriotic glory, a rant for England's improvement is quickly quashed by Graeme's unfeeling 'there isn't time for that!' Commercial pressure calls for a bit of advertising. Goodlop QC Radicals sees a dragged-up Tim and Bill munching of inflatables while schoolboy Tim listens to his Rice Crunchies breakfast and almost has his head blown off from the explosive force. Leaving dear old Harry H with a Vic inhaler rammed up his nose the lads are straight into action. Their travelling hospital is a quick and easy conveyor-belt, whipping through operations in a blink of an eye, using a rickety tent for an overprotective maternity ward and allowing artistic freedom via plaster casting – some poor bloke is turned into an armless Venus de Milo by Graeme and Tim. This is also the sequence which produces my favourite opening credit gag – Graeme frightened by a skeleton emerging from behind the X-ray machine. Slap dash it may be, but the country is cured by the trio's efforts – and the National Health Service is unmasked as an incompetent, outmoded system. Harry H has completely lost the plot by now, playfully blowing his nose on an endless supply of sooty hand puppets and hounding the lads via sneeze-ridden telephone banter. The plot thins out and it's an excuse for Oddie musical, leading The Goodies Medical Show with Graeme's slick, wise-cracking hip doctor salesman flogging wonder cures and Tim's sheepish 'poor suffering boy' staggering onto the stage for some mercy medicine. It's all worth it for Garden's rigorous boasts (this stuff will cure sunburn, heartburn and Tony Blackburn... now that's powerful!) and the joyous union of the three selling their wares through song. There's just time for a much welcome return from Harry H brandishing a witch doctor's skull stick and threatening to strike the Goodies from the General Medical Council. But this supposed bogus medicine works, the aged council members are immediately sucked into the jubilant celebrations and our heroes ride off on an outlaw quest to cure the country, springing the patients held captive in government-controlled hospitals like Robin Hood in a

THE CHIEF DAMBUSTING GOOSE TAKES FLIGHT WITH A LITTLE HELP FROM THE PRODUCTION CREW

white coat. This liquid is so strong that Egyptian mummies walk free from museums and the dead rise from coffins. Having made the NHS obsolete and brought the waiting list down to nothing, the job is done. Problem is, after three million Brits, the Goodies are exhausted and wracked with pain from overwork and there are no doctors to help them. Hoisted by their own petard, the cure has gone, plastered Tim and Bill swing precariously on their traction weight contraptions and, somewhere off camera, that glorious nut Harry H Corbett has the last laugh.

HARRY H CORBETT, THE FRED TOMLINSON SINGERS. Episode Three, recorded Tuesday 24 April, broadcast Saturday 15 December 1973, 8.10–8.40pm, BBC2.

SPECIAL: THE GOODIES AND THE BEANSTALK

This is the one everybody remembers. Justly regarded as a comedy classic, this has 'very special' Christmas special written all over it. Pitched in the middle of Series Four's run, the trio move into the realms of traditional Christmas

THE DAMBUSTING GEESE OFF DUTY, SANS HEADS AND WITH UMBRELLAS

family fun with an added budget, longer screen time and the chance to deconstruct cinematic style. Showcased as a film experience in your living room, the usual credits are abandoned in favour of a British Board of Film Censor panel heralding the fact that the Goods have all passed domestic studies. The paint by number, play the game, avenue of happy-go-lucky Chrimbo fare is sent up by the legend 'Based on the traditional fairy story… *Snow White and the Seven Dwarfs*'. Self-deprecation of the group is also embraced with the credit, written by Graeme Garden and Bill Oddie with Tim Brooke-Taylor's biro. The laughter is uneasy and the irony is clear – Timbo wasn't writing as much as the other two and, before long, his writing credit would be dropped completely. But here, in these early, fresh, vibrant times, the lads are at full power – from the joyfully mixed-up photo captions (with bursts of enthused studio laughter), pass the wagon's ho! parody of a burning Wild West map and rants about the 1837 Indians versus Custer home match, it's on to normal territory with the Cricklewood, 1973 setting. Blessed with the extra screen time and allowing themselves the luxury of plot establishment and characterisations, the trio inject plenty of slapstick visuals and pathos-driven moments into this, near wordless, opening sequence. Money's too tight to mention and our hapless trio stroll through a myriad of visual comic bits of business for a slice of 'life on the street' reality. It goes on for an age and some of the jokes are so old their pension books have evaporated but that's the

whole point – this is Seventies' silent comedy homage and if it all plays like groovy Buster Keaton then it's achieved the desired effect. There's the delightful corn of the three fruit machine parking meters, the begging war veteran pleading for generous donations and receiving a leg and, best of all, Oddie's hard to calm down musical obsession, with a busking jazz quartet of grannies and Bill on drums. The usual targets (gay advances from pin-striped businessmen/policeman) form a back drop for the poverty-stricken Goods and, again as per usual, Graeme is still enjoying the scientifically easy life of Riley. As the sounds of a blues guitar set the scene for Bill and Timbo, Gray Bags is happily relaxing on his park bench, blowing up his paper bag pillow, reversing his clothes for night wear, chilling his champagne in a litter bin and reading his book by the light of a near-by flower. Oddie's plaintive song, *Poor*, echoes through this make-shift comfort as Tim's equally money-starved but less effective night arrangements act as contrast, giving pained looks into camera as his paper bag pillow explodes and having his problems compounded with a load of camp fire logs bashing his bonce. Oddie eventually breaks the long radio silence with braying wolf howls and finally offers up his only option – the sale of his beloved three-seater bike, Buttercup. Bill lovingly makes sure the bike's tyres are comfy and bucket-loads of emotion are paraded before looks of weird amazement from his fellow Goodies. Bill's pathetic offering is shamelessly mocked by the punters and the single exchange rate, a tin of baked beans, sees the deal signed sealed and delivered. Feel that lump in your throat as Oddie's tears know no bounds. Even the studio audience give an enforced 'Aah!' of sympathy. But then Graeme has a wild idea, he plants the last bean from the tin and this sends the show into homage overdrive for the manic beanstalk chase. It's a glorious mixture of comic textures, crossing over into surreal Benny Hill chasing of sexy girls, contrasted with futuristic musical overtones of *2001 – A Space Odyssey* and Oddie's oh-so-catchy little ditty, *Come Back*. There's a feel of Fifties' monster flick, some more glam ogling with a beanstalk bath invasion and plenty of self-mocking television fun with Woodall's ever so straight newscaster. It's all very Goodies – and before long xenophobia, more bare flesh and a breakneck world tour, finally finds the lads employing snake-charming techniques to conquer the infamous stalk. It's instant access to the lofty, mystical peak of Mount Everset. But the boys only want to get home and with plenty of Wild West splendour and mule hitch-hiking, the delights of Cricklewood allow a bit of respite, more low-level luxury for Graeme with his fountain bathing, a dash of homosexual angst ('let's have a look!') and a big dollop of gutter journalism with The News of the Sun's hyped up competition. Typically basking in animal abuse and glorious tastelessness, the newspaper's prize, 5000 puppies, are heading off to the nearest Indian restaurant if nobody enters. As if by magic, the air of small screen competition bursts into that monumental of cool, xenophobic kitsch, *It's a Knockout*. With the familiar title sequence, an enthused 'Wow' reaction and the familiar faces of regular punters Eddie Waring and Arthur Ellis, it's business as usual for the squad with this contest from Kathmandu. Suitably for Christmas, the expected and much welcomed attack on the madness of the foreign Johnny, is based round pantomime conventions, so the stereotyped contestants (the manic Spaghetti Brothers from Italy who wind up shooting each other / the German crowd, Hans, Nees and Bumpsadaisy) plough through papering the parlour, tackling daisy the panto cow, waking up the sleeping beauty, avoiding the blacked up and coconut tossing Man Friday on Robinson Crusoe's island and, ultimately, shooting up the butter-coated, 200 foot beanstalk. Waring's typically babbled, racist and endearingly uncultured delivery fits the Goodies' parody perfectly, political satire is spread thickly with the Ted Heath Joker card and the pleasures of patriotic victory are brought to life via Graeme's effortless paper hanging and the team's all-round jolly good egg devotion. All this and the German's suffer piranha-consumed failure at the watering hole... But it's soon up the beanstalk and into echo city with yodelling fun. The location looks like a *Dr Who* quarry pit, those pricelessly dodgy special effects come straight from Pertwee's budget allowance and that eerie whistling emptiness creates an effective atmosphere of impending doom for our comic heroes. It's only heightened with Oddie's bewitched, obsessed luring to the daunting castle and an Indian, sub-George Harrison version of the Shadow's *Man of Mystery* before the show's third act of comic greatness kicks in. All is revealed with the Dr Frankenstein, foaming laboratory, stuffed with contented chickens and 22-caret gold eggs. The Keaton/Sellers prat-falling of Oddie's buddies merely acts as a comic bridge between the expected slapstick and this gloriously twisted bit of panto folklore. Tim's laid-back,

THE MAKING OF *THE GOODIES AND THE BEANSTALK* #1

effete comment concerning the 'nice airy room' is the perfect introduction to the Land of Giants concept. Oddie, meanwhile, is far too busy with wide-eyed instant wealth, while the imminent arrival of the show's chief guest star follows an obvious, but no less effective for it, read through his huge recipe book – shepherd's pie: first peel two shepherds. Of course, only the Goodies would create the expectation of a fierce giant and then cast that diminutive character acting legend Alfie Bass in definitive Jewish tailor, *Fiddler on the Roof*, mode. Ashamed of his normal background and hiding away behind the booming voice, Bass pathetically relates his past life at London Zoo's Snowdon Aviary, perfecting his multi-pound production line, cutting himself off for tax purposes and embracing the iconography of fee-fi-fo-fum ('as we giants say!') for protection. Bass is stunning, throwing himself into the manic rants, sheepish grins and sublime craziness of the part – 'there's more to being a giant than size you know!' Naturally, he doesn't stand a chance against Garden's all-conquering, logical knowledge, but greed is more than enough to tempt the trio into a brief life of giant slavery. Amazingly, Bass enjoys a very brief time on screen, but that image of the tiny chap munching on a giant cake, sipping from his mug marked 'Lofty' and stomping round the oversized place in a giant boot, is indelible from the mind. Besides, not only does this masterly written section have a bit of Snow White clout with a *Whistle While You Work* spring clean but it also basks in the delights of the towering

THE MAKING OF *THE GOODIES AND THE BEANSTALK* #2

dam-busting geese that pelt the Goodies with eggs, soar majestically to Eric Coates' stirring theme and back up Alfie's bizarre, boot-encased warlord, desperately trying to finish the boys off. Naturally, the gang get away, the naughty but nice villain mistakenly wins the Knockout stakes and role reversal sees Alfie's eye-rolling charm walk off with the prize. Admittedly it ain't much, but that climax allows some painfully shy glam girl eye contact, Eddie Waring's life-affirming rugby try after years of merely commentating on the game and Alfie's low-key comeuppance with a fate sealed of flogging puppies on the street corner. But you can't go back to your port and mince pies just yet Granddad. For just when you think it's all over, Tim has a quick rub of his baked bean tin, a further panto convention is spirited up in the shape of Aladdin's wondrous genie and, surprise, surprise, the chief rival, John Cleese, steals the thunder with a snatch of *The Liberty Bell*, as a turbaned version of his familiar 'And now for something completely different…' Python newsreader. In the most cutting moment of Goodies' history, he utters two words: 'Kid's programme!' Despite Cleese already being an ex-Python, on television at least, this is a magical crossing of the two most important and influential small screen teams of the post war years in the same year that saw their reunion on radio's *I'm Sorry I'll Read That Again*. Of course, *The Goodies* was far from a kid's programme, but Cleese joyously voiced a common thought and finished this Christmas special with a real seasonal bang. Ex-Cambridge buddy, Brooke-Taylor, has the last laugh as he shouts 'push off!' and covers the tin, but the genie's had his say.

rendition of *Who Wants To Be a Millionaire*. Accompanied by more talented animals than a Dr Dolittle convention, the Goodies relish their major musical number with cheerful mugging and pleasure in their own perfectly tuned team work. Oddie lands a less showy Chico moment, Brooke-Taylor endearingly goes all coy and mop-headed for his Harpo impression and, by far the most praiseworthy attempt, Garden goes all Groucho with a spirited dance, the exact eye movements and cigar-touting cool. This Thirties flashback notwithstanding, our main men are simply playing for time to escape the clutches of Alfie's wee giant. The plan is to get away with all his eggs in their basket. The resulting, tightly directed, menacing, comic and surrealistic battle of wits, is a comedy masterclass to rival any other television series. Bass, with his *Wizard of Oz*-like flying army, sends out the nerve-wracking collection of geese to chase the lads. Indeed, the hushed tip-toeing through an ocean of birds, with no soundtrack save the disconcerting babble of the geese themselves, is a stunning piece of work. It's all very Hitchcock and there's a portly Hitch figure tossing the birds on from the sidelines and a snatch of the *Marionette's Funeral* to ground it in the master of suspense's territory. Some of the bird madness is wonderfully inventive, notably the firing squad conventions and war time unity. But all pales in light of the

Did You Know? This special was commissioned by the BBC on Monday 23 July 1973. Originally dubbed 'The Goodies Christmas Show', the huge project was made entirely on film. Suitably for a show which momentarily basked in the shadow of Alfred Hitchcock, the Beanstalk episode was mapped out in detailed fashion before filming. Location shots took place in London, Dorchester and Weymouth during the Autumn. The flying geese effects were achieved via mechanical models with flapping wings attached to invisible wires. The show was among the first batch of classic BBC videos which burst on an expectant audience in 1983. The price was an astronomical £50 plus and all the happy punter got was one, albeit special length, episode of The Goodies. Bill Oddie, cynical, bitter, but with more than a fair point, considers that some chap at the BBC filed The Goodies away as a television show that doesn't sell on video and decided to leave the great trio languishing in the vaults for another 11 years — before the Beanstalk episode was re-released alongside two other choice shows. However, for rarity value alone, the original 1983 video release is well worth tracking down — not only as a vital piece of Goodies folklore but also, for Dr Who completists, the nifty BBC trailer: News flash — The Video Tasties, is presented by an irresistibly grinning Tom Baker. His own Revenge of the Cybermen, The Two Ronnies, Butterflies, Ripping Yarns, Blue Peter Makes… Target, Grange Hill, The Good Life, The Fall and Rise of Reginald Perrin and all, stand in line as the BBC's first home viewing selection. The glorious politically incorrect front cover for the 1983 release depicts the gold-bikini clad, stunning figure of Helli Louise wrapped round the huge, green, phallic symbol beanstalk with the three lads superimposed on it. The reverse pics were later adopted for the reissue tape in 1994. A clip from the show was featured in the Ronnie Corbett hosted seasonal comedy fest, All the Best For Christmas in 1997.

ALFIE BASS, EDDIE WARING, JOHN CLEESE, CORBETT WOODALL, ROBERT BRIDGES, MARCELLE SAMETT, TONI HARRIS, HELLI LOUISE, MARTY SWIFT, ARTHUR ELLIS. Filmed Monday 24 September–Thursday 18 October, broadcast Monday 24 December 1973, 5.15–6pm, BBC2.

THE STONE AGE

Very few comedy shows could spend almost half their running time encased within a Tyrannosaurus Rex's stomach and make it funny: *The Goodies* can. The concept relies on viewers' knowledge of Disney's *Pinocchio* and the Monstro the Whale dilemma. Oddie's eyeball experience links in with Jimminy Cricket's legendary umbrella float past the whale's eye in the 1940 classic, but there's much more to this sublime Jurassic lark than that. It's a long and winding weekend in darkest Cricklewood and while studious Garden gets even more studious, Oddie and Brooke-Taylor carry on like spoiled brats. Oddie taps into his own obsessions – a combined hobby fest of music, football and bird-watching. Brooke-Taylor's tap-dancing ping pong practice goes into surrealism overdrive but each spoils the other's fun and the day cascades into the doldrums of total boredom. Like a couple of twins, they cry for parental guidance for a bit of light relief. However, the diverting bit of mechanical wonderment – a TV set which acts as a record player, a keyboard and a washing machine – may impress the bickerers but Garden's heart simply isn't in it. His obsession is reaching back to prehistoric history but his colleagues inject comic mockery – Oddie, again eager to pinpoint dubious sexuality, questions the legality of being 'into Neolithic man'. Timbo, meanwhile, cheerfully undermines the whole thing with gloriously silly comments about the Post Office Tower falling over if you dig under it and undermines Garden's stone age lecturing: 'Palaeolithic age, megalithic age…' 'The budgie cage!' But never a man to see his scientific

CAMELOT? NOPE, *THE GOODIES AND THE BEANSTALK*

THE MAKING OF *THE GOODIES AND THE BEANSTALK* #4

pontificating ridiculed, Graeme proves his huge hole theory correct by falling down one in the Goodies office. A load of obvious, but no less funny for all that, delayed reaction hollering, keeps the comedy level high as the loggerhead duo of Oddie and Brooke-Taylor take a full three weeks of pothole book consulting and fashion accessory stuffing to make the perilous descent to save the bespectacled one. Tim as the man who skilfully avoids fear like the plague, names himself the chap who stays above ground to look after things. Oddie is the reckless loony, careering down the hole at a rate of knots. All things being equal and all ropes being attached to Brooke-Taylor, the blonde lad's trousers are quickly whipped off, before his entire body and most of the pad's furniture hurtles down the hole as well. After some hasty skeleton discussion ('Hello cheeky!'), some mock ventriloquism business and some quite bizarre, irrelevant references to Sir Alec (Guinness?), Garden reveals himself as alive and well, and the trio are reunited in their fascination for the ancient collection of bones contained within Goodie Hole. The lads get away with stone me comments and a rock cake diet, discuss a tiny ape with a huge brain who became extinct because it kept falling over, before Bill and Tim's rendition of *Dem Bones*. The halfway commercial break gets topical, with a plug for Stones Linament and Bristo Gravy which rids you of Rolf Harrises fast. Graeme is excellent as the destructive Rolf, causing mayhem in Grannie Tim's kitchen before succumbing to a dose of poisoned Bristo, but it's dinosaurs the public want. There's time for slightly off-tune ramblings to bewildering intellectual comment as Scary and Posh point score with shared historical knowledge, Tim revels in the O-level archaeology he almost passed and proves a point with very teeth-like stalactites, before everything goes pear-shaped and the team find themselves trapped in the mouth of a dormant T-Rex. True to form, Garden is totally rational, Oddie just takes the mickey (using the dino's tonsils for a punchbag) and Brooke-Taylor patriotically panics. The stomach set looks like it was left over from *The Three Doctors* and lengthy discussion of the strange potholing chap who loved cheese and chutney sandwiches, merely wastes a bit of time before the lads accept their fate. A life within the prehistoric beastie. Naturally, there's surprisingly little to do within a huge stomach and Oddie's painstakingly created Home Sweet Home sign is impressing no one. Thus, it's time for one of the Goodies' sublime flights of illogical fantasy.

Within the structure of isolated madness, Bill and Tim play out a bizarre football match between Derby County and Chelsea. Sheer genius is touched as Timbo cheats, Oddie's international selection of subs come on and, surprise winger, Steve McQueen, allows Hayley Mills to get the winning hat trick. By now, Oddie has dished out the slap-up feast of a single bean each, been discovered as a secret, cunning, chicken-eater (his self-indulgent, unrepentant admission bringing on a touch of corpsing) and resurrected his on-going battle with Tim from the show's start, with bitchy battling and Susan Hampshire name-calling. Poor old Tim huffs off to the spleen for a well-deserved sulk and Garden, taking no prisoners, polishes off Bill's tuck, wipes his hands on the long Oddie hair and formulates a way out of the mess – to get up the dinosaur's nose. It should be a piece of cake, he's already got up Bill's. The huge vocal chords of the creature are used, while Oddie gleefully throws himself into a brilliantly naff bit of dummy talking which goes on for ages ('She was only the caveman's daughter but you don't know what Dina saw!'), and gets more and more hilarious the more desperate he gets. But regardless of the billions of years that have elapsed since King Rex walked the earth, all this illogical mucking about with his bits and pieces causes the thing to wake, a burst of *Dick Barton* accompanies the lad's hasty exit, a back-stabbing bit of business concerning Oddie's insurance is quickly forgotten and the trio say their farewells before, literally, all hell breaks loose and the far from dead dino emerges from under the Goodies office.

Did You Know? Industrial action at the BBC severely disrupted this season. Four episodes were in the can before the trouble began, while *Goodies in the Nick* was hastily allotted studio time a few weeks after the original schedule date. However, this episode wasn't recorded until November, almost six months late and just under two months before its first broadcast. Purposely written as a tight-knit, non-guest star, cheaply-set vehicle to balance the huge budget expense of both the Christmas special and earlier Series Four episodes, the effect was both funny and inexpensive and clearly pointed the way towards soul-searching classics *The End and Earthanasia*.

Episode Four, recorded Friday 2 November, broadcast Saturday 29 December 1973, 6.30–7pm, BBC2.

GOODIES IN THE NICK

With time on their hands and tension in the air, the Goodies relax over a card game of Happy Families before their office is invaded by the fuzz. Like Sid James in those *Hancock's Half Hour* days, Oddie's first reaction to the boys in blue is mad panic, but the hasty search and heavy-handed manner are merely pale remnants of police brutality. In contrast to Paul Whitsun-Jones and his evil authority figure from Series One's *Give Police a Chance*, here the head bluebottle is friendly, naïve and bumbling – brilliantly brought to life by relative new boy to the *Carry On*, Jack Douglas. Injecting the Northern innocence of his celebrated Alf Impititimus characterer, there's no room for the legendary twitch but enough comic scope for Jack to pile on the pathos among the slapstick. Childlike and eager to please, his 25 years in the force seem to have been for nothing as he whips out his notebook and tells his woeful tale. He's only arrested two criminals in all that time! Having promised not to laugh, the helpful trio can't keep their promise for long as Jack's touching, violin accompanied, 'Dear Goodies', letter unfolds. Afraid of criminals and desperate for promotion, this policeman's lot is certainly not a happy one but with the promise of two tons of certain substances and a cart load of dirty mags, Bill, for one, is eager to be of assistance. Police corruption is hinted at rather than satirised this time and most of the comedy comes from Jack's simpleton performance, while the lads happily run comic rings round him. The Goods are hired to stage a bank robbery and fall into the long, wrong arm of the law – undercover coppers headed by a uniformed, and proud of it, Jack Douglas. Suddenly, it's back to the Roaring Twenties with our playacting Goodies taking on the mantle of Al Capone's boot-legging, bar-smashing, tax-evading American. That legendary hunch-shouldered, violin case carrying trip into the Dogger Bank – which later featured in the opening credits – sets up a great bit of comic business with *Godfather*-style musical accompaniment and Jack's mistimed, mistaken attempts to arrest the gang carrying out the heist for an age. Finally, the safe is cracked but the money is gone – Jack, clearly tipped off by the Goods has removed the loot and ruined the plan. Hey, but have no fear, a cheque – for the princely sum of two million quid – is written out and it's Goodnight Vienna as the trio make haste out the door. A wonderfully staged slapstick chase ensues with Oddie handing the musical reigns over to the Twenties' jazz classic *Tiger Rag* – familiar from Robert Youngson's Sixties silent film compilations. The scene memorably combines Goonish cries of delight with something akin to Norman Wisdom's police steeplechase from *On the Beat*. Following mock plugs for Henson and Bedges tobacco and Longbow Cider, the narrative returns with the reappearance of Douglas at The Goodies office. But things have changed. The lads are now cigar-chomping hoodlums, the crown jewels, Mona Lisa and other valuables are scattered around the room and the comedy actor formerly known as Tim Brooke-Taylor is now the big, big Boss, dubbed 'the Goodiefather', spluttering with mouth-full Marlon Brando-isms and acting tougher than tough. After protests of innocence and the usual Cagney chatter about pinning wraps, being given the dough and spilling the beans, it's down to the cop shop and heavy, corrupt interrogation. Poor old Eric Chitty, as blind as the proverbial bat, Mr Dennison, is dragged in for the identity parade and just about picks out the Goodies. It's an unfair cop and time for some quality time at HM's pleasure in Strangemoor Scrubs. Under wraps for three years, bearded Goodies emerge blinking in their cell and immediately decide to get out. After some half-hearted Royal business – the wardrobes of the Queen and Prince Phillip, Bill's lavatorial Royal Flush groaner – it's through the wall and into another manic chase, this time to Oddie's old stand-by *Run*. Losing the facial hair thanks to a handy hedge clipper and semi-fooling the police with drag and little boy disguises – cleverly concealing their ball and chain as everything from balloons to a pregnancy bump – it's quickly back into the law's embrace and a face the music appearance in court. That glorious sitcom favourite Tommy Godfrey does his usual poor man's Sid James act as a boxing booth barker keeping order in court while puns (QC, Issy Bent, the judge, Justice Once) keep the laughs flowing. As opposed to the police-biased judgements of *Give Police a Chance*, this time the balance is addressed and the Goodies take control. There's room for a bit of referential forelock tugging to Hancock's *Twelve Angry Men* with 'the quality of mercy' banter and Bill adopts funny glasses and big nose in the judge's chair (banging his gavel and winning a huge teddy bear, fairground style), while Jack's ambitious corrupt rozzer is completely overcome by the even more corrupt legal system – he's now with M15 and boasts 5000 arrests. By now, Bill's gone power mad, finally realising that the only way to beat the system is from the inside. A prison sentence is casually dished out to Edward Heath and a classic bit of auctioning is played out on Mary Whitehouse. Gloriously paying her back for condemnation of the show, The Goodies – and everybody else for that matter – scream for a prison sentence of 50, 60 and even, cheekily, 69, years, as the show comes to a close.

Did You Know? *A very brief sequence from this episode – that of Tim vowing never to squawk and Jack goosing him for the desired result – featured in the comedy compilation The Laughing Policeman, first broadcast as part of BBC2's theme night Cops on the Box. Bill Oddie bought his hoodlum suit from the BBC costume department – the only suit he has ever owned!*

JACK DOUGLAS, TOMMY GODFREY, ERIK CHITTY. Episode Five, recorded Friday 1 June 1973, broadcast Saturday 5 January 1974, 6.45–7.15pm, BBC2.

THE RACE

Ten years after *It's a Mad, Mad, Mad, Mad World* kick-started Hollywood's renewed obsession with outlandish slapstick, explosive prat-falling and comic wreckage, *The Goodies* tackled the format in this low-key effort. Not a great deal happens, but there's more anti-French jibes per square foot than any other comedy around and the essence of *Wacky Races*, *The Great Race* and *Those Magnificent Men in Their Flying Machines* is captured. Indeed, the majority of the race sequences are dominated by a Terry-Thomas-style baddie, Baron O'Beef, continually sabotaging the other vehicles, grinning madly from within his black, Gilliam-esque, teeth-adorned bumper logo and enjoying the company of equally black-clad girls. You almost except him to break the silent slapstick pantomime and utter 'Blast!' at any moment. Deeply rooted in continental stereotype, the episode kicks off with the Goodies inadvertently winning the Tour de France. It's all striped sweaters, onions over the handlebars and black berets, as the official competitors gain on our heroes – the epitome of Brit cool, dark-shaded, hang loose, flared and laid-back hip – and force them into speed mode. As a throwaway hook to hang this half hour on, it works fine, allowing a champers-swigging Timbo to comment about plans to find Skegness and loads of Oddie francophile food delights with proffered plastic frog and crunchy snails. The motives may be different (Brooke-Taylor's all out for patriotic glory / Garden wants the money) but that powerful mix of instant wealth and putting one over the foreigners is enough to unite the team for any international race going. The flag-waving, red, white and blue, stirring diatribe from Tim is one of the series' highlights, every xenophobic comment, name calling and 'we are best' bulldog spirit put-down is distilled into 30 seconds, as the Churchillian bubble is skilfully burst with his 'we'll cheat!' coda. Garden throws himself into a pidgin French, Maurice Chevalier-seasoned explanation of the British way of life (the Queen, football and a bit of intertextual Eddie Waring from the *Beanstalk* adventure, *That Old Black Magic*, *I'm Sorry I'll Read That Again*

et al.), while Oddie just sits around and waits for the action to begin. The seed of plot is sown and the lads are entered into the 24-hour Le Mans race – the only problem is, they haven't got a car and none of them can drive anything more sophisticated than a trandem. Naturally it's Tim, everybody's favourite cowardly custard, who is instructed in the art of driving from TS Eliot's ultimate guide book. Oddie injects great swathes of deliciously unsubtle working class oikness into the proceedings, Garden does his best with the poor student in front of him and Brooke-Taylor, embraced in the ethos of *Toad of Toad Hall* with his goggles and Rupert the bear scarf, happily plays up to his childish image – mocking all knowledge, poking fun at the jargon and sheepishly offering his disobedient hand for teacher smacking. Within the eager smut ('pull what out!') and playground howlers (congratulating the engaged gears), Brooke-Taylor and Garden succeed in creating a real sense of Sid Field / Jerry Desmonde class here, allowing Oddie's homosexual references, fear of nether region abuse and giggling suppression to enhance the routine. Garden's scientific bent is once again brought into the open with his rather dodgy-looking jaunty jalopy. Tim is none too impressed, his higher/lower seating arrangements cause concern and the overactive windscreen-wiping Sudsy Wudsy spray dominates the proceedings. Still, alongside all the visual nuttiness, cat abuse and blind panic, Oddie's earthy smut is allowed full reign – notably doing the classic three tier Italian-made, German-made, French maid business. The 'check your points' comment could have come from Peter Butterworth's *Carry On* canon. However, on to the race itself, with heaps of anti-foreign stuff (the diminutive Japanese entrant using an Ever Leady battery) and various slapstick interludes (including a tinkering balletic segment and the bizarre, *Jake the Peg* mechanic moment for Oddie), as the bearded one delivers with another class ditty, *Motorway Madness*, performed in laid-back Latin beat. After plenty of nasty mucking about from the Baron the race seems set to a corrupt close, but 'weep not fearless track ace' for that beloved crackpot Garden has worked his weird magic and made The Goodies office into a roadworthy vehicle – leave all credibility at the door as you come in! With a spot of hand grenade volleying, the Baron is hoisted by his own evil petard, our out of control heroes face the turmoil of white knuckle back projection, an open air Can Can competition, a lack of brakes in their vehicle, slurs on Tim's driving and a *Starsky and Hutch* leap

THE GOODIES ARE FORCED TO SHARE ONE DIRECTOR'S CHAIR BUT NOT ONE DIRECTORIAL VISION FOR THIS RELAXED MOMENT DURING A BREAK FROM FILMING THE OPENING EPISODE OF SERIES FIVE, *MOVIES*

on to their fast-moving home before it's *Chitty, Chitty, Bang Bang*-like, metamorphosis into a flying machine. Winging its way into a perfect sunset and a stunning Fin, as the French, and those French-mocking Goodies, say.

Did You Know? This episode was the only time Graeme's motivation mode in the Goodies' accommodation was used since its unveiling in the opening programme of Series Three, The New Office. It's simply a tarted-up lorry in disguise. Keeping up the official railway signifiers, the set is adorned with a poster concerning the withdrawal of freight services from Strathclyde Station. Although the entire Series Six episode, It Might as Well Be String was packed with commercials as part of the narrative, it was also the last episode to feature a mock break, here advertising air hostesses and the 'What I Like Best To Eat' Tim Brooke-Taylor Heinz Meanz Beanz spot finally delivered correctly only to be ruined by the scenery falling on the poor lad's head. Having been a near-permanent

fixture through Series One, more recently these had been faded out – only to return, unmocking but sometimes almost as funny, when real breaks were included in The Goodies' Series Nine.

BILL WESTON. Episode Six, recorded Thursday 3 May 1973, broadcast Saturday 12 January 1974, 6.45–7.15pm, BBC2.

SERIES FIVE

By common consent this is the finest series put together by the Goodies. Made in the immediate wake of the televisual demise of Monty Python, the 13-episode season was resurrected with every entry a classic. The BBC's Robin Scott fought for and won the coveted 9pm slot and, although, initially, the trio were less than impressed, this broadcast time became the breakthrough. It resulted in several letters of complaint from younger fans – the time change put *The Goodies* after their bedtimes – but many kids were allowed to stay up late and share the 'family' feel of *The Goodies* and the show suddenly rocketed into mainstream success. The ratings jumped from three million viewers to 10 million, *The Goodies* books and records made the team multimedia favourites, and they were even named top telly comedians by readers of the *Sun* newspaper – Eric and Ern were second and the two Rons third! 1975 was clearly *the* year. The episodes were originally commissioned as two series, one of six and one of seven. Dubbed *The Goodies 1974* in BBC correspondence, industrial action struck again. Location filming for the series began at Wareham on 2 April 1974 but by the middle of June only two editions had been completed. The remaining four programmes were postponed. As a result, the purposed two series collections were destined to be broadcast at a later date and it was decided to bunch them all together into a 13-strong season. Work on the second batch of programmes began in earnest on 22 September with location filming in Cornwall and London but, now, amazingly, the Goodies had to really get their skates on and complete 11 programmes in the time allocated for only six. Latching on to the creative immediacy adopted by John Lennon – when tracks like *Instant Karma* were conceived, written, recorded and released like musical newspaper – some of these later Series Five episodes were recorded as little as three days before broadcast. Also, of note, this series was the first to feature Tim Brooke-Taylor donning one of the ultimate signifiers, the Union flag waistcoat. It was the finishing touch to Bill Oddie's outlandish vision of Tim Brooke-Taylor. Oddie explained that Tim was, fundamentally, 'pro-Royal and I'm not!', but Brooke-Taylor, in reality, has often been uncomfortable with his Goodies image. Bill's claim that he is the sort of bloke who looks like he should always be in a suit has led to Tim's frequent 'I've never worn a suit in my life!' rant but, eventually justifying himself in 1999, Bill commented, 'I'm afraid Tim suffered entirely from having a double-barrelled name – I'm sorry, you've got poncy blonde hair and a double-barrelled name, you're going to have to be the posh one who bursts into tears! Somebody had to do it.' The series also saw the debut of a more upbeat version of the theme song.

Film cameraman John Tiley. Film editor Ron Pope. Visual effects Peter Day and Len Hutton. Costume Rupert Jarvis (Episodes 1–12) and Andrew Rose (Episodes 4–13). Make-up Rhian Meakin (Episodes 1–5, 11) and Jean Steward (Episodes 3–13). Lighting Alan Horne. Sound Jack Sudic (Episode 1) and John Howell (Episodes 2–13). Music by Bill Oddie and Michael Gibbs. Design John Stout (Episodes 1–8, 10–13) and Austin Ruddy (Episodes 7, 9, 10 & 12) with Lesley Bremness (Episode 1 & 2), Ian Rawnsley (Episode 3), Colin Green (Episodes 5 & 12) and Tom Carter (Episode 8). Production assistant Peter Lovell. Produced by Jim Franklin.

MOVIES

The opening episode is a glorious celebration of the slapstick silent cinema and animated classics. At home in the Cricklewood office, Bill is indulging his passion for old comedy movies – killing himself at the grand tradition of custard pie fights, pratfalls and police chases. Tim is less amused. Sitting quietly, quizzically and with a faint smile on his face, the camera need not illustrate vintage material for this scene to work. Graeme's earnest, cod American narration – perfectly in the style of those Sixties' Robert Youngson silent film compilations – builds up the comic moment for Bill's no holds barred reactions. He can't get enough of it – Chaplin, Langdon, Keaton, Lavatory Meadows… ah, WC Fields. Yep, the lads get away with that old gag. Meanwhile, Graeme is doing a bit of Goodies' product placement by reading his treasured copy of *The Goodies File* – available now in all good book shops. Besides, he's done the movie thang already by inventing the pocket movie camera. A huge mother of a thing, the special, copiously pocketed trousers are also required for the full benefit – but what's the point? The British film industry is dead in the water. That grand bastion of film-making, Pinetree Studios, is in financial ruin. A 99-year lease is up for grabs for 25 quid, the industry is safe in the knowledge that The Goodies are there to get the cameras turning. Pathé News covers the events with typical gusto, with three big-nosed, big-cigared Goodies setting off on their chauffeur-pulled trandem and into movie-making glory. All the great directors are foregathered for their work to be marked and as any good, ex-schoolteacher should, Tim Brooke-Taylor rips into their handiwork with a vengeance. The artistic boredom of Death in Bognor is as nothing compared with Russell's The Life of Pablo Casals complete with flaming cellist, bleeding nun striptease and worryingly white-faced clown imagery. Despite Graeme's skill at building up this work as a masterly piece of surrealist genius, Bill's 'load of old cobblers' dismissal gets the thumbs up vote from the team and it's time to make the directors face the music. Tim shines brightly here, condemning Kubrick, telling Zeffirelli off for giggling and barking at Fellini – 'Yes, I am looking at you!' With a portrait of Diana Dors looking down on the Goodie, the golden age of Fifties' cinema is subtlety provoked. Cannes success and Andy Warhol's cinema verité filming of Tim's rant, doesn't cut any ice either and the entire lot are sacked in a flurry of talcum

GRAEME GARDEN, TIM BROOKE-TAYLOR AND BILL ODDIE REFLECT ON THE LIFE OF A CIGAR-SMOKING MOGUL IN *MOVIES*

powder – much to the emotionally exhausted, devastated, tear-stained chagrin of poor, precious old Tim. Mind you, it does mean that there's a gap in the market. The trio are all powerful and the director's job is theirs for the asking. Sharing a three-seater chair and dishing out the assignments – Tim directs for this turn, Graeme's on camera (allowing a painful but still worryingly funny 'camera running' visual gag) and Bill's a lowly clapper board boy – the lads embark on a glorious, much censored, cleaned up and very, very short treatment of *Macbeth*. It's just an opening scene, with the glorious old ham walking out of a door. But the poor 'mutt and jeff' lovie can't manage it, Tim's outrageously eccentric and potent cries of 'Action' can not penetrate and the whole cinematic splendour ends up more like a damp squib. All this is hopeless, so, with no directors save themselves, the Goods go for the Orson Welles meets Charlie Chaplin

syndrome, dismiss the actor and take on the thespian mantle as well. The new, improved blockbuster, Macbeth Meets Truffatt the Wonder Dog, is the motion picture to put Pinetree back on the map and it's a grand Goodies' production. Immediate post-filming delight goes straight to their heads. Tim minces about à la Mae West, Graeme's donning a sparkling version of his boring suit and Bill's right off the deep end with a Richard Harris-style Irish hell-raising attitude, swearing, boozing and falling all over the place. There's an invaluable moment as staggering Bill collapses and sits on Tim's beloved poodle momentarily skips out of character and chucks in a priceless ad lib – 'Have a drink…' – as he forces alcohol down the doggie before merrily tossing the pooch away. Behave like stars they may do but act like stars on the silver screen they most certainly do not, with the long-awaited private viewing of their work running like badly edited out-takes,

THIS IS WHAT THE *CLOWN VIRUS* DOES TO YOU!

line fluffs and set falling over moments. Tim's glorious 'damn spot' speech is on the floor hilarious, finally ending up with the offending curse on the end of his nose and failing miserably to locate it. The ghost is a real dead loss and as for the wonder dog of the film's title, he's so knackered and camera shy (pre-Bill's attachment to a bit of raw meat), that a pathetically inept, toy dog on wheels is pulled into vision. A real stinker, a fight breaks out between Bill and Tim in the screening room, Bill happily screams his less than original plan to get drunk and all three prima donnas vow, Greta Garbo-like, never to make another film. But, with more come-back promises than Frank Sinatra, the trio are quickly back in the mad business of show, each with different ideas for the picture to make. Tim, in fetching loin-cloth and carrying a very unconvincing lion under his arm, naturally yearns for the muscle-bound epic of a cracking Samson movie. Gray Bags, meanwhile, pre-empting the *Bunfight* classic yet to

come, opts for a Western. While, best of all, Bill has set his heart on a back to roots silent, black and white, slapstick comedy, painstakingly painting the room black and white and celebrating the legends like Keaton. A squabble breaks out in the group – brilliantly Bill plugs his idea with a non-verbal hand-held sign screaming 'My silent classic', but eventually the trio combine with less than happy hearts, resulting in a slapstick bombardment of comic ideas. Graeme sets the ball rolling with a *High Noon* fashioned gun fight with slow-motion, Sam Peckipah-style death scenes, hastily invaded with marching centurions, epic movie music and a cheerful Timbo still lugging that killer lion around with him. But the real genius comes with Bill's sad-faced silent clown. Pure magic is guaranteed as he runs out of his Twenties' world into the colour reality of the other films. Pursued by, naturally, black and white Keystone Kop clones, the genres merge with rival camera crews battling it out, the custard pie ethos invading biblical grandeur and a stone tablet prophet emerging from the Epic Department, and hitting Bill over the head. But Bill finds solace in the archive department with departed heroes, Chaplin, Keaton and Stan and Ollie strolling to his defence, throwing themselves into nostalgic slapstick glory and even picking up a few hints. Contrasted with a gloriously sick visual as Tim's Indian brave sends an arrow zinging right through the heart of a 'hills are alive' belting Julie Andrews, the lads borrow from the great Keaton as the comedy moves away from the actual making of films and on to watching them. Heavily inspired by Keaton's brilliant 1921 film, *Sherlock Jnr*, Tim can sit watching himself on the screen and the comedy legends pelt him with rocks. Frankenstein's Monster gives poor Tim a shock in the next seat and creates a strong link with 1942's madhouse masterpiece *Hellzapoppin'* with Olsen and Johnson. The huge cinematic Bill latches on to *King Kong* power with a quick Rent-a-Fay Wray grab at Tim, while feuding Goodies can do nothing about the huge The End which signals imminent closure of the physical, three stooges battle. Grabbing on to The End and being whisked up out of the top of the screen into infinity, the familiar theme music is abandoned in favour of an epic sweep and, ingeniously, the familiar credits spiral upwards in big screen fashion.

Did You Know? *The start of this monumental fifth series warranted the second and final Radio Times front cover appearance for the Goodies (8–14 February 1975). Basking in the glory of the Beanstalk classic, it was a masterpiece by Lyn Gray, featuring caricatured mountaineering Brooke-Taylor and Oddie climbing up the green beanstalk of Graeme Garden. The legend read, 'The Goodies' Ascent — Goody, goody, they're back' and in the same issue, Michael Wynn Jones took a detailed look at the various off-shoots from Oxford and Cambridge from Beyond the Fringe to Monty Python. The article, entitled 'The goods on the Goodies' was complimented with a family tree chart detailing the Goodie connections with such programmes as At Last the 1948 Show and Twice a Fortnight with caricatured heads of Tim, Bill and Graeme. The piece also included Allan Ballard's behind the scenes photos from location work on Rome Antics as well as fascinating storyboard images from the episode. This episode won the team their second Silver Rose at the Montreaux Festival held in May 1975. The Australian Broadcasting Commission had a field-day with the scissors here, editing references to 'knockers', 'sex, perversion and violence' and various Bill / Tim screening room insults from 'clapped out old queen' to 'bitch'.*

MELITA CLARKE. Episode One, recorded Friday 14 June 1974, broadcast Monday 10 February 1975, 9–9.30pm, BBC2.

CLOWN VIRUS

A real back to basics corker, the Goodies are actually hired for an actual assignment like the old days. And like the old days, a timely comment on the dangers of nuclear and germ warfare is tossed into the comedy for extra bite. John Bluthal as the Yankee military high-flyer Charles M Cheeseburger storms into view like Sterling Hayden in *Dr Strangelove*. He's totally untrustworthy and totally unconvincing in his attempts to hide the fact that this secret conversation is being recorded – dual ashtrays cum reel to reel tape decks spin, as do Jane Fonda's breasts on a pin-up picture and a couple of plates. A flower doubles as a microphone and Bluthal even does the 'Peter Piper picks a pickle…' testing, testing, one, two, three line, which he had delivered 10 years earlier for *Carry On Spying*. Playing along with all this recording business, the Goodies face the job in hand – dumping a huge can of nasty waste stuff masquerading as a can of tomato soup. There's a nice Anglo-American dispute about the pronunciation of 'tomato' but business is business. Graeme, satisfied with the 'no fishing' and, more importantly, 'no fish' sign, finds the perfect watering place to do the deed, ultimately getting Tim – Slim Pickens-style from *Dr Strangelove* – to ride on the tin's back and into the water. Besides, they have Bill's *Boomeranger* to help, but failure greets every attempt even with the ultimate in hardware aid – the ACME Flipper. Fun with a one-ton weight, the useless flipper and the tin sees Graeme squashed on several occasions as Tim casually whistles his way away from the scene of the crime. The only option is consumption, and donning his chef's gear, Timbo serves up the dodgy stuff as if it was… tomato soup. The fact that it's green and tastes revolting doesn't enter in to it – Graeme gets away with an unsubtle urine reference in a very subtle aside, 'Perhaps it's pea…', before the moment is invaded with Tim's lavishing of red paint into Bill's bowl for the desired visual effect. Delicious it ain't but with fond memories of really awful service station grub on the M1, Graeme hits on the brain wave of a lifetime – flog it to the swines. Thus, instant rid of the nasty stuff and a few quid besides. The trusted driver's friend chain, Thirties (as opposed to Fortes, get it?) seems the ideal mugs to take it. The coffin symbol on the welcoming sign outside says it all. The chef – happily rearranging lettuce from the dustbin for the salad – takes a revolting mouthful, gobs it out with gusto and gives the thumbs up. The deal is done and across the country various places are serving up the muck as various stuff – coffee to petrol, it doesn't matter. The Goodies have achieved their mission. But wait, you know what's going to come. After all, what's the name of this episode? Embracing the world of surrealism and good old-fashioned entertainment, it's the ultimate die laughing ailment – the clown virus. First it's Tim, inventing *Comic Relief* and sporting an expanding red nose. Bill's hilarious comment that he's becoming KoKo the Clown doesn't make Graeme laugh. He takes all the most implausible facts and figures from the episode and smugly mutters, 'It all makes sense…' It doesn't, of course, but the clownish facts are as plain as the very red nose on Timbo's face. With a painted smile, unfolding shirt front and fuzzy wig, Tim's case is getting worse. Bill, meanwhile, finds his trousers expanding to comical proportions as the lads approach the dreaded military base. Hastily, Gray Bags is dragged into this mystic world of sick slapstick and becomes the beloved sad-faced clown with fly-away hair. The three, in full make-up, staggering away from the camera at high speed, has become one of the greatest images in the series – it would recur many times in credit sequences to come. The race is on to find out exactly what that chemical concoction was – it's gonna take ages but the Goodies ain't got the time to hang around. Just as the search begins, Tim calmly says, 'Found it!' But being the good, God-fearing, patriotic, I may not have signed the official secrets act but I love what it stands for, sort of bloke, he refuses to read it – after all, it's marked 'Secret'. Graeme is not so precious about all that and grabs it for inspection. It's CV 70 nerve gas, the material that turns you into a clown, but this is compounded with an ultra weird compulsion continually to act like a clown. Thus, fun with water squirters and the like are the order of the day and in the episode's best moment, mock Italian clowning Bill desperately attempts to set up mock Italian clowning Tim with the classic 'whip the chair away before the victim sits on it' ploy. Tim's coy, knowing, walk into the trap, followed by, 'No, I not sit on the chair…', is charm itself. But things are worse than just the Goodies camping it up in full big top regalia. The exhaust from cars pumped full of the mixture instantly turns innocent passers-by into Charlie Chairoli types. He may look totally silly but Graeme knows it's rather serious. This is no mere accident or twist of fate. The big guy in the States, General Pentagon, beams in *Dr Who*-like and

promises invading American forces to capture little old England. The plan – to claim it as the 51st state. The BBC News hosted by Corbett Woodall, stone-faced and disparaging, relates the chronic case of clown virus throughout the land. The State Opening of Parliament is literally a circus and the Queen's regally detached wave is accompanied by the less than regal party blower. Corbett, in twirling bow-tie, sets up the impending, invading might of America with perfect understated gloom and as the Glenn Miller formation gets into action, Bill's song, *Here Come the Clowns*, and the Goodies – suitably attired in clowning dudeness – signal the battle cry. With the perfect collapsing trandem, the Goods use every clown trick in the book to keep the US folk at bay – from Yankee food missiles to playful bucket antics via tiptoe-reacting landmines. With nowhere to go save the end credits, the blown to bits troops, black and burnt, are treated to some good old Southern hospitality, rounded up like slaves by Ramsay Williams as a white-suited Colonel Sanders spin off, and forced away in mournful, sing-song, slave-song style with *Ain't Gonna Study War No More*. The Goodies end the show in full clown garb but, fear not, before Radio 2 takes hold next week, the lads will be back in shipshape shape.

JOHN BLUTHAL, PETER DYNELEY, CORBET WOODALL, RAMSAY WILLIAMS. Episode Two, recorded Friday 7 June 1974, broadcast Monday 17 February 1975, 9–9.30pm, BBC2.

CHUBBIE CHUMPS

All is not well at the Cricklewood offices. Graeme returns from a less than fruitful fishing trip with nothing but a carrot suit-clad Bill Oddie complaining about his use as bait. The thought of a pleasant, Timbo-cleaned place of work is the one bright spot on the horizon. But, shock and gasp a plenty, that lazy ratbag is tucked up in bed. The place is a pig sty and Tim's snorting sleep noise only clarifies the point. And it's all the fault of that damned Radio 2. Jimmy Young rabbiting on about the state of the nation and glorious cooking tips for fat-laden recipes are all that Tim is bothered about. Suet, buckets full of lard and whale blubber till it comes out of your ears are the name of the game and a very fat Tim is the result. But while one presenter piles it on another is there to burn it off. Terry Wogan's Fight the Flab campaign is remorselessly ribbed with fat Tim struggling to touch his toes – he resorts to touching Bill's instead – and hanging on every word the grand Irishman mutters. Answering back, reflecting on his profound thoughts and really getting involved, Bill is amazed at this blind devotion. But Tim's not the only one, a host of housewives are, pied piper-like, forced out of their front doors by the smooth-talking devil, jogging along to their heart's content, being joined by the butter ball Timbo and ultimately being lead to the health and beauty farm, The Lazy DJ. The methods may be dubious – fat-reducing techniques include brutally beating the fatty, while Bill's *Lay Weight on Me* song, weight-lifting sessions and very limited food supplies are also part of the regime (poor Tim is reduced to consuming the bowl). But the results are stunning, after a quick five-minute hair wash and brush-up, Tim and the female heavy weights are transformed into drop dead gorgeous babes. Yep, even Tim's donning a shapely figure-hugging dress, blonde wig and come to bed expression. Back at base, Graeme and Bill seem surprisingly upset that their third number is not among them. Bill mutters, 'I'll miss him…' just before Gray Bags bursts the emotional balloon, allows the dart to come into shot and comments kindly, 'Not if you aim carefully!' Bill aims very carefully. Still, the housework has gone to pot without Tim's loving touch. Bill's shampooed the joint of meat and stuck the cat in the oven – and even that's not cooked properly. Sending up the washing-up liquid ads, the two go into demonstration mode. Now with smooth hands and the reappearance of Timbo, things seem to be going wonderfully, but Tim's not just had his hair done, he's beautiful and Bill and Graeme are dumbstruck. For Tim, the final of the Miss Housewife of the Year is the only matter on the agenda. But Gray Bags is not happy. Deconstructing the non-fatty housewife line-up down to the cattle market mid-feminist mentality of the beauty contest, Graeme talks up for the ugly, horrible people who never get a look-in at such competitions. Crossing the boundaries of total reality with ease, 'Tel' comments back and, openly on air, speaks against an audience of nothing more than 'a load of old crones'. Wogan's silence, on-air shutdown and Beeb job description for a new presenter forms a nice, hasty chain reaction for Graeme to face his future, clear out and tackle life at Broadcasting House. Lax security, Gothic atmosphere and bird-nest dereliction is the name of the floundering radio game but Gray's a fighter. And fighting past the dust and *Psycho*-style musical score, he takes his seat in a studio scrawled over with hits of yesteryear. As if gripped by the spectre of his radio, multifaceted personality performances, Graeme dives into his legendary collection of impressions. Walter Gabriel from *The Archers* is greeted like an old friend, there's the

trendy BBC relaunch of Eddie Waring's babbling, ever-chuckling, reporting style and a spot of manic Jimmy Saville – by this time Gray's lost the plot a bit and starts donning costume accessories for radio – wiggling his cigar, getting all clunk-click and dishing out entertainment which is perfectly 'far out and embarrassing'. Tony Blackburn makes a guest appearance as a bubblegum music-loving ventriloquist's dummy – check out Graeme's corpsing as the lines go awry – while dreamy old Fluff rounds things off with his usual hip, cool and laid-back enthusiasm. Power mad by now, Radio 2 has become the characterisation domain of one man – Graeme Garden – and if Tim's fooled by that dubious 'Terry Wogan' then Bill certainly isn't. Reversing that slim regime of the Irish dude, the new improved Graeme cum Terry plays *Food Glorious Food* full blast and urges all his lovely housewives to stuff themselves stupid. The power of radio is great indeed and a food-eating binge runs through the nation. Tim – or Timalina – is tempted, but Bill thinks he knows the score. Surely, good old Graeme is knobbling all the other contestants to allow Tim to win. And if he isn't, Bill certainly isn't going to stand by and let the delicious Tim ruin his figure. The local Zoo has its dolphin and elephant stripped of edible meat by these raving housewives. For the big showbiz bash, Bill allows himself a gloriously self-indulgent musical number, crooning *Les Girls* and camping about like a good 'un, before Graeme's Wogan takes over and introduces the line-up of milkman judges. The fat glam pageant is enough to curdle the milk, Miss Liverpool even bemuses Graeme – 'Lord have Mersey!' – and slim-line, stunner, Miss Cricklewood, Tim, easily romps home to victory. Meanwhile, Michael Aspirin (with Michael Aspel himself actually stepping out for a couple of seconds to play his *Goodies'* host name corruption created for Series Two's *The Baddies*) has staggered off stage and shot himself rather than facing the thought of embracing the contestants. But corruption – comic or otherwise – is never looked on favourably, and the male winner, still in drag, is chased out of town by his fellow beauties. With Gray and Bill for company, Tim's quickly back into his Union flag waistcoat but still the outraged wannabe beauty queens are in hot pursuit. It's all pin-ball machine mayhem as the Goods bounce for Britain, Tim discovers that hiding under a bath proves no safe option, while Bill is mercilessly flattened by the gals and hastily rolled up by Graeme. Pumped up via a garage gas dispenser, the other lads grab aboard an expanded Bill, float into the sky and escape. By the time the girls finally catch up with them, it's like a fortnight at the Lazy DJ has happened over a minute. Stunning and sexy, Bill's cough miraculously relieves the girls of their clothes and the Goodies magically don Benny Hill berets and dirty macs. The chase reverts, the Goods try to fondle the girls and the 'Benny Hill chases women' myth is compounded forever. A vastly undervalued comment on the power of media and the nationwide clout of Terry Wogan.

MICHAEL ASPEL Episode Three, recorded Friday 20 December 1974, broadcast Monday 24 February 1975, 9–9.30pm, BBC2.

WACKY WALES

Another unsung entry for Series Five, it all begins with dear old Tim packing his case, dropping in his pet goldfish sans water and merrily singing *There'll Be a Welcome in the Hillside*. The genius for cornball gags is established from the outset, with Tim's longing to go to the Eisteddford reverberating down to Bill's happy quip about the time when 'I stayed for dinner!' A practice of Welsh pronunciations (complete with umbrella to protect one from spittle), a chance for Graeme to resurrect his *I'm Sorry I'll Read That Again* 'no idea what I'm talking about' Welsh nonsense punctured with familiar Clive Jenkins reference, beloved show biz targets (Rolf, Des and Max B), a bit of stereotypical dismissal ('Taffy druids'), a charming moment of three-part folk singing and the like, and it's off to the Rev Cllewellyn Cllewellyn Cllewellyn Cllewellyn of Llan Dlubber. Dryer and more devout than an Oliver Cromwell convention, the place seems closed to everybody, and nothing, absolutely nothing, is allowed to take place. The clever visual gags on the way – a road sign reading Drive Caerphilly, a class optical illusion with huge hats seemingly billowing smoke and the direction for Snowdon panning across to reveal the regal photographer snapping away – work as a perfect build up for the ultimate, interior arrival in Wales' abstinence city. The train journey conjures up an obvious gag as the Welsh place name looming large outside the window spans the entire trip. But it's the Gothic, alcohol-free domain of the Reverend which really kick starts the action. Bellowing from behind the scenery and looming large with greased down hair and staring eyes is the one and only immediate post-*Who* Jon Pertwee moaning and groaning 'boyo' for all he's worth. Graeme remembers the guest star with much affection, 'Jon was wonderful. 'I can only do stage Welsh' he announced, which was true, but was very funny. He also

introduced us to the ideas of 'Freebies' or as he called it 'Tut'. Do a gig for someone who makes suitcases, and get a couple of free cases out of it!' A truly wild eccentric, he's God's gift to the scriptwriting Goodies. In this glorious place of the Seventh day repressionists, booze is a clear no-no and even tea is maniacally condemned as the 'foul potion of the orient, stimulator of the flesh and inflamer of the senses!' Bill is corpsing at this point but Pertwee masterfully continues to twist the knife of outlandish performance. The low birth rate for the area is obviously explained but even a request for sandwiches – 'voluptuous indulgence of the carnal appetites' – and lavatories – 'temples of Beelzebub!' – sends Pertwee into a fit of puritanical fever. 'The hot seat' is no place for a Welshman and Bill's desperate 'dying for a s…' makes him no friend to the black-clad religious crusader. The name of the game is being as bored stiff as possible. Pleasure, in any way or form, is shunned, and all attention is dedicated to the impending International Festival of Gloom which Pertwee, needless to say, is a past master at. But with the Goods in town, things could be slightly different. The overpowering scream of Welsh opera leaves even the natives cold – the desired effect – with one stage-view blocked chappie asking for the lady in front to remove her hat and, almost immediately, leaning forward again to ask if you would kindly put it back on again. Into the breach come the lads with their twist on the old format. A scantily clad girl – what else – is tossed in for immediate kapow, the boys turn on the Fred Astaire tap-dancing charm, Bill goes for his cowboy whipping trick with lovely assistant Tim losing a fag from the mouth, the almost pre-requisite rock interlude with *Welcome in the Hillside* done with Led Zeppelin proportions, the balloon-stripping babe has her cover popped down to three well-placed blow-ups, the fan-dancing stunner becomes Tim for later opening credit inclusion and Graeme's magical Wazir pulls out all the stops. The result, despite a bosom-clasping curtain call babe in the Barbara Windsor tradition, is silence from the totally unimpressed audience. It's just the hook Pertwee needs to put the religious boot in. Preaching to his obedient brethren, the mere mention of the word bosom brings on a shocked, rehearsed 'ooh!' from the congregation and working his crowd like an orchestra leader, Rev Jon asks whether these Goodie people entertained. Sweeping his arm upwards for the desired chorus of 'No!' from the auditorium, Pertwee condemns the very nature of the show, branding laughter as sinful. It's down to the Druid's Stone for our heroes and a bit of ritual humiliation. Bound and whipped on the way – with Tim, sinfully, enjoying it rather too much – Pertwee goes for full-on, delicious overacting mode, blabbering away and muttering 'b, b, bthese are humble offerings' all over the place. It's the start of a glorious scene with Pertwee going into 'boyo!' Welsh overdrive, protecting his blood-stained good name with unsubtle comments, 'We all have to make sacrifices', and setting up the 'What's it all about…' moment for the assembled masses helpfully to chorus 'Alfie!' But Wales being Wales, rugby is the thing. The only true sort of faith. To the tune of *Sunday Night at the London Palladium*, a gold rugger ball is revealed on a revolving mini-stage, just before the impending slaughter of three Goodies to its greater glory. Not fools and having seen the male-bonding Road movies, the Goods are not slow in protecting their own skins. Hands may be tied and patter cake patter cake may be ruled out but there's always desperation acting, throwing themselves into the Welsh salute and joining in the singing. Pertwee is wide-eyed with astonishment. Amazed these heathens know the ancient, sacred lyrics, the Goods inject a flamboyant dose of Welsh mannerisms into the chatter and dumbfoundedly laugh about the national identity being in their blood boyos… 'Oooh…', Shirley Bassey, Tom Jones and, to a less impressive extent, Mary Hopkins ('Who…' bless her) is name dropped to stoke the fire of subterfuge, before Graeme goes quietly insane and leads the lads in a quick rendition of *The Abadadabdaba Monkey Song*. By now, of course, it's almost all good pals together and the Pertwee 'leek boyo' business is merrily countered with a cry of 'I've just been'. Cries of 'We Are the Champions' cut the scene just at the right moment and set things up for the religious slanted Ecclesiastical Seven-a-Side Rugby Special coverage. There is throwaway delight to be had in the Quakers versus Derek Nimmos fixture, terminology twisting with a conversion from the Church of England and a nasty dig at the Goodies' major opposition, with Mary Whitehouse as the unthinkable – a hooker! Television convention is thrown into the mix with commentator clarification for those not watching in colour. Bill referees, the Druids speed around like Billy Whizz, rugger kit is proudly displayed under the religious finery and even the Pope comes on as the Catholic sub for a spot of divine intervention. Naturally, the Druids are victorious but their patriotic, beer-swilling celebrations are hardly the actions of religious followers. Lo and behold, an international team of professional players have assisted Pertwee and the boys. Tim shockingly disqualifies the winners and almost immediately lives to regret it. To the strains of Bill's groovy *Play the Game* number, Tim is used as a rugger ball, Bill hilariously dislodges a fisherman from his bridge-based position, Graeme paints white lines à la *Vision On* to create holes, trapdoors and escape hatches akin to the Warner cartoon classic *The Whole Idea* and the gang literally move the goalposts for a culmination of the physical comic abuse. But a new idea is a new idea and the religious Sunday League has taken off. Bill's not quite pious enough with his Bishop-clad chappie screaming, 'Easy Almighty!', while Tim and Graeme start out dignified before throwing in with the fandom attitude, shouting Ahems and rattling their rattle for the good of the Lord.

Did You Know? Several dubious references were edited by the Australian Broadcasting Commission including mentions of 'indecent exposure' and virgins, a 'get stuffed', a scene featuring Bill flashing at Tim and, not surprisingly, the Welsh rugby player, Brother Ignatius, mouthing, 'Why don't you fuck off, bitch?', to 'Mary Whitehouse' after a particularly rough tackle. Due to the major upheaval in filming schedule over industrial action at the BBC, the original choice for the Reverend was unable to appear. Before Jon Pertwee was signed up for wide-eyed rant, the more obvious but less potent choice of Windsor Davies was due for the Welsh madness. The new recording dates clashed with previously arranged working commitments for Davies and Pertwee was drafted in as a last minute sub.

JON PERTWEE, MARCELLE SAMETT, ALUN WILLIAMS, THE FRED TOMLINSON SINGERS. Episode Four, recorded Friday 28 February, broadcast Monday 3 March 1975, 9–9.30pm, BBC2.

FRANKENFIDO

Will mad scientists never learn? Graeme Garden is quietly and secretly pioneering the latest in genetically modified pets. Hard at work in a disused church, Gray Bags has his detailed breeding process in progress. Nutty dog breeds are the fad and his nurse feeds the huge Dulux Sheepdog a tin of deluxe paint. A toy St Bernard ('barrels of fun') and other wannabe freak show exhibits, are unveiled. With his hormone spray in one hand and a collar in the other, this is Graeme's big time business, and it's all in aid of the hotly awaited Crufts Showday: the unusual breeds section. Tim and Bill, never ones to let such an opportunity pass them by, have applied for a very special breed for the competition and a parcelled up, novelty breed is whisked to their Cricklewood base by special delivery. According to the paperwork, it's a Long-Haired Pug but Bill is less than convinced, he mutters, 'There's nothing in there'. Admittedly, it does resemble the top of an old mop but Tim is willing to give the creature a sporting chance. Naming him Rover and instructing patriotic, never known to fail commands – 'Dive for the Queen!' – Bill is still having none of it. Graeme, the twister, has flogged them a dead dog. This is quickly disproved when the beastie bites Bill, or, at least, does something to Bill, for the mouth, apparently, is round the other end. Whatever, there's enough cheek and gall in the Goodies camp to dash through the old 'My dog has no nose' gag, before stuffing the white ball of fluff with milk and a pork chop. His tricks are limited to a rather fetching begging motion. But Tim tries to push the little creature further, tempting him through a hoop, getting a wee instead and charmingly muttering through gritted teeth, 'near enough…' Tired out and groomed, the wee thing does exactly that – and it's a rather off-putting green-coloured liquid. But it is a novelty breed and Bill's cruelty to animals at all times policy allows him to wring the wet doggie out, stick it through the mangle and make urgent plans to visit the Graeme Garden Kennels with all due dispatch. The muted interest in their dog is not the issue any more. Graeme has been found out. Everybody is ordering novelty breeds for Crufts and Gray Bags is raking in the dosh. To put it frankly, he's a 'miserable breeder' and his fellow Goods want answers. The man in glasses has plainly gone mad. He's even crossed a dog with a mouse – yes, huge holes in the skirting board. There's the dog tortoise – memorably lifted out for a brief visual gag and quickly discarded (much to the BBC prop department's chagrin I'm sure). A French Poodle is crossed with a frog for some hopping mad mayhem and a pitiful failure with the mixture of Cocker Spaniel and parrot is quickly hidden away. The aim was to get a talking mutt but Gray ended up with a flying one instead. Still, as he gleefully admits, 'You can't win them all…' and scientists never give up. Spraying hormones and telling the poor wee doggie to 'close your eyes and think of Crufts', the cloning, cross-breeding experiments continue. But it's that Long-Haired Pug that Tim and Bill are concerned about. A novelty breed it may be, but with novelty breeds flooding the market what good is it? Well, not a lot really, particularly after it's obviously been having a bit of fun with a sexually active mate and produced a darling string of mini-white mop things. Chasing the full

speed collection of babes all over England, they playfully attack Tim like a ferret down a rabbit hole and create all sorts of visual antics to the classic *Kitten Kong* number, *Come Back*. Lacking the sheer inventiveness of that Series Two masterpiece, the knockabout interlude is quickly curtailed in favour of interior discussion as to the parentage of these little tearaways. Bill pleads his innocence and, after a bit of thought, Tim is fairly confident it wasn't him either. Graeme discovers the truth, a common duster was the father in question and if that's the case then dog and inanimate object could get together for all sorts of amazing new possibilities. With that in mind, one poor doggie is encouraged to get amorous with an armchair, with the right, soft atmosphere and Sinatra musak used to get the desired results. It's all a disgrace but the Crufts Ideal Dog Exhibition wants that sort of thing and Graeme is never one to disappoint. A barking toilet (Royal Flush King Charles) and spot-covered oven (North Sea Gas Dalmatian) are part of his wondrous menagerie but Tim holds the trump card – Bill Oddie fetchingly disguised in a dog suit and able to do just about everything. Acknowledging the fans with gusto, showing a keen sense of humour with the 'heel' moment, playing the flute and begging successfully with heart-wrenching violin tunes, Bill is a wonder dog. Indeed, Cuddly Scamp Hairy Legs of Cricklewood, to give him his full name, romps home during the motor car assembly test, picks up the cup and allows gloating Tim to gloat over a less than chuffed Graeme. A genius in the making, his obedience and intelligence are second to none and a nationwide obsession with Cuddly Scamp is heightened with his high prestige appearance on *Mastermind*. Magnus Magnusson happily goes along with the joke, asking canine clad Bill four questions on his route to victory. Bill, cross-legged in that famous black chair, timing the four simple words – woof, arf, howl and ruff – to success, it's hilarious stuff. Tim's over the moon but Graeme needs to work fast. Suddenly remembering the title of this episode, he turns to the ideals of Dr Frankenstein and aims actually to make, rather than simply create, something. The result is unspeakable – it never says a word. With an impatient 'get out of my light' the mad genius grabs for his Needlework for Beginners book, glances down his 'Chopping List' and gathers together remnants and celebrity bits 'n' pieces for the job in hand. Mind you, like a demented Dwight Frye or Marty Feldman, the idea is good but the selection is wrong –

picking out Donny Osmond's teeth, the mini brain of Nicholas Parsons, a hair (supposedly pubic) from Yul Brynner and the suitably bespectacled and bow-tied leg of Robin Day. Tim is appalled – 'You've been using people… and Donny Osmond!' Going to the gloriously Gothic roots of the book and the James Whale film, lightning plays its important part in life creation and the Champion of Champions is unleashed on the world. A six-legged *Sesame Street* reject is the result but, seriously, would you argue with it on a dark night in Oxford Street? Predictably, all hell breaks loose at the Crufts bash. Armchairs and dogs alike attack the new entrant, the show's host screams openly that he 'can't stand dogs!', the Goodies go in hot pursuit aided and abetted, once again, with the legendary *Come Back*, Frankenfido makes a speedy getaway on the trandem and a delicious opticians 'can't believe my eyes' sequence pre-empts the *Not the Nine O'Clock News* lamppost visual rearranged, reheated and revitalised by Rowan Atkinson. Before long, the panic is over, Dr Garden has dismantled and parcelled up all the Frankenfido bits and things get back to normal – or, at the very least, as normal as they can get with Bill still trapped in his doggie costume. Traumatised after his bare-back riding experience with the huge monster and having been locked away with the beastly 'bitch' for three days and nights, the anguish takes years to get over. Still unable to come to terms with his human identity and emerge from within the Cuddly Scamp persona, Bill weakly responds to his old Goodie pals and finally has to face his parental duties when a Frankenfido meets Bill Oddie puppy comes a calling.

Did You Know? The Australian Broadcasting Commission wiped the line 'Feeling sexy?' from the show.

MAGNUS MAGNUSSON. Episode Five, recorded Friday 7 March, broadcast Monday 10 March 1975, 9–9.30pm, BBC2.

SCATTY SAFARI

The team were always ready to name drop and name check variety celebs and telly legends for a good, cheap laugh at someone else's expense, and this episode is the ultimate example. Travelogue narration is a frequently used technique and the whole thing kicks off with Graeme's presentation of The Goodies Star Safari Park – with a myriad of Seventies' small screen look-a-likes, including a flea-picking Steptoe and Son, manic Tommy Cooper, limp-wristed Liberace, an interview-hungry pack of Parkinson, Harty and Frost, a trouser-dropping Brian Rix and a peacock-style Danny la Rue. The racist content of the Black

and White Minstrels is indelicately handled with an attack by the singing troop à la baboons on the safari jeep, while the arch rival *Monty Python* is mocked with a quartet of grumbling Gumbies herded away to the refrains of *The Liberty Bell*. Even in a *Python*-free age on BBC television, the Goodies couldn't resist a subtle dig at their old cohorts. The unity of comic double acts (Morecambe and Wise/Mike and Bernie Winters) is shattered with frantic fighting – note the use of Eric and Ernie's old sig tune, *Following You Around*, as accompaniment – while the intro is curtailed with the sight of Mary Poppins sinking slowly into the West. With idea established, the team can let rip with a stunning diatribe on the problems of keeping famous people in captivity. Bill has just survived a very pleasant session with a particularly frisky Eartha Kitt and merrily heaves a load of pig swill in the general direction of Oliver Reed. Pet targets – Des O'Connor, Max Bygraves, Ronnie Corbett – are tossed around the place, Graeme is less than chuffed with all the hard work and even Tim seems totally despondent. His one shining light in a miserable world is the prized star attraction – Tony Blackburn. Lavished with luxury food and drink, it's a dark hour when the famous Tony is found near death's door in his stable. Bill isn't bothered, fighting to get at his last, untouched meal and practically falling over himself to do the poor old thing to death with a shotgun. Tim, the softy with a heart of gold and respect for dumb animals ('I swear he can understand every word I say!') can't face to pull the trigger, realises he's pining – not for the fjords but for pure freedom – and bravely decides to release him back into the wild. Now, Tony is the only 'celebrity captive' to play the Goodies at their own game and actually appear on the show. Happy to send himself up rotten, Tony's brief, wordless cameo is a classic – sprinting away in slow motion to the theme of *Black Beauty*. A touching wave of fond farewell brings on Timbo's water works but the moment can't get too bogged down in pathos so a Michael Palin-style DJ-culling squire, shoots him down in cold blood and heads off in search of Jimmy Young. Poor old Tim is still blubbering back at the compound, but it's not the loss that is getting to him ('Stuff Tony Blackburn!' 'That's an idea!'), rather a Graeme-like obsession with the financial decline the death of their star will bring. A hasty replacement is required but nobody seems willing to risk the boredom of the hunt at Max Bygrave's Palladium show. Besides, Bill's heart seems set on the unknown sex goddess Doris

FORGET THE A TEAM, WE HAVE THE ECKY THUMPERS, IN A PUBLICITY SPIN-OFF FROM THE 1975 EPISODE, *KUNG FU KAPERS*

Newbold. Gray Bags has the solution, but never one to give away his genius at the first hurdle, he drags the other two down a long and winding question game. Bill and Tim struggle gamely with the clues – Australian and black beard eventually leads to the close suggestion of Rolf Atkinson, before Tim has another desperate attempt with Brenda Atkinson – and even the rhyming clue: 'Plaster of Paris', doesn't quite get to the correct solution. But once Rolf Harris is agreed on, Bill looks up his Observer's Book of Stars. Dismissing Anita, Chopper and Richard with a winning, suppressed giggle, he drives home the comedy with a summary of the great man's opinion of himself ('I'm an all-round entertainer') and almost breaks up with the classic throwaway statistic – 'number of legs – variable'. Bill is less than impressed with the onslaught of abos, dingos and upside-down jokes. Still Tim's outrageous Aussie accent brings on an amazed and hilarious reaction from Oddie, a load of stock footage (Sydney Opera House, leaping kangaroos *et al.*) sets the scene and a quick, *Mr Benn* excursion into the nearest Poms' Outfitters soon sees our

heroic lads kitted out in huge sun hats with corks (and in Bill's case, wine bottles as well) attached. It's Aussie cliché city with unsightly females spouting 'Fair dinka day', salubrious locations like Kangaroo Avenue and the entertaining prospect of wallabies wrestling in mud. But before long, the Goods are trekking through the outback in pursuit of your one and only Rolf Harris – some bloke in glasses, a beard and a very Seventies' sparkling waistcoat. Once the beast is caught (note the kindly arm rub before the misplaced injection, akin to *Kitten Kong*) and transported back home, the heat is on to keep the fellow on peak form. Graeme, allowing his body to react to the faulty thermometer – 'By gum it's hot in here!' – has a plan to bring fame and glory and a load of dosh, to the Goodies. While Bill and Tim partake in a bit of *Take Your Pick* banter (all open the box and take the money), pondering on flogging the new captive to Lew Grade and, finally, on hearing the plaintive cries of *Two Little Boys*, agreeing to keep the box closed, Graeme has cooked up his plan. He enjoys a wonderful, surreal colonial spiral, remembering the old days when thousands of Rolfs roamed the countryside before white hunters got at them for their valuable beards – ideal for lavatory brushes apparently. The only other Rolf, from Moscow Zoo, is drafted into Graeme's unsophisticated breeding programme (chucking him in the same basket as the Aussie one!) One year on and the experiment bears fruit – there's another naïve, wonderfully detailed newsreel interlude narrated by Tim. Like a *Jurassic Park* with additional facial hair, the baby Rolf is a no show at first, before staggering out of his hut, falling over himself, having a mistimed bash at painting and gingerly avoiding the dreaded watering hole before being pushed in by his lazy father. The moment when he's hit on the head by a swiftly chucked tube of lager is hilarious, but it's Bill who's laughing all the way to the bank with his fund of merchandising opportunities. Repeated visits are guaranteed by the act of nailing Baby Rolf's feet to the floor and assuring his absence from the public's gaze. Car stickers promote the little bearded rascal, there are packets of plastic Rolfs complete with a free cornflake, inflatable Rolfs guaranteed to burst and walking, talking Rolf dolls who mumble 'Tie Me Kangaroo Down Mammy!' before their heads fall off. Not only that, but in addressing the Chi Chi panda phenomenon, Bill's dug out the old cuddly bears and stuck the Rolf facial traits on to them. Clever eh! Well, no not really, for just as Bill's plan for making even more baby Rolfs for the pet market is taking space, a speechless Graeme bursts in with a bit of *Give Us a Clue* charades. It doesn't take a genius to work out that the Harrises have scarpered, although it's worth all the frantic mime just to have Tim's confident guess 'Tie me kangaroo down... tennis!' trail off into self-doubt. Another year whizzes by and the Rolf invasion is at its peak. Six million of the swines are careering round the country, playing their wobble boards and creating the new blight of graffiti with the place full of rotten paintings. Enoch Powell holds his hands up and moves to Jamaica and the BBC is over-run with Rolf – with every programme from The Dick Emery Show with Rolf Harris to Sports Night with Harris over-run by the bearded entertainers. A pied piper climax is the answer – with charmingly attired Goods and a quick rendition of *Waltzing Matilda*. Sheila Stefal's wonderfully discreet Queen Elizabeth II dishes out the promised rewards and Garden's lilting narration tells the dreaded plague tale in rhyme as the Goodies, dressed to kill and didgeridoos at the ready, tempt the Rolfs playfully away to the other side

– onto ATV. One Rolf survives, of course, the lame, Jake the peg specimen – Bill and Graeme are swamped with a thousand OBEs and blushing bride Timbo marries ever so eligible bachelor, Prince Charles.

Did You Know? *The extensive section based in and around Australia reflected the fact that The Goodies enjoyed huge success in that country. When the show was scheduled for family audiences several more adult moments were edited from the broadcast tapes with Graeme's first line of dialogue, 'I'm knackered!' biting the dust. The line was simply dubbed out, leaving a silent mouthing entrance for the bespectacled one. Several further cuts were made for the Australian video release on the Polygram label, BBC53912 and the re-issue on ABC Video 17884. Check out the almost subliminal plug for The Goodies up-and-coming hit single, Funky Gibbon – just before the lads face the Rolf Harris television take over, the back wall on the office is adorned with the lyrics 'Come on it's gibbon time'. Goon nut, Goodie fan and all round Royal good egg, Prince Charles was initially going to make a special guest appearance in this episode as himself. As part of the narrative, the Milligan-esque 'anonymous Queen' announces that her eldest son will marry who ever rids the land of Rolfs – in the end, of course, this is Tim Brooke-Taylor and, indeed, he is seen marrying the Prince via rather unconvincing archive footage and back of the head shots. The Palace decided at the last minute that Charles's real appearance would be ill advised (another tentatively agreed spot on The Morecambe and Wise Show was also curtailed), although the Royal seal of approval promoted the team to close the show with an official crest and the legend – The Goodies, By Appointment. For the only time the closing credits are backed by regal red and written in fancy, gold letter type.*

TONY BLACKBURN, SHEILA STEAFEL, DAVID WILLMOTT. Episode Six, recorded Friday 14 March, broadcast Monday 17 March 1975, 9–9.30pm, BBC2.

KUNG FU KAPERS

One of the handful of classic episodes which everybody seems to remember, it all starts with Graeme and Tim indulging in the ancient art of karate, turning on the slow motion, face contortions with realist intent before Gray stops the martial art exhibition to consult page three of his little instruction book: 'raise two fingers... no, not like that!' as Tim goes for the common denominator, but it's not all Bruce Lee and television violence. Graeme knows the secret of delayed reaction and with a few ticklish taps and fondles Tim's completely dead – well, near enough. His outlandish, pained reaction delights the audience and there's even room for a quick Funky Gibbon motion in there – a later plug for the single comes with the office wall graffiti, 'It's still gibbon time'. But Bill Oddie is none too impressed with all this phoney baloney oriental stuff, he's a master at that Northern deadly art, Ecky Thump. Intrigued and anxious, the lads listen to this wry old black pudding-consuming bloke as he flashes back through rippled screen effect to the glories of Rochdale. Andes pan pipes merge from ancient tunes to the refrains of *Ooh, I Do Like To Be Beside the Seaside*, as Bill's Lancastrian mythology is related. The road t'enlightenment was a long and painful one, searching out the Mystic East – a delightful fish 'n' chip shop – and being cleansed for the battle of mind over matter to follow with the heavily scented luxury of Ajax… Size does matter where Ecky Thump is concerned and, starting out with a wee cloth cap, the goal is to the giant cap of the Grand Master – and, eh, he was grand. Complete with Grasshopper eyes and an air of mystery, the main man leads his disciples through black pudding eating, chip buttie eating and throwing up synchronisation, before our Bill finally lands his black belt and braces. Tim and Graeme, blood thirsty and eager to improve their skills – want a demonstration of all this Northern business but peace-loving Bill refuses. The art is far too dangerous for the likes of those two and no amount of name calling and provocation will make Oddie's sap rise… he would rather commit Harry Corbett! Not even Graeme's heartless taunt about him being a Chelsea Supporter provokes him. But finally, with relatives from all over the world name dropped (from Uncle Taffy's 'Yaki-Da!' to Uncle Izzy's Golders Green 'Oi Voi!') and martial art justified, Bill declares war, names Primrose Hill as the site and prepares to beat all comers with his Ecky Thump technique. As per usual, Tim's dulcet tones are dubbed for the boxing barker as Bill simply rules the roost via a swift wallop on the head with his trusty black pudding. Graeme and Tim take it in turns – playing various incumbents of ancient skill without any success at all. Tim's Frenchman, complete with stick of bread, and Scots Bagpipe expert, both feel the weigh of Bill's pudding. No one is safe and the Ecky Thump craze is the result. Bill's cashing in at 10 quid a lesson, *Nationwide's* Michael Barratt reports on the all encompassing trend for pudding bashing and a seemingly never-ending session of big screen adventures invade the cinema – ranging from Big Pud to the immortal Disney classic Ecky Thump Meets Mary Poppins. The nation has gone pudding mad and it's up to Tim and Graeme to save the day. Bill, playing the *Coronation Street* theme, enjoying a Rank Gong type bloke bashing his tin bath and sitting, lotus position, in deep,

Northern concentration, welcomes the lads in for the ancient tea ceremony. Tim is in plaster and stuck in the karate chop position so spillage is on the cards but Bill's not bothered about that. He's hell bent on world domination with his little Chairman Mao inspired red book and pudding devotion. But Graeme spots his weakness. As he says, 'He's useless without his pudding…' and after a nice innuendo from Tim ('Who isn't!'), it's off to sabotage the pudding mixture at Peckinpah's Perfect Puddings. After a dramatic fall in the mixture, Graeme's radio-controlled receivers gum up the works with scientific genius and Bill's march for the common man – black and white, Einstein homage merging into colour Goodies slapstick – sets up the final battle. Flying leaps, raining puddings, angry chops and cunning plans all get thrown into the musical, visual climax which culminates in a youthful *Last of the Summer Wine*-like tea trolley descend down a slope and over a mountain. With nowhere else to go, the Goodies seemingly dead and gone and the Ecky Thump trend gone with them, Tim's earnestly serious BBC voiceover chappie intones the dangers of practising the martial art without full knowledge and the show ends. Just to enforce the coldness and mysteriousness of the climax, the credits are played out over a clouded sky as the Ecky Thump legend fades away.

Did You Know? This classic episode sprang from two separate suggestions for the new series – one, an affectionately mocking tribute to Bill's Northern roots, and the other, an all-out parody of the Martial Arts craze cooked up via the David Carradine television series Kung Fu. The genius was in bringing the two together. When this episode was first screened in 1975 the hilarity proved too much for one viewer. Scots bricklayer, Alex Mitchell, was so tickled at the sight of Tim defending himself with his bagpipes that he started laughing uproariously. Once he had started he just couldn't stop and the laughing convolutions continued throughout the programme. The strain was too much for the man's heart and with a final huge laugh just before the closing credits, the poor chap passed away. Reported in the newspapers as Man of Fun Dies Laughing, the BBC expressed their deepest regrets to his widow but Mrs Mitchell penned a letter to the Goodies thanking them for making her husband's last moments so happy. Comedy that can kill you – that's powerful.

MICHAEL BARRATT, RICHARD PESCUD, WILLIAM F SULLY. Episode Seven, recorded Friday 21 March, broadcast Monday 24 March 1975, 9–9.30pm, BBC2.

LIGHTHOUSE KEEPING LOONIES

The Goodies delivered their tightest scripts when they were locked in a room together and allowed to talk about life, the universe and everything. The definitive example is *The End* which rounds off this series, but this episode is a wonderful dry run packed with banter teetering on the edge of insanity and a catastrophic setting which tests the trio's tolerance to breaking point. Where better for a load of tight-knit isolation than the Jolly Rock Lighthouse – a five-year assignment misunderstood by gallant Graeme who read the advertisement as a little light housekeeping! Bolshy Bill is complaining from the outset but Tim, a born chinless leader with a very unstiff upper lip, immediately takes charge of the situation. His whistling, authoritative barking and job allocating to his designated 'number twos' really does the trick before Bill throws a hefty spanner in the works and almost gets tempted into some expected back chat. Mind you, Gray Bags has already swallowed the bait and set to work on the light. He turns on the radio for a bit of light relief and gets *A Walk in the Black Forest*. Clearly, Radio Goodies is still running from Series One and they still haven't found another record to play. Garden's visual bit of business (reading his book by following the light round and casting a wonderfully unconvincing silhouette on the white cliffs of Dover), ushers in its own musical gag with a burst of *Carousel*. But while Graeme has hours of fun with hand shadows, Bill is stamping his little feet in starved frustration – was there ever a time when Bill wasn't hungry? His drop into Northern mannerisms results in some ungraceful mickey taking from Tim, a sarcastic invitation to do Jimmy Cagney and a bit of unsuccessful fishing. The show's highlight comes in extended bickering between the worker and the toff. There's always a sense of danger round every corner when Oddie and Brooke-Taylor get at each other's throats and in the confined, suffocating atmosphere of a lighthouse there's a real powder keg about to explode. Although having been incarcerated for just over five minutes Bill is already cracking up. Obsessed with the roundness of everything he starts smashing records and, even, shock, horror, turning down his food – a rounder than round hamburger. Breaking out of mere anger into childish, bemused muttering ('The shape of the tray is round!'), it's a spiralling performance of twitching madness modified only by the calming ritual humiliation of Timbo – a round lemon meringue pie nestles nicely into his face. Out of the script for far too long, Graeme staggers back into the action in moth-attacked clothing to keep this wonderful, purple patch going. A jolly sea shanty is the name of the game and the lads are delighted to find a cheerful little ditty dedicated to their very own light. *Don't Go to the Jolly Rock*

may start off full of energetic, arm-swinging gusto, and the lads even proudly do a little Shadows (sans guitars) step routine, but the murderous references, censored nasty bits and deathly threats quickly sap the happy-go-lucky passion from the upbeat chorus. Bill and Graeme are playing cards with a round deck, Tim is soon down with the mumps screaming 'Can you hear me!' to little avail, the fuel is down to nothing and the gag quota is doing its best to join it, but there's some effective mincing messages from the shipping forecast, Bill enjoys his own 'Cross channel fairy!' comment and the old-fashioned ways come into their own with a return to candle power – with Bill strapping one to his head. Desperate times need desperate actions and after some hopeless rocket prat-falling and fine against wind mime business, Graeme becomes a human fog horn (by swallowing the mechanism) and dishes out polite, warning announcements to anyone who cares to listen. Tim, by contrast, is not calm at all. In fact, he's very, very uncalm indeed, even reciting Status Quo hits ('down, down, deeper and down') in his brain-addled state. A regal wave and two finger salute from Prince Philip as the Royal barge inches by, sort of perks him up. But it's burrowing Bill, digging for North Sea oil, who saves the tedium. Turning on the cocky unionist attitude, Oddie rants on about bad conditions, hard hat regulations and capitalistic desire to get a slice of the financial action. However, he may find oil (as well as North sea coal), but a foolhardy lighting of his can sets the stuff ablaze and any amount of kitsch, oh so Seventies, hole-bunging, can not save the day. Woodall's dead pan news report juxtaposes the UFO fever with the missing lighthouse story without connecting the two, and includes a flash of Swedish nudity (the last naked breast to grace a *Goodies* show), very unsubtle royal photo fits and, best of all, a totally out of his head bit from series favourite Patrick Moore, merrily leading the nation down a twisting, turning search for space objects. Careering around at 150,000 feet above the earth, Tim's rubber duck and bath water are in for a bumpy ride as Graeme and Bill try and get the flying lighthouse under control. A little fuel shortage speeds things up with the plummeting missile making a soft landing on top of Nelson's Column. Tim's mumps are cured – he's passed them on to his two fellow Goods – but panic stations are still at red alert as the Central London stranded lighthouse succeeds in attracting a seriously off-course ship to sail through the streets of London.

Did You Know? *The Australian Broadcasting Commission edited the naked lady out of the Woodall news report. The lighthouse lamp room set had previously been used in the Dad's Army episode Put That Light Out.*

CORBETT WOODALL, PATRICK MOORE. Episode Eight, recorded Friday 28 February and Friday 28 March, broadcast Monday 31 March 1975, 9–9.30pm, BBC2.

ROME ANTICS

Coming between *Carry On Cleo* and *Monty Python's Life of Brian*, this is the Goodies having a bash at the Roman Empire, reassuringly adopting elements of innuendo and surrealism. The outlandish, Max Wall-like arena entrance, circus-based mayhem and, in particular, Tim's dangerous battle with the killer, rather inanimate, stuffed sheep from *The Lost Tribe* – to the sound of fledgling *Funky Farm* grooves – is certainly in the *Monty Python* mood. The explanation that all the lions have been consumed by the Christians and that, now, in this sheep-fearing environment, the threat of being thrown to the old grass chompers can send grown men – well, at least, the Goodies – into total shock, is a memorable one. However, for all that, the unseen hand of Talbot Rothwell is most at play here. Phallic symbolism, high camp and a trio of luscious slave girls are all major parts of the narrative and Tim – determined to out do Charles Hawtrey's single musical variation on 'home' to 'Rome' – injects snatches of song throughout. *Carry On's There's No Place Like Rome* gets in, as does Sir Harry Launder's early classic, *Roman in the Gloamin'* and the immortal *Rome Cooking!* Graeme's 'hail' comment allows Tim the 'no time for a weather forecast' joke and even the armless and headless Venus de Milo is shown to be the result of careless coat hanging. Further comic signposts are included, George Formby-a-like playing primitive uke in the Roman band and a couple of sightings of the Goons' Mukkinesse Battlehorn – cropping up first of all as Bill Oddie makes his initial appearance bravely trying to play *The Goodies Theme*. Rome AD55 is our eventual setting, with Graeme Garden's earnest voiceover setting the scene. Cricklewood's finest are open for business and Bill's in full rant mode. Contemporary concern for Britain's failing might, the common market and immigration is played out by Bill's militant aggressor. It may be the dark ages when opening a window dictates knocking a hole in the wall and Graeme's glasses are still in primitive square style, but Bill's concerns are bang up to date. The country has gone Rome mad, with motorways ruining the countryside, traditional English delights being whittled away and an influx of Roman Johnnies, smelling differently – that's clean, as

Graeme cannily points out – talking differently and behaving differently. Bill's passion for the familiar way of life latches on to Tim's patriotic glory with more bite thrown in, but even Bill can't stomach Brooke-Taylor's heartfelt, Rule Britannia stance on the situation. Bill's hilarious reaction, 'God, here we go...' mutes the full flow of passion but Tim's main interest is his new container of blue woad. Party time is here but Bill's not happy. Despite Tim's glorious lapsing into corny song and pun – Keep Right on 'til the End of the Woad, Roman Woad and the like – Bill's dismissive of the new Britain solely based round Roman tourism and the interest in new culture. What seems like light years before John Cleese ranted about what the bloody Romans had done for us, Bill condemns the beauty of Stonehenge and, unwittingly, reveals the centuries-old riddle concerning what it is – 'it still doesn't fly!' – but each and every one of the lads pulls their weight when the Roman messenger comes a'calling. Spouting Latin like a native and even confusing the genius that is Graeme Garden – he settles for a few moments of gibberish, a grab of the message and a brilliant embrace of Frankie Howerd's *Up Pompeii* performance supremacy with a hasty, 'Get off!' to the support player. Message received and understood the Goods are off to meet Nero. After the primitive wooden trandem collapses, it's a case of long straight roads (all of which do indeed lead to Rome), into trees, down slopes – that immortal trio drop that would later enhance the opening credit sequence – and even under the sea, the boys make their way to work and, ultimately, an audience with the great Emperor – or should that be Queen Nero. Roy Kinnear goes for it as Nero. Camp in the extreme and obsessed with copious amounts of fruit, particularly the old variety, unsurprisingly he delights in sexually fondling an over-ripe pear and squeezing the juice down his arm. Check out Bill cracking up as Roy mutters on about pears and their 'soft sensuous bulbous botties!' Making his first appearance surrounded by fruit, glam girls and singing *It's a Good Life*, Roy storms through his brief appearance, delighting in his kinky reputation, taking a shine to the overtly heterosexual Bill and dishing out the 'chucky boots' name calling with relish. Latching on to sub-Bona chat, Roy is wounded that his subjects dismiss his fruit and market gardening-based entertainments and calls in Gray and Tim, listening outside the door, to liven things up a bit. All that sheep-based circus stuff doesn't hit the spot, Roy is pelted with fruit and –

TIM DOES HIS MOOSE IMPRESSION FOR GOODIE PUBLICITY!

much to his renewed interest, intriguingly shaped veg. He's unsatisfied. Fed up with the never-ending line of ruddy orgies, his weaning affection for the decadent lifestyle has already been pinpointed when jelly, cream and a cherry on top lovingly placed on his bare chest and licked off by his three girls, is boringly labelled 'the same old tongues!' But Tim's quite keen on the job description and happily takes over the asses milk and massage life of a great ruler. Gray Bags, the newly appointed entertainment manager, has the answer to the Emperor's problem by recreating the place in the style of 20th Century Blackpool. A winning sales pitch jokingly sets the scene and ancient Rome goes all seaside with a Pathé newsreel – dubbed Partheon News. Tim's joyous narration taps into all the usual, heavy-handed smutty gags. Nudge, nudge, wink, wink reaction to a beautiful pair is finished off with 'of breasts' to rip the Max Miller double entendres away. Gray's done wrong, invited all the worse elements of society to Rome and like Brighton's mods and rockers invasion, the resort is about to be over run by Attila the Hun and his smash and grab

vandals. Bathing beauties, Blackpool musicians and the fun of the fair are all swept away by the sinisterly grinning, bearded nut-case, and to the tune of Bill's unvalued *Big, Brave, Bold Hunk of Man*, the place falls to the ground, the lads fight back and, in so doing, invent the Olympic Games – right down to the five hoop-la hoops forming the five rings and Tim's huge burning ice cream paving the way for the sacred flame. Tim's smashing of an In Case Of Fire cabinet to find his fiddle for when Rome burns is a great visual. As the three make a hasty retreat, the road sign for Pompeii is spotted and clear warning for subsidence is ignored as the lads fall into the volcanic pit and face another adventure.

Did You Know? *The team had great fun with guest star Roy Kinnear, returning after the delightfully corny banter of The Lost Tribe to excel as Nero. Tim remembers working with the gloriously undisciplined actor, 'What was frustrating about Roy was that he was such a generous guy he would never do the same performance twice! Every rehearsal was different and on the show it was just luck if you got a good one or not. He always felt he was letting people down if he did something similar.'*

The Australian Broadcasting Commission cut a great chunk out of the Roy Kinnear attempted seduction of Bill Oddie. Even more interestingly, in a twisted reflection of the later reinstatement of Laurence Olivier's attraction to Tony Curtis in Stanley Kubrick's Spartacus, these missing scenes were replaced for screenings from 1987. In 1996 a poster campaign for vodka used an image of stone-age, fur clad Goodies from this episode with the caption, 'Good Clean Fun'. A brief clip from this episode – as Graeme explains the Blackpool-style Rome – was featured in the opening episode of the BBC comedy retrospective, Laughing For Ages introduced by Stephen Tomkinson in January 1999.

ROY KINNEAR, OLIVER GILBERT. Episode Nine, recorded Friday 4 April 1975, broadcast Monday 7 April 1975, 9–9.30pm, BBC2.

CUNNING STUNTS

In this the *Goodies'* greatest series, even those episodes which, on the surface look fairly routine, bristle with complex sub-text and potent comic references. The best example is this often neglected gem which launches a three-pronged narrative attack on the senses, shifting gear constantly, tossing in subtle intertextuality and sexual role reversals with an almost throwaway grandeur that's too much for a mere half hour. The major plot hook is our lad's busy, busy newspaper – The Goodies Clarion and Globe – brilliantly latching on to all the *His Girl Friday* reporter clichés with Tim's action-packed chief at the city desk and Graeme's eager beaver reporter, wise-cracking, talking 10 to the dozen and dishing the dirt on anything that moves. The telling touches are the typically British slant on Thirties' US print hounds, delving into the sleazy underbelly of society, feeding an all-consuming compassion for 'big bosoms' of any variety and, most telling of all, stripping bare the fast, efficient workings immediately to highlight the overworked truth that Tim mans every department in a pathetic attempt to impress the outside world. But then again, the real office drag is Bill, sitting around the place in a bewitched, lovesick trance, unable to respond, full of dreamy, impossible thoughts of romance and totally hopeless. His lonely, dumbstruck stroll through the killing fields of Cricklewood – with robbers, murderers, Cheeky Charlie giving a regal flash and burning houses going unnoticed, makes no impression at all. The poor little rich girl who has captured his heart – Muriel Makepiece as brilliantly played by Tessa Wyatt – is caught in a fairytale situation, with a rich uncle, plenty of admirers and plenty of ambition. Her employment in the Goodies office sets up a finely crafted section of sexual tension, power performance and genre stereotype twisting. Tim gamely defends the enrolment of a blonde, leggy, shapely, pert bum possessing young lady. Tim's sexual attraction is a shameful, suppressed urge which is, very unsuccessfully, masked by copious amounts of praise for her work. But being a man, obsessed with a bit of the other, he can't help dropping into more and more extreme speeches of admiration for her physical qualities. One can almost see the feminist hackles rising as the scene is played out, particularly when the experienced Bill clarifies Wyatt's sexual prowess and the charming lovely in question doesn't even register the conversation shooting round about her. But the whole issue is turned completely on its head within minutes. With Bill out of the way and the office running like a well-oiled machine, Wyatt turns on the hard-nosed authority and barks out orders as if she owns the place. Not only that, she takes on the obligatory sexual clichés of the male boss in authority, treating Tim and Graeme like the sex toy girlies in the typing pool. A career-orientated, power-dressing bit of 'crumpet' with sexual predator written all over her, she pinches the bum of Tim, flirts with the pitifully rejected Graeme and cockily projects a persona of good time fun. Branded a 'female chauvinist sow' in one of Tim's moments of bravery (his sudden, hands on hip bark of 'Women!' instantly fades to a tearful, gibbering wreck), the super cool Wyatt dismisses him as nothing more than a 'pretty little thing' and pulls Graeme through the hoop in a priceless, knee-trembling moment as he gingerly sits on her lap. However, the constant thematic target throughout this episode is even better. Bill must make his lady love's miserable father, Sir Joshua Makepiece (*Goodies* regular Ronald MacLeod), laugh in order to win her hand in marriage. With Tim's headlines and circulation figures buzzing in his head, Bill's quest to land his wealthy babe, is ably assisted by his old chums, journeying down to Makepiece Mansion to provide a crash course in the art of joke telling. Heralded by Timbo's cheerful, rousing rendition of *Make 'Em Laugh*, repeated feed lines from Tim and Graeme attempt to impart comic timing to a sheepish Bill. He's clearly no Max Miller, he's not even a Bernard Manning, so the tone is lowered in favour of more obvious comedy. Funny noises and visual humour are brought into play – donning Oddie in ginger fright wig, glasses and buck teeth. Problem is, it makes him a mirror image of the humourless Makepiece and hardly makes the best conditions for a laughter fest. Bill's failure leads to the very deconstruction of the sainted

Goodies team. Their mainstay of visual humour has already been condemned as 'unsubtle' by Graeme and now the three-man team become two looking for a replacement. Little echoes of past glories pepper the show, Oddie's constantly healthy appetite is addressed: his parting gift – a piece of cheese inscribed with his full name, William Edgar, although misspelling the Oddie bit – sets his working class loser in *Goodies* mythology. Tim and Graeme's speech looking down on him is a reference back to the legendary Cleese/Corbett/Barker class system from *The Frost Report*. Even more cutting is the dismissal of his *Goodies* persona – not only is mainstream talent like Ernie Wise considered but the ad strictly forbids 'stuffy, hairy, frustrated pop stars!' Royal approval is again lavished on the team, with Prince Charles trying to get in on the act, while Goonish tradition is highlighted by Tim's dubbing of the Prince as 'Bluebottle'. Even the Monty Python boys, having delivered their five-man strong last season just the previous year, seem to want to get involved. Graeme's outraged reaction to *The Liberty Bell* gets an instant laugh before the comic relevance is stripped away with his 'Band of the Coldstream Guards' identification. In the end, pathos seems the funniest thing around and not just comic tragedy but real-life tragedy. Bill's tale of woe to Wyatt's father results in fits of shared laughter – check out Bill's trouser patch 'Kiss My Ass' – and the return of the singing, lovesick fool, tossing flowers all over the place, laughing at Tim's loveable jokes (putting the paper to bed) and grabbing Graeme's fuzzy chops with real affection. Of course, the hurtful truth (that he's been replaced by his girlfriend) and the timely portable mood music, results in a barrage of unsuccessful suicide attempts before he does something silly and puts himself up as the sole entrant for The Eurovision Raving Loony Contest. The Katie Boyle parody (Karin MacCarthy's Katie Pimple) and the reading of the *Radio Times* dig ('who the hell does!') acts as a perfect introduction to the self-destructive mugging of the competition. Bill (out to win, i.e. kill himself) is protected all the way by his two track-suited pals (as the Rest of the World team), whose manic mugging (falling all over the place as Fritz and Fratz) and selfless attempts to save him merely result in all the hidden dangers hitting them. The ultimate visual joke – banana skin slipping – and Oddie's classic song, *Crazy Man*, just add the finishing touches of greatness. The celebrated collapsing ladder sequence would later be adopted for the opening credits. A

touching, airborne reunion, with Bill emotionally commenting 'we had some good times together didn't we!', pulls the unit back together again in a glorious fashion. But previously heartless treatment of loveable Bill results in their, serves them right, joint winning of the contest – bandaged, battered and bruised, Tim and Graeme have learnt their lesson and, cartoon-like, will return to normal health for business as unusual next week!

Did You Know? *Copious cuts were enforced by the Australian Broadcasting Commission with references to bosoms, crumpet, 'upside-down with a goat', Tim's sexist remarks about Mildred's body in terms of her work ability and the 'up yours' being removed. And how the lads got away with that very risqué Spoonerism title heaven alone knows! The monthly newsletter published by The Goodies Rule OK Fan Club is named The Clarion & Globe after the newspaper published from the Goodies office in this episode.*

TESSA WYATT, ROLAND MacLEOD, KARIN MacCARTHY. Episode 10, recorded Friday 11 April, broadcast Monday 14 April 1975, 9–9.30pm, BBC2.

SOUTH AFRICA

The most maligned episode of *The Goodies*, this is, ironically, one of the funniest, cleverest and most politically challenging efforts from the team. It also showcases universally excellent work from the trio and their guest star and delights in a prime slice of old value upper class Englishness from Garden and Brooke-Taylor which echoes their glorious sparring from *Broaden Your Mind*. So why is this classic so hard to come across? Well, it's obvious really. The dreaded question of racist comedy rears its ugly head and, to be fair, although the entire point of the show is to illustrate the ridiculousness of racism and, as with admittedly, less subtle comedies like *Mind Your Language* and *Love Thy Neighbour*, the racist question is addressed and tackled with understanding, there are a lot of derogatory terms flying around in the early part of this programme. Philip Madoc's bombastic figure of authority is the most Sarth Efrikkan South African ever captured on film, Tim's black-faced minstrel mugging injects plenty of tongue-in-cheek references to the black situation in the oppressed country and Graeme Garden's funny, albeit, slightly uncomfortable, trawl through racial stereotypes would raise a few eyebrows today – all fuzzy hair comments, a sister called Topsy and a father who was a bus conductor. However, the whole point of the show is to highlight the racist situation in South Africa as totally unacceptable and if that means starkly bringing prestigious and unpleasant terminology into the open then the satirical joke benefits fully from it. Madoc gives a towering comic performance, barking out threats to Garden's reasoning enquiries ('Kill 'im!'), reacting with shocked outrage as his hand takes on a darker hue through his shades and frantically painting everything white, even down to Gray's rather suspect brown tie. He is desperately press ganging whites from British streets and carting them off for African immigration while his office is a white haven, full of coffee with milk and milk, a piano (with the black and white keys separate) and a front door sign spelling things out completely – 'Through door and turn white'. The joke is laboured to the point of extreme but the playing is peerless and Madoc's dead pan answer to Garden's black and white film query ('Just white!') may be obvious, but the sincerity and cynicism of the intonation is breathtaking. The Goodies are hired to make over South Africa's image and attract white supremacy back to the country. Tim's thigh-slapping, Al Jolson-fashioned fun seeker proclaims the land of the free, business opportunities (Sambo enterprises no less) and the joys of nature – Graeme's knowing host celebrates the dodgy lion (a dog with some wild hair) and the Springbok, only to suggest the glories of shooting and throwing in 'but only with a camera'. The film isn't exactly what the racist ordered and Madoc isn't a bloke to flow with the humour: brutal threats see the trio packed off to the land of apartheid. Surprise, surprise, Madoc is there to greet them, reduced to immigration officer thanks to the influx of British blacks flocking into South Africa, not really liking what they see and suggesting all the native blacks sample the delights of the land of hope and glory. Madoc reveals his human side with some perverted Wordsworth-style poetry and his blubbering admission that he'll miss the coloured Africans – simply, it has to be said, because he rather enjoyed the blanket abuse he thrust on them. But now it's down to the real heart of the comedy. Oddie's sherbet-sucking, carefree racist sees poor old Tim tripping over Garden with his broom as he takes on the lowly, slave labour chores of the departed coloured population. Ever ready to stand tall and pontificate on nationalist issues, Tim becries Oddie's outrageous clichés and off the cuff remarks to defend the man behind the skin colour, laudably protecting the individual against abuse by other nations. The fact that he falls into Bill's jokey trap about doing all the work because the nig nogs have gone, not withstanding, this is the core of the script, decrying racist remarks and sending up the idea of segregation with a replacement notion. At a time when the BBC had heavy connections with the country, trade sanctions were being imposed and international concern over South African's mentality was at its height, this was also cutting edge comedy of the bravest type. Madoc's gleeful re-entry à la Tarzan, ushers in the new repression for South Africa. She has suffered apartheid, now it's a case of apart-height, and that mouthy little devil, Oddie, is at the centre of the torment. Folk who come in under a recognised height chart are now the new second class citizen and Bill, bless him, just doesn't have the inches! The rest of the episode runs with this new minority situation, setting up small people in the same, looked down on light as the old coloured residents. The notion of separation becomes ridiculous – and that my friends, is the powerful point behind this entire half hour of classic Goodies comedy. In the funniest sequence in the show, the team go through the new motions via instruction manuals. Meanwhile, Tim lords it as the upwardly mobile 'Big un' population as Oddie cowls and boot licks as the gravel-voiced 'Little un', reading from the booklet and delightfully accepting his 'kick up the bum'. There's one moment of revenge as Tim reacts to the 'great white Queen' comment but, by and large, it's all doom and gloom for Oddie's all singing, all dancing slave – receiving death threats from Madoc, forcing out 'it will be an honour, bwana!' and finally seeing Garden succumb to the colonial ways. It's a wickedly funny and important piece of comedy. A WWII air raid siren calls curfew for the tiny ones but Oddie, ever the rebel, decides to let his legs do the walking and his mouth do the very fast talking. Accompanied by his undervalued song, *Run!*, Oddie bombs through the South African police state with a myriad of visual hiding tricks. Despite the rather obvious pleasures of little Bill encased under a tall shop dummy and the split screen business at the swimming pool, the most effective laughs come from the infiltration of the new discrimination into the high street with various anti-small posters – Snow White's Seven Dwarfs and Ronnie Corbett are banned from the country. Sadly, freedom never lasts for long particularly in a half-hour comedy show, and Bill's soon herded into the compound – just him and a load of pseudo-jockeys employed by the Beeb between panto seasons. On the other side of life's rich pageant, Tim and Gray are whooping it up in their nice clean white jackets, their upper class, semi-bickering hunting chat, abuse of their jockey houseboy, Lester, and free for all mosquito slapping. A day-time trek through the sinister African plains is peerlessly heralded with Tim and Graeme's mood music interlude, as Oddie, leading the battle from the front, goes into tiny but beautiful attack backed by another of his songs, *I'm Small*. With arrows and step ladders, the little 'uns make their stand and win the day. In the heat of glory, Madoc literally loses his head, Oddie ushers in the respected Prime Minister and a bit of body mutilating pantomime banter sees the lads shipped back to England, with the sainted Oddie in tow. But pity them, dear reader, for Tim is wide of the mark when he bravely utters 'England will never change!' The coloured population have completely taken over, the whites are now the second class citizens, Enoch Powell (as played by Oscar James) is ranting about keeping Britain Black and, shock, horror, even the Queen has been sucked into the situation. The Goods, holding their hands up, head for the nearest boot polish and blend in, baby. Now, this may offend some people, certainly at the time it merely fitted the bill of a comedy show within a BBC that prided itself on *The Black and White Minstrels*. But the whole issue at stake is whether the Goodies are mocking or reinventing. Clearly, it is the white population who are questioned and mocked, simply following any notion of minority as long as their supremacy is rock solid. In terms of the black situation, all this programme does is tell it exactly how it was – if we laugh then we also accept the conflict of interest and the responsibility to change.

Did You Know? *Even 20 years on and in the aftermath of 1980's political correctness, the satirical edge to this classic episode was still misread and misunderstood. When the team's back catalogue proved a popular time filler on cable television, this show was permanently left on the shelf – indeed, it was labelled 'Racist – Do Not Use For UK Gold'.*

PHILIP MADOC, OSCAR JAMES, ALBERT WILKINSON. Episode 11, recorded Friday 13 December 1974 and Friday 11 April, broadcast Monday 21 April 1975, 9–9.30pm, BBC2.

THE BUNFIGHT AT THE OK TEA ROOMS

This is the show where Graeme Garden falls off that forlorn stuffed mule – an image later used in the show's opening credits. However, this pleasure is yet to come as we see sad old Tim mending his hankie with parts of his trousers and Bill freezing by an open candle. In the wake of the *Beanstalk*'s beginning, one would think the Goods have been as poor as poor could be, but this is, apparently, rock bottom. As per usual it's all Graeme's fault, throwing away all the spare cash on a load of gold prospecting gear. The stuff obviously works because it

picks out Tim's gold teeth in a flash and tempts the dubious twosome to follow the bespectacled one on his 'Go West Young Man' ego trip. This show is visually top heavy with gallons of slapstick, silent movie sight gags and plenty of ribbing against the wild wilderness of the West. And what better for musical backing than that Oddie composition, *Walking the Line* – and this is the Bill solo mix not available on any record. The mule's a dead donkey and a huge carrot is hardly the winning formula to perk him up but those prospecting boys are doing their stuff, with Tim's traditional panning technique producing gold jewellery and Bill's frying pan offering up tasty sausages. It's an uncomfortable night under canvas for our two lakeside gold diggers and all this comic Western business needs is a rude, British culture shock awakening. For this is not Arizona but the West of England, namely, Cornwall… and clever old Gray Bags has discovered a very rich stream of Cornish cream. Any excuse for some wonderfully corny gag telling ('Gold Ore!' 'Ore!' 'Or Something else!') and the dream of untold riches, leads the lads into hard, hard work for some more visual delights as Graeme takes things easy, his wacky, labour-saving inventions see him enjoy the life of Riley and the other boys do all the work. Unionist revolts and threats of downing tools cut no ice with Mr Cool Graeme, the Cornish cream fever grips the nation (plenty of archive footage and sepia Timbo in the best Butch Cassidy tradition) – but in Camp Goodies, the message goes out to trust no one. Hatred stirs within the ranks, Garden reveals Oddie's attack on Brooke-Taylor's beloved Royal collection and the shall we sleep or shall we wake now routine leads things down an ever more cunning path. The comic highlight comes with gullible Timbo succumbing to the evilly intended lullaby, only to break out of slumber at the last minute and join the team together in a rousing, sleep-inducing climax. Always one to break away from the Goodie unity, Garden slips into his nasty Western baddie mode with ease – he notably masks the early attempt to hoodwink his pals with a throwaway 'but worth a try…' comment. But it's his Garden with no name, Clint-esque persona, that really digs in deep. He may have trouble keeping his donkey between his legs, but this black-clad swine is the full comic business, filing his cream claim, alienating his old pals and schemingly spying on their strawberry jam strike. Scones are discovered close by and the British class struggle is effortlessly injected into the raw Western ideal with the hilarious, ever-building and on-going battle over scone pronunciation. But the town of Pinnenick, quietly enjoying its cream teas, is well prepared for the Western show down – cream cakes are consumed in the garish atmosphere of a two bit saloon, the shapely waitresses whiz the steaming cups down the bar. The scene is set with a Groucho-like piano banger, Tim's nasty but nice chair kicking and the onslaught of *The Sting* ragtime score to add musical tension to the card game – based round the notion of cream tea at Dodge City. Garden looks every inch the gambling dude, rolls dice with sugar cubes, shuffles his toast playing cards and whips out his cookie chips. Things get far too rich for Tim's blood, with the emergence of fruit cakes and Cornish pastries, Gray's notorious cheating (getting a fresh hand via a none too cleverly concealed toaster) is dramatically discovered, and the final gun slinger show down is captured with pounding cowboy boots, mysterious shadows on the wall and Oddie's nerve-jangling *Ballad of the OK Tea Rooms*. The nonchalant sight gags (the poor bloke boarding up his home only to find himself on the outside trying to get in) and the crazy Western names (Wild Bill Oddie and Texas Tim), add extra comic sweep to this terrifying, heartless, Sam Peckinpah-style, tomato sauce battle. But this is not just a landmark *Goodies* moment and it's not just a case of permanently setting a Seventies' food dispenser in comic context. No, the three quite clearly, also invent the phenomenon of paint balling in this sequence as well! Light among the shade, Tim's sheepish grin into camera when his squirter fails to deliver is a mere glint of relief from the realistic Western carnage performed in foodie terminology. At the end of the shoot out, the place looks like the climax of Hamlet. Bodies litter the street, Garden's money-grabbing villain finds life without love futile and the closing seconds are reassuringly unreassuring. There isn't an ounce of redemption or upbeat comedy before that oh-so-familiar theme tune jars the imagery and plays into eternity. Even the closing credits are painted in blood red paint – what a way to go!

Did You Know? Forget paint balling and fast food, look out for an early, cunning example of product placement in the opening sequence. During Garden's gold rush rubbish, the blackboard behind him clearly bears the legend 'Buy Funky Gibbon' – the single was already riding high in the charts when this show first aired.

Episode 12, recorded Friday 18 April, broadcast Monday 28 April 1975, 9–9.30pm, BBC2.

THE END

This is Goodies comedy in its purest sense, just the three in a single set for the entire half hour – only the usual disconnected voices of authority, broadcasting (Woodall) and regal (Steafel), penetrate into the plot. The rest is the Goodies bickering, bantering, bonding and battling their way through a lifetime of imprisonment. Everything starts with bird-watching Bill eulogising on the glories of Kew Gardens before, ironically, turning the tables and blowing the tranquil sight to kingdom come. Graeme doesn't really care either way, for he is in league with the notorious Harry Highrise, fiendish property developer intent on covering our green and pleasant land with tons of concrete. The scientific chap, bombarded by the offer he couldn't refuse of £50,000, has come up with a wicked scheme. Tim is rather cross. In fact, he's at his most impassioned, patriotic and royal – sparks are going to fly and it's poor old money-grabbing Graeme that's in the firing line. Of course, Tim, bless him, is so fired up he's a tad confused, he forgets the Queen's address (room for plenty of homophobia– Grayson, La Rue – and footie – Park Rangers) before he is calmed down enough to dictate a letter which Garden eagerly scribbles down. Still the penny doesn't drop and Graeme, after years of having his name remorselessly misspelled, joyously sends it all up as Timbo clarifies the spelling ('that's G. R. A. E. M. E!') and he angrily crosses out his previous attempt. Outraged and bemused, but still able to make polite inquiries for three OBEs, Tim hardly has a chance to fume before the office is encased in a load of concrete. Things are looking pretty bleak for the boys. The days tick by, Tim's beloved Monarch lets them down and the Ministry of Works call a strike at the crucial second and leaves Graeme hanging on the telephone for six months. In another Garden masterpiece, he explains away the myriad of road works to complete, wins at noughts and crosses and feverishly announces the long wait in front of them. It's getting far from a joke when the new figure of one year, seven months, four days, three hours, five minutes and 10.3 seconds comes into play. Panic is the name of the game and Timbo wastes no time in claiming his place as the office teapot. Will power and self-respect desert Bill and Tim, who noisily drink away their blues ('turps for burps!'), sport newspaper hats and project an attitude of alcoholic-enhanced friendship – the fuzzy-chopped Garden, of course, facing the chopping block for his outrageous design, is less than chuffed.

Everyone takes it as read that Tim's request for heroic OBEs and head whipping off for the developments has got through to the Queen. In fact, even assuming she would act, the note hasn't even been sent. But hey, no matter, the Goods are convinced and that's all that's needed for Garden to get blind-folded, Oddie to get blind drunk and Brooke-Taylor to fuss about finding a decent shirt – Bill, ever the bloke to lend a hand, happily provides him with a flower pot hat. But slow down lads, there's no need to panic – nothing happens, the phone disintegrates, the BBC announce a complete curtailing and all contact with the outside world is snuffed out. Fundamentally, the Goodies office becomes a new state and authority is dished out between the three inhabitants. The scientist, the landed gentry and the working class are divided for duty. Tim's Queenly 'Here! Here!' is effective and Oddie gets all shirty with typical comic overtones. He shows himself in true colours, condemns Garden as a 'four-eyed git' and by-passes Tim as a chinless wonder. There's no denying that, but Bill is hardly going to stand by and do the shoe cleaning – it's a case of sizism all over again and he didn't get out of South Africa to continue with all that! Besides, here is a perfect chance to create the unionist, utopia of new, non-class-lead society. Well, that's Bill's plan and he's sticking to it, even if no one else gives it house room. Wisely, he smashes Tim's record of the *National Anthem* just before the ruling classes start to talk through their ruling arses, but merely sees the comic impossibilities in Tim's desperate desire for a son and heir. Even Garden's medical genius can't help the situation but Bill milks the awkwardness with plenty of camp sexual advances, Liza Minnelli look-a-like suggestions and knowing mockery about exercising things as much as he likes, with no usefulness whatsoever – much to Tim's disgust. Everything comes down to name calling and pompous bubble popping – with Bill mocking Tim's surname and Tim coming straight back into the game with a pleasing 'Oddie! – Billoddie stupid!' – it clearly tickles Graeme as much as the audience. There's no clear way out of this back-stabbing nonsense so Garden nips off to the lav for a fortnight, decides to become a Monk and discovers that Tim, in the interim, has casually converted to the Jewish faith. Feverishly constructing a miniature synagogue out of matchsticks. Meanwhile, and with any excuse to turn on the 'black man' excess, Bill bursts out as Rastous Watermelon with boot-polished face, Mohammed Ali poetry and bucket-loads of 'honey child,

honey lamb' chatter. But after religion fails, what's left? Well, in this case it's grub, or more to the point, lack of it. Bill's sacred, solitary cornflake has been consumed by Timbo's friendly pet mouse, Gilbert. The tension becomes so great that a furry, whiskered chappie effortlessly slips on to Tim's menu before caring Graeme talks him out of it and pops the sweet rodent in his own mouth. There's time for some *Kitten Kong* memories as the inanimate mouse becomes playful with Garden, before he scurries away into the concrete wilderness. But desperate men face desperate decisions, and cannibalistic tendencies are breaking through. Poor, innocent young Bill merrily picks the long straw and it's eager preparations for frying tonight! In the end, Tim's new found belief curtails the bean feast and the butchers aprons are removed for a tasty bit of home furniture cooking. But by now the three have cracked, seeing imaginary friends all over the place and facing the humorous, comforting words of Dr Garden. Garden's rational textbook reading is simply revealed as yet another hallucination as all hope is abandoned. A further 70 years whiz by (even the David Cassidy and David Essex posters have grown long beards) and aged Tim and Gray quietly battle through an exhausting, albeit obvious, game of I Spy. The two enjoy another priceless, rambling conversation, wistfully remembering the old days of rain in the face and a woman on the arm – the memory plays tricks and allows Tim to get confused and inject a bit of smut. Endearingly bizarre, the fun is interrupted by Bill, looking not a day older, breezing in for his 106th birthday celebrations. Bless him, he doesn't do much else each year, but coming round next to a couple of skeletons (one complete with glasses and the other sporting a Union flag waistcoat) is the final, death knell with the already departed bony ones pulling a sheet over the bodies. Timed to perfection as always, futurist man breaks through the crumbling rock to rescue these three brave chaps and, of course, it's a younger, trendier, *Star Trek* fashioned trio of Goodies – even down to Tim's modernised, portable *National Anthem* chorus – and this is sort of where we came in… a never-ending, recurring nightmare of catastrophic party games and enforced cohabiting.

Did You Know? *Check out the similarities between this legendary Goodies episode and the classic Warner Brothers cartoon, One Foggy Evening, featuring an endearingly buoyant singing frog. As an all-time favourite of the team themselves, The End was hand-selected for a video release in 1994 on The Goodies and the Beanstalk tape. The Australian*

THOSE PATRIOTIC GOODIES

Broadcasting Commission edited out the 'pissed' banter between Tim and Graeme, latterly included on the Australian release of the BBC video, ABC BOO100. Out-take bloopers exist for this episode, broadcast on American television within a Dick Clark presentation, Lynn Redgrave hosted a British telly interlude featuring the Goodies. Tim's patriotic speech is interrupted because the Rule Britannia record starts to early — 'I haven't put it on yet!' The scene grinds to a halt for a second time when Bill notices the music is playing but the record isn't spinning, and finally, Bill cracks up and gives in when his attempt to smash the offending record fails. Immediately after the show's first broadcast, the BBC switchboard received dozens of calls from anxious viewers distressed that the corporation had killed off The Goodies. Naturally, Sherlock Holmes-like, the team were back within the year! Although the team relished building up their eccentric characters and scripting dialogue rather than falling back on oceans of visual mugging, with a huge chunk of the special effects budget already swallowed by a special effects heavy series, this half hour was purposely written to avoid outside filming, guest star expense and costly technique.

CORBET WOODALL, SHEILA STEAFEL. Episode 13, recorded Friday 25 April, broadcast Monday 5 May 1975, 9–9.30pm, BBC2.

SPECIAL: GOODIES RULE OK?

As a crowning glory for their most successful year, the Goodies presented this 50-minute special just before Christmas. Having its finger on the pulse of changes in both British music and politics, the show is a tightly knit, cleverly written and passionately performed piece of work. And it's the one with the giant Dougal in it! Amazingly, that image appears extremely briefly and right near the end, but its power has somewhat overshadowed the rest of this episode. Starting with a deliciously mock Pathé Newsreel with a distinguished narration put on by Barry Cryer, the year is highlighted as 1961 and pop's young dreams are kicking in big time. There's Cliff, Cilla, very, very, young Bay City Rollers – still in their cot – and, of course, the Liverpool sound from the Cavern, the Bootles. The Goodies have a wonderful dig at The Beatles and claim their crown like never before. Graeme as the Lennon-like Don, Tim as nice as pie Saul and a big-nosed Bill drumming at the back as Bingo, are aided and abetted in their black and white rocking storm, by a shop dummy George. Reeling through *She Loves You* with the Jewish impresarios crawling around and, then, ultimately, tossing cabbages, stock footage of Paul McCartney looking less than impressed is perfectly slotted into the mix to prove the Goods a real failure. But three rockers in the audience, obviously intrigued with the sound, pick up the discarded Goodie wigs, put on the gear, unearth Eleanor Rigby by Graeme Garden and I Want To Hold Your Hand by Tim Brooke-Taylor and Bill Oddie, and feel confidant enough to have a go. Ringo seems keen and the action cuts to screaming fans worshipping at the feet of the Beatles performing… *She Loves You*. The Goodies look on, gutted. 1968 rolls in with the Goodies now going under the name of the Confirmed Bachelors – performing *Silence* from *I'm Sorry I'll Read That Again* – before the Bachelors themselves find fame. 1970 is the same – the Goods are doing *Baby Love* as the Extremes just before the Supremes hit the big time, and by 1974 even the much-awaited announcement of 'The Three… ' is cut off with a chorus of 'fed up with it all' boos! 1975 and the glam era ushers in a half-hearted rendition of *Nappy Love* which goes nowhere. The lads are on skid row and in a monumental piece of writing and performing, Bill and Tim discuss the entertainment scene. Bill laments that they always seem so far ahead of their time. The Goodies are too new and too original. Mind you, everybody seems to be suffering – in the most subtle of Python back-handed mentions, a couple of low-key Gumbies ferret through the dustbins as Bill wanders pass and mutters, 'All right John, Eric!' There's even time for a u-bend humiliation attack on the way Indians are depicted in *It Ain't 'Alf Hot, Mum*. But good times are on the cards for the Goodies. Graeme has worked out a plan to take elements from all the big Seventies' names and stick 'em all together. Thus we have Donny Osmond's teeth (cue Bill and Tim adopting sunglasses to avoid the glare), Gary Glitter's Welcome Mat of a chest hair display, Kojak's hair – or lack of it, the Bay City Rollers' checked trousers, the Wombles feet, Roy Wood's make-up and the whole scene. The stunning mish mash leads to pop chart domination and the concert of the millennium – The Goodies playing Wembley. So hot are the tickets and so tense the predicted atmosphere, that no members of the general public are allowed. The place is so well guarded by police that coppers make up the entire audience – screaming undying love to Tim, invading the stage, and smoking pot. Miming to the recorded release of *Wild Thing* – note Tim turning his back to avoid lip syncing the start of the complicated spoken bit – the Goodies are musical successes at long last. All 10 top places on the *Top of the Pops* countdown are Goodies records and an off-camera voiceover reveals that the trio are raking in the dosh. More to the point, the country is in a very bad way indeed. National debt is at an all-time high and England expects her Goodies to do their duty. After all, there are three OBEs in it. The date is set – 12 May – for the Royal Garden Party and the grand Goodie OBE presentation. Despite Tim's never-flagging optimism – 'sunniest day of my life!' – the rain doth fall down and the party becomes somewhat waterlogged. With the Queen submerged and the OBEs delivered, the Goods make off in a row boat, punting dramatically outside Buck House and receiving a watery command from the PM – they can tell it's him because he is using his pipe as a periscope! Graeme translates what old Harold wants and the Goodies are made Pop Group Laureate, the government is nationalising them – after all they are the only British company making any money – and, by royal decree, the trio are instructed to cheer up the country. Tim is delighted, and with all three donning the Union flag waistcoats and proudly displaying their 'By Appointment' drum-kit logo, the team rip into the patriotic morale booster *Bounce*. And everybody does. Babies in cots, Maggie Thatcher, Barbara Castle, Harold Wilson – via mucked about with stock footage – and *Nationwide*'s Michael Barratt in the studio. A special Crisis Edition reveals the irresistible curse of bouncing as the worst threat to Britain since the Black Death. The Goodies – at home watching all this on their television set – are not impressed, and nor, it seems is Harold Wilson. He bounces off the top floor of a very tall building and a General Election is called for and Terry Wogan, in the flesh, hosts the whole thing from the Lyceum Ballroom. The Goodies, naturally, are representing the Bouncing Party, old time dance is catered for with the Waltzing Party and there's even a bizarre, breakaway collection of Max Walls doing the rounds. Roland McLeod – in the briefest of brief cameos – prances about as swing-o-meter king Robert McKenzie before the BBC cameras cut to the returning officer announcing the victor at the Hammersmith Palais. The Goodies are up against stiff opposition – mainly from the bowler-hatted, shop dummy candidate, literally standing for parliament and advocating absolutely no movement at all. A great dig at DJ John Peel, in the shape of Sir Jonathan Peel of the Funky Gibbon, and the Goods themselves, lose to this inanimate man of the people, and the *Sun* headlines laments a Day of Gloom for Britain. Slowly trudging through a nuclear winter situation, with the wind howling and Norman Mitchell's bellowing town crier delivering the news, things are looking bad for fun lovers. The lads may ignore Mitchell's legal cries of non-fun making and anti-chat concerning free and easy funky chickening (a cry of 'Cobblers…' is the result), but this Cromwellian situation has evil law-enforcers waiting in the wings. The Myth Inspectors. Like a cross between the WitchFinder General and Robert Helpmann's Child-Catcher from *Chitty, Chitty, Bang, Bang*, these masked men ride on horse-back through England's green and pleasant land. Burning guitars, copies of the *Dandy*, records, film cans and the like, popping children's balloons and unleashing Myth Inspector ventriloquist's dummies to beat up entertaining ventriloquist's dummies, Mitchell's rant continues throughout, winding up with a quick look at the weather forecast. But the dye has been cast and the Goodies are on the case. The ethos of Robin Hood is resurrected with fun and games in Sherwood Forest – a trio of Lincoln green, sing-a-long chaps riding through the country, warbling their new theme song *We're the Goodies* and insisting of going against the 'Keep Britain Gloomy' regime. Coming across a down-in-the-mouth couple residing in a house called Dunchucklin, the lads go into full cabaret mode. Tumbling antics with Tim and Graeme result in that legendary credit opener as a tin barrel lands on Graeme, Bill and Tim turn on the Gypsy charm – with Timbo stalling his wind up organ and, eventually, being run over by it. Bill puts Graeme through the fear barrier with knife, axe, and even, machinegun bullet throwing. Graeme's black-clad wazir saws Tim in half – and sticks him back the wrong way for some hilarious visual helplessness. Gray goes into hopeless balloon bending routine, Bill licks into electric guitar riffs and a *Wild Thing* reprise – complete with policeman fan

attention. The whole thing closes with a conjured-up chorus line and the entire cast saying farewell in *Sunday Night at the London Palladium* revolving stage style. All the time, Mr Yokel has been binding, gagging and generally restraining his good lady wife from laughing. Once the show is over and she's stuck there with a bag over her head, he finds the sight so funny that the Myth Inspector picks him out for a good head bashing. In fact, this masked nutter is none other than Graeme, or at least, Graeme's alter ego, gingerly explaining his failure to the dummy PM and receiving a beating. Britain now has to take a leaf out of the book of Twenties America. Entertainment is prohibited, so Hootleggers are needed for illegal laughter. The Goodies again step into the breech, dishing out old comedy routines for the starving masses, doing some nasty, custard pie business on St Valentine's Day and putting on the hoodlum style in secret Joke Easys. Rumours of Harry Secombe, Cilla and, even, Eric and Ern (so exciting Tim's hat blows off), keep the entertainment black marketeers thirsty for more. To the strains of Oddie's *Where Are They Now?*, old telly favourites are rounded up for the good of the country. Tommy Cooper is a traffic warden, Ken Dodd is a dustman and Rolf Harris is a house painter. All are called, although Tony Blackburn, happily sending himself up again, is idly leaning on a lamp-post and hastily ignored by the laughter-seekers. The problem is that once the stars are caught, they can't remember how to do the business. The funny voices are gone for good. In a bristling bit of work, Graeme Garden romps through his impressions with ease, desperately trying to teach Tommy Cooper the 'Just Like That' stuff, hoping to help the real Eddie Waring change from an Arthur Mullard sound-a-like to his usual eccentric babble, coaxing a camp Telly Savalas, tempting a Rolf Harris from Scots chatter to Ozzie pant and putting on the full Jimmy Saville for the 'not himself' broadcaster. Eddie Waring turns on a bit of Frankie Howerd – thanks to a Bill Oddie voiceover – Patrick Moore goes from female sky-watching to Eddie Waring rugger commentating, Eric and Ern are dumbstruck by Graeme's perfect encapsulation of their act – complete with Jimmy Durante plastic cup nose business and energetic face slapping – and Sue Lawley eventually turns on the Ken Dodd 'By joves'. But it's hopeless. Real live entertainers have clearly had their day and Bill has the solution – a puppet government. Or more to the point, a hand puppet government. Back to Michael Barratt and *Nationwide*, with Prime Minister Sooty and

Home Secretary Sweep, squeaking for the country, suggesting xylophone playing and generally letting their corrupt strings show. The Goodies – bizarrely watching *Today In Parliament* on a screen stuck in the side of a tree – see the puppets going power mad and a particularly chatty clanger shouting the odds. Things are not looking good, the people have no trust in the puppets and a secret visit to Chequers is required. Cue the sinister music and our three heroes infiltrating the dark, brooding world of puppet control. A Punch and Judy guard on the front door is fairly low-key – and Bill even pinches their string of sausages – but the Cabinet Room is more of a problem. Barging into the inner sanctum, Tim sheepishly lays his cards on the table. Pussy footing around, Graeme bellows 'Get on with it…', but however Tim tries to sweeten the pill with niceties and gags ('Out of hand…') the puppets don't take kindly to threats. Hector from *Hector's House*, Sooty, Paddington and all the mob, fly in for the kill. Making a run for it, a sinisterly oversized Pinky and Perky attack from above, while giant Andy Pandy, Loopee Lu and Teddy turn on the menace. In an attempt to convince the huge puppets that they are part of the furniture, the Goodies turn on the Gerry Anderson walk and paint on rosy cheeks. Tangled strings sort out the Andy Pandy Three, while a very ropey-looking Grouch from *Sesame Street* gets Tim into his bin, an off-camera burp results and Brooke-Taylor happily emerges with a bit of green fur hanging from his well-filled

mouth. Bill and Ben storm into the battle, engaging the lads in a sword fight, and eventually, being defeated via Graeme's unsportsmanlike string severing. Bill, meanwhile, finds himself ambushed by the Wombles and thrown into a lawn-based, rough and tumble brawl with the Wimbledon boys. Back in Bill and Ben land, a late starting Weed is no match for Tim's single swipe, while Uncle Bulgaria falls at the first hurdle as Bill boots his stick away. But now it's the moment everybody remembers. The puppets seem out for the count but what's that rumbling. Yes, it's a massive Dougal, turning the bend and on the look out for Goodies. Luring the huge dog into the trees, his bouncing *Magic Roundabout* pal Zebedee bounces into view as Dougal literally runs poor old Tim over. A round and about, bareback riding bit of madness is accompanied by a burst from *Carousel* and keeps Graeme occupied as a 'Get out of it!' screaming Bill is grabbed from the trees by the springing fiend. However, with a booming 'Time For Bed!', Zebedee crashes into the puppets domain, Dougal ram-raids the ground floor and the entire thing crumbles into dust. The Goodies quietly emerge from the rubble and walk away. Naturally the News – with priceless Corbett Woodall making a late appearance, embracing the earlier celebrity hopelessness and losing his female voice with a hasty glass of water, reports the change in power with Dougal destruction footage and info on the new collision government. Tim longingly looks forward to the good old days but it's all puppets again, with Margaret Thatcher, Harold Wilson and Jeremy Thorpe strung up and ready for government. Luckily for the nation, the hands who are pulling the strings are none other than the Goodies. With a wicked look into camera and their credits emblazoned over the image, that's the end of the show and the Goods are in control… Or are they. With the show effectively over, the production credit of Jim Franklin is pre-empted with three puppet Goodies and the puppet master – Franklin himself – controlling the entire Goodie universe from up in the Gods.

Did You Know? *In between the end of Series Five and this ground-breaking special, BBC1 had kept The Goodies very much in the public eye with another lengthy repeat session. In fact, this special was originally conceived as a two-parter, thus 60 minutes of material had to be tightly condensed into a 50-minute slot. Instead of the familiar opening credits, the show starts with extracts from The Goodies Rule OK? itself. Having adopted his legendary beard since Series Two, Bill Oddie appeared clean shaven for this special all-film episode. Although it was* *back, loud and proud for the start of Series Six the following year. This special, like the Beanstalk, was made entirely on film. Roger Wilmut in his essential book From Fringe to Flying Circus considered the show packed with invention but 'perhaps too much for its own good.' As a matter of fact, there is probably more invention in any single half-hour classic from Series Six, but this special is a brilliant testimony to the skill, awareness, music and pure slapstick heritage of the Goodies. During publicity for this special, the Goodies – thanks to major support from Tim – were involved with the Derby Festival and took part in a tea party at Paddington Station in aid of Action Research for the Crippled Child. An oft-seen shot of the lads with the Paddington Bear mascot was the result. That legendary giant Dougal was, in fact, 16 BBC props men in a skin! The final scene – Franklin with the Goodie puppets – was a delicious in-joke from the team. It was common knowledge that Franklin would have loved his stars to have been puppets and done exactly what he wanted, when he wanted with absolutely no complaint whatsoever!*

MICHAEL BARRATT, TONY BLACKBURN, SUE LAWLEY, PATRICK MOORE, EDDIE WARING, TERRY WOGAN, CORBET WOODALL with NORMAN MITCHELL, RONALD RUSSELL, ROLAND MacLEOD and the voices of BARRY CRYER, SHEILA STEAFEL. Punch and Judy JOHN STYLES. Written by Bill Oddie and Graeme Garden. Music by Bill Oddie and Dave Macrae. Graphic design Bob English. Costume Dee Kelly. Make-up Jean Speak. Visual effects Peter Day. Design John Stout. Production assistant Peter Lovell. Sound Les Collins and Alan Dykes. Lighting cameraman Reg Pope. Camera operator Brian Easton. Film editor Ron Pope. Produced by Jim Franklin. Filmed from Monday 22 September–Friday 17 October, broadcast Sunday 21 December 1975, 7.25pm–8.15pm, BBC2.

SERIES SIX

Due to the fact that the shows from Series Three and Four had been conceived and commissioned as one set of episodes, Series Six was, rather incongruously, referred to at the BBC as *The Goodies: Series V*. Filming on the six episodes began in the Spring of 1976 and, as with the Special, Tim Brooke-Taylor's writing credit was dropped. From now on, *The Goodies'* scripts would be totally in the hands of Graeme Garden and Bill Oddie.

Film cameramen Reg Pope and Brian Easton. Film editor John Jarvis. Visual effects Peter Day and Tony Harding. Costume Andrew Rose. Make-up Jean Steward. Lighting Alan Horne. Sound Jeff Booth. Music by Bill Oddie and Dave McRae. Production assistant Peter R Lovell. Design John Stout with Peter Blackner (Episodes 2, 4 & 6). Produced by Jim Franklin.

LIPS OR ALMIGHTY COD

What better way to start a series than a comment about the fishing territories and cod wars, a stunningly low-budget but hilarious version of the previous year's Hollywood blockbuster, *Jaws*. The scene is a BBC news report with the 9 O'Clock logo adding journalistic weight to Barry Cryer's brilliantly 'cod' cod news item. Those dirty Eskimo swines have given us the cold shoulder and extended the fishing boundaries by some 2000 miles, in order to take in British rule and the rich pickings of The Serpentine. The poor old Brits are quite unprepared for watery legal wrangles. Happily extending his rod, listening to *Rule Britannia* on his tinny wireless (Barry's civilised 'good fishing gentlemen' is the calm before the Greenlander storm), Tim casually exchanges quips, football castigating of Chelsea and the usual foreign Johnnie humouring of misunderstood languages ('quarter past three…'). But, when funny words and deadly looks suddenly become a gunfire attack it's time to make tracks. Meanwhile, down on the Dr Graeme Garden Fish Farm, the main man is taking the 'farm' aspect a bit far with full welly boot kit, herding terminology and 'proud beauty' cries to such beloved cow-style watery livestock as 'Buttercup'. The cod are his pride and joy but Bill isn't very convinced by this unique and bizarre system of fish farming. Besides, his hands are full with the tiny, wee fish eggs practically vanishing in the great expanse of his standard egg cup, and literally being crushed out of existence as he struggles to stamp the little lion on them. Problems are instantly forgotten with a rousing chorus of Gershwin's *Summertime* – 'and the fishes are jumping…' Indeed they are, as one hurtles out of his tank, the dogfish gets a tasty bone and the ultra-playful pike gets a good grip on Graeme's arm and refuses to give up. Shocked and stunned Tim reappears and he's got bigger fish to fry: irritant Eskimos with big guns and a cod obsession. It's war and although the thought of big guns doesn't exactly put Bill and Tim at ease, Graeme is confident. After all, the lads 'have cod on our side!' Graeme goes into battle with a huge cod as protection. His slant-eyed opposition has a tiny tiddler as defence which proves little or no match. With victory in sight and the fur-laden ones on the run, the trio throw their entire cod supply at their foe. Unwounded and underwhelmed, the Eskimos have what they want (the cod) and the Goods are left with caviar on their faces. Back at codless base, Bill's doing his best to convince the nation that a pumped-up haddock is the match for any cod. With a frenzied, 'it's working!', Bill is over the moon with his handiwork but scientific Graeme knows that, sadly, it's just full of wind. Tim's battered goldfish – 'crisp, golden and crunchy' – is hardly going to feed the 5000. Besides, it's poor old Bill's beloved pet, Gilbert. Tim was only trying to cheer up his friend Graeme, so Bill's going to cheer Tim down by frying his friend Graeme in leftover batter. Graeme needs a miserable, happy or wooden-legged cod – just any cod in fact – in order to rejuvenate his floundering organisation! But England is completely codless. The only thing to do is nip over to Eskimo country and pinch one. Revelling in their Englishness, the disguise for the three is as MCC North Pole tourists, flogging cricket stumps to an Eskimo for a handy ski set and resurrecting the old Warner cartoon *Whole Idea* ideal of portable black holes. Bagging a tasty cod through the ice and covering their tracks with Bill's removal of the portable hole, the lads are off to the customs. It's a case of is that a cod in your sports bag or are you just pleased to see me, as the water leaks out with gusto, the concealed fish makes waves and the X-ray machine reveals all. British to the end, the cod provides Graeme with a perfect substitute cricket bat, Tim skilfully bowls a snowball and fielder Bill gets an icy one right in the mouth. Laughter cures everything and Oddie's distress causes enough comic confusion to make enough time for a speedy escape back to Blighty. Beatlemania worship awaits the Goods on their return, with airport adoration rocketing them to culinary national heroes. Graeme's aim is to rear the biggest cod in captivity but, as with dear old Kitten Kong, fondness for dumb animals breaks down the scientific barriers. Tim, meanwhile, is more concerned with international distribution. The world waits for something to put next to its chips and Tim's got it all worked out. Bradford wants curried cod, the French can have the overpriced, undertasty head, while the best stuff goes to the three lads themselves. But Graeme's reasoning has totally deserted him. He doesn't know what Timbo is talking about but Bill's got a fair idea. Storming into the scene in full fishmonger mode, Tim sings his devious plans of chopping the fish in two and serving it up with loads of lovely chips. Graeme sees the Cod – lovingly named Brian – as 'one of us', while all Bill sees is a thousand fish fingers. Brain food or not, Brian is safe from the Oddie fillet knife as Gray takes him for watery walkies, bemuses a female dog walker with his stick-fetching antics and even uses a waterlogged lamp-post for relief. Bill's knowing comment that the cod is being spoilt is even more unkindly echoed in Tim's condemnation of distinct cissy elements creeping into the fish. Fear tactics have to be employed and the most fearful thing Bill can come up with is a Nicholas Parsons mask. But that's no good – any fool and Tim Brooke-Taylor knows that Nick is huge down Greenland way. His game show, *Whale of the Century*, is a major winner. The only thing the trio have to do is get these fish to lose their temper. With a cardboard cut-out Eskimo and a self-bashing mallet arm designed to outrage Brian the cod into

action, the plan for killer Britfish seems to be more dead than newspaper-wrapped haddock. It's down to Timbo to try to save the day. A fin, when none of us thought it was safe to go back in the water, is enough to terrify anybody. That is, unless, Tim, in fetching bathing suit, isn't discovered underneath it fighting for breath. No, it has to be the fish, and armed with the essential fish-miffing manual, A Thousand and One Ways to Make You Cross, Graeme is still going for it. But still, megaphone-bellowed mentions of *Radio Times* popularity and the simple, heart-stopping words, Tony Blackburn, do not cut any ice with these cold fish. Facing defeat and trying to relax, the side-burned boffin turns to musical comfort and the powerful musical performance of Max Bygraves's *Tulips From Amsterdam*. The golden throat of Maxie drives fish wild with anger… even camp cod Brian himself. With a huge pair of false choppers and Graeme's quick, unprepared dive into the water tank, the ultimate underwater missile is ready to launch. Hold your horses, what's that frightening fin in the water, it's Lips, with a beautiful pair of nashers, a Max Bygraves bloodlust and evil in its belly. Tim and Bill's hapless escape is in a Lenny the Lion boat and a hilarious hook, line and sinker dragging of the huge fish round a boating lake. Elements of Pinocchio's Monstro the Whale come into play when Lips swallows the gramophone player still belting out Max, Graeme's angst at not reaching the off button first is brilliantly expressed and Tim's sweet, cod glove puppet – almost as convincing as the Lips costume – perfectly sends up the cheapo special effects, the BBC costume department and the exterior monster movie genre. Tugging on the line for all their worth, the false gnashers finally come soaring out and cascade towards a shell-shocked Bill. Brian crashes into the jetty, miraculously toppling over huge cans of batter and oil. A flame sets the whole thing off at regulo seven and, bingo, instant fish fingers falling on your head.

Did You Know? *The opening credits for Series Six use bits of Frankenfido running through the streets, Cuddly Scamp dancing to Tim's playing, Bunfight close-ups, the cliff top fall from Rome Antics, Tim's clown virus and the immortal clowning trio running away from the camera as the closing, writing credit, image. With the huge international success of Jaws in 1975, Bill thought a Goodies version was essential. However, by the time Series Six came to fruition in early 1976, Graeme considered the Jaws theme well and truly outdated. A clever emphasis on the cod wars convinced him. The comic strip character, Gums, featured in Monster Fun, helped to keep the Jaws myth fresh in young minds for years after as well. For screening between 1976 and 1987 the Australian Broadcasting Commission cut Graeme's cod-aimed insult 'You great poof!' As well as the radio broadcast, Barry Cryer also croons the Max Bygraves material. The giant fish was called Brian due to the fact that both Graeme and Bill shared an agent named Brian Codd!*

The voice of BARRY CRYER. Episode One, recorded Friday 4 June, broadcast Tuesday 21 September 1976, 9–9.30pm, BBC2.

HYPE PRESSURE

The 'bored in Cricklewood' office set-up sees Graeme struggling with his Tony Blackburn guide to Play Guitar My Way and Other Jokes, while Tim perches on his throne engrossed in his copy of *Variety*. However, Bill is desperately pacing up and down trying to write a number one hit record – he toils with the near legendary 'eck, eck, funky ferret', quickly discards the remnants of *I've Got a Brand New Combine Harvester* and is convinced that his *Tomorrow* song has been done before. Well those, 'all my troubles seemed so far away' lyrics do have a familiar ring… Hard at work for three minutes, Graeme isn't impressed in the slightest. He clearly remembers the days when Bill could have whipped off nine or 10 chartbusters in that time. Bill readily agrees, happily recalling the glories of *Black Pudding Bertha*. Graeme is having none of this self-gratification. Not with 'ironic' world-beating lyrics like 'By gum, shake your bum!' And as for their greatest, inspirational hit, the *Funky Gibbon*, Gray's computer – allegedly – came up with that one. Bill's Gershwin meets Lennon via Bolan talents have left him and it's a career away from music that is the only option. Bill's going to become a folk singer! His ambition to write sick-making sounds, burst your bladder and cause various other internal nasties, even upsets Dr Garden, but all that one hand over the ear cat-a-wailing stuff sees Timbo emerge from behind his paper for the first time. He may not know the difference between a quaver and a cheese crisp snack, but that strange, haunting howling is music to his ears. And what's more, Graeme can do it as well. 'Two of 'em!': Country Bill and the other one. Money in the bank, all in the name of corrupt self-promotion. Tim hosts *New Faces* as a black-clad mortician eager to heap ritual humiliation and go to your grave glances on any unsuspecting contestant. But nothing can stop Bill and Graeme ploughing through a number called *The World Is Full of Men and Women*. It reduces the judges to tears and starts a nation-wide madness. Tim, pelted with cabbages, losing his blonde wig and foaming at the mouth with panic, is not a happy bunny. Next seen staring dumbly into space with Gray and Bill forcing smelling salts under his nose, nothing seems to jolt him out of his brain dead coma. The great silent one was merely thinking. If Showaddywaddy and *Grease* could do it, why not the Goodies? Rock 'n' Roll is back so dig that sound Daddio, grab your gal and spin that platter. Tim's regressed to 1956 when, according to Graeme, he was 37. It's the new trend and Britain is turned back 20 years. Teddy boys and Brylcreem rule, footie shorts get bigger – Tim and Bill can even share a pair – Tim's beehive hair-do attracts the honey, Concorde is scrapped and royal interest is shown with tourist pleasing re-enactments of the Coronation – once a day at 2.30pm and twice on Saturdays. A stunning recreation of Fifties cool, Bill's lead singer curls his Elvis Presley lip with passion, Tim dons checked jacket, mounts his double bass and pays homage to Bill Haley's Comets. He later chisels his piano, gets out the paint-roller, screams out the number and sends up the genius of Little Richard with passion. Graeme, on the other hand, quietly and effectively, swaps his usual specs for the black, thick-rimmed variety and plucks his guitar like Buddy Holly. His lazy, have a cup of tea interlude while a false arm keeps the rhythm hot, is a classic and, unable to retain the Fifties' pace completely, there's a glorious, heavy rock, insane Jimi Hendrix riff with string-biting antics to spice up the sound. The two gum-chomping, hip-swirling, bobby-sock sporting Fifties girls go through the motions with an attitude of total boredom but the fans at home – namely Graeme himself – don't let the influence fail. As long as that rocking sound plays at a certain frequency, Graeme rips up his seats like a teenager watching *Rock Around the Clock* at the local Odeon. Bill does the sensible thing and turns the set off. Immediately bringing Graeme to his senses he faces the truth – 'I really shouldn't be doing this should I!' Bill condemns the music of the devil, but it's potent stuff. Britain has been transformed. *Porridge* and *Fawlty Towers* have gone. It's now endless *Prudence Kitten*, *What's My Line* and *Muffin the Mule*. Graeme may enjoy his fix of Annette Mills and wooden puppets but Bill is quick to point out that 'you can get locked up for that you know!' But things are about to get worse. Tim has passed the Fifties and has ended up in the Forties. He's the definitive spiv, waddling round like George Cole's Flash Harry (and, momentarily getting Graeme to follow his lead), talking through the side of his mouth and by-passing the ever ready fag, sporting a snappy zoot suit, trilby and thin tash, and casually flogging nylon stockings to anyone who cares to listen. He has also resurrected the death penalty as a sideline. What's more, Bill and Graeme have been called up – National Service is back in play. But once a spiv not always a spiv. Tim has ambitions to be a television director, going on about the glories of military life at Aldershot, revelling in the renewal of the death penalty and screaming 'bless 'em all… ' from here to breakfast time. With a longing for the past and nostalgic obsession gone completely mad, Tim is now a sort of contemporary bloke with a Sergeant Major attitude to small screen entertainment. Tim seems determined to milk the fad dry, Graeme seems convincingly stuck in Forties' war-torn Britain, while Bill has time-jumped into the flower power Sixties. Not for him war, obedience, songs about blind learner motorcyclists and their pet hamsters… no, he is a child of peace with flowers in his hair. Love and understanding is the name of the game, although a swift knee in Tim's groin is always an option for total clarity. But Tim being the arch villain that he is, tempts these poor unsuspecting souls into the evil world of Independent television – check the ATV logo on a Beeb show – cackling the most cunning, heartless laugh since Dick Dastardly and unleashing himself as the ever so camp director of music spectacular Super-Ficial. Bill and Graeme – or William and Grayfunkel in this flowers in the hair, head-band wearing, groovy baby peace trip guise – perform their moving song of flowers. The whole number finally embraces class, near smut, swinging cuddly chimps distracting the warblers, *Top of the Pops* style foam and wind effects, landmines and an ever so explosive conclusion with dynamite destruction. In between, the weather forecast has been scuppered by Tim's 'cue the snow', Corbet Woodall's news report is rocketed away and Moira Anderson's *Stars On Sunday* rendition of *Bless This House* has been floored by a cascade of bricks. Telly viewers Bill and Graeme watch in horror as Tim cues himself and begins his latest and greatest epic, World War II. Going totally insane in the nicest possible way, Tim orchestrates land attacks and airborne dog fights, bags the entire British armed forces as extras and prompts his two colleagues to hire another loony director to sort him out. Tim cues Hitler but the other two Goods are ready for him. An Alfred Hitchcock-a-gram calls on the birds for an egg attack on the hun, Vanessa Redgrave's nun's habit comes in handy, black and white Red Indian footage piles on the manpower and Tim desperately cues Kitten Kong

and Bill cues Dougal. Thus bringing together the two most important, best remembered, oversized foes of the trio for an all too brief battle of the giants. The minature models are hastily revealed with Beeb technical staff pulling the strings but in that few seconds an entire British comedy legacy is reviewed. But Gray and Bill have one more ace up their sleeve that even Tim, the mad director, can't handle. Cue the Party Political Broadcast and more to the point, cue Mrs Thatcher. Indians, troops and Tim himself can't face that. The battle is won through television power. Run the credits.

Did You Know? *This episode was never offered for broadcast outside the UK and only resurfaced on Australian pay television in 1996.*

McDONALD HOBLEY, MARY MALCOLM, CORBET WOODALL, JAKE ANTHONY, RICHARD PESCUD. Episode Two, recorded Friday 11 June, broadcast Tuesday 28 September 1976, 9–9.30pm, BBC2.

DAYLIGHT ROBBERY ON THE ORIENT EXPRESS

The latest Cricklewood wheeze – Goodies Hols – is set to revitalise that boring fortnight by the sea. Fed up, like dear Bill, of being stripped to the waist and wearing a handkerchief on your head, well now you can try deep sea fishing, brain surgery (check out Bill's crazed expression), dodo rediscovering (establishing Series Seven's *Dodonuts*) or even missionary work with a boiled alive option and free funeral thrown in. The latest commercial presentation from the team, this is Graeme's loony scheme. The adventure holiday is the future so long as you don't want to go further than six miles from Goodies' control. Bill, donning his tree costume for a couple of owl comic banters with Tim, a scone pronunciation battle over the wordplay gag 'stone's throw' and a brief chat about the Cricklewood Loch Ness, reveals the assured sighting of the weird, mysterious and legendary tree monster – Bill in disguise – and Graeme's tasty, tartan Scottish Oat Cakes. Episode One is sort of revisited with Graeme's *Jaws* impersonation and the scaled-down Mount Everset is sold as a major attraction. Tim's not convinced but he gets to wear the hostess hat with 'I try harder' written on it. What's more, he's allowed to make the tea and seductively answer the phone for potential business parties. Injecting kind, lovely and almost 'come back to my place big boy' invitations, Tim unwittingly and independently agrees to cater for The Detective's Club Annual Outing. Like *Murder by Death* meets a cloning machine, the detective enthusiasts come in droves for this stunning Orient Express journey designed to arrive back in time for *Police 5* on the telly. Four Sherlock Holmes arrive in pairs – without Watsons. Four wheelchair bound Ironsides file in, there are seven Hercule Poirots and seven lolly-sucking Kojaks greeted with a cheery 'Who loves ya, baby!' from Timbo. Graeme's the guide, Tim's the sex interest and Bill is the station master, whistle blower and special effects bloke making the never-changing scenery from a motionless train seem like a gallop through Europe and beyond. Cranking up the steam locomotive gramophone record and shifting the station lamp-post, he kicks off the journey into mystery and suspense. With Bill and Tim restricted to, albeit, very funny quick changes and visual moments, this is Graeme's opportunity to shine bright. Building up the very dubious props passing the window, that tree becomes a tourist site of interest as the one which Dick Turpin was hanged from, gulls (with their strings clearly visible) signal the seaside and some unsteady playacting from Graeme convincingly creates an atmosphere of a cross-channel ferry. Cannes is depicted with tin cans, a mini Eiffel Tower makes Graeme desperately search for the plot and a leaning tower of Pisa falls down and miraculously reappears again. Tim, of course, is quick changing for all he's worth, bringing in onions and bread sticks as a saucy French maid, grapes and plastic-wrapped spaghetti and finally stumbling in as Yugoslavia's finest wench just as that part of the tour comes to a close. With nothing of interest save that tree again and a dodgy dead, stuffed cow, the pleasures of Yugoslavia are few and far between. Miss Marple, Father Brown and the other assembled 'tecs seem happy enough, particularly when the tour gets back on track, the full presentation of that 'boring' epic *Murder on the Orient Express* kicks in and Tim does a quite stunning impression of Ingrid Bergman. And still the new locations come. Gray thinks it's Torquay but it's obviously Egypt, with that same cow masquerading as a camel. Finally, it's the land of the midnight sun, Lapland, depicted by Bill's reindeer, complete with stick antlers, red nose and touchingly shivering persona. Time for bed and the Kojaks are cared for – 'Lollies out, bottles in, polish the head and tuck 'em in…' But time and tide wait for no Goodie. Tim's in the middle of changing into an oriental Geisha girl, Gray grabs literally half a second of sleep and wallows in randy feelings of giving glam Tim a good seeing to. Bill, bedraggled, sodden and smelly, blames the livestock for the pong before facing the truth – he has crawled under the train and been covered in sh… shomething very nasty. But the train record is in Graeme's hand and the train noises are still churning away. Obviously

the train is actually moving. Tim gets hysterical, Graeme slaps him, Tim slaps Graeme, and Bill, sensibly, jumps off the train and checks out the view. It's moving alright and any amount of bareback riding of a stuffed cow will not get him back on board. Bill chases, chases and chases the runaway train, grabbing, missing and trying again for a slapstick thrill. Tim indulges in a bit of *Just My Bill* lyric recognition from *Carousel* before breaking into full song and lamenting his little lost buddy. In full hostess uniform and slit skirt, the sight is one to warm the cockles of the coldest heart but all hope seems lost. The train's headed South and gone under the Ocean. Poor brave Bill is drowned. Well, actually, no he isn't. Like any self-respecting silent comedian or cartoon character, Bill Oddie is indestructible. The fact of the matter is though that the entire train and its occupants have been stolen. Just the sort of thing the Detective's Club were after. Graeme reveals that some of his questions may be painful (Tim asking 'Why?' soon finds out when he's bashed on the head by a mallet), but no one seems to be to blame for the crime but the Goodies themselves. A pair of glasses, a Union flag waistcoat and a beard are the only clues. These fiends are false Goodies, cunningly revealing the real heroes tied up in the back room. Graeme's escape solution ('Try the goat!') doesn't really interest Tim ('Not now thanks!'), although he has a jolly long think about it. But to try the goat biting through the ropes is the plan and try that they do. The whole kidnap, train-stealing operation is aimed towards Cannes legendary Le Boring Festival. A mind-numbing collection of the world's biggest bores competing for their country. With stock footage of celebs backing up the gags – Clement Frued and John Peel are in the solo bore stakes, Liz Taylor and Richard Burton see their crown lifted by newcomers Rod Stewart and Britt Ekland, the House of Lords and Welsh Choirs go for the Formation category, Madeline Smith's in the figure section and the like – the audience is non-amused into stiffness with the display. Things liven up a tad when the Orient Express – a very quick, model shot – breaks into the anti-fun, and the false Goods go for the crown. Fiendishly clever and suicidally boring, the bad trio don chilling white masks and go for the full six and a half hour presentation of *Murder on the Orient Express* in French mime. With the festival rose almost won, the real Goods break free and spice up their lives with music. Escaping thanks to Gilbert the Goat, Graeme and Tim are free and easy. Graeme castigates Tim for suggesting Gilbert help Bill and then reverses the sensible option by biting through Oddie's ropes himself. However, once out and about, the lads grab their instruments and play. Tim's on drum, Bill blows his saxophone and Graeme plucks his banjo thing but the mime Goods are having none of this. Miming innocent snowballs and, subsequently grenades, destruction is rife. Tim is suitably golfed down by an imaginary club and Bill's walking against the wind performance is blown away. But the train bound and, now all wheelchair bound, detectives, come to the rescue. With a score reflecting each of the crime-busting greats (note the charming, brief use of Ron Goodwin's *Miss Marple* theme from the Margaret Rutherford movies), the pros are joined in the wheelchair stakes by the Goodies and, indeed, Gilbert the Goat. Fooled by mime banana skins, invisible panes of glass and the like, riderless chairs and defeated bodies litter the place. There's even a cameo for Tim's Lady Constance as Miss Marple goes for a burton. But Gilbert comes to the rescue. Chair-bound and ready to butt, he hoists one baddie Goodie into the waiting getaway boat and wrecks it. With a score of 00.03.01. on the boring scale, the Goodies swell with pride. Who can blame them?

Episode Three, recorded Saturday 3 July, broadcast Tuesday 5 October 1976, 9–9.30pm, BBC2.

BLACK AND WHITE BEAUTY

If you ever wanted the comic ideals of the dead parrot sketch given a more penetrating treatment, then the first half of this *Goodies* episode is the place to be. The taxidermist terror to come is softened by charming countryside music, a merry Tim and Bill cycling through the pastoral scene and shared plucked heartstrings all round with the first viewing of Graeme's Pets Corner for clapped-out animals. It's a touching collection of aged, infirm, hearing aid equipped creatures, including the obligatory gibbon and that rock solid donkey from *Bunfight*. With camp mincing and flamboyant affection, the lads steep praise on their selfless, dedicated, bespectacled chum. But all is not as it seems in the Graeme Garden hideaway, in fact, these beloved animals are stuffed and frozen for preservation purposes. It's a guilty secret and one Gray Bags is rather keen to keep. Besides, with the lads having brought a basket of tasty tit bits how can he hurt their feelings! So, with frantic panic and unconvincing speed, he introduces them to the collection – all called Kenneth and all very dead. Naïve Tim baby talks and prods a stuffed budgie who falls from his perch and a rather more

TIM BROOKE-TAYLOR'S FLASH *GOODIES* PHOTO AS USED IN THE SHOW *ALTERNATIVE ROOTS*

cynical Bill senses Kenneth, Kenneth and Kenneth are looking a tad poorly too. Graeme tries every desperate attempt to convince him the creatures are still in the world of the living. Once Kenneth the flying tortoise takes to the air, hilarity ensues. Tim eagerly searches for the clever-shelled one, unaware that the shell of its former self has soft landed on his head. Relentless Bill mercilessly grabs the thing, places it on his own head, smugly tries to force feed a kipper to a stuffed cat and triggers a fidgeting Gray Bags into playfulness with a fluffy hamster. Bill's cocky 'come here mate!' is priceless and, defeated, Graeme faces the shame of his deceit. That nasty, anti-animal, pro-

155

experimental edge to Garden's character is enhanced with his pitiful explanation. The creatures are on their last legs anyway and don't last long – 'not the way I treat them!' – but business is business and the owners, human fat cats with far too much money for their own good, keep dipping their hands in their pockets every time visiting day comes around. Whatever, the animals may be dead but the illusion of life is enough to keep the owners happy and the money-mad Graeme ecstatic. As always, money talks to Tim and Bill as well. Beloved cats are booted into touch and sickly stick insects are machine gunned, all in the name of animal welfare – with a jolly whistle and tilted hat Graeme effortlessly changed from caring doctor to wheeler dealer. By now, Tim and Bill, unfamiliar and uncomfortable with the ice box conditions of Graeme's establishment, are going blue round the gills and another load of dogs are humanely required to boost the fire. Seemingly running out of ideas on the stuffing front, the show suddenly changes gear. Gone is the dead animal magic of cushions stuffed with hamsters, dogs stuffed with boxes of sage and onion, and Tim stuffed with terrapins in the mistaken belief they are pickled walnuts, and in its place stands a sub-standard, lip-smacking children's adventure yarn. Without a doubt, a show of two clear halves, the arrival of a mysterious package containing Kenneth the pantomime horse grips the imagination and rockets the trio into the clipped, ever so melodramatic world of *Black Beauty* meets *National Velvet*. Seemingly altering from their usual comic characterisation to children's book heroes and villains, the Goods run with the overplayed notion till the show's climactic race. Graeme is all wistful, charming and full of continued animal abuse (lighting matches on cats and reading James Herriott's latest, How To Drown Kittens), while Tim delights in a picture of wild-haired, leg-flipping foppishness, submerging himself in the essence of Enid Blyton's frightfully British universe with gleeful excitement and wonderfully shocked reactions. Best of all is Bill, effortlessly going from dismissing his pals as 'a pair of nuts!' to an instant vocal change, challenged to find his own runner for the Grand National and deliciously kicking Black and White Beauty with heartless contempt. Within the space of seconds he's latched on to an Olivier-proportioned villain, storming round the place like a grouchy bear, injecting 'bah humbug!' rants and wickedly laughing at his own nastiness. Moving into Honest Farmer Jolly's stud farm, Bill has a whale of a time with cunning

plans to pinch the horse and whipping the poor, defenceless thing once it is caught on his land. Tim and Graeme plan to steal the beast back – disguising themselves as gypsies for an easy, get out of trouble, policy. Their obvious, 'Hello, we are the gypsies coming to steal the horse…' is a great moment. Making enough noise to wake the dead or at least give nasty Bill plenty of time to almost catch them red-handed, Tim and Graeme clamour into the horse suit to avoid detection. With Bill still in scenery-ripping, overacting mode and the lads breathing life into the horse suit, the time is right to corrupt the Grand National, big time. Riding in on rock bottom odds of 10,000–1, Bill's mare is set to clean up if it wins and our man isn't going to stand by and leave things to chance. Tearing a page out of the book of Terry-Thomas, the evil Oddie dopes the other horses and makes certain of race failure by filling their water buckets with booze. Tim and Graeme, meanwhile, are more keen on reassuring their fellow contestants that they have no worries about winning. With gentle tones and friendly banter Tim gushes that 'we're only two fellas in a suit!' and 'you'll murder us!' but the tampered-with nags are bunged to the eyeballs with certain substances and copious amounts of Tequila Sunrise. Tim offers Graeme a sniff, before angrily clarifying that he should remove himself from the back half of the pantomime horse before the actual sniffing – but with one puff of the joint Garden is falling over like a high Groucho Marx – 'Hey, where'd you get the stuff man!' Suddenly, the fake accents, mugged performances and earnest delivery are curtailed. Bill's whip happy nutter is simply back to his gambling, money-mad self. Having bet a bit of his own money, some of Tim's and all of Graeme's, the team is once more united for victory – throwing themselves into a Grand National completely populated by pantomime horses. Egotistically posing for the photo finish picture, the lads lose and plunge into poverty. Bill's rag 'n' bone man gees on Black and White beauty as the familiar *Steptoe and Son* theme fades into goodnight Goodies.

Episode Four, recorded Friday 10 July, broadcast Tuesday 12 October 1976, 9–9.30pm, BBC2.

IT MIGHT AS WELL BE STRING

Longing for the early days when an episode was balanced with mock commercials, this edition is given over entirely to a deconstruction of the advertising man mentality and an ocean of parody ads. As an opening assault, Bill as friendly expert 'Joe' tries to sell the brilliance of Mold washing power. With a typical housewife refusing to give up her usual stuff, Bill urges ('You should!') before stopping the raucous laughter in the throat, in an instant, with a brutal, out of the blue, smack in the mouth. Threatened with rolling pin beating and the boys coming round, the poor lady unwillingly plugs the powder and Bill can go home happy. Graeme's not much better. Masquerading as Captain Fishface, he serves up the grub with sea-faring jolliness. The horror sets in with child abduction and ransom terror – 2000 packs of Captain Fishface grub must be sold and the wrappers sent in for the safe return of the little ones. This is all too much for sweet Timbo. Shocked and stunned at the new commercial campaigns, a heated, camp conversation with himself convinces him that Graeme and Bill are simply bad eggs. All three are advertising men extraordinaire, sporting red and white striped shirts and the full businessman clobber. Even Bill, of all people, has gone capitalist. Tim is not chuffed at all – he relishes in calling Bill, B.O., and ultimately clubs them both together as B.O.G.G. Potential billboards, taking the milk slogan 'Are You Getting Enough?' and juxtaposing it with a shot of Maggie Thatcher, are simply not acceptable. Tim, longing for the good old days when, as Bill points out, ads told lies, hardly gets a chance to complain before Graeme gets his wall chart out and runs through the system. An A–D scale is in operation with the Dumb housewives at the bottom and the Advertising men at the top. The target is those thick, bless 'em, 'goodnight ladies, goodnight…' housewives, but things ain't as easy as they once were. Raz washing power clearly makes clothes grey and/or rot so it's brute force and impossible dreams that count on Harvest Moon Perfume. The stuff must be bought else Bill will get cross ('Harvest Moon, the scent that lingers. Buy some… or I'll break your fingers!'), while promises of becoming Pope or Heavyweight Boxing Champion of the World tempt punters to buy Kenny's Cornflakes. Eager illusions of little kids with the charming, 'she's a wonderful mum…' break into the classic comment with Graeme's follow-up, 'and a terrific lay!' It's the fool-proof bully and trick system, but Tim, having lived this commercial lie for far too long can take no more. The bread sales pitch relating nine out of 10 doctors believe that the product will stop the punter being squashed by elephants may have taken Graeme a long time – to find the loony doctors and the willing elephants – but Tim's defensive to the end. He calls for the truth, presenting the

toothless antics of sticky, sweet, blackcurrant mixture Vibena with veteran drinking mum, Janice Thormby, and her dentist-ignoring daughter. There's Graeme's Scots dog handler, Jock McPhee, feeding his pooch a choice of Nosho, nails, broken glass or manure. Meanwhile, Mr Rudyard has no knowledge of what goes in his almond Regency Slices thanks to his 'ruddy great factory' and exceedingly large amounts of money. Sales plummet as a result of all this honesty. More to the point, a rather nasty smell – which certainly isn't fried chicken – wafts in and takes control. B.O. is convinced it's B.O. but it's certainly not his arm pits that pong. A less than subtle attempt to check out his colleague ('All those in this room called Graeme Garden raise your arm!'). But, it's neither of them. It's product-denying Timbo who staggers in. Graeme, delicate as always, makes a tentative comment ('You appear to have dressed carelessly… '). Soap, toilet paper, toothpaste, mouth wash and every other body cleaning luxury is off Tim's shopping list. He's a walking, smelling advert for the denial of advertising campaigns. Bill and Graeme can't help themselves. The mention of stains lets Graeme rip into his 'hard to budge' removal pitch, there are products 'just right for you' and all manner of tempting, untruthful promises. But the all-powerful smell is too much to ignore. The marketing-obsessed Bill and Graeme need to advertise something and, strangely, need Tim's agreement to go for it. Embracing every sales cliché in the world, Gray goes through the 'run it up the flagpole and see if the cat licks it up' business in order to suggest the ultimate in safe advertising products – Bread. Tim admits that people like bread and even he eats it but the 'Bread is Nice' slogan is dismissed as 'too racy…' and leads to a further suggestion. Water seems a fair bet but Tim's sex-obsessed mind conjures up erotic images of wet T-shirts ('the damp, almost transparent fabric clinging to her every contour') that sends him off in orgasmic fits before regaining his calm – 'at least, that's what springs to my mind!' Tea allows Tim a 'little perforations' moment before Graeme scuppers that notion due to its involvement of water. Tim inadvertently hits on the winner and before long, string is most definitely the thing. Plans are a foot for The String Marketing Board and Bill goes off into a delicious musical rendition of I'd Like to Teach the World to String. The ads may be mocking familiar set ups and stereotypes but everything is alright –

TIM, BILL AND GRAEME AS CONVICTS – *GOODIES IN THE NICK*

it's only string. Bill's limp, Heineken-drooping manhood can not be tempted by his low-cut, in your face cleavage, companion. That's where string comes in, it 'refreshes the parts beers have reached!' Tim's super smooth, Bondian, white dinner-jacketed cool dude, calmly eyes a wet T-shirted nymphet running across the beach. She stops to offer him a string cigar and gives the stressed chap a chance to 'unwind…' Tim's as pleased as punch. After all, clad in his string vest, eating his string on toast and not being able to tell string from butter, this entire boom industry is down to his genius. However, something's not quite right with Bill and Graeme – there's a distinct possibility that dummies have taken their place to conceal their absence. But poor old Tim, even tossing a string dumpling at 'Graeme's' head and twisting it askew,

doesn't get any danger signals. He's far too busy holding power over housewives and revelling in the worship of himself. *Tomorrow's World* with Raymond Baxter, complete in string underwear, presents a report on string's success. Safer and cheaper than any other industrial tool for one simple reason – 'it doesn't work…' Rock guitarists are silenced with string strings, string umbrellas are as much use as a wet weekend in Bognor, operation scars are stitched with string, it's used to replace leg cartilages in very wobbly patients and even the BBC studio is totally reliant on the stuff. Thus, the cameras, stool, table, and entire set, collapses around our hapless host's ears. Tim is still loyal ('it's honest!') and besides, fear not, string is still the thing and another glitzy small screen programme, The Wonderful World of String, is here to prove it. With Graeme's narration, business isn't quite booming but the Brits just can't get enough of the stuff. A string-covered Dougal is dragged through the street, the stock exchange predicts a huge slump and the average housewife in the studio echoes the narrator and wonders, 'Why can't we import it?' The truth, of course, is that Graeme's the housewive, Graeme's the supplier and Graeme's the money-pinching crook in all this affair… alongside Bill, naturally. The Arabs have reams of the stuff, destroying ancient carpets to redistribute string, sending it down an elaborate pipe system. Arabs Bill and Graeme (in heavy disguise but fooling no one except, possibly, Tim) have control of the huge string mountain and want a fortune for it. String bags are losing potatoes and tennis rackets are next to useless, while dummy Graeme and Bill keep Timbo's insane babblings happy with recorded 'Yes Tim' and 'Most certainly' stock answers. But realisation that the bad Chelsea result didn't raise a titter from Bill causes concern, an in-depth look (he lifts the back of Bill up) reveals robots and the manic, laughing head of Bill forms a sinister, funny and potent image to cut from. The silhouetted Arabs on television are clearly the two Goodies gone bad but Tim's attack reveals merely cut out stand-ups. Chasing the two villains out of the tiny shoebox of a BBC studio past the stunning independent glories of ATV, Tim stumbles into the world of adverts. With Bill and Graeme's irritatingly catchy, 'Everybody loves string, everybody needs string' campaign ringing in the ears, desperate Tim tries to suppress interest with cold reasoning and anti-string lectures. Squashed from beneath the screen and from the sides, Tim breaks into his heartfelt pleas before he's side-stepped into a huge pot of margarine and ultimately re-introduced to himself in the shape of the vintage Beanz Meanz boy. This time plugging string like a good 'un, Tim sticks a plate of beans in his own face and scurries off after Bill. The Kung Poo aftershave interlude employing the original Valerie Leon to reprise her man-hungry High Karate performance, sees Tim finally give in to her well-endowed advances, pucker up for a kiss and receive several well-timed karate chops for his trouble. The evil duo make their escape within a huge tin of Dulux which, went infiltrated by Tim, spurts out great amounts of non-working non-drip red paint. Meanwhile, Bill's Milk Tray guy delivers an explosive box of chocs for Tim. Reaching fever pitch with Tim's forcible entrance into a washing machine for a rinse with Bubble X, the lather goes haywire, the ATV studios are awash and even the television set at home fills up and breaks with the pressure of suds. The Goodies — out of context of the episode and happily wiping away the soapy mess from their, and the nation's screen, happily sit down to watch the closing credits. With the cast and crew listing reversed to reflect the trio looking towards the viewer, the lads don't seem to understand what their own show has been about. Bill's beginning to crack up as a stony silence is required through several seconds of backward credits. Supping tea and watching bemused, finally the giveaway, Jim Franklin's name pops up, 'He's to blame!' Tim reckons he's 'trying to win a prize', Graeme confidently predicts 'he won't!' Reaching forward he switches off the TV and the episode is finished.

Did You Know? *The Australian Broadcasting Commission edited out Graeme's line, describing the perfect advert mother figure as 'A terrific lay'.*

RAYMOND BAXTER, MARCELLE SAMETT, VALERIE LEON. Episode Five, recorded Friday 18 June, broadcast Tuesday 19 October 1976, 9–9.30pm, BBC2.

2001 AND A BIT

With Stanley Kubrick's futuristic vision as their starting point and a contrast between the violence rules the sportsfield ethos of Rollerball and the gentle, pleasant boredom of cricket, this is a fascinating episode. With aged Goodies all staggering round the 60 mark, this edition is also painfully close to where the legendary three really are today. However, unlike The Beatles, in heavy disguise for *Help*, the Goodies are not bloated, long grey hair sporting fogies, quite yet. The terrific three play their own, mixed up at birth, and rearranged, sons. Thus, Bill injects Tim's

patriotic mincing, Tim has Graeme's cold scientific reasoning and little Graeme has Bill's full-blown bloodlust. One longs for a more detailed sketching of these intriguing, swapped characterisations, but the first half is packed with irony and comic asides. By this stage, the trio's identities were so firmly etched on the public that character twists and mannerisms merely enriched the comedy. It all starts with Graeme's less than futuristic sounding announcement that 'The year is 2001 and a bit' with gruff old Tim Brooke-Taylor OBE, now with a beer belly and that manic hairstyle retained from *Hype Pressure,* frankly chatting to his beloved son, Bill Oddie in Union flag waistcoat and suit. Lightening his voice, sporting a ribbon in his hair and proudly up-holding the Goodies name, the old firm is finally placed in his hands. What, might you ask, happened to Bill and Graeme? Well, Tim got rid of them for various reasons: Bill for being Bill really and, of course, biting people, while, Graeme was absented thanks to detention at the Crown's pleasure through an unnatural relationship with his computer. A real Brooke-Taylor (he's a right little crawler), Bill tugs his metaphoric forelock, calls his father 'Sir!' and meekly fights to keep his facial fungus because of its 'butch' effect. Handing over the reigns, befuddled old Tim shows the old Goods as they were. There's also a shot of Tim's wife and the mother of all three new Goodies, Raquel Welch! With the notion that each are really playing each other's children with the enforced attitude from their surrogate father shining brightly through, Graeme, er, sorry, Tim, can amble into the scene complete with glasses, side burns and biting putdowns towards Tim, er, Bill — get it! But this new brave set of Goodies, led by Bill in Tim mode, must start as they mean to go on… with a rousing, patriotic speech. Bill's first attempt is ruined by Tim's interjection and there are tears. Now Tim's father may have been a 'great raving loony' but that doesn't stop his offspring knowing a thing or two about logic. With an anything-goes society, the Goodies are archaic and useless. The old days of father nipping off for a quick look at his *TitBits* have gone. In the glorious kingdom of Jolly King Charles, it's a totally free, do what you want, attitude. Everything considered a bit off in the old days is legalised now, kids turn off from *The Beano* and *The Dandy* in favour of The Porno and The Randy ('gives Biffo the Bear a whole new dimension!') and the television, sanitised with Mary Whitehouse-killing violence and filth, has gone so far there's nowhere else to go. The point is that total openness is boring, as Graeme's lacklustre telly announcer proves. BBC3 hopes to get your attention with an in-bred, multisex beast sitcom, while on the side you're watching, it is Sportstime. The thought of this is far too much for any sane man (Graeme shoots himself off camera), with Arab Jimmy Hill, getting his oats as he boringly trails chess and non-football. Cue the new improved Bill-influenced Graeme Garden, complete with beard and frantic passion for Rollerball. He stomps round the place in protective shoulder pads and mouths off how proud his glorious dad Bill would be (after the real Bill worries himself of what Mr Oddie would think of it all, reverses his picture on the wall and reveals the back of his head on the flip side). But all this violence is getting duller by the minute. Audiences are so immune to it all that Gray needs to spice up the action a tad. The new brighter Rollerball goes down the unpromising route of mixing the old style with an egg and spoon race, resulting in Dodo destruction, death of players and general apathy from all concerned. Rants to include tanks or audience acid-spraying interludes are conjured up, but Tim – being decisively Tim-like in his Graeme mode – longs for the good old days. Bill, naturally, is all for it. Something genuinely boring will knock the crowd out… but what? What else but cricket? With his 1976 guide to hand, Tim rediscovers the ancient rules. Lovingly relating the art of preparing a grass pitch then waiting till it rains, covering it over, digging it up, writing George Evans Is Innocent and spending time in prison, cricket seems the answer to everybody's prayers. The police seemed to be continually victorious via these rules but Bill's dad should know what's what. Young Bill vaguely remembers going to a match as a little lad and falling asleep. A telephone call to father is required, although Tim Senior is no better, muttering something about Lord's and dropping off himself. But Young Tim sees the light. Of course, Lord's is the cricket world's ancient Stonehenge-like place. It's not a temple for sun worshipping, those pitches weren't rice fields and the MCC wasn't Roman numerals. Cricket is the key and Bill and Tim are on the job. With an enthused confused rendition of the old theme song, 'Goodies, goody, goody… thing, thing!', the lads are off. Bill and Tim Senior, strap on their painfully slow, ultimately high-speed Acme Power Boots and head off on an expedition to round up the MCC bods, while little Tim is off to Lord's. Unknowingly tipping out the ashes, donning a jock-strap as

shoulder gear, a box as a cap and a couple of caps as tassles, he slowly pieces together the grand art of the game via Tim's Theory of Cricket book. The *Cricket Box* publication was to come 10 years later! Bound and padded, he lays a ball – chicken and egg style, sets up a couple of stumps as a sling affair and blasts one through a bat, onto the pitch-roller and through the window. Meanwhile, as Tim learns the hard way, Bill and Tim Senior, puffing his cheeks like Donald Sinden in *The Island at the Top of the World*, arrives at the MCC Sanctuary where these vitally important, ultra-rare creatures are preserved for the nation. Bill Oddie the birder clearly takes over the scriptwriting here, retaining class political satire (the five-pound notes have Maggie Thatcher's head on them) alongside indulged bird references ('these game birds', the golden pullover, the camp little ring pullover, old coots, the willow warbler with its duck call – 'Owzat!' – and the like). Touchingly, and surprisingly, aged Graeme and aged Bill have been sucked into the cricketing ethos and Tim Senior – initially mistaken for Nicholas Parsons and pelted for his trouble – is all misty-eyed and emotional, reunited with his two old pals. At least, there's more air time than *Television's Greatest Hits* provided, and sexual memories ('After his mother' 'Weren't we all!'), throwaway jokes and real emotion, ignites this sequence. Best of all is a shared conversation about the good old days, 'The three-seater bike, you remember, the good old days!' 'Ooh yes, the giant kitten!' 'The giant beanstalk!' 'The Ministry of Silly Walks!' 'Yeah… I don't remember that…' But all these happy memories are as nothing as the job in hand – to resurrect cricket for a jaded generation. Young Bill, his heart full of Timbo-like flare, relishes his inspiring, rebel-rousing poem *The Pride of the MCC*. Juxtaposing aged hopelessness with rampant xenophobia ('We'll show them all with bat and ball, in spite of our lumbago. We're not caught out by frog or kraut, nor greasy wop nor dago!') If the aim is to bore them stiff – and I think it is – then cricket is back with a vengeance. A computerised host of Sportstime yawns along with everybody else, as Bill and Tim desperately try to make things thrilling in their commentary. A debate about whether one of the MCC lot is breathing or not gets heated and a speeding pigeon stuns the crowd into muted grasps of amazement. But even Bill concludes it's all a load of rubbish before Graeme breaks into the playing area with Rollerball gusto. The old boys get destructive and spinning googlies fox the opposition. Bashing balls down at a rate of knots, a communal, protective suit for the Rollerballers is less than useless for batting purposes. Wickets fly, get cracked, whittled and wrenched from the ground, while the Rollerballing bowling doesn't even dent the oldies. Graeme's spiked ball sticks to aged Bill's bat, bad sportsmanship and tripping gives Timbo a sitter for six and those wonderous Power Boots make running between the wickets a pleasure. Knocking down Graeme's fielder with mechanised gusto, poor old Gray Bag's removal of the helmet, only to get a crack on the bonce from a cricket ball for his trouble, is a masterpiece. Employing tanks and grenades to finish off the match, Tim's final pitch of an atom bomb is momentarily hit by Graeme's bat, the universe goes into slow motion and the mushroom cloud erupts. The end of civilisation… not on your life. The MCC inherit the earth and retain the ashes. Chilling, hilarious and eerie all at once, the three aged Goodies and their colleagues stroll through the credit sequence merrily singing *We Are the Boys of the MCC* like demented, twisted remnants of *Dad's Army*.

OLIVER GILBERT. Episode Six, recorded Fridays 18 and 25 June, broadcast Tuesday 26 October 1976, 9–9.30pm, BBC2.

THE GOODIES ALMOST LIVE

It may not be unplugged but it's certainly pre-MTV. This is the definitive record of the Goodies as pop stars, taking one step beyond the usual three-minute *Top of the Pops* appearance and presenting a half-hour concert within the context of the television series. Packed full of Bill Oddie's greatest tunes, he is clearly having the time of his life. Although, despite this reassuringly and openly, not being a live concert (Graeme's opening announcement gets stuck in the groove and repeats into infinity), the entire collection was re-recorded for this very special presentation. Thus, mimed and minced they may be in parts, there are plenty of subtle differences between these performances and the released versions. For the *Sgt Pepper*-like flow to work, Tim stands alone at the outset, starting *Please Let Us Play* and suffering Graeme and Bill condemnations from the sidelines. Gray even encourages the live audience. Sort of convincing (on occasions) his hands usher in cries of 'no, no, no', but soon enough, backing vocals and Beatles head shakes are the name of the game. Bill drums, Gray strums and Tim sheepishly plays the triangle, brilliantly transforming from 'normal' Goodies attire to Rock Gods. Belting out the number, it allows Bill to relish real clout behind a drum kit and Tim

(revealing the nerves behind the glam) to give a sigh of relief as his triangle finale goes off without a hitch. Graeme lets rip on electric guitar – although most of the instrumental licks and bits are played in-house by the studio musicians. Graeme, in full country and western gear, ambles through *Good Ole Country Music* with Bill providing sound effects and ultimately an ironic backing vocal. Reading from sheet music blessed with a single, never-faltering note, Graeme's relentless howls finale reduces the songwriter to a laughing wreck, hiding behind his music for comfort. The natural progression is into Tim's camp as a row of pink tents, midnight cowperson's stunning rendition of *Cactus in My Y-Fronts* with Bill's cool backing vocal and female interjection aided and abetted with Graeme's coconut horseshoe effect. Note the absence of the 'horn-swaggaled' line at the close, replaced here with Tim's semi-humble reaction to the applause of the crowd – 'I deserve some of it, not all of it…' But now, with the show in full swing, Bill can step out front in his groovy pink disco suit, grab a little soul, bask in a couple of glam backing singers and strut the funky chicken. With Pan's Grannies doing their thang, Bill can get all funky before Graeme ('I don't want to do no funky chicken!'), gets on stage in his pink disco suit and kick starts the slimy toad. The Grans follow along until Tim, in his pink disco suit, changes course towards the Loony Moth – rejoice in Bill's bearded granny crashing straight into the camera. Getting more and more outlandish (staggering through everything from the festering ferret to the disgusted three-toed sloth via the belligerent bee) this brilliant build-up reaches a climax when, having gone along with everything else, even the two girls refuse to get involved with – shock, horror – the *Funky Gibbon*. With a saddened, pleading look into camera, Bill utters those immortal words, 'Come on everybody, it's gibbon time…' and the full force of three G-emblazoned dungaree-wearing Goodies do the business. With stock footage reversed, speeded up and generally mucked about with, gibbons, chimps and orang-utans get in on the act, Bill crouches in an amazed loony reaction to Tim's gibboning about and even the audience get the bug. Another version of the Goodies classic, this retains the 'yellow ribbon' close from the single release. Backed up with its original B-side, Graeme's mini narrative on the history of the blues leads into the almighty, sepia-presented *Sick Man Blues*. Bill goes seriously mellow while Tim hams it up. Graeme hands out sick bags to the audience. And note the ad-lib 'makes you sick...' off camera from Tim at the end. With a Goodie theme interlude and the legendary 'One More Time' the lads storm through a winning medley, turning on the superhero garb for *The Inbetweenies* (with Bill rocking it up and the other lads donning square/hip costumes for the 'too old and too young' chorus). It's ecky thump, huge flat caps and *Black Pudding Bertha* next, with Tim and Graeme's baby glove puppets assisting Bill's touching croon through *Nappy Love*. Perched on a stool and proudly wearing his 'Billy' badge, Bill does a charming job but it's Graeme's deep throat interjection which really hits home. Tim rallies the patriotic troops for *Bounce* – with all three in Union flag waistcoats, a glorious Union flag back projection and red, white and blue balloons floating through the audience. Graeme's Scottish and Nazi moments are priceless and mucked about footage even gets Harold Wilson and his dog doing the bounce for Britain. Graeme's dapper orchestra leader sets up *The Last Chance Dance* with Bill, again in loosened tie and stool-seated Sinatra mode, giving a peerlessly emotive performance. With Tim acting out the lyrics with hopeless ineptitude and Graeme's madcap conducting, Bill tends to lose the plot at stages but the entire, triple-strength presentation is blinding. Even HRH takes to the floor. But, the best is kept till the end. With the lads clad in pin-striped business suits and bowler hats, a familiar, almost inaudible, tune wafts from the audience. It is uneasily picked up by Tim and gradually blossoms into Bill grabbing the microphone and belting out *Wild Thing*. The bristling rendition is electric and Tim's toe-curling smooth talking to a very embarrassed female audience member is unforgettable. Chucking his coat into the crowd, getting ready for Series Eight John Travolta cool and letting rip with knowing looks and flashes of leg, Tim milks the comedy, while Bill hits home with the rock, as the closing credits roll and the Goodies sing the short snatch of their legendary theme... live, well almost.

Episode Seven, recorded Friday 17 July, broadcast Tuesday 2 November 1976, 9–9.30pm, BBC2.

SERIES SEVEN

Jim Franklin relinquished directing duties for this series handing the reigns over to Bob Spiers, later to direct the second series of *Fawlty Towers*, *Absolutely Fabulous*, two episodes of the Australian Colin Lane comedy *The Adventures of Lano* and *Spice World: The Movie*. A month-long filming schedule began on 9 September.

Film cameramen Reg Pope and Richard Gauld. Film editors Glenn Hyde and John Jarvis. Visual effects Dave Havard. Graphic design William Blaik. Costume Andrew Rose. Make-up Jean Steward. Lighting Eric Wallis. Sound Jeff Booth and Peter Edwards. Music by Bill Oddie and Dave McRae. Stunt adviser Stuart Fell. Designers John Stout and Pauline Harrison. Production assistant Tony Ravenscraig. Producer Jim Franklin. Director Bob Spiers.

ALTERNATIVE ROOTS

Bill had been allowed to indulge his Northern roots for a bit of Ecky Thump. For this thought-provoking opening episode for the new series, all three Goodies backtracked to primitive tribes. Risking controversy and, indeed, misunderstanding akin to the *South Africa* programme, the Goodies finally debunked and berated that perennial television favourite *The Black and White Minstrel Show*. Condemning its racist content and giving the minority attack a comedy voice, the real genius of the programme is its brilliant use of strange bedfellow television reference to *Roots*. Hugely popular at the time, the stark realism of slavery drama used in terms of innocent, happy, showbusiness entertainment, makes this a richly interesting piece of work and a real social document for changing attitudes in broadcasting. And it's 10 years before political correctness kicked in. The show starts, typically enough, with Tim preening himself for an instant photograph. Bill's entrance ruins the moment, 'You made me flash before I was ready!' and the image is all hair akimbo and blind terror. But, never one to let the bearded swine get him completely down, the framed pic goes on the walk next to his ancient limp-wristed ancestor – the massive-chinned Beau Brooke-Taylor. He came across with William the Conquerer (as Bill comments, he looks like he would come across with almost anybody). Chins, apparently, run in Tim's family but with selective breeding and sheer determination the plan is afoot to create the ultimate chinless wonder. Bill is convinced that mission has already been accomplished and ponders on how far and convex the breeding can go in the future. Eager to promote his heritage, Tim presents his proud family coat of arms. Again, Bill is having none of this – a flick of the wrist and a different angle highlights Tim's family as nothing more than sheep stealers (the coat of arms is all villain masks, dead rams and gallows). Even his priceless family legacy is a bag marked SWAG. A debate on the pros and cons of digging up the past is just about to erupt when Graeme's entrance stops the scene. In full traditional Scottish dress the others don't recognise him – Tim is convinced he's come to the wrong place ('Madam!'), engages in simple, loud, 'these foreigners don't understand sense', communication, before vowing to get the immigrant swine deported. Unbeknown to Tim and Bill (who thought Gray had been in the loo for the last three weeks), the canny Scot had returned to his beloved roots for a soul-searching interlude. Tim's not bothered. Having waited all this time for the convenience to be free, he's got an urgent visit to pay. In television-mocking mood, one man's search for highland heritage or Hoots!, sees Graeme pinpointing the Scots' appalling sense of humour – with a myriad of punning sign posts for Loch Jaw, Glen Ford, Ben Doon and the ultimate destination, Dunghill. With simple needs and roulette wheel pleasure, these tartan chappies go about their day. The tribe's elder, holding a wee baby aloft embraces *2001: A Space Odyssey* with a snatch of classical music. 'Old and bent' with a camp motion, he wanders off to leave his offspring to it. The offspring is, eventually, Graeme or Celtic Kiltie as he is known. With fireside initiation into the ways of the Scots, porridge, money and traditional dress ('What's worn under the kilt?' 'Nothing… it's all in perfect working order!'), the ultimate hunt for the wee haggis is begun. A hilarious speeded up chase through the highlands ends in Graeme's capture of the adorable creature (it's tracked to its tree-bound lair and Gray chucks a rock at it). Skinned and enjoyed – with the fur the only bit worth eating – Piper Andy McPrevin plays out the action as Graeme's story comes to a close. But Tim's, still desperate, worsening by the second, lavatorial requirements, must wait… for Bill has a tale of Johnny Applefarm, cider-drinking yokels and the ancient Ooh Ahh Ooh Ahh tribe in his own telly presentation, Froots! A recognised man of the tribe when you can suck the straw and do the funny voice, these simple people sing, dance and frolic to their heart's content before idyllic innocence is shattered by the arrival of the dreaded tour bus. Bryan Pringle, in evil mood, plays out this corruption of Marty Feldman's quick march sight-seeing tour, with the added sinister element of slave trade overtones. Herded aboard, whipped and humiliated, only the fit, young men and Kinda Kinky aka Bill Oddie (much to his parent's champagne-celebrating delight), are chosen, with before long, Graeme's Scots brigade and Tim, as County Cutie, with his band of sheep robbers, joining the nightmarish trip to London. Desperately trying to bond – Bill and Graeme's almost impossibly thick accents and hilarious attempts at communication go right over the head of Tim's frightfully British bloke – 'quarter past three!'

Repeating each others phrases – Tim's 'Jolly good show!' is a classic and even the sheep gets its 'baa' in on the act – the lads struggle to agree on the tune for *We Shall Overcome*, as these slave-destined chums suffer the dreadful conditions and, even worse, dreadful packed lunches, of the hellish coach company. Tim's less than keen to get too close to Bill's camp glances, but adversity makes them loyal friends, with the whistle stop, Dick Barton tune accompanied, tour of London Town, leaving the lads in a real spin – particularly after a madly spinning spot of lunch in the Revolving Restaurant of the Post Office Tower. But the ultimate humiliation is yet to come… BBC Television Centre and the slave market. Forced to flash their fetlocks and show those sparkling teeth, lot 75, or the Goods and their clansmen, are enlisted by bald-headed, cigar-puffing producers for such terrors as *Seaside Special* (which the Goodies had just appeared on) and even, *The Max Bygraves Show*. The solitary chosen apple farmer is given total, knowing respect from the three remaining specimens – yep, you guessed it, the Goodies. Pringle's desperate attempt to flog them for *Rolf Harris and Friends* on their very friendliness alone, fails (particularly with Bill earnestly mouthing 'Piss off!'). But the evil Pringle is not prepared to trek over to ATV. He's going to break these swines in personally, at The Cotten Fields. Dragged over to this fiendish place, dance routines are constantly in progress with the ritual humiliation of cockney knees up Mother Brown, there's nothing like a damn sailor horn-piping and straw-hatted country ho-downing. Good for nothing and nothing but Goodies, the lads may think they have won – but no, still worse is to come… *The Black and White Minstrel Show*! Bill wants respect, wears a painted white mouth sneer and sports snappy dreadlocks. Graeme tries, unsuccessfully, to sneak in his Scottish headgear but, shockingly, Tim seems very happy. After all, it hides the dirt, sets off his eyes, the bow tie is so Frank Muir he has a bash at introducing *Call My Bluff* and he can sing patriotic songs all day long. His high-pitched rendition of *Land of Hope and Glory* is condemned in light of Graeme's book on How to Rap Minstrel. But Bill and Graeme – stoking the already lit fire of degrading contempt for the series – try to convince him that a white and white minstrel show would be better. Tim, of course, isn't convinced, believing this to be racial prejudice. Indeed, the Black and Whites are so popular, he thinks, because it caters for both races. An experiment to do it without the make-up resulted in half the audience switching off – quite clearly the coloured viewers! Television programmers trail the new season and, desperate to win huge audience figures, everything is in blacked-up make-up – from *The Six Million Dollar Man* to *Kojak* (renamed Cocojak), *Blue Peter* (sorry Black Peter) to Sooty and Michael Darkinson interviewing a white-washed Mohammad Ali. All three are outraged now, and the opening number of the show is disrupted by Bill's 'revolting' stand against racism, passionately turning on the Martin Luther King-style delivery. Backed with a protected array of multicoloured minstrels, people shall no longer be oppressed merely because of the colour of their make-up! The minstrel Goodies are on the warpath and a cell of their blacked-up colleagues are released into television centre. Treated like animals with a 'Do Not Feed' sign over their door, the freed slaves go ape. A 'minstrel loose' warning is sounded, BBC parking attendants brandish 'Car Park Full' signs and the place is over-run by the BBC dogs… well dog, actually. Absailing down the front of the BBC, Graeme tempts the pooch with a huge bone, hits him through the window golf club style and beats a dog impersonating attendant over the head with it. A blacked-up Angela Rippon (typically flashing her legs post-Eric and Ern), Robin Day and even Enoch Powell, distract the chase, and unconvincing moving scenery back projection is revealed, as Tim is bashed over the bonce, and his count out on the canvas is accompanied by the flickering count down on a film strip. The twittering bird sound effects of the knocked out Timbo are immediately traced back to Bill, intently listening to the bird song within the archives of the sound department. Rolling the discs towards uniformed foe and creating apt accompanying musak (thus the locomotion vinyl spins along the floor to train effects), the fun and games soon become a shared laugh, but the guard's smile is quickly wiped off when the tick, tick, tick of an explosive record blows up in his face. The chase continues, the climax is needed quickly and, with the trio and a Beeb bod falling into a vat of film department developing negative fluid, the Goodie minstrels are transformed into black-suited white chappies and the dark-suited white guard becomes a minstrel clone. With a grin into camera from the boys, one of the many watching Jewish television producers intones, 'Great… give those boys a series'.

Did You Know? *The line concerning young maidens licking off a coating of porridge was edited by the Australian Broadcasting*

Commission. *The Black and White Minstrel revolt sequence was included in the documentary* One Million Years PC *part of BBC2's themed* Politically Incorrect Night, *on Easter Monday 1998.*

BRYAN PRINGLE, CHARLIE STEWART, STUART FELL, MAX FAULKNER, THE FRED TOMLINSON SINGERS, JOHN MELAINEY, BRIAN ROGERS, KENNETH WARWICK. Episode One, recorded Thursday 28 October, broadcast Tuesday 1 November 1977, 9–9.30pm, BBC2.

DODONUTS

One of the sweetest Goodies episodes is, ironically, full of excrement and vomit gags with an insane desire to kill the endangered creatures at its centre. Shifting gear from cruelty to animals humour, Bill becomes the Bill Oddie of reality with his 'eco-freak' conservation of God's menagerie. While Tim and Graeme stagger round the country in Colonel Blimp eyebrows and moustaches, Bill quietly tries to enjoy his off-Goodie passion of bird-watching and focuses the madness of society through a looking glass of his comic expression. For his two cohorts, the kill anything that moves ethos is just a bit of playacting. Destroying a weather vane, filling Tim's tossed cap full of shot, exploding a pigeon coop and literally stamping a sparrow into the ground, once back at the Endangered Species Club – everything eaten, drank, sat on or played with is made from remnants of dead animals – Tim reverts to normal and complains that the character 'voice hurts the throat!' Comfy pandas, flamingo-legged sitting sticks, darts with stuffed birds and head-warming baby seals are not the sort of things to impress Bill. However, crying anti-hunt and inhumane slogans from within his obvious hide, the club society rejects his protest. Despite the odd mistake (the squashed sparrow), it's only the very rarest and most precious creatures the hunters are after – but that's Bill's point. Tim tries to explain that there just isn't any fun in killing budgies, before he suddenly doubts his own words ('is there?') and Graeme, off camera and with plenty of gunfire, proves it – 'none at all!' Dismissed as a loony conservationist who would rather starve than eat harmed creatures, the delicious club menu (with red and white – squirrels and rhinos that is) leaves Bill cold. Handpicked as a potential endangered target himself, Bill runs off with a cloud of buck shot behind him. With a burst of the Goodies tune, a caption card details the months that have passed and the wounds that have healed. Back at Cricklewood, Bill has successfully gathered about him the entire remaining collection of hit list rarities. He even has the dwarf gibbon. But, more importantly, Graeme Garden-like, he has fiendishly designed ways of protection for the poor things. An armadillo without his armour is, naturally enough, a illo. Completely wiped out and often used as catapults, the armour saved the day. Hence, armoured shrew, armoured rabbits, a porcupine grass snake which doubles as a loo brush, exploding slugs, vulture-beaked pulvets, boxing kangaroos, a duck that claws back and Clara the chicken who launches a jet-propelled egg attack in self-defence. He may be a crank but he's a very clever one. But the old master, Graeme, is even cleverer. Fuelling his passion for the rare and wondrous, his local pet shop provides the last, remaining specimen from the ultimate discontinued line – the Dodo. Tim isn't being fooled by that. What about that legendary phrase 'as dead as a...', but the proof of the pudding is in the waddling, and large as life and twice as cute, is the bird in question. Forget Dougal, forget the flying geese, forget even the mini London skyline destroyed by kitten power, the Goodies Dodo is the finest prop in the show's history. Cheeky, smelly, noisy, hilarious and, above all, strangely convincing in the right light, the Dodo squawks away all over the place, causing a mess and generally living on borrowed time. Introduced with the truly punful, 'Going cheap?' 'No, going aggrhhh!', exchange between Tim and Graeme, the dear, fat bird soon settles in as resident irritant. Of course, it could all be a dreadful dream. Bill and Tim wake up to the squawking commotion, Graeme – leaving behind a rather feeble action man double – is not in sleepy land and something is certainly very odd in Cricklewood. Three in the morning is no time to bang home the going cheap gagline but it ain't Gray, it's the Dodo. Popping up with superb comic timing from behind the sofa, attacking Graeme and dragging him down, the bird makes his way towards Bill's tantalising dangly bits and, worst of all, throws up in one of Tim's jubilee sneakers. The filthy, bean-stuffed thing has done its business on Tim's regal throne. Posh initially thinks it is a new cushion and, later, a gardener lovingly shovels some on his prize roses only to see the blooms instantly wither and die. A dollop of baked beans is blamed, but Bill doesn't care about the pong. This is scientific and humanly precious. Conservation is the future. The Endangered Species Club is none too happy, an emergency closing down meeting gets under way once the facial hair completes the members' character and Tim, shockingly, explains that Bill's protection act has

DIB, DIB, DIB. THE GOODIES GET OUTRAGEOUS FOR *SCOUTRAGEOUS*

denied them all the fun. All the animals were kept in a big box and have now eaten each other. Goodbye, good hunting. Of course, Graeme remembers one final target worth having a bash at... the Dodo. Tim's stirring patriotic climax is hastily curtailed and the lads head off to Bill's sanctuary. Life with a Dodo is no fun, Bill's at his wit's end, his lunch is pinched, the window is permanently closed, the smell is overpowering and that bleeding squawk could drive a man to distraction. Bill doesn't know whether it's good for the bird or not, but 'it certainly isn't good for me, I'll tell you!' Fresh air is the answer and, in order to convince the Dodo that the outside world is safe, Bill dons his own unique Dodo suit. Unique? Tim's got his own Acme Decoy Dodo to tempt the real feathered prize out. The coy courtship between the mock Dodos is one of the most hilarious bits of visual magic featured in *The Goodies* and Bill's bird-loving passion informs the scene further with the Walt Disney Wildlife camera crew (the reel holders double as the operator's Mickey Mouse ears) and Oddie's spot on, comic, laid-back narration in the true-life adventure style. The delectable Doris (Tim) and dirty old Dennis (Bill) find love, sexual attraction and wedding plans ('I dodo do!') before beak-to-beak dancing and close-hugging tango, rounds off the fun. However, Bill is quickly revealed as a fake and the real one is required. Tim bursts into the shed, shouting 'Where is it!', and is nearly throttled by the bird jumping from out of a cupboard. Graeme cunningly dismisses the bird as 'inferior' due to its lack of flying and with Bill enthused, the race is on to launch Dodo into the wild blue yonder. For the hunters it's merely an excuse to create a moving target, but Bill takes on Peter Cook's legendary and impossible ravens underwater attempt and tries to get those old Dodo wings flapping. The bird unconvincingly falls off a wall, is tossed from Goodie to Goodie, fired from a circus cannon and finally rugger touch-kicked by Tim. Little seems to helps the matter. Tim, just too eager to wait, finally lets off a shot, wounds the bird's beak and allows Bill introspectively to do his bit. Biggles Dodo, flying ace, is the result, taking to the air in his veteran plane, soaring along with the *Dambusters* theme and generally scuppering the evil destruction attempts of Tim, Graeme and the other mindless killers. Nets and bombs may back fire but the faithful old trandem equipped with anti-aircraft gun is no match for the flightless wonder. Crash landing on to Bill's safe haven, the dejected soul sits among the ruins as his two cohorts try to comfort him. But, at least, the secret of the Dodo's extinction is revealed – their taste is delicious. In fact, they're finger-lickin' good. A powerful comment on man's inhumanity to animals, an extended advert for Kentucky Fried Chicken or somewhere in between… you decide.

Did You Know? This was the most censored of all Goodie episodes with the Australian Broadcasting Commission cutting almost two minutes of material. The Endangered Species menu item 'barbecued badger balls' was removed as was the Dodo sex-obsessed 'at it like knives' observation during Bill's Disney-style film commentary, a knee in the groin, a 'bloody' – although a later one concerning the sausage that makes up Bill's grub gets through the net – and many comments on the sex-mad, breaking wind, crap-dropping habits of the endangered bird. Before presenting the effect on film, the BBC special effects department fashioned a five-foot biplane for the Biggles dodo to fly in. Showing the trio how well the working model could fly and do loop-do-loops, the idea was for smoke to pour from the craft for a stunning aerial display. The button was pushed for action and the plane immediately blew up in mid-air! There were two Dodo models – one a more expressive hand puppet and another, mechanically operated one, for the walking scenes.

BARNEY CARROLL, EDDIE DAVIS, ERNIE GOODYEAR, JIMMY MAC, JAMES MUIR with PERCY EDWARDS as the voice of the Dodo. Episode Two, recorded Friday 4 November, broadcast Tuesday 8 November 1977, 9–9.30pm, BBC2.

SCOUTRAGEOUS

Tim's got a secret, for the last 16 years, Bill and Graeme have idly sat by, gone along with his bizarre, off-camera ritual (raincoat on, trousers down, bin bag on head) and seen him patter off into the night. But tonight is the night when two pursue one, and with Tim unusually late for a very important date, the guard of nervous protection is slightly lowered. The rousing chorus of *I'm Late* from Walt Disney's *Alice in Wonderland* is justified with Tim's jittery, scurrying progress through the dark streets, while comic close-ups of the three pairs of Goodies feet criss-crossing with Hitchcock tension is effectively delivered. In the darkness, Tim is joined by more of these shameless, bizarrely clad figures, eventually finding solace in their tightly guarded hut and revealing themselves as the lowest of the low – wanton boy scouts. This group of old boys in short uniforms avoiding dirty thoughts, are led by young Timbo himself, while Bill, who as usual, has the courage to succeed, takes on the boy scouts' regime on its own terms. Graeme comes along for the ride, sporting the shortest pair of shorts in the world and joining in with the mutual cold shower ritual every time sex rears its ugly head. Bill is immediately into send-up mode, mocking the mini Union flag the lads are expected to salute, going into a 'let's go down the pub' suggestion in response to the sainted dob, dob, dob, and finally succumbing to the cause only because of his greedy, commercialistic desire for badges. Tim is the model of refined duty, dismissing any ideas that the movement is full of shirt lifters, proudly revealing his 'Brown Owl' handle – deliciously misrepeated later by Graeme as both Brown Ale and Brown Trousers – and informing the new boys that woggle jokes are right out: 'He does not indulge in woggle jokes, such as 'Have you seen his woggle?', 'No, but it's a good trick if he can do it!' Back at Goodies camp, the scout thing is tackled and those glorious, tempting badges are flaunted about. Bill and Graeme are hatching a cunning plan and a bit of scout line towing is the name of the game – of course, line towing doesn't last long with the boys, and their scouting duties disintegrate into a visual kaleidoscope of sight gags and authority baiting. Helping old ladies across the street soon turns into a human game of pool, employing a terrifying Nicholas Parsons cut-out face on a stick for shock tactic wig spotting and even crafty techniques to pinch Maggie Thatcher's bloomers – the world's first, pre-prime ministerial, Mrs Thatcher gag – finally pinpoints the outrageous truth that these two boy scouts in the hood are bucking the system and making up scout badges for their own ends. Bill is rather keen to go for the Cheering Up Lonely Housewives Whose Husbands Are At Work badge! The two are ceremoniously drummed out of the organisation. But revenge is sweet, Bill and Graeme are never ones to let a personal grudge go unanswered and poor old Timbo's washing day Ging Gang Goolying is suddenly disrupted by the scout hard men. It may be reminiscent of an old Python sketch but this joyful juxtaposition of bob-a-job week terminology and bovver boy tactics is irresistible. Besides, there is no one who could make a heavy duty scout more painfully hilarious than Graeme Garden in full flow. Donning black masks alongside their scout gear, the rival nasties offer 3500 quid a job deals, get to work with two fire sparking sticks over Tim's hat and dump his shorts accidentally, on purpose, into a bowl of starch – 'ho, ho, ho, whoops!' Tim's shoes are shone so bright he can see his face in them. But it's Graeme's evil scheme of whittling Tim's staff that drives the point home. These guys mean business and no one's jubilee mug is safe! Their scout protection racket dominates the neighbourhood and, played out in Lone Ranger style, the two's trail of knot tying – in everything from lamp posts to a giraffe's neck at the zoo – results in the official dubbing of the scouts as an illegal organisation. Being everybody's favourite coward, Tim scarpers off to burn the evidence of his scouting allegiance but the, by now, very wealthy Graeme and Bill inject a bit of 'less than chum-like behaviour' and tip off the dreaded Scout Finder General. Combining the Vincent Price witch hunts and some chilling Nazi-like attitude, special guest Frank Windsor twists a lifetime of playing friendly coppers on the edge to deliver a cold-hearted, dedicated picture of determined domination. His cunning realisation that even one dob from Tim's accused is a pretty scouty thing to say, comes across with a refined job satisfaction. Windsor's cheerful, tuneful trapping of the scout troupe is a masterclass in underplaying – simply tapping the table and leading the incognito lads in a rousing chorus of *Riding Along on the Crest of a Wave*. Tim's been caught but this half hour is fast running out and there's little or no time to construct a sequence of imprisoning, springing and revitalising Brooke-Taylor for his head-on clash with the duo of evil scouts – instead the glorious English class system comes to the rescue and Tim's released without fuss and off camera simply because he went to a public school. Hurrah! Bucking his ideas up and going for the jugular, Tim joins the – wait for it – Salvation Army… latching on to military might in terms of black bonnets and tambourine slapping. It's a Person's Life with the Sally Ann and Tim's regimented Drilling Sergeant runs

THE LADS GO PUNK FOR *ROCK GOODIES* PUBLICITY

his recruits through their paces, ridiculing those who are after a 'crafty kip' and yelling the 'orrible ears off this brave fighting unit. It's a stunning characterisation, called into action to stop that dreadful duo achieving the World Domination badge and emulating Julius Caesar, Alexander the Great and – in another dig at their old ringmaster – David Frost. The basic plot, sticking Graeme's home-made atom bomb under Oliver Reed and only detonating it if the money is forthcoming, is the ultimate McGuffin here. For, it's just an excuse for Tim's army to cross old-fashioned tea and sympathy with five rounds rapid and machinegun warfare. Tim's wild-eyed, war-crazed expressions are priceless but the battle ends in the anti-climactic defeat and unmasking of the renegade scouts. The bomb is a flop, a simple lie allows the crooks off scott free and, just at the moment of glory, Tim reverts to the gullible creature we know and love. At the end of the day, he reassuringly lacks the true killer instinct.

Did You Know? *The Australian Broadcasting Commission cut a 'bloody' and two lengthy sequences – the cold shower scout ethos and the Maggie Thatcher bloomers-pinching badge plan. The outrageously sized Scout hat wore by Bill is an uncorked reappearance of his Australian hat from Scatty Safari. Bill's sparkling green and blue jacket had previously been wore by John Inman in Are You Being Served?: The Old Order Changes.*

Special Guest FRANK WINDSOR with MICHAEL BARRATT, IRIS JONES, PEGGY MASON, PAT MONTROSE, NORMAN BACON, ERNIE GOODYEAR, JAMES MUIR. Episode Three, recorded Friday 18 November, broadcast Tuesday 22 November 1977, 9–9.30pm, BBC2.

ROCK GOODIES

'God Save the Queen!' was on everybody's lips, whether it was the bunting-decking patriots preparing to celebrate Elizabeth II's Silver Jubilee or the gob-splatted safety pin wearing punks screaming along with Johnny Rotten. The Goodies, with fingers on the pulse as always, tackled elements of both with this and the following edition. With their own recording career well behind them, Oddie's singer–songwriter can gleefully send up the new musical trends. The show bursts into life with our three singing used-to-be's desperately trying to entertain a tough audience of leather-clad, zip-ridden grannies, with a tasty, sweet and innocent little thing called *Shiny Shoes*. The team members get a hasty name check within the lyrics, the past, flared, *Top of the Pops* look is masked with a new group title – The Little Laddies – and the psychedelic, splitting graphics, gives the whole thing a far-out Seventies sense of excess. The boys turn on the niceties, soft shoe shuffling and gradually allow their footwear to extend to clown-sized proportions. The reaction is not great, in fact, it's down right dissatisfying and, backstage, bewigged, bemused and bewildered, Bill is not chuffed. This three-way camp bitch fest highlights the ego-mad performer within the Goodies grouping. It's all talk of fairy cakes and the fraud of punk with Tim acidly dubbing Bill 'a poor man's muppet!' Tim is proud of his nice, glam image, complete with hitting the spot aftershave and act-making 'old feet'. Graeme simply goes on and on about the really bad reaction received, while Bill is plain fed up. Everything seems to be 'out' in the cultural circle at the moment, so it's a change of direction and a change of style that's needed. It's time to get back on the road and back to the fans. Bill, taking the road idea a bit too far, belts out his rocking *On the Road* number in the middle of a very busy road indeed. *Let It Be*-like, the police turn up, get a bit groovy and drag them away to an unfulfilling life of police balls and benefits, while Bill laps up the pretentious scribblings of trendy journo, Caroline Kook – a reflection of real-life punk journalist Caroline Coon who was stepping out with The Clash's Paul Simonon. The police van back projection convention is mercilessly mocked with standard scenery passing by before ultimately inducing severe facial close-ups, a bit of Winston Churchill and even clips of the BBC broadcast war-stretching Mickey Mouse short, *Mickey's Gala Party*. Revealed as a stationary vehicle with coppers enjoying movies projected on to it, it's a quick, visual which works as the perfect backdrop for Goodie punk revolution. Graeme throws himself into the smelly sock spirit of things, but, naturally, it's Bill who's to the fore, renaming himself Willie Snot and mixing the new with hippie old in a cry of 'Go punk, man!' Tim, struggling to impose Tim Normal as a fresh image, finally has the very objectionable Tim Brooke-Taylor retained. But it doesn't really matter. Oddie sacks his two co-Goodies and the split sends shockwaves through the national press. Well, no it doesn't actually, because everybody seems wrapped up in the punks. It's the kind and gentle people of Tim's nature that are depicted as the weirdo ones in this twisted, parallel universe, with the essence of spit and swearing invading small screen convention. *Nationwide*'s Michael Barratt – a Goodies favourite – dons the gear and bleeps the bleeped-out obscenities, while a greased and gritty Patrick Moore presents the ultimate Seventies version of *The Sky at Night*. Roland McLeod as *Tonight* presenter Bill Grumpy, dares to stare controversy in the face, and invites Timbo to speak his mind, in a brilliant parody of the infamous Sex Pistols interview. Tim's outrageous lobbying for nice ways, plug for his 'Keep Britain's Shoes Shiny' and complaints of 'awfully uncouth' behaviour, are surely unforgivable. The average common decency of friendship and respect is frowned on and the entire sparkling clean persona of Tim is forcefully denounced as 'sick'. The times have certainly changed… with smart and sophisticated Timbo trying to woo and impress style expert Kook – stunningly played by Jane Asher – the glorious atmosphere of his favourite restaurant has been transformed in a matter of hours. Gone are the soft lights and sweet music, in their place graffiti-strewn walls and 'get stuffed' service. Waiter Graeme Garden – shockingly jumping on the spit in yer face and two-fingered salute bandwagon – delights in the non-service. Taking Tim's coat, only to wipe the table clean with it, retrieving a severed ear from Tim's seat just before he sits on it, setting up the juke box which systematically smashes all the records and serenading with punk violining, the actual food is so disgusting Tim can't even bring himself to finish. The menu, cheerfully used as Garden's nose wipe before consultation, throws up (literally) the least offensive, easiest to semi-keep down concoction, number 23. Garden brings on the bucket of grub, treats the lady with gentle respect but eagerly dumps copious amounts of slops over ever so elegant Tim. But it's the money and fame that impresses Asher. The 'ackers' are what counts and mocked marriage proposals and feverish screams of 'Consider me punked!' from poor old Tim don't cut any ice, or jugular veins, with her. Graeme, back to his usual scientific persona with medical overtones, is officially turning folk freaky for the Trendsetters Ball. Punk is old hat and the media world wait for the next new thing. Bill's happy with his huge, safety-pin pierced head, cracking up at his exit and desperately trying to get through the door without wrenching the prop off. Freakology is the future, man, and with typically punked-up nurse and sheepish, expectant Tim ('Don't kill me!'), Dr Gray Bungles at St Punk Hospital can pull out all the stops and pull out one of his client's legs – ('Go to the Hop!'). By this stage, Bill's gone into ugly sister mode and Tim minces about in typical Cinderella fashion, christening his companion housefly, Buttons, and squashing a charmingly squeaky, almost convincing mouse for its helpful, agreeing re-enforcement of Tim's required ugliness. Beauty is a thing of the past. It's total bizarreness that will get you noticed and Gray's the Fairy PunkMother to make your Walt Disney meets Sam Peckinpah wishes come true. Ball invitations are guaranteed, speech gets down and dirty ('lamb's wotsits!' are cheerfully promised) and the freak of the week award is winging its way towards Tim's pumpkin-headed, rats and lizard customised, stranger. The old 'home by midnight' business here centres around the prospect of Tim's feebly re-arranged leg conking out and dropping off, but the entire Punkerella ball sequence seems ill at ease and uncomfortable. Only Frank Thornton's gloriously refined, punk barker, with his immortal instruction, 'Gentlemen, you may spit!', is class. Tentatively embracing the bisexual community (it's ladies, gentlemen and a knowingly drawn out, and AC-DCs), spiritedly standing tall with great dignity through all the punk madness and delivering a cameo of finely etched skill, Thornton's second and last Goodies assignment –

having served in *Farm Fresh Food* – is a masterpiece. Musical ability isn't part of the fun, as a panel (including Asher and a heavily disguised 'John Peel') sit through Rev Rotten head abuse, protesting ferret trouser-dropping and Bill's smartly attired, dwarf gibbon protecting, manic fit jerking, garbled rendition of *I'm in Love for the Very First Time*. It's all really 'amazing' or near enough, but drags on a tad and, even, the unexpected, centre of attention appearance of Tim's Punkerella conjures up yet more campery. With the clock striking midnight, Asher's interest up and Timbo's Union flag socked leg going the way of all flesh, the obvious 'so, who ever this leg doth fit the blonde babe will wed' business, goes into overdrive. Wannabe punk heroes saw off their legs for a chance and Bill's cunning devil – his delicious, 'Gray Bundle Old Fruit!' line is one of my all-time favourites – cleverly adopting Long John Silver antics for a leg bash. Ultimately, Bill is revealed as faking the uni-peg look ('me spare!') and suggests his parrot should be considered. But, naturally, it's one-legged scrubber Tim that fits the limb and, in keeping with punk tradition, gets the hand of Jane Asher – literally and only. Garden gets the looks and Oddie, seemingly delighted, gets the all important body bit. Oh spit!

Did You Know? *The fragile relationship between the Goodies and the BBC was getting more and more fragile with each passing series. Demands were made radically to restructure this punk pantomime, throwing up the rather bizarre situation of anarchist Bill Oddie mediating between the usually reserved Tim Brooke-Taylor and the Head of BBC Comedy. The powers that be considered the show took the far too 'nasty' subject of punk and, by pushing it beyond the reality boundary, made the subject even more distasteful. In the end, a compromise was made and slight re-writes were made to the original script. The Australian Broadcasting Commission wiped the phrase 'Yeah, you bitch' from this episode. This episode is alternatively referred to as both* Punkarella *and* Punky Business. Rock Goodies *was screened as part of an evening of Cult Comedy at the National Film Theatre on Tuesday 11 May 1993, from 7.30pm.*

JANE ASHER, FRANK THORNTON, MICHAEL BARRATT, PATRICK MOORE, RONNIE BRODY, ROLAND MacLEOD, VICKI MICHELLE, SELINA INGRAM, JAMES MUIR, NORMAN BACON, BARNEY CARROLL, EDDIE DAVIES, ERNIE GOODYEAR. Episode Four, recorded Friday 25 November, broadcast Tuesday 29 November 1977, 9–9.30pm, BBC2.

ROYAL COMMAND

A right royal boot up the Union flag-emblazoned behind, the monarchy had been a beloved Goodies target since the first episode and a vital part of Tim's persona for just as long, but this is the ultimate jubilee attack. Finally, having been clutched to the regal bosom, Tim is the host for the

Royal Command Performance, dragging out the usual array of stars doing ever so slightly twisted versions of what they usually do – a brief snatch of rocking chair-encased Val Doonican crooning *Danny Boy*, Dickie Henderson and the Charles Laughton playing golf routine, Mike Yarwood impersonating the Red Army Choir, Bernie Delfont's fund of no-name novelty acts, Lena Zavarony going low for *Old Man River* and Charles Aznavour blessed with a bit of Bill's *Charles Aznovoice* track. Throughout, Graeme and Bill, desperate to keep the royal special guests awake, fire off guns, ring alarm clocks, pelt them with veg, throw water over them and generally make a bleeding nuisance of themselves. A final helping hand and helping wave for an (allegedly) legless Princess Margaret, sees the show off to a thundering anti-climactic reaction. Back at Cricklewood, Tim's decked up in Earl robes or, as Graeme describes it, 'comedy garb!' Honestly, the two even get away with the vintage Earl/OBE = earlobe gag and stagger into Thank Heaven for Little Earls, I'm Just an Earl Who Can't Say No and the like! The joke isn't overplayed thanks to the hasty, mail-bag smothered, entrance of good old Bill. Bearing an important regal message, the main family are less than chuffed with Tim's feeble efforts. With all the noisy distraction, this has been the first Command Performance they haven't slept through. Having seen what rubbish the show really is, they demand, by Royal Command, another one. Cue Graeme Garden mugging it as a *The Good Old Days* barker. With the bloodlust baying crowds, entertainment sacred cows are put to the sword – Max Bygraves has time for one 'I wanna tell you a story' before the trap-door gets him, Rolf Harris ties down his kangaroo but the Queen insists Bill 'Cut off his didgeridoo', Rod Stewart changes the *Sailing* lyrics for I Am Stretching, 1976 Eurovision champs Brotherhood of Man find saving your kisses leads to death by hangman's noose and culture interlude Rudolph Nureyev finds the *Nutcracker Suite* a tad painful. Finally, politician Willie Hamilton is boiled in oil, Bill holds a loft a 'Frying Tonight' placard and the enthused audience sing *Happy Days Are Here Again*! Tim is appalled by the wild behaviour but, amazingly, Graeme's gone all patriotic and regal. With a Union flag false nose he celebrates his new position as the Queen's Own Master of Entertainment. He plugs the new listing journal, Royal Radio Times, and announces the royal takeover starting in a small way – 'they're taking over the BBC!' Suddenly, it's horse crazy. Horse of the Year Show, Horse of the Day

Show, Horse of the Minute Show, Racing from Newmarket, Racing to Newmarket, Rock Fillies, Dobbin Day and the like. The Goodies proudly present The Amazing Tumbling Royals. Tim can't face it. Thoughts of breaking every bone in their bodies turns him off completely, Graeme denies it can happen but a hasty burst of the Goodies theme and an on-screen message – but they did! – proves him wrong. Tim's 'nervous nerk!' can hardly face the completely plastered Royal quartet. As Bill explains, 'One is not amused… and two are bloody furious!' While a Harry Secombe autograph would appease the Goonish youngster, plans are made for official Royal stand-ins. The only guys I know who could do that are already in the ward. Tim bags the Queen's job, Graeme can't decide between horsey female or naval husband so goes somewhere between the two, while Bill goes for the easy option. He's dug out his old Cuddly Scamp gear from *Frankenfido* and gone for the corgi look! Clearly, not amused, Queen Tim makes an official complaint and, thus, tapping into the young Prince's surrealist comedy passions, Bill is Charlie – in a dog skin! But Tim will stand for no jokes – no son of hers is going to look silly, even if he does have to wear a crown complete with huge, stick-out ears. Tim's powerful, impassioned speech about the family having flipped their lids, screwed up and, now, desperately in need of a chance in public image, is probably more cutting and relevant now, some 20 years later. The resulting Royal Command rehearsals are less effective but still hilarious. Still, the elongated horse-jumping version of *Stars on Sunday* from Hickstead with Moira Anderson faulting and the like, tends to drag a bit. An urgent newsflash sees the Chancellor of the Exchequer doing the horse thang and revealing major plans for a tourist money-sucking wheeze – a re-run of the 1953 Coronation to mark the 25th anniversary. The Queen is all for it. Via a grovelling telephone conversation with Timbo, she gives the Goodies the Royal blessing to take control of the day, looking forward to watching it on the telly having missed it last time round! A production line of Timbo Coronation mugs flash across the screen, the Buckingham Palace crowds are eagerly awaiting a sniff of regal cool and poor old HRH Timbo has laddered his tights getting in through the window. The real Majesty forgot to leave the key. Graeme's in the mood with continuous, 'One' this and 'One' that and 'beastly' indignation at the pomp and circumstance, while Bill, hiding behind a suspiciously regal cloak turns on the wacky Charles with red nose, spinning bow-tie and clownish street wear. Graeme indulges his skill for impressions with a knowing look to the audience as he struggles through the deliciously satirical Pam Ayres ode and Tim – all tight, tense arms, Union flag waistcoat and pre-coronation nerves – insists Bill does the Queen waving because he's got the beard for it. The crowd go mad, Graeme brilliantly and subtly chucks an irritating corgi over the balustrade and dummies/puppets are brought into to flesh out the three fake in the flesh royals. The trio, live on air, realise that they are in and that the old Royal lot are out. The plastered originals jump from their hospital beds and aim to fight for their own valued heritage. A rather drawn out but funny chase results, with Tim feverishly trying to get crowned at Westminster Abbey, cost-cutting attitudes revealing cut-out choir and dignitaries, a thought that the real Maggie Thatcher has turned up before there is a correct realisation that she too is a dummy and polo-like antics to claim the crown. The horse-racing commentary almost labels Graeme's female impersonation as an official crack at Princess Anne with a fumbling, 'Princess Ann... Yes, it is the Princess!', Graeme's horse refuses to jump the Thatcher dummy, Bill clobbers the dummy head of Prince Phillip all over the place, the Archbishop is mounted by the Princess and a bow-tie spinning, flying, Oddie crashes in for the kill, spins out the crown, knocks a Royal into the Royal Free Hospital and ultimately sends the bejewelled headwear winging towards Tim's depressed, bench-seated, down and out wannabe ruler. The Royals are out, the Goods are in, but Tim's old heroes are still very much in a job. With the Goodies in the Palace, Tim can settle down to his favourite telly show, those crazy, four-seater trandem-driving clowns, The Royals... Royal, Royal, Yum Yum! Check the awarded and crossed-out OBE for director Bob Spiers in the closing credits.

Did You Know? *Problems with the BBC at script level came to a head with this right royal bombardment. With two Royals in hospital at the time, the BBC had decidedly cold feet about the project. For a starter, the Goodies planned to include actual archive footage of the regals dramatically falling off their horses for The Tumbling Royals section. This was completely out of the question. Their excuse that using newsreel footage out of context for entertainment wasn't allowed didn't fool anybody – they had done similar when That Was The Week That Was had requested Harold MacMillan material in 1963. Further more, Royal Command was originally planned to be broadcast on the day Princess*

Anne was due to give birth to her first baby. The Goodies, however, saw their idea curtailed by a cold-footed BBC who quickly rescheduled the programme towards the end of the series. In an infamous example of how out of touch with the comedy the corporation were, Graeme Garden remembers, 'one administrator said 'I've got a solution – instead of putting this one out, why don't you put out the one you recorded last Friday?', we said, 'This is the one we recorded last Friday!' Alasdair Milne had decreed that if Princess Anne's child was born before 6pm – three hours before the show was due on air – then the episode was not to be broadcast. In the end, the child arrived at 11.30am. As a result, the scheduled broadcast, 15 November 1977, slotted between Dodonuts and Scoutrageous, was plugged with a hasty repeat of the Series Six programme 2001 and a Bit. Royal Command finally aired in the sixth-week slot reserved for the culminating Series Seven edition, Earthanasia, dictating that that earth-shattering show was found a new, independent broadcast slot just before Christmas.

RICKY NEWBY, TERRY DENTON, ERNIE GOODYEAR. Episode Five, recorded Friday 11 November, broadcast Tuesday 6 December 1977, 9–9.30pm, BBC2.

EARTHANASIA

'Can't think of a punch-line... blow up the world!' Bill Oddie.

The Christmas comedy special, traditionally packed with silly hats, parties, excess drinking and carol-singing. That is, of course, unless you are Brooke-Taylor, Garden and Oddie. Oh sure, all the necessary elements are in place but *Earthanasia* is unique. Arguably the team's masterpiece, it embraces the close-knit angst of *The End* with a sense of total destruction. Played out in real time, we share the final half hour of *The Goodies* with the Goodies trapped together in the Cricklewood office and with nothing to do but talk to each other. Starting with the innocence and joy of a normal Christmas edition, Graeme cheerfully decks the halls and decorates the tree. Cheekily flashing under the tree fairy's tutu, his intricate paper tearing results in the perfect, coloured decoration and its final placing across the door completes his *It's a Wonderful Life* climax before Bill bursts in and ruins it. The embodiment of tearaway youth, his by-words are speed, violence and destruction. All of which are helped on their way by his Christmas present to himself – a skateboard. Bill and Graeme, each getting more and more fraught, map out the agreed plan to avoid rows over Yuletide this year and Gray's present to himself, a Skateboard Destruction Kit, calms him down. Smashing it, shooting it and blowing it up, the problem is solved, Bill pinches the gun and shoots the robin on the chocolate log. In contrast

SKIFFLE WITH GARDEN IMPLEMENTS, BILL, GRAEME AND TIM HAVE TO BLOW THEIR OWN WATERING CAN IN THIS PATRIOTIC PUBLICITY SHOT

to the carnage, the charming, smoothing choir service from St Martin's in the Field sets things up for a happy seasonal holiday. Unfortunately, an urgent BBC newsflash takes the gilt off. World leaders, fed up with the dreadful state of the planet, have all agreed to call it a day and combine co-operating military forces for the climactic big bang. At midnight the world will be exploded for the good of all. Gray's convinced it's a hoax but the all hearing radio chappie assures him that it isn't. This is no Orson Welles *War of the Worlds* affair. No, it's the truth, guv. In 30 minutes the world will come to an end. Everybody may be dead by midnight but it's all for the best. The world's in a right old state, he intends to enjoy his last golden half hour and Graeme, quickly recovering his financial brain, telephones his insurance company to see if his claim can cover this unforeseen occurrence. To the continued seasonal broadcast, final plans are fleshed out. Bill's in high spirits indeed – wallowing in his joyous rendition of *Enjoy Yourself, It's Later Than You Think* – he's got plans for his last 27 and a half minutes. Taking the advice of Graeme and taking time

out to consider his options, Bill's creature of the flesh makes his mind up pretty damn quick. Passion with a ready and willing Jane Fonda, licking the choc off two dozen Mars Bars, his guitar and skateboarding down to Wembley to score a hat-trick, should just about sort him out for eternity. Graeme, on the other hand, is less easily pleased. Muttering, 'I've done it all!', he ponders on the giant kitten, monster cod and Eddie Waring impressions. Suddenly, the panic of gratification is blown away and the reality of having to tell Tim hits them. Bill insists it's Graeme and both hope he already knows, but, of course, he doesn't. Staggering in with a 'The End Of the World Is Nigh' sandwich board and gleefully flogging his chestnuts – 'Tim's nuts are nicest!' – a real sense of joy is upon him. Delighting in the wonderful, magical time that is Christmas Eve, Tim's child-like charmer skips through, desperately searching for the right stocking to hang up for presents and joyfully listening out for Santa's sleigh-bells. Bill goes completely ape, rants in the finest piece of acting Oddie contributed to the series and sets this episode on its fateful journey to inner reflection and destruction. Bill has had enough – 'D.E.D.D. DEAD!' just about convinces Tim. After a few seconds of silence and Bill's drumming home of the truth – empty pages in the Christmas *Radio Times* after 24 December – the scream of the helpless nightmare breaks in. Tim's manic burst, 'My life, my life!', allows Bill the observation, 'He's gone Jewish now!', but insane is more to the point. Resurrecting 'I'm a teapot' babbling from *The End*, desperate to die, with his shiny shoes on and longing for a close, friendly Goodies togetherness Christmas, the final wish is granted with Graeme's forward planning notion. A four-minute Christmas is officially set for 11.56pm but Bill isn't interested. Tim, in desperation, needs the reassurance and his dream of festive joy and cries of 'Billy Willy!' are heart wrenching. Bill's callous, 'Happy Christmas. Goodbye!' seems all the more hurtful and cruel. Suddenly having an attack of mortality, Tim ponders the eternal questions and debates the prospect of heaven and hell, but Bill's heard enough. He's off for his 16 minutes of Jane Fonda and skateboarding while his two colleagues close their eyes and contemplate their sins. Graeme, sniggering at the glorious memories, is a smirking, 'Oh, yes!' chuckling, foot-jerking, treat, while poor old Timbo fails to recall any misspent time. Tucking his shirt into his underpants and breaking wind in the bed sort of just about count and besides it's worth all the fuss just for Bill's radio-based quip, 'Sin something simple!' Nervously, Tim must come to terms with the fact that his internals are about to be torn away – and that means revealing, for the first time, what exactly lurks under that legendary waistcoat. Bill's gleeful shock is a picture. The truth is a red, white and blue A-string (like a G-string but a little higher up) to mask his shameful belly button. Tim, now with a waste paper bin over his head, is shamed, and Bill wants to get out for some of that final action. He's even begged Graeme to turn Tim into Jane Fonda to save him the taxi fare, but the inner soul of the manic Brooke-Taylor proves to be of continued interest. Grudgingly, Bill has to stick around for the childhood regression session. Not hypnotised by his own watch (although Gray goes for a second), Tim finally is put under with a triple arm wave from a desperate Graeme. Turning the clock back 15 years, Tim starts twisting again like we did last Summer, further back he's still rocking, 30 years gone he's tellingly warbling '21 today…' and ultimately, as a 10-year-old, he's a self-conscious, upper-class schoolboy with a problem mother. Bill, in shawl, plays the part for added effectiveness, dubbing her son a 'bad 'un!', mocking the Hovis ad conventions, ordering a man's life future for her offspring down t'pit and finally revealing the root of the problem with chat about Belly Button Sunday. Condemning Tim's namby-pamby ideas of being a 'hair artiste' and getting ready to wipe the fluff from his shamed private indent, Tim breaks down. The beard, voice and social history is all true, schoolyard taunts of 'jowl to jowl carpeting' come back to haunt the poor lad, and Bill takes a touchingly saddened turn towards sorrow and compassion for his distressed fellow Good. But long-standing pain about not being tough and hairy can't get in the way of the more important things. The world only has eight minutes left and Timbo's got some urgent ironing to do! The actor indulges distress at the end of Derby County Football Team as the character feels for the departing Muppets. Graeme, seizing on Tim's childish devotion and belief in Kermit and company, strips away the truth with a bundle of laundry and a mini-Muppet Show in the office. A green sock becomes the frog, a pair of Y-fronts and a mop transforms into Miss Piggy, a brown jumper and a hat starts cracking Fozzy Bear gags and a huge number of the cast make split-second cameos, until the crucial, all-conquering *Halfway Up the Stairs* interlude from Kermie's little nephew. Tim, worryingly convinced, finally loses control, runs off screaming and attacks Gray with a cooker. End of the World revellers are storming through Trafalgar Square, last minute shoppers are on the look out for great bargains and the Royals are rocketing away to safety. Comically, a changed Bill emerges in smart suit and clean shaven style. Revealing the real him, just for Tim, Graeme's telling comment ('You vicious swine!') cuts no ice with the new, square Oddie. The removal of his long-haired Gerbil pet wig reveals the 'closet Kojak' truth, explains the little saucer of milk on his pillow, explains hair-cutting appointments with the vet and almost clears up those little funny noises from his bedroom. But if Bill has veered towards Tim ideals, than Tim has most definitively veered towards Bill's. Singing *The Stripper*, prancing about in a bellybutton-exposing body stocking and enhancing the sense of freedom with a myriad of arrows pointing to the once sensitive spot, Tim's gone nasty. Plain speaking and flashing it, Bill is ashamed but Tim is going to have his say. Bill is denounced as a baldy 'dreary little wart', Graeme is dubbed 'Buggerlugs!', Christmas is mocked as nothing but too much telly, and grub and booze is consumed by the new, blonde violence-monger. But with four minutes to go and a speedy Christmas in the offing – frantic turkey plucking to reveal a sparrow-sized bit of meat and a seamless medley of all the great carols – presents are dished out and exchanged with Tim chucking over his fresh from the foot Union flag socks ('not to be sniffed at!') and rounding off with a string of corny sock word plays ('No socks please we're British!'). But with seconds to go, Tim and Bill go quiet. Desperate to have something nice said, Tim can't help Bill and Bill can't help Tim. Both have no crumb of solace for Graeme but, in crisis, the two-people nation turns its lonely heart to him. Winding up for a 'perfectly frank' total condemnation of his Goodie partners, the clock strikes 12, the lads hold their breath… nothing happens. Cracking up with laughter, Graeme's 'silly joke' is revealed. But, sadly, it isn't that silly. You see, the world is still doomed. He's just put the clock back a bit – half a minute to be exact. Lovingly allowing his pals to go with a smile on their faces. A white blast and civilisation is wiped out. The spinning BBC globe explodes to add symbolic weight to the ending and no closing credits or closing theme are included. Although the lads would re-appear, this seems to cap *The Goodies* for a generation.

Did You Know? One longs that someone at the BBC would have thought of the Orson Welles notion of screening this episode at 11.30pm on Christmas Eve 1977, but no. They certainly could have done, thanks to the series rescheduling hassle over Royal Command. This masterly episode had almost two minutes edited by the Australian Broadcasting Commission including 'I'm knackered', Bill's Jane Fonda-obsessed sex plan, Tim's bath wind-breaking revelation and the Timbo knee in Bill's groin. The Radio Times really built up the tension with '…is this really their last 30 minutes?' The ultimate sacrifice for Bill Oddie was, of course, shaving off his beard. However, just as Bill was halfway through trimming his facial hair, the director rushed in with news that the previous shot had to be filmed again. A boom microphone was in shot and the crew needed a re-take. Oddie's attitude was 'Tough!' The beard was gone and the boom remains in the finished programme. Worst of all, Bill's clean-shaven persona failed to get a laugh. The audience were more shocked than amused!

Episode Six, recorded Friday 2 December, broadcast Thursday 22 December 1977, 9–9.30pm, BBC2.

SERIES EIGHT

Jim Franklin and Bob Spiers shared the production credit for this final *Goodies* season for the BBC although, as with Series Seven, Franklin was producer and Spiers director. Weary and wary of the hassles over Series Seven, the Goodies and the production crew decided to get ahead of the game and film the majority of material well before the broadcast dates. Filming began in the Autumn 1979 with the very last BBC episode, completed in January 1980. During this final flurry of BBC activity, clips from *The Goodies* were showcased in the retrospective celebration *The 70s Stop Here!* Hosted by Penelope Keith it was the final programme of the decade, broadcast Monday 31 December 1979, from 10.40pm to midnight. An accompanying *Radio Times* article rather half-heartedly commented that 'The Goodies go on being good.' Perhaps, the Goodies were only destined to shine during the Seventies.

Film cameraman Reg Pope. Film editor John Jarvis (Episodes 1, 2, 4 & 5) and Glenn Hyde (Episodes 2, 3 & 6). Visual effects Tony Harding and Andy Lazell. Vision mixer Angela Beveridge and Bill Morton (Episode 5). Graphics Linda Sherwood-Page. Costume Andrew Rose. Make-up Jean Steward. Lighting John Green. Sound John Holmes and Keith Gunn (Episode 5). Dubbing mixers Dave Simpson and Ken Hains. Sound recordist Bill Wild. Music by Bill Oddie and Dave McRae. Designer Andrew H Davies with Bryan Ellis (Episode 2). Technical managers Harry Bradley, Jack Walsh and Rod Litherland. Production team Jennifer Hunter, Katharine Paxton (Episode 6), Jill Heaver and Mark Williams. Production assistant John Kilby. Production Jim Franklin and Bob Spiers.

GOODIES AND POLITICS

The Goodies stormed into view in a new decade. The BBC had sent a shot across the Goodies' bow, denying them more money for special effects and keeping them under a non-playing contract to stop the rival channel head-hunting the trio. However, the team were back with a vengeance, proving straightaway that their satirical sights were as finely tuned as before. Indeed, the radical upheaval in the political landscape provided them with an unbeatable target for show number one. Maggie doesn't hang around for long once she is in power – just a few months after winning the election she's on the next plane to the Bahamas. All political representatives vote themselves a massive pay rise and join her in a sun-drenched paradise. Hence, what's a beleaguered and government-less nation to do – the Goodies, as always, can help. Graeme's already proved his corrupt pedigree via his wealth of cheesy, easy adverts (ranging from a half-hearted poke at American Express flasher David Frost to a bizarre Keep Britain Tidy campaign) with his outrageous advertising agency, Snaatchi and Snatchy. However, with his political creation having fun in the sun, it's down to battling Tim and Bill to get the country back in order. It doesn't take an expert to work out which political side the two feuding Goodies fall back on – with Bill surrounded by revolutionary images of Lenin, Jane Fonda and David Essex… sorry… Che Guevara. While Timbo, ferociously patriotic, royalist and a true blue, cavorts his harmless fantasy of stepping out with Maggie Thatcher and shamelessly worships his image of Fonda with Maggie's head superimposed. Up to their knees in serious debate, there's a moment for smut as Tim defends the Thatcherite policy of the 'man with a small firm' before Bill lowers the tone with the retort, 'small firm what?' But it's Garden's money grabber that sits at the centre of the intrigue (even his shirt is not what it seems, with the stripes added by black marker pen while he awaits the arrival of his clients). Tim enjoys a glorious comic moment when he enters in full Thatcher mode, Graeme dishes out less than subtle satirical references with the addition of an Adolf Hitler moustache and builds up 'her' ego with plans for making the lady in blue the Empress of the World before collapsing into bemused exclamations of 'How did I sell you!' Of course, it hasn't quite sunk in that Tim is, in fact, standing in for the Iron Lady, and needs a fresh, vote-winning image to combat pseudo-Vanessa Redgrave candidate Bill Oddie. There's much eyebrow-raising ribaldry between the performers and Bill's brown-skirted, bumbling leader of The Workers Revolutionary Party staggers in and breaks down on the line 'standing against you!' with an impromptu, 'with difficulty I admit'. But if anyone can convince the electorate, it's Graeme – Thatcher was transformed from a Hylda Baker sound-a-like and ripped to victory with a majority of just 35, so a slightly camp chap in blue and a bearded unionist should prove no problems. The battle lines are drawn with Tim's angelic features promoting the upper class glories of a cleaner, nicer Britain with the flat-capped and handkerchief-adorned working classes regularly culled on the rocks. These Oddie-style oiks must also administrate their own medical care and suffer the death penalty for walking behind the bowler's arm at Lord's! Bill's ideals are dismantling the royal family and selling the Queen to Disneyland for a Brit History attraction, worshipping at the radical, sexy feet of Jane Fonda and refusing all icons of commercial labelling, particularly Oscars. Having embraced the new girl on the political block in the shape of Thatcher, the Goodies simply tap into the old political girl on the new West End map in the shape of *Evita*. Bill had already injected a brief mention of the Andrew Lloyd Webber blockbuster via his David Essex reference, but now the two female authority icons are juxtaposed in one of Tim Brooke-Taylor's most outstanding and unforgettable performances – Timita. Not to be out done, of course, Bill adopts the combat gear of Che Guevara, dismisses Tim's wannabe leader as both Miss Piggy and the Tin Tranvestite, before seeing this queening, sharp cookie take television by storm with a Graeme Garden-fronted political address. Descending from the skies on a golden moon, Tim delivers a lovingly calm comment to a couple of shorthand typists by the names of Marge and Tina. Full of worries and concern about the future of Britain, they break down with heartfelt fear for their beloved Timita, Tim takes a deep breath and goes for it: 'Don't cry for me Marge and Tina!' Television's coverage of election night is always ripe for parody and the lad's don't miss a trick with self-mockery from a face-stuffing David Dimbleby, mucking up his lines, gleefully plugging all manner of BBC publications and happily going under the tongue twisting handle of David Dimblemblm. The whole thing is a sham, with the television coverage so entertaining that only the candidates themselves have bothered voting – thus, despite a myriad of recounts, it's a hung parliament and the two political rivals join forces for a doubled-handed, doubled-headed, doubled-quilled attack on the voter. With nowhere else to go and political satire pretty much exhausted, it's

down to Graeme to liven things up with his back catalogue of television personalities. Falling into something the team really knew about, sending up television itself, the two leaders suffer the camp excess of Garden's Larry Grayson of *The Generation Game*, a burst of Nicholas Parson's *Sale of the Century* (with the ever-glam Penny Irving returning from the typing pool seductively to pose in front of weapons of mass destruction), some mouth-watering Frank Muir mumbles for *Call My Bluff* (complete with token bimbo crumpet and United Nation antics) and Terry Wogan's *Blankety Blank* microphone bending madness. Finally, it's back to that useful comic stand-by, *It's a Knockout*, with a more politically geared parody. Garden stands in for the gurgling Eddie Waring, the Joker is Cyril Smith and the ever-laughing Stuart Hall is a blow-up dummy. The name of the game is European domination, with plenty of national stereotypes along the way, comments aimed at the wasteful butter mountain and the horrors of the Berlin wall. Tangible threats come from minefields and nuclear destruction, while the playful cliché of bursting those pesky balloons sets the entire parody in context. At the end of the day, Tim and Bill, now united as hopeless, battling Brits, stagger through the drunken wine drinking and end up last for the home country. The booby prize, naturally, is the return of Margaret Thatcher to take over government.

Did You Know? *Hilarious out-takes of Bill and Tim cracking up with laughter during the filming of this episode are in existence. Penny Irving's sexy comedy career included fun with Benny Hill, a role as one of Joan Sims's Birds of Paradise in Carry On Dick, some naughty romping with Leigh Lawson in Ralph Thomas's Percy's Progress and temperature-rising poses on Young Mr Grace's lap for the television series and film version of Are You Being Served? This episode briefly reunites the Goodies with old I'm Sorry I'll Read That Again playmate Jo Kendall.*

DAVID DIMBLEBY, CORBET WOODALL, JO KENDALL, NICHOLAS McARDLE, ROSEMARY FAITH, PENNY IRVING, MARIA ELDRIDGE, JOAN BLACKHAM. Episode One, recorded Thursday 8 and Friday 9 November 1979, broadcast Monday 14 January 1980, 8.10–8.40pm, BBC2.

SATURDAY NIGHT GREASE

Time for a send up of Mr Cool, hip and funky himself, John Travolta . The Goodies tackle three movies, *Grease*, *Saturday Night Fever* and *Staying Alive*, in one episode. The idea may be better than the execution and the team seem to run out of ideas after about 10 minutes, but the first portion of American style in frumpy British terms is outstanding. It's the embodiment of uncoolness, Tim Brooke-Taylor, who is sucked into the world of Bee Gees records, glittering balls, sparkling flares and easy women. With an establishing shot setting up the Travolta link immediately, Timbo struts in, shows his natty Union flag socks, waistcoat and dark, heavily greased wig, while balancing his affection for the Queen and a lust for that Aussie temptress, Olivia Newton-John. With hair full of axle grease, an open to the waist shirt, gold medallion, oversized shoes and an attitude that says 'Give it to me!', Tim strolls down Cricklewood High Street looking for action. He's booted out of his local disco and returns to find solace in the company of his chums. Bill and Graeme are hardly the most understanding of people and so Tim's ego is squashed by snide comments and laughter. Tim's squeaky voiced, Bee Gees jive talk hits the spot but Bill knows the solution, undoes Tim's zip and allows him to talk with his own voice. The funny side is not seen by Timbo, his pride and ego may be wounded and his girl obsession may be out, but his dreams are in place, ditching royals in favour of his blonde *Grease* baby. His Britishness shines through, bemoaning his persona as a proud MCC member, while Bill squirts the tomato sauce dispenser, over a huge mound of grub. Bill and Gray Bags happily launch into the do wop 'Tell me more!' chorus as Timbo goes all Seventies meets Fifties cool and merrily slaughters the final note of *Summer Nights*. There's an untypical moment of Bill Oddie naïvety as he considers the delights of 'a real woman!', Dame Edna Everage, and a bemused Graeme himself ponders whether he should reveal the truth about Barry Humphries. Uniquely for this series, there's even time for a couple of new Oddie compositions and the first of these, *Grease Cycling* is a real winner. The lads prance about in sparkly overalls, the old three-seater is given a make over and the white-washed background brings a Fifties shine to the rocking song. The dancing craze is embraced and backdated by Oddie, who flourishes into view done up like a poor man's Fred Astaire – he even includes a nice golfing touch by injecting the essence of the 1938 routine from *Carefree* – while Garden goes all pink and feminine for his strutting bit of stuff. An irritating and uncommon bit of script by-passing, with Bill's obvious, plot device pondering on the great idea of opening his own disco, folds away to allow a less than impressive dancing lesson from Graeme. Tim, despite being the Travolta of Cricklewood, eagerly tries to pick up the new grooves and, with a little help from vomit-inducing Max Bygraves records, grasps the rudiments of the Disco Heave. Bill's got a snappy new song for the occasion, Tim's all set to catch some totty in his tempting babe trap and the early Eighties' period piece of stuffy, no-contact discos literally reeks throughout the sequence. The essence of ballroom dancing and the modern ideal of dancing miles apart is mocked, with the Goods taking things that one comic step further with a major raid and the arrest of our hapless hero. With a chunk of comedy behind them, the lads take their foot off the pedals and freewheel, allowing corrupt and corruptable Garden and Oddie to dream up a crazy, perverse idea about a mixed disco dancing championship. Television gets in on the act and there's a £5000 BBC-funded prize. Gray Bags plays to form and plans to double double-cross his bearded partner in crime, while trust in the prison service is tested and found happy to help with a phone call to spring Timbo. Even the tart without a heart outside the disco refuses to lower her standards and take part in mixed dancing but a few bovver boys heavy handedly drag her in to scoff and handbag bash various half-hearted dance propositions from Oddie. Despite a very funny *Rivers to Babylon* moment, it's all in vain, for Tim's, Tim Revolta (complete with ball and chain and straitjacket) staggers on to the dance floor in partnership with Graeme's worryingly attractive stab at Newton-John (all tight, figure hugging black trousers, blonde wig and playful tongue action). Their painful rendition of *I Get Chills* is hilarious, culminating in shared cries of 'Ooh! Ooh! Ooh!' in agony, before Gray Bags is defrocked and the mixed dancing carnage goes ape. Tim's escape from his shackles effortlessly leads into a heartfelt plea on behalf of the beautiful freedom of mixed dancing – backed with a stirring underscore of *Land of Hope and Glory*. The dissenters are impressed, the Goodies are back together again and everybody grabs all sorts of nutty partners for a quick spin to *The Tennessee Waltz*. Sadly, the police, always a group of chaps behind the times, break up the fun and send our three chaps rushing off into a cascade of musical reference points. Choreographer Flick Colby has a field day, using the team's visual comedy with a condensed history of popular dance in a few minutes of sheer joy. With crouched finger clicking and gritty angles of some mean Cricklewood streets, *West Side Story* is at play here, counter-balanced by Mack Sennett knockabout police doing a slapstick chorus line routine. An air of camp is added with a Village People policing variation on *YMCA*, while the ideal of dance as recognised currency is embraced with the sign 'Do Not Dance on the Sand' – immediately broken by the Goodies presenting a classy soft shoe shuffle and the boys in blue going down the expected, hammed, Wilson, Keppel and Betty route. After a very effective rain dance, movie history is plundered with a Busby Berkeley meets Alfred Hitchcock's *Foreign Correspondent* umbrella routine, an incorporation of *Singin' in the Rain*'s centrepiece and a delightful arm in arm, *Wizard of Oz* romp down the yellow brick road, before a Goodies cum Police conga through a 40p car wash ends up in *Paradise – Hawaii Style* territory (with the wipers standing in for grass skirts and inner tubes hung round our heroes' necks like garlands of flowers). Things come to a head at the Fred and Ginger Café with coppers grabbing the lads, chairs flying in perfect sequence and a final, pyramid of umbrellas showcasing the beaming faces of the Goodies.

Did You Know? *Although ex-series admirer Mary Whitehouse had been a long-standing campaigner against the dubious quality of The Goodies, it was this episode that really got her blood boiling. Famously she wrote, 'Tim Brooke-Taylor was seen undressing, mocking John Travolta in an exceedingly tight pair of underpants with a distinctive carrot motif on the front…'*

MARIA ELDRIDGE, CHRIS EYMARD, SPENCER SHIRES, OKON JONES, SANDY STRALLEN, MARK WHITE, DAVID MACHIN. Episode Two, recorded Friday 16 November 1979, broadcast Monday 21 January 1980, 8.10–8.40pm, BBC2.

A KICK IN THE ARTS

Been there, done that: another Goodies mockery of Britain's feeble sporting record. This episode delivers nothing original. But with the 1980 Moscow Olympics just months away, the time for more sporting nonsense seemed right. Tim's celebrity campaign in aid of the British Olympic team, using Cyril Smith hang gliding, Basil Brush boom booming his way through a fox hunt and Rod Hull's Emu in clay pigeon shooting, produces the not so grand sum of three pence. British sport is represented this time by ex-*Fawlty Towers* resident Ballard Berkeley. Sports officials drop like flies and Berkeley gives one final patriotic rant about running for Queen and country before he, himself, pegs out and hands the reigns over to dear old Tim. With his three pence in his pocket and dreams of super-dooper training facilities, Brooke-Taylor heads for the sporting wilderness, only to find those scheming ratbags Gray and Bill, fleecing the entire athletic world with their crafty indoor games centre. Bill, the king of the con, and Graeme, the not so honest bookie tempt fresh-faced Brooke-Taylor into dodgy games of scrabble (check out Bill's cool Sinatra *Luck Be a Lady Tonight* wrist action), a very suspect bit of point scoring at ping pong and a bash at

I Spy. Tim's impassioned 'You don't care about Britain!' falls on less than bothered ears, his clothes are stripped away like some campy jeans advert and, left with no dosh, he throws himself on the mercy of the court and becomes a British sportsman. Crime is the only answer for the ragged, starving, wreck of a British team – led by Tim's undercover alter ego, the Masked Shotputter. The major Goodies' idea in this episode comes with Timbo held at Her Majesty's Pleasure and his two sparring partners establishing an international cross-section of sporting legends to represent England. Garden as Kerry Thwacker, blessed with a manic Australian accent is a highpoint, and despite the fact that packaging of celebs and subsequent treating of them as if they were thoroughbred horses, complete with cleaning out duties, had already been done in *Scatty Safari*, there's a real sense of comedy here. Throwaway references to John and Chrisie Lloyd getting it on and Joan Collins going through the entire Arsenal football team merely act as cover for Timbo's earnest attempt to buy athletes, while Garden hatches his money-making plan to take over the 1980 Olympic games for the good of Britain. Forget the fact that truth became stranger than fiction with Zola Budd's South African roots being ignored, Greg Rudeski suddenly finding his tennis racket stamped with a British insignia and the Premier football league being awash with foreign players and managers – where Chelsea can field a team with only one British bloke, 1980 was a time when British was British and British meant losing with pride and dignity. Graeme has the solution – all the foreign blokes are to marry Virginia Wade and all the foreign girls get anglified by Bill Oddie! Of course, with wires crossed and alliances under fire, the shared patriotic aspirations fly out of the window and that miserable pleader Brooke-Taylor louses up the operation with some clandestine alterations to the games programme of events. The sporting antics smack of Chapman and Cleese with myriads of weird, British-slanted events, forged with usual Olympics business. There's the nice touch of the flame carrier hanging around and lighting his fag with the sacred glow. The assortment of look-a-like British dignitaries – from Sir Alec Guinness to Alec Douglas-Hume – wandering through heights of sporting strangeness and even a bit of actual, backwards footage, seems to grate across the comedy. But the Hamlet diving, dead sea scroll relay, operatic swimming, poetry weight lifting and literary long jumping, squeezes out the

TIM BROOKE-TAYLOR (WITH LINE IN VISION) PLAYING THE SUPERHERO IN *U-FRIEND OR UFO?* GRAEME GARDEN LOOKS ON WITH DELIGHT – HE'S HAPPY NOT TO FLY!

humour. There are some pleasures along the way – the 'JB Priestley' pipe-gripping grin of success is endearing and Norman Mitchell eagerly throws himself into the boxing barker announcements for the match between Barbara Cartland and Bill's drag queen, Dame Wilhemina Oddietta, in the novelist mud-wrestling. There's even room for a spot of Graeme's medical bull fighting. Graeme loses both his wager and his dignity, while the regal wrangling seems light years from the satire of earlier shows.

BALLARD BERKELEY, ROLAND MacLEOD, NORMAN MITCHELL, GUY DEGHY, CYD CHILD, BARRY CRYER, TONY GUBBA, MARIE SUTHERLAND. Episode Three, recorded Friday 7 December 1979, broadcast Monday 28 January 1980, 8.10–8.40pm, BBC2.

U-FRIEND OR UFO?

This science fiction romp taps into the late Seventies' obsession with alien pictures. A few months earlier, Ridley Scott's dark, isolated parable, *Alien*, had hit the cinema screens and this touches the mysterious threat aspect while embracing elements from *Close Encounters of the Third Kind* and *Star Wars*. There's even a guest appearance from R2D2, masquerading as EBGB (Electronic Brain of Great Britain), a labour-saving device invented by Graeme which serves as pedal bin, washing machine, teas maid, spin dryer and door blaster. There's even a chance for some contemporary BBC sci-fi antics when the cute little robot goes all war-like, produces his familiar black eye stalk and rants the Dalek's

death cry, 'Exterminate!' More interestingly, *U-Friend or UFO?* – apart from getting away with an uncouth bit of bad language in the title pre-empts the nation's obsession with *The X Files* 15 years before the series. This X farce has all the gossip on alien abduction, there's plenty of green mist clogging up the atmosphere and Bill's performance is intense. Apart from all that, it's very funny – with Oddie dumbfoundedly witnessing the disappearance of trombonists across the land. But Bill's weird ramblings are not to the liking of Timbo – trapped in his Union flag pinny and trying to see his Knutters Knoll Knite Spot eatery get a spanking good opening night. Graeme's detached radio report sets the whole thing in comic context (with a 76 trombones reference), but Garden's 'in office' persona is hard at work maintaining his mad scientist label with the unveiling of the amazing, helping round the house, *Stars Wars* refugee. How they got away without Lucas's copyright lawyers suing their arses heaven alone knows, but it's full steam ahead into Cricklewood's alien territory and Bill's trombone-playing bait for extra terrestrial interest. Bill goes it alone for a spooky trek through Cricklewood park, complete with Roger Brierley's manic jobsworth attendant controlling the nocturnal weirdos in strictly time-scaled batches of druids, flashers, UFO obsessives and the like. By now, even the ever-contrary Tim knows something is decidedly up – Bill, face to face with the alien destiny he has been seeking, suddenly gets cold feet and scurries back to the sanctuary of home, Tim cowers behind the counter like the eternal coward he has been for a decade and Graeme successfully elevates the delicate situation with a manic, sub-Fred Scuttle appearance. Jabbering on about spaceships, cataloguing his vast array of UFO equipment and adopting the archetypal, train spotter, Peter Cook drone of the sad obsessive, Graeme delivers a telling cameo. Enjoy the elongated chat between sado Graeme and sado Tim as distressed Bill is sucked into the alien craft, checked out off screen and unceremoniously rejected from ET's master plan. United again, Graeme digs in his heels, adopts the whining vocals of the UFO obsessive again and aims to make contact with the outer space visitors. Tim's bemused, panic-stricken reactions to the threatening green spludge on Graeme's computer screen are perfectly pitched and almost Chapman-like in their power – there's also yet another excuse for Brooke-Taylor to break down completely in to 'I'm a teapot' mode. Everything begins to make some sort of sense once our heroes deduce the aliens are learning everything about mankind from television. Following the obligatory Nicholas Parsons shock reaction gag, the *Close Encounters* influence comes into play with the Cricklewood landing mound (sign posted in the Sally Army bonnet and Bill's possessed culinary offering). The solution is simple: Graeme's notion that, if television is the source of inspiration then television must promote a race of Supermen. It has merit. Besides, it's the expected excuse for some honky tonk, underscored, slapstick business from the boys with plenty of phone booth changing antics – complete with Timbo's Moss Bros top hat appearance – and loads of muscle-pumping action from Bill's overzealous superhero. After a very short burst of, short on ideas, visual material, the Goods throw in the towel on several levels – a World Ambassador of Peace is required and by the look on Tim's face, he's favourite for the religious make over. In an echo of those experimental, brain-storming days of 1970 and the original Goodies conception of Super Chaps Three, the team go into Gerry Anderson terrain with SuperNun. The opening credits shamelessly embrace ATV convention, Tim's holier than thou appearance is a comic treat and, despite passing similarities to *Python*'s The Bishop, the physical abuse of Archbishops, jet-propelled flying, and the energetic

TIM BROOKE-TAYLOR AND GRAEME GARDEN: SUPERHEROES!

flapping habit of his ever-flapping habit, make this an interlude to treasure. But Graeme, for all his utterly convincing pleas that he isn't a mad scientist, has gone down that utterly mad scientist path and stuck a nuclear warhead on Tim's bonce. With heavy contemporary overtones of up-and-coming space shuttle missions and ambitious launching experiments, this minor space opera sees Tim's destructive nun become little more than a pawn, whacked between Bill's Super chappie and the impressive tennis arm of the alien space ship. Tapping into the hip, new, groovy world of primitive, pioneering computer games, Graeme's screen becomes the archaic but addictive tennis game, Brooke-Taylor bellows out a request for 'new balls please!' and the entire scenario allows for a healthy rooster of nun gags performed on screen by the show's writing team ('I didn't know the nun was loaded!') Destruction is diverted as an impassioned Bill communicates with the aliens via trombone playing – there's an impressive and probably expensive, landing effect in the best *Close Encounters* tradition. Oddie's musical peace-making latches on to a burst of Hitler (who only had one!), the haunting theme from *Coronation Street* and, most warming of all, *The Goodies* theme itself. Bill seems to have cracked it, and basking in burning white light, delivers a powerful speech of isolated life forms, the reality that, besides earth's population, the inhabitants of this space ship is the entire sum of living creatures in the universe, and begging for a totally peaceful understanding between everybody. But before Bill can stroll on forever, Tim's five megaton explosive religious icon storms into view and the earth disappears in a giant mushroom cloud. A bleak ending to an excellent show, but while the *Dr Strangelove* credits had Vera Lynn singing *We'll Meet Again*, this episode revels in the juxtaposition of total destruction with the pleasure of *The Goodies Theme*.

Did You Know? During location filming in 1979 at Portland Bill Bird Observatory, Bill Oddie spotted the ultra-rare American bird, the Yellow Billed Cuckoo, and predicted an invasion of twitchers – he was right and impressed Tim Brooke-Taylor for the only time... allegedly. Graeme's robot, EBGB, works as a prototype for the regular robotic helper in Series Nine.

ROGER BRIERLEY, MARCELLE SAMETT, ERNIE GOODYEAR, RICHARD SMITH with PATRICK MOORE. Episode Four, recorded Friday 14 December 1979, broadcast Monday 4 February 1980, 8.10–8.40pm, BBC2.

ANIMALS

Here, several years before Nigel Planer's Neil got groovy with 'vegetable rights and peace!' in *The Young Ones*, meat-eating crusader Bill Oddie defends the rights of carrots and spuds. More to the point, in the first flush of *Not The Nine O'Clock News* success, this episode recruited lead player Mel Smith as a high-profile guest star. Unlike *Dodonuts*, which wallowed in Bill's ultra-conservationist persona, here it's Timbo that's all kind and considerate. With Brooke-Taylor's Beast Boutique and Animal Actors' Agency, his system for the gentle and meaningful use of furry creatures is totally against the bloodlust ideals of bearded Oddie. Bill makes his appearance as a wannabe nice old granny, attracting a group of pigeons with a bag of bread and then shooting one for his breakfast. Dead pig, dead baa lamb or indeed, dead hot dog, is a worthy menu substitution but Tim's outraged and offended. Poor Raquel the Tortoise doesn't know which way to turn and all the creatures are clearly traumatised by the conversation. Actually, they all seem fairly calm, even if star-struck Tim wants to bask in the reflected glory of his artistes – plans for a wart hog to become the next Oliver Reed are on the cards, but the telephone just doesn't ring. Begging, pleading and lovingly

cooing at the receiver, Tim yearns for a ring, ring, ring, before Graeme Garden's 'near enough!' knock comes to the rescue. As Captain Grayboots the Fearless Lion Tamer, his circus act is all raring to go, with one problem – no lions. Of major importance, Gray wants six, Tim hedges his bets with an offer of one and a masterpiece of banter takes off with Brooke-Taylor finally facing the fact that lion stocks are quite low, in fact, they are zero. But, like Michael Palin in a famous sketch from 11 years earlier, Tim desperately works at customer satisfaction with the suggestion of a bowl of shebunkins. Harmless, beautiful, swimmy swammy fish things, Graeme is none too convinced, even with Tim's earnest ripple of the water. Besides, Tim hates the cruel notion of circus animals. In a subtle battle of the printed word, Tim holds aloft his 'Kindness Costs Nothing' message, quickly counterbalanced by Graeme's 'Cruelty Is More Fun' pledge. But Tim's animals have a veritable host of skilled activities. There's Terrence the tap-dancing dog, uneasily wearing the shoes, doing absolutely nothing and allowing Tim to dive headlong into a sparkling rendition of *Stepping Out with My Baby*. There's Buster the bicycle-riding budgie and some nose antics with the rare Patagonian nose vole – which makes several hilarious reappearances throughout the show. In a 'back to the fans' tour, Tim grabs his dog and steam organ, attempts the dance routine once more, gives up and does the dance himself, to the dog's playing. Finally, admitting defeat he heads back home to Cricklewood Central. Shock, horror! All the animals have vanished, but not so, those money-making, cruel-mongering swines Bill and Graeme who used the entire wildlife stock. Marlon the Three-Toed Sloth makes a fab peg bag, crabs make pretty good pegs, Ollie the Octopus is let loose on the washing-up and even Henrietta the Hedgehog has been turned into a brush. Gray can hoover with a snake while dogs can double as mops and self-powering, oven-heating, timer-setting, snack treats. The future of mankind rests on the major plan, an animal-driven power station. It can't last, and the suitably entitled *Not the News at Ten* Mel Smith newsflash details equal rights for animals. Reversing the BBC's exploitative programming, the hilarious *Life On Earth* parody, Life On Presenters, showcases a stunning impression from Graeme Garden as he hushes and whispers his way through natural history. Tracking down the fossilised remains of Michael and Armando Dennis and recovering the ultra-rare Hans and Lotte Hass 'still alive

DISCONTENT DURING THE MAKING OF *ANIMALS* FROM THE FINAL **BBC** SERIES. GRAEME SEEMS HAPPY ENOUGH BUT TIM AND BILL ARE SUFFERING ON LOCATION IN RABBIT SUITS IN THE MIDDLE OF NOWHERE

and still filming', more common species are discovered and examined. There's a dozen basking Jacques Cousteaus on the Galapagos Islands, a short-sighted Patrick Moore, a destructive family of David Bellamys ripping plants from the ground and, recreating that landmark television moment, of Attenborough and the gorillas. Away from the box, Graeme and Tim charmingly chat about the programme's finer points, wondering what a Bellaburger – a cross between Bellamy and Attenborough – would taste like. Meat-hungry Bill isn't bothered, he's starving. He tries to consume a nose vole sandwich, sticks Tim's hand in a bun ('on the other hand!') and ultimately threatens to shoot him dead for a proper meal. With Tim's notion of compulsory vegetarianism, veg has a right as well and Bill aims to relate it. He's already on the telly before the other two can blink. Having bounded over to the studio to help their bearded pal, Tim and Graeme and the herd of

presenters, make a quick exit from wood-tearing, snarling, hairy-pawed beasties. With *Watership Down* fresh in the memory and sporting huge rabbit skins, the trio go all uneasy, slow, softly spoken and endearing. Capturing the essence of the animation, they bound off, worryingly look out for each other, try and stop Bellamy picking the flowers, go through cartoon violence road accidents and ultimately face their maker via fake television cameras. All this sequence is touchingly blessed with the emotive *Bright Eyes* song, a Sam Peckinpah sense of slow motion death sees the exit of Timbo as the camera fires bullets and the dark climax is a masterpiece. With the lads dead and the animals inheriting the earth, a dog mouths the announcement that it's the last of the series and trails its replacement – The Doggies. Complete with their own Doggie Doggie theme song and a white poodle sporting a Union flag waistcoat, the credits roll.

181

Did You Know? *Although the penultimate episode of Series Eight, Australian television screenings on the ABC Network would often show Animals out of order thanks to the misleading 'last of series' conclusion. With the ITV shows a whole different ball game, the slaughter sequence would conclude the Goodies for some viewers. Not only is Mel Smith inspired casting for the newsreader but another association with the new wave of comedians came about when one of the Goodies rabbit costumes was recycled for The Young Ones. It was worn by Dawn French for her role as the Easter Bunny.*

MEL SMITH, PATRICK MOORE, RONNIE STORM, ERNIE GOODYEAR. Episode Five, recorded Friday 21 December 1979, broadcast Monday 11 February 1980, 8.10–8.40pm, BBC2.

WAR BABIES

Although no one realised at the time, this was the final burst of Goodies greatness for the BBC. As the *Radio Times* put it: '1940 STOP Britain besieged STOP How did Churchill win the war QUERY Only now can it be told STOP And only three small boys can tell it SEMI-COLON – Reuters.' The scene is 1939 and young Bill pops out into the world a fully formed, bouncing, bearded baby boy, ready to suck his huge milk dispenser dry. The wartime era is set with vintage newsreel footage boosted by Tim's earnest voiceover. Speeded camerawork, backwards cranking and unsubtle new black and white inserts, allow Adolf Hitler to dance to the music of the band and Neville Chamberlain to perform a magic trick in between holding aloof his immortal 'no war today' declaration. But it's Bill's amazing and amazed Lancashire parents who cover the newspapers – Bill's arrival takes the front page while the outbreak of war sneaks in somewhere at the bottom. His mum is nursing a bump the size of the Albert Hall, journos go crazy with flamboyant, headlines about developing a football team and the cliché of speeding clock hands depicting the father awaiting the event, breaks down into the comedy of a faulty, out of control, timepiece. Oddie's coy entrance, with a full-bloodied 'Hello Daddy!', is priceless. But soon, after a myriad of early training antics, it's off to school with a bus full of clever kids and the *Dad's Army* technique of employing Forties' musak to capture the era. And if you miss the subtle parallel with the classic BBC situation comedy, a little later there's a burst of *Who Do You Think You Are Kidding Mr Hitler?* just to drive the point home. Oddie tackles his two-year-old in a 40-year-old body with relaxed acceptance. Nervously creeping past the young geniuses already settled in the school transport, he finds himself a seat, only to whip out his pipe and grab the chance of a few chapters of *Lady Chatterley's Lover* on the journey. Ironically, for the team's last outing for the corporation, we get to see the first meeting of the Goodies, as 'eager to please and willing to make a friend' Bill chats to equally oversized, conker champion Graeme. Tim is a stupid baby, gurgling at all and sundry, pushed throughout his carefree life in a pram and covered in labels detailing everything as Tim's property. The trio are incarcerated in a special intelligence school, Highbrow Hall, ruled by straight-laced Headmaster Geoffrey Palmer, gamely trying to cope with six-year-old students so advanced they can disprove the existence of God to the school chamberlain. Oddie, always a bloke with an eye for all sorts of birds, gives the green light to the school's sexy blonde bombshell of a Matron. The Goodies get cracking on bomb disposal and listen to Churchill's radio plans for enemy line infiltration. Timbo has trouble slotting coloured blocks into the right holes, although this babbled patriotic speech gets the other two fired up! But this is not the brave derring-dos of John Mills, no, the Goodies' mission is simply to break through into Germany to buy Winston Churchill a box of cigars! The entire senselessness of warfare is condensed and delivered with a sharp, satirical edge. And if the whole notion is sort of lifted from *Python*'s Princess with Wooden Teeth then so be it, the Goodies transfer the idea and give it teeth of metal. Exactly as it should be, the condemned children's show enacted by the stars as children tackles issues rooted in the British psyche. Richard Attenborough's shamed cowardice from *In Which We Serve* is comically expanded to reflect the bitter, anti-fighting mentality of the British Tommy, gathered round the wireless for Mr Churchill's speech and vehemently refusing to fight them on the beaches or anywhere else come to that. The adamant babbling of the Prime Minister, about him not doing the fighting but leaving that to the great British public, is sweetly timed and potent. All the intriguing business involving the parachute jump and Brooke-Taylor's dismembered body acts as a comic touch of pathos before the most delightfully written moment of the show, featuring telling cameos from Graeme and Tim as Hans and Fritz, a couple of Nazi soldiers. Learning from *Monty Python's Life of Brian* and the idea of playing several characters within the same narrative (only Tim had previously attempted this, in *Hunting Pink*), the wistful, humanised delivery from Brooke-Taylor leads to a barrage from Garden tapping into war movie conventions which dictate that all such 'damn this war' monologuers meet with sudden death.

Current television heroics are reflected in Tim's six million dollar baby – being recreated by scientific Garden (already, at the age of two, a whiz with mechanics) and storming off in a slow-motion jog. It sets things up for the show's most dangerous joke – Andrew Ray's excellent cameo as Winston Churchill, hiding behind the groaning voice due to his uncanny similarity to Adolf Hitler. Morale is low and Ray won't lose his moustache and black, sweeping hairstyle, so, that never-idle boast that the Goodies could do anything, anywhere, comes into play to save the face of British, war-mongering politics. Tim's wind-up decoy does all the movements, delivers the dialogue and interacts with bounding energy. Ray's priceless dramatic pauses and long, drawn-out speeches are sublime contrasted with Garden's impatience, 'The war's gonna be over by the time you're finished!' First World War mythology juxtaposes with Forties' mentality as *The Match of the Day* theme signals a football match between the battling Brits and the gritty Germans. The injury list takes things beyond satire into a darker area of comic observation, but soon it's Python-esque nuttiness as Tim's Churchill bounds on, dishes out two-finger salutes before Graeme reverses his hand, passes to himself, and on to himself and then, hey, back to himself. No score after extra time dictates that the war must be decided on a penalty shot-out, the German tank threatens to block the Brits and Tim's painfully slow tap towards goal ends the match with a hold your breath moment. Like Geoff Hurst's classic, a debate rages about whether the ball crosses the line or not and, as with Sir Geoff, the ref gives the old thumbs up. A glorious commentary from Brooke-Taylor's newsreel chap ('Give that man a coconut Grandma!'), allows shared memories of 1966 to invade the seriousness of war, while the final, abrupt ending – Churchill getting a knighthood and historic glory, the Goodies getting lollipops – is as cool an ending as the team could hope for. A bit of confectionery is pretty much equated to a worthless medal in the team's eyes, and who was the real heroic element of the war? A final, affectionate, knowing two fingers to authority, the BBC door was closed on *The Goodies* from this point on and a new outlet was needed. The other side made an offer the three couldn't refuse… But for all their irreverence, Tim's final line of dialogue in a BBC *Goodies* episode, is 'So long suckers!' – it drips with irony.

GEOFFREY PALMER, ANDREW RAY with SHARON MILLER, ERNIE GOODYEAR. Episode Six, recorded Friday 25 January, broadcast Monday 18 February 1980, 8.10–8.40pm, BBC2.

SERIES NINE

Between 1977 and 1980 the trio had been frustrated and unimpressed with the corporation's resting of the series. Their insightful form of comedy, unappreciated and misunderstood by the BBC, was labelled as children's programming. However, the major argument was the vast cost of special effects for *The Goodies* in light of the BBC's commitment to their flagship production *The Hitch Hiker's Guide to the Galaxy*. The importance of that Douglas Adams' epic has been some what blown out of proportion in the eyes of fans of *The Goodies* looking for conspiracy theories. True, *Hitch Hiker's* bit deeply into the BBC effects budget, but Mary Whitehouse complaints and a new breed of comedian quickly usurped the established guard and made the corporation less than keen to renew the trio's contracts. Oddie and Garden were increasingly disenchanted from the late Seventies, but Brooke-Taylor stuck out for BBC loyalty and the team eventually landed an eighth and final series. However, a verbally promised agreement to commission a Goodies Christmas special for 1980 was curtailed at the last minute and problems were immediately resurrected. Besides that, Bill and Graeme were both going through bitter, expensive and messy divorces and needed money quickly. When the offer from ITV came, Tim was pressurised by the other two to take it. Another petty BBC knock-back broke the proverbial back of the camel and the trio hitched their legs over the trandem and pedalled into commercial television. The rumblings between the BBC and the Goods had reached the ears of the 'other side'. As with Morecambe and Wise, part of the temptation package was the promise of a feature-length film version of the show. In the end, Eric and Ern got *Night Train to Murder* – finished just before Eric's death – and the Goodies saw themselves launched with the 25-minute 'film' special, *Snow White 2*. But money was the crucial factor, and a lot of it as well. The Goodies were offered a three-year contract, delivering more money than the entire BBC run put together. It cost LWT almost twice as much as the BBC ever paid to make the programme and nobody at the independent station seemed to know what to do with *The Goodies*. At their peak of inventiveness they were still often perceived as nothing more than children's entertainers. Indeed, for their opening ITV effort they were expected to be just that. A seasonal pantomime, the show was given a primetime early evening Christmas Eve slot. However, the continued programming of the series at early evening through January and February didn't suit and, after a popular beginning, it failed to keep audience figures high. With just one year of their contract completed, *The Goodies* was unceremoniously dropped by Michael Grade from the LWT schedules. Having burnt their bridges at the BBC, the Goodies were without a straw to clutch at. In fact, the BBC repeated three episodes from Series Eight – *Saturday Night Grease*, *War Babies* and *Animals* from 7 to 22 January 1984. Shortly after, the ill-fated ITV season was repeated from 10 June 1984, nestled in at an even earlier time, from 5–5.30pm. It was the last regular exposure for *The Goodies* on British television. Sadly, the team weren't given the chance to call the shots, stop when they felt the time was right and finish with a special edition. Bill Oddie believes they 'could have gone on for years', while Tim Brooke-Taylor is convinced the show could still have been running today.

Film cameramen Tim Piper and Ian Howes. Film editor Ray Weedon. Videotape editor Graham Roberts. Special effects Peter Hutchinson with Bob Harman (Special & 6) and Peter Pullen (1, 3 & 4). Vision mixers Terry Kinane (Special & 2) and Kay Harrington (1, 3–6). Vision controllers Richard Cooper (Special, 2 & 6), Terry Pyrke (1), Frank Parker (3 & 4) and Don Furness (5). Graphics Tony Oldfield, Brian Terry and John Tribe. Costume designer Brenda Fox. Make-up Sandy MacFarlane with Wendy Brown (Episode 4). Lighting directors Brian Pearce (Special, 1 & 2) and Chris Bartlett-Judd (3–6). Film sound Bill Cross, Tony Anscombe and Anne Parsons with Jon Matthews (Special). Sound supervisors Graham Hix (Special, 1, 2 & 4) and Graham Thor-Straten (3, 5 & 6). Music by Bill Oddie and Dave Macrae. Vocals Bones. Choreographer Ali Minto (Special). Stunts Sadie Eddon, Sue Crosland, Ken Barker and Stuart Fell. Location production managers David Fitzgerald (Special & 5), Alan Woolfson (1, 3 & 4) and Peter Hall (2). Casting director Nikki Finch. Floor managers Peter Hall (Special, 5 & 6) and Simon Holder (1–4). Stage manager Tony Crutchley with Caroline Brill (Special). Cameras Martin Bond (Special, 2, 5 & 6), Dave Taylor (1), Mike Paterson (3) and Phil Lofthouse (4). Production managers Brian Penny (Special, 1–3), Mike Hack (4) and Glen Jennings (5 & 6). Production assistants Glynis Jones and Marion Poole. Designed by James Dillon and Roger Hall. Executive producer David Bell. Produced and directed by Bob Spiers.

THE GOODIES CHRISTMAS SPECIAL: SNOW WHITE 2

As the *TV Times* warned, 'just when you thought it was safe to go back to the pantomime… the Goodies, Tim, Graeme and Bill, bring you Snow White 2.' A brilliant, if short, realisation of the Goodies' plan to create an anarchic pantomime format taking in elements of traditional panto experience and twisting it. The result, landing squarely within the *Snow White* story succeeded in remaining essentially a prime slice of family entertainment. However, the team inject enough surrealist and adult comedy to tip the balance. This is certainly not Mike Reid or Jim Davidson, but the Goodies fashion a biting deconstruction of pantomime technique and cliché. Basking in the light of blockbusting cinema – both *Jaws* and *Star Wars* are referenced – the show begins with a cinema trailer. As their first effort for the other side, the beginning is aptly dramatic, heralding the Goodies House of Humour and galloping through the gamut of nasty panto traditions from grotesque dames, enforced sing-a-longs of

I Lift Up My Finger and I Go Tweet, Tweet (complete with Graeme leading 'the miserable lot' in the stalls) and the boredom of the xylophone player brought in to fill in time during set changes. A stunning image has the Goodies – alone in a theatre auditorium – in full BBC costume surrounded by empty chairs. The aisles spookily fill up with Jaws-like fins which are ultimately revealed to be the hats of the seven dwarfs. As narrator Richard Briers explains, this is where the story proper really begins. The dwarfs are sharing a place with the less than white Snow White (check out the thumbs up from one of the highly sexed little fellows). The Goods are the shocked neighbours, reacting to the good time girl's antics with the small seven and, again, turning on the shocked amazement at her running off with the 'so-called Prince!' As is the norm, the Prince is a woman and much thigh-slapping and thinly veiled lesbian disapproval is brought in. As Briers observes, Snow White is clearly a weirdo and her nutty tenancies are developed via the high life. The dwarfs are cruelly used as skittles and garden gnomes. Two die from overexposure and one is gobbled up by a goldfish thus leaving vacancies for three out of work chaps. Although the BBC is not mentioned, the Goodies were clearly in need of employment. Snow White's less than cheerful attitude – 'stuff em!' – is hardly the best recommendation and the little people are not immune to being bashed on the head by tossed away story books, but a job is a job and the lads slip into place. The small problem of being a bit on the big side doesn't seem to bother the remaining four dwarfs, although the Goods rendition of the *Heigh Ho* rip-off *Hay Ho* causes the trio to bash their heads while those about them are preserving theirs. Memories of *Scoutrageous* are provoked with a saucy shower scene (Tim is surprised by a dwarf's loofah in a most personal place) and the oversized trio squeeze into tiny costumes for the full panto effect. The head-banging comic motif is continued and the Goodies edge is injected with David Rappaport as the fag-smoking leader. A stunning support turn, parallel with sterling work in Terry Gilliam's *Time Bandits*, he goes through the motions like a union leader, addressing the new boys as 'Soppy, Grotty and Tim…', mysteriously mentioning that impostors are among their number and suspiciously commenting that some of the group are not dwarfs. One of the actual dwarfs breaks down and confesses at this point before Timbo faces the music and bravely admits his deceit, 'I'm not a dwarf!' Bill is less keen to give up the job, insisting that 'I nearly am…' before breaking into banter about unemployment and discrimination against big people getting the work. Rappaport is completely insane as well as very helpful – offering to make them dwarfs by chopping off their legs at dawn. Dressed as three little Lord Fauntleroys, the Goods play *Babes in the Wood* for an instant, twist the *Snow White* 'can't do it' woodcutter scene with the dwarf really not being able to do the evil deed because he falls down due to the weight of the axe, and ultimately break out of the danger zone with *Dick Whittington* spotty hankie iconography and a desire to get to London. A newsreel interlude of a busy, red bus and underground, sets them in London and Bill has already sent up the pantomime format with Tim's lament about lack of beans, faithful cow etc… greeted with the resigned, 'Well we're screwed then, aren't we!' Tim's Fairy Godmother – using the old Lady Constance vocals – offers to show them round London with a helpful A–Z, goes all Jewish Mama after Bill's frustrated dismissal and leaves the lads stranded in Battersea Park with nothing but the tube for travelling purposes. The Park reverts to pantomime tradition almost immediately, with doom, gloom and unfortunate skeletons surrounding our heroes. Bill explains that the path back home has been picked out and retained by dropping the spots from his hankie bundle but a quick burst of snow (looking exactly like the hankie spots) soon makes that plan hopeless. Tim throws himself into an impassioned monologue about the dangerous forest and receives a round of applause from the trees for his performance. Graeme is less than impressed simply muttering, 'Very good!' before purchasing an *Evening Standard* from a dispensing tree, relishing a helpful forest lamp provided by Bill and earnestly looking for likely work. A call for a trio of dwarfs is hastily ignored, genies are out of the question (they must have their own lamp and Bill insists he will never be able to get into one), and every other job seems to be dedicated to women – from Prince Charming to Huntsmen. Bill's off again, moaning about sexual discrimination before the fox hunting, black tight-clad huntsmen break into the scene and carry the lads – bagged stag style – back to the castle of women. Ruled by the fairer sex, Snow White, Princesses and Princes sit around the place, boozing, singing and humiliating men. Brilliantly pointed and scripted, these happily ever after women are seen to abuse the panto situation and treat men

shamelessly. In the midst of the Woman's Lib movement, the Goodies highlight pantomime as the opposite extreme and a song and dance number is the result. With the Goods initially clad in Buttons uniform and the dancing girls doing the full Busby Berkeley bit, Bill warbles the number with all the gusto of the old days. Leading the chorus in a panto spelling of M.A.N. and what that word means to the females – W.O.R.K. – the Goods rip through a load of panto characters to illustrate the point. Going through the custard pie routine, doing a bit of plank-bashing slapstick and donning bear skin rugs for some painful stepped on expressions, the Goods are well and truly put through the hoop. They don genies' garb and perform the Wilson, Keppel and Betty sand dance, find themselves within geese suits, struggle to produce the golden eggs and finally black up for some racial business as grinning Man Fridays, before the girls get fed up and throw them out of the castle and on to the scrap heap. The idea may be a variation of the Female Castle from *Monty Python and the Holy Grail*, but the Goodie routine is inspired and the gospel chorus of Bones even fades in to compliment *The Goodies Theme* heralding the advert break. After real commercials for the first time in a Goodies episode, the boys are still on the scrap heap, firing up the unwanted panto men for a castle invasion. The union is not happy, Graeme calls everybody 'Brothers!' and Bill is in his element. There's room for a bonding between the dwarfs and the big boys with a we/wee men misunderstanding corrected with Rappaport's supportive 'neither are big men!', while the awful drag tradition is condemned as making cool blokes look like Barbara Cartland. The virginity of the less than pure Snow White is brought into question – a matey moment between Bill and Rappaport when Oddie nudges him knowingly with a 'You remember…' The attack plan is set but Tim's cold logic immediately dampens the passion. His 'How we gonna get in?', however, is counted by Bill's 'Cows!', a general agreement that that's exactly what the female foe are and finally a fashioning of a Trojan Cow notion to find a way into the castle without detection. The irritating xylophone player is chucked over the wall at this point and the Goodies head off to Panto Lane – the Petticoat Lane of Christmas theatre – in search of aid. With plenty of *Oliver!* musak and tasty wares (from custard pies and pumpkins to dead rats and ear plugs), the lads finally find a cow suit seller and prepare for battle. Finding one with six legs was probably the hardest thing but the female huntsmen like what they see, take the creature round the grounds for a quick ride, use a rather large couple of house bricks to persuade the lads to jump over a wall and finally leave the boys stranded and failed outside the castle. A quick crawl up the side soon rectifies things and the dead loss and dead weight of Tim sleeping in the rear allows Bill and Graeme to lapse into dive-bombing jargon. Graeme's 'What the hell's going on!' is a joy as the duo grab Biggles iconography (leather flying cap and goggles) and latch on to war banter, clipped delivery and *Dambusters* accompaniment. Reading the garbled, cryptic and rhyming note from Tim, the dreaded foe of Timbellina is established – Tim, out of the skin and out of the special effects floating bubble, looking lean and mean, doing the snake eye, carrying her wand in a violin case and embracing Mafia ideals with the sinister theme and in her stance as the Godmother. Bill's disgruntled rhyme injection – 'Up yer leg!' – is a winner, before counter culture is embraced with Tim's wand cum *Stars Wars* light sabre and an epic battle akin to the climax of *Don't Lose Your Head*. Bill and Graeme illustrate that all that panto thigh-slapping actually hurts, Bill helpfully provides a pad for added protection, skilfully performs a fire-eating trick with the light sabre (which immediately reappears out his rear end) and ultimately defeats the female with help from a frantic attack from the outsiders who are no longer outside. A fluttered eyebrow and a hint of leg is more than enough to turn the Goodies off course. With seductive promises of doing anything for them, Graeme leads the male troops in a sing-song through the *Say Tweet Tweet* number and runs off for a pampered life with the women. Bill and Graeme – back in Goodie garb – are treated like Kings and eagerly await the thing that boys like best of all. But Tim's Fairy promise is not all it's cracked up to be – the ladies throw themselves into a xylophone rendition much to the lad's chagrin.

Did You Know? ITV were really building up their latest signing. The trio – in dwarf costume – were featured on the Christmas highlights photograph montage and an article. Despite being the first ITV venture screened, this was in fact, the very last Goodies episode ever made. It was completed just weeks before its broadcast, after the six LWT programmes were already completed.

DAVID RAPPAPORT Chief Dwarf ANNETTE LYONS Snow White SYD WRIGHT Xylophone player. Dwarfs: KENNY BAKER, PETER BURROUGHS, GEORGE CLAYDON, MIKE COTTREL, MALCOLM DIXON, MIKE EDMONDS, TONY FRIEL, JOHN GHAVAN, RUSTY GOFFE, JACKIE PURVIS, GERALD STADDEN. Princes/Princesses: JACKI BARRON, CAROLINE DILLON, JANE FIRTH, CAROL FORBES, JACKIE HALL, NOLA HAYNES, CHRISSIE KENDALL, CHRISSIE MONK, WANDA ROKICKI, JANE WINCHESTER. Narration RICHARD BRIERS. Recorded Wednesday 9 December 1981, broadcast Sunday 27 December 1981, 7.15–7.45pm.

ROBOT

The first of the new ITV series sets the Goodies within a familiar context. Things haven't changed, with Tim and Graeme stooped over a hot computer and Bill breezing through life playing air guitar along to his headphone-encased universe. Modernity is the thing: the result is a Robot – very Eighties – and the perfect replacement for the scruffy, loud mess that is Bill Oddie. Less than happy with his irritant status, Bill's off, he's packing his stuff for the long journey into nowhere. Tim's delighted with the clean job he's made of the place, but Posh Good's frantic fidgeting leaves the bearded one wondering. Is an urgent trip to the loo required, or is Tim simply distressed to see him go… Neither, Tim is playing the expectant father to expectant mother Graeme Garden! There follows a pointed torrent of abuse on the fact that Tim always liked Graeme better, 'because he's got less hair than you!' – and questions of over-friendliness, hidden sexuality, thoughts of unnatural acts and misunderstanding flicker over Bill's face as Tim time-warps back to the old days with a spot of teapot panic. Graeme emerges clutching his bundle of robotic joy in a blanket and a new, very short, era of Goodies history begins. Bill is less than impressed. Apart from being far too little for the job, he's got a tin head! But Graeme knows the little chap will do the job, castigates Tim's gobblegook speech as unnecessary, before happily joining in with the diddums chatter. Bill, considering the duo completely round the twist, faces defeat ('I know when I'm licked… because it feels lovely!') and wanders off. The scene cuts to night, the baby sleeps in its cot and the two remaining Goodies are, likewise, in slumber land. That is, of course, before the screaming starts. Tim's shaken out of his Thatcher fantasy, 'Not now Maggie!' and a sequence reflects those endless, restless nights with baby. The writing wallows in marital pressure, name calling, thinly disguised attempts to explain why the other partner should deal with the problem, complaints of ruining the figure from mother Graeme and indignation at the prospect of breast feeding. Tim almost lands the job – even though Graeme warns the thing will bite his nipples off – but it's Tim's loving coos of affection, and thoughts that baby responds better to Graeme which, really sets this in the comedy mould. The only solution for baby is the employment of au pair. Tim doesn't want to know. Graeme meanwhile, playing the housewife to perfection – with baby duties, washing line grabbing and ironing skills as

BILL ODDIE DRAGS HIMSELF THROUGH THE MECHANICAL ANTICS OF THE OPENING EPISODE OF SERIES NINE, *ROBOT*

'father' reads the paper – is all for the scheme. So is Tim once a line-up of lovely girls turn up… oh, and Bill as the Swedish anti-babe Helga. Tim's cries of 'Get 'em off…' fade as Bill's bearded beauty rolls his eyes, does the sing-song Swedish talk and cracks up under the pressure. Graeme suggests hiring the ugliest one, Tim goes along with that, settles for the one on the end and grabs the really stunning cutie nearest him. Beauty, as he unconvincingly tries to explain, is in the eye of the beholder and check out the hideous 'boat race' on his choice. Actually, she's drop dead gorgeous and Bill's Helga gets the job. Bill's on a mission to destroy the enemy and takes the babe to a government health-warned playground. Backed with his own song, Bill whizzes the defenceless robot through roundabouts and the like before chucking him in a box and hoisting him on a crane. Amazingly, the robot himself is driving the vehicle, Bill gets hoisted by his own petard and is trapped in cement before the metallic chap's crushing ball lets him free. But music is always Bill's strong point and

TIM AND BILL POSING, OFF-DUTY, DURING THE MAKING OF *ROBOT*

FOOTBALL CRAZY – BILL ODDIE – FOOTBALL HOOLIGAN GETS NASTY FOR THE CAMERA

a saxophone lullaby sends the baby to sleep – a hasty escape into the commercial break and Bill's achieved his goal. He can't get away from Tim's punishment, however. This involves plenty of bum slapping for the naughty, absent-minded 'Helga' with Tim's robotty, botty, botty antics reaching a frenzy of perverted pleasure. Graeme's outraged that this 'girl' arouses Tim so much and casually catalogues the history of mistakes – losing the baby 25 times in just two weeks… By now, Bill can slip back into Bill Goodie persona. While still adopting the blonde wig and large falsies, Graeme's clocked that the accent has gone and the Oddie swagger has returned. The home movie footage of the little robot is sweetness itself – Tim cuddles the thing, sets him off on his first steps and sees the poor kid fall flat on his face several times. Contrasting Tim and Graeme's loving comments is Bill's aggressive commentary, mirrored in the film with the robot squirting water into his au pair's face from the bath and throwing up over him. Bill is seen deliberately to turn away as Tim tosses the babe towards him! Bill angrily goes to smash the camera and Tim proudly displays baby's potty full of nuts and bolts – but the charm of infancy is rudely shattered by

the arrival of the big, bold and laddish Robot, as voiced by the marvellous David Rappaport. Graeme's homing programme chip obviously works, but the Robot is not the sweet thing he once was. He's hardly without sex either – dragging in a pink robot for a bit of the other. Tim's parental order to go to his room is just what he wants to hear – 'You said it baldy!' – and the usual teen angst for parents sets in. Suddenly, thoughts of nice furry little Bill seem appealing as the robotic sex fest starts to ruin both Tim's life and his ceiling. Bill's rant about the parents being to blame ushers in glittering Gray Bags as a good, instructive and role-model robot, but the tin wonder doesn't want to know. He's became a metal Bill Oddie – playing loud music (*Funky Gibbon*), growing long hair and a beard. The real Bill has had enough of all this business, defending the old Oddie ways and finally revealing himself behind the Helga disguise and giving an impassioned speech on human power, the influence of robots and the conflict of flesh over metal. Did Shakespeare give Metal Mickey a cameo in *Hamlet*? No! Where are the robotic greats to rival human achievement – nowhere. Bill pleads for the melting down of R2D2, K9 and all that mob before the militant robot (very Bill) gets the lads out and leads a mass strike of kitchen appliances. Resurrecting Bill's class song *Come Back* the chase is on, as Tim tackles the toaster and takes time out for a nibble, get punched by the robot's concealed boxing glove extension and gets charmed by a snake-charming vacuum cleaner. Back at the office, Graeme's tamed his robot (now a mangled mess muttering 'Sorry Mummy!') and found a much better way round the financial problem. An emotionless Bill whisks the grub, acts as a hoover and does everything else round the place. As Graeme proudly declares… 'Bring in the Clones!' The genius of Gray Bags has achieved the miracle of the age – loads of Bill Oddies!

Did You Know? Ironically, this opening edition of the ITV series saw the Goodies get their highest viewing figures ever! The opening credits are a joy – using a lot of footage from *Change of Life* and thus including black pudding, geese and trandem iconography from the old days. The theme tune is an even funkier variation on the old, with robotic interludes, while the first appearance of the lads – doing their thing with their new image stagger – allows Bill's aggressive boot into nothingness to drop kick *The Goodies*' title. As with the *Snow White* special, the entire LWT series was also blessed with the very American legend – 'Created by Tim Brooke-Taylor, Graeme Garden and Bill Oddie.'

DAVID RAPPAPORT as the voice of the robot. Episode One, recorded Friday 12 June 1981, broadcast Saturday 9 January 1982, 6.45–7.15pm, ITV.

FOOTBALL CRAZY

A cross between two contrasting ideas – football and ballet – is given a lacklustre treatment by the Goodies. There's some great guest stars and delicious impressions from Graeme Garden, but the magic is missing. Bill has a ball, opening the episode as a thick-skulled, thick-eared, loud-mouthed bovver boy yelling at the referee, moaning about nancy-boy players not taking injures like men and proudly standing for the worse side of society. Bill's rant machine follows the fouled footballer into the operating room and, finally, to an atmospheric funeral scene where the silence is broken with one more 'Get up!' taunt. British sport has taken a violent turn, *The Big Match* is considered so awful that Tim covers his teddy bear's eyes and, indeed, Fred Dinenage's hosting of the programme centres on the hooligan activity in the crowd rather than the game. The gentle art of football is gone and Tim longs for the glorious days as he blurs the edges between actor and character and surrounds himself in the colours of Derby County. On screen, the Twerp of the Week is analysed, Graeme Garden lapses into comic ad mode to down a pint of neat scotch and the legendary Kenneth Wolstenholm (who said 'They think it's all over!' in 1966) is reduced to interviewing King of the hooligans – Bill Oddie. Surprisingly sheepish and shy, Bill delights in his infamy, embraces the jargon ('I just seem to be getting 'em right!') and hints at taking a Continental offer to become the first million pound vandal transfer. Back at base, Tim calls for action and interacts with himself on the television screen. Tim the Goodie and Tim the newly appointed police officer in charge of footie crime, have a mutual appreciation society chat before Bill bursts back into Cricklewood Central. Tim frantically ad-libs ('Hang on!… Wait for it… Nearly there…') as he struggles to reveal the police costume under the Goodie Timbo garb, Bill breaks in and breaks through the wall and Graeme casually sits back with a look of extreme disinterest on his face. He's been like that since the episode started and one can hardly blame him. However, on with the plot and with Bill caught by the fuzz, Tim exposes the disgusting spectre of sexual tension within football. Getting himself more worked up than most over the thought of tight shorts and sweaty thighs, he vows to turn back the clock – *Hype Pressure* anybody? – and bring back long shorts and good manners. Long hair is banned and if you can't show a bald pate than hats must be worn. As for the hooligan problem – the new ruling allows just one fan to attend each match to contain the anger. Bill's bovver boy looks on as the newsreel treatment of the match is played out. Tim's narration is hilarious – Grandad references and clipped Forties delivery – while copper Tim referees with well-timed 'hello, hellos' and instant arrests. Once a goal is scored all hell breaks loose, with bald caps removed for flowing, exposed locks, romantic music, slow motion and some suspect embraces between the players. Bill's supporter goes loopy on the terraces, invades the pitch and ends up nicked in the back of the net. After the break we return to Cricklewood with Graeme doing his scientific bit, experimenting with mice in a mini football viewing situation. Tim is too busy kneeing Bill in the groin and getting him cracked up over his delayed reaction to bother about Gray's business, but a quick Stan Laurel-like cry, a promised gift and a presented box of favourite hankies, gets things back on course. The point of the experiment is to prove that the game itself is not to blame – the mice have done nothing but go eek and wash their whiskers, while a Millwall hamster hooligan is going berserk in the concealed box. Tim isn't impressed with the crackpot scheme and Bill's bit of eeking and whisker washing seems to prove his point. Still, culture calls and Tim dons his glad rags for a night at the ballet. Sinisterly followed by a group of mad ex-football hooligans (and resurrecting memories of *Scoutrageous*' secretive late-night scurry), Tim's theatrical box is invaded, the tension mounts and, finally, Tim himself joins in the rant with an unlikely cry of 'Get up yer great nancy!' Back at the office, ballet has replaced football and cliché corner is packed. Tim's 'over the parrot' with the result, Bill – in knitted outfit and camp, ballet-obsessed persona – minces around the place with a rendition of 'Ballet Crazy' while Graeme, the voice of reason as ever, considers the whole thing a waste of time. Tim's plan for a Cricklewood Ballet Team is dampened with Graeme's highlighting of an entire ballet league in the offing. The show glides to its climax with Manager Tim on the sidelines and Garden and Oddie ('a strong combination') keeping the Cricklewood end up. The strong Villa side – featuring impressive work from the young Wayne Sleep – takes on the lads in a *Romeo and Juliet* Match. The sequence is well orchestrated, while football terminology breaks into the Covent Garden mentality with the perfect pitch of comic expression. Looking for the gap to make their move, getting it in the back of a hair net and handing over to a masterly split screen with three Graeme Garden footie/ballet punters discussing the game, all builds up to a classic close. Bill's moaning dancer is yellow-carded, Cricklewood's 'Kevin Keegan' spins into infinity and the *Swan Lake* free kick wall is arguably the funniest moment in the show. Garden makes use of his physical comedy skills with a bit of limp-armed, dying swan business, while the magic sponge brings him round just in time for the human penalties – 'Pele' is tossed and saved and Oddie crashes pass the goalie to get a dodgy, questioned and crowd-rousing winner. As the voiceover comments 'it's a funny game…' and a stage/pitch invasion leads into the closing credits.

Did You Know? This second episode was heralded with a TV Times cover and in-depth Bill article, Oddie Man Out, by Alex Coleman. The closing ballet sequence was filmed at Wimbledon Theatre, while the football scenes were recorded at the Crystal Palace ground.

FRED DINENAGE, KENNETH WOLSTENHOLME, WAYNE SLEEP, JOHN CROSS, ALAN FORRESTER, KIM GAVIN, TREVOR WILLIS. Episode Two, recorded Friday 29 May 1981, broadcast Saturday 16 January 1982, 6.45–7.15pm, ITV.

BIG FOOT

One of the best episodes from the last series, this is an ingenious, fun-packed offering almost to equal the days at the BBC. The boys parody television to great effect, with Tim and Bill nervously watching the mysterious world of Arthur C Clarke. Graeme does an impression of the great writer and 'inventor of the digital lawn-mower', with great swathes of out of focus photographs and outlandish theories explaining away myths and superstitions. To him it's all a load of old rubbish – as space travellers land and fill up on petrol from Stonehenge, frogs rain down on him from a great height and a quiet trip to Loch Ness results in the monster craftily looking over Graeme's shoulder at an unconvincing explanatory image of a rhino holding a French loaf in its mouth and balancing a tortoise. Skipping round the world and delighting in dismissing everything, Graeme's 'Arthur' finally tracks down the Yeti. The whole Big Foot thing is cobblers to him but he cleverly sets down a book to tempt the creature out. Tim and Bill – from the comfort of their sitting room – engage in television banter, calling out the 'behind you' lines in earnest. Graeme's kind 'teasing old Arthur' arrogance is a classic moment and even the half consumed book bait is flippantly explained away as the result of mice chomping. Part 97 is heralded, Graeme delights in the dosh he is making out of this garbage and the skull logo – vivid from the real Arthur show– mouths 'Night, Night!' as the watching Goodies relax. The show takes on the premise of 'to believe' or 'not to believe' and combines a pre-*X File* obsession with joyous Goodie

comedy. Besides, there's even Oddie's classic *They'll Never Believe It* song. Graeme is sheepish about all the interest, after all he is Arthur C Clarke and after a hasty 'me… him' recovery sets up all sorts of obstacles for the discovery of further information. However, the other lads are in earnest, setting out to prove that the great television presenter and mystery pundit does actually exist. It's two against one, but while Graeme wants real proof – like droppings – Tim's small screen documentary, The Quest For Arthur C Clarke – Man or Myth, sets things up for a narrative battle. Decidedly Python-esque, Tim's roving reporter talks to a person who actually witnessed Arthur on the box – he saw him briefly, fell asleep and when he woke up, Arthur was gone! Tim's reactions as the witness gets more and more mad (revealing his passion for eating spiders and tapping into references from *Dracula*) are hilarious as Tim's documentary effort leads into the Goodies reality. The battle lines between science and myth have been drawn. Tim and Bill are set for an expedition and Graeme must go with them to protect his 'Arthur' alter ego. Off to the Rockies, Tim is hardly sensibly dressed in sunny weather gear (he was planning to start looking in Africa), but Bill's mountaineering garb finds room for the gag – 'Haversack… have another a sack!' – before he gets down with copious amounts of beans, a silencer (which triggers off the audience and the cast), a bit of capons/crampons confusion (Tim's shoes are equipped with poultry), ice hooks, a *Generation Game* homage in the shape of a cuddly toy, a port-a-loo and a bit of rhyming comic observation with a rifle and a trifle. Graeme almost lets the cat out of the bag again when he comments that he has to be there if the boys want to see Arthur, but with his identity still protected, the trio head off to Mystery Park in search of the unexplained. Safe in their observation hide and even enjoying the comfort of a turn-off-able log fire, Bill is spotting mysteries like a good 'un, while Graeme sees nothing at all… it's hardly surprising, considering that he's playing all the parts – including tossing up dinner plates for UFOs and allowing his wig to slip during an 'Arthur' sighting. A recreation of the famous Big Foot film is revealed as nothing more than a man in a skin – and that man is Graeme, doing the lumbering walk, looking round towards the camera, having a crafty pee, displaying a rather obvious zip and even lapsing into chimp tea party mode. The truth is out as Graeme admits to everything – creating mysterious creatures for a couple of million quid – but as the advert break looms and the tension seems to fade away, the Goods hut is circled with huge footprints and another, real mystery rears its ugly head. After uncertainty as to whether the big-footed thing came from within the hut and is there or is outside trying to look in, Tim the brave goes off to follow the tracks. Speeded up and tapping into *Benny Hill* land, Tim whizzes round the hut, round the mountain and round the bend, dropping down a mountain à la *Rome Antics*, injecting *Roadrunner* 'Beep! Beep!' sounds into the fun and finally returning to the hut. Concluding that the creature must be nearby, the lads stay in the hut all day and face night with terror. The show's greatest scene is the result, with Bill nervously hearing a strange, elongated 'OOOOh!' noise and desperately trying to work out where it comes from. Graeme hears it too and the confusion of what was the noise and what was the noise Bill was making to illustrate what the noise sounds like ('No, that was me!') is class. Realising there is something else in the room, Tim is revealed as the culprit. Sleepwalking in his pursuit of strange creatures and gaining one leg shorter than the other thanks to continuous mountain walking, Tim's foot expands from all the walking and becomes the mythical, singular, Big Foot. Tim, of course, doesn't know what's going on and, waking up suddenly, sees the huge foot, believes it to be five nude midgets and whacks it! A torrent of foot gags burst out... no soul/sole, corny, heel, put a sock in it, shoo, hop it etc... Hurt and wounded, Tim stomps off to the hills and, blessed with Bill's hillbilly *Bigfoot (They Call Him Bigfoot)* sing-a-long narration, Tim's plight is documented. The more he walks the bigger the foot grows and the sight is so comical that folk die laughing just to look at it. A kindly soul with just a huge foot, Tim tries to hide the thing to avoid mass murder of the local population – a Dougal dog skin is used briefly as a walkies device – but an Indian squaw squeals and her baby pops out of its holster: danger is rife in the mountains and a price is put on the foot. Tough Mounties are called for and stepping into the breech are Bill and Graeme. Now rather proud of the enlarged appendage, Tim paints his nails and goes all hairy for the real Big Foot look. The skin is wonderfully unconvincing and Tim minces through the forest with high spirits, setting up a *Snow White* woodland animal musical interlude and attracting a bear-disguised dance routine from the other two Goods. Cleverly hiding behind a rock, allowing the lads to walk and walk and walk round the mountain and finally flattening his foes, Tim sees Graeme

and Bill lose their disguise and get struck down by the dreaded swollen foot business themselves. Wandering into the mountains for salvation, the Oddie band continues to play as the shamed Big Feet stomp away. Roll the credits.

CHARLIE STAFFORD. Episode Three, recorded Friday 19 June 1981, broadcast Saturday 23 January 1982, 6.45–7.15pm, ITV.

CHANGE OF LIFE

The finest ITV episode, all three Goodies are facing the thought of being 40. It's Bill's birthday and Tim and Graeme – comfy in their very comfy jumpers – are preparing a special party surprise. Bill's off camera and elongated stomping up the stairs sets things up for a tense and nervous confrontation. He's not fit, he's not happy and he's certainly not grateful. Condemning his pals, ordering them to shut up and wrecking the birthday bunting, Bill is less than impressed. Facing the facts without liking them very much, he fumes round the place screaming 'I'm older...' to all and sundry, shouting down the corridors, phoning though the bad news on his Mickey Mouse telephone and turning the atmosphere sour with anger. Tim and Graeme – by now donning hard hats for added protection – present the cake boasting 75 candles, and invite Bill to blow them out. Forty, fat and unfit, Bill can't muster the puff and needs oxygen to recover, before Graeme extinguishes the flames with a pucker of the lips. The birthday card simply rubs in the bad news – 'Your birthday's here, so give a cheer. You're lasted through another year. Be sure you have some birthday fun. You might not get another one' – and Bill culminates his fury covered in his own cake. Bill regrets his advancing years, dismisses his middle-aged spread and removes his cream-soiled t-shirt as the vanilla icing drips off his beard. Tim clocks the beer belly 'Oddie body' and titters for England. With cries of Moby Dick, there she blows, 'wibble, wobble jelly on a plate' and comparisons with elephants, Bill's fatness becomes an issue. Bill, the laughing on the outside, crying on the inside, mournfully faces his weight problem and bemoans the memory of girls laughing at him – 'everybody laughs at you...' corrects Tim. Helping the situation less and less, Tim offers to squeeze his pimple-like nipple, displays his Graeme-invented, hand-shaped male bra and signals the appearance of Garden's medical alter ego, Dr Gray Boots. A return to *Doctor in the House* antics, Graeme examines his patient and tries to inject modernity with face-lift, body-lift and everything-else lift suggestions. Bill's whine about being raddled seems to fall on deaf ears as Graeme tries the soft soap approach, 'You're only as old as you feel… and you feel pretty old!' He offers the possibility of a face-lift so powerful Bill will have eyes in the back of his head and a belly button displaced to form a Kirk Douglas-like chin dimple. A mud face-pack is employed simply to hide his ugly face, before talented Timbo is used as a *Generation Game* display area to highlight the different, celebrity-based looks on offer. Combinations of Telly Salvalas and Prince Charles, Barbara Cartland and Lord Grade and, even the expected cuddly toy, all flash by. But, even though Bill selects his favourite, the entire team are heading for a make-over. Graeme may not want to believe it – when Bill complains about being too old to chase girls the good doctor mutters, 'You speak for yourself… and possibly Tim!' – but eventually the trio don their new images, and to the tune of *You're Only As Old As You Feel* (sung not by Bill but female backing singers, Bones), the Goods take on the world. Well, they take on three overactive, over-sexed and over-fun loving old biddies. Bill is all Teddy Boy, Graeme looks like Groucho Marx meets Kevin Keegan and Tim turns on the teeth and charm persona of a camp Johnny Mathis but it's all to no avail… the pub is far too much, the cinema showing of *The Texas Chainsaw Massacre* leaves them throwing up and the groovy disco leaves them exhausted. With the 'girls' picked up by some leather-clad bikers, the Goodies return home. A 'Closed Due to Old Age' sign says it all. Gray's about to jump out of the window and making his will in a rush, he dishes out his childhood teddy bear, bequeaths his set of clubs – not the golf kind but the clubbing kind with which Tim plans to get his own seal skin hat – and his stamp collection – a display of squashed kittens. Graeme jumps but all he's done is stamp on Tim's pet tortoise, Gilbert – another one for the collection. The office robot is keeping quiet as Graeme's Plan B is put into operation. The trio are forced back to see if they really are fit to still be considered Goodies. It's The Goodies Standard Test and the start of the most potent Goodies back referencing. Down at the Centre, the lads are set against the wannabe robot Goodie and once Tim collapses from the shock of the starter's pistol, things seem to go from bad to worse. Within the test, all the glorious memories of Goodies past are brought back. The lads, having struggled in to their ill-fitting old costumes, face the ultimate challenge – the spectre of their own lost

success. Tim gamely tries to deliver a feeble patriotic speech as the Robot employs Union flags and fireworks to enhance his diatribe. Given 30 seconds to record a hit record, the old G-logo dungarees are slipped on and the 'give me an oooh!' is stumbled through. The computer, asking 'Put 'em together and what have you got?' gets the also inaudible mutter from Tim 'Three ooohs!' Meanwhile, the robot runs through a brief extract from *Funky Gibbon*, just as the latest model in the *Kitten Kong* range is unleashed. There's a reprise for Bill's song, instructions to avoid the wires and off-camera stage directions to the lads to stop running too far to the left. The Seventies' special effects are sent up, while the Ecky Thump sequence features a big-hatted Robot bashing the lads all over the shop and Bill's blow-up black pudding exploding in his face. A hasty scurry past the beanstalk and some wonderful silly running, sets up a cameo from the *Beanstalk* goose, a request for a freeze-frame moment (to receive the full effect of the exploding egg) and a call for the dummies for the mid-air after effects. The illusion is shattered with the Goodies remaining in shot while the dummies are present and the quick cut from landing dummy to recovering Goodie is ruined when Bill returns a lifeless dummy, ultimately pops back into life in the wrong place and sheepishly marches off when the computer cries, 'Get the dummy out!' The flying goose is revealed as nothing more than a model on the end of a crane and the appearance of a cut-out, mobile Nicholas Parsons ('Nicholas is after you!') results in a five-point penalty for Tim for overacting. The robot, meanwhile, is bashing away foe with ease as the ageing Goods try to clamour on to the trandem only immediately to fall sideways and into the gutter. Autograph hunters don't bother the trio but surround the robot, although the final score – the mechanical marvel with 53 is just beaten by the combined score of Tim's 24, Graeme's 28 and Bill's 2. Perhaps it was easy to rest on the laurels of the past. Perhaps it was ill-advised to wallow in classic moments when they overshadow anything in the LWT shows. It really could have been the episode to call the whole series a day. Full of references back to the golden years, emotionally acted and written with Bill and Graeme's sharpest pencils, this show is the perfect goodbye. Sadly, it was screened slap in the middle of the ITV batch, but as a legacy this should be treated as *The Goodies'* swan song and a mighty fine one at that.

Did You Know? *The Goodie stand-in dummies created for this season and used extensively in this show proved useful for personal appearances. A 1981 charity assignment for the team was under threat because of Tim being unavailable. In the end, Bill, Graeme and Tim's dummy did the gig!*

DAVID RAPPAPORT. Episode Four, recorded Friday 5 June 1981, broadcast Saturday 30 January 1982, 6.45–7.15pm, ITV.

HOLIDAY

Akin to *The End* and *Earthanasia* this effort sets the trio in a single location and allows them to talk, argue, bicker, play games, sing songs and have a pretty awful time. Tim starts the show doing the housework, surrounded by Union flags and bemoaning his fate, as the bowler-hatted Bill and Graeme return from a hard day at the office and simultaneously miss the hat stand with their objects of office conformity. Bill settles down to drum bashing, Graeme turns to high-tech science for tea, massage and cosy slipper relaxation, while Tim rants about the queues at Sainsbury's and the workload. Bill dismisses 'her' complains as 'boring and dull' and even turns his nose up at the pig's head lovingly prepared for dinner. The relationship isn't working and Tim has the notion that the three should spend more time together, away, on holiday. Rows will be a thing of the past when they arrive at their bungalow on the coast at Dunsquabblin! But the British weather lets them down. Arriving in waterproofs and complaining about the rain, that's about as far as the story goes. The rest of the episode sees the trio desperately searching for something to do. Graeme strolls in with a summer suit and an umbrella hat attachment. Bill can't get musical for fear of disturbing the sheep. The house rules are clearly detailed in the room, including the 'No sheep after 11 O'Clock!' Any breakages result in the offender being shot and even Bill's disgruntled removal of the warning notice incurs a huge fine – resulting in its hasty return. Tim and Graeme, meanwhile, are inspecting the very cosy bathroom – with the toilet and sink halfway up the wall and the almighty flushing causes earth vibrations which leaves Posh Good a nervous wreck. Tim's solution is for nobody to use the thing. Bill can't imagine not going for three weeks, although Tim proudly tells him that the Royal Family never go – 'That's why they're Royal!' Graeme is bored, Tim's optimism is fading and Bill moans about the rain. Bill begins to lose it which explains why his character takes an unexpected and unwelcome nose-dive into self-pity. The t-shirt is perfect – featuring the single word

'TWIT' and a finger pointing to who ever may be to his right (usually Tim) – but his sad admittance that he has no friends to send a postcard to is just not like him. There's more of the same when Tim and Graeme settle to play the card game Spat. Bill sheepishly mutters that he can't play cards and gets all upset and tongue-tied when the team captains fumble, stall and finally begin picking chairs as team mates over the small bearded fellow. The game itself is a joy, shared knowledge between Tim and Graeme and abuse for Bill. Shouting 'Ratbag!' and 'Prig!' in unison, chucking tea over Bill, bashing him with mallets, they even threaten to kill him for the completion of the game. Graeme's been going through his own pockets, Bill reads a pound note he's already read before, Graeme paints a charming coastal scene within the cupboard to brighten Tim's day, Tim moves in and is uncomfortably locked in the cupboard by a giggling Graeme. Tim rediscovers sanity by introducing the boffin to the delights of making a cup of tea. Tim explains the principle of putting one in for the pot and nervously reveals that a teaspoon has no switch to turn it on. Gray is hooked and churning out tea like a good 'un. There's nothing much else to do but drink it and Bill's bloated as a result. He tries to count sheep, gets mad, allows them to count him for a bit before getting sick of the business and screaming 'mint sauce!' to them. With the card game a shambles, the sheep asleep and even Graeme's cupboard sunshine picture soaking Tim with realist weather, the 'holiday' is going from bad to worse. Days have drifted by, the rain is making *Bambi*-like music as it drips into the accommodation and Bill gets groovy to the beat. The other lads aren't impressed. Seventeen days into the break, non-stop rain having hounded their outdoor pursuits and Bill forever 'not tired' because of his continuous bed sit-in, Tim and Graeme are miffed to say the least. Bill's 'creature of the outdoors!' speech is greeted with Graeme's 'ferret' comparison, while Tim gives in and promises that tomorrow will be dedicated to Bill's passion, bird-watching. Bill, far too excited to sleep now, gets even more keen when Graeme notices that the rain has stopped. Sadly, the rain may have gone but snow has replaced it as a flurry bursts through the window, a block of compressed snow barricades the door and an unconvincing sheep pokes its head through the white, icy mass. Indoor bird-watching is called for and Tim, complete with muted 'quacks' and a rubber duck tied to his head, tries to fool Bill and his beloved Spotter's Guide. Tim's cover blown (Bill observes that he's a tit!), he frantically blows out air (Puffin), cries in mock pain as his trouser zip gets caught (Fly-Catcher) and, by request, tries to emulate a crane by using his arm as a mechanical lifting device. Graeme, emerging from a spot of snorkelling in the bathroom, is much more like Bill's crane description. Playing along with the idea, Graeme performs a hilarious comic mating dance, turns on the motorcar-like horn call and goes into a mini *World About Us* interlude with slow-motion flying, Tim's pan pipe accompaniment and Bill's earnest narration. Graeme avoids the sharp points of the Alps and finally gets shot at by gun-happy Italians – Tim and Bill sporting black tashs. With the snow being snow fun at all, Tim gets all patriotic and proud, delivers a speech, reminds the assembled masses of their Britishness and cracks up completely as the world seems to reach the pinnacle of boredom. Graeme amuses himself with a huge Rubic's Cube – although his tension is revealed when his hands continue to do the motions when the cube is put down – while Bill and Tim are allowed to lie down and relax on flimsy sun-beds. Graeme's uncomfortable, dangling business on the sun-bed is a masterpiece of visual comedy and with floppy legs suddenly going stiff, his tension is faced, his cube crumbles to pieces and the holiday becomes a living hell. He has no gadgets, Bill has no noise and Tim can't go shopping! The result – a return to the good old days or, more to the point, a musical evening akin to the telly show *The Good Old Days*. Graeme takes on the mantle of host Leonard Sachs, Bill dons Queen Victoria garb for added clout and Tim nervously warbles *I Do Like to Be Beside the Seaside*. Graeme and Bill happily throw themselves into the chorus, inject frantic, camp, Twenties vocals and dance movements and inject real nonsense. Grabbing tennis racquets for guitars, turning on the cockney twang and bursting forth with *Top of the Pops* gusto, the trio round off with a Sex Pistols' version of the classic song, smash up the place, include bleeps to mask their explicit lyrics and collapse in a mound of rubble. Tim, a picture of joy, mutters, 'That's the best holiday I've ever had…' and the credits roll.

Episode Five, recorded Friday 23 October 1981, broadcast Saturday 6 February 1982, 6.45–7.15pm, ITV.

ANIMALS ARE PEOPLE TOO

Historically important, this episode was the very last of *The Goodies*. Very similar to the penultimate BBC effort – it is often also called *Animals*. The show starts with Graeme Garden proudly placing a Sold Out sign outside his Gray

Bags Pet Shop. Tim – the new owner of a Barbara Woodhouse Dog Training Kit – strolls into a men's convenience and, Superman-like, reappears almost immediately from within the next door ladies convenience, kitted out in the Woodhouse garb of grey wig, sensible shoes and heavy skirt. A national icon at the time, Woodhouse seemed to be everywhere, and although her eccentric behaviour and beloved catchphrase – instructing a dog to 'Siiittt!' – was ripe for *Goodies* parody, the notion seems dated in a way many of their Seventies' targets do not. Fresh in 1982, Tim's parcel-wrapped dog seems to take little notice, although a passing Bill Oddie certainly sits on demand as does any other person who happens to walk into shot. Soon, these people are coming here, there and everywhere, fetching sticks and begging like good doggies. Graeme, watching through his binoculars, is more than intrigued and thinks up another money-making scheme – selling people as pets. That's the plot then. The writers use the abuse and treatment of animals as a mirror to show how mean we can be to our pets and livestock. Some of it works very well, even if the Tim/Graeme pet shop banter plays like yet another very poor relation to the Dead Parrot Sketch. Graeme, dumping the unwanted doggie into a dustbin, displays his collection of dog-like men. 'Almost a dawg…' in Tim's clipped dialect, the big, brown, sad, ugly eyes of Bill Oddie melt the heart and a sale is made. Obedient and happy to frolic – if threatened with a stick – this little scamp pricks up his ears and chases cars at the drop of a hat, shows real interest in a lamp-post (hilariously standing up and undoing his fly) and finally finding a home in an uncomfortable basket in Tim's house. The best scene has Tim (cuddled up with his teddy) woken from his slumbers by a frisky Bill jumping on to his bed and trying to settle down next to him. Tim over-reacts (crying rape), ordering him off and making him get back in the basket. Continually on heat, Bill's sex-mad gaze, dreaming of chasing more interesting things than rabbits and struggling to get comfy within his allotted bed, bemoans his fate as a pup. Sitting on something unpleasant, his dismissal of the job description – chomp on slippers, chew socks, get tied up in toilet roll – leads to another bout of self-pity. Facing the fact that Tim's now bored with him, doesn't find him cute anymore and refuses to call him pet names, Bill gets a bit overamorous, tries to recapture the old days and offers seductively to lick his face. Even the prospect of a

GRAEME GARDEN TREATS HIMSELF TO A NEW MOTOR FROM HIS **BBC** GOODIE REPEAT FEES!

wet nose in the ear doesn't turn Tim on, as Bill's nose is now as dry as a prune. A hassle in a collar, the cuddly Bill now insists on walkies, complains that his litter tray is full and annoyingly howls and bays to Tim's rendition of *Rule Britannia* on the violin. Bill gets a bash on the head for his troubles – causing his false nose to slip a bit – and Tim is seized with the unhealthy desire to destroy the creature. Staggering round to the water's edge, Bill nervously pokes his head out of his sack, Tim himself is dragged into the water by the weight of the brick attachment and Bill's soft old brown eye trick works its magic for a last minute reprieve. Tim sees the light and vows to protect all unwanted humans. A short trailer, along the lines of a human is for life not just for Christmas, sees Bill treated like a King, given love and affection, and fed with steak and chips washed down with champagne. However, the life of Riley with a copy of *Playboy* soon fades to a life as a mistreated plaything, with schoolkids taunting him, throwing food over him and even pulling back his false nose for some painful fun. Brooke-Taylor's new mission – Tim's Society for the Prevention of Cruelty to People, rounds them up from bomb sites and rubbish tips and gives them warmth in Battersea Man's Home. Like a

charity ad itself – ending with Tim lovingly licked by a couple of human dogs – the advert break comes in at this point, returning us to the Goods with Graeme collecting animals and chomping ideally on a tortoise. With that look of another great idea hatching, Gray's new restaurant, The Rumbling Tum, opens for business and the best customer seems to be none other than Tim. Enjoying hamster burgers and gerbil dumplings – with a tail sticking out of his mouth as he chews – Tim is horrified to find that the names are not just nasty gimmicks but accurate descriptions of the content. As Graeme comments, the burgers are '100% Nigel and Kenneth!', selected by Tim simply by saying hello to them as he came in. Not feeling too well at this point, Graeme's other offerings (including 'Special Fried Mice') don't help the situation, nor does Tim chewing on a twiglet (stick insects) or the thought of some pickles (the dog's name which Graeme is willing to cook up a treat). It's the carnivores backlash. Doggie bags have real doggie in them nowadays and thanks to this trend, animals are getting very thin on the ground. Tim's problem is, of course, what to do with his unwanted people and Graeme's suggestion and news report point the way forward. Humans can replace animals. With a food parcel gift from Japan – of a panda – Tim finds time to voice his realisation of Graeme's cunning plan. Besides, Tim's wearing shiny shoes, so everything he says has clout and meaning. Animals are scarce – and getting scarcer, with Tim shooting a low-flying duck – but police human dogs, guard hooligans, homing people and Royal human horses fill in the gaps. London Zoo proudly exhibits the accountant's tea party and an out of work BBC Symphony Orchestra, while Tim's lawn is ruined by an escaped community of Welsh miners. However, Graeme's real motive is revealed in the shape of Graybungles People Farm. With a new Oddie song as backing, the penny drops and Tim realises that these defenceless humans are being fattened for slaughter. Bill – with little to do but put on silly costumes and be abused – is now part of the livestock, sensing rain and, with his cow duty hat on, sitting down in the field. It doesn't take Bill long to get worked up, and, seizing unionist power, he faces Graeme's management head on. With a 'me and the lads…' opening comment, there is time for a corny innuendo ('Cows…' 'Bullocks') before the real business hits in. Bored out of their tiny minds, the bullocks want the same sort of treatment as the Japanese give their livestock. That boils down to beer, music and sex, and once that's been agreed on, Bill seems pretty happy. But Tim breaks up the cosy meeting and exposes Graeme's plan. The prospect for the bullocks is nothing more than slaughter and although Tim is weakened by the thoughts of delicious steak and onions, Graeme's power is overthrown. He's amazed that just because one of their Goodie number may end up dead at the end of the scheme, Tim doesn't seem to like it, but, taking the hint, he jumps for it and makes his escape. The lads follow and Tim slips back into Barbara Woodhouse to control the human animals. Staggering past female chickens and a big black bull, Graeme unsuccessfully tries to blend into the bullock community, is bombarded by low-flying ducks dishing out egg splatter treatment and is ultimately herded into a sheep dip. Attacked from all angles, the boffin holds his nose and goes under! A quick cut shows Tim and Bill relaxing and having the time of their life chomping on a huge Desperate Dan sized pie in the countryside. The discovery of Graeme's glasses creates a worrying few seconds before Bill assures his pal that the third Good is very much alive. Confined in a kennel bearing the legend 'Beware of the Loony', Graeme emerges to fetch his specs and, with a summing up of

cartoon violence, the show ends with the rousing Warner Brothers conclusion of 'That's All Folks!' That really was all from the Goodies. An enforced ending rather than a well-rounded conclusion, the Goodies were no more as a working unit after this. British television was far the poorer without them.

Episode Six, recorded Friday 30 October 1981, broadcast Saturday 13 February 1982, 6.45–7.15pm, ITV.

THE GOODIES ANNUAL 1974

Reassuringly not a 'kid's programme' from the outset, the fledgling Goodies skilfully enjoyed a double life. Stripping away the political and social awareness of the television series to embrace puns and slapstick, a series of comic strip appearances in *Cor!* comic and this 'based on the hilariously funny television series' collection of further comic strips, stories and brainteasers endeared them completely to a younger audience. There is no cynical edge to this publication aimed at children, although the Goodies themselves would later send the style up in *The Goodies Book of Criminal Records*. Nor were they competing with Monty Python's deconstruction of the publishing industry. This was jolly good fun for all, pure and simple. *The Greatest Story Ever Told or how did three silly people like the Goodies ever get their own show on television*, tells the pre-1970 life stories of the trio proudly relating their Cambridge experiences and primitive small screen successes. Interestingly, there's also much pride in relating their early connection with the Monty Python boys. The Reunion, a tasty little comic strip for starters, sees the mad professors Voltage, Noon and O'Reilly, side-tracked by the Goodies – there's even time for a quick 'O'Reilly' 'Oh, really!' gag and a delicious fish-based pun rant from Oddie before he's turned into a mouse for some scientific nightmares. A more structured story, along the lines of an actual *Goodies* episode, is *And For My Next Invention*, which sets up the usual plot device of a client in need of help – Mr Pimmington of Grimsdyke-by-Sea – and includes a nod to the social consciousness of the TV shows with the lads' assignment designed to prevent the pollution of a million motor cars on a near-by motorway. It's all really an excuse for the Goodies trandem to go through *Wacky Races*-like alterations – from aqua-trandem to rocket-trandem – all illustrated by Graeme Garden's detailed pencil sketches. A later story, *Sureshots Steal*

Show, is less typical, with Oddie's love of football orchestrating an FA Cup team made up of a gorilla, a giraffe and, of course, the Goodies. *The Hobbymobile* sees our listless heroes with nothing to do and sweltering in a heat wave. The answer, Graeme's wonderful machine that allows Tim to play chess and Bill to indulge his musical talent. Keeping that idea off the screen and on the written page must have saved the Goodies production team pounds! The comic strip, *Hiram's Holiday*, is a standard tale of an American antique collector who, via a handy magic lamp, transports the gang to the manic Kingdom of young dictator, Ahtishooma. At least there's a telling remark from Graeme Garden directed to a saucy female belly-dancer – 'I might add that we've a small part for a ravishing beauty in our next series!' The spirit of the lost tribe of Tonka is alive and well in the strip *Safari So Goodies*, desperately trying to flog hamburgers to King Gobblemup and his tribe, but almost ending up on the menu themselves. *Sprechen Sie Serbo-Croat?* – a bit of a mouthful for any five-year-old – reverts to business, with the team setting up a translation service, Goodtrans, and causing problems at a UN meeting. While the best comic strip, *All A'Bored*, tells of the totally bored Lord Bored of Leet Lodge. Pick of the fun is a delightfully naff Lord Bored dummy act from Bill and the vengeful sacked butler, whose unmasked roving monster thing, Bulboso, turns the whole tale into a well-judged *Scooby Doo* experience. Other features include *From a Trandem to a Unicycle* – some interesting facts about the Goodies mode of transport, Graeme's Multipurpose Spectacles, Bill's crossword, *Just Jokes* and *Just a Few More* if you can take them, an odd word quiz and a *Kitten Kong*-inspired board game, *The Search for Mighty Mice*, with copious images of the lads in mouse disguise. There's even a comic strip commercial break interlude – plugging the Common Market burger from Heinz and the talk challenge ad, now with 10% more mutter – and *The Goodies by the Goodies*, three sketches by each of our heroes depicting the spirit of the team. Naturally, Graeme's is a work of art, Bill muses on the 'away from Goodie life' hobbies of the team and Tim's stick creation sees himself, typically, topped with a halo. But it's the behind the scenes insights into the Goodies at work which really hit the spot. *All Together Now* is a photo record of the lads recording their first album, *Big Problems for the Goodies* is a one-page plug for the glories of *Kitten Kong*, the Goodies at Le Mans covers the filming of *The Race* and a Special Effects section goes behind the scenes at work on the office building visual gags concocted for *The New Office*. All in all, a charming and priceless little toe in the waters of publishing.

World Distributors 1972.

THE GOODIES BEASTLY RECORD

This was the team's last original recording and failed to make much headway in the charts, only a couple of compilation releases would follow. The problem may have been down to the series not being on air. The album was released in 1978 and the trio wouldn't see their new season screened until 1980. Apart from that, there's none of the classic pop hits fans remember and all the best songs are re-recorded versions of titles previously heard in *I'm Sorry I'll Read That Again*. These are definitive renditions and easily outweigh the other, rather less satisfactory, inclusions. Indeed, this album plays like a Goodies answer to The Beatles *White Album*, with several musical styles and genres grafted over the familiar sound to create a unique package – there's even Oddie's equivalent of Lennon's *Revolution No. 9* in the shape of *Funky Farm*. The opening track, *Melody Farm*, is a typical country and western number, featuring Graeme Garden's usual 'yee haa!' persona. Celebrating the natural musical talents of animals – 'there's even a donkey who can croon like Bing' – Garden is rather more affectionate about the old Groaner in the light of Crosby's death in 1977 as opposed to his cheery dismissal in *Good Ole Country Music*, while Oddie delights in the blues singer convention with a one-eyed turkey blessed with soul. Graeme turns on clipped romance for his *Oyster* song with Bill and Tim hamming it up for *Spring Spring Spring*. A favourite of Oddie's, it made a third appearance in the 25th anniversary edition of *I'm Sorry I'll Read That Again* and perfectly sums up the 'do anything, say anything' style of the team. Tim delivers the main body of the piece like Noel Coward on speed, snootily looking on as Oddie interjects with deadly one-liners and obvious word-plays. The five-bar gate/sheep joke interlude is a masterpiece, but even more cornier than before sound effects continually hit the spot, from sun beating (cue beating drum) to bluebells ringing. By far the greatest inclusion on the album is Oddie's *Terrapins*. Arguably the finest Goodies recording, the concept is mad but Bill's upbeat performance is peerless. Graeme buts in with off-kilter responses à la Lennon on McCartney's *She's Leaving Home* and his 'munchable! – crunchable!' comments are outstanding. Tim's there with an overplayed 'pangalin' chorus repeat, Bill takes the song to new heights with insane brushes with lupins, nappy pins, drawing pins and the like, while even taking time for a bit of banter about gibbons which 'always get a grin!' The chant-a-long ending, 'What a wonderful song!' says it all. Even the Formby-esque poultry-bonding of *A Man's Best Friend Is His Duck* can't touch it. *Spank That Hamster*, one of the few totally original songs written for the album, is less cool, primarily because Oddie performs it in disco Bee Gees high pitch. As a result a lot of the offensive animal abuse lyrics are lost in whining. Mind you, 'castigate the hound!' is audible and funny, and there's a complete back-tracking name-checking salute to the first album's *Stuff That Gibbon*. And what's more, Tim's sadomasochistic hamster screaming 'spank me, spank me!' is worth sticking around for. Bill indulges his love of reggae for *Rastashanty* and Tim, in demure domestic mode, pours out his heart for *Ironing My Goldfish*. One of the best album tracks, there's plenty of time for corny fish comments and Tim's winning ambition to get his fish as flat as a tobacco leaf is class. Another one to wallow in time and time again. *Funky Farm*'s cornucopia of moos, barks and clucks drags on to the Thirties *There's a Walrus in My Soup*, featuring a frightfully well-mannered Oddie explaining his problem to an uncaring waiter. The format is a load of animals rhyming with food on the menu. *Why Doesn't an Elephant...* features an earnest Tim, surprised to find animals in the zoo and set on a relentless, time-wasting rant about the various noises creatures make. His final disgust at humans merely being able to talk and sing signals a whole wealth of beastie bickering. Although there's a certain amount of charm in Tim's performance, this new number soon pales in the light of a *I'm Sorry I'll Read That Again* revisit. *I Am a Carnivore* is a glorious religious celebration of the shameless meat-eater, bursting forth with stirring church organ effects and a corrupt

rendition of *All Things Bright and Beautiful*. Again, full circle from the debut album, *The Goodies Sing Songs From The Goodies* , this gathering of a like-minded congregation joining in with the spine-tingling chorus is a real treasure. Full of tasty bits 'n' pieces – Tim's 'I should say so!' and the notion of consuming Graeme's wife, are highlights – Bill's ever-mounting meat-loving sermon ('surloin, it's been good to gnaw you!') is the pinnacle with Graeme's score-counting references to animal flesh culminating in '14 – it's a record!' The 'eight and a half' unease about the veggie option 'stew' is a masterstroke. There's really nowhere else to go after such a classic, and thus it's falling back on groan-worthy jokes for the record's climax. This was the last hurrah for the squad on vinyl and a fitting epitaph if ever there was one.

Did You Know? *Funky Farm was released as the B-side to EMI's Goodies single, M.I.C.K.E.Y.M.O.U.S.E. That track wasn't included on the album because of contractual ties with Walt Disney but acted as a prelude to The Goodies Beastly Record. Incidentally, that is the correct title. Despite the spine reading Beastly Record – The Goodies, the front cover (with The Goodies in usual Goodies font) and the record label (featuring 'The Goodies Beastly Record' by 'The Goodies') promotes the full title. Note the ominous credit – The Goodies are (at the time of recording) – on the back cover. A parody of Let It Be bickering which resulted in the end, or the real thing! As well as boasting the finest Goodies recordings, the album also features the best front cover design – a cartoon version of the team with familiar trademarks to the fore (Union flag waistcoat, thick glasses and beard) on a Tim fox, a Graeme rabbit and a Bill dog. Oddie's lyrics were again included as part of the package, although this time they were printed on the actual inner record sleeve.*

Side One: Melody Farm, Taking My Oyster for Walkies, Spring Spring Spring, Terrapins, A Man's Best Friend Is His Duck, Spank That Hamster. **Side Two:** Rastashanty, Ironing My Goldfish, Funky Farm, There's a Walrus in My Soup, Why Doesn't an Elephant Go Tweet Tweet?, I Am a Carnivore, Elephant Joke Song. All songs written by Bill Oddie. All arrangements by Dave MacRae. Produced by Miki Antony and Bill Oddie. Engineered by Steve Levine. Second Engineer Graham Dickson. Featuring the gentlemen musicians of Le Hot Club de Cricklewood, the Cricklewood Rhythm Boys and The Finchley Funketeers with the Hendon Horns (all under the direction of Dave MacRae). Cover design Feref. Caricature by David Anstey. YAX. 5509 EMI/Columbia Records 1978.

THE GOODIES' BOOK OF CRIMINAL RECORDS

A direct sequel to *The Goodies File*, this book takes the form of another 'concept' publication detailing the legal court case between the Goodies and the publishers of *The Goodies File*. A positive celebration of the trio's eccentricities, it forms the brief to

A SIGNING SESSION FOR *THE GOODIES' BOOK OF CRIMINAL RECORDS* AT BOOTS, BRENT CROSS, ON 18 NOVEMBER 1976, WITH THE TRIO FACING A HOARD OF DEVOTED FANS – DO YOU RECOGNISE YOURSELF?

counsel for the plaintiff from solicitors Terribly, Terribly, Boring and Dull at the deceptively named 987 Short Lane. As with the previous book it proved hugely popular. Brooke-Taylor, Garden and Oddie saw this volume shoot to number one in the *Times* best-seller list. Beginning with a publishers note thanking those who returned copies of *The Goodies File* which, due to the paper shortage, have now been recycled to produce *The Goodies' Book of Criminal Records*, it's on to Dr Garden's Funny Farm and exhibit A – The Loony File. Graeme's foolproof guide, *So You Think You're a Loony*, puts the threesome through rediscovered documents, questionnaires and pulse rate tests but finds out little except Tim's secret ambition to be Queen of England – which most of us knew already! Bill's failed rock nightmare is a telling moment and there's pure joy with Tim's Royal Variety Show with the royals doing all the entertaining. Graeme gets technical with his loving, *All About Computers* section, including easy to follow instructions on how to build your own, while a

historical breakthrough is unveiled with *The Case of 'Cricklewood Man'*. Helping out the strapped for cash British Museum, the Goods prove the existence of this Piltdown clone via a special edition of the archaeology magazine Times of Old, with artist's impressions, dwelling details and historical context. Of course, shock, horror, the entire thing is revealed as a fake after the bods at the British Museum have given the dosh. But fear not, the Goods' reputation is not spoiled as their visitor's book testifies – with contributions from Marilyn Monroe, Tom and Jerry, the Marx Brothers, Louis Armstrong, Winston Churchill etc... The team's unique mode of transport, the trandem, is revealed with an *Auto Test* article and full mechanical details of its working, before we head straight into the *Political File*. Initially promoting Graeme as potential Prime Minister, soon it's every Goodie for himself with Bill's Little People's Revolutionary Party appealing to the common dominator with a naked woman and promises of no hard work. The situation between the lads gets tense as illustrated through notes answered with forthright dismissal from the bearded anarchist – 'Dear Tim, Get stuffed! Love Bill.' Brooke-Taylor's response is typically subtle – 'Oscar Wilde strikes again! TB-T.' But, as with most things, the team's political ambitions are short-lived. Soon it's on to the glories of *The Goodies Book of Art* as devotion to the masters gets comical, and Dr Garden explains How We Revived A Fading Masterpiece by going deep under the surface of *Whistler's Mother*. The Goodie Green Stamps catalogue is a whiff of Seventies' nostalgia with the load of old guff displayed with delicious irony. A major highlight is the long-awaited musical collection, *The Tim Brooke-Taylor Song Book*, presenting, for the first time, the finest works of Mr Brooke-Taylor with recommendations for albums, Bridge Over Tim Brooke-Taylor, Tony Bennett's I Left My Heart in Tim Brooke-Taylor and Sgt Pepper, with Tim, rather chillingly, replacing John Lennon in the Beats line-up. But it's the songs that count, including such timeless classics as, to the tune of *Rule Britannia* – Tim Brooke-Taylor, Brooke-Taylor We Love You, to the tune of *Chicago* – Brooke-Taylor, Brooke-Taylor, That Toddlin' Tim or, best of all, to the tune of *Camptown Races* – Oh Tim Brooke-Taylor Sings This Song, Timbo, Timbo. But still, there's no pleasing some people. The lad's biggest foe, Mary Whitehouse, complains about the filthy top-shelf magazine business and pleas for the trio to present a clean version. The result, *Old Maid Only*, is reproduced for our inspection, plugging milk stout for the old dears, revealing the raunchy poses of the Nudist Vicar, allowing Timona (guess who) the roving reporter to test the gentry and, last, but by no means least, a saucy, seasonal pin-up calendar with Graeme, Bill and Tim alternating for the months – culminating with Tim's Santa proclaiming 'Mr December is always jolly, but careful where you put the holly!' The spirit and conventions of *The Beano* and, indeed, that old Goodies-endorsed comic *Cor!!* is gloriously sent up with *Goody Goody!!*, a ham-fisted attempt to make the traditional swot character a *Dennis the Menace*-style cool hero. *The Biffo the Bear* clone, Boffo Bore, avoids a banana skin and returns a discovered sweetie to the police station, Dennis the Vicar is right-on for religion and Cecil the Swot refuses all temptations of

the flesh to study – an action condoned in the *American Graffiti*-like character round up at the panels close. *Merry Graeme's Page of Phacts 'n' Phun!* finishes off a neat little parody, with a suggestion to amaze your Mum and Dad – come down to breakfast drunk – before the reigns are handed over to Tim's scientific, historic and religious load of old guff about his theory concerning the ultimate question – *Was God an English Astronaut?* With an uneasy recommendation from Dr Garden, realms of heart-felt research open to ridicule and a rejection letter for his follow-up effort, The Chariot of the Dogs, the firm decides to save the money to publish *The Goodies File* instead… and thus, start all this legal problem in the first place. And so, to the heart of the matter, the head-to-head battle with the publishers, and the ultimate piece of evidence, *The Crisis File* – Tim's red, white and blueprint for a cheaper Britain. With factions of children, television cut backs (it's now Monty Python's Flying Puppet Show and The Goodie), reward schemes and self-help, it all looks very new age, new values, even new Labour? But the ultimate is Bill's Animal Power, making cats, hedgehogs etc… fulfil their complete potential in the community. PM Harold Wilson takes their ideas on board, the country is saved and the Goodies are the best kept, lowest paid, secret in the land. Pages from the subsequent trial are reprinted for inspection but Tim gets uppity, the judge insists on putting himself forward as an exhibit and the final rant 'it's not so much a matter of being out of' – (continued on page one) – flip back to 'Paper shortage'. So, read the whole thing again or go completely insane – tick your chosen option.

Did You Know? On the back of the Sphere re-issue, a timely plug was made for the previous publication, 'Have you enjoyed *The Goodies Book of Criminal Records?* If so, you'll like The *Goodies File* – a fun-spilled, totally insane compilation of Goodies material: songs, pix, letters, competitions. It's impossible to describe – read it instead.' Note the incorrect grammatical correction by inclusion of an apostrophe on the title Goodies' File.

Weidenfeld & Nicholson, hardback, 1975. Sphere, paperback, 1975.

THE GOODIES FILE

Having branched into publishing with *The Goodies Annual*, this second effort moved towards a more anarchic style to form a collection of letters, photographs and documents. A sordid attempt on the part of 'a good for nothing old ratbag' of a charlady, Mrs Edna Tole, to discredit her former employees, the Goodies, and make a huge sum out of the book rights. With a lengthy 'This book belongs to…' check list and a disclaimer from the publishers explaining that 'on reading the file you may find it boring.' It's on to the dirt dishing: a collection of photographs, including scenes of the trio at their exclusive club, taken from *Caught in the Act*, and Tim's virginal pose from *That Old Black Magic*, try to provide an insight in their secret life! The poor lads are even branded coots, before an insert of the Goodies brochure by Bill Oddie and published by Tatty and Cheap (Prunter), is included for inspection. Supposedly the piece of literature prospective clients are forwarded, a snatch of The Beatles song *Help!* is reproduced, highlighting that Lennon and McCartney might have been writing about the Goodies but weren't, before the Sixties legends are mocked via Bill's delicious grouching about all those lyrics concerning 'teeth in a jam jar or something'. The knife is further twisted with comments on the disbanded Seventies Beatles, with that 'heavy rubbish John's into these days or, indeed, those soppy tunes Paul sings now' before embarking on *Who are the Goodies?* A glowing five-year track record – mapped out with pics from *Camelot*, *Scotland*, *Hunting Pink* and *The New Office* – and handy identikit guide to the three workers – later reproduced for the 1994 video release of *The Goodies and the Beanstalk* – sets the scene, before plans for the future and facilities available, are detailed. Easy access to the lads entails 'wearing a Goodies t-shirt', 'waving a Goodies LP and shouting Goodies For Ever!' A letter to the Goodies from the Head of MI9 and Tim's magazine love questionnaire, 'So you think you're pretty naughty?', simply adds power to Mrs Tole's ammunition, while the touching collection of animal love poems, *Garden of Verse*, illustrates the lads' sensitive sides. Although Tim's soppy and wet intro is counterbalanced by an ingenious *Ode to the Tax Collector*, £35.70. Bill delights with a more forthright effort, *Love Is*: 'There's a girl in 3C, With a wart on her knee, And a pimple upon her behind, I gave her 3p, And she showed it to me, Don't you think that was awfully kind? P.S. Wonder what she'd do for a quid!' Graeme's

Readers' Digest offer for a Nobel prize draw and various legal correspondence with Geronimo Boots, solicitor for Boots, Boots, Boots, Boots, Marchinup and Downagain, leads to interest from the Metropolitan policeman, PC Bent. Criminal records, intricate information and mug shots line up the Goods as potential baddies, while further evidence for Graeme's cleverness is illustrated via detailed design for the lad's trandem. Meanwhile, the stupidity of the policeman is heightened via the ramshackle IQ test of a certain PC Bent. More Goodies information is provided with the *Things To Do* brochure, cheekily deconstructing comic strips with a Draw It Yourself section complete with voice bubbles and blank spaces, a cookery corner – How to cook a leather armchair – and a ballroom dancing interlude with Graeme and Tim dressed up as Norman and Norma Higginbottom demonstrating the step-by-step routine to the *Goodies Theme*. With a hasty plug for the single and Bill's original manuscript – complete with Tim and Graeme interactions – poor old Britannia is embarrassed as Tim teaches the world to sing and play *Land of Hope and Glory* on milk bottles. The Goodies Annual Prize-giving dinner grudgingly acknowledges the national clout of *Morecambe and Wise* in the laughter stakes and celebrates with The Beatles giving a special farewell performance. The custard pies by the way, are not to be eaten… Three near-naked Goodie clothes dolls and various different costumes could provide hours of fun for those daft enough to cut the book up, while a double-page spread of ultra-rare, early pics of the lads illustrate Bill's bad tendencies and the angelic innocence of young Tim. A Kleeno Smalls Laundry bill shows the dirtiness of the trio, while Bill's ultimate achievement – pop stardom – is documented in the Top Secret file *The Rise and Fall and Rise of the Goodies Feb 1st–Feb 12th 1974* which includes a cover shot of their first LP and a *Melody Maker* report suggesting they have already broken up – 'rumours that Graeme Garden is going to go solo were described by the others as xxxxing ridiculous.' Pop agent Izzy Bent is just part of the collected evidence showing the team's path to pop success. Appeal to the tiny tots – in Under 5, the *first* fab-mag for the baby-boppers – sees the Goodies as 'baddies more like' and condemns them as the Chelsea Pensioners of Pop. But that doesn't stop their original cast recording of Pious XIV Super Pope

(He's Divine) hitting the top of the charts – with Bill in the title role, Graeme as Cardinal Wolsey and Tim hamming it up as Joan of Arc. Recreated from *Superstar*, there's support from Pan's Nuns and the Mincing Monks. How could it fail? It even reaches a higher position than John Lennon's immortal 'xxxx to the lot of you'. A minor 'stop press' announces the Goodies getting back together again – the fools – and with success behind them, Tim writes a grovelling letter and we are privy to their rather corrupt tax returns. With his musical passion indulged, Bill then presents a short book, *How to be a Bird-watcher*, which justifies his hobby in the most aggressive, clear off and leave me alone, sort of terms. He's not interested if you are not interested – 'You can stand on your head and sing *Ave Maria* for all I care' – but this is merely a hilarious prelude to the most secret of all files – *The Case of 'The Royal Command'*. Contained within is a letter from Prince Andrew inviting the Goodies to brighten up the annual boredom fest, the Royal Variety. Affectionately sending up their illustrious predecessors and illustrious contemporaries, the Goons prove unwilling – Sellers wants too much money – and Monty Python are a bit uncool, really. The Prince writes that they are 'a bit past it now aren't they?', so it's the cheap and cheerful Goods who break into Buck House, save the crown jewels, pick up a few OBEs, recreate the spirit of *The Tower of London* on the written page and get away with it. A wallow in artistic style in *The Goodies' Tradition*, sees them within the Bayeaux Tapestry, as depicted by Picasso, and Da Vinci's pioneering designs for their trandem. Following an ad heralding New Year's Honours up for grabs, the 'so-called self-style clever dick Goodies' trial is presented via exclusive notes from the court house. Finally, Mrs Tole's manuscript, including a favourable comment from David Frost, rejected by the powers that be and the British Army intelligence, becomes the scandalous, unofficial book you hold in your hands. The resulting legal wrangle formed *The Goodies Book of Criminal Records*… but that's another entry.

Weidenfeld & Nicholson, hardback 1974. Sphere, paperback, 1975.

THE GOODIES FUN BOOK

As part of a 1977 Cadbury's chocolate promotion, lucky sweetie-eaters could collect 100 used wrappers and send in for this special Goodies' activity publication. Two versions were produced – one for tiny tots and one for older children – and included pages of fun and laughter similar to *The Goodies Annual*. Bill Oddie promoted the pleasures of nature, there was, gulp, Graeme's Garden Tips and a host of comic strips, stories and puzzles.

IPC Magazines for Cadbury's, 1977.

THE GOODIES GREATEST

A strange Goodies album. Despite its title and the fact that all the group's Top 20 hits are featured, this isn't really a greatest hits compilation – new material is also included. And, on the other hand, it can't really be considered an original album release because the vast majority are reissued tracks from the singles chart. All six A-sides of the Goodies singles released between late 1974 and early 1976 are gathered together, along with four of the B-side numbers. The additional tracks are a fresh outing for the 'new' *Goodies Theme* and a completely new piece for the Goodies musical selection, *Charles Aznovoice*. This was originally written by Oddie for radio's *I'm Sorry I'll Read That Again* and broadcast in the fifth show from Series Seven. Akin to that classic closing burst from *An Audience with Kenneth Williams*, the lyrics mainly consist of pidgin English–French phrases frequently used in Britain. With gentle piano and drum accompaniment, Oddie's lead vocals drip with growing sexual passion, screeching through the non-sequential material until his voice drifts away into a pitiful croak. It's a one-gag stab at Charles Aznavour. Following hot on the heels of *The New Goodies LP*, Bradley's records were clearly trying to milk the pop star status of the trio before the bottle turned sour. As it happens, this record was the crowning glory of the Goodies' reign in the charts and acts as an interesting cross section of their most popular recordings. The cover is an effective inclusion of both the Goodies themselves and illustrations depicting the songs on the album, within a garish snakes and ladders game board. The back cover photograph of the lads has a cheery Tim, a bemused Graeme (sans glasses) and a concerned Bill (looking like something out of Jefferson Airplane), astride their immortal three-seater.

Did You Know? *The track listing has Make a Daft Noise For Christmas incorrectly abridged to Make a Daft Noise For Xmas.*

Side One: Goodies Theme, Funky Gibbon, The Inbetweenies, Nappy Love, Last Chance Dance, Father Christmas Do Not Touch Me. **Side Two:** Black Pudding Bertha, Bounce, Panic, Make a Daft Noise For Xmas, Charles Aznovoice, Wild Thing. All titles written by Bill Oddie except Wild Thing, written by Chip Taylor. Music arranged by David Macrae (Side 1: tracks 1 & 5, Side 2: tracks 2, 4 & 6) and Tom Parker (Side 1: tracks 2 & 4, Side 2: tracks 1 & 3), despite interference from Bill Oddie. Produced by Miki Antony. BRADL 1012 Bradley's Records November 1976.

THE GOODIES GREATEST HITS

Now, this really is the greatest hits album – a wonderful and pretty damn definitive collection of the finest songs from the Goodies. Released in the wake of ITV's reappraisal of the television series in October 1981 before the screening of *Snow White 2*, the cover boasts a terrified mug shot of Tim, Graeme and Bill from *Big Foot*. All the old classics, from 1975 chart hits to *Beastly* gems, were featured, along with the first album appearance of the 1978 single, *M.I.C.K.E.Y. M.O.U.S.E.*

Funky Gibbon, Black Pudding Bertha, Father Christmas Do Not Touch Me, Nappy Love, Rock With a Policeman, I'm a Teapot, Spring Spring Spring, Good Ole Country Music, Wild Thing, The Inbetweenies, Cricklewood, M.I.C.K.E.Y. M.O.U.S.E., A Man's Best Friend Is His Duck, Melody Farm, Last Chance Dance, Charles Aznovoice, Taking My Oyster For Walkies, Make a Daft Noise For Christmas, Baby Samba, Rastashanty. NTS 233 EMI 1981.

THE GOODIES SING SONGS FROM THE GOODIES

An album that does exactly what it says on the side of the tin. The first vinyl offering from the Goodies is a treasure. Less comically geared than subsequent offerings – most of Oddie's lead vocals are played straight, while Brooke-Taylor and Garden keep the humorous fires stoked with their contributions – the production values, musicians and lyrics, create a classic addition to any collector of Seventies rock. From that count in for *All Things Bright and Beautiful*, it's clear Oddie is firing on all cylinders. *Ride My Pony*, originally featured in the Series Three episode *Hunting Pink*, benefits from another stonking Oddie performance. Relating his life-enhancing obsession of weekend riding – 'slip a horse between my legs' – and making his boring pencil-pushing office job in the city bearable, there's an energy that's electrifying. There's more tasteless animal abuse in *Mummy I Don't Like My Meat* from the show, *Superstar*. A pathetic and heart-breaking two-hander between Timbo's pathetic and heart-broken little girl and Bill's sensitive, hard-up mother, it's played

as a mournful lament. Out of work for two years and driven to desperation point, the family menagerie of pets is gradually consumed – and what's worse, the dewy-eyed child dislikes the cooked remnants of her furry friends. Just feel that lump in your throat when 'she' enquires about the budgie – 'Why don't he sing Mummy?' *Show Me the Way* – a powerful piece which accompanied Bill's sleep-walking madness in the second episode, *Snooze*, rounds off Side One. Slowly building up from nothingness, a stunning steel guitar performance from Brian Cole gives a subdued country feel which perfectly moulds with Oddie's lead vocal. A serious song with totally helpless connotations of begging for religious assistance in getting through life, it's a brilliant number reassuringly pulled kicking and screaming into comic line by Tim's sleeve note comment – 'It's at the end of the corridor on the right.' Dismissed by Oddie's 'Oh that old thing', Side Two begins with a humdinger recording of the original *Goodies Theme* before handing over to Garden's composition – *Sparrow Song* – which appeared in *Superstar*. With an endearing feel of anthology-like rehearsal track, Graeme humbly apologises in advance for the ramshackle, unfinished quality of the ditty. With nervous coughs, Tim's tentative introduction and unconvincing technician banter – 'wax this one now…' – it's off, off and away into the granddaddy of all corny birdie songs to follow. The 'tweet, tweet' choruses have to be heard to be believed! Despite Garden's rather biased 'Excellent' comment, please be prepared to leave all hope behind you with this little gem. The song is given even more clout thanks to its cunning juxtaposition with the whirling guitar blast introduction for Oddie's outstanding *Taking Me Back*. As Graeme hilariously comments the song 'Takes you back'. Featured in Series Four's *Camelot*, Bill is in full voice with this tribute to the 'peasant and pages' days of yore. Sick of the ways of the 20th Century, it's a wish list of historical escape, brilliantly performed. *Sunny Morning*, an original number for the album, changes the pace completely. With a dreamy piano backing and Oddie's vocals with love in mind, this clearly takes its influence from Randy Newman with stunning results. Again, Bill delivers the lyrics dead straight, injecting potent passion into the 'take me away!' pleads. But Tim and Graeme are never too far behind to stop the wannabe rock star getting too serious. An uncredited variation of *The Sparrow Song* theme – *The Butterfly Song* with awkward 'flutter, flutter' scansion – is quickly usurped by Tim's delicious *Winter Sportsman*. Using the medium to its full advantage, the unseen hand of Oddie is clearly at work when the performance is unceremoniously interrupted by the needle being clumsily yanked off. It settles on Oddie's own performance of *Spacehopper*. Sending musical aspirations up with a delighted grin, the piece starts as a wheezing, piano-based rock 'n' roll jam before flowering into full blown cool with the 'Ladies and Gentleman… Bill Oddie' introduction. Mocking the pretentiousness of the music industry, Tim mucks about as the host of an all-star celebrity bash – welcoming Mick, Elton, Elvis, Lulu etc… receiving multitrack greetings from the Osmonds/Jacksons and twisting the knife with the Little Jimmy Osmond/Jimmy Clitheroe interlude. Finally, the Goodies turn up to their own promotional party and are quickly shown the nearest broom cupboard. There's a very half-hearted attempt to get the *Sparrow/Butterfly* guitar riff up and running again but somehow it's lost all importance – with a dejected 'No!' the lads give up and the record grinds to a halt.

Side One: All Things Bright and Beautiful, Ride My Pony, Stuff That Gibbon, Mummy I Don't Like My Meat, Show Me The Way. **Side Two:** Goodies Theme, Sparrow Song, Taking Me Back, Sunny Morning, Winter Sportsman, Spacehopper. All compositions by Bill Oddie except 'All Things Bright' (Oddie, Antony, Jackman) and 'Sparrow Song' (Garden). Drums Clem Clattini. Bass Les Hurdle. Lead guitar Mike Morgan. Rhythm guitar Eric Ford. Percussion Tony Carr. Keyboards Dave Macrae & Andrew Jackman. Steel guitar Brian Cole. Alto Sax solo Pete Zorn. Additional percussion and Penny Whistle W Oddie. 'Taking You Back' personnel John Marshall (Drums) Chris Spedding (Bass) Gary Boyle (Lead guitar). 'Sunny Morning' personnel John Mitchell (Keyboards). Arranged by Andrew Pryce Jackman except 'Taking You Back' by Mike Gibbs. Produced by Miki Antony. XZAL 12585P Decca January 1973.

GRAEME GARDEN

Not the man but the radio show. On Wednesday 23 July 1986, the day Sarah Fergusson married Prince Andrew, BBC radio and television was in disarray and broadcaster John Dunn saw his regular Radio 2 spot filled by guest presenter Graeme Garden. It was the usual mixture of chat, music and witty banter, made even more chatty, musical and witty with the ex-Goodie in charge.

GRAEME GARDEN'S COMPENDIUM OF VERY SILLY GAMES

If your party lacks that essential fizz you could do a lot worse than dig out this handy guide to some bizarre, time-consuming games. Collected in easily digestible chapters, Graeme Garden drags the reader through a collection of fun for all the family. Card Games tackles such popular past-times as Greengages, where the winner is the first one to ask, 'Wait a minute, why is this game called Greengages?', and Icelandic Roulette where the severe penalty dictates the player must swallow a frozen herring in one gulp. Children's Games span the lavatorial to the terminal – the original Ring a Ring O'Roses which results in the spread of black death. Graeme's helpful suggestion for a going home present is a copy of The Ladybird First Book of Diseases! Games of Skill include Shooting the Walnut (from a player's mouth), Shooting Crap (which is self-explanatory and illustrated with a dice on the end of a loo chain), Ploo (a mixture between Pool and Polo) and Dining Table Snooker which uses food instead of balls. Requirements include a small white turnip, a black prune and 15 red tomatoes! Party Games presents Rhyme Time which provides hours of rhyming fun with players having to rhyme with the previous player's word. The short version starts with the first player saying 'Orange'! Dickens is played by putting a complete set of the great Charlie's work in a bag, asking the players to pick a book, read it quietly and see who finishes first. The I Went to Market and Bought a Fat Pig game – leading to a pig-based conversation along the lines of 'Did you?' 'Yes' – is less taxing. Spooky Games plunders the rich vein of Gothic novels with the likes of Vampire (using Stoker's rules, of course) and Monster Monster! where the player must make his own creature from bits of dead bodies. A full set of rules are available from Mrs Shelley in Switzerland and players are advised to have a crowd of peasants carrying flaming torches on stand-by if things get nasty. Finally, the baffling section on Games of Chance includes Dingo (Bingo with an Australian accent) and Welwyn Garden City which is not a game at all, simply an excuse to provide a brief potted history of the place and lamenting the fact that no game has, as yet, been named after it. The book rounds off with a symbol guide as the gauge, equipment needed and danger level for each game included, a glossary of terms and a suggested further reading list. A masterpiece of nonsense.

Methuen 1987.

GRASSHOPPER ISLAND

An unfairly forgotten children's 1972 adventure show from ITV concerning the antics of the children named X, Y and Mouse – the cheese-lover of the group. Its acting credentials alone make it worth searching out. Tim Brooke-Taylor played the dominant voice of authority, donning three or four disguises along the way and even including a bit of Lady Constance, while there was a rare 'Oh! Hello!' from the legendary Charles Hawtrey as the mysterious old man.

THE GREAT BIRD RACE

Bill Oddie indulged his passion for bird-watching in this one-off special which presented two teams of dedicated twitchers trying to see or hear as many different varieties as possible in the space of 24 hours. Bill made sure fair play prevailed.

Producer Major Steadman. Directors Tom Hulsh and Major Steadman. Saturday 14 May 1983, Channel 4.

THE GREAT ROCK 'N' ROLL TRIVIA QUIZ

Basking in past glory of rock stardom, Bill Oddie had a bash at this fun and fruity musical nostalgia question fest.

Producer John Leonard. Sunday 1 January 1984, Radio 1.

THE GRIFF RHYS JONES SHOW

Graeme Garden was a guest on Griff's Radio 2 show broadcast on 3 July 1999.

GROW BIG QUIZ

A special Christmas edition of the gardening television quiz hosted by Alan Titchmarsh. Bill Oddie sharpened his wits and handled the spade, fork and a hoe, hoe, hoe with ease. Trevor Harrison as Eddie Grundy attempted to confuse and bemuse the team with his unique brand of festive fare.

Produced and directed by Nick Pattern. Thursday 22 December 1988, BBC2.

NEWSCASTER JAN LEEMING MEETS UP WITH BILL ODDIE, GRAEME GARDEN AND A DUMMY TIM BROOKE-TAYLOR WHO WAS UNABLE TO ATTEND THIS 1981 PUBLIC APPEARANCE

GROWING PLACES WITH PENELOPE KEITH

In the last of this series, Bill Oddie wandering on for a guest spot and discussed the uses, dangers and advances of employing chemicals in the garden. He also cast an eye over the final developments of the garden in progress through the series.

Produced and directed by Alice Harper. Thursday 1 June 1989, ITV.

HARK AT BARKER

Springing from an April 1968 episode of *The Ronnie Barker Playhouse* written by Alun Owen, this series starred the ever versatile Barker as the seedy, sex-mad Lord Rustless, as well as a galaxy of other grotesques along the way. The first series of eight episodes featured scripts by Alan Ayckbourn and Ronnie Barker, as well as individual contributions from Graeme Garden and Bill Oddie.

Lord Rustless RONNIE BARKER Mildred Bates JOSEPHINE TEWSON Badger FRANK GATLIFF Dithers DAVID JASON Cook MARY BAXTER. Director Maurice Murphy. Producer Humphrey Barclay. **Series One:** Fridays, 11 April–30 May 1969, ITV.

DAVID HATCH

Born in May 1939, Hatch read history at Cambridge, meeting Tim Brooke-Taylor and Bill Oddie via the Footlights group. He appeared and wrote material for the revue *A Clump of Plinths* and stayed with the show through its successful West End transition to *Cambridge Circus* and the BBC radio cult *I'm Sorry I'll Read That Again*. Eventually graduating to series producer, Hatch chaired the radio programme *Information Please*, hosted *Quiz International* for the World Service and became the Head of Light Entertainment for BBC radio. He managed to secure an entire cast reunion for the 25th anniversary in 1989. Tim Brooke-Taylor is godfather to one of Hatch's sons.

HAVE I GOT NEWS FOR YOU

Legendary satirical banter for the small screen which delighted in pitting politicians, journalists and new-wave comedians against politicians, journalists and old-wave comedians. Sixties survivors such as Peter Cook, John Bird, John Fortune and a certain Graeme Garden showed there was still satirical bite left in the old dog yet. Old Gray Bags joined regular Ian Hislop in a head-to-head battle with Paul Merton (milking huge laughs through his recent ditching of the smoking habit) and Kirsty Young (whose front of desk Channel 5 presentation was equally milked for maximum comic effect). Garden, laid back, clever and totally charming, tapped into glorious bad taste with a lengthy diatribe on the use of human ashes in egg timers, provided a winning missing word suggestion for the 'chip' headline, pondered the fate of barn owl impersonators,

laconically wandered through the Labour party tobacco sponsorship embarrassment and, best of all, cheekily muttered on about the Spice Girls. Besides, it was an admirable excuse for chairman Angus Deayton to provoke memories of Graeme's own pop super stardom with *The Goodies*, ushering in the familiar *Top of the Pops* reminiscences. Glorious. Oh, and there was a brilliant, throwaway about Cannon and Ball finding religion: Cannon and Canon. Well I liked it!

Director Paul Wheeler. Producer Richard Wilson. Friday 14 November 1997, BBC2.

HELLO CHEEKY

Just before the long-awaited return of *I'm Sorry I'll Read That Again* in 1973, Tim Brooke-Taylor branched out with this gloriously jam-packed, groan-worthy and quip-stuffed half hour offering with Barry Cryer and John Junkin. Denis King and his trio provided the musical interludes. Any pun was fair game, the cornier the better, and it was mainly due to his writing and performing commitment to the lengthy run (1973–79), that Tim dropped out of writing for *The Goodies*. On radio, the relentlessness of the show soon won huge audiences and attracted media stars such as Frank Bough for mild ritual humiliation. A BBC record, *The Least Worst of Hello Cheeky*, was released in 1976. In between a concentrated assault on the airwaves, Yorkshire television tempted the team onto television in 1976. Light years before *The Fast Show* this was the fastest show on the box. The recipe was the same – barrel-scraping jokes and beautifully mugged performances – but despite concurrent screening during the broadcast of radio's hit fourth series, the reaction was less than impressive. The terminal second television series appeared before the end of the year radio special. Edited highlights of the television series were commercially released on the record, *The Seedy Sound of Hello Cheeky*.

Radio. Series One: Sundays, 7 April–16 June 1973, Hello Cheeky, Hello Christmas: Tuesday 25 December 1973, (60-minute special), Radio 2. **Series Two:** Sundays, 10 February–19 May 1974, Hello Christmas: Wednesday 25 December 1974 (90-minute special), Radio 2. **Series Three:** Sundays, 9 March–1 June 1975, The Least Worst of Hello Cheeky: Sundays, 25 January and 1 February 1976, Radio 2. **Series Four:** Sundays, 7 March–29 August 1976, Cheeky Whittington and His Magic Ballpoint: Saturday 25 December 1976 (45-minute special), Radio 2. **Series Five:** Sundays, 7 October–11 November 1979, Radio 2. Producers David Hatch and Bob Oliver Rogers. **Television. Series One:** Mondays, 19 January–22 March 1976, YTV. **Series Two:** Wednesdays, 26 May–23 June 1976, YTV. Executive producer Duncan Wood. Producer Len Lurcuck.

HIS AND HERS

A standard situation comedy, whose basic premise of husband and wife role reversal was rather better investigated in the BBC series *You Must Be the Husband*. The acting link, Tim Brooke-Taylor. Here he ridicules the domesticated bliss of Ronald Lewis that he would himself later embody. Ronald Lewis starred as Rupert Sherwin, a freelance journalist with time on his hands. Happy to throw himself into his new found place as house husband, his dedicated wife, played by Sue Lloyd in Series One, continued her successful job as an accountant in the city. The best dialogue was reserved for dumb-founded, pithy comments between the odd couple's next door neighbours, Tim Brooke-Taylor and Madeline Smith. When the series returned in 1972, Barbara Murray had been drafted in to play the wife figure and, most importantly of all, the Burgesses from Series One were completely removed. Perhaps, even more strangely, Tim Brooke-Taylor was invited back for a one-off appearance as a different character in this 13-episode run and nobody from Series One seemed to recognise him! The spooky world of sitcomland…

Series One: Rupert Sherwin RONALD LEWIS Kay Sherwin SUE LLOYD Toby Burgess TIM BROOKE-TAYLOR Janet Burgess MADELINE SMITH Dorothy JANIE BOOTH. Written by Ken Hoare and Mike Sharland. Directors/producers David Mallet and Graham Evans. Tuesdays, 23 June–28 July 1970, ITV. **Series Two:** Directed and produced by Ian Davidson. Fridays, 7 April–30 June 1972, ITV.

HOAX!

A sort of radio pioneer for the cable game show, *Pull the Other One*, in which a panel of celebrity guests related tall, shaggy dog stories to each other. A rather bemused Tim Brooke-Taylor was in the chair and it was down to him, the listener and the studio audience, to spot the fib-telling performer. *Hoax!* provided easy entertainment and allowed Tim to shine as the slightly uneasy, completely bewildered, host. Interviewed for the *Radio Times* Tim explained, 'I don't know which is true or false either, so I can at least use my legal training and get in a bit of penetrating cross-examination!'

Series One: Fridays, 24 October–14 November 1986, Radio 4. **Series Two:** Thursdays, 17 September–1 October 1987, Radio 4. **Series Three:** Saturdays, 6 February–12 March 1988, Radio 4. **Series Four:** Saturdays, 4 August–8 September 1990, Radio 4. **Series Five:** Thursdays, 21 November 1991–16 January 1992, Radio 4. **Series Six:** Tuesdays, 10 August–28 September 1993, Radio 4. Devised by Ian Messiter. Produced by Edward Taylor.

THE HOFFNUNG FESTIVAL OF MUSIC

In celebration and memory of that great musical wit and raconteur Gerard Hoffnung, Bill Oddie joined the fun in 1988. Typically, Bill contributed his wind power as one of the Vacuum Cleaner Players during 'A Grand, Grand Overture'.

Performed 12 and 13 February 1988, Royal Festival Hall, London. Double CD 444 921-2 Decca 1988.

HOLIDAY QUIZ

This spin-off from the BBC's *Holiday* programme presented by Anne Gregg invited star guests to spar with the regular presenters in what became a light-hearted geography trivia test. In the last of this series on Monday 2 January 1989, Tim Brooke-Taylor played along with the resort questions and guessing games.

HORIZON

Before Des Lynam revealed all, this 'How on earth did they do that?' Special took an in-depth look behind-the-scenes at the tricks of the film industry. Broadcast on BBC1 on 23 December 1973 the show concentrated on slapstick comedy technique, visual business and special effects with clips from such films as The Golden Voyage of Sinbad. Naturally, it turned to one of the Beeb's contemporary favourites, The Goodies, to illustrate some of the points. After all, the lads used old, familiar ideas, the clips were cheaper to use and the off-screen antics of Brooke-Taylor, Garden, Oddie and crew gave the show a real sense of cool clout. Out-takes and production footage from Series Five classics, *Rome Antics* and *Cunning Stunts*, was included.

HOTEL PARADISO

Stage production starring Graeme Garden.

HOW TO IRRITATE PEOPLE

The final stepping stone between *At Last the 1948 Show* and *Monty Python's Flying Circus*, this was David Frost's final hold on his Cambridge team before their stardom overshadowed him. Written by the four *1948* principals with Feldman's acting contributions plugged by some sparkling work from Michael Palin, the programme was designed to catapult the Cleese style into America (via Frost's contact with the Westinghouse Network). It successfully resurrected old favourites as well as echoing others: the Palin/Chapman car repair sketch is commonly acknowledged as the fledgling 'dead parrot'. Cleese, lecturing and linking the interludes, makes an imposing, suitably irritating host and historically speaking, with three Pythons on board, this is a vitally important piece of television. Usual targets (restaurants, television discussion programmes, parties and, of course, mothers) are hit for the comic effect, although Tim Brooke-Taylor is rather underused and features in just three pieces, two of which see him in 'pepperpot' drag. The term, actually used in the narrative here, sets off Chapman, Cleese and Brooke-Taylor to gabble, chatter and gossip in a cinema, succeeding in winding up poor Michael Palin who only wants to enjoy the film. Commenting on the smallest detail, repeating everything each of them says, hilariously responding to bedpan humour and shockingly intoning 'Well I never!' when their actions are questioned, Tim doesn't have to do much except go with the over-the-top flow to help make a mini-comedy classic. For his second 'pepperpot' appearance, Tim abandons the squawking, primitive Python variety and reverts to his old *1948* crone. Giggling, muttering and blinking his way into the irritated subconscious of Cleese's false smooth television quiz master, Tim whines and muses on simple questions, longingly hopes to win the star prize, a battleship, and, best of all, continually rambles on about her big family and great age... 'I'm a 103 today!' By the close, she's succeeded in reducing Cleese to a nervous wreck, won the contest and reached the ripe old age of 640! Finally, Tim clad in more sensible clothes, recreates another old *1948* sketch with Cleese: The Job Interview. Both these vintage classics were re-done within Python but this remains the definitive record, with Tim's ultra-nervous wannabe trainee reacting with wild panic to John's sinister bell-ringing, musically geared cries of 'Goodnight!' and ice-skating styled scoring for his interview technique. Primitive but potent.

Did You Know? *For some reason the show was recorded in broadcast order, thus Cleese had to change out of his smart presenter suit, into his sketch costume and back again. Capturing the spirit of the ground-breaking but depleted At Last the 1948 Show, having the added bonuses of Michael Palin in the cast and having been filmed in colour, this was a*

CLIVE ANDERSON, JEREMY HARDY AND GRAEME GARDEN TRY TO TAKE CONTROL IN *IF I RULED THE WORLD*

natural choice for video release. It emerged in 1990, hot on the heels of A Fish Called Wanda, Python's 20th, the death of Graham Chapman and continued Goodies silence. With Cleese preferring not to get involved, Palin cast an eye over the tape and incorporated longer edits to make the show a 65-minute package.

JOHN CLEESE, TIM BROOKE-TAYLOR, GRAHAM CHAPMAN, MICHAEL PALIN, GILLIAN LIND, CONNIE BOOTH, DICK VOSBURGH. Script by John Cleese and Graham Chapman. Additional material by Marty Feldman and Tim Brooke-Taylor. Executive producer David Frost. Directed by Ian Fordyce, 1969.

I

I CAN'T GET THROUGH / BECAUSE SHE IS MY LOVE

A couple of serious songs. Writer–performer Bill Oddie remembers them as 'a sort of poor man's Gene Pitney and how poor can you get!'

R5433 Parlophone April 1966.

I SUPPOSE YOU THINK THAT'S FUNNY

Well, not really no! In the new digital age of television, ITV launched its second, over-spill channel, repeating recent hits and commissioning other exclusive time-fillers. One such time-filler was this thrown-together comedy quiz hosted by Lisa Tarbuck and kicking off with the rather disconcerting sight of the legendary Tim Brooke-Taylor flanked by Little and Large.

Monday 14 December 1998, ITV2.

IF I RULED THE WORLD

Another in that seemingly endless conveyor belt of satirically edged television panel games from HatTrick Productions, this politician play-acting pitted team captains Graeme Garden and Jeremy Hardy in a battle of lies, half truths and downright corruption. Trendy comic guest stars included Doon Mackichan, Richard Wilson, Griff Rhys-Jones and Andy Hamilton. Graeme's blue team and Hardy's red, never officially represented the Tories and New Labour, but with a torrent of counter-discussion, scandal, heated debate and often shared ideals, the comparison was never a million miles away. Bemused, acidic host Clive Anderson refereed both teams and the studio audiences voting interludes, through various rounds ranging from Soap Box, allowing a non-stop rant through song lyrics delivered in the style of a party political broadcast, to an adaptation of the Golden Gong game where any answer was good apart from 'Yes' or 'No'. Perhaps the highlight came with the I Couldn't Disagree More session which requested blanket denial of anything your opponent expressed. Garden's laconic and methodical approach was a major asset, packed with pithy comments, Colonel Blimpisms, corrupt vote grabbing and, occasionally sensing a Radio 4 audience in the vicinity, rushing through gloriously bad rhyming answers for a major point building session. However, the peak of Series One came with the third show. A masterpiece in every way, not least, because of Tim Brooke-Taylor's guest appearance on the red team. The programme's major joy is of the simplest form, with both Tim and Graeme helplessly breaking up at each other's comic observations and, most treasurably of all, shamelessly celebrating the legacy of *The Goodies*. It's a tricky one for Graeme. Tim's I Couldn't Disagree More proposal, 'as a fan I believe *The Goodies* should be repeated!', ought to get a negative response from the other side. With deft touch, Graeme couldn't disagree more, 'they should have been repeated 10 or 15 years ago!' Anderson holds his hands up, suspects the show of being hijacked and allows the masterly comic duo to bask in deserved audience applause. Although condemned by some critics as nothing more than radio on television, Graeme returned for a second series in 1999. Memories of the good old days were recaptured once more when he was asked to name the star of *The Goodies* during his Seventies awareness round. Graeme's muttered 'that bloody kitten' was only bettered by his bemused reaction to the correct answer: Bill Oddie.

Did You Know? A pilot edition of the show was recorded on Sunday 20 April 1997. This remained unscreened due to the fact that Graeme Garden was simply a panel member and not Team Captain. Future regulars Jeremy Hardy and Fred Macaulay were also involved. For the second show of the first series Rebecca Front quickly replaced Pauline McLynn following the sad news of the death of her Father Ted co-star Dermot Morgan. Promoting the programme The Mail on Sunday's programme supplement (15–21 March 1998) featured the Mavis Nicholson interview with Graeme Garden. Graeme's smiling mug even appeared on the front cover, alongside none other than the five Spice Girls intertwined with Ruby Wax. The series kickstarted Radio Times interest in Graeme Garden with the beginning of Series One highlighted with a questionnaire with the man and Series Two pondering on a world ruled by the ex-Goodie and Seventies icon, predicting a land of 'black pudding wielding Ecky-Thumpers and a giant cat and a funky gibbon on every corner' (9–15 February 1999). A third series was planned but axed in January 2000.

Series One: Fridays, 27 February–3 April 1998, BBC2. **Series Two:** Mondays, 8 February–13 March 1999, BBC2. Executive producers Mary Bell and Jimmy Mulville. Director John FD Northover. Series producer Anne Marie Thorogood.

JUNE WHITFIELD POSES WITH THE TEAM AFTER PRESENTING THE 1995 SONY AWARD – BARRY CRYER, JON NAISMITH, GRAEME GARDEN, TIM BROOKE-TAYLOR, COLIN SELL AND WILLIE RUSHTON

I'M SORRY I HAVEN'T A CLUE

Bethnal Green. Regent's Park. Waterloo. Dagenham Heathway. Holborn. Kilburn... Mornington Crescent. Oh, and by the way, main-line stations were wild there. Should have mentioned that! One of the glorious cornerstone monuments of Radio 4, *I'm Sorry I Haven't a Clue* has deservedly become a vital part of the national fibre, a beloved cult favourite and award-winning masterpiece. It only took 25 years! Wallowing in ripping apart radio convention and using the medium for glorious self-mockery, the show in its prime, delights in a unique combination of treasures. There's the ultra-sexy, sadly fictitious, scorer Samantha, whose raunchy, anyone at anytime, persona gets the contestants temperatures rising. Colin Sell's piano skills are severely sent up. The high-tech, laser display board revealing the answer to the studio audience has all the glamour and style of a piece of cardboard with hasty scribbles adorned over it. Chairman Humphrey Lyttelton growls with

frustrated boredom and, most importantly of all, the players, with Graeme Garden and Tim Brooke-Taylor prominent among them, tear through corny gags at a rate of knots.

SERIES ONE

Originally conceived by Graeme Garden as the 'antidote to panel games', shows which were literally flooding the airwaves in the early Seventies, the resting *I'm Sorry I Haven't a Clue* production team, and Garden in particular, decided to deliver their own twisted version full of the wonderfully groan-worthy puns that had made Radio Prune such a popular programme. Sophisticated refinement was personified in ex-*Daily Mail* cartoonist, ex-Grenadier guardsman, jazz trumpeter and respected bandleader Humphrey Lyttelton. His selection as the Kenneth Horne-like authority chairman proved perfect for the galley of grotesque and farcical interludes from the full roster of the Goodies and selected contributions from Jo Kendall and John Cleese. Sadly, Bill Oddie, physically

GRAEME GARDEN, BARRY CRYER AND WILLIE RUSHTON IN ACTION FOR A SHOW SPONSORED BY TAYLORS PORT

sick before and after recording, couldn't face the pressure of non-stop improvisation. Future player Barry Cryer chaired the series on five occasions.

Tuesdays, 11 April–4 July 1972, Radio 4.

SERIES TWO

The classic format was beginning to come together when Cleese and Kendall opted out of more programmes and Barry Cryer took his regular seat on the panel. He joined the Goodies to complete the show's resident line-up of funsters.

Mondays, 30 April–23 July 1973, Radio 4.

THE GOLDEN YEARS

Bill Oddie decided against appearing in the third series and allowed the ultimate dream team of Brooke-Taylor, Garden, Cryer and Willie Rushton to fall into place. As Humphrey Lyttleton described them, 'a veritable 'who's that' of British comedy!' With only occasional substitutes, the quartet would run gentle riot through radio comedy for the next 20 years, structuring the series into the thing

we now all know and love. Wittily scripting limericks, puns and monologues in a desperate, fooling no one attempt to showcase spontaneous gems and, as often as not, finding their purple patches with informal bits of actually ad-libbed near nonsense. Mornington Crescent, its rules, past masters and etiquette, became a part of the national heritage. The self-explanatory round, One Song to the Tune of Another, reduced fans to a heap of collapsed laughter and the biting parody of Just A Minim ruthlessly 'borrowed' from *Just A Minute*'s 'repetition, deviation or hesitation' avoidance, only this time with songs. Predictably, impossible titles like *There's a Hole in My Bucket*, *Old MacDonald Had a Farm* and *The Twelve Days of Christmas*, were chosen. Rounds with some sort of sense to them – historical postcards from the famous, newspaper reports on great moments in world history or completing legendary quotes with comic intent – were juxtaposed brilliantly with moments of pure surreal insanity. Panellists would labour for minutes trying to identify a motorway merely from a brief snippet of recorded traffic noise from

CHECKING THE RULES OF MORNINGTON CRESCENT – THE DEFINITIVE LINE-UP, GRAEME GARDEN, BARRY CRYER, TIM BROOKE-TAYLOR, WILLIE RUSHTON AND HUMPHREY LYTTLETON

the stretch of road in question. Authors were pinpointed merely by the sound of a clacking typewriter at work, while Sound Charades reinvented the classic mime game immortalised by *Give Us a Clue* with the added help of sound, as well as movement, for the benefit of radio audiences. Often past glories were lovingly incorporated as with the time when, during the Tell a Fairy Tale round, Barry Cryer's continuation of the basket of goodies perennial resulted in the wares being put down because 'Tim Brooke-Taylor, Graeme Garden and Bill Oddie weigh a hell of a lot!' Later, in a November 1996 edition, Tim suggested The Godies with Bill Oddessius during a Greek-flavoured round of Ancient Radio Times, and Barry Cryer further added to the tradition when introducing Tim, Bill and Graeme at an Australian Party as The G'Days! The spectre of *I'm Sorry I'll Read That Again* was, also, fully embraced with the closing late arrivals at the Ball for medics, morticians, solicitors or whatever. It was cue for the most outlandish puns or wordplays: hence Mr and Mrs Roids and their daughter Emma. Various film clubs for

certain professions threw up such gems as the bird-watching group screening Sean Canary in Licence to Trill or Warders of the Lost Ark and the sublime suggestion from Tim for the banker's film club: North By NatWest. Celebrity Answer phones even prompts Humphrey Lyttleton into action with the classic, 'Hello, this is Tim Brooke-Taylor, I'm not in at the moment, but whatever it is I'll do it!' Swannee Kazoo delights in musical renditions featuring the, rather limited, instruments swannee whistle and kazoo, while Cheddar Gorge, an audience favourite, had our hapless panellists, desperately trying to compile a sentence, a word at a time, without actually completing it. Things were made even more complicated by the added rule that all words had to start with the same letter! Mornington Crescent, of course, is the ultimate crowd-pleaser, prompting cries of foul, support and deviation. The location was altered from the London underground to the Scottish system, Morningside Crescent, when the team travelled North of the border, but still the rules could confuse the most intellectual of types. Positive and negative critic discussions, depending on Humphrey's hooter, allows contradictory comments to merge into one, Name That Toupee and Spot the Ostrich take bizarreness beyond breaking point, and the treasurable shared song performance has created true radio magic. The legendary rendition of If They Could See Me with Graeme and Barry alternating words, is one of the finest examples. Even dear old Hump, whose usual lacklustre, sarcastic mutterings reach the minor excitement level of 'Well that was fun!', was in awe for the first time in 20 years! This is what classic comedy is all about.

Series Three: Wednesdays, 28 August–2 October 1974. **Series Four:** Tuesdays, 29 July–16 September 1975. **Series Five:** Sundays, 6 March–10 April 1977. **Series Six:** Tuesdays, 22 August–24 October 1978. **Series Seven:** Mondays, 16 July–17 September 1979. **Christmas special:** Monday 24 December 1979. **Christmas special:** Wednesday 24 December 1980. **Series Eight:** Saturdays, 22 August–24 October 1981. **Christmas special:** Friday 25 December 1981. **Series Nine:** Saturdays, 20 March, 27 March, 10 April–29 May 1982. **Series 10:** Saturdays, 26 February–30 April 1983. **Series 11:** Saturdays, 7 April–9 June 1984 (TIM BROOKE-TAYLOR missed shows 9 and 10). **Everyman's Guide To Mornington Crescent:** Sunday 23 December 1984. **Series 12:** Saturdays, 4 May–6 July 1985 (GRAEME GARDEN missed shows 3, 4, 7 and 8). **Series 13:** Saturdays, 26 July–27 September 1986 (TIM BROOKE-TAYLOR missed shows 7–9, GRAEME GARDEN missed shows 5–10). **Christmas special:** I'm Shorry I Haven't A Cluesy Woozie Thursday 25 December 1986. **Series 14:** Mondays, 17 August–19 October 1987 (TIM BROOKE-TAYLOR missed show 4). **Series 15:** Saturdays, 7 January–11 March 1989 (GRAEME GARDEN missed shows 5 and 9). **Series 16:** Saturdays, 13 January–10 March 1990. **Series 17:** Saturdays, 17 November–22 December 1990. **Series 18:** Saturdays, 22 June–27 July 1991 (TIM BROOKE-TAYLOR missed shows 1 and 2). **Series 19:** Saturdays, 19 October–7 December 1991 (TIM BROOKE-TAYLOR missed shows 3 and 4, GRAEME GARDEN missed 1–6). **Series 20:** Saturdays, 23 May–27 June 1992, (GRAEME GARDEN missed 1 and 2). **The Best of I'm Sorry I Haven't A Clue:** Compilations, Mondays, 3 and 10 August 1992. **Series 21:** Saturdays, 14 November–19 December 1992 (TIM BROOKE-TAYLOR missed 3–6). **Christmas special:** Saturday 26 December 1992. **Series 22:** Saturdays, 6 November–11 December 1993. **Christmas special:** Saturday 25 December 1993. **Series 23:** Saturdays, 28 May–2 July 1994. **Series 24:** Saturdays, 5 November–10 December 1994 (TIM BROOKE-TAYLOR missed 1 and 2). **Series 25:** Saturdays, 27 May–1 July 1995. **Series 26:** Saturdays, 11 November–16 December. **Christmas special:** Monday 25 December 1995. **Series 27:** Saturdays, 1 June–6 July 1996 (TIM BROOKE-TAYLOR missed 1–4). **Series 28:** Saturdays, 9 November–14 December 1996. Producers Geoffrey Perkins, Paul Mayhew-Archer, Paul Spencer, John Magnusson, Jon Naismith.

AFTER WILLIE

'Graeme Garden, Barry Cryer, Willie Rushton and Tim Brooke-Taylor were being given silly things to do by Humphrey Lyttelton.' A heart-warming phrase which had rounded off so many glorious 30 minutes of quick fire, free-wheeling radio comedy. Sadly, it was a line silenced on 11 December 1996 when Willie Rushton died at the tragically early age of just 59. The 28th series, which featured his last work, was still being broadcast when the news came and Ned Sherrin's stirring introduction before the final show was aired, brought a sense of loss to every listener. Travelling through Mornington Crescent on the Northern line, I always spare a thought for Willie. Ill for some time, the fourth man place on the panel had already been occasionally filled by sharp-witted ad-libber Paul Merton, a comedian who had taken over *Just a Minute* witticisms on the death of Kenneth Williams. The decision was whether or not to continue with *I'm Sorry I Haven't a Clue* in the wake of losing such a major player of the game.

Ironically, the show had never been so popular and, at long last, official award recognition was beginning to shine through when the series won Best Radio Comedy at The 1996 British Comedy Awards. Guest stars (including John Junkin, Jonathan Lynn and Kenny Everett) had been used in the past, so it was agreed to retain the three principal wits, Colin Sell at the piano and chairman Humphrey Lyttelton, while interspersing the old favourites with younger comedians like Jeremy Hardy and Tony Hawks. The new boys were more than eager to prove they could cut the mustard with the best of them. Owing to the affection and sheer gusto of the veterans, this transition period went off without a hitch. Eerily, shortly after Rushton's funeral, a show was being recorded during a heavy storm. Suddenly, Barry Cryer made a joke at Willie's expense and a huge clap of thunder silenced the audience. Barry sheepishly apologised and the storm calmed. The old boy still refused to allow the last line to go to somebody else. As I write *I'm Sorry I Haven't A Clue* is even more popular than ever before, a reassuringly familiar point in a rapidly changing world of radio station policy. Here's hoping there is much more life in the old dog yet. A new series was recorded from 22 May 2000.

Did You Know? A continuous game of Mornington Crescent is being played on the internet site. After 26 years, the series finally won not one, but two, radio awards. One from the listeners and one from the critics. I'm Sorry… was also embraced by BBC television as a radio comedy flagship: Tim's suggestion during Barcodes, a game in which contestants have to identify super market products from their bar codes, 'it's lillets with wings…', was used as a plugging sound bite for the glories of the BBC wireless output in 1998. Radio Times put the show into Goodies context with the article 'The Only Sense Here Is a Sense of Fun' by Roland White. Tim, Barry, Graeme and Willie recorded an unscreened television pilot edition of the show.

Series 29: Saturdays, 8 November–13 December 1997. **Series 30:** Mondays, 27 April 1998–1 June 1998. **Special:** I'm Sorry I Haven't Got a Desert Island, a compilation of favourite moments from past series selected by celebrity fans Jim Broadbent, Jack Dee, Dame Judi Dench, Stephen Fry, Germaine Greer and Neil Kinnock, Monday 11 January 1999. **Series 31:** Mondays, 1 December 1998–4 January 1999. **Series 32:** Mondays, 24 May–28 June 1999. **Series 33:** Mondays, 8 November–13 December 1999.

I'M SORRY I HAVEN'T A CLUE: the BBC audio collection

One of the smash hits on the BBC audio cassette range, at the time of writing there have been five best-selling titles. The first release contains four compilation half hours culled from the many miles of taped Brooke-Taylor, Cryer,

Garden and Rushton material. The first issue intriguingly promises that it 'includes the rules to Mornington Crescent!', but fans, don't believe it! To make amends, Volume Two, features just three 'best of' editions, plus the lengthy, historical look at the ground-breaking mind game, *Everyman's Guide to Mornington Crescent*. A two-part celebration, tackling the cultural significance of the game and the complete understanding of the rules, the programme was introduced by ex-*Tomorrow's World* host and *The Goodies: It Might as Well Be String* guest, Raymond Baxter, with additional, convincing comments from Brian Johnston. Beryl Bainbridge and the ever-popular man in the street sing the game's praises, Brooke-Taylor, Garden and Rushton re-enact a game played at the Court of King Henry VIII, Cryer does Peter Sellers doing Laurence Oliver doing Shakespeare's Richard III delivering a monologue version of Mornington Crescent, while Garden highlights a heartfelt, academic setting of the rules within Chaucerian England. Rushton delights with a music hall geared, the Western Brothers-style, 1929 recording of Lord Mornington Crescent, aided and abetted by stunning harmonising from his fellow team members. Ken Livingston gloriously sends himself up, Claire Rayner offers some helpful counselling and Graeme Garden creates a comic masterpiece as a grand master sacked from his far too tempting, game-dominated employment as an underground ticket seller. A wonderfully cheeky documentary, the mist begins to clear! Volume Three presented three complete shows with the regular quartet and a half-hour compilation showcasing the noted guests through the years, Denise Coffey, Jeremy Hardy, Mike Harding, Tony Hawks, John Junkin, Paul Merton and Bill Tidy. The fourth volume, released in 1998, broke the mould for the better, and featured four complete programmes, the last shows Willie Rushton appeared in, recorded at the Everyman Theatre, Cheltenham, Northampton's Royal Theatre, the Liverpool Playhouse and, finally, a coming home session for Tim and Graeme at the Cambridge Arts Theatre. Sherrin's opening memoir was also included. Willie and, indeed, great swathes of *I'm Sorry I Haven't a Clue*, were further saluted with the release, *Willie Rushton at the Beeb*. A Radio 2 series presented shortened versions of this BBC audio collection range and *At the BBC: Willie Rushton* was first broadcast, Thursday 25 March 1999.

ZBBC 1388 I'm Sorry I Haven't a Clue 1993. ZBBC 1698 I'm Sorry I Haven't a Clue 2 1995. ZBBC 1888 I'm Sorry I Haven't a Clue 3 1996. ZBBC 2125 I'm Sorry I Haven't a Clue 4 1998. ZBBC 0563 I'm Sorry I Haven't A Clue 5 1999.

I'M SORRY I HAVEN'T A CLUE: the book

Just after the seventh series of everybody's favourite panel mickey-taker, the accompanying book, *I'm Sorry I Haven't a Clue*, was published.

Written by Tim Brooke-Taylor, Barry Cryer, Graeme Garden, Humphrey Lyttelton and Willie Rushton. Robson Books, hardback, 1980. Unwin Press, paperback, 1981.

I'M SORRY I HAVEN'T A CLUE: the official limerick book

A choice selection of hilarious limericks lifted from the show's lengthy history, lovingly dedicated to the irreplaceable Willie Rushton.

Written by Tim Brooke-Taylor, Barry Cryer, Graeme Garden, Humphrey Lyttelton and Willie Rushton. Orion Media, hardback, 1998. Paperback, 1999.

I'M SORRY I'LL READ THAT AGAIN

Billed as 'A radio custard pie thrown by...', those legendary guys and gal from *Cambridge Circus* achieved the treasured ambition of its key writers to became the Sixties' equivalent of the totally influential radio masterpiece, *The Goon Show*. When I was a youngster I seem to recall twiddling through the stations on my parent's radio set and suddenly hitting on a burst of laughter and applause. It was a welcoming invitation, even at that tender age, and my finger faltered on the knob. What followed sounded both very familiar but completely new at the same time – I recognised the voices – it was certainly Bill Oddie and I was pretty certain that it was Tim Brooke-Taylor as well. The jokes were corny, obvious and totally infectious: all historical puns and schoolboy howlers. To my ears it sounded like *The Goodies* reworking a *Carry On* movie for the radio... and I guess that is as good an encapsulation as any as to what *I'm Sorry I'll Read That Again* is all about, with a lot of irony lavished on it of course. Pre-*Monty Python*, television's sacred cows such as *Dr Finlay's Casebook*, *Dr Who* and David Frost were put to the sword, while songwriter extraordinaire, Bill Oddie, continued to produce an alarmingly prolific selection of original numbers for the series, penning over 140 by the close. Although on occasions Eric Idle, John Cleese and Graeme Garden would contribute songs to the show, the musical signature was pure Oddie. He successfully repackaged many titles for single and album release while, later, improving on the originals via cover versions within *The Goodies'* releases. Despite room for improvement, Oddie's performances

BILL ODDIE, IN HOUSEWIFE MODE, PLUGGING HIS LATEST COMIC SINGLE IN HOMAGE TO THE SMOOTH DISC JOCKEY JIMMY YOUNG

and the musical assistance of Leon Cohen and Dave Lee (later to work on *The Goodies*' records), made sure that these 'live' recordings in the studio were of the highest quality, funny and capturing of the unique style being parodied, like a comic Beatles *White Album*. As comic actor, Bill Oddie hammed it up as a continually misrepresented

Hughie Green and the aged crumbling old soak Grimbling. Graeme Garden created a couple of unforgettable radio monsters in his flamboyantly uncanny Eddie Waring ramblings and the dithering charm of Walter Gabriel. Tim Brooke-Taylor delighted an entire nation as the sex-mad, screaming old crone, Lady Constance, deviously and

215

THE DEFINITIVE CAST LINE-UP: GRAEME GARDEN,
BILL ODDIE, DAVID HATCH, JO KENDALL,
JOHN CLEESE AND TIM BROOKE-TAYLOR

outlandishly over-performed from the humble roots of *A Clump of Plinths*'s Oscar Wilde sketch. Tim played the autobiographical Tim Brown-Windsor and could get huge rounds of applause, affectionate 'Ahh's, and major laughter, by merely barking his beloved Spot the dog dialogue. This surely was comic genius... With healthy obsession with gibbons, teapots, fish, ferrets and the worthlessness of, but embittered desire to be awarded, an OBE, the *I'm Sorry I Haven't a Clue* squad developed from post-graduate, post-satirist funsters in the early Sixties to the most polished purveyors of Christmas cracker puns a decade later. Every gag known to man, and a few that weren't, finally found their way into the series somewhere. The concept of a Wombat being something you play wom with, or the relentless gag fest of Fish 'n' Quips, was fittingly balanced with censor-bypassing risqué gems like the announcement of a Mr and Mrs Farquar and their daughter Martha – get it? The show also proved an invaluable training ground for the future Goodies to establish and refine their recognised alter egos for television stardom. Ooh, what a give away...

THE PILOTS

Stemming from the radio presentation of *Cambridge Circus*, broadcast on Monday 30 December 1963, producer Humphrey Barclay got the green light from the BBC to record the first of three semi-successful attempts at launching the Footlighters as a recognised radio comedy team. The initial programme was recorded on Sunday 10 March 1964 (with the two further pilots following over the next couple of Sundays). Originally given the title, *Get Off My Foot* – a pleasing reflection of the team's music hall styled jokery (the line had been a Frank Randle catchphrase as well as a 1936 film starring Max Miller), these broadcasts were finally released on to an unsuspecting nation as the typical newscaster apology for an incorrectly delivered line: *I'm Sorry I'll Read That Again*. Heard today, the opening programme sounds uncertain and tentative, with the performers quite clearly gauging reactions from the uncertain and tentative audience. Most of the material was re-worked or re-performed *Cambridge Circus* sketches with John Cleese and the boys in good spirits for Top of the Form, a rather lacklustre stab at Jack and the Beanstalk, Bill Oddie energetically hamming it up for his rigorous Scots master of Inward Bound and the frightfully British Tim Brooke-Taylor stealing the Cricket Commentators interlude with some stuffy misunderstanding. Graeme Garden was allowed to play his trump Eddie Waring card early, while Jo Kendall serenades the PM with Jim, some fresh News comes in and there's the decidedly Python-esque Performing Hamsters scene. Was Terry Jones tuned to this I wonder... The opening pilot's highlight comes with rant-a-thon Cleese dishing out the wine-tasting challenge to a totally inept Tim, with the poor chap finally crumbling into a frenzied guessing game, culminating with a manic burst of beverages, all of which are wrong! Of course, it's really steak and chips – the difficult ones first! Northern banter is wonderfully sent up with the Butterworth Lads, Bill and Tim have some fun with the somewhat pointless charade of Horrible Hairy Spiders, while the Bank Manager and Bill's celebrated London Bus song, conclude proceedings. This is clearly performers still finding their feet and, indeed, the following two broadcasts proved similarly useful grounding for the lengthy series to come. Again these represented *Cambridge* classics, with the third show featuring Secret Service, You Say Tomato and the Headmaster sketch, although sadly, their quality or otherwise can no longer be judged as these second and third pilot episodes have been wiped from the BBC archive.

TIM BROOKE-TAYLOR, ANTHONY BUFFERY, JOHN CLEESE, DAVID HATCH, JO KENDALL, BILL ODDIE. Written by Humphrey Barclay, Tim Brooke-Taylor, Anthony Buffery, John Cleese, David Hatch, Alan Hutchison, Jo Kendall, Elizabeth Lord, Bill Oddie and Chris Stuart-Clark. Music by Burt Rhodes and his Quintet. Produced by Humphrey Barclay and Edward Taylor. Fridays, 3, 10 and 17 April 1964, BBC Light Programme.

SERIES ONE

Almost immediately after the three pilot editions were broadcast, the *Cambridge Circus* cast were whisked off to New Zealand for a tour of the show. This resulted in a further four radio programmes being made for the 'down under' market. A Broadway beckoning, cast changes (Tony Buffery dropped out, Jonathan Lynn and Graham Chapman jumped aboard) and various other work commitments, meant that the first series proper of *I'm Sorry I'll Read That Again* was missing several notable performers. Jonathan Lynn proved reluctant and unavailable, while both the pre-Pythons were also out of the running. John Cleese, still in America following *Cambridge Circus*, was now appearing in *Half a Sixpence*, while Graham Chapman (who would never return to the cast) was busy with his medical training. In an attempt to plug the gap, another medical man, Graeme Garden, was drafted in to join his fellow future Goodies, themselves having just returned to England following the American touring stage version of *That Was The Week That Was*. Although the bulk of material was still written by the cast members, others like Eric Idle and Clive James were brought in to help. The rehearsal and recording for the first edition of this first series proper took place on Sunday 28 May 1965 and a legend was undoubtedly born.

SHOW ONE

The team start as they mean to go on with media mockery of the Weather Forecast, Ins and Outs, Bill Oddie happily slaughters Nashville with the Howling Country and Western Song, a frightfully stiff upper-lipped RAF Briefing from 1942 wallows in ground-breaking memories of Peter Cook and the *Beyond the Fringe* revolution, traditional jibes are twisted with the Mother-in-Law on Bus sketch, Bill's back with another number, She's Gone, pre-Python convention is established with the TV Complaint, there's madness with the Giant at the Marriage Bureau and the team get hilariously anal for The Critics.

SHOW TWO

Cleese enjoys another rant for Universal Challenge, Masochistic Monks, the Noel Coward ideal of Brits is parodied with Stately House, Bill admits to musical short-comings with the song I Ain't Got Rhythm, Ug's Fashions, Louis Armstrong, Artistic Specimens, Cricket Spectators, The Animals in terms of the pre-Goodies for The House of the Rising Sun and more snobbery for Swan Lake Commentary.

SHOW THREE

Thick policemen unveil the latest wonder of modern technology: Audible Road Signs. Kenneth Moore heroics are put to the sword with Reach For the Sky, Second Lieutenant Fellow-Smith, High Spot, Black Magician, Dwarf Warning, Bill gets all domesticated for We're Gonna Knit, The Stolen Banana, Yokels, Oddie croons by the letter but the message gets confused during BLIMPHT and a Holmesian mystery, The Singular Case of the Workington Shillelagh.

SHOW FOUR

American Settlers and the Red Man.

SHOW FIVE

The major Dickens spoof Martin Copperwick.

SHOW SIX

The Inventors, Customs, Lover of Things, Movie-Go-Sound, featuring the song After the Fall, Dickensian gentility with Lord Clumpwit's Appeal, Bill gets musically embarrassed with The Wind, life before the television and even the wireless, for an Old Evening's Entertainment, another Oddie number, The Freedom Day, and hard-bitten criminality with Mike Spanner – Private Eye.

SHOW SEVEN

Interlude, incomprehensible nonsense with Smurtot Yach Proxl, Insurance Policy, cool romantics with the song Don't Let It Rain on My Baby, News with a very vocal audience, Prehistoric Flight, a hasty repeat of the refined work song: The London Bus, and typically tongue-in-cheek patriotism via England Our England.

SHOW EIGHT

Looking well ahead with Long Range Weather Forecast, Nature Study, the song Let There Be Love, primitive memoirs from Prehistoric Woo-man, HMS Dreadful, featuring the song, Dowan at the Bottom in a Submarine and vintage, William Hartnell tail-ender, Dr Who fun-poking, with the sublime Dr Why and the Thing.

SHOW NINE

A special examination of the History of Radio, featuring send-ups of perennial favourites: Mrs Dale's Diary, Family Favourites and The Archers, the BBC gets in a flap during the Censorship sketch, we go Down My Way with Wilfred Pickles, Come Into the Garden Maude gets the audience nostalgically misty-eyed and contemporary arts discussion is shown the door with The Late Late Late Show.

TIM BROOKE-TAYLOR, GRAEME GARDEN, DAVID HATCH, JO KENDALL, BILL ODDIE. Written by Tim Brooke-Taylor, Brian Cooke, John Esmonde, Graeme Garden, David Hatch, Eric Idle, Clive James, Jo Kendall, Bob Larbey, David McKellar, Johnny Mortimer, Bill Oddie and Peter Vincent. Music by the Dave Lee Group. Producer Humphrey Barclay. Mondays, 4 October–6 December 1965, BBC Light Programme.

SERIES TWO

The shows were already attracting huge audience figures and a loyal following so it was hardly surprising when the team returned just over three months later for a second series of more of the same. Importantly, there was one addition to the cast – Humphrey Barclay having signed up John Cleese on his return to Britain. For one season, at least at the present, the classic *I'm Sorry I'll Read That Again* line-up was in place. As a result, Cleese and Kendall resurrected their celebrated John and Mary characterisations from *Cambridge Circus* for the first time, regular fixations with ferrets and rhubarb raised their comically enchanting heads and, most intriguing of all, Angus Prune made his debut. Prune was the cast's idea of what the regular home listener was like and pretty soon the catchy opening and closing theme music would be given lyrics and dubbed, not surprisingly, *The Angus Prune Tune* – 'I sit in my bath and I have a good laugh…'

SHOW ONE

Relaxation, BBC Statements, Rat Exterminator, Hypothetical Plane Crash, Eastern Chant, Off His Food, Sensitive Hearing, the cockney knees-up song Old Boutique and Ireland.

SHOW TWO

Another bash at the Brain of Britain mob with the Round Britain Quiz, the Friendly Inn, I Love You, Bill's upbeat suicidal chap sings Drown All Your Troubles Away, things get heated with Biology for Schools, the legendary Johnny Cash meets Ronnie Biggs for the country classic Train Robbers in the Sky, Moll Flounders.

SHOW THREE

Consult the Diary, the Zookeeper sketch, Secular Religious Pop Song, Small Airlines In-flight Entertainment, Reincarnation of Genghis Khan, another foot-tapping number: Just One of Those Things and Ali Baba.

SHOW FOUR

Radio's beloved soap, The Archers, goes through the mill, there's no pain on earth like Pregnant Man, Radio Strip Club, a Musical Journey, Fairy, Pride and Joy, Lord Nelson.

SHOW FIVE

The amazing Gothic tale of Dr Heckyl and Mr Jibe.

SHOW SIX

Stereo Sound, a Traffic Inspector for human traffic, the almighty Oddie lovesick song Stop It – I Like It, Jerusalem, Do You Love Me?, the These Foolish Things number and, at long last the full story of Angus Prune – Soccer Legend.

SHOW SEVEN

Auctioneer, Archbishop of Canterbury, Animal Question Time, a musical tribute to the dog – A Man's Best Friend, Housemaster, Isn't Nature Wonderful?, Opportunity Flops, Flat Inspector, another touching song: Tomorrow, Rogue Budgie, Five Little Emergent Nationals.

SHOW EIGHT

Soldiers, the BBC Animal Service, Red Sea Safari, it's not Norman Wisdom but Bill Oddie with Don't Laugh at Me – oh go on, he wants you to really. Three Babies – the first of many sketches written by David Hatch and invariably casting himself, Cleese and Brooke-Taylor as bickering babes with ever-patient mum Jo Kendall. Museum Attendant, the Beatles-esque Day Tripper featuring the song My Old Age Pension, World of Sport.

SHOW NINE

Rat Catchers' Strike, Compulsive Knitter, Traffic Warden, Promenade Concert featuring the song There Was a Ship That Put to Sea, The Doctor, rustic law-enforcer charm with the West Country folk song The Lawman, Marriage Guidance Bureau and fun and games with Julius Caesar.

SHOW 10

More mockery of their own backyard with the Radio Quiz Game, Police Message, Old Dark House, the dreaded musical eulogy to the Rhubarb Tart Blues, The Supernatural, the Occult and the Unexplained featuring the spine-chilling number Meet Me in the Churchyard, Nellie.

SHOW 11

Defusing a Bomb, diminutive antics at the Dwarf Olympics, the Play Little Piccolo-Man song, Girls' School Address, Show Jumping, Oddie's My Baby's Become a Folksinger lament and the usual gang get camp, dish out dodgy gags and go all Lincoln green in Robin Hood.

SHOW 12

Beethoven's Audition, John and Mary Alone in the Country, criminal musical love with Identikit Gal, alright already as the Bard gets a Jewish slant in Kosher Hamlet, the End of the World, a bit of music hall with Take It Off and Flashman whips it off during Tim Brown's Schooldays.

SHOW 13

In reflection on the international Mersey Beat invasion, a special edition – It is Liverpool – featuring Lennon, McCartney and Marsden homage songs, Ferry Cross the Mersey, and Liverpool.

TIM BROOKE-TAYLOR, JOHN CLEESE, GRAEME GARDEN, DAVID HATCH, JO KENDALL, BILL ODDIE. Written by Tim Brooke-Taylor, John Cleese, Graeme Garden, David Hatch, Eric Idle, Jo Kendall and Bill Oddie. Music by the Dave Lee Group. Producer Humphrey Barclay. Mondays, 14 March–6 June 1966, BBC Light Programme.

SERIES THREE

No sooner had the dream-team six pack of writer–performers been assembled than their number was depleted for the third batch of programmes. Graeme Garden, who was still training for a medical career, was unavoidably detained on a midwifery course in Plymouth. However, thanks to regular correspondence with Bill Oddie and Humphrey Barclay, Garden still kept his connection with the series, frequently contributing to the scripts by scribbling dialogue on the back of envelopes and sending it to Broadcasting House. Of equal importance was a definite shift towards the classic format of the show, allowing half the time to present a torrent of puns while finishing each edition with a good 10 or 15 minutes of sustained comic drama or pantomime. The first of these popular serials, The Curse of the Flying Wombat, was featured as the second half of all 13 editions. Apart from mixing Sir Arthur Conan Doyle suspense and Biggles adventure with *I'm Sorry I Haven't a Clue* style barrel-scrapers, it also presented the debuts for Oddie's old family retainer, Grimbling, and Brooke-Taylor's legendary screaming man-hunter, Lady Constance de Coverlet.

SHOW ONE

What Do You Know?, Cricket Commentary, Italian Letter, Vet, The Good News from Ghent to Aix, The Ferret Song, Three Babies 2.

SHOW TWO

Sitar Player, Bonnie Scotland, Business Marriage, Oddie's self-mocking song I'm Small, amaze your friends with Bird and Animal Impressions, Honeymoon on a Sloop, Making Horse Racing More Attractive and a poignant closing number, My Mum Had Lost My Dad.

SHOW THREE

The unspeakable horror of Cleese's Bath Night, Children's Tour of an Art Gallery, the tortured experiences of a Film Actor Specialising in Military Roles, Alice Through the Looking Glass, the Footlighters push their luck with the corporation with the tongue-in-cheek chant We Like Working for the BBC, the frightfully restrained John and Mary in Bed, Great Big Waterproof Boots, The Minister of Fuel and a rousing chorus of My Smile.

SHOW FOUR

Glasses of Water, East German Trade Exhibit, Beethoven's Fifth, The Family's on the Rocks song, William the Conqueror.

DAVID HATCH, BILL ODDIE, GRAEME GARDEN, JO KENDALL, JOHN CLEESE AND TIM BROOKE-TAYLOR HAVE A QUICK RUN THROUGH THE LINES

SHOW FIVE

New Show, espionage thrills with The Spy with My Cold, Gentlewomen's Protection Action Group, Bill quietly croons his way through One For My Baby as his audience ignores him, a heartfelt Appeal for Distressed Bumblebees, pubescent yearnings with Kendall's young lady at a school for boys, PC on Traffic Duty and the song Just to Keep Me Warm.

SHOW SIX

Colour Radio, Music for Schools, A Welcome in Ireland, Outside Lavatory, Managing Director and Employee, the Animal Child song.

SHOW SEVEN

The Fastest Show on Earth, a delicious poke at Peter Noble with Movie-Go-Flat including the decidedly Disney-esque song Antibellamlaudidartaarmomutatorum, John and Mary bluff their way through a legal wrangle with a Policeman, Prime Minister's Speech to French, Are You 21?, Oddie gets hip and into Pete 'n' Dud land with De Blues and All Dat Jazz.

SHOW EIGHT

Drum Beat Message, tomorrow's science today with The Day After Tomorrow's World, more backward-looking forward nonsense from The Clapham Mystery Trial of 1960–Now and the splendidly Coward-esque musical interlude The Ferrets of Old England.

SHOW NINE

Radio Oscars, International Cabaret, John and Mary and the Burglar, Hush Now Baby song, the hilarious Shakespeare Joke, Bill's anti-Rolf Aussie ditty What Can a Didgeridoo?, Bonzo Angus Prune Experiment.

SHOW 10

Air My Grudge, the Royal Navy, the Sick Song, Warning.

SHOW 11

Those hotly contested results from Show Nine's Bonzo Angus Prune Experiment are revealed, a certain Galton and Simpson rag 'n' bone sitcom should sue over For Better or For Worse and Son, Oddie moves his musical celebration from four-legged to two for the future Goodies classic A Man's Best Friend Is His Duck. It's all deep, meaningful and incomprehensible for Blues Song, the Bee-keeping sketch and a step back in time to the golden days of Old Time Radio including the foot-tapping number Benjamin Disraeli.

SHOW 12

Animal Round-Up, The Fawcetts with the Elimination Dance song, Driving Test, Three Babies 3, Did You Know?, Yodel Song.

SHOW 13

Builders, a celebration of the classic Broadway musical with The Rise and Ears of Cole Hammerstein III, including the show stopper: I Love a Show, Petula Clark Sings.

TIM BROOKE-TAYLOR, JOHN CLEESE, DAVID HATCH, JO KENDALL, BILL ODDIE. Written by Tim Brooke-Taylor, Graham Chapman, John Cleese, Graeme Garden, David Hatch, Eric Idle, Jo Kendall and Bill Oddie. Music by the Dave Lee Group. Producer Humphrey Barclay. 3 October–6 December 1966, BBC Light Programme.

SPECIAL:

JACK AND THE BEANSTALK PANTOMIME

The *I'm Sorry I'll Read That Again* team kick-started the new year with a special programme, a corny rag-bag of puns and songs culled from Series Three and re-performed for the post-Christmas blow-out audience.

TIM BROOKE-TAYLOR, JOHN CLEESE, DAVID HATCH, JO KENDALL, BILL ODDIE. Written by Tim Brooke-Taylor, John Cleese, Graeme Garden, David Hatch, Jo Kendall and Bill Oddie. Music by the Dave Lee Group. Producer Humphrey Barclay. Monday 2 January 1967, BBC Light Programme.

SERIES FOUR

There was still major upheaval in the cast, with John Cleese missing one edition due to ranting assignments elsewhere, Graeme Garden, ironically, getting away from delivering babies for the edition that Cleese missed, and, the then Mrs Bill Oddie, Jean Hart, enjoying a one-off substituting turn for Jo Kendall. The unique mix of Cambridge cool, bad puns and hilariously constructed songs remained the same.

SHOW ONE

John and Mary in Magic, M.O.T.H., Three Babies 4, Are You 6' 5"?, clipped harmony with There's a Walrus in My Soup and a camped-up romp through The Knights of the Round Table.

SHOW TWO

A stroll through Spring including the debut of Bill's groan-worthy song Spring Spring Spring – five-bar gate and all, John and Mary on Humpty Dumpty, the characters from Series Three's mini-serial The Curse of the Flying Wombat revealed in full gory glory, Champion the Wonder Mouse.

SHOW THREE

A Concert of Modern Music, Crime Prevention, the faithful Faith Healer, I've Forgotten the Words to this song, Estate Agent, a back-handed salute to Doris Day with the musical philosophy What Will Be Will Be, William Tell.

SHOW FOUR

Calypso, Greyhounds, If I Were the Only Girl in the World song, John and Mary discuss the Car, The Rabbits and Land Hour, Work Song, Dr Clubfoot in the Antarctic.

SHOW FIVE

Helpful tips for Motorists, Drilling for Moles, Garden Club, The First of May song, Toy Shop, I Like Singing in the Bath Tub… and why not?, The British Army.

SHOW SIX

Television discussion on Did You Miss It?, Bank Manager, Bill gets musical and dripping with Underwater Underwear, Folk Dancing, John and Mary on Tibbles, Drinking Song, The Decline and Fall of the Entire Roman Empire featuring a long overdue bash at Cleopatra.

SHOW SEVEN

To the ultimate shock of everybody bar Mr Cleese, it's the frightful Vulture Song (No, John, No), Horrible Hairy Spiders yet again!, the Russian Eurovision Song, the Gas Meter Reader, Late Cricket News, how to attract the waiter via song – Garçon, Garçon and the very, very grim Grimm fairy tale: Princess Goldilocks and the Perverted Goblins.

SHOW EIGHT

Club El Caraway, let's take safe sex on board with the Pill, Wales Travelogue, A Very Sad Case, I'm Gonna Live song, The Operating Theatre, another burst of music with the charming Spit, All Hands on Venus.

SHOW NINE

The British Courts of Justice, 25 Guinea Tour of Britain,

John and Mary on Moles, Bill gets aged for the humbling song William Grimbling, Three Babies 5, the Cricket song, and, middle and off-stump, way out West Tales of the Old Wild and Woolly Peter West.

SHOW 10

Please don't panic but your radio could explode, Film Censorship, I Can Hear the Wombats Dancing, The Dentist sketch, Portuguese Love Song and spooky goings-on with The Ghost of Objectionable Manor.

SHOW 11

Osteopath, Round the World Query, Buying a Stocking, a Music Hall comedian tries to get his point across in song with No, No, But Seriously Though, and blacked-up actors are out for a further bash at the bard in Othello.

SHOW 12

Memory Lane, Zoo Time including the Animal Noises song, House On Fire, the peerless meat eater's chorus I Am a Carnivore and the Inimitable Grimbling acts in his inimitable way.

SHOW 13

Radio Circus introductions, the hip hit show Record Spin, that Oddie could make the phone book sound good, oh, he has, with the absolutely outstanding Directory (Dial 999) – why no Goodies resurrection!, John and Mary on Jumbo, elephant obsession and corny gags – go for it Cleesy, I Do Like to be Beside the Seaside and a Greek tragedy gets even more tragic with the team's version of Ulysses or The Bill Odyssey or Up the Greek with Humphrey Barclay, Tim's slightly iffy hero and a stunning, very brief musical interlude into Have You Even Seen a Cyclops Blink?

TIM BROOKE-TAYLOR, DAVID HATCH, BILL ODDIE, JOHN CLEESE (missed Show 12) GRAEME GARDEN (Show 12 only) JEAN HART (Show 8 only) JO KENDALL (missed Show 8). Written by Tim Brooke-Taylor, John Cleese, Graeme Garden, David Hatch, Jo Kendall and Bill Oddie. Music by the Dave Lee Group. Producer Humphrey Barclay. Fridays/Sundays, 23 April–23 July 1967, BBC Light Programme.

SPECIAL:
THE SOUND OF MY FAIR SEVEN BRIDES FOR CALAMITY POPPINS AND I ON THE ROOF

Surprisingly, a merciless parody of the classic Hollywood musical and there's more than just Julie Andrews' nuns and flying nannies, Audrey Hepburn English lessons, Doris Day thigh-slapping, bald Oriental Kings, loads of brothers and warbling Jewish milkman on thatched cottages, here my friend. If that wasn't enough...

TIM BROOKE-TAYLOR, JOHN CLEESE, DAVID HATCH, JO KENDALL, BILL ODDIE. Written by Tim Brooke-Taylor, John Cleese, Graeme Garden, David Hatch, Jo Kendall and Bill Oddie. Music by the Dave Lee Group. Produced by Humphrey Barclay. Sunday 23 July 1967, BBC Light Programme.

SERIES FIVE

Humphrey Barclay relinquished hold on the production reigns to allow David Hatch to step into a triple role as performer, writer and producer. As it happens, Series Five was the first really classic run. All six essential team members were finally and, more or less, fully, in place, while the bulk of punning scripts were in the more than firm grasp of Graeme Garden and Bill Oddie. While Brooke-Taylor, Hatch and to a lesser extent, Cleese, would still contribute, the break-neck speed and gritty bite of Graeme and Bill saw the programme confidently stroll into cult comedy classic mode.

SHOW ONE

Dave's Diary, Bill goes Beatles mad again for I'm Sorry I'll Read That Again (Magical Mystery Ball), Firm of Solicitors and gangster convention ripped asunder for Bunnie and Claude.

SHOW TWO

A fresh angle on Listen with Mother: The Rabbit Family, Going for a Burton, more mockery of Sports coverage, Bill gets embroiled with a shell fish in the sentimental ditty Taking My Oyster For Walkies, a pre-Python edition of Blackmail (or Fishpaste), Jack Mulberry, a pre-Goodies Rock with a Policeman, Dentistry.

SHOW THREE

The Army Sense of Humour... or lack of... during Drilling, Pots and Puns, The Good Old Days and Kirk Douglas swashbuckling with The Vikings.

SHOW FOUR

Roy Plumley reinvented for the laughter-starved: Desert Island Jokes, a Report on Schools, the You'll Feel Much Worse song, Police Message, Reunion, Ole song, and Incompetence, the failed life story of the Arkwright Family.

SHOW FIVE

Experiments in Sound, Joke Swapping report, Bill's sublime sing-a-song, finger-clicking, finger-licking Here Comes the One-Man Band, the John Cleese Recipe, Bank Loan, Keep Fit Class including the I'm Tougher Than You song, 10,000 BC.

SHOW SIX

Bits and Pieces from various comedy shows or cheaper and cheaper laughs, Sir Ruddy Shame, The Facts of Money, the I Wish You Love song, Let's Hear About It: Cauliflower, Bill's post-dentist number Has Anybody Seen My Teeth?, The Ghost of McMuckle Manse.

SHOW SEVEN

Graeme tries to deliver the Football Results but Bill's rowdy supporter breaks in, Squealbase Motoring Show with Tim and Jo bantering over the best vehicle, Cleese resurrects Frost's courier material for a speedy Continental Coach Trip, Bill's love letter to singing nun Julie Andrews, Operation Chocolate.

SHOW EIGHT

Forgotten Folklore, Theatre Bar, a touch of the Tom Lehrer's with the song Persecuting Pigeons in Trafalgar Square, John and Mary Have Breakfast in Bed – the filthy swines, operatic antics with El Budgerigar and a foreign legion romp through Beau Legs.

SHOW NINE

GPO Spokesman, The Kevin Mousetrap Show, Louis Armstrong again with the song What a Wonderful World, a reprise of At Last the 1948 Show's Take Your Clothes Off, a musical walk around the talented animal inhabitants of Melody Farm, Warning to Motorists and Macbeth according to Garden and Oddie.

SHOW 10

Facetious Patient, Problem Corner, The Doctor: Bad Eyes, Bounce, Bounce, Bounce, gets the nation singing and, indeed, bouncing, the one thing the show didn't need: a Spot the Joke Competition, and the beloved Angus Prune is reinvented for a castaways adventure in Robinson Prunestone.

SHOW 11

Puzzle Corner, The Countryside in Spring, Cows Talking, We're Going to a Football Match musical number, Controversy: Pacifism and the Roaring Twenties.

SHOW 12

Just half a minute with the Thirty Second Theatre production of Retribution, Oil Riggers in the Desert, The Headmaster's Daughter, Chartered Accountant song, the Doctor on getting fat, and bare-faced, bare-back riding with Lady Godiva.

SHOW 13

A Tribute to Cinema including the song Let's Laugh, Censorship by Dubbing, a belated but much welcome revival of The Curse of the Flying Wombat and the seemingly endless showbiz song The Show Must Go On and On and On and On and On.

TIM BROOKE-TAYLOR, GRAEME GARDEN, DAVID HATCH, JO KENDALL, BILL ODDIE, JOHN CLEESE (missed Show Six). Written by Graeme Garden and Bill Oddie. Music by the Dave Lee Group. Produced by Humphrey Barclay and Peter Titheradge. Sundays, 14 April–7 July 1968, Radio 2.

SPECIAL:

DICK CINDERELLA UP THE BEANSTALK… OR SOMETHING… AND HIS CAT

A classic hour-long Christmas pantomime from the team including a healthy round-up of classic series five songs, Spring Spring Spring, We're Going to a Football Match, I Love You and Julie Andrews, alongside new items, The Music of the Dawn, We're All Going to Die and the seasonal offering, Hope You're Had a Very Merry Christmas.

TIM BROOKE-TAYLOR, JOHN CLEESE, GRAEME GARDEN, DAVID HATCH, JO KENDALL, BILL ODDIE. Written by Graeme Garden and Bill Oddie. Music by the Dave Lee Group. Produced by David Hatch and Peter Titheradge. Thursday 26 December 1968, Radio 2.

SERIES SIX

So successful were the team that television beckoned with bigger pay cheques and wider exposure. The reality of Python and the Goodies was just months away and spelt the end for *I'm Sorry I'll Read That Again* and, as such, the end of an era for the major popularity of comedy on radio. As it was, the gang had already tackled the small screen with the likes of *Twice a Fortnight* and *Broaden Your Mind*, and this new-found experience gave them acres more confidence and a polished sheen to their comedy. The BBC radio bods were none too impressed. If Bill Oddie's scripts called for certain, unusual requirements an oft-repeated phrase would be, 'There once was a programme called *The Goon Show* and they don't work for us any more, so don't get uppity with us!' So there! The familiar Goodies personae were more or less intact now with, notably, Tim Brooke-Taylor milking audience reaction and gaining mock, and as often as not genuine, frustration from Cleese. More importantly, Brooke-Taylor could drag the audience on to his side with heartfelt pleas of helplessness. To the patriotic strains of *Rule Britannia* he would profess himself as merely an actor who only needs to act. Cricklewood was just round the corner. In fact, his most decried character, Spot the dog, featured in the serial, Professor Prune and the Electric Trousers, which closed each edition of this series – the team returning to *Dr Who* territory just as Patrick Troughton rounded off his tenure.

SHOW ONE

New Rules, Dave's Diary with the Knees song, Three Babies – the Majorca sketch.

HAIRDRESSING CAMP FOR THE NEW YORK MARKET – DAVID HATCH, TIM BROOKE-TAYLOR, BILL ODDIE, JOHN CLEESE AND JEAN HART IN *CAMBRIDGE CIRCUS* OFF BROADWAY

SHOW TWO
Pick of the Bunch, Army Report, the Late Football Result, the Hovercraft Ride song.

SHOW THREE
Global Time Check, Population Explosion, Fog Warning, a musical tribute to the world's favourite disc jockey – We Love Jimmy Young, The Psychiatrist, down the folk song path with On Ilkla' Moor Baht 'At, Party Political Message.

SHOW FOUR
Tommy the Tuba, Hobbies, the Oliver Cromwell song featuring lead vocals by your own, your very own, John Cleese, Reuben the Farm Hand.

SHOW FIVE
Bill turns on the Hughie for a Talent Contest, Transport through the Ages, the song She's Gone, a TV Quiz host can't shake his media personality while relaxing at home, from Franco-romantic to whispered croak singing with Charles Aznovoice.

SHOW SIX
The Petticoat Whine, Report on Industry, Bill's impossible tartan dream song If Mao Tse-Tung Were a Scotsman.

SHOW SEVEN
Dramatised German Lesson, Survey on Money and the Baby Samba.

SHOW EIGHT
All My Yesterdays, Sports Yawn, street directions set to music in Marcella's Lane, John and Mary get confused with a chat about children, a Paranormal Message, Here Are the Nudes.

SHOW NINE
And now a choice of listening, the introduction of a new concept in broadcasting history – Radio Prune, Bill's 1967 Radio One retro retread of the Move's Flowers in the Rain produces the cheerful breezer Listening to the Flowers, The Big Quiz.

SHOW 10

Shopping News, Report on Housing, Carry Me Back to Europe song.

SHOW 11

The Great Cities travelogues: London, the Reptile Joke, the Auto Destructive Rag.

SHOW 12

Going For a Gong, The Aristocrats, Shakespeare gets heavy with the rock version of Henry V.

SHOW 13

Love, Sex and Marriage, Denmark Street song.

TIM BROOKE-TAYLOR, JOHN CLEESE, GRAEME GARDEN, DAVID HATCH, JO KENDALL, BILL ODDIE. Written by Graeme Garden and Bill Oddie with additional material from Tim Brooke-Taylor, John Cleese, David Hatch and Jo Kendall. Music by the Dave Lee Group. Produced by David Hatch and Peter Titheradge. Sundays, 12 January–6 April 1969, Radio 1 and 2.

SPECIAL:
THE I'M SORRY I'LL READ THAT AGAIN CHRISTMAS SHOW

A no frills Christmas rampage with the team, sending up carol singers with Tim's angelic cherub and Bill's gloriously ranting protestor – 'Shut up!' – and the sainted traditions of Christmas at the BBC with recorded message after recorded message after recorded message – even Bill's miffed listener is on a loop tape. A vote of confidence for the veggie movement comes from Graeme's deceptively relished plug for dead turkeys and Bill continues the ghoulish educational programme with the priceless Old Turkey Strangler song. They just don't make 'em like they used to as Christmases of Yesterday proves with the post-*1948* Yorkshiremen, post-Buffies from *Broaden Your Mind* and stuffiness of the future Goodies, (complaining about all these 'modern, long-haired pansy hens!' and the like), while the tail-end of the decade *Give Peace a Chance* motto from Lennon, is comically reflected in the John and Yoko sketch. Christmas Round the World takes a whistle stop journey through the changing face of Yuletide across the globe including another Lennon-like number Hari Krishna, and while the *Carry On* gang were doing the low-brow version, Tim, Graeme, Bill and the rest presented their own slant on Charles Dickens with a Christmas Carrot. Tim's breaking up at his awful lines is a moment to cherish.

TIM BROOKE-TAYLOR, GRAEME GARDEN, DAVID HATCH, JO KENDALL, BILL ODDIE. Written by Graeme Garden and Bill Oddie. Music by the Dave Lee Group. Produced by David Hatch and Peter Titheradge. Thursday 25 December 1969, Radio 1 and 2.

SERIES SEVEN

By common consent the finest series of *I'm Sorry I'll Read That Again*. This season was billed as 'A New Improved Whiter-Than-Blue Radio Wash-Out'. With the fiendish creation of a concept pirate radio station, Radio Prune, the programmes did for radio what *Monty Python's Flying Circus* and later *Rutland Weekend Television*, would do for television. With moans from the BBC, the dreaded spectre of commercial radio, all the expected celebrity impressions and an even thicker spread of puns per second, these were non-stop 30 minutes of pure insane genius. Cleese, as was his wont, wasn't available for all the recordings, but the famous five kept a tight ship and the scripts were arguably the best of all. Importantly, in terms of the Goodies development, November 1970 was fast approaching and the ideas for the new television series were already in place. Tim's patriotic, Bill's anarchistic and Graeme's scientific boffin stormed through Radio Prune's full frontal radio policy, even previewing the classic jingles and Garden 'Boom's!' later featured in *Radio Goodies*.

SHOW ONE

New Look Radio Times, BBC Cutback, get out your jingle for the Full Frontal Radio song, Radio Prune reveals its audience manifesto, the BBC stuffed shirts rant on about censorship, a lavish, limp-wristed stab at The Taming of the Shrew.

SHOW TWO

Radio Prune Goes commercial with Tim's Fairy Puff Man Advert just before appearing in Episode One of *The Goodies*, the entire varied radio audience of England is catered for with the religious hip funky beat of Home This Afternoon a Go-Go, the stupidity of the British housewife is unmasked with a two-for-one soap powder swap ad, Commercial News, Sing Us a Song, Chaucerian antics with t'Graeme Garden's t'grouchy father and t'Bill Oddie on t'crest of t'camp wave as an incognito Prince for t'Canterbury Tales meets t'ducking stool witch-finder general play.

SHOW THREE

Top of the Charts, Countrywide, the garbled News with Eddie Waring, another Fairy Puff ad, Letters, Soap Opera, El Tarantula advert, Commercial Trial, the very noisy salute to the Barron Knights: Silence with Bill and Goodie chorus, an exposure of the General Post Office.

SHOW FOUR

Contrary to popular belief, the previous programme didn't exist, Soap Opera 2, Nudes Room, Forthcoming

Programmes, the peerless song Ironing My Goldfish, Tales of the Circus.

SHOW FIVE

David Hatch aka Patrick Bore and The Stars at Night, Tim gets literal as the Wireless Doctor, The 9 O'Clock Honours List, Graeme staggers through the News in Welsh, Minority Programmes, the classic beyond words Musical Football Results – check out that Arsenal score, the sublime *Sgt Pepper* response: Nigel Carter-Smith's Society Band lets Bill loose on a fab musical trip, and loads of tuck, sexual references, food gags, overplaying, Hatch outbursts and flagrant camp for Billy Bunter of Greyfriar's School. Interestingly, when the Goodies reformed for a Radio 2 *Bunter* serial, Graeme played Squeal, as here, and Bill, of course, toned down his stunning Bunter. What a wheeze…

SHOW SIX

The boundaries of expected programming are discussed with the common thought about the listening people we will be offending, Motoring Flash, Complaints, the Rolf Harris Dirty Song Book, Three Babies and the NSPCC Inspector, Tonight it's the uncertain celebrity guest show: Is This Your Life?, If You Have Seen This Man, the musical masterpiece Stuffing the Gibbon, The 3.17 to Cleethorpes.

SHOW SEVEN

Militant Tim gets them all out for the Listeners' Strike and to make sure you don't have it on for 30 minutes it's heralded by the Angus Prune tune, Listeners' Oath. Tim pleas for the rights of the little old lady listener much to Bill's disinterest. The Cooking Segment, David Hatch in the Nudes Room, a bit of Bill satire as army ads are allowed but smoking ads aren't, Bill's old soldier gets Blimpish about the battle fields of cricket with the rousing number We Are the Lads of the MCC. Bill's irritating singer, Jimmy Saville, is finally shot for the good of mankind and the glorious reign of Henry VIII gets the full treatment with Graeme's huffed and puffed King Hal stealing the scene, Tim reinventing that screaming biddy Lady Constance as a sex-starved Lady Anne of Cleavage and Bill hamming it up with 'ooh!'s and 'Noooo!'s all over the place as Katherine 'Frankie' Howard. Glorious.

SHOW EIGHT

There's No Business Like Show Business, Common Market Committee, International Music Hall, the censored version of Tom Jones, It's a real knockout with Guerres Sans Frontiers, Honours List, Wonderful Noises song, Jorrocks.

SHOW NINE

Critics, Ashamed, Weather Report, Set Up a Sketch Competition, Rearrangement of Programmes, Dublin Folk Song Dance and Drinking Society Song, Horror Story.

SHOW 10

The racist question arising from the Black and White Minstrels prompts an oriental version (Yellow and White) and British (Pink and White), Cleese's whining David Frost hosts the Radio Prune Awards and flogs the latest headline, General Flies Back to Front. Bill's sublime Beach Boys meets Northern By 'Eck angst song Bradford Girls sets up elements of *Black Pudding Bertha* and delights in wonderful close harmony from the team, The Harder They Fall the More They Hurt Themselves.

SHOW 11

Teapot, Review of the Pops, the Julie Andrews Dirty Song Book, The Money Programme, the Kenneth Wolstenholme and Andy Pandy song, Captain Nemo goes from hero to zero in 20,000 Leaks Under the Sea.

SHOW 12

Combined Holiday, Night with the Stars, Holiday News, Hogmanay, Cleese comments on an hilarious Brian Rix Farce in terms of a sporting event commentary, while Tim is possessed by the ghost of Christmas yet to come as he mocks the medium he would later excel in, Bill's Tillybourne folk and madrigal society present Football Chant, more Eddie Waring and the complex tale of Oedipus 'my feet are killing me!' Rex.

SHOW 13

A represented compilation of classic songs from the past with the ethos of Prune entertainment being put to music for Full Frontal Radio and the epic Raymond Nostril Story featuring The Ferret Song, Stuffing the Gibbon, Silence, Nigel Carter-Smith's Society Band, The Rhubarb Tart Song, Sing Us a Song, I'm Gonna Make It and We Are the Lads of the MCC. The end of the series, the end of the road, the end of the station with Radio Prune Close-Down.

TIM BROOKE-TAYLOR, GRAEME GARDEN, DAVID HATCH, JO KENDALL, BILL ODDIE, JOHN CLEESE (missed Show Seven). Written by Graeme Garden and Bill Oddie with John Cleese and David Hatch. Music by the Dave Lee Group. Produced by David Hatch and Peter Titheradge. Sundays, 15 February–8 May 1970, Radio 2.

SPECIAL

Between the end of Series Seven and this End of Year

Special, *The Goodies* had hit the television screen. With Cleese busy as a Python, the central trio busy on a trandem and, more to the point, the writing core of Bill and Graeme wrapped up in their own series scripts, *I'm Sorry I'll Read That Again* was fast coming to a close. This flirty revue featured the delights of Radio Prune's full frontal radio in drag, catchphrases and the controversial Miss World contest featuring the song Les Girls. Bawdy Christmas songs are censored, there's a lengthy retrospective of the year 1970 and a full-blown reinterpretation of David Lean's *Dr Zhivago*.

TIM BROOKE-TAYLOR, JOHN CLEESE, GRAEME GARDEN, DAVID HATCH, JO KENDALL, BILL ODDIE. Written by Graeme Garden and Bill Oddie. Music by the Dave Lee Group. Produced by David Hatch and Peter Titheradge. Thursday 31 December 1970, Radio 4.

SERIES EIGHT

David Hatch, now a fully on-board BBC back-room boy, managed the almost impossible and reunited the entire cast for one last season at the end of 1973. Three years since the squad had gone their semi-separate ways, Tim, Bill and Graeme were now firmly established, Cleese had just temporarily abandoned life as a Python to team up with Les Dawson, and the only reason a new series was considered was due to gaps in all six performers' schedules coinciding, much against the odds. In many ways, the references to each other's work in the interim, notably Tim's rival radio venture *Hello Cheeky*, joyful mockery of the radio medium and a healthy disregard for each other's feelings, gave this a wonderful sense of the experienced slumming it for old time's sake. The scripts were also of the highest quality. Cleese rants at his fellow cast members and audience like never before, much hautiness is made of the lad's panel game rip-off – condemned as I'm Sorry I Don't Have a Script by Cleese – and even Tim's ever-popular Lady Constance cannot make her scripted appearance because the actor has forgotten how to do the voice… even though he'd been doing it almost every other week somewhere in *The Goodies*! An emergency throat operation is essential for the great Lady to make an electric appearance at the close of the opening episode.

Did You Know? As with other national favourites like The Goon Show and Hancock's Half Hour, BBC Transcription Services issued 74 episodes of I'm Sorry I'll Read That Again on long-playing records to various radio stations for broadcasting outside of the UK. As well as the Goodies and the Pythons resurrecting musical numbers from the series, Bill Oddie issued a solo album of his I'm Sorry I'll Read That Again

numbers entitled Distinctly Oddie. Also during the life of the series, between 1964 and 1970, Oddie released four singles (Nothing Better To Do, The Knitting Song, Jimmy Young and On Iikla Moor Baht 'At) which used I'm Sorry… songs as well as original compositions. In 1976 he reunited with John Cleese for the Bradley single Superspike.

SHOW ONE

The old team is back together again, including the singing brillo-pad, Bill Oddie, found somewhere in Hampstead. The All-Purpose Sitcom, BBC Controller of Programmes, the resurrection of Radio Prune, Bill is convinced the word terrapin is funny and he's got a little ditty, The Terrapin Song, to prove it, epic adventure with Oddie's 'ecky thump Nanook of the North and Lawrence of the Antarctic – On Ice!

SHOW TWO

Cleese gives Robert Robinson lessons as the chairman of *Ask the Family*, comedy formulation is mocked with So You Think You've Got a Feed Line. Prune Forum, Tim presents the culture discussion programme A Kick in the Arts, Twerp Special, Bill adopts a limp-wristed stance for a pre-Tim rendition of Cactus in My Y-Fronts and the 'so good they did it twice' Sherlock Holmes meets Jack the Ripper Victorian nightmare…

SHOW THREE

One Channel Stereo, Radio Mindless, Saville's Travilles, Fight the Flab, a competition, Square Table, the almighty Sick Man Blues and a legal loop-hole skipping science-fiction parody – St*r Trek.

SHOW FOUR

Audio Porno Fair, What's My Kink?, the Masochist's Rag, Search for the Nile.

SHOW FIVE

The finals of the Miss United Prune competition, a radio scriptwriter is fired, Festival of Light, Toy Symphony, The Song of the South.

SHOW SIX

By-Election Results, New Programmes, babyish longings in Nappy Love, Oklahoma.

SHOW SEVEN

The Royal Family, The Wedding of the Year, Eddie Waring makes a meal of It's a Cock-Up, Russell Harty Plus, Alice in Wonderland.

SHOW EIGHT

Ministerial Broadcast, Childhood Remembered, enough of prunes it's now the station for that ultimate funny word Radio Terrapin, the Just My Bill song,

David Hatch Down and Out, Chloe musical moment, The Colditz Story.

TIM BROOKE-TAYLOR, JOHN CLEESE, GRAEME GARDEN, DAVID HATCH, JO KENDALL, BILL ODDIE. Written by Graeme Garden and Bill Oddie. Music by the Dave Lee Group. Produced by David Hatch and Peter Titheradge. Sundays, 4 November–23 December 1973, Radio 2.

Cult status

When the final ferret was put to bed and the team went on to other things, *I'm Sorry I'll Read That Again* became one of the BBC's most valuable radio classics. Frequently repeated with the likes of Roy Hudd, David Jacobs and, even, David Hatch himself, resurrecting it for Radio 2's irregular *Smash of the Day*, *Comedy Hour* slot and various other nostalgia interludes, the Angus Prune fan base was vocal indeed. But that wasn't quite the end of the road…

SPECIAL

Just when the world thought it had heard the last of Radio Prune, the 25th anniversary in 1989 was marked with an extra special hour-long edition broadcast on Christmas Day. For Cleese is was the culmination of a long year, marking another celebrated anniversary – 20 years of Monty Python – and saying farewell to his closest writing partner, Graham Chapman. For everybody else, it was one last chance to don silly voices, talk about ferrets and get paid for a huge reunion party. It all starts with the one and only David Hatch tackling his Bond dialogue, 'The name's Hatch…' and introducing the sound nobody wanted to hear again: The Second World War air-raid signal wailing into the Angus Prune tune. One of the most spine-tinglingly, effective moments ever heard in a BBC comedy show… Back to the plot and Hatch faces an emergency meeting of the BBC Governors. Nothing's changed, the news is still comic, the *Today* programme resurrects Oddie's classic Spring Spring Spring (complete with John's totally disgruntled five-bar gate reaction) and the swords of satire are as sharp as ever – old favourite *The Clitheroe Kid* is reflected against today's answer, *The Krankies*… But, at the end of the day, a decision is needed and only one thing can save the BBC from total collapse: the recycling of old *I'm Sorry I'll Read That Again* scripts. Writers Graeme Garden and Bill Oddie are tracked down to a block of flats recently converted into a disused warehouse in London's Docklands. Eager to please – Hatch dismisses them as merely a doctor and a bird-watcher now – Graeme, never one to say die, has already written something this morning: a prescription! Keen on a reunion, the lads are not convinced that Jo Kendall – alias, as she now is, award-winning star Meryl Streep – will be willing to return. In a gloriously ad-libbed moment of high-pitched campery Graeme gets Bill cracking up. Convinced he's turning into some recognisable character Graeme pleas – 'Let's hope it's somebody funny!' John Cleese, of course, multimillionaire Python and *A Fish Called Wanda* sex symbol, is now an eccentric recluse, trying to console himself aboard the space shuttle Ferret 1. But he seems happy to have a bash if he can do an audio version of the silly walk and perform the Ferret Song… Besides, he wants to perform a new John and Mary sketch, Eleanor and Armadillos. Demands met, it's just down to Tim Brooke-Taylor for the complete case reunion. Bill seems to have forgotten him but Graeme helpfully reminiscences – naturally Bill is only pulling his partner's leg, 'Just my little joke!' 'That's him!' Allegedly having left comedy far behind – you remember, we did 10 years of *The Goodies* with him, he gave it up just before that… Tim is now resident of Milton Sitcom, a dreaded place where vicars and bosses are always arriving for tea and every entrance must begin with 'Hello darling, I'm home!' The gang back together proper, Bill and Graeme deliver the new script – an almost word for word repeat of the 1973 classic Jack the Ripper. All the beloved groaners are in place – Cleese and Garden discussing the fog 'A real pe… pe…' 'Peasouper?' 'No thanks I've just been!' and relentless musical lapses into China Town – and all's right with the world. But it's not enough to save the station. A humbled Cleese is mocked and ridiculed by his old chums, the 'hilarious' sound-only silly walk is grudgingly allowed to go ahead and the show grinds to a close… but wait… the BBC is in trouble, it's up for sale at auction and only a mad bloke with more money than sense can save it – John! With Cleese in charge and broadcasting no longer an endangered specimen, he indulges in a ferret barbecue and proudly launches into a tuneless rendition of I've Got a Ferret Sticking Up My Nose. A further helping is promised in 25 years' time, Cleese says, 'I'm Sorry I'll Read That Again… again' for the last time and that, my friends, is how to end a radio treasure on the highest note possible. An emotional and hilarious 60 minutes, it practically begs for another series but that, I suppose, was the point. It was all from a very different age but still pricelessly funny for all that. God bless 'em.

TIM BROOKE-TAYLOR, JOHN CLEESE, GRAEME GARDEN, DAVID HATCH, JO KENDALL, BILL ODDIE. Written by Graeme Garden and Bill Oddie. Music by the Dave Lee Group. Produced by Richard Wilcox. Monday 25 December 1989, Radio 2.

I'M SORRY, I'LL READ THAT AGAIN: the records

Choice extracts from Series Two and Three of 'the wonder show of BBC Radio' were first released in arrangement with the BBC in 1967. The record has been re-released twice since. Classics like John and Mary are joined by an extract from the Bill and Graeme serial masterpiece The Curse of the Flying Wombat and several priceless Oddie musical interludes. The sleeve notes were written in suitably proud but ever so slightly tongue-in-cheek style by producer Humphrey Barclay and the original issue included tongue-in-cheek, thumb-nail biographies of the cast. Extracts from Series Six and Seven with an apologetic sleeve note from David Hatch were released in 1978.

TIM BROOKE-TAYLOR as the auctioneer, Robin Hood, Baby Cyril, Bill, Tim Brown-Windsor, Lady Constance de Coverlet and Wong the Supply-keeper. JOHN CLEESE as the Doctor, Mary's John, Little John (Little John!), Sir Angus of the Prune, the MC, Baby Rupert, Captain Cleese and Wong Tu. GRAEME GARDEN as Alan a'Gabriel and the Sheriff of Nottingham. DAVID HATCH as Will Scarlett, Baby Hugh, Mr Hatch, Colonel Clutch-Featheringhaugh and all the dull bits. JO KENDALL as John's Mary, Maid Marion, Cyril's mother, Jean, Fiona Rabbit-Vacuum and all the other female parts except those played by Tim Brooke-Taylor. BILL ODDIE as the patient, Friar Tuck, Grimbling and Nosebone, and he sings the songs. THE DAVE LEE GROUP. **Side One:** The Auctioneer: opening (written by Tim Brooke-Taylor), The Day After Tomorrow's World (written by Graeme Garden), The Doctor (written by Bill Oddie and John Cleese), BLIMPHT (written by Bill Oddie), John and Mary (written by John Cleese and Bill Oddie), Robin Hood (written by Graeme Garden and John Cleese). **Side Two:** Identkit Gal (written by Bill Oddie), Baby Talk (written by David Hatch), Family Favourites (written by Tim Brooke-Taylor), The Curse of the Flying Wombat (written by Graeme Garden and Bill Oddie), closing announcements and Angus Prune Tune (written by Dave Lee, Lizzie Evans and Humphrey Barclay). Music by Dave Lee. Production team Len France, Tony Wilson, Andy Cartledge and Lizzie Evans. Edited by Bert Fisher. Musical arrangements by Leon Cohen. Front cover photograph by Lewis Morley. PMC 7024 Parlophone. AX 701433 EMI/Axis. OUM 2119-OC One-Up label. 054 97394M EMI 1967.

Did You Know? The News In Welsh was featured on the comedy charity record We Are Most Amused (RTD 2067).

TIM BROOKE-TAYLOR, JOHN CLEESE, GRAEME GARDEN, DAVID HATCH, JO KENDALL, BILL ODDIE, THE DAVE LEE GROUP. Written by Graeme Garden and Bill Oddie. Songs by Bill Oddie and Dave Lee. Arrangements Leon Cohen. Sound Max Alcock. Edited by Bert Fisher. Special thanks John Cassels and Bob Oliver Rogers. Record production by David Hatch. Opening Credits Tim, Graeme, David, Jo, Bill and the Dave Lee Group, Full Frontal Radio and Prune Manifesto and Buffers, Critics, Motoring Flash – David, Quickie – Cleese/Hatch weather report could do better, Honours List and News in Welsh and Minority Programmes – Graeme, David, Jo and the Dave Lee Group, Home this Afternoon A Go Go – John, Graeme, David, Bill and the Dave Lee Group, newsflash – David, Listening to the Flowers – Bill, cast chorus and the Dave Lee Group: You're Dancing On My Heart Bryan/Meyer-Feldman, Opening – John, David and the Dave Lee Group, Talent Contest – Bye, Bye Blackbird – Henderson/Dixon – FDH, Half A Sixpence – Heneker/Brittania, The Sound of Music – Rodgers/Hammerstein/Williamson, Side By Side – Woods/L Wright, Eddie Waring Impersonation – Graeme, David and the Dave Lee Group – Bill: Kern/Wodehouse/Hammerstein – Chappell, Sick Man Blues – Bill, cast chorus and the Dave Lee Group, Taming of the Shrew – John's I've Got a   Feeling I'm Falling Link/Waller/Rose – Campbell-Connelly and Closing Credits. REH 342 BBC Records 1978.

I'M SORRY I'LL READ THAT AGAIN: the BBC audio collection

On the demise of the BBC record label, the corporation were quick to include *I'm Sorry I'll Read That Again* on the new, cassette-only audio collection. Counting the three pilot broadcasts, six specials and 95 regular editions, *I'm Sorry I'll Read That Again* ran to an amazing 104 programmes. Bill Oddie and Tim Brooke-Taylor appeared in all of them, while Graeme Garden notched up 74 appearances. The only surviving tape from the first batch of

three programmes has already been released by the BBC while a further 14 editions have been issued to date. Although the BBC archives have several gaps in their library (Shows Four and Five from Series One and Show Five from Series Two), there are currently 86 editions still available to the BBC for commercial release.

I'm Sorry I'll Read That Again (ZBBC 1100), released 31 December 1990: editions from 9 June 1968, 22 March 1970, 5 April 1970 and the very last original programme. I'm Sorry I'll Read That Again 2 (ZBBC 1329) released 1992: includes the first pilot episode, an edition from 9 May 1966 and the hour-long 25th anniversary special. I'm Sorry I'll Read That Again 3 (ZBBC 1723) released 4 September 1995: editions from 26 May 1968, 22 February 1970, 3 May 1970, 11 November 1973. I'm Sorry I'll Read That Again 4 (ZBBC 2005) released 4 August 1997: editions from 1 March 1970, 19 April 1970, 4 November 1973, 2 December 1973. *The Clown Jewels* (ZBBC 1752), a compilation of great comedy moments released in 1995 hosted by Ken Bruce features an extract from the second volume. An *I'm Sorry* extract was included on the 1998 BBC double cassette and compact disc release, *Sporting Laughs*, in which commentator John Inverdale trawled through the Beeb's sporting comedy archives. John Cleese at the Beeb 1999.

I'M SORRY I'LL READ THAT AGAIN: the classic scripts

The writer's choice, as Graeme Garden and Bill Oddie present the pick of their celebrated radio scripts. Tellingly, four of the selected episodes come from the final, most polished series, with complete scripts for editions broadcast on November 4, 11, 18 and 25 of 1973. The main sketch material from the New Year's Eve special from 1970 is also included.

Javelin Books, paperback, 1985.

IN PURSUIT OF EXCELLENCE: AN AFTERNOON FOR THE JOHN F KENNEDY LIBRARY

A one-off performance by the *Cambridge Circus* team in Connecticut on 15 November 1964.

TIM BROOKE-TAYLOR, GRAHAM CHAPMAN, JOHN CLEESE, JO KENDALL, JONATHAN LYNN, BILL ODDIE.

IN CONVERSATION WITH...

An informal radio chat show format with Paul Jackson, BBC Controller of Light Entertainment, chatting to some key comedy writer and performer figures within BBC Light Entertainment. The major coup for the series of six shows was the gathering of half of *I'm Sorry I Haven't a Clue* and more importantly, two-thirds of the Goodies in the shape of Tim Brooke-Taylor and Graeme Garden. The two discussed Cambridge, Goodies and all that with perception and good humour.

Thursday 14 October 1999, Radio 4.

IN SICKNESS AND IN HEALTH

Alf's trick with his late wife's old wheelchair and his new jacket full of military ribbons leads him and Arthur into the money… for a short time at least. Graeme Garden turned on the sophisticated charm as a political chappie a decade before *If I Ruled the World*.

Alf Garnett WARREN MITCHELL Rita UNA STUBBS Mrs Hollingbery CARMEL McSHARRY Arthur ARTHUR ENGLISH Winston EAMONN WALKER Political candidate GRAEME GARDEN Gate-Keeper RON PEMBER Mr Kiltel RENU SETNA Invalid MICHAEL RIPPER. Written by Johnny Speight. Director Richard Boden. Producer Roger Race. Thursday 20 August 1987, BBC1.

AN INSPECTOR CALLS

Graeme Garden starred as the Inspector in this 1986 production of JB Priestly's classic play at the Royal Exchange Theatre, Manchester.

IT RUNS IN THE FAMILY

A touring production of the classic farce with Tim Brooke-Taylor starring alongside Lionel Blair. The production played the Grand Opera House, Belfast, from 25 September until 30 September 1995.

IT'S MARTY

Having been considered *At Last the 1948 Show*'s weak link by David Frost, it was ironic when Marty Feldman proved him impressively wrong by almost immediately landing his own series. Head-hunted by the BBC and rejoicing in his comic independence, his *1948* co-stars Chapman and Cleese were busy working out Python, while Tim Brooke-Taylor was invited to form part of Marty's supporting team. Akin to Spike Milligan's *Q* shows, Marty was the star here, gathering a hand-picked cast and crew around him before the ensemble madness of Python and Goodies usurped him within 18 months. Indeed, Chapman and Cleese had several submitted sketches for the Marty programmes rejected because they were *1948*-style team efforts rather than focused, individual pieces. John Junkin filled in very credibly for the bewildered authority figures of John Cleese, Roland MacLeod played the Terry Jones game as insane bowler-hatted businessmen and disconcerting officers, while Mary Miller succeeded in combining glamour with a real flare for absurdist comedy. But it was Tim Brooke-Taylor who shone brightest opposite Marty's bedevilled expression. As well as contributing written material, Tim threw himself into his bizarre character work assignments. Most memorably of all was the continually whining, insane, doddery old lady, Cynthia, alongside Marty's aged rant machine. One watches the material today and gets an inkling where Harry Enfield's Wobbly Old Ladies came from, while the entire concept of old people milking society's respect for

mischievous play is a less malicious parallel of the Old Gits. In the Travel Centre sketch John Junkin quietly faces Tim's mounting frustration, screaming that her husband 'died in the war for people like you!' The irritating couple resurfaced for a Marriage Guidance sketch and later, in Series Two, the classic Post Office encounter. Junkin's assistant again faces deliberate misunderstanding (orders of tea or light ale) and wild memories (Tim's losing appearance in the 1923 Olympics Long Jump). This character was Tim's finest work for the series but in a diverse, surprisingly brief run, Tim played distressed young men, television presenters, a pompous 'clothed' nudist, a member of the 1966 World Cup Squad and even a fly. Tim played the stilted host of Film Parade celebrating the ultra-bizarre expressionist, propaganda and biopic career of German genius Fritz von Angst. Thanks to the 'star' policies and also Feldman's Buster Keaton fixation, dictating that a vast quantity of material was inspired, very expensive (allegedly the biggest budget for any BBC comedy show), self-contained, silent slapstick vignettes, Tim's appearances are often minimal. The Vet's Waiting Room sees him turning on blind panic as Marty's seedy bore drones on about the huge creature he has concealed in his basket. Tim need do little but react with terror-stricken face – but there's no one who can do it better. In Friend or Foe, Tim's nervous Bedrock Nuclear Research Centre sentry, Godfrey, goes through the 'halt, who goes there…' stuff with John Junkin's frightfully smooth baddie, while Flies delights in Tim's Northern Harold opposite Marty's cockney George. Clad in fly suits, chatting about life, the universe and everything, conversing on the ceiling and reflecting human pub talk in thoughts about the neighbourhood going to seed – with a family of black beetles moving in – all the major points are addressed: Why are we here? Why do flies jump about all the time? And where do humans go in winter? Marty's the leader, suggesting a go at the milk jug and some cheese creeping, before John Junkin's newspaper ruins the party. An intriguing, reflective bit of writing, performed with gusto – check out Tim's gloriously sustained pork pie line fluff. Father and Son equally illustrates Marty's skill away from self-indulgent mime, with Tim facing a bumbling, sex-shy explanation on the birds and the bees before, finally, admitting he's got a lady pregnant. The Headmaster sketch again calls on Tim's nervous performance, as the shot and wounded Master Thompson desperately trying to

BILL ODDIE PROUDLY WEARS THE SWEATER TO ADVERTISE HIS LATEST SINGLE, *THE KNITTING SONG*, ON AN APPEARANCE ON *THANK YOUR LUCKY STARS*

cast breaking away from a medical skit and addresses the audience for a curtain call – this was ground-breaking stuff. It may have steered Tim away from Monty Python but allowed him to sharpen his craft opposite a master and prepare to launch himself into *The Goodies*.

Did You Know? *Although the original tapes of the show sometimes have the title of* It's Marty Feldman *or simply* Marty, *the Radio Times and collectors settle for* It's Marty *as the all-encompassing title for the 12 classic half hours. Indeed an April 1968 Radio Times featured an article heralding the new Marty Feldman and Tim Brooke-Taylor series. This and subsequent pieces in the journal called the show* It's Marty. *Only two complete editions – Series One, Episodes Two and Five – survive intact, although the Montreaux compilation and several independent sketches are also retained. Pye records released a compilation of Series One on the album* Marty.

Series One: Mondays, 29 April–3 June 1968, BBC2. **Series Two:** Mondays, 9 December 1968–13 January 1969, BBC2. Written by Marty Feldman and Barry Took with Tim Brooke-Taylor, John Junkin, Graham Chapman, John Cleese, Terry Jones, Michael Palin, Terry Gilliam, Tom Clarke, Peter Dickinson, Dennis King, Phillip Jenkinson and Michael Seddon. Producer Dennis Main Wilson. Director Roger Race.

IT'S MARTY: Montreux compilation

With *It's Marty* having won the Writer's Guild of Great Britain Award for Best Light Entertainment Series and a BAFTA for Best Script, the BBC thought it was a safe bet for the illustrious Montreux Festival. However, this priceless collection was just pipped at the post for the Gold Rose Award, picking up Silver. Obviously for the international market, it concentrated on Marty's visual pieces. As such, Tim Brooke-Taylor appears in just one sketch, the Vet's Waiting Room, with the rest of the show highlighting gems like the Coach Trip, Stuntman 1, the Golfer and A Hard Day's Night.

Did You Know? *The 1968 Christmas Night with the Stars featured a new sketch. The 1969 edition contained a previously broadcast contribution from* It's Marty *Series Two. Although almost forgotten in later years, the BBC repeated the Montreux compilation as part of the Patrick Allen linked* A Day in the Sixties *and further fired up* Marty *interest in 1995 with a specially produced compilation programme hosted by fan Jonathan Ross.* It's Marty Resurrected: Some of the Best of Marty Feldman *was screened on Tuesday 4 July 1995, just before the first ever video release of* It's Marty *material which featured Brooke-Taylor in* Bishop, Travel Agency, Wine Treading, World Cup 1966, Vet's Waiting Room *and* Battle of Britain's Taxis.

With ANN LANCASTER, DENNIS KING, VICKY RICHARDS, SONNY FREEMAN, STEPHANIE HEESOM, MAGGIE LYNTON, MICHAEL PALIN, TERRY JONES, BOB MURPHY. Written by Marty Feldman, Terry Jones, Michael Palin and Barry Took. Monday 17 March 1969, BBC2.

get Marty's sympathetic attention. A Film Noir-style interlude provided a sense of impending danger, shadowy threats, mysterious footsteps and suspenseful music give poor hunted Tim Brooke-Taylor a real fright in this Fritz Lang-esque nightmare. Marty's Sydney Greenstreet-style boss adds to the terror before breaking into camp mode and revealing the set-up as a game of tag! Battle of Britain's Taxis is an ingenious resurrection of World War II RAF banter via a battle of drivers versus pedestrians with Tim as the Richard Attenborough type – young, ambitious and with a young girl to go home to, he looks to the future he doesn't have with real poignancy. But perhaps the most unsung sequence is the seance with Marty's unconvincing spiritualist, Madame Arthur Aldridge ('afternoon believers!') and Tim as the dodgy assistant running through the gamut of play-acting from an Indian warrior to a possessed Mary, Queen of Scots. Like the best of *It's Marty*, it's fall-off-the-chair hilarious. Beating the path towards Python's door with challenges against sketch show conventions – Show Five of the second series ends with the

J

JACK AND THE BEANSTALK

Tim Brooke-Taylor proved a hit during the 1998/1999 pantomime season. For the Goodie fan, it was a treat to see Tim involved with the legendary Beanstalk 25 years after defeating Alfie Bass, and Trevor Bannister added extra comic clout to the production. Rosemary Ford made a fetching principal boy and Robert Powell a deliciously, lip-smacking villain. Tim provided perfect comic relief as the bumbling Simple Simon, the incompetent brother of the hero, making his entrance to *The Goodies Theme*, leading the audience sing song, reading out the birthday cards and dishing out the sweeties.

December 1998. Yvonne Arnaud Theatre, Guildford.

JACKANORY

The perfect voice for this priceless slice of children's story telling, Bill Oddie brought life to the deliciously off-kilter world of Roald Dahl's *The BFG*, aided and abetted by the mighty Bernard Bresslaw as the big fellow himself.

Adapted and directed by David Bell. Monday 14–Friday 18 November 1983, BBC1.

JIM HENSON'S ANIMAL SHOW

Bill Oddie wrote material and four songs for this educational BBC puppet show in 1998.

JIMMY YOUNG/IRISH GET OUT

A Bill Oddie single featuring two reworked numbers previously performed in *I'm Sorry I'll Read That Again*.

F 12903 Decca April 1969.

JOKERS WILD

The ultimate refuge for dreadful jokes, this long-running panel game of sorts recruited the great, good and the well below average comedian and comedy actor to crack a seemingly never-ending collection of funny stories on a given subject. Two teams of three battled it

A YOUNG BILL ODDIE WITH FAG, STRAWS AND A DROP OF THE HARD STUFF

out with outstanding regular contributions from treasured old-timers, Arthur Askey and Ted Ray, ably supported by the droll monologues of Les Dawson and the Jewish, camp queen stumbles of Ray Martine. It was never high art but the succession of class guests – Clive Dunn, Alfred Marks, Milo O'Shea, Jack Smethhurst, Norman Collier – makes it a cherished nostalgia fest. Tim Brooke-Taylor bravely stepped into the wise-cracking forum for several back-to-back filmed appearances. Great turn your brain off and chill entertainment.

Chairman BARRY CRYER. Directed by David Millard, 1971.

JUMBLE

Corny ITV celebrity-based game show hosted by Jeff Stevensen. Faith Brown and Tim Brooke-Taylor went through the motions on Wednesday 20 March 1991.

JUST A MINUTE

Without hesitation, deviation or repetition, Graeme Garden joined regular players Kenneth Williams, Peter Jones and Clement Freud on four of the Radio 4 programmes on 28 October 1975, 7 January and 10 November 1976, and 9 February 1977.

K

L

THE KENNY EVERETT TELEVISION SHOW

Almost 20 years after supporting the manic antics of Marty Feldman, *Hello Cheeky!* chums Tim Brooke-Taylor and John Junkin were together supporting his natural successor in the small screen zany stakes, Kenny Everett. Tim made several guest starring appearances, notably being covered in dubious substances during the What Do You Goo segments, but, arguably, the all-time classic sketch appeared in 1981 and featured Everett as a wild-haired, disgruntled Beethoven, feverishly bastardising his musical art for the two wise-cracking, commercial-geared publishers of Tim and John. Through rants, taunts, musical misunderstanding, bitching about Mozart and continual secondary pep-talking from Tim's Marvin, Everett finally latches on to the advertising glory of selling soap on a rope and presents his *1812 Overturn* with lyrics, 'Soap on a Rope!' The finished plug, with Ken playing the piano with passion and a quartet of naked bathing beauties, including Cleo Rocos of course, is a winner. The clip was included in the BBC's comedy compilation series *Laughter Through the Ages*. A BBC video of Everett material was released in 1999.

Written by Ray Cameron, Barry Cryer and Kenny Everett. Produced and directed by Bill Wilson.

THE KNITTING SONG/AIN'T GOT RHYTHM

An *I'm Sorry I'll Read That Again*-inspired single release from Bill Oddie.

R 5346 Parlophone October 1965.

THE KUNG FU YEARS

A BBC2 evening of martial arts programming hosted by Peter Sellers' man servant, Burt Kwouk, on 24 May 1997, literally kicked off with this documentary. Contributor Bill Oddie, described as 'ornithologist and former comedian' in the press release, discussed the Goodies show *Kung Fu Kapers* and recalled the chap who died laughing at the episode.

THE LADYKILLERS

In the wake of Colin Baker and Robert Powell bringing *Kind Hearts and Coronets* to the stage, this 1999 touring production of the 1955 Ealing black comedy starred Tim Brooke-Taylor as sinister baddie Professor Marcus. As played by Alec Guinness in the film and inspired by the ghoulish persona of Alastair Sim, Tim had two major acting mountains to climb and reached the top with consummate ease. Delightfully injecting the edgy, slightly unhinged, insanity of Guinness, Tim's physical comedy, peerless reactions and continually darting eyes behind his pair of glasses, created a disturbing, humorous and powerful comic villain. Spine-tingling moments permanently etched on the memory from the film – the brilliant call box conversion with the Major, complete with Bocarenni snatch and pleading with the anxious military man to press button 'A', persistently straightening the unstraightenable portrait of the late Captain Wilberforce, the impassioned 'windows are the eyes of the soul' speech, the cricket score/robbery sum newspaper confusion and an underplayed point upstairs as One-Round frantically tried to track down teddy boy Harry – were stunningly recreated on stage. A breath-taking performance within an ensemble cast of great skill. Dulcie Gray, bluffed and bewildered her way through the delightful 'Mrs Lopsided', *Coronation Street*'s slick con-man, Owen Aaronovitch, was brilliant as the fiery, temperamental Herbert Lom figure and *The Brittas Empire*'s Tim Marriott followed in the footsteps of a young Peter Sellers with real bird-loving gusto. Brian Murphy presented a touchingly, believable twist on the nervous, cowardice of Cecil Parker and, best of all the supporting gang, Martin Herdman *was* Danny Green. Bashing his way through the charming, atmospheric set, man-handling most of his fellow cast members and mixing comic stupidity with a real, powerful threat, it was a stunning, hilarious performance. Great for those, like me, who had seen the film far too many times to care to admit, and great for those who had no idea the film had been made.

Did You Know? *A six-page interview with Tim Brooke-Taylor, conducted by Lucie McGuire, was published on the Ceefax Spotlight section at the end of February, plugging the play, paying tribute to Derek Nimmo, celebrating Tim's ex-Goodie pride and still wondering why the BBC have never repeated them! ITV's TeleText service and Victor Olliver for TV Plus, 2 March 1999, also interviewed Tim, while the actor did the radio plug rounds with appearances on Radio 4's Live From London in January, Radio 5 in February and Talk Radio in April.*

Professor Marcus TIM BROOKE-TAYLOR The Major BRIAN MURPHY Mrs Wilberforce DULCIE GRAY Louis OWEN AARONOVITCH Harry TIM MARRIOTT One-Round MARTIN HERDMAN. Director Richard Baron. Performances on tour from 1 March to 22 June 1999.

LARRY GRAYSON'S GENERATION GAME

Campery was rife after Bruce Forsyth and before Jim Davidson, when that dear old queen, Larry Grayson, minced through this hugely enjoyable slice of Saturday evening family fun. Tim Brooke-Taylor was roped in to adjudicate – in the guise of some boffin-type from the ministry – on some outlandish word game in the Eighties.

THE LAW GAME

A baffling legal Radio 2 panel game hosted by *Police 5*'s Shaw Taylor. On 26 March and 2 April 1985, Bill Oddie joined in the tricky case cracking fun with witty verdicts and jolly quips. On Boxing Day 1988, Graeme Garden had a crack and in 1989 the Goodie connection was completed when Tim Brooke-Taylor appeared on the show on 14 and 21 November. Graeme returned on 15 and 22 June 1991.

THE LEAST WORST OF HELLO CHEEKY

A BBC Records release for the very best of the Radio 2 Tim Brooke-Taylor series, *Hello Cheeky*.

Did You Know? *The track Simultaneous Broadcast was featured on the 1977 best of the Beeb collection, Comedy Special – Highlights From the Top BBC Comedy Shows (REH 294 BBC Records).*

REH 189 BBC Records 1976.

LIFE WITH COOPER

The last episode of the first of three seasons for the beloved Tommy Cooper, these scripted, sitcom-format programmes showcased the riotous past of our accident-prone hero. In this edition, it's the problems, hassles and red tape of the Royal Mail that causes all the headaches. In a very early television acting assignment, a young Bill Oddie is featured in support.

Saturday 4 February 1967, ITV.

LIFELINE

Bill Oddie appealed on behalf of SUSTRANS – builders of car-free urban routes for cyclists, walkers and disabled people.

Sunday 31 October 1993, BBC1.

LIFT OFF WITH AYSHEA

The Goodies made a guest appearance on 3 December 1974, promoting their single release of *The Inbetweenies*.

THE LITTLE BOOK OF MORNINGTON CRESCENT

At last, the truth about that most celebrated of parlour games written by the *I'm Sorry I Haven't a Clue* boys. Well, actually, it's just an excuse for even more confusion and great laughs, but buy it anyway.

Did You Know? *The original title for the book was The Official History and Rules of the Game of Mornington Crescent.*

Written by Tim Brooke-Taylor, Graeme Garden, Barry Cryer and Humphrey Lyttelton. Orion 2000.

A LITTLE HOTEL ON THE SIDE

Graeme Garden starred in the National Theatre production of this classic Feydeau farce during 1984 and 1985.

THE LIVE SIX SHOW

Sky One's magazine programme hosted by Jenny Powell and Richard Orford. Tim Brooke-Taylor guested on 9 April 1998 and revelled in an archive clip of him and Sir Cliff Richard singing together from *The Case*. Cliff footstep-follower, Darren Day, was a fellow guest.

LONDON TODAY

Irrate resident Bill Oddie contributed his opinions on Camden Town's rubbish disposal and recycling needs in a brief on-screen interview in 1995.

THE LONG HOT SATSUMA

A short, cool, non-citrus fruit of a show… the long-awaited sequel to *My Darling Clementine!*, Graeme Garden wrote and starred in this inventive, unfairly forgotten radio comedy revue show with *I'm Sorry I Haven't a Clue* co-star Barry Cryer. The *Radio Times* heralded the series with an article, *A Pithy Classic* but the mix of corny gags, surreal interludes, gratuitous wackiness and one or two jokes,

BILL ODDIE IN, HIS OWN WORDS, 'A LONG TIME AGO…'

failed to gel despite sterling support from Alison Steadman. The second edition was a Time Travels Special, giving the listener another chance to hear the programme you heard next year!

Written and performed by Graeme Garden, Barry Cryer, Paul B Davies. Producer Dirk Maggs. Thursdays, 25 May–13 July, 1989, Radio 2.

LOOK ALIVE

Teeny bopper ITV magazine programme which lightly sprinkled features, things to do and star guests. Basking in their pop world cool, the Goodies appeared and performed the B-side of their current single *Wild Thing* on Tuesday 11 November 1975.

LOOKS FAMILIAR

Tim Brooke-Taylor made a guest appearance on this ITV nostalgia entertainment panel game on Tuesday 17 August 1982.

LOOSE ENDS

Tim Brooke-Taylor was question master testing the wit of the wittiest and the general knowledge of the generally knowledgeable. Old pals John Junkin, Barry Cryer and Willie Rushton were among the players.

Producer Roy Ronnie. Director Roger Castles. Tuesdays, 12 February–9 April 1985, BBC1.

LOOSE ENDS

The other, more famous, Radio 4 *Loose Ends* was a brilliant

trawl through contemporary popular culture with Ned Sherrin. Plugging *If I Ruled the World*, Graeme Garden appeared on Saturday 14 February 1998, explaining that *The Goodies* was halted by choice… 'just not ours!'

LOOSE GAGS. SONGS & SKETCHES Or a Night at the Old Gaff Salty Comedy

A music hall celebration of the Clement Brothers who performed their comic shows at Skegness between 1902 and 1932. Performed at the Bristol Old Vic, that lush *Man About the House* babe Paula Wilcox and Tim Brooke-Taylor cracked the jokes and sang the songs.

Also with JULIA HILLS, CHRIS HARRIS, ROBERT AUSTIN, JOHN TELFER, THE SKEGGY SYNCOPATORS. Written and presented by Tony Staveacre. Directed by Alec Reed. Monday 26 December 1988, Radio 4.

LORD PLUMFIELD VERSUS WELLES

A hilarious commentary on the eccentricities of British stately homeowners from masterful film-maker Orson Welles. Described as 'a small puzzle in two parts and from different times', this short comic gem was never commercially released and, as often with Welles, a labour of love filmed when money was available. Welles himself plays the haughty, financially embarrassed Lord Plumfield as a variation on Peter Sellers' frightfully British nob from the *We Need the Money* recording. Many years later, Welles again played a bush-encased interviewer linking the earlier footage. The first selection of material – filmed during the late Sixties – features Tim Brooke-Taylor as Welles's upper class, twit of the year son, Algeron. Begging for biccies like a faithful lap dog and twittering on with a burst of 'Hellos', 'Gollies' and 'Goshes', Tim is stunning good value. Imagine being able to put worked with Orson Welles on your CV, cool or what! It is also of note that the second narration voice used on the project was Graeme Garden. Welles, having been impressed by *Broaden Your Mind*, had contacted Garden's agent and phoned the man himself to arrange a meeting. Graeme turned to Tim and muttered, 'That was Orson Welles!' to which Brooke-Taylor sighed, 'And I'm the Pope's mum!' Tim went on to became a regular Welles player and is proud to boast that 'I've been on *Top of the Pops* and directed Orson Welles!'

Did You Know? Extracts from this and Tim's other Welles' film were featured in The Lost Films of Orson Welles. [See One-Man Band entry.]

Produced, written, edited and directed by Orson Welles.

ROLAND MacLEOD

Character actor whose connection with the Goodies stretched back to Series Two of *Broaden Your Mind*. Playing the third, aged eccentric in the Buffies interludes opposite Graeme Garden and Tim Brooke-Taylor, the association with Tim continued in 1968 when he joined the supporting cast of Feldman's sketch success *It's Marty*. MacLeod went on to make seven appearances in *The Goodies*, stretching almost the entire BBC run from Paul Whitsun-Jones's thick copper cohort in *Give Police a Chance* in 1970, to *A Kick in the Arts* in 1980. He featured in Series Two's *Wicked Waltzing*, Series Seven's *Rock Goodies* and the classic 1975 special, *Goodies Rule OK?* His finest contributions came with his rabbit-transforming scientific boffin in *Invasion of the Moon Creatures* in 1973 and, best of all, the totally comic and eccentric depressive of *Cunning Stunts*, 1975.

MAKE A DAFT NOISE FOR CHRISTMAS

The fifth and final Top 40 Goodies single came exactly a year after the first. Reassuringly, it was another 'silly season' seasonal sing-a-long. Boasting a funky intro beat and an outstanding glam rock lead vocal from Bill Oddie, this is a salute to Marc Bolan's T-Rex sound, with daft chanting interludes, plenty of boogie on down rhythm and an interesting poverty row, depressed Britain, subtext. The Goodies are here to cheer you up with some good-natured nonsense, and cheer you up they do with a delightfully nutty number. Bill's pied piper leader of the gang instructions to 'come along girls and come along boys' and a delight in singing songs of love and joy ultimately breaks down to shared madness. Repeating a wealth of daft noises into infinity, there's an essence of *April Showers* from Disney's *Bambi* and an *All You Need Is Love* musical cornucopia before the long, drawn-out conclusion. *The Last Chance Dance* is the pitiful saga on one man's failure in the disco pulling stakes. A country and western ballad of rejection and desperate searching for love, this brilliantly kicks off with a wailing guitar and Graeme Garden's laid-back announcement for the last dance. Bill Oddie's angst-ridden delivery piles on the emotion and is well served by

Tim's throwaway comic comment – 'I suppose a (blank)'s out of the question!' – as the action almost hots up. Again, as with the best Goodies' songs, Oddie takes his part very seriously and allows the lyrics and his fellow Goodies to inject the necessary comic touches.

Did You Know? *The B-side classic The Last Chance Dance was listed as A Goodies Disco Special on the original single release. Hardly living up to the name in musical content, its addressing of love failure on Saturday night on dancefloors across the land surely made it more relevant in 16-year-old British youth than a bucket load of Bee Gees material. Released in November 1975, it entered the charts on 13 December 1975 and stayed for six weeks. Its highest chart position was Number 20.*

Written by Bill Oddie. Arranger Dave Macrae. Producer Miki Anthony. Bradley's Records BRAD 7533 1975.

THE MAKING OF... BILL ODDIE

As part of the BBC2s late night *Learning Zone* programming, notables were interviewed about how they started and what made them tick. Bill Oddie took part in a four-part inspection of his career, tackling his early days, a magical *Funky Gibbon* moment and life as a Goodie in the opening edition, selecting Bill Haley's *Rock Around the Clock*, a bit of cool Chris Barber jazz and Revel as his mixed musical inspirational favs in Show Two. In part three Bill discussed his Cambridge days, comedy influences and post-Goodies bird-watching – when a hobby became a career. The final instalment was a very brief but fascinating insight into comedy as a living. Bill insisted that team-work is essential and revealed the Oddie/Garden writing technique – quiet Graeme being forced into idea action because 'mine are really bad this week!' There was also room for some choice clips from *The Goodies: It Might As Well Be String*.

Monday 6 October–Thursday 10 October 1998, BBC2.

THE MAKING OF THE GOODIES' DISASTER MOVIE

The fourth and final Goodies book, this is arguably their printed masterpiece. With more than a little inspiration from the trio's own, short-lived, ill-fated attempt to launch a feature film, this pinpoints and mocks with malice the anal, corrupt, gloriously blinkered world of British cinema. Above all, it's really funny as well which helps a lot. The cartoon cover itself is an awe-inspiring incorporation of elements from every classic Seventies' disaster movie – the towering inferno is being trampled by

King Kong (from the 1976 version) as the *Airport* Concorde crashes into the ape, *The Poseiden Adventure* liner sinks in the background and several pals of *Jaws* poke their heads into the fun. In the middle of all this are the Goodies, trembling as they balance their trandem on a highwire. Mocking the written convention from the outset, with the contents page listed in alphabetical order (ie chapter eight to two) a Biggles-style, *Boy's Own* adventure story involving Germanic intrigue and a murderous combine harvester, kicks off the story, although this, and another tale of a bloke mending his exhaust pipe in Northampton, has absolutely nothing to do with the main bulk of the book… apart from a very tenuous link. Still, it's the Sixth Annual General Meeting of The Goodies at the Albert Hall, 5 May 1977 from 7.29pm, that really concerns us. Tim's the chairman while Andre Previn and the London Symphony Orchestra fill out the place. The minutes are reproduced in the book alongside the articles of association, pinpointing things to do within the Goodies' reign and ticking off some items (fight giant kitten, climb beanstalk) and hoping to tick off future ones (peerage – Tim only, appear on *Morecambe and Wise Show*, Goodies split). With best-selling author credits, a silver rose of Montreaux and recording stardom, it's only a feature-length film that really eludes the Goodies multimedia regime – hence this book's attempt to promote them as film stars. Tim seemingly longs to be wearing dark shades, while Graeme has a boys' edition of Lord Baden-Powell's Making Films for Pleasure and Profit. Tapping into the humour of *Scoutrageous*, this boy scout slant on movie-making recommends cold showers and is used to form a brief, jokey, naïve, racist opening to each of the following chapters. First things first and the boys need an agent – after advertising in a shop window next to women of easy virtue, they are approached by the flamboyant Louie Bunce of Wardour Street. Having proved his skill with Charles Bronson's Macho! – about an evil man who lends out his pen and doesn't get it back – he begins plugging his latest epic, Robin Askwith in Confessions of Dorian Grey – this time it's a portrait of the hero's bum that gets old in the attic in this high-brow celebration of Oscar Wilde. Even with the poster detailing the special guest appearance of Nicholas Parsons, the trio are not put off and sign an agreement on the menu of the local Indian Restaurant (the Teepee). A proposed movie form is filled in with The Goodies Film (title to be announced) and a heavily disguised Roger Moore standing

in for all three stars. Chapter Three, Raising the Money, dismisses the use of commercial marketing tools (as with the Texas Chainsaw Mascara) and opts for the Jaws-style jumble sale to make some dosh. The resulting wave of funds is subsequently spent on a lavish thank you party at the Playboy Club and, back to square one, the Goods receive pledges from interested parties. Bryan Forbes gives £200 to play the able seaman who cracks under pressure while Richard Attenborough tops that with £5000 to play Bryan Forbes. The fourth chapter sets out to find the director. Naive and loveable Tim sends an offer to Walt Disney – giving his love to Thumper – but receives a correspondence from Mr Michael Mouse's people explaining that Walt's 'like, dead, see'. A lavish, Disney rip-off illustration from Ken Cox milks the Disneyland way of audience participation but Graeme has already fleshed out a storyboard with Alfred Hitchcock. The great director even provides a poster tagline: 'The Goodies Are Coming', but Tim's not taking any chances. It may be non-art but it's 'just good clean English smut' so he's off for a chat to director Peter Rogers (taking over from Gerald Thomas for one day!) on the Shepperton set (away from Pinewood for one day!) for Carry On Christ. A delicious send-up of the films with Orson Welles, guesting as the Voice of God, the poster caricatures of Bernard Bresslaw, Peter Butterworth, Charles Hawtrey, Kenneth Williams and Barbara Windsor are spot-on. Away from this low-brow comic romping, Bill's delving deeper into the strange world of Ken Russell and Oliver Reed via Roger Vadim and the delightful Bridget Bardot. Chapter Five, Casting, brings in sexy Rita Acapulco (thanks to a wopping big pledge from Sheikh Yafist) while Bill is playing Bill (for the time being) at least! The female Dustin Hoffman, Frank Sinatra – no sole agent – Reggie Bosanquet, Rod McKuen, Bing 'Two-Ears' Laybelle Crosby and skeleton remains of Buster Keaton and Rudolf Valentino are all sort of considered from the pages of the Stage and Spotlight. However, there's no doubt that sexy Beverly Hills is to be included, having thoroughly impressed the producer, twice, and been built up like a great sex starlet by the *Daily Mirror*. A child star and, naturally, technical equipment, is also considered essential for the mix. This signals a search through The Kid Breeders' Gazette and copious film mags adorned with nude ladies much to the pleasure of Graeme's mad boffin. Meanwhile, Tim's Royalist begging and, more to the point, their producer's threats, secures

BEHIND THE SCENES WITH GRAEME AND BILL POSING FOR THE AQUATIC, SHARK THRILLER AS FEATURED IN *THE MAKING OF THE GOODIES DISASTER MOVIE BOOK*

the help of the Queen's Own Armoured Photographers. The costume and make-up departments get the ball rolling with designer Little Willie fashioning Who drummer Keith Moon as a replacement for Bill and costume sketches for Graeme's stunning attempt at Nina Mouskouri. The Bolshoi Ballet's potential performance as Bill is also catered for and there's a less than subtle ad for Wot Wig wig hires. Locations form Chapter Eight, with a helpful trackers guide to recognising snow footprints (including the Goodies – six prints – and Keith Moon – a collapsed body and bottle print). Naturally, Bill's location suggestion includes that major, essential film shot requirement – milk – 14 crates of Gold Top from the Cricklewood Deli to be precise – and, naturally, a lengthy bird-watching cum movie-making tour of the world. Due to expense and the fact that Tim's granny has moved there, the location is finalised as Weston-Super-Mare. Indeed, a very fine choice as a reproduced ordnance survey map details the area's rich filming tradition from Weston Side Story to North By North Weston via the immortal Hamm Farm named after Laurence Olivier. Things are getting to the nitty gritty with Chapter Nine, The Call Goes Out, with the artiste's call sheet, Tim's casting as Tim, Graeme and Bill's casting as Tim's stand-in and the final selection of Ken Russell as director. The one major problem they face – there is no script! And there's only 11 hours to go. An ominous THE END spreads a double page before Chapter 10, Writing the Script, sees Bill leap into action and remember an old correspondence course he once enrolled on. Lesson One, in which Frank Muir shows the best way to tie a bow-tie, is unhelpfully included. Tim's solution is a visit to the library with a scream-ridden selection from *King Kong* and

237

THE NAÏVE GOODIES FACE SHARP-TALKING MOGUL LOUIE BUNCE

an extract of Graham Green's *At It Again* perused for inspiration before Graeme's computer whiz-kid comes out on top with his multiple choice print-out. Although the selected route keeps the Goodies busy acting and singing in Cricklewood, I rather fancy the ignored 'fiancée with *Magnificent Ambersons*', but still, on with the plot, past an ad for the Hammer Blood Chart and into Chapter 11. The First Day, 21 June and wannabe stars line up – the Yugoslavian Army, Jon Wayne and Bert Lancaster – ready for action. Bill's more interested in photographing the Arctic Tern but nothing is more serious than the escape of Keith Moon. Chapter 12 is a stunning one-page illustration from Ken Cox with Moon as Kong, proudly standing on a skyscraper constructed from a drum kit. Things get worse and worse through the suitably named, thirteenth, chapter

of disasters. Director Ken Russell clears off, Graeme takes over, the kitchen scene in Cricklewood is attempted and Charles Bronson replaces most of the cast. What's more, the crew are behind schedule, Bill stands in for the shark attacking Graeme, Graeme himself stands in for Nana playing Graeme during this dangerous sequence and those temperamental stunners, Beverly and Rita, refuse to get into their Nun gear without a closed set. Having been naked through six movies, they sit naked waiting for their demands to be met… Problems like that, we can handle. Chapter 14 offers uncensored morsels from the censors to spice things up a bit – the funny three seconds from *Confessions of a Window Cleaner*, the bang bang from *Chitty, Chitty, Bang, Bang* and the bit in *Mary Poppins* where Julie Andrews takes her umbrella and stuffs it up her… (cont.).

This is later clarified and cleaned up in the text as 'chimney', but that first, ultra-risqué thought is class comedy. Chapter 15 sees the lads facing action stations time, with an emergency committee deciding to 'forget the art – where's the ackers', while Chapter 16 details The Final Day, with the arrival of the Shiekh, a distressed rant at the lack of Rita's equipment and outraged reaction to the surfeit of camel jokes. Threatening to put the price of oil up at every turn, things get to such a crisis that he declares war on the West Country and provides the perfect platform for the Goodies realism, 'as it happens', fly on the beach motion picture, All Quiet on the Weston Front. The climax to The Goodies: Hype Pressure is heavily plundered. The press reviews are certainly encouraging with the Times publishing the stand-out report, headed No, Not a Lovely Bore. Surprise is shown at the inclusion of an, admittedly funny, moment of Confession comedy, the complete story is revealed immediately after mentioning how annoying that can be, while Tim Brooke-Taylor's performance as the bitchy, waspish failure who resents being told what to do character, Tim Brooke-Taylor, is suitably praised. As a climax to the book we disconcertingly return to the climax of that combine harvester adventure at the start and we note the British Board of Book Censors has awarded the publication C minus – must try harder. A hilarious two fingers to the film business, this is a Goodies gem well worth searching out.

Designed by Anthony Cohen. George Weidenfeld and Nicolson Ltd, hardback, 1977. Sphere, paperback, 1978.

MAN OF THE YEAR

Bill Oddie appeared in this 1964 ITV programme.

A MAN'S BEST FRIEND IS HIS DUCK

A three-track Columbia single release from The Goodies Beastly Record which failed to chart but includes some of the best work from the team. As with the previous single, Blowing Off, Graeme Garden and not Bill Oddie takes centre stage at the microphone. Two of the numbers feature Garden's lead vocal and the principal track, A Man's Best Friend Is His Duck, is an endearingly innocence evocation of Thirties George Formby comic romance. Chuck in a load of cheeky cockney rhyming slang for a more modern day twist and you have a Goodies classic. Delivered with music hall gusto, Garden is accompanied by Tim and Bill on backing vocals, throwing in energetic 'Ahhs!' and various other interjections. Tim's non-sensical,

AN ULTRA-RARE, UNUSED SHOT OF GRAEME GARDEN FROM THE MAKING OF THE GOODIES DISASTER MOVIE PHOTO SHOOT

mystical rant about his grandfather is only one of the gems. Basically, the story tells of Graeme's friendly, obedient pet duck which faithfully acts as a substitute guard dog – after all you can get a 'very nasty suck' from a duck. As with Formby's My Little Goat and Me, a number recorded in 1937, the bonding between man and his pet is charming. Besides, it's worth digging out purely to hear rock star Oddie reduced to well-timed 'Quack, Quack' responses… sort of like Lennon and Harrison whistling on McCartney's Let It Be! Taking My Oyster for Walkies is similarly stuck in a Thirties' time warp with Garden getting all love-struck over an oyster. Performed in semi-Noel Coward terms, it's a jaunty little ditty concerning a dignified British gentleman and his weird obsession with shellfish. He sheepishly admits to other affairs with molluscs but this oyster is the real thing. As with the duck, Graeme adopts this tasty morsel as a pet. This narrative ploy sets up the legendary line concerning the difficulty of taking the sweet thing for walkies: 'a oyster has very few feet… if any!' Classic stuff. A touch of pathos is injected at the close as uncontrolled snogging results in the consumption of Garden's object of desire but that sinister 'Oh dear!' is a masterly way to end the tale. Finally Rastashanty, allows Oddie back in control to present, as the title suggests, a winning mix of reggae and sea shanty. Made famous by Bob Marley and the Whalers, and, no, not that Bob Marley as the sleeve notes explain, this is really upbeat stuff. Garden provides some hilarious come backs – 'a bloody freezing!' – while Oddie delights in the corniest of gags – penguin chocolate biscuits, frozen dreadlocks used as cork screws and the like. However, the funniest moment comes with simulated backing vocals from the surrounding aquatic life – the bubbling mackerel harmony is a classic. The last Goodies single to date.

Did You Know? *Rastashanty is the only original song on this single, with the other two offerings first having appeared in radio's I'm Sorry I'll Read That Again – A Man's Best Friend Is His Duck in Episode Eleven from 1966's Series Four and Taking My Oyster For Walkies in Episode Two, Series Six from 1968. The unique picture cover release reused the animal cartoon from the Beastly Record cover.*

Written by Bill Oddie. DB 9053 Columbia Records October 1978.

MARRIED WITH CHILDREN

Long-running (over 250 episodes in 10 years) American situation comedy which unashamedly contrasted the pathos-ridden, domestic format with its family of poor white trash. Along with *The Simpsons*, it provided Fox with audience-grabbing clout, and before *Friends* launched their high-profile trip to London, the series enjoyed three editions set in Britain – the birthplace of 'Shakespeare… Churchill… Benny Hill!' Although packing in a bit of Brit-bashing, a mutual hatred of the French is the major xenophobic comic kick. Airing in the States during May 1992 these, predictably, were dubbed 'The English Shows' and guest-starred Bill Oddie as the frightfully nice Winston… apart from wanting to kill the two male members of the Bundy family, of course! Bill remembers the experience as frustrating, 'Every time you did a line, five or six producers had an opinion on how you should deliver it. It was impossible! The only satisfaction Alun Armstrong and I got out of it was by being incredibly efficient. The Americans would do lots of takes. We would turn up at 10 in the morning, do our lines in one take and go. You could almost hear them thinking, 'Bloody English!' That was great!' Basically, the plot revolved round an old British-based curse, from 1653, still cursing our hapless hero in 1992 Chicago. The entire village of Lower Uncton has been plunged into darkness ever since and local historian (Bill) arranges to lift the curse by killing the man at its centre. Lured over to England with the promise of an all-expenses paid trip, the family are driven round by Bill, see the sights, spend pots of money and encounter Alun Armstrong and his right-hand man (from Lower Uncton and determined to kill the folk in London to preserve the darkness and their lucrative, neighbouring tourist attraction). Bill overplays his part to perfection and fits in well with the no-nonsense, pathos-avoiding, knowing (the climatic battle scene is held in Upper Uncton because it's too dark to film in Bill's village) comedy. Indeed, the closing scenes are Bill's finest – deliciously trying to riddle out of cannibalistic insinuations (blaming the darkness and not being able to see what he eats), flogging 'Al Bundy' merchandising t-shirts and ultimately facing the fate that, with the curse lifted, village life has became drab, realistic and normal. A brilliant slice of bitter Yank comedy – a real-life *Simpsons* if you will – these special shows are well worth tracking down… if only for the stunning, self-promoting stupidity of Christina Applegate as she finds her way round London. For Goodie fans, it's essential.

Al Bundy ED O'NEILL Peggy Bundy KATEY SAGAL Kelly Bundy CHRISTINA APPLEGATE Bud Bundy DAVID FAUSTINO Marcy Rhoades AMANDA BEARSE Jefferson D'Arcy TED McGINLEY Winston BILL ODDIE The Executioner MARK ADDY Trevor ALUN ARMSTRONG Igor STEVEN HARTLEY Mayor TONY STEEDMAN Customs Officer CHRIS LANGHAM. Created by Michael G Moye and Ron Leavitt. Producers Barbara Blachot Cramer. Director Gerry Cohen. Written by Ellen L Fogle, Stacie Lipp and Kevin Curran. Fox/Embassy Communications, May 1992.

MARTY

Just to confuse the *Marty / It's Marty* debate over Feldman's 1968–69 BBC2 programmes, Astor records licensed a bunch of Series One *It's Marty* pieces from the BBC and released them on an album entitled *Marty*. A valuable and hotly sort-after audio archive of classic Feldman. Regular supporting player, Tim Brooke-Taylor, appears on six tracks, playing sexual innocence in Father and Son, religious bod on God, creepy grub Woodworm, thinly-veiled camp on Funny He Never Married, aged whine on Travel Agency and further religious mugging on Bishop.

PLP 1294 Astor. NPL 18258 Pye 1969.

MARTY AMOK

An Easter special for Marty Feldman which is an extended *It's Marty* in all but name. With writing, directing and cast connections – Mary Miller, John Junkin and Tim Brooke-Taylor provide their usual flawless support in the sketches – the inspired choice of cherry-on-top guests enhanced the typical goings-on. Vivian Stanshall played the game on his own terms and an international flavour was added with the French comedian and Feldman influence Robert Dhery. The surviving highlight is probably Marty and Tim's resurrection of the aeroplane-confined, passenger-terrifying, *How to Irritate People* classic, Cockpit. The resurrected lost gem is Bookshop – a Marty/John Junkin retread of the *At Last the 1948 Show* sketch. The Tim Brooke-Taylor Fish Restaurant sketch was featured on the BBC video release, *It's Marty*.

MARTY FELDMAN, ROBERT DHERY, JOHN JUNKIN, TIM BROOKE-TAYLOR, VIVIAN STANSHALL, MARY MILLER. Written by Brian Cooke, Marty Feldman, Terry Jones, Johnnie Mortimer, Michael Palin and Barry Took. Restaurant, Bookshop, Long-Distance Bowler, Judge, Royal Handicap, Cockpit, Atilla the Hun, Buying a Double Bed, Changing Cubicles and Reality in the Cinema. Producer Michael Mills. Director Roger Race. Monday 30 March 1970, BBC1.

THE MARTY FELDMAN COMEDY MACHINE

Having proved Marty Feldman's key stooge during the glorious BBC days, Tim Brooke-Taylor returned to the fold for these Lew Grade ATV specials created for the American market. Now an active Goodie, Tim's contribution was limited to selected written sketches. The spectre of Monty Python was embraced with Terry Gilliam employed to create the opening credits and linking animations, while the old man himself, Spike Milligan, was a constant writing and performing crutch. The 14 shows also attracted mega guest stars such as Orson Welles, Groucho Marx and Roger Moore. Due to a personality clash between Feldman and producer Larry Gelbart, a second series was curtailed. Indeed, Gelbart tried to suppress the first series. A half-hour compilation was screened on 15 February 1972 and scooped the Top Comedy Award and the Golden Rose at Montreux.

MARTY FELDMAN, SPIKE MILLIGAN, BOB TODD, HUGH PADDICK, CLOVISSA NEWCOMBE, RUDY de LUCA, BARRY LEVINSON, FRANCES de la TOUR, VALENTINE DYALL. Written by Chris Allen, Tim Brooke-Taylor, Marty Feldman, Larry Gelbart, Sheldon Keller, Barry Levinson and Rudy de Luca. Executive Producer Colin Clews. Producer Larry Gelbart. Director John Robins. Fridays, 1 October 1971–14 January 1972, ITV.

MASTER CHEF

Graeme Garden was a guest judge in a 1997 edition of this Lloyd Grossman-hosted foodie challenge programme.

THE MATING MACHINE: Flo and Monty and Harry... and Harry

While Sid James and the gang were making light of the new computer dating system in *Carry On Loving*, producer Bill Turner and director Harold Ross constructed a series of seven comic half hours based round the idea. Writers ranged from Ray Galton and Alan Simpson to John Esmonde and Bob Larby, with this second programme scripted by Graeme Garden and Bill Oddie. Starring Miriam Karlin as a bored housewife, the surreal plot involved an ill-fated trip to a dating agency and the resulting appearance of 10 different wannabe suitors, all called Henry, all clad in cloth-caps and long coats, and all sporting an identifying red carnation. Hand-picked matchmaking through the eyes of a comic Fritz Lang, the show culminated in all these cloned fellows chasing the dissatisfied Karlin through the mill and beyond and right back into the cosy, predictable, comfortable arms of her husband.

Did You Know? *In an assignment the actor prefers to forget about, one of the multitude of Henries was David Suchet in his first television appearance.*

Flo MIRIAM KARLIN Monty NORMAN BIRD Henry ROGER BRIERLY Henry DAVID SUCHET. Written by Graeme Garden and Bill Oddie. Producer Bill Turner. Director Howard Ross. Friday 16 October 1970, ITV.

ME & MY GIRL

Tim Brooke-Taylor went from active Goodie to beloved situation comedy actor in one leap with this long-running, undemanding and charming domestic romp. The series starred Richard O'Sullivan as the widower Simon Harrap, looking after his young daughter, Sam, promoting himself as a sexed-up raver and trying to balance the books of his promotions company, EyeCatchers. The actor wallowed deep in tried and tested sitcom convention with healthy irony. The characters, and above all, performances, were so endearingly played that even the corniest banter was welcome, while slight, underlying pathos was allowed to emerge with a subtle, unsugary style which made the whole thing believable and emotive. Joan Sanderson, television's favourite harridan since the *Fawlty Towers* episode, *Communication Problems*, was O'Sullivan's dogmatic, aggressive but ultimately warm-hearted mother-in-law and business associate. Tim Brooke-Taylor, comic nervousness personified, carried the bulk of comic business as O'Sullivan's brother-in-law and business associate Derek, facing problems from unseen wife and children, bumbling through life and generally keeping the show hilarious even at its lowest ebb. Initially delivered at an astounding rate – 26 programmes were broadcast in just 16 months – this was mainly due to the production team's concern over the young leading lady, Joanne Ridley. Naturally, a 14-year old girl is bound to develop over the period of four years and the makers wanted to capitalise on naïve, dawning sexual awakening plot lines before she outgrew them. Mind you, as the series went on and Ridley became a very accomplished, full-figured, actress, the emphasis merely shifted to sex chat and troubled relationships. Tim was called on to do everything from wearing a poultry suit in 'Let's Talk Turkey' to playing heart-breaking pathos opposite Patricia Brake in 'Thinking About Fluffy' but most of the time he simply enlivened the show with bemused expressions and silly antics. Perhaps the most sustained of Eighties' ITV sofa sitcoms which, although isn't saying a great deal, isn't half bad either. Besides, it was a huge hit in Iceland… and Tim's got the fan letters to prove it!

Did You Know? *The creator of the series, Keith Leonard, had himself looked after his own daughter – from the age of three – having lost his wife through divorce rather than early death; her name was Samantha.*

Simon Harrap RICHARD O'SULLIVAN Derek Yates TIM BROOKE-TAYLOR Nell Cresset JOAN SANDERSON Samatha Harrap JOANNE RIDLEY Maddie LENI HARPER Liz JOANNE CAMPBELL (Series One and Two) Isobel McClusky SANDRA CLARK (Series Three to Six). From an original idea by Keith Leonard. Written by John Kane, Colin-Bostock Smith, Bernard McKenna and George Layton. Produced and directed by John Reardon. ITV.
Series One: I Love You Samantha, Design For Loving, A Clean Slate, Jobs For The Girls, Lost and Found. Fridays, 31 August–5 October 1984. **Series Two:** Love and Kittens, Let's Talk Turkey, Sticky Fingers, The Kids Are Alright, Leaving on a Jet Plane, Swings and Roundabouts, You Tak' the High Road. Fridays, 18 January–1 March 1985. **Series Three:** On Approval, Wild About Harry, Dangerous Corner, Goodbye For Ever!, A Woman of Taste, Put Yourself in My Place, Sam Who?, One Wild and Foolish Moment, A Picture of Harmony, An Inspector Calls, Faraway Places. Fridays, 6 October–27 December 1985. **Series Four:** Love's Young Dream, Marriage in Haste, The Rhinoceros and the Pussycat, Poor Uncle Derek, The Lost Weekend, Kissing Cousins, French Leave, A Single Night of Love, A Star Is Gorn, Pulling Power, An Offer You Can't Confuse, Waiting For Adrian, Like an Old Time Movie. Saturdays, 10 January–4 April 1987. **Series Five:** Thinking About Fluffy, Question Time, A Couple of Rough Nights, Play Your Cards Right, Love Thy Neighbour, I Wonder Who's Kissing Him Now? Fridays, 8 January–12 February 1988. **Series Six:** My Second Best Friend, The Story of Foxy-Features and Melon-Head, Mundane Monday, Only the Lonely, When You're Smiling, A Little Overtime. Fridays, 23 September–4 November 1988. TIM BROOKE-TAYLOR missed one episode in Series One, two in Series Three and one in Series Six.

MEGA SUPERTOT AND THE ROBOTTY POTTY PLOT

A children's story book co-written by Bill Oddie and relating the awe-inspiring case of an ingenious baby combating an alien invasion on earth.

Fantail 1989.

M.I.C.K.E.Y M.O.U.S.E.

After their major chart success, the Goodies were roped in by the Walt Disney corporation to record a straightish version of the *Mickey Mouse Club* theme song, *M.I.C.K.E.Y. M.O.U.S.E.* Basking in the mouse's 50th anniversary in 1978, the disc kicks off with some funky drum beats, guitar licks and Bill Oddie's rousing chorus of *Happy Birthday* before the funked-up version of the familiar tune comes in. Bill delivers a stunning lead vocal, although the comedy content is pretty limited. Mind you, Tim enjoys a Mickey-like squeak appearance and all the lads relish the corny not a… Field Mouse, Dor-Mouse, Hippapota-Mouse, anony-mouse, fa-mouse business. The picture cover ditched the chart-busting trio in favour of old round ears

THE GOODIES POSE WITH THE MOST FAMOUS MOUSE IN THE WORLD FOR THEIR ILL-FATED 1978 SINGLE RELEASE

himself – with a charming, bubble-speak 'Hi' emerging from his mouth. Released as a prelude to *The Goodies Beastly Album*, copyright restrictions prevented it being featured on the record. However, the single's B-side did appear. *Funky Farm*, a sort of 1969, John's just settled down with Yoko, experimental noise thing, is a hip cornucopia of woofs, baa's and clucks set to music. Its groove is in the right place but after a while it's just a confused noise – the *Revolution No. 9* of the album.

M.I.C.K.E.Y M.O.U.S.E. written by Jimmy Dodd and Marc Ray. Arranged and produced by Miki Antony. Funky Farm written and arranged by Bill Oddie. Produced by Miki Antony. EMI 2784 EMI Records May 1978.

THE MIKADO

The major musical elements of *Monty Python* (Eric Idle) and *Beyond the Fringe* (Dudley Moore) had done it, then why not the major musical element of the Goodies? Thus was the sound reasoning of the English National Opera when offering Bill Oddie the chance to prove himself in the celebrated comic role of Ko-Ko, the Lord High Executioner during 1988/1989 season – 'They only cast me because I could fit into Dudley Moore's suit!'

MILLIGAN'S WAKE

Influenced by late night television satire and pioneering the sketch format which would fully blossom with the *Q* series, Spike Milligan presented this important, largely forgotten piece of surreal programming. Following a season of four, Galton and Simpson-scripted episodes during 1964, the Godfather of alternative comedy was back the following year with seven more editions. More politically geared, thanks to new script contributor John Bird, these still wallowed in Spike's own unique brand of humour. From *Cambridge Circus*, Tim Brooke-Taylor was brought in for comedy ideas, sketch structures and to serve as editor for the written material. However, at all times Milligan was the leading creative powerhouse, as Tim remembers, 'I learnt very early on that Spike wanted his writers to provide a beginning, middle and end for a sketch and also to add a few jokes. The rest of the scene would be his to add to, improvise and rearrange. I did this thing about a Peer who's fallen on hard times and now lives in a council house, shooting the ducks off the wall and all that. Well, Spike worked from that original and eventually had the butler coming out of a wardrobe saying, 'Time for your heart attack, Sir!' that was the genius of the man.'

Did You Know? Tim recalls a later encounter with the unpredictable comic genius, 'I was doing a musical, bizarrely enough in Perth in Australia, and Bill Kerr was in the cast. We both went to see Spike doing his one man show and Spike said, 'Knock, Knock!' and without a second's pause Bill shouted out 'Who's there?' and Spike stopped and said, 'Is Bill Kerr in the audience?' He was a true feed!' The album, Milligan's Wake (NPL 18104 Pye), and the accompanying single, The Olympic Team / The Epilogue (7N 15720 Pye), features only material from the first series.

Written by Spike Milligan, John Bird, Tim Brooke-Taylor and Reuben Ship. Producer Anthony Firth. Director Gordon Reece. Series Two, Saturdays, 3 July–14 August 1965, ITV.

MONTY PYTHON

'We were the Bay City Rollers, they were the Beatles!'
Bill Oddie

Beatles or Stones, Keaton or Chaplin, Oasis or Blur, Goodies or Python, when ever two major forces come along with similar baggage at a similar time the media circus pulls into town with the battle of the giants' rivalry. Usually, within the groups and fans in general, it doesn't matter if you like, love or loathe each with equal passion, but in the papers you can't sit on the fence, you have to celebrate one and decry the other. With the

Goodies, the connections and shared experiences with the Python boys is clear cut. The two met and worked with John Cleese and Graham Chapman at Cambridge, did the Footlights together and created *A Clump of Plinths*, *Cambridge Circus* and *I'm Sorry I'll Read That Again*. Graeme toiled with Eric Idle on the revues, *Stuff That Dreams Are Made Of* and *My Girl Herbert* and subsequently, Idle's material was included in both radio's *I'm Sorry I'll Read That Again* and the American presentation of *Cambridge Circus*. The Oxford boys, Terry Jones and Michael Palin, also contributed. Back at home, joint contributions to *That Was The Week That Was*, *The Frost Report*, *Twice a Fortnight*, *Broaden Your Mind* and *It's Marty* pointed the way forward, while Tim Brooke-Taylor had already performed with Chapman and Cleese to great television acclaim on *At Last the 1948 Show*. The American special, *How To Irritate People*, resurrected the trio, with Michael Palin in tow, and the pre-Goodies and Cleese were still churning out radio gold-dust through *I'm Sorry I'll Read That Again*. Of all the Goodies, the only one who was a potential Python was Tim, thanks to the *1948 Show* but he comments that, 'Python considered themselves a writing team. Graeme and Bill were the same. I couldn't write quick enough or well enough to be a Python!' The success of *Monty Python's Flying Circus*, from October 1969, shifted the emphasis from pure sketch comedy and turned Brooke-Taylor, Garden and Oddie towards *The Goodies*, broadcast from November 1970. The nine had found their respective niche and were forever after linked, Pythons and Goodies for life. Both groups found cult stardom on television, diverted into publishing and recording and created a very vocal war of the absurd. Fundamentally singing from the same hymn sheet, *Python* was considered cool while *The Goodies* was cosy. Reassuringly adult in their targets and style, John Cleese's infamous gag appearance at the close of 1973's *The Goodies and the Beanstalk* put the debate into perspective. His muttered, 'Kid's programme!' spoke volumes. Perhaps more interestingly, while Python happily mocked their old ringmaster, David Frost, despite name checks for Tim Brooke-Taylor in both *Monty Python's Big Red Book* (1971) and *The Brand New Monty Python Bok* (1973), they never bothered to mock *The Goodies*. The Goodies on the other hand, mocked the Pythons continually, whether it be 'Prince Andrew's' consideration that the Pythons are past it in *The Goodies'*

Book of Criminal Records or several references in the television episodes – the Liberty Bell and gumby waddlers in Scatty Safari, potential replacements for Bill in Cunning Stunts ushered in with the Liberty Bell, the relentless screen coverage in Invasion of the Moon Creatures, the alien signal in U-Friend or UFO? It gave the impression of protesting too much or, at the very least, keeping the Python/Goodies rumbling going. Despite retaining their BBC series longer than the Pythons, in the wake of Cleese's departure before the six episodes of Monty Python in 1974, the trio presented their brilliant Series Five. By the time the Goodies were left high and dry by the corporation in 1980, the regrouped Python six had managed to break into feature films and, as a result of Monty Python and the Holy Grail, crack the American market. Live shows, solo movie popularity and international respect resulted. Although the link was always maintained with Tim Brooke-Taylor acknowledged for use of 1948 material in Monty Python Live at the Hollywood Bowl, Tim and Graeme's involvement in Cleese's Video Arts films, Cleese's return to the fold for the 25th anniversary broadcast of I'm Sorry I'll Read That Again and Tim's attendance of Graham Chapman's memorial service, singing Always Look On the Bright Side of Life for the departed 'Brian' (footage of which was featured in Omnibus: Life of Python, 1990), the two groups were light years apart in terms of profile. With no repeats and limited celebration at home, the Goodies must look with dismay at Python's complete video availability, feted discussion and commercial ability – with everything from calendars to CD-Roms. Interestingly, Python fame seems to have lasted longer around the world. When filming Around the World in 80 Days, Michael Palin was greeted by a Yugoslavian sailor with, 'You are Monty Python!' while a Bill Oddie-semi-lookalike cameraman was met with, 'And you do those bird shows!' Bill Oddie always sums up the difference with a stable attitude, 'I think in comparison with Monty Python's Flying Circus, their highs are higher than ours, their lows are lower than ours. I think we're more consistent.' While I must agree that Monty Python's Life of Brian is the Oxbridge generation's finest achievement, this line of thought does tend to underestimate the power of The Goodies. At their best – a level they sustained with alarming frequency through a decade – the trio presented a staggering collection of structured, challenging and endearing comedy. Tim

Brooke-Taylor believes that 'Python was more like a pop group – it appealed to the young and almost annoyed the old. The young fans fought for Python, as they should do, but when their parents said, 'Oh! I prefer The Goodies!' it almost made The Goodies bad! We are different, people can like us both and I think we both did some excellent work.' While never decrying the undeniable genius of the Pythons, it was simply clever and potent marketing forces that made the popularity difference. For me, the nine writer–performers are of equal stature and deserve equal recognition. Besides, their long and winding roads crossed paths so many times, it's only fair isn't it?

MONTY PYTHON AND THE HOLY GRAIL: the trailer

The cinema trailer for Monty Python's classic 1975 medieval romp featured a very brief sequence with Terry Jones pushing a custard pie into the face of none other than Graeme Garden. Both were clad in suitable historical clothing and it is believed this extract came from either Twice a Fortnight or Broaden Your Mind. Some, however, believe it could be the much more potent possibility of an edited sequence from the Python film. Eric Idle's 1976 publication, The Rutland Dirty Weekend Book, sent up the situation with a mock mention for the forthcoming Goodies' version of Monty Python and the Holy Grail.

MORRIS MAGIC

An affectionate and touching tribute to Johnny Morris who simply was wildlife television. Bill Oddie via voiceover narration and front of camera intros from Whipsnade celebrated the unique skills of Johnny, his lasting legacy in the shape of Animal Magic and the sheer warmth of the man himself. Tony Soper, Terry Nutkins and the late Desmond Hawkins, founder of the BBC Natural History Unit, were among those paying tribute. Oddie's playful antics with a camel and a few star-struck lemurs would have brought a smile to Johnny's face.

Producer Hilary Jeffkins. Sunday 23 May 1999, BBC1.

MURDER MOST HORRID

Confessions of a Murderer is an episode from the fourth series of Dawn French's deliciously dark comic tales of death. Here, she played the ultra-sad, detective telly-obsessed (her cats are called Inspectors Frost and Morse, and Bodie and Doyle, the doorbell plays the theme from

Z Cars), pebble glasses wearing, Harriet Snellgrove, continually crying wolf and confessing to every crime known to man. She is the bane of Nutley Police Force, with *Poirot*'s Phillip Jackson doggedly correcting the University-educated Inspector, Hugh Bonneville, on his confused onslaught of clichéd, Cops on the Box banter. Graeme Garden is enlisted for a marvellous cameo role as the entire journalistic talent of the Nutley Chronicle and Advertiser, Alex Docherty. Making full use of his skill for swift vocal changes, Garden goes frightfully posh for the politics, broad Scots for the Sports and gravelly cockney for the crime desk. A priceless performance. The moment when his isolated little world of pub quiz injuries and the like suddenly throws up murder confessions and police corruption results in a potent 'Sounds like a real story!' With an earnest click of his ballpoint, the scene explodes into action. His enthusiasm is, of course, short-lived. After stoking French's fire, recording her wild rant and suggesting the head copper is to 'do nothing at all!' in wonderful, gutter journalism style, the line-up sees his case fall away and he wanders off sheepishly, concerned his pager is receiving no messages. The final twist is clever and avoids the obvious wonderfully, while the direction combines Film Noir interest with sitcom confinement.

Harriet Snellgrove DAWN FRENCH Police sergeant PHILIP JACKSON Inspector Dawson HUGH BONNEVILLE Alex Docherty GRAEME GARDEN Police constable PAUL PUTNER Barman RICKY GROVER. Written by Ian Hislop and Nick Newman. Producer Sophie Clarke-Jervoise. Director Edgar Wright. Friday 19 March 1999, BBC2.

MY FAT FRIEND

A 1978 Australian stage production of the camp comedy starring Tim Brooke-Taylor as the gay friend continually advising on the weight situation of his portly female companion.

MY FIRST, MY LAST, MY EVERYTHING

Bill Oddie guest-starred on this UK Arena select-a-disc programme in February 2000, picking Bill Haley's *Rock Around the Clock*, Joni Mitchell and Miles Davies. Bonnie Langford admitted her 'first' was *Funky Gibbon*.

MY GIRL HERBERT

The 1965 Cambridge Footlights revue largely written and performed by the year's president, Eric Idle. Graeme Garden, who had left the previous year, had some of his left-over sketches included in the show.

MY SUMMER WITH DES

An essential experience for anybody with a healthy obsession for football, beautiful women, Nineties' Goodies-spotting and *My Fair Lady*, in that order. This may lack the total, gut-wrenching, passionate tension of *Fever Pitch* – that was Arsenal after all, here it's merely England – but this is still powerful stuff. The God-like Des Lynam comments on the situation, on and off the pitch, via actual BBC interludes or newly recorded pearls of wisdom, John Gordon Sinclair does his usual charming Scottish bloke act to near perfection and the stunning Rachel Weiss is every red-blooded Brit's ideal woman: intelligent, gorgeous and with a devotion to footie. Cutting gag appearances come from publican Tony Selby, surprisingly effective Ned Sherrin, bemused Peter Shilton and totally awesome David Seaman, while Neil Morissey – the greatest small screen lad since James Bolam – injects pathos and dignity into his expected beer, birds and fags persona. Musical soundbites from David, Frank, the Lightning Seeds and Oasis give the chilling use of actual archive Euro '96 footage a real sense of time and place. You almost think Southgate might just stick that penalty home and in the lead-up to the French World Cup of 1998, this was potent telly indeed. However, our major concern is an ultra-rare BBC television acting assignment: the first since *In Sickness and In Health* for Graeme Garden. Restricted to just a handful of scenes, Garden's tight-lipped, melon-arsed Scots boss is a towering performance of cold, incisive venom. Like Henry Daniell in *The Philadelphia Story,* he seems to delight in building up hopes merely to dash them even more soundly, with charming snake-like words of sweetness on the phone, cheery footie banter and even a delightful snatch of 'Football's Coming Home…' before fully terminating Morissey's career. Cold, clinical and straight to the point, Graeme delivers a stunning cameo. Wrapped up in his record company, conferences, the delights of female-heavy treasure hunts and basically cutting Morissey's pleasure off at the wrist, Graeme does a powerful job in a pretty powerful slice of television comedy drama.

Martin NEIL MORISSEY Angus GRAEME GARDEN Rosie RACHEL WEISS Cameron JOHN GORDON-SINCLAIR Barbara ARABELLA WEIR Anna TILLY BLACKWOOD. Written by Arthur Smith. Producer Joy Spink. Director Simon Curtis. Monday 25 May 1998, BBC1.

N

NAPPY LOVE

In a natural response to Seventies heart throb Donny Osmond and the youthful slush of *Puppy Love*, songwriter Bill Oddie took the notion to comic extremes with this pre-school counter blast from the Goodies. Another number in the Fifties' do-wop style, the opening 'Boop-Sho-doop!' chorus sets up Oddie's infantile lead vocal perfectly. A tragic tale of a two-year-old Romeo devoted to his 'Queen in plastic panties', the Fifties' teen-angst feel is heightened thanks to Graeme's booming, bass responses and a classic spoken verse in his best Elvis *Are You Lonesome Tonight?* mode. An endearing, catchy tune, Tim's shocked reaction to the 'free' (from nappies)/'three' (a child on the way) misunderstanding is cleverly milked for maximum comic effect. The B-side is an altogether different kettle of haddocks, however. The only occasion the Goodies played the cover version game and recorded a number not penned by Bill Oddie, this is a rousing, rocking outing for Chip Taylor's seminal classic *Wild Thing*. Originally a massive hit for The Troggs in 1965, Oddie maintains that the Goodies version was a tribute to Jimi Hendrix, whose bristling recording from 1966 remains one of rock's true highpoints. While *Sick Man Blues* or *The Inbetweenies* is more quintessentially Goodies, this track perfectly sums up why the group were so damn cool for a glammed-out generation. First and foremost, Bill Oddie has a wonderful rock voice. And more importantly, on *Wild Thing* he plays with a totally straight bat. Ripping through the lyrics, roaring out the chorus and giving a hip scream almost worthy of Tom Jones, this guy is good. Equally important, Tim and Graeme are on hand to comic-up the rock atmosphere. Tim – playing the typical shy Brit akin to Peter Sellers turning on the charmless charm for Sophia Loren on *I Fell in Love with an Englishman* – does a Rex Harrison spoken delivery with added coy reserve attitude… 'Hold me tight, not quite that tight!' Oddie's raucous vocals clearly bolster Tim's potent 'you make my heart swing!' lines and the effect is stunning. Tim, seemingly coming in too early for the second 'you move me' bit, just adds to the overall ham-fisted innocence of the performance and his irritated acceptance of unwanted female attention is sheer perfection. Roy Orbison-style 'Grrrs' are slotted in for extra humour and Graeme's bland, disinterested, speedy repeat of 'You make it so groovy!' is a masterstroke. All in all, the track to initiate the uneducated rock journalist into Goodies music. It's a familiar, legendary number, treated with respect by the main man and wonderfully Goodied up by his cohorts in crime.

Did You Know? This Goodies single advertises the two tracks as coming from 'their forthcoming LP Almost Live'. That title was subsequently changed to The New Goodies LP, with the 'recorded almost live' teaser on the back cover. The single entered the charts on 27 September 1975 and stayed for six weeks. Its highest chart position was Number 21.

Nappy Love written by Bill Oddie. Arranger Tom Parker (despite interference from Bill Oddie). Producer Miki Antony. Wild Thing, written by Chip Taylor. Arranger Dave Macrae (despite interference from Bill Oddie). Producer Miki Antony. BRAD 7524 Bradley's Records 1975.

NATIONWIDE

Before host Michael Barratt became a familiar Goodies guest player (*Kung Fu Kapers*, *The Goodies Rule OK?*, *Scoutrageous*, *Rock Goodies*), Tim Brooke-Taylor, Graeme Garden and Bill Oddie appeared on *Nationwide*. Celebrating the fact that the BBC had selected *Kitten Kong* for the Montreaux Festival, the interview was broadcast on 17 February 1972, nine days before filming began on the up-dated version.

NATIONWIDE

The Australian show of the same name for ABC featured Bill Oddie's Odd Team during the Good's October 1989 Oz-based charity twitch-a-thon trip.

THE NATURAL WORLD: TOUGH DUCKS

Bill Oddie narrated this fascinating investigation into the truth behind ducks: a savage, vain, angst-ridden, parental protection-based community of bad-tempered dudes who do not turn up their beaks to a meal of dead seal meat or killing their own in the line of duty. From the Common Eiders in the Arctic via the Pink-Eared Duck of Australia and on to the tight-knit duck situation in a village pond, Oddie's delivery was at its usual enthused, passionate, joke-peppered best. Even chucking in some wonderfully corny puns, Johnny Morris-style vocals and an endearing on-screen appearance at the close, this was class wildlife entertainment.

Producer Mary Colwell. Sunday 21 February 1999, BBC2.

NEEDED

The greatest Goodies song never recorded for commercial release, *Needed* perfectly captured the good, do anything for anyone, attitude of the team. Apart from *The Goodies Theme* itself, the song was the most oft repeated in the series. Used in the very first show, *The Tower of London* it reappeared in every episode of Series One. It was further used for eight Series Two editions, *Scotland*, *The Commonwealth Games*, *Kitten Kong*, *Farm Fresh Food*, *Women's Lib*, *Gender Education*, *Charity Bounce* and *The Baddies*, before being abandoned for good.

THE NEW GOODIES LP

Jimi Hendrix and Queen may have wowed them at the Rainbow Club but the Goodies, never ones to be outdone in the rock 'n' roll stakes, delivered this stunning album release 'recorded almost live at the Cricklewood Rainbow June/July 1975'. After their initial album's reflection of songs heard within the television series, this second Goodies release was the first really to promote the team's pop chart success. It set out the Goodies stall of rock hand-in-hand with comedy. The back cover features Oddie living out his show business dream: belting out a rock song on his knees. Graeme and Tim, unconvincingly strumming guitars either side, give him maximum musical accompaniment but the auditorium isn't full of screaming fans. Only one person sits quietly and listens, the theatre's cleaner, gagged and bound to her seat. It was a serious business to Oddie, after all, his 'lyrics and words' are included on a separate official song sheet with the album (make sure it's there when you find this at your local car boot sale). But even these are given a perfect comic edge with Bill's hand-written 'invaluable notes and insights into author's intentions, social messages, hidden meanings etc...' Double-edged, these pinpoint the cleverness of Oddie's work, while delighting in self-mockery at his own song-writing pretensions and revelling in back biting at his fellow, interfering Goodies. As such, the whole package is an archetypal comedy rock album and kicks off with the only suitable track – the 'new', funkier version of *The Goodies Theme* which had happily usurped the old favourite (featured on *The Goodies Sing Songs From The Goodies*) on television and now committed to vinyl in a specially recorded take. It's still the grooviest telly tune of all time

ORIGINAL PROMOTIONAL MATERIAL FOR *THE NEW GOODIES LP*

and guaranteed to get those hairs on the back of your neck standing erect. The refrains of the theme fade away as the banjo introduction of *Please Let Us Play* kicks in with Tim pitifully muttering a lament about wanting to be a rock star. This is Oddie's comment on everybody else's reaction to the Goodies cutting ice as recording artists – echoing the 'what a load of rubbish!' cries of derision and proclaiming an innocent ideal of simply having fun. That stuff about not even wanting money certainly doesn't sound like the Goodies from the television show I remember, but there's a real endearing charm about the need to spread a bit of good-natured pleasure through the pop world. It's unpretentious, fun and harmless, with Oddie relishing the final emperor's clothes verse when success bites, people suddenly want them and fair-weather friends emerge from the woodwork. The album experiments with *Sgt Pepper*-style track merging here with the successful pleas to have a chance seamlessly cross-fading to an imaginary concert and Graeme's earnest Billy Shares-like, 'Ladies and Gentlemen...' introduction. With rock excess heavy in the air, the groovy guitar riff and promise of 'eternal happiness', the lads break into the ultimate musical tribute to that perennial comedy favourite: the custard pie. Again, contrary to the telly persona, Bill seems to decry booze and drugs as the secret to inner discovery and instead celebrates the definitive way to get high as a well-placed custard pie. Musically and lyrically this is probably the weakest track on the album – lifted from the old *I'm Sorry I'll Read That Again* rhubarb tart lament – but there's real feel-good energy at work with Graeme's down, down,

BILL ODDIE GLEEFULLY GETS INTO THE SPIRIT OF THINGS WITH *THE NEW GOODIES LP*, OBVIOUSLY INSPIRING ROBBIE CARLYLE'S LOOK FOR BEGBY FROM *TRAINSPOTTING*

deeper and down bass interlude, suitably sploshy sound effects and a chant-a-long spelling lesson all adding to the wacky pleasure. Setting up a musical running joke which continues with the new version of *Funky Gibbon*, the number closes with a bit of nursery rhyme fun, 'Mummy's little baby likes shortening bread', before Bill screams a final, defiant 'Pie!' and proves once and for all that he's a Rock Star with a capital Rock. An infectious tinkering piano outro makes way for, arguably, the best track on the album and frequently the Goodies song I tend to pick as my all-time favourite. *Cricklewood* is a classic evocation of the Goodies' adopted home, lovingly ridiculed and cheekily allowing the self-proclaimed pop master firmly to grab the reigns from the defunct Beatles. Oddie's throwaway sleeve note comment has tongue placed in cheek as firm as it would go, while, if the spiralling musical chords and psychedelic elements fail to signpost things clearly, the lyrics bask in references to *Penny Lane* and *Strawberry Fields*. It's a sort of *Balham – Gateway to the South* set to a Sixties' beat combo backing with Tim dreamily pondering on the boredom of the place with spine-tingling harmonies in *The Turtles* style

adding musical weight to the piece. All that 'looking for the sun' fabness and 'Ahh' chorusing owes a debt to everybody from the Beach Boys to the Byrds and it's brilliantly brought down to mundane British life with Graeme's droning travelogue, explaining the bus route through Cricklewood and embracing Sixties hipness with a *Mission: Impossible* 'this is a recording' loop tape. With a seemingly endless rhyming conclusion covering everything from the ageing rock stars ('we're going grey!') to desperation sing-a-longs ('Whey hey hey hey!'), an Irish jig arrangement gently leads the listener into Graeme's wailing country music memories before baby Timbo tells the tall tale of three tiny Goodies making beautiful music together. Striking a blow for youth culture (dubbing his mother boring) and plugging *The New Goodies LP* as part of her shopping list, his proud narration allows pet hatred for Bill to seep in and an, unconvincing but endearing, latch on to hip jive talk – 'we got a whole thing going!' Indeed, once the thing does get going, Bill takes over the lead vocals and the Samba-style melody drags the ditty along with a feel good energy. The talent of Oddie is ribbed and berated by Tim's disgruntled narration – Bill can play the tin whistle long before he could talk – while the endearingly sweet 'That's the song of the baby!' backing chorus adds extra warmth to the piece. Girl-shy and sounding, for the life, like Sellers as Bluebottle, Tim's cutesy pie 'One more time!' will melt the coldest heart. For the closing track on Side One, Oddie pulls out a little cracker. Heaven knows why *Rock with a Policeman* wasn't released as a single. This is a three-minute musical version of the Series One episode *Give Police a Chance*. Taking its rhythmic influence from Elvis's *Jailhouse Rock*, this is pure genius all the way. Oddie's rocking 'Owws!' are electrifying, the great thick copper chorus chugs along with style and, best of all, Graeme Garden's monotone 'Evening all...' lapses into 'May I have this dance!' niceties without a waver in pace or emphasis. It's packed with treasurable bits with 'You got my number!' resulting in Oddie's screamed '999!', a blue suede boot stomp backing beat like something from Lennon's *Power to the People*, simpleton confusion ('Call the police!' 'We are the police!' 'Oh Yeah!'), and cheeky inclusion of the *Dixon of Dock Green* theme as Garden mutters 'And now will you kindly accompany me to the flip side!' Without doubt another one for The Goodies Desert Island Discs. Side

Two kicks off with *The Cricklewood Shakedown* which is a less successful, Seventies disco answer to Side One's peerless *Cricklewood*. Mind you, the opening gambit, 'One, two, three, four, where's the place that we adore? Doing it right, doing it good, we're all going to Cricklewood!', is a winner and the 'wobbling, wobbling' jelly chant always makes me laugh. A bit of a funk on down, one can imagine the disco babes bopping to this one and it does make an effective prelude to Oddie's baby angst *Nappy Love* and the sublime *I'm a Teapot*. Latching on to a comic motif used in both *I'm Sorry I'll Read That Again* and *At Last the 1948 Show*, the hip 'What are you?' intro paves the way for Tim's frightfully posh upper class twit, rabbiting on about his teapot obsession – 'I don't worry coz I'm OK!' Cool, happy and self-contained, Oddie's sleeve note points out the social comment lyrics, faces an ever-mounting crisis and reveals the comically profound subtext of protecting innocent minorities whatever they want to do. There's even some gibbon jibbering during the 'Go ape' section and Tim's perfectly refined 'if it's not too much trouble' in answer to the hippie, happy question 'Shall we show you the way', is classic indeed. The only song actually to feature in a narrative *Goodies* episode, with the exception of the opening track, is the brilliant *Working the Line*. Originally in the Series Five *Bunfight at the OK Corral*, the wailing guitar introduction and tambourine set up Oddie's seriously intended American labouring song, continually 'mucked up' by Graeme and Tim's comic last line of each verse. There's nothing to touch Tim's effete 'I got terribly hot!', but it's all pretty great stuff. Finally, the 'she promised to bring me a bunch of blue gibbons' version of that legendary hit single, *The Funky Gibbon*, links into the climatic *Wild Thing*, leaving a rocking, funny album at its peak.

Side 1: Goodies Theme, Please Let Us Play, Custard Pie, Cricklewood, Good Ole Country Music, Baby Samba, Rock with a Policeman **Side 2:** The Cricklewood Shakedown, Nappy Love, I'm a Teapot, Working the Line, The Funky Gibbon, Wild Thing. All titles written by Bill Oddie except Wild Thing, written by Chip Taylor. Arranged by Dave MacRae (Side 1: tracks 1, 2 and 7, Side 2: tracks 1, 3–6) and Tom Parker (Side 1: tracks 2, 4–6, Side 2: track 2), despite interference from Bill Oddie. Drums Clem Cattini, Tony Carr, Billy Rantim, Barry Morgan. Bass Brian Odges, Tony Campo. Guitars Alan Parker, Joe Moretti, Bernie Holland. Pedal Steel Gordon Huntley. Keyboards Dave MacRae, Tom Parker. Percussion Tony Carr, Bill Oddie. Horn Section Chris Hughes, Bob Burtles, Derek Watkins, Tony Fisher, Geoff Wright. Flute Bill Oddie. Vocal Backing 'Bones' (Joy Yates, Jackie Sullivan, Sue Lynch), Miki Antony. Produced by Miki Antony. BRADL 1010 Bradley's Records, October 1975.

THE NEWS QUIZ

The Radio 4 inspiration for *Have I Got News For You*, Barry Took hosted the topical fun with his usual wit and charm. Graeme Garden guested on Saturday 3 October 1992.

NIGHTLINE

Bill Oddie recorded an interview with Phillip Brady for this 3AW Melbourne radio show hosted by Bruce Mansfield. Bill, talking from London, was broadcast on 15 January 1999.

NO, THAT'S ME OVER HERE!

Under the David Frost banner and making his first solo mark on television, Ronnie Corbett starred in this domestic situation comedy as the definitive minor businessman, complete with bowler hat, rolled umbrella and faithful copy of the *Times*. Full of self-importance, self-promotion and huge ideas like a variation on Tony Hancock's *The Rebel* persona, he battled with his wife (Rosemary Leach), pompous next-door neighbour (Henry McGee) and life's little irritations, in general. The first series, broadcast in 1967, was jammed full of behind-the-scenes Frost familiars and the final episode welcomed a one-off appearance from Tim Brooke-Taylor in the immediate wake of *At Last the 1948 Show*.

Ronnie RONNIE CORBETT Laura ROSEMARY LEACH Henry HENRY McGEE The Boss IVOR DEAN The Secretary JILL MAI MEREDITH with TIM BROOKE-TAYLOR, MICHAEL NIGHTINGALE, VICKY DELMA, BARRY CRYER, GRAHAM CHAPMAN. Written by Barry Cryer, Graham Chapman and Eric Idle. Executive Producer David Frost. Producers Marty Feldman and Bill Hitchcock. Tuesday 19 December 1967, ITV.

NOEL EDMONDS PRESENTS MULTICOLOURED SWAP SHOP'S ROCK GARDEN PARTY

Multicoloured Swap Shop was a Saturday morning delight, with the cuddly dinosaur Posh Paws (try it backwards!), cuddly Noel Edmonds and the awe-inspiring chance to exchange your X-Ray vision Action Man for a Cruise Missile (nearly). Essential youth television, the Goodies appeared on a special early evening Bank Holiday edition shown on 29 May 1978. Celebrating the Mouse's 20th anniversary they performed their latest single, *M.I.C.K.E.Y. M.O.U.S.E.* and several other hits, for a live broadcast from a garden in Central London.

NOEL EDMONDS, SHOWADDYWADDY, DARTS, THE GOODIES, PATTI BOULAYE. Producer Crispin Evans. Executive producer Rosemary Gill. Monday 29 May 1978, BBC1.

NOEL'S HOUSE PARTY

Noel Edmonds' live Saturday evening package of messy games, public humiliation and mugged rushing about, this was the show that gave us Mr Blobby, the Gotcha and endless Crinkley Bottom jokes. Mind you, it became compulsive viewing during the early Nineties if only for its continued embrace of national treasures like Bernard Cribbins, Spike Milligan and Jon Pertwee. During this era Graeme Garden was frequently called on to liven up the script with some painfully punful jokes and, rather unwisely getting involved on a higher profile, Tim Brooke-Taylor was occasionally spotted cringing in the quick-fire Joke Corner where the likes of Frank Carson popped up and cracked a less than cracking cracker.

NORMAN GUNSTON

Pioneering the British work of Alan Partridge, Gunston was the nightmarish show business creation of actor Garry McDonald. Tim Brooke-Taylor was interviewed on this mock Ozzie chat show on 3 August 1976 plugging *The Goodies* and taunting the host with thoughts that the show is aired far too early. Tim appeared on the second show of Series Three, with headlining guest Michael Caine.

NOT NOW DARLING

Tim Brooke-Taylor starred in a production of this classic John Chapman and Ray Cooney farce in a 1980 tour.

NOTHING BETTER TO DO/TRAFFIC ISLAND

Bill Oddie single release of two *I'm Sorry I'll Read That Again* numbers.

R5153 Parlophone 1964.

NOTHING TO DO WITH US

'Musically the best record we ever made… by a mile!' Bill Oddie.

Having changed record labels from Bradley's, the Goodies would never again enjoy the chart success of 1975. However, this album, released by Island records in 1976, was a more mature, thought-provoking piece compared with their catchy hit singles. As with *The New Goodies LP*, Oddie's lyrics are included on the album insert. For this more progressive rock collection, everything is fully geared to near the knuckle comic mode as opposed to Oddie's few semi-serious rock numbers. Mind you, beginning the record with an ambitious operatic response to Queen's *Bohemian Rhapsody* which weighs in at nearly 12 minutes, this is Oddie's musical pinnacle. *The Policeman's Opera* is a staggering achievement, revisiting the territory of Series One's *Give Police a Chance* but addressing the issues with comic-focused clarity. From the opening 'Hello, hello, hello' chorus and stunning guitar breaks, this is classic stuff with Oddie taking centre stage as the ordinary policeman depressed at his big flat feet and bald head. Giving him a complex about taking his helmet off, the piece follows his plight. 'Pig's Lament…' forms an emotive overture with Oddie's confused admittance about beating up old ladies receiving the unforgettable echo from his fellow boys in blue, 'Well, what's wrong with that!' With a guitar solo from Bernie Holland almost worthy of George Harrison, the lads intend to cheer up Oddie and usher in another guitar interlude joyfully ripping off Brian May's unique sound. The 'Dreadcop's Comin'' section showcases Graeme Garden's chilled copper dishing out certain substances, Bob Marley bootleg recordings, self-mocking references to their own label, Island Records and test match tickets in a reggae-style funk fest. The corrupt force element is brilliantly addressed and Garden's performance is peerless, but the more shady side of law-enforcing is dismissed in the 'Third Bit' when the scum-busting Chief Inspector elbows weed in favour of love. Within the narrative operatics of this work Oddie drops in a number which could have been a single in its own right. 'Photofit Love' boasts a funky, sexy saxophone backing, a hip, disco beat and Oddie's obsession with a vision of loveliness in the mysterious, fictional face of a photofit glam. His 'She does not exist!' whining leads into the Aria, sending up the flamboyant flourishes of *Bohemian Rhapsody* with Oddie desperately trying to top the operatic responses of the Rozzers Ensemble. The spell is broken by the appearance of Bill's dream date, Policewoman Edwina Crump, as played by Tim Brooke-Taylor in *I'm Sorry I'll Read That Again* old crone mode. The shrieked 'Hello!' is arguably the funniest moment on the album and 'Rhapsody in Blue' elaborates on the ill-fated romance with sexy urges and coy innuendo. (Oddie is still concerned about his big feet but he need not worry for Timbo cries 'The bigger the better, feet that is!') The 'Finale' is a sober, low-key affair, Oddie's bald, egg-like head causes nothing but hilarity, the boys in blue kick in with an endless chorus, an authentic siren gives the closure clout and Tim is allowed to ad-lib insults into infinity. A towering achievement and a flawless way to start a vastly under-rated album. Tim camps it up rotten for the second track, *Cactus in My Y-Fronts*, playing the gay cowboy with relish and riding in with limp-wristed elegance. Dying for a leek, he nips behind a cactus and gets pricked in a delicate place, his 'I knew the meaning of a prickly pair... Ouch' is the stuff of comic legend. Accompanied by cool country fiddle, his talented horse hoofing out the rhythm and a yodelling coyote, Tim milks the effeminate mincing for all it's worth. While Jerry Lee Lewis may blame too much whiskey for making 'a loser out of me' Tim faces cactus in his... oh you know where! Oddie's earnest desire to take Queen Elizabeth II away from the boredom of Christmas speeches closes Side One, while Graeme's unsubtle *Blowing Off* gets Side Two off to a flying start. Both tracks made up the unsuccessful single from the album but pale instantly in light of Bill's rocking 'n' reeling track *I Wish I Could Get High*. Certainly the most upbeat and marketable number on the album, it's about Oddie's favourite subject, the music industry, and his inability to join in the drug-induced haven with the roadies, groupies and musicians. Revelling in rock excess and boasting Jimi Hendrix-style riffs, Bill laments his feelings of dullness through a totally unforgettable rock anthem. Trying everything from old bananas to coke (the bubbles get up my nose), the entire concept of drugs equalling great musical skill is mocked wonderfully with gob-smacked reaction to Holland's guitar genius. But drugs don't enter in to it – 'I just practise a lot actually!' *Synthesiser Man* is another one from the rock inner sanctum, bursting forth with a funky beat and reeling out the modern need for thousands of wires, speakers and voice distorts. There's nothing very funny here and the idea can hardly sustain the running time but that doesn't matter, Oddie is in great voice and his 'do it if you can!' wails are fine indeed. *She Wouldn't Understand*

sees Bill back on comic course, playing a mournful, sex-obsessed chap ashamed that his nine and a bit year old marriage is corrupted by affairs with everybody he meets. He's 'got a thing going on...' with schoolgirls, secretaries, bus conductresses, cleaning women and a couple of barmaids... to name but a few. Raspberry yoghurt and a lady wrestler come into the equation along the way in this private confession to the listener. Indeed, his wife wouldn't understand but there's so much overflowing lust in Oddie's 'have the time of our life' that you can't help giving the guy a big thumbs up. Finally, we have Tim Brooke-Taylor running through a little ditty which plays like a cross between a Fred Astaire ballad and Brotherhood of Man's *Save All Your Kisses for Me*. The Eurovision Song Contest connection is further promoted with a communication problem moment and the deadening award of a big fat zero to the Great Britain entry. Still, there's huge charm in Tim's upbeat desire to think of a worthy lyric to deliver and more than a touch of maliciousness in Bill's cutting 'no you can't' interaction after the 'and I can play' repeat. With no copper-bottomed hits and a concept album with no real concept, it's easy to dismiss this effort – don't! It's a compact, brilliantly realised effort of a singer–songwriter and his comic cohorts at their peak. Oh, and get a load of the cover: Victorian law-enforcing via contemporary vandalising with the Goodies caught red-handed painting the album title across a bill poster plugging the 'host of hits' on the record. The reverse images of Tim and Graeme lovingly blowing each other a kiss is only bettered by Oddie's totally suspicious, sideways glance.

Side One: The Policeman's Opera (A Major Work in four movements with a few bits in between), Cactus in My Y Fronts, Elizabeth Rules UK! **Side Two:** Blowing Off, I Wish I Could Get High, Synthesiser Man, She Wouldn't Understand, I Wish I Had Something To Say. Words and Music by Bill Oddie. Produced by Dave McRae and Bill Oddie. Arrangements by Dave McRae (despite interference from Bill Oddie). Female backing vocals 'Bones' (Joy Yates, Jacquie Sullivan and Stevie Lange). Male backing vocals Russell Stone, Chas Mills and Tony Burrows. Famous Voices Charlie Dore. Keyboards (Piano, Electric Piano, Clarinet, Synthesisers, etc) Dave McRae. Drums and Percussion Jeff Seopardie. Extra Percussion Bill Oddie and Dave McRae. Bass and Artificial Flatulence Bill Kristian. Guitars Chris Rae, Ray Flack and Bernie Holland. Guitar solos on 'Policeman's Opera' and 'Wish I Could Get High' Bernie Holland. Trumpets Derek Watkins, Henry Lowther, John Huckridge and Paul Cosh. Trombones Chris Pyne and Geoff Wright. Saxes Ron Aspery (Solos) and Geoff Dailey. Personnel on 'She Wouldn't Understand' Tony Carr (Drums), Alan Parker (Guitar), Brian Odges (Bass), Strings The David Katz Strings. Hot Fiddle Graham Prescott. Engineered and Mixed by Geoff Calver. Engineers Mark Demeley, Mike Silverstein. Special thanks to Terry... Illustration by Mick Brownfield Photography by Gered Mankowitz. ILPS 9452 Island Records, November 1976.

BILL ODDIE INDULGING HIS PASSION FOR THE DRUMS

BILL ODDIE

'I didn't realise I'd done so much, no wonder I feel knackered!' *Bill Oddie*

Writer, actor, composer, bearded anarchist, unbearded anarchist, drummer, birder, campaigner, Goodie and comic genius, William Edgar Oddie was born on 7 July 1941 in Rochdale, Lancashire. Comedy was the young Bill's escape route and he attended the Lapal Primary School and Halesowen in Rochdale, discovering his skill for writing comic songs in the back of the school's rugby coach. Bill progressed to King Edward's School, Birmingham, and met Nat Joseph, later the head of Transatlantic Records. Joseph wrote a school review which Bill performed in and its success led to a second show which featured Oddie's vocal prowess again, as well as written musical contributions. Restructuring the school's rugger songs indulged both his passions for music and sport. The young Bill had been rugby Captain at school, a member of the Warwickshire school cricket team and an avid supporter of Chelsea Football Club. But it was his delight in the written word which helped shape his future career. Reading English Literature at Cambridge's Pembroke College, he subsequently joined the Footlights alongside Tim Brooke-Taylor, John Cleese and Graham Chapman. The musical content of the revues had usually been Gilbert and Sullivan-style stuff but Oddie's contemporary ear for pop music brought new zip to the productions. Despite never having learnt to read or write music, Bill had a natural talent. Of most note was his Adam Faith audience with the Pope piece which was included in the 1962 revue, *Double Take*. His first actual appearance came with the 1963 show *A Clump of Plinths* by which time William Oddie BA had found a new home in Hagley, Worcestershire. The huge success of *Cambridge Circus*, at home, in New Zealand, in America and on radio, proved an invaluable training ground for the performer. The spin-off BBC radio cult series *I'm Sorry I'll Read That Again* kept Oddie busy for much of the Sixties and this popularity saw him move to London in 1965. As well as performing and writing the scripts, Oddie composed all the show's songs, used in several single releases during the decade and the 1967 album, *Distinctly Oddie*. 'I had made some records with Gee Martin as producer and even did a radio Luxembourg broadcast with a pre-stardom David Bowie with me singing some ridiculous Gene Pitney-esque ballad! But I had come back from doing *Cambridge Circus* in America and had to find work. I was a contract writer and sometimes performer for *That Was The Week That Was*. That was my main job and I was paid to write a song and two or three minutes of material every week… but I was also farmed out to other programmes. I wrote for Tommy Cooper and Ronnie Barker. I did a special song for Lulu and Alan Price which I was rather proud of.' He made a mark on television with appearances on *BBC3*, *Twice a Fortnight*, *At Last the 1948 Show* and *Broaden Your Mind* before co-scripting *Doctor in the House* and its various sequels for Thames. He had married performer Jean Hart, with whom he had two daughters, Bonnie, a choreographer and dancer, in 1972, and actress Kate Hardie. From 1970, Bill co-wrote and acted in *The Goodies* for BBC television, pioneering the intrinsic use of music in the comedy and revelling in pop stardom with the team from 1975. He had ambitions of 'becoming the oldest teenage pop idol on the scene!' and, with Tim and Graeme, achieved it with Top 10 records and regular *Top of the Pops* appearances. At the time he indulged his love of football by playing in the Top 10 Eleven Sunday league team and delighted in his musical street cred. At the height of *Goodies* fame, he would often sit in as drummer with top-name bands for University gigs and in 1973, he attended the party where Tim Rice announced plans for the musical *Evita*, like most people Bill considered the idea a dubious one. 'I did do solo gigs. Tim and Graeme came and saw my show at the Rainbow Club in Highbury. That was wonderful: Jimi Hendrix, Queen, Stevie Wonder, the Jackson Five and me have played that venue! It was actually not the right place for my kind of stuff. What was far more appropriate, was over a dozen campus gigs, which were great fun. I played Glasgow on a Saturday night and lived! Looking back, I fell under the spell of doing the rock act for real. I was doing all the silly songs but dressing in that glam rock fashion. I was a lot slimmer in those days and dangerously bordered on a rock image. I should have just done a Billy Connolly in t-shirt and jeans but it was the glam era. I got those t-shirts made by the same people who worked on the series *Rock Follies* (based in Cricklewood as it happened) with 'Wild Thing' and the like emblazoned across them. My daughter sometimes borrows them to this day!' Bill had long planned to write his own musical and he appeared opposite Roger Daltry, David Essex and Vivian Stanshall in a Seventies' stage production of *Tommy!* But it was as an active Goodie that Bill found lasting fame, alternating between quite tubby, clean-shaven working rant monster to a lean, mean, laughing machine, bearded, working rant monster. Throughout, his diminutive (5 foot 4 inches) bag of angst-ridden, sherbet-sucking, girl-chasing dudeness, was an essential part of the Britcom experience. Comically obsessed with his weight from an early age, his notes on the *Distinctly Oddie* album proclaimed his weight in socks as 10 stone, 8 ounces and the weight of his socks as 10 stone. By the time *The Goodies* had moved to ITV he was actively involved in the *TV Times* weight-watcher regime (February 1982), tackling the Full Choice Plan Diet alongside Jill Gascoine. Typically, he had cited his favourite foods as the contrasting delights of lemon meringue pie and celery. After the Goodies' short-lived association with independent television, they regrouped for *Bananaman* and Oddie co-wrote the ITV series *Astronauts* with Graeme Garden. Successful ventures into children's television (*Saturday Banana*, *Tickle on the Tum*, *From the Top*, *The Bubblegum Brigade*) kept Oddie busy as both actor and, with second wife Laura Beaumont, writer. Heavily involved in nature charities, Bill is proud of his

A Seventies publicity shot of Bill Oddie

connection with The National Trust and is Patron of the Children's Tropical Rain Forest (UK). In 1994 he launched the Southampton-based Look Lively Television to further young broadcasting and an ambition to get behind the camera and that same year he could be spotted enjoying ITV's *An Audience with Bob Monkhouse*, but it was his passion for bird-watching that took up much of his time. He combined birding with children's television when he popped up in the *Ed the Duck* video. One of his proudest achievements is mentioned in the 1976 listing of Rare British Birds sighting which records his glimpse of the Thrush Nightingale on Shetland. Since then, Bill has became a prolific author on the subject, publishing such notable books as *Bill Oddie's Little Black Book of Birds*, *Follow*

BILL ODDIE FURTHER INDULGING HIS PASSION FOR THE DRUMS

That Bird and *Bill Oddie's Gone Birding*. In 1985 he wrote the foreword for Hamlyn's *Bird Behaviour* by Louise Dawson and *Bird Habitats and Conservation* by David Chandler. He is President of the Sandwich Bay Bird Observatory and a council member of the RSPB. On television, he has birded on *Good Morning Britain*, *Bird in the Nest*, *Birding with Bill Oddie* and *Bill Oddie: Bird-watcher*. Thus, it was unsurprising when a familiar broadcasting bird, Alan Partridge, alias comedian Steve Coogan, name-dropped Bill Oddie in each of the six sublime editions of *I'm Alan Partridge*. Continually phoning without leaving messages, co-hosting charity after dinner speeches or suggesting suitable corporate video jobs, the mentions were gloriously throwaway and subtle. Oddie even wrote a note in green ink offering to guest appear as himself on the show! His frequent trips to Australia resulted in a load of birding and the odd radio interview, often appearing on JJJs radio with Merrick and Rosso. His love of all styles of music has made him a popular guest broadcaster, notably on the BBC and Jazz FM. In 1998 Bill's *My Kind of Day* for *Radio Times* reflected his multifaceted life – a meeting on the British Trust for Ornithology in Berkely Square, London, for a protection policy for nightingales – and comic business, playing a robot insect voiceover for a corporate video. In September 1999 (Monday 6, Wednesday 8–Friday 10) he

hosted a themed week of birding documentaries on BBC Choice. The *Radio Times* (2–8 August 1997) revealed Bill's favourite films as *Purple Rain*, *West Side Story*, *Close Encounters of the Third Kind*, *ET*, *Field of Dreams* and *This Is Spinal Tap*. His cinematic heroes are Buster Keaton and Mickey Mouse, while the finest scene remains Donald O'Connor's *Make 'Em Laugh* routine in *Singin' in the Rain*. Bill is married to former *Sale of the Century* hostess, writer and illustrator, Laura Beaumont, with whom he has another daughter, Rosie. Kate Hardie has presented him with a grandson, Lyle. His new BBC series, *Bill Oddie Goes Wild*, is scheduled for September 2000.

ODDIE IN PARADISE

Three-part bird-watching programme unleashing the ex-Goodie in Papua New Guinea on the look-out for the fabulous birds of paradise. Show One had Bill struggling up a mountain, getting drenched in tropical rain and prancing round a maypole with a golden crown on its head! Show Two saw the bird of paradise search continue through mountain terrain where rhododendrons and kangaroos do play. Bill tracks down a parrot which looks like a vulture and a bower bird which decorates its nest with red and blue berries. Even more amazingly, some of Bill's photographs actually come out! Show Three concluded the fun and games with a trip into the open grasslands. Bill travels down the River Bensbach, encountering spoonbills, cranes, magpie geese, wallabies, crocodiles and even a deer that wears a hat to impress its rivals.

Did You Know? Radio Times plugged the first episode of the show with an article, 'A Birders' Eye View', 22–28 June 1985.

Producer Richard Brock. Wednesdays, 26 June–10 July 1985, BBC2.

OMNIBUS:
the film of Reeves and Mortimer

This comic documentary dedicated to Vic and Bob saw a brief extract of a pub-based version of *Shooting Stars*. Television panellist Bill Oddie can be spotted doing the business for all of 10 seconds.

Sunday 21 September 1997, BBC2.

ON IIKLA MOOR BAH'AT/HARI KRISHNA

A Bill Oddie single release on the John Peel label for a couple of *I'm Sorry I'll Read That Again* songs.

4786 Dandelion. EPC 3793 Epic January 1970.

ON THE AIR

A light-hearted nostalgic Radio 2 quiz game recruiting radio celebrities to recall golden classics of the wireless age. Graeme Garden, basking in *I'm Sorry I'll Read That Again* memories, appeared in two editions on Tuesday 26 August and 23 September 1986. On Tuesday 26 July 1988, Tim Brooke-Taylor took part.

ON THE BOX

For the second in a series of Glyn Worsnip chats with television celebrities on BBC2, Bill Oddie, who as the *Radio Times* commented 'was one of the Goodies and is now an enthusiastic bird-watcher', was the second guest on Thursday 26 May 1988.

ON THE BRADEN BEAT

Peter Cook had made a huge impact as EL Wisty on this show before another leading comic light from Cambridge, Tim Brooke-Taylor, was drafted in as replacement. Having started work on the show as a researcher, Tim became a regular performance fixture during the 1965 series playing a self-opinionated, pompous, bowler-hatted London businessman who ranted on about life and British society in a highly prejudiced manner while considering himself a liberal man of total understanding and compassion. The satirical edge, of course, as with Johnny Speight's Alf Garnett, was often lost on the viewer. While Tim's creation was a mockery of the liberated Brit whose fundamental beliefs are abhorrent, many viewers agreed with the supposed thoughts of the actor and celebrated him accordingly. This right-wing, racist bigot became a hero of the people he was attacking, as Tim recalls, 'I found people were beginning to agree with my obnoxious character: 'They work like blacks, er, slaves, er, extremely hard', pre-dating Prince Phillip!' Tim remembers one show very well: 'The night Kenneth Tynan said 'fuck' on David Frost's programme at the same time I was being censored on the Braden Beat. I was doing a piece about Princess Margaret who had been misbehaving in the West Indies. My advice was along the lines of 'she must remember at all times that she is British, at least on her mother's side.' This I had to re-record as 'she must remember when she's in Mustique, she's not just abroad, she's a princess'. Fairly feeble I agree but still there were objections, there was no time to re-edit so they debased the sound on transmission so no one could

hear it. As with Cook before, Tim wrote his own material and Bill Oddie also contributed to the scripts for the programme. Bill also appeared under the guise of folk singer 'Hooligan' a send-up of Bob Dylan and Donovan.

Saturdays, 2 October–25 December 1965, ITV.

ONE FOOT IN THE GRAVE

The final show-down for the Nineties' best-loved situation comedy is a real case of getting together loose ends, looking with emotive nostalgia on the programme's past and celebrating classic comedy in a whiz bang seasonal feature-length finale. Richard Wilson and Annette Crosbie are their usual uniformly excellent selves with Victor forced into a story line concerning a temperamental, haunted caravan and the unintentional kidnapping of a wealthy Indian lady by the name of Mrs Khan (airport confusion setting the farcical ball rolling with style). But it's the supporting cast that really interests us here for, apart from *George and Mildred*'s old next door neighbour in the shape of blunt copper Norman Eshley, there's a new couple of next door neighbours for the Meldrew's to bemuse with their eccentric behaviour. With Angus Deayton opting out of the show, Tim Brooke-Taylor brilliantly stepped into the vacant property with TV wife Marian McLoughlin. A gloriously hesitant, nervous chap by the name of Derek McVitie, Tim — with glasses almost permanently perched on the end of his nose — mutters, giggles and frets his way through his role. Spelling out mild swear words — much to the dry, puncturing amusement of Wilson — Tim proudly plugs his newspaper cartoon strip, McVitie's View, the hilarious antics of an aged bloke who complains about everything. 'Where do you get your ideas from?' Meldrew innocently enquires. Anyway, apart from McLoughlin spotting the old nut from next door apparently having sex with a radiator (he is in front of it drying his wet trousers), the couple embark on a dream fortnight in a rented cottage in Norfolk. Another sitcom misunderstanding sees the Meldrews arriving at the same place and a classic BBC comedy moment as Tim sleepily thinks he spots the main man in bed with him. Usually in sitcomland all the problems and dubious occurrences are skilfully ironed out (off screen and by the ladies), so Tim can gently get over his angst, calm himself down and relax for one second before the police break in and arrest him for Mrs Khan's kidnapping — Meldrew having used his telephone for the supposedly innocent call to Khan's wealthy son. A

BILL ODDIE DOWN AND OUT AND SINGING THE BLUES

wonderfully orchestrated piece of radical comic tension, Tim's only briefly spotted twice more, facing hard interrogation down the cop shop and being whisked through the hospital ward in hot pursuit by the police. Touching, beautifully acted and hilarious enough in large swathes to allow the pathos to work perfectly, *Endgame* is a perfect close to a landmark television comedy. Such a great pity that Tim didn't have a longer crack at playing the next door neighbour to Britain's favourite old grouch... Maybe he will return!

Victor Meldrew RICHARD WILSON Margaret Meldrew ANNETTE CROSBIE Derek John McVitie TIM BROOKE-TAYLOR Betty McVitie MARIAN McLOUGHLIN. Written by David Renwick. Produced by Esta Charkham. Directed by Christine Gernon. Thursday 25 December 1997, BBC1.

ONE-MAN BAND

Later considered for the title of his autobiography, this stunning comic autobiographical film from Orson Welles takes the form of a tongue-in-cheek London travelogue. Peter Sellers and *Balham, Gateway to the South*-like, Welles tackles all the London eccentricities, from a portly Policeman earnestly singing the title song to a less than coy violet seller happily pursuing her sideline trade in dirty postcards. Tim Brooke-Taylor hosts this hilarious short, donned in British businessman bowler hat and suit.

Embracing the new found, cool and hip attitude of swinging Sixties' England with bursts of 'Wow!' all over the place, Tim's bumbling Brit starts his guide to London with nose-pinching pain from the clapper board and uncertain knowledge of the recording equipment 'I say, this thing is on isn't it?' Desperately trying to locate Carnaby Street without much success, Tim is finally brought into the seedy world of Soho striptease. Removing his hat, he reveals a long blonde wig underneath and mincingly dances off into the sunset.

Did You Know? *Long hidden in the Welles vault, this and Tim's other late Sixties collaboration with the great director, Lord Plumfield Versus Welles, was featured as part of the 1995 documentary The Lost Films of Orson Welles from producer Pit Riethmuller and director Vassili Silovic. It was broadcast on BBC2 in 1997 as part of the TX series, edited by John Wyver. The title song was written by Bill Oddie for I'm Sorry I'll Read That Again (Series Six, Episode Five) and used again for the fourth show in Series Two of Broaden Your Mind.*

Produced, written, edited and directed by Orson Welles.

OPEN AIR

Tim Brooke-Taylor was interviewed by Janet Ellis for this live 1988 phone-in. Sporting a *You Must Be the Husband* evil spirit sweater, discussing his latest sitcom success and tackling Goodies questions from the great British public. Tantalisingly mentioning new rules for Mornington Crescent and accepting a culminating cuddle from the host, Tim's thoughts of comedy, law and the female sense of humour were stimulating and entertaining.

Producer Rachel Purnell. Director Alan Yardley. BBC1.

OPEN HOUSE WITH GLORIA HUNNIFORD

On Wednesday 6 February 2000, Bill Oddie was interviewed about birds and lack of *Goodies* repeats on this Channel 5 chat show.

ORSON'S BAG

A television special show-casing the unique genius of Orson Welles. Having seen and enjoyed *Broaden Your Mind*, the great man personally asked for Graeme Garden and Tim Brooke-Taylor to write for the show in 1969.

OUR SHOW

Tim Brooke-Taylor was interviewed for this television programme on the 13 May 1978.

PAUL HOGAN'S ENGLAND

With the fledgling Channel 4 having scored a hit with compilation shows of Paul Hogan's Australian programmes, the Nine Network liased for two specially made editions for the English home market. Fashioned as comic postcards to back home, the second headlined Tim Brooke-Taylor. Sketches included Harry Butler, the dangerous London Bobby, Conan the Barbarian and Charles Bronson but Tim's appearance – greeted with a huge round of applause – was as Mr Rhys-Jones, possible British emigrant for Oz. Hogan's doctor delighted in this 'chinless wonder' and tested loyalty to English cricket, reaction to a sexy blonde nurse, potential liquid intake and whinging capacity. The results find Tim out as a sherry-drinking, patriotic, possible poof and twit… with no sense of humour when it comes to fake funnel web spiders!

With PETER CLEALL, DIRE STRAITS, PAUL YOUNG. Friday 30 December 1983, Channel 4.

PEBBLE MILL AT ONE

Treasured early afternoon BBC magazine programme broadcast from the Birmingham studios and wallowing in cool guests, gloriously naff graphics and a sense of regional telly. In an edition steeped in nature with Chris Baines launching the 1986 Conservation Awards, outside broadcast presenter Paul Coia journeyed with Bill Oddie for some binocular action on Bird Island, the Seychelles. The following week, Bill Oddie was dragging Coia on a nifty bit of 'island hopping', checking out the alleged Garden of Eden at Praslin Vallet de Mai and skipping on to La Dique before the pubs shut!

Mondays, 10 February and 17 February 1986, BBC1.

THE PERSUADERS & OTHER TOP SEVENTIES TV THEMES

A stunning, double CD collection headlined by John Barry's super cool title music for the classic Roger Moore/Tony Curtis adventure series. Bill Oddie's Theme from The Goodies taken from The New Goodies LP was included as Track 11 on Disc One. Forty-eight other selections, a complete remaster, groovy design and articulate sleeve notes from Michael Richardson made this an essential package.

NEMCD 424 Sequel Records 1999.

THE PHILANTHROPIST

Tim Brooke-Taylor starred in this stage production alongside Edward Fox. A bitter–sweet Christopher Hampton play revival from 1970 dealing with a couple of Oxford dons and the dangers of nicety, the 1991 tour took in Bradford, Sheffield and Birmingham.

THE PLANK

The classic cinema-released version of the trials and tribulations played out by builders Eric Sykes and Tommy Cooper with, the star of the show, a wooden plank. As usual Sykes, the Orson Welles of comedy, attracted great star names to join in the fun – notably, Jimmy Edwards as the policeman and Jim Dale as a bemused house painter. A young Bill Oddie appears briefly as a window cleaner working outside a pub. Due to the plank manoeuvring, a punter's pint ends up in Bill's bucket, he looks around in wonder while gripping the empty glass and is quickly whisked into the establishment – through the open window – for a massive, off-screen, beating.

Producer Jon Penington. Written and directed by Eric Sykes. 1969.

PLAY IT AGAIN

A sort of Desert Island Discs for the cinema, various celebrities were invited to select their all-time favourite film moments and discuss their importance. Comedian, writer, actor, teacher and film producer Tim Brooke-Taylor delved into his passion for classic Walt Disney animation with a clip from Snow White and the Seven Dwarfs, while revealing the visual comic influences on The Goodies with knockabout banter from Abbott and Costello and breath-taking genius from Buster Keaton's Sherlock Junior. Other selections included the 1933 King Kong and Wages of Fear.

Producer David Jones. Director Bernard Preston. Wednesday 3 November 1982, ITV.

PLEASURE AT HER MAJESTY'S

The invaluable film recording of the first Amnesty International concert A Poke in the Eye (with a Sharp Stick), this features brief appearances from the Goodies both on stage and behind the scenes. Originally made for a BBC Omnibus special, it was later given a limited cinema release and, made rather more commercially viable in America where is was released as Monty Python Meets Beyond the Fringe.

Director Roger Graef. Wednesday 29 December 1976, BBC1.

A POKE IN THE EYE (WITH A SHARP STICK)

In 1975 John Cleese was approached to support a theatrical venture celebrating 15 years of Amnesty International. Indeed, in a reference to many of the cast's past history, Cleese suggested the concert be called An Evening Without David Frost. However, before long, the proposed Sunday evening performance had been changed to a three-performance, late-night, gala charity season. Cleese had vowed to take an active part in the show as well as promising to rope in 'a couple of friends' to perform. Those friends included four-sixths of *Monty Python*, three-quarters of *Beyond the Fringe*, all of *The Goodies* and other notables from the Oxbridge satire boom. Unlike Python, the Goodies as a unit, had not performed on stage together and, thus, had no tried and tested routines to perform. More to the point, whereas Python had recognisable, self-contained sketches that could transfer to stage with ease, *The Goodies* had always been fashioned as a 30-minute piece. Besides, a recreation of their most famous bits would have needed a huge beanstalk, a giant kitten and a huge chunk of the BBC Special Effects department budget. Therefore, the contribution from the Goodies boiled down to a performance of four of their hit recordings, *Mummy I Don't Like My Meat*, *Cactus in My Y-Fronts*, *Sick Man Blues* and, of course, the hit single, *Funky Gibbon*. In a return to the glories of *Cambridge Circus* on Broadway, Bill Oddie also resumed his place in the Jones/Palin slapstick lecture alongside the Python boys, while all the Goodies joined the rest of the cast in backing Michael Palin's climactic rendition of *The Lumberjack Song*.

Did You Know? Tim Brooke-Taylor was not in the best of spirits for this show. His beloved Derby County had just lost to Sheffield Wednesday in the semi-final of the Cup and he was nearly hoarse from yelling.

ALAN BENNETT, JOHN BIRD, ELEANOR BRON, TIM BROOKE-TAYLOR, GRAHAM CHAPMAN, JOHN CLEESE, CAROL CLEVELAND, PETER COOK, JOHN FORTUNE, GRAEME GARDEN, TERRY GILLIAM, BARRY HUMPHRIES, NEIL INNES, DES JONES, TERRY JONES, JONATHAN LYNN, JONATHAN MILLER. BILL ODDIE, MICHAEL PALIN. Director Jonathan Miller. Produced by Peter Luff and David Simpson. Thursday 1–Saturday 3 April 1976, Her Majesty's Theatre, London.

A POKE IN THE EYE (WITH A SHARP STICK): the record

Boasting a stunning Terry Gilliam-designed cover of a head split asunder with David Redfern photos from the concert bursting out, Transatlantic Records put together a brilliant recording of the show's highlights. Described as 'The Comedy Album of the Century', the Goodies connection is embraced on just one track – their spirited performance of *Funky Gibbon*. With the Gibbon already having been a successful A-side single and Oddie considering the performance inferior, the Goodies actually campaigned for *Sick Man Blues* to be included on the album. However, producer Martin Lewis insisted on the hit being included. Appearing by kind permission of Bradley's Records, it was nearly 20 years before the other three tracks were made commercially available.

THE RE-ISSUE... THE COMPLETE A POKE IN THE EYE (WITH A SHARP STICK)

In the CD age, every classic album was cleaned up and repackaged and *A Poke in the Eye* was no exception. In 1991, Castle communications took up the Amnesty course and issued an essential two-CD set from the first charity concerts from 1976. The first disc was an exact resurrection of the original album with the second featuring further gems from the Pythons, Neil Innes and, of course, the Goodies, performing *Cactus in My Y Fronts*, *Mummy I Don't Like My Meat* (incorrectly credited in the listings as Mummy, mummy, mummy) and *Sick Man Blues* (also mistakenly dubbed Sick Man's Blues on the album).

THE PRESS GANG

Glyn Worsnip hosted this radio celebration of newspapers, gutter journalists and outrageous headlines. Guest Bill Oddie denied a compulsive ornithologist slur and brightened up the half hour with his usual anarchic wit on Friday 14 October 1988.

PRIVATES ON PARADE

A 1981 National Theatre of Western Australia stage production of Peter Nichols's autobiographical account of wartime military camp entertainment. Tim Brooke-Taylor took the lead.

BILL ODDIE POSES WITH BIG ROBIN PAL FOR AN **RSPB** PROMOTION

PULL THE OTHER ONE

A cheap and cheerful down-market Carlton Select cable television variation on *Call My Bluff* with host Paul Coia, flanked by an unconvincing library back-drop, setting two teams of three celebs off on a battle to fool each other with true or false tall stories. Somehow Bill Oddie managed to stumble into a couple of editions in 1998 and, even more laudably, retain his dignity throughout.

PUNCHLINES

An energetic celebrity ITV panel game hosted by ever-grinning Lennie Bennett. Supposedly a test of initiative, memory and various skills, the contestants would be aided and abetted by a collection of famous faces and given an extra clue from a surprise guest star. This untaxing piece of television asked its general public contestants to remember 'What they heard and where they heard it!' Tim Brooke-Taylor gritted his teeth and twice went through the motions on 7 March 1981 and 26 February 1983.

Q

QD – THE MASTER GAME

An interesting experiment from Channel 4, spreading five, live, early evening programmes over a single week and challenging six contestants to surprise practical tasks, sports activities and memory tests. Sort of like Richard O'Brien's far more successful *The Crystal Maze*, this slice of enjoyable fun was hosted by the ever-charming Tim Brooke-Taylor and Lisa Aziz who willed the players on through 20 gruelling rounds and on to the final chance to win £5000.

Producer Rod Natkiel. Director Juliet May. Monday 29 July–Friday 2 August 1991, Channel 4.

A QUESTION OF ENTERTAINMENT

An unambitious BBC1 celeb fest tackling trivia posers, classic clips and witty one-liners through Tom O'Connor's sharp control. Bill Oddie joined the panel for a single 1988 appearance on Sunday 3 July.

QUICK ON THE DRAW

A classic ITV game show, later resurrected in the shape of the Bob Mills time-filler, *Win, Lose or Draw*. In a nutshell, it was a celebrity game of *Give Us a Clue* using drawn clues rather than mimed ones. Goodie and cartoonist extraordinaire, Graeme Garden, unsurprisingly took to the fun with the style of a duck to wet stuff and on one, early occasion on 7 July 1977, fellow Goodie and cartoon admirer, Bill Oddie, had a bash as well.

QUICK ON THE DRAW: the book

The programme proved so popular that Denis Gifford was commissioned to compile some of the funniest moments from the shows in an Arrow publication through *Look-In* comics. Several of the key players were roped in to help, including Graeme Garden.

Written by Denis Gifford, with help from, Graeme Garden, Michael Bentine and Bill Tidy. Arrow/Look-In publications 1977.

RADIO TIMES COMEDY PARADE: CIRCUS CIRCUS

As part on a BBC initiative to discover fresh writing talent, five lucky competition winners won the chance to have their play produced, performed and professionally broadcast on Radio 4. For this third presentation, Graeme Garden starred as the Scottish circus owner, Hector McVie, in a chillingly hilarious tale of murder, passion and burnt sausages, set under a big top community threatened by a serial killer in 1951. Lots of post-war angst, delicious black comedy and a stunning central performance to enjoy.

Hector McVie GRAEME GARDEN Betty BRENDA BLETHYN Charlie GREGOR FISHER Raymond GARARD GREEN Mrs Umberto JENNIFER PIERCEY Bimbo PHIL NICE Mirabella AMANDA SWIFT Moto NEIL MULLARY. Written by Bill Brennan. Producer Mark Robson. Saturday 1 November 1986, Radio 4.

DAVID RAPPAPORT

Britain's best-loved dwarf actor, Rappaport injected a street-wise cool into his little men, most notably stealing the limelight in Terry Gilliam's *Time Bandits*. He did more of the same as the militant Chief Dwarf in the first Goodies venture for ITV, *Snow White 2*, and appeared twice during the LWT series. Providing the cheeky vocals for the office Robot in both the opening episode, *Robot*, and the in-joke ridden classic, *Change of Life*. A former schoolteacher, Rappaport was proud of his short stature, explaining that God's greatest gift was to be 30 and be able to look a child in the eye. However, typecasting took its toil and this fine actor committed suicide in 1992.

RATTLE OF A SIMPLE MAN

A Cambridge Theatre Company presentation of the celebrated play, starring Graeme Garden.

ROLAND RAT: THE SERIES

The saviour of *TV-AM*! A street-wise, shades-wearing rat with the most irritating laugh in the world was awarded his own headlining BBC children's series. Like Rod Hull and Emu he was allotted his own, fictitious station, BBC3, and basked in his cool dude appeal as the sewer-dwelling Superstar. Regular scriptwriter Colin Bostock-Smith, of *Me & My Girl* and *You Must Be The Husband,* attracted favourite actor, Tim Brooke-Taylor, to appear in the very first episode.

Written by David Claridge, Colin Bostock-Smith, John Langdon, Sean Carson and Daniel Tomlinson. Produced and directed by Marcus Mortimer. Friday 31 July 1987, BBC1.

RORY BREMNER

With the impressionist skills of Mike Yarwood and the satirical edge of Peter Cook, Rory Bremner revolutionised impressionist comedy on television. It was no longer good enough to do a fair Tommy Cooper or Frank Spencer, your characters had to be funny within themselves, comment on current issues and sound totally convincing, all at the same time. Bremner was helped by two great satirists from the Sixties, John Bird and John Fortune, while another force from the past, Graeme Garden, contributed additional material to the scripts.

THE ROUGH WITH THE SMOOTH

An English slant on *The Odd Couple* or a more subtle *Men Behaving Badly* for the Oxbridge generation, call it what you will, this situation comedy premise was a hasty collaboration by Marty Feldman cohorts John Junkin and Tim Brooke-Taylor. The basic premise was two confirmed bachelor flatmates — the rough and ready Junkin and the smooth-talking Brooke-Taylor — whose sole interest was sex. The comedy boiled down to anxious desperation in trying to out do each other in the female pulling stakes. A pilot episode aired in 1971 but it wasn't until four years later, and after success together with BBC radio's *Hello Cheeky*, that the duo were invited back for a single, six-part series. The hilarious situations were further enhanced by several notable guest stars who wandered into the action.

Harold King JOHN JUNKIN Richard Woodville TIM BROOKE-TAYLOR. Written by John Junkin and Tim Brooke-Taylor. **Pilot:** Producer Leon Thau. Thursday 22 April 1971, BBC1. **Series:** Producer Harold Snoad. Wednesdays, 16 July–20 August 1975, BBC1.

ROY KINNEAR: AN ACTOR'S LIFE

Introduced by satire babe and *Help!* co-star Eleanor Bron, this was a hilarious, touching and warm tribute to the much-loved comedy actor in 1988. During a break from recording *I'm Sorry I Haven't a Clue*, Willie Rushton recalled *That Was The Week That Was* days and Goodies Tim Brooke-Taylor and Graeme Garden remembered Roy's peerless Emperor Nero and the painful Boom-Boom tribe escapade.

ROYAL VARIETY SHOW

Following two ground-breaking series of *It's Marty* and the special *Marty Amok*, Tim Brooke-Taylor teamed up once again with Marty Feldman for the 1970 Command Performance screened on BBC1 on 15 November.

RULE BRITANNIA: THE WAYS AND WORLD OF THE TRUE BRITISH GENTLEMAN AND PATRIOT

As the great Bo Diddley once said, 'You can't judge a book by its cover…' Mind you, no book could possible deliver the ultra-patriotic cool that this cover conjures up. Our Union flag waist-coated hero proudly taking his best, hands on lapels, legal stance and sticking his stiff upper lip and stiff British chin out a mile. As Tim explains in his Cricklewood-based, immediate post-Goodies, introduction, the book details the best and worst aspects of the true British hero. Eccentric, often pompous, convinced of their God on Our Side righteousness and eager to tackle anything for the betterment and promotion of the nation. As Sir Claude Champion de Crespigny is quoted as saying, 'Where there is a daring deed to be done in any part of the world, an Englishman should leap to the front to accomplish it'. That statement just about sums up the glorious Brits celebrated and gently mocked within these pages. Each chapter heading is ingeniously fashioned in such a way that the first letter of each spells out B.R.I.T.A.N.N.I.A. R.U.L.E.S. T.H.E. W.A.V.E.S. allowing Tim to guide the reader through such monumental topics as Births, Deaths, Marriages to the Stiff Upper Lip. Along the way there is a ponder on the British in India, the treatment of servants, a rather useless 'lingo by jingo' glossary to help one understand 'toff', and a charmingly naïve look at Victorian attitudes to sex. Explorers, soldiers, politicians and etiquette requirements of the 19th Century are all included, with each chapter hilariously illustrated by a quite spiffing cartoon from David Farris. Although protesting against being stereotyped as a fully paid up member of the Brits Rule Club, you get the impression that Tim is wallowing in the manic antics of the book's true patriotic legends. An attitude

TIM BROOKE-TAYLOR – GOODIE, ACTION MAN, YOUR LAST LINE OF DEFENCE!

perfectly captured in Field Marshall Montgomery's outrage at the 1965 Homosexuality Bill: 'This sort of thing may be tolerated by the French, but we are British, thank God.'

JM Dent & Sons Ltd 1983.

RUN FOR YOUR WIFE!

A man has to keep two separate lives and two separate wives apart as a vicar, a camp next door neighbour, his sheepish, covering up, best pal, and a bombastic Policeman, all get involved in trouser-dropping, door-opening, door-closing, domestic farce. A high-pitched, ultra-fast stage romp from the prolific pen of Ray Cooney, one production, during March 1984 at the Criterion Theatre, Piccadilly Circus, delighted in teaming *Me & My Girl* stars Richard O'Sullivan and Tim Brooke-Taylor as the bigamist hero and his nervy friend, Stanley Gardner. As an extra bonus, Bernard Bresslaw turned on the suspicious menace as the law-enforcer.

S

SATURDAY BANANA

While golden Saturday mornings of my youth had *Tiswas* and *Multicoloured Swap Shop*, we also always had Bill Oddie, *Saturday Banana* and copious amounts of blow-up yellow fruit. A huge banana was erected in the car park at Southern Television and was often spotted during serious news reports from the area. The show was the usual live marathon mix of star guests, cartoons and messy games, with the ultimate prize being a Super Banana Bike, awarded to each week's winner in the ultimate contest, Bananas. If anyone has an original model for sale let me know... please!

Did You Know? Bill Oddie claims that the show was meant to be called *The Saturday Bonanza* but somebody misheard and dubbed it 'Banana'. Bill can be spotted wearing a Saturday Banana badge in several of the later Goodies episodes – a rare BBC/ITV cross-over endorsement.

Producer Anthony Howard. Saturdays, 8 July–30 December 1978. Special: Saturday Banana Christmas Fayre, Saturday 23 December 1978. ITV Southern and Anglia regions.

SAYS WHO?

Graeme Garden hosted this Radio 2 impressionists' comedy debate. The pilot was recorded on Thursday 10 February 2000 with Ashley Blake producing.

SCHOOLDAYS

A new comedy play by JV Stevenson bringing together celebrated Cambridge Footlighters, in leading actor Graeme Garden and director Jonathan Lynn. Ian Lavender, scoring in the ratings with *The Glums*, was also in the cast.

Performed for one week from Monday 17 March 1978, The Cambridge Theatre Company.

THE SCIENCE SHOW

Plugging an Australian based bird-watching Twitch-a-thon, Bill Oddie was interviewed by Robin Williams on this ABC Radio National programme in October 1989. He chatted about *The Goodies*, *The Mikado* and, most potently of all, memories of Graham Chapman just days after his death. Considering Chapman the 'most human' of Pythons, Bill remembered the last time he had seen him, a couple of years previously at a Guy's Hospital Revue marking the 20th anniversary since the Cambridge boys had performed there.

BILL ODDIE HAPPILY POSING ON A HUGE BANANA FOR HIS FUN-FILLED SATURDAY MORNING SHOW, *THE SATURDAY BANANA*

SCOOP OF THE YEAR

Barry Norman presented this light-hearted look back at the people and events that shaped 1981. Graeme Garden was part of the panel put through the memory test.

Producer Colin Goodman. Monday 28 December 1981, BBC2.

SEASIDE SPECIAL

The Goodies made a guest appearance on this BBC1 Summer variety show on 19 June 1976.

THE SECRET POLICEMAN'S OTHER BALL

For this, the fourth hugely successful Amnesty International comedy concert, an injection of fresh talent was included with notably the *Not the Nine O'Clock News* team joining forces with their idols and a more prominent emphasis on musical entertainment ushered in via such rock gods as Phil Collins, Eric Clapton and Jeff Beck. Of the old timers, John Cleese rounded up John Bird, John Fortune and Neil Innes, as well as one fellow Python,

THE SECRET POLICEMAN'S OTHER BALL: the book

With an introduction by John Cleese and production notes by Terry Jones and Michael Palin, this featured scripts, lyrics and Michael Putland photographs from the shows.
Metheun 1981.

THE SECRET POLICEMAN'S OTHER BALL: the record

A companion record featured highlights from the musical performances, but this collected together the best of the comedy and included Tim Brooke-Taylor on just one track, Top of the Form.
HAHA 6003 Island 1981.

THE SECRET POLICEMAN'S THIRD BALL

A decade since *A Poke in the Eye* had started the whole Amnesty comedy tradition, this charity concert handed the reigns almost completely to the waiting in the wings *Comic Relief* generation. Again, comedy stood hand-in-hand with pop performers, resulting in two video releases directed for film by Ken O'Neill, and two records, covering comedy and music independently. Only pioneer John Cleese and Cambridge pal, Bill Oddie kept the old campaigner flag flying this time round. A book and record, The Secret Policeman's Third Ball – The Comedy, were released.

JOAN ARMATRADING, CHET ATKINS, JOY BEHART, PAUL BRADY, RICHARD BRANSON, RORY BREMNER, JACKSON BROWNE, KATE BUSH, JOHN CLEESE, PHIL COOL, ROBBIE COLTRANE, ANDY DA LA TOUR, DURAN DURAN, ERASURE, CRAIG FERGUSON, DAWN FRENCH, STEPHEN FRY, PETER GABRIEL, PAUL GAMBACCINI, BOB GELDOF, DAVE GILMOUR, GARETH HALE, LENNY HENRY, JOOLS HOLLAND, NIGEL KENNEDY, NIK KERSHAW, MARK KNOPLER, HUGH LAURIE, WARREN MITCHELL, YOUSSO N'DOUR, BILL ODDIE, NORMAN PACE, EMO PHILIPS, COURTNEY PINE, LOU REED, GRIFF RHYS JONES, JONATHAN ROSS, ANDREW SACHS, JENNIFER SAUNDERS, MEL SMITH, SPITTING IMAGES, LOUDON WAINWRIGHT III, WHO DARES WIN WORKING WEEK WORLD PARTY. Director Paul Jackson. Thursday 26–Sunday 29 March 1987, London Palladium.

SEEDY SOUND OF HELLO CHEEKY

An EMI record release of classic moments from Yorkshire television's 1976 series, *Hello Cheeky*.

Miserable Song, Moon Over Romford, Your Third Leg, Wrong Love Song, Soda Syphon Baby, Road to Plaiston, I'm Growing a Beard, I'm in Love with the Girl, Carrots for My Lady, Don't Say Goodbye, Tickling Mrs Adcock, Pie and Chips, Hymn to Cockroaches, Rock Cake Rock, Transistorised Sweetheart, Sweet Old Fashioned Thing, Love Song for Agnes, Belle of Chalk Farm, South of the Ankle, Edith Cosgrove, Smashing Year, Love is Ranember in Dumfries, Crossbar Katy, Tram Ride to Romance, Money Song. EMC 3112 EMI Records 1976.

IT MAY BE WORKING BUT WHO WANTS TO GET UP EARLY ON SATURDAY MORNINGS! – BILL POSES FOR THE SATURDAY BANANA

Graham Chapman, one Fringer, Alan Bennett, and one Goodie, Tim Brooke-Taylor. In fact, Tim was really embraced as part of the vintage *At Last the 1948 Show*, with three of the original gang involved, fleshing out vintage fare with contributions from the *Not* performers. Clothes Off! reunited Brooke-Taylor, Chapman and Cleese performing the fully clothed naked Cha Cha Cha dance rountine ('They are naked and they do dance!') alongside Pamela Stephenson, while the programme's show stopper was an elaborate staging of Top of the Form with Cleese in the chair surrounded by Tim Brooke-Taylor's Tracey, John Bird and Graham Chapman on the girls team and John Fortune, Griff Rhys Jones and Rowan Atkinson on the boys team. The best bits were captured on film by director Julian Temple for a video release.

CLIVE ANDERSON, ROWAN ATKINSON, JEFF BECK, ALAN BENNETT, MARTIN BERGMAN, JOHN BIRD, TIM BROOKE-TAYLOR, JASPER CARROTT, GRAHAM CHAPMAN, ERIC CLAPTON, JOHN CLEESE, PHIL COLLINS, DONOVAN, JOHN FORTUNE, BOB GELDOF, BARRY HUMPHRIES, NEIL INNES, TERRY JONES, CHRIS LANGHAM, JIMMY MULVILLE, DAVID RAPPAPORT, GRIFF RHYS JONES, TONY ROBINSON, ALEXEI SAYLE, PAMELA STEPHENSON, STING, JOHN WELLS, VICTORIA WOOD. Executive Producer Peter Walker. Producer Martin Lewis. Directed by Richard Eyre, assisted by John Cleese. Wednesday 9–Saturday 12 September 1981, Theatre Royal, London.

GRAEME GARDEN FINDS A SENSE OF THE PAST
AND A SCENT OF THE FEET

A SENSE OF THE PAST

Immediate post-Goodies presenting assignment for Graeme Garden, examining Britain's rich and varied history with an enthusiastic, informative style. Despite the rather naff opening credits, with dear old Gray Bags in silhouette wandering through rough sites of historical interest, the actual programmes were brimming with good, non-mocking, fun.

Series One: Thursdays, 28 July–1 September 1983, ITV. Series Two: Thursdays, 16 January–20 February 1986, ITV. Producer David Wilson. Director Ann Ayoub.

A SENSE OF THE PAST: the book

A tie-in publication with the popular Yorkshire television series, Graeme Garden is given major writing credit for the project, although the copyright mention for his co-writing Graham Nown suggests the lion's share was out of the Goodie's hands. Retelling facts, feats and fascinating folklore revealed in the television episodes, many chapter headings are lifted from the series (The Power and the Glory/Fortress Britain/Dirty Old Town), while others tackle the same ground under a different name — the funeral tradition of *A Celebration of Death* is dealt with under the chapter *Great Gardens of Sleep*, while *And Now… a Short Intermission* becomes *The Ad-Man Cometh*. The book is a wealth of information from the outstanding opening piece, *It's the Fourth Leg Which Causes the Wobble: History Down at the Local*, to the 11th and final essay, *The Age of the Train*. Copious photographs illustrate sights of historical interest, Graeme enjoying a pint, Harrogate's Turkish Bath and a Hyde Park cinema. The book's major purpose is to celebrate and preserve Britain's history, encouraging protection and interest via comedy connection long before Tony Robinson's excellent Channel 4 blitz with *Time Team*.

Written by Graeme Garden with Graham Nown. Ward Lock Limited 1985.

7.30 REPORT

Bill Oddie was interviewed for this ABC programme during his October 1989 Australian bird-watching break. Trying hard to plug the Oxford University Press bird books, conservation and Oddie's Oddballs charity Twitch-a-thon team.

THE SEVENTH MAN: MY PART IN THE DEFECTION SCANDAL

Double Orson Welles plus one, this is a witty, incisive, eloquent and compact — I once read it on a return train journey to Bath — parody spy thriller novel by Graeme Garden. Based on first person, flash-back, hand-written manuscripts from the bewildered, naïve, charmingly incompetent hero, Geoffrey T Alsop, the piece is set within the corrupt intricacies of British Intelligence, Russian defectors and the Kim Philby scandal… although the names of the most famous players are kept incognito until a halfway point author's disclaimer. Reassuringly British, the plot takes in Alsop's delicious narrow-minded, business-first mentality (complete with detailed maps and hilarious, winding footnote explanations of code-words and initials). The flustered, disconcerting affair his wife is enjoying, rife homosexuality in the department and the alcoholic lesbian, Agnes, keeping a less than firm grip on the record files, all seem to pass by unnoticed by the central character. A gentle comedy theme underlines the espionage believability and state of the nation at the time. The book skilfully contrasts the decline of the

264

nation and prophetic narrative concern about impending problems over the Falklands, with troubled pondering on the Tip-Ex situation and continued referencing of A roads used for destinations. A understated satirical piece of work, the only really farcical scenes involve a rain-sodden uncovered stake-out resulting in pre-offered lavatory paper and a drunken Western cat-call session when our main man masquerades as Mr Roy Rogers. A cracking read and an intriguing cover which perfectly captures the low-key, secretive, very British coup story of death and deceit (a black wall with six flying ducks and one terminally falling to his fate). Besides, there's a character called Spiers after *The Goodies'* director Bob Spiers and anything that gives a name-check to Basingstoke has to be worth a glance…

Eyre Methuen 1981.

SHADES OF GREENE: THE OVERNIGHT BAG

Tim Brooke-Taylor appeared in this TV presentation of a celebrated Graeme Greene story. Typically dipped in acidic, black humour, Tim played a bemused nervous man who desperately tries to get pass the customs at Heathrow Airport. The story takes a darker turn when his mother – brilliantly played by Joyce Carey – gaily recalls a restaurant meal which contained a human finger. Displaying perfect British manners she calmly left it on the side of the plate and the play develops into a delicious two-hander of mounting amazement.

Did You Know? Tim discussed this dramatic role as well as his current ITV hit Hello Cheeky and, of course, The Goodies in the TV Times article 'Straight Acting for Naughty Eyes' by Jane Ennis.

Henry TIM BROOKE-TAYLOR Airport girls DIANA BERRIMAN and DAPHNE LAWSON Woman on Plane ELEANOR SUMMERFIELD Customs Officer NEVILLE PHILLIPS Hire-Car Driver DUDLEY SUTTON Mother JOYCE CAREY. Dramatised by Clive Exton. Producer Alan Cooke. Director Peter Hammond. Tuesday 3 February 1976, ITV.

SHANG-A-LANG

As a youth culture showcase for those Seventies tartan boppers, The Bay City Rollers, producer Muriel Young put together this camp, glorious pop music programme which captured the zeitgeist perfectly. The Goodies made a guest appearance on the series on 22 April 1975.

SHOOTING STARS

Although *I'm Sorry I Haven't a Clue* had been mocking panel games for what seemed like light years, this spin-off from Vic and Bob's sketch series *The Smell of*

Reeves and Mortimer, took the game show format, stuffed it through a mincing machine and deliciously treated its roster of celebs with almost total contempt. In 1996, mega-fan, Tim Brooke-Taylor, happily wandered into the camp pseudo-Sixties madness and nonsensical brain teasers, creating at least one classic television moment when Bob whips away a pair of Union flag underpants and proudly claims the flag of the Goodie. Bill Oddie also found his way on to the anarchic programme with Vic's flamboyant opening statement: 'It's the bloke from *The Goodies!*' resulting in head-in-hands embarrassment from Oddie. A photograph of Oddie billed as Ugly Bill the bird-spotter appeared in the 1996 BBC *Shooting Stars* book.

THE SKYLIGHTERS

A wonderful collection of brief but sweet Graeme Garden poems dedicated to that uncelebrated labour force who build, paint and restore the atmospheric colours and objects. With a delightful phrasing and a collection of cowboy workers, Garden fashions a makeshift, experimental collection of small folk tackling the vast job in hand. My favourite piece is *Moon Gang* with Norman O'Gorman the Foreman facing the militant revolt of his craftsmen, while *Fog Blind* has a touching poignancy and *Old Mr Blue*, a magical air. Garden's words are brilliantly illustrated by dazzling, full-page art work from Neil Canning

Methuen Children's Books 1988.

SMITH & JONES

As *Beyond the Fringe* begat Cook and Moore, *Not the Nine O'Clock News* begat Smith and Jones and although, at their sketch-bound worse, they wallowed in Little and Large terrain with added bite, Mel and Griff consistently delivered fresh, funny, dangerous comedy for a decade. Pinnacles came with their *Morecambe and Wise*-like introductions, Stanley Rogers the hopeless film score composer and Clive Anderson's sublime head-to-head discussions. Graeme Garden contributed several sketches to the series.

Did You Know? The classic first series won a British Comedy Award. Two Ronnies-like, Smith & Jones was compiled into an eight-week season of classic sketches and BBC videos, while Radio 2, represented television favourites as Smith and Jones Sound Off.

SMITH & JONES IN SMALL DOSES: THE WHOLE HOG

Probably the finest use of Mel and Griff, these playlets were short-lived and unpopular while presenting brilliant, perceptive writing and some of the most hilarious acting from the duo. Perhaps the most chilling came from this opening episode written with malicious glee by Graeme Garden. Smith is a nervous, business-stressed employee in a doll factory facing the future under the perverted, sadomasochistic doll regime of Griff Rhys Jones. If things weren't bad and bizarre enough, Griff is Mel's ex-wife following a sex change operation. Series potential surely...

Giles MEL SMITH Maurice GRIFF RHYS JONES. Written by Graeme Garden. Produced by Peter Fincham and Trevor Evans. Director Mike Newell. Thursday 19 October 1989, BBC2.

SOME OF THESE DAYS

Cliff Michelmore hosted this nostalgic Radio 2 quiz looking at the people, places, events and music that were leaving a mark on the world on this day in years gone by. For the last in the series on Tuesday 6 August 1991, Graeme Garden took part.

SPID

An enchanting children's story narrated by Bill Oddie for a Chivers Children's Book audio release in January 1991.

SPILLED BLOOD: 10 MURDER MYSTERIES

A Telstar talking book, two-cassette collection of crime stories and thrilling heists featuring one tale read by Bill Oddie.

SPIN-OFFS

Tim Brooke-Taylor could make drying paint interesting and, although the resulting series was a fascinating historical travelogue of Britain, the basic premise of this show almost meant he had to. Proudly, Thames television presented the ex-Goodie's personal journey through the M25, the orbital motorway. Thrilling stuff ahh! Well, yes, actually...

The Orbital Motorway, The Dickens Connection, Surrey & the Tillybourne, Hertfordshire, The Darent Valley, The Thames Valley. Produced and directed by Edward Joffe. Wednesdays, 12 November–17 December 1986, ITV.

THE STATUE

A manic load of old tosh with Mr Sophistication, David Niven, struggling through gamely as a distinguished inventor of a Universal language, whose commissioned, 18-foot statue for the outside of the American Embassy in Grovesnor Square, is ultimately revealed as a nude study. More to the point, scandal erupts when everyone tries to work out who was the male model for the lower region... Writer Denis Norden, knowing full well that the script was spiralling out of all control, took the wise decision to spice things up a bit with a load of class Cambridge performers. Thus, John Cleese, Graham Chapman and Tim Brooke-Taylor were drafted in to lend a hand for this feature-length film.

Professor Alex Bolt DAVID NIVEN Rhonda Bolt VIRNA LISI Ray Whiteley ROBERT VAUGHN Pat Demarest ANN BELL Harry JOHN CLEESE Hillcrest TIM BROOKE-TAYLOR Sir Geoffrey HUGH BURDEN Mouser ERIK CHITTY Sanders DEREK FRANCIS Newsreader GRAHAM CHAPMAN Mrs Southwick SUSAN TRAVERS Mr Southwick DESMOND WALTER-ELLIS. Written by Alec Coppel and Denis Norden. Based on the play, Chip, Chip, Chip by Alec Coppel. Producer Anis Nohra. Director Rod Amateau. 1970.

THE STEVE JONES GAMES SHOW

Later re-named and relaunched as *The Pyramid Game*, this was an intricate, mind-numbing ITV celebrity game show which embraced a certain Bill Oddie during a rest from *The Goodies* on 7 July 1979.

STUFF THAT GIBBON

My favourite track of *The Goodies Sing Songs From The Goodies* album, *Stuff That Gibbon* originally sprang from the track, *Stuffing the Gibbon* from *I'm Sorry I'll Read That Again*. Indeed, the original working title during recording was Stuffing the Gibbon, only being changed in post-production. The song found immortality when it resurfaced in *The Goodies* canon in Series Three's *That Old Black Magic*. Featuring Graeme on lead vocals with some wonderfully off-kilter studio banter, 'Moonshine' and the like, it touches the musical soul with a funky fiddle introduction from Don Harper and milks the situation for all it's worth. Surely the prime candidate for a forthcoming compilation CD, The Funniest Songs About Taxidermists... ever! It's a masterpiece of overplayed, hilarious bad taste. If anything, an even better celebration of the furry ape than the group's more revered *Funky Gibbon*, the groovy 'ooh, ooh, ooh!' choruses are already in place, the poor defenceless creature is bounced round like a rubber ball – sans Bobby Vee – and Tim does his expected posh, chinless Brit act, politely turning the thing into dance hall banter and requests for stuffing action à la ballroom jiving. But, best of all, is the eagerly embraced 'Stuff It!' rant, initially delivered with embarrassed unease by Brooke-

Taylor before fully finding his confidence. The B-side, if one can call it that, is, of course, the famous original version of *The Goodies Theme Song*. All in all, six different version were produced for the opening credit sequence and even by 1975, when Decca released this single in the wake of Bradley's records' Goodies success, the new, improved, groovy version was being used on the show. That rocking version was recorded by Oddie on Wednesday 8 November 1972 and remains the most familiar rendition, but this earlier take is an invaluable record of the fledgling Goodies and their promise to do anything, anywhere. Within the lyrics, old *I'm Sorry I'll Read That Again* obsessions with OBEs are referenced, while circuses and seaside piers are promised like a mini alternative to *Challenge Anneka*. There is a sense of nostalgia about this old 'take a little good advice!' version. With the familiar 'yum, yum!' choruses belting out of your speaker, Oddie's virtuous playing of a penny whistle giving it an air of the Troggs's *Wild Thing*, and even an embrace of Lennon philosophy with the 'all you need's a little love!' line, this is reassuring class.

Did You Know? In the Nineties, when Tim Brooke-Taylor's son attended Bristol University, a student band included The Goodies Theme in their set, emphasising the Good E's / 'it's what ever turns you on!' drug references. The lad even asked his father whether he and the other two Goods would mind! 'Of course not!' The song's composer, Bill Oddie, remains very proud of the team's signature tune, 'people recognise those opening notes everywhere today, every time you hear a train go by with 'Daa-Daa' it starts The Goodies Theme song!' The song was Bill's ultimate example of bringing music used in comedy programmes out of its familiar rut – 'Comedy music had been all tuba or bassoon, somewhere it had been written that those are funny instruments! I hated all that stuff and wanted to move completely away from that for The Goodies. I put together some dream bands. They were brilliant. Music aficionados would tape the background incidental music because it would include people from Soft Machine and Jack Bruce, really good musicians. We would just record great chunks of stuff. I would write a song and say, 'Look, this is going to be shoved behind some ridiculous visual thing. You won't hear a word of it but I need 10 minutes of material just to be safe. So I would dish out solos to various people and it was brilliant. We all got off on this great jam session. In a way we reverted to what those Twenties' pianists were doing for silent movies at the cinema. Just improvising music which suited the mood of the image. There was a great sense of freedom and release.'*

F 13578 Decca 1975.

BILL ODDIE WAVES THE FLAG FOR THE WORTHY SPORT CHARITY RECORD *SUPERSPIKE* IN 1976

STUFF WHAT DREAMS ARE MADE OF

Graeme Garden's major credit for the Cambridge Footlights. He wrote some of the sketches and performed throughout this 1964 revue. Recent graduate Bill Oddie contributed musical numbers to the show but did not appear himself. ATV presented an edited television version, *Footlights '64*.

JOHN CAMERON, GRAEME GARDEN, DAVID GOODERSON, SUSAN HANSON, SUE HEBER-PERCY, FLICK HOUGH, ERIC IDLE, MARK LUSHINGTON, JONATHAN LYNN, MIRIAM MARGOLYES, GUY SLATER. Written by Jim Beach, Anthony Buffery, John Cameron, Robert Cushman, Richard Eyre, Graeme Garden, Brian Gascoigne, David Gooderson, Susan Hanson, Jimmy Heal, Sue Heber-Percy, Flick Hough, Eric Idle, Mark Lushingham, Jonathan Lynn, Miriam Margolyes, Andrew Mayer and Bill Oddie.

SUPERSPIKE

Forget *Comic Relief*. What with *A Poke in the Eye (with a Sharp Stick)* and this bit of vinyl, 1976 was the year that saw the dawn of comedy stars pitching themselves as multimedia fundraisers. *I'm Sorry I'll Read That Again* sparring partners, John Cleese and Bill Oddie, joined forces to help form The Superspike Squad, a gang of celebrities collecting funds for an International Athlete's Club. Released on the Goodies' record label, Bradley's, this is a continuous track, consisting of part one and part two on each side of the disc.

BRAD 7606 Bradley's Records February 1976.

QUESTION MASTER GRAEME GARDEN PLUGS THE CHANNEL 4 PROGRAMME, *TELL THE TRUTH*

SURGICAL SPIRIT

A rather cheerless Granada situation comedy created, and, in the main, scripted by, Peter Learmouth, the series made a brief star of Nichola McAuliffe who ranted, raged and scowled her way through life in Gillies Hospital with the acidic angst of Peggy Mount on a very bad day. Contemporary comment on lack of medical funds, domestic hassles with a teenage son and on–off romantic flirtations with mild-mannered Duncan Preston were at the root of most of the humour. A surprising hit, the series ran for 50 episodes broadcast over seven series from 14 April 1989 to 7 July 1995. The underused but effective masterstroke was producer Humphrey Barclay initiating a *Doctor in the House* reunion by commissioning five scripts from Graeme Garden under the direction of old *Doctor* director David Askey.

Dr Sheila Sabatini NICHOLA McAULIFFE Dr Jonathan Haslam DUNCAN PRESTON Joyce Watson MARJI CAMPI George Hope-Wynne DAVID CONVILLE Neil Copeland EMLYN PRICE Sister Cheryl Patching SUZETTE LLEWELLYN Michael Sampson BERESFORD LE ROY Giles Peake SIMON HARRISON. Written by Graeme Garden. Created by Peter Learmouth. Executive Producers Andy Harries, David Liddiment, Al Mitchell and Antony Wood. Producer Humphrey Barclay. Director David Askey.

T

TABLE MANNERS

Tim Brooke-Taylor starred in a 1990 tour of this Alan Ayckbourn comedy.

TAKE ME TO YOUR READER

Short-lived radio situation comedy starring Tim Brooke-Taylor as nervous, shy and ineffectual publisher Colin Luscombe. The series set up the promising premise of an established publishing house, Roache and Brewer, facing the Eighties' 'greed is good' ethos and battling between cultural quality and commercial viability. The second edition saw Tim turn on the expected fraught panic when the latest potential blockbuster, an explosive war memoir, goes missing. *Me & My Girl*'s Joan Sanderson poured on the withering rant in the fourth episode and class guest star, Carry On legend Kenneth Connor, was a delight as an aged Western writer with a story line block in Episode Five. By common consent with those who heard the series, *A Change of Medium* offered Tim his finest moment. The star-struck versus traditionalist dilemma faced Tim's anti-television chap after he has been offered a spot on a high prestige television book programme.

Colin Luscombe TIM BROOKE-TAYLOR. With GLYN HOUSTON and EVE KARPF **1:** The Trouble with Billy with EDWARD JUDD, JOE DUNLOP **2:** The Old Man and the Sea with NELL BRENNAN, AUBREY SALLIS **3:** A Change of Medium with JON GLOVER JOHN GRAHAM **4:** I Thought I'd Never Stop with JOAN SANDERSON **5:** Writer's Block with KENNETH CONNOR. Written by Andrew Palmer. Producer Edward Taylor. Saturdays, 8 March–7 April 1986, Radio 4.

TAKE NOBODY'S WORD FOR IT

A sort of *Tomorrow's World* meets *How Do They Do That?* presented by Carol Vorderman and Professor Ian Fells. Bill Oddie helped Carol launch into DIY aerial photography via the use of his kite.

Producer George Auckland. Director Hendrik Ball. Thursday 26 January 1989, BBC2.

TELEVISION'S GREATEST HITS

Another one of those cut and paste BBC shows designed to celebrate classic BBC programmes. Gaby Roslin was perfect as an informative guide through the television archives when the Goodies were reunited for, apparently, one night only. The section 'Truly, Madly, Goodie' was introduced with wide-eyed excitement and spine-tingling 'Goody Goody Yum Yum!' from

Roslin, before a brief but concise compilation of vintage clips captured *The Goodies* heritage in seconds: paint by number identifications, *Nappy Love* singing, the kitten, Dougal, Graeme's Jimmy Saville from *Chubbie Chumps*, a *Royal Command* poke at the monarchy, Julie Andrews done to death in *Movies*, *Funky Gibbon* on *Top of the Pops*, those titles, that theme tune… Then the moment we all were waiting for, Tim Brooke-Taylor, Graeme Garden and Bill Oddie bounding on to the stage to a huge audience reaction. Praised as 'very intelligent' by Tim, Gaby seemed keen to let these old comic codgers know that people not only still knew who they were, but also that deep affection remained for them. So, if that's the case, and this heavily plugged reunion is all so important, why were the Goodies rolled out like an ancient exhibit, given three and a half minutes out of a 30-minute show and wrapped up just as the comic juices began to flow? Bill rattled out the old story of how the Goodies became the Goodies, Tim lamented that Australian Television screen the programmes all the time and people under 24 in Britain have no idea who they are, while Graeme was given the familiar anecdotal tit-bit about doing *Top of the Pops*, fearing middle-aged rejection and discovering all the other teenage idols were middle aged as well. Despite the expected self-mockery with Tim pleased to be dragged out of retirement and Bill undermining his new career in 'flipping wildlife' programmes surrounded by 'flipping birds', there's no doubting real pride is generated between the three. There's certainly an intangible magic about the sight of the trio together again on that cheap BBC sofa. Tim's 'I wouldn't mind doing it again' is poignant indeed, but the piece was so brief as to be an insult, Gaby's good-natured, heart in the right place treatment couldn't redeem the wasted opportunity and Bill's quizzical glance to his two cohorts coupled with a disbelieving shake of the head spoke volumes. His, 'Christ, 18 years away from the Beeb and that's all we get' look summed up the entire spot. More to the point, Terry Wogan, who pops up somewhere at least every 20 minutes, was greeted like the second coming and given almost half the show's entire running time… It's a disgrace! Mind you, three minutes of cool, class, priceless television is better than nothing. Here's to bringing the lads back for a *Parkinson* Special.

Producer Paul Rezini. Director John Rooney. Monday 24 August 1998, BBC1.

TELL THE TRUTH

A sort of *What's My Line* variation with four dial-a-celebs (at its best regrouping a couple of old *Doctors in the House* and *in Charge*, Robin Nedwell and George Layton) questioning a line-up of three people, one of whom has a strange, interesting, or hopefully both, quality. The object of the exercise was to guess which one was the right one. Punters revelled in such bizarre claims to fame as being the model for *Juliet Bravo*, finding pleasure from helping toads across busy roads or believing that Cliff Richard records should be saddled with a compulsory tax. Chairman Graeme Garden kept things ticking along with quiet restraint.

Series One: Sundays, 26 October–18 December 1984, Channel 4. **Series Two:** Fridays, 6 September–22 November 1985, Channel 4. Producer Brian Wesley. Director Noel D Greene.

TEN OF THE BEST

VH1's excellent desert island discs for pop videos has invited the great, good and indifferent to select their 10 favourite pieces of music on film. The show has spanned classic editions from Sir Paul McCartney to the Rutles. The king-pin in the musical legacy of *The Goodies*, Bill Oddie, was a perfect choice for the programme. His informed and enthused selection on Saturday 17 May 1997 included the stonking Ricki Lee Jones and Dr John version of *Makin' Whoppee*, *Tutu Medley* from Miles Davis, Little Feat's *Let it Roll*, *Don't Stand So Close to Me* by the Police, *Little Sister* from Ry Cooder, Stevie Wonder's *Superstition*, Julie Fordham's *Where Did Time Go*, The Jacksons' *Blame it on the Boogie* and Frank Zappa's *Peaches En Regalia*.

THAT WAS THE WEEK THAT WAS

With the gusto of *Beyond the Fringe* in its sails and the Profumo scandal just breaking apart political stability, *That Was The Week That Was* was a live, late, satirical sketch ground-breaker which made stars of its youthful satirists, while embracing old war-horses like Frankie Howerd for a comment on the budget, and Michael Redgrave's reading of *Waxworks*, to startling effect. David Frost was the self-promoting focal point, and with the early Sixties' explosion of Beatlemania, Carnaby Street cool, the mini skirt and Britain's immediate post-war austerity slowly being debunked by the hip attitude of youth, *TW3*, for its very short lifetime, touched a major nerve. Almost as quickly as it

BILL ODDIE PUBLICITY POSE FOR THE CLASSIC 1963 SATIRE SHOW *THAT WAS THE WEEK THAT WAS*

had started, the decline of MacMillian, General Election caution, a new Labour government, the dawn of the really swinging Sixties and the assassination of JFK, saw the series pulled from the schedules. The show's importance can not be over-stressed. Not least because a very young Bill Oddie, fresh from Cambridge, was recruited into Frost's large harem of class comedy writers, contributing musical items and, ultimately, by Series Two, often joining forces with Robert Lang in cod Gilbert and Sullivan performances. The music was in the safe hands of future *I'm Sorry I'll Read That Again* and Goodies' man Dave Lee, while Oddie would later tour America with the stage version, *David Frost's That Was The Week That Was*, alongside Tim Brooke-Taylor.

Directed and produced by Ned Sherrin. **Series One:** Saturdays, 24 November 1962–27 April 1963, BBC. **Series Two:** Saturdays, 28 September–28 December 1963, BBC.

THAT WAS THE WEEK THAT WAS: the record

Written material by Bill Oddie was included on this 1963 release, supervised by George Martin.

PMC 1197 Parlophone 1963.

THAT'S ENTERTAINMENT

For the first in a new series of the tacky but cheerful show biz quiz, Tim Brooke-Taylor twice joined in the antics with brilliantly unpredictable team captain Kenny Everett and cool dude *Me & My Girl* pal Richard O'Sullivan.

Producer John Kaye Cooper. Director Peter Hamilton. Saturdays, 20 May and 1 July 1989, BBC1.

THIS IS YOUR LIFE

The eternally popular 'man with a red book surprises a celeb and starts a reminiscing party' format sprang from the States, settled into a Sixties' BBC niche with the mild-mannered charm of Eamonn Andrews, switched to ITV for the Seventies and then enjoyed a BBC revival with the mild-mannered charm of Michael Aspel. Towards the tail-end of the Nineties, it had become one of television's most respected, revered sacred cows. When Barry Cryer was caught, Tim Brooke-Taylor happily remembered good times on *Hello Cheeky,* while *I'm Sorry I Haven't a Clue* partner Graeme Garden strolled on to comment on a pantomime he had written which featured Cryer, during a throaty cold, as the only Dame to sound like Lee Marvin. On the edition broadcast Monday 18 January 1999, Bill Oddie completed the Goodies connection with knowingly dismissive thoughts on *Doctor at the Top* and distress at the vast quantity of dodgy sitcoms the show's focus, George Layton, had penned. Tim Brooke-Taylor was the show's subject in 1981, an episode ranking as the 88th most-watched British television programme of all time!

THIS WON'T HURT

A Radio 2 comedy panel game based on all things medical. Graeme Garden was the perfect host for this pilot edition on Saturday 28 June 1997 which failed to lead to a series. Philip Pope set things in a Goodies context with a mention of Ecky Thump.

THOSE TV TIMES

A neat idea for a time-filling television show, allowing beloved small screen favourites to battle it out in a test of small screen knowledge. Memories of fine, past, great shows and stars added to the overall feel good, warm-hearted, nostalgic pleasure. Two Goodies jumped aboard, with Tim sparring with *Goodies in the Nick* guest star, Jack Douglas, on 27 June 1977, and Bill Oddie endorsing the programme with an appearance on 7 July 1978.

3-2-1

Saturday nights were simply not complete without a fix of Ted Rogers, Dusty Bin and the most complex, nonsensical collection of cryptic clues known to man. Somehow, it was compulsive stuff for ITV viewers. Into this melting pot of harmless tat, Tim Brooke-Taylor appeared in Tea on 12 February and Sea Cruise on 9 April 1983.

THREE MEN ON A BIKE: A JOURNEY THROUGH AFRICA

As if finally to put *The Goodies* to bed, the BBC Props Department included the legendary trandem in a 1984 auction. A gentleman by the name of Hugh Spowers bought it and immediately used it for charitable purposes. Between the years 1989 and 1993, Hugh's brother, Rory Spowers, and Bill Oddie would ride the trandem round London for all manner of good causes. A more ambitious journey from the mouth of the Ganges river to the Himalayas resulted in a television documentary, and a further bit of pedal power across Africa produced a book, *Three Men on a Bike*. Bill Oddie provided a useful foreword contribution, giving a first-hand account of the perils of riding the trandem.

Canongate Publishing 1995.

THROUGH THE KEYHOLE

David Frost slums it between high-profile interviews with this celebrity ITV panel show which satisfies the nation's bizarre curiosity for what other celebrities homes look like. It allows the irritating Lloyd Grossman to wander through a mini, clue-ridden guided tour and leave the guests open to make wide, question-asking, stabs in the dark. The wild audience reactions were often more hindrance than help. Bill Oddie reunited with the old *TW3* chairman for one programme on Friday 10 March 1989. Tim Brooke-Taylor played the game on Friday 25 June 1993.

TICKLE ON THE TUM

A long-running ITV children's favourite with Bill Oddie becoming a semi-regular fixture as the delightfully dotty Dr Dimple.

Measles, Monday 7 October 1985; Doctor in the Well, Monday 2 December 1985; Nurse Knightly Can't Sleep written by Laura Beaumont, October 1986; Dr Dimple in the 20th Century written by Laura Beaumont and Bill Oddie, Monday 1 August 1988; Mysterious Doings at Tickle Hall written by Laura Beaumont and Bill Oddie, Tuesday 29 November 1988.

TIM BROOKE-TAYLOR'S CRICKET BOX

This is an essential, hilarious and mind-spinning celebration of the noble game. Wallowing in the devotion to the sport of his Goodie persona, Tim unwraps astounding facts and figures, the etiquette of the Gentlemen Players, the game's grand tradition and a deliciously black slice of humour to take cricket 'out of the Long Room into the lunatic asylum' through 21 chapters. The book opens with Tim's earnest claim that he has a secret English cricketing life, semi-proved by a dodgy-looking Barbados newspaper report and a charming photograph of old Timbo in the national colours. The book is a result of his frantic search for further evidence. My 10 Favourite and Most Unusual Cricket Grounds, presents a illustrated celebration of the strangest fields of play, while grading County conditions with the spongy, green and tickle factor at work. Extracts from the 'Teeny Weeny Very Very Much Shorter Companion to Cricket' relates an A to Z... well A to W, listing of terms and phrases explained with a healthy comic slant, of course. Helpfully, it warns against the use of 'I do declare…' as in 'I do declare it's a nice day'. The Umpire may get the wrong idea. Cricket Through the Eyes of the Camera selects some choice photographic proof of such amazing events as Mark Thatcher catching himself out and the infamous, Mr Bendo, seen upside-down for an entire match in 1951. A look at Shanghai Clicket unveils the full impact of this half-forgotten, surely against the rules, martial art attitude for certain victory. Chapter Four presents four earth-shattering articles which changed Tim's life, while the following offering, I Was Mike Brearley's Guru takes the reader through three hilarious, overheard telephone conversations with the English captain and his spiritual advisor, forever incognito and finally adopting a Cornish accent and explaining unavailability due to a five-year shopping session: 'he's got a lot to get'. Seeing Is Believing spots discrepancies in team photographs, including the 1934 Windies squad of 12 men, while Cricket As Art delights in masterpieces like the Venus de Milo from the Gasworks End and, my personal favourite, Dali's (signed 'Dalivered') The Persistence of Cricket complete with melting bat, ball and ant infestation. The Arnold Turner Collection of Quite Outstanding Cricketers and Their Unique Achievements is a long-winded explanation for classic mini biogs of players such as Garfield Twitty who, as well as once bowling himself out, scored an amazing 126 from a single ball. How? Read the book and weep, sucker… Some Controversial Teas are discussed before Chapter 10 helps cover up the cricketless boredom of October through to April with a time-filling, cricket-flavoured calendar. There's hints on the toss, the supporter and directions for inspecting a wicket, while a charming scratch 'n' sniff card reassuringly reminds the pining nostrils of great cricketing venues. All that, leads to the sublime one-act Wisden's meets Agatha Christie play The Selector Calls. Set in Maltravers Hall, with a cricket-obsessed detective (casting Richard Attenborough and creating memories of the first production of The Mouse Trap), other casting delights include Denis Compton and Irene Handl. Brighter Cricket unearths the lost findings of the 1981 International Committee for Brighter Cricket held in Scarborough. Topics under discussion included vintage use of the six and out rule (featuring opposing fans willing boundary attempts), and the one-handed batting technique, as well as new suggestions like the better the batsman the less protective clothing allowed, dictating nudity in some cases. Cricket Tactics looks even deeper than the bodyline to encourage sudden bowling (when you are making your way back to your mark) or the dignified beauty of Synchronised Cricket. Umpire: Fiend or Foe? tells it how it is, dismisses sexual favours, promotes financial bribes and details how to get your enemy disorganised. Cricketobilia delights in presenting rare objects to the reader, including the bat of schizophrenic JH Lancing with which he scored 2451 not out against himself, and the Geoff Boycott Board Game promising hours of fun and amusement for everybody. Etiquette to and from the Pavilion makes that long walk easier via reprinted extracts from Potter's A Day in the Field and Peter Risedale-Forest's the Gentlemen's Game, which helpfully recalls ES Turner's mistaken facing of three balls before he realised he had left his bat behind! Some Other Ashes pays tribute to many cricket loving souls who died in the field of action as well as a resurrection of I'm Sorry I'll Read That Again's Spot the dog, squashed by a pitch roller and scattered over the site Spot's Spot. A Short History of Ladies' Cricket is a spine-tingling, brilliantly feminist piece of prose highlighting such greats as glam model Candice Heatman who would turn on the sexy pout for the audience. Schools' Cricket, hopes to find the stars of the future, although, St Rentums' under-14s tend frequently to go out for under 14 runs. Another Book of Records rounds up amazing bits of overlooked or underestimated info, including the most famous batsman called Donald Bradman, the greatest number of pads on one leg, the longest period without moving for a batsman and the surreal, Goonish, notion of the greatest number of centuries off one ball. Finally, Cricket Today, embraces the glories of both one-day cricket and 10-day cricket, as well as sponsorship. This notably throws up the Andrex toilet tissue campaign which failed for getting wrapped round the bat at inopportune moments. A plug for the Official MCC Cricketer's Diary rounds off this classic, cricket-loving, comedy celebration. Oh… and wallow in that cool cover representation of Player's cigarette cards with the author getting one in the old Niagaras.

Did You Know? Tim's cricket knowledge was employed by the Radio Times (22–28 May 1993) when they asked the question 'Who is in your England side?' Tim wrote 'Although I'm a Derbyshire supporter, I would still pick Devon Malcolm as he is one of the few genuinely quick bowlers we have. I, myself, of course, should open the bowling with him. I think I might sneak a couple of wickets before the Australians realise how bad I am!'

Stanley Paul & Co Ltd 1986.

TIM BROOKE-TAYLOR'S GOLF BAG

A follow-up to Tim's masterly cricket book, this volume, written during the Winter of 1987–88, shifted further towards the writer's own personal sporting passion rather than that celebrated by his Goodies personality. Writing in the same, bizarre, gently mocking style, this is a delight for the golf clubhouse bore and casual reader alike. Ingeniously structured like a round of golf with 18 chapter holes, strokes instead of page numbers and the opportunity to score enjoyment through each bit of play, the book charmingly opens with the local rules: covering natural hazards like unreadable or missing pages by allowing a page from a different, similar length, book to be read instead. Permission is also granted to use the volume as a fly swat as long as the bits are removed before returning it to the library. Tim's witty introduction, distilling the golfing term 'good' down to its fundamental meaning of impossible, and a fond comment about his favourite course, Swinley Forest, is the perfect opening swing before teeing off proper with Golfing Around the World. New-fangled equipment and innovations, notably an endearingly

THE SPORTING GOSPEL ACCORDING TO GRAEME GARDEN, 'TIM BROOKE-TAYLOR ENJOYING A GAME OF GOLF, I THINK!'

profound conversation about the *Horizon* programme on AIDS with his talking golf ball, is countered by revelations about new developments in the game with our very own writing Goodie displaying the one-legged golf technique. Celebrity-handled tournaments are brought down to earth with suggestions for the Ali from *EastEnders* Pro-Am and the Girl Who Drapes Herself Over the Prizes in *3-2-1* Round Robin Event. The Golfer's Hall of Fame features Tim's personal choice of unsung heroes like the legendary TJ Whitworth, father of the knitted golf club head cover, while also looking at the forgotten golfing inventors and taking a glance at unusual golf. The Toughest Course I've Ever Played, is Tim's breath-taking, mountain-trekking tale of playing the dreaded Annagurna: so dangerous that one hole has never been played and completed, while the deceptively easy 18th can lure an over-powerful putt and send you shooting down the other side of the mountain.

Your fate? The nightmarish prospect of playing the course all over again! The Rules of Golf is a stunning piece of writing and, arguably the most sustained piece of prose in either of these brilliant sporting collections. Taking the story back to its real origins with Milligan-esque detail, Tim explains that 'In 1823… there were no rules. In 1811 even fewer…', before exposing the bloodless coups and overzealous fellows who swamped the pleasure of the game with unfathomable intricacies. It's a masterpiece, capped with extracts from the official stuff before the battle, after the brave fight, in the wake of the give in, and, eventually, getting itself totally lost in the menu for a very reasonable Chinese restaurant. Golf As She Is Played is the bluffer's guide to winning, through fair ways (as in honest play rather than the actual fairway) or, mainly, foul. The noble art is recommended, through the likes of being very rich, very pathetic or the rarest of all, voodoo, which

TIM BROOKE-TAYLOR'S GOLF BAG—TODAY'S THE DAY

allows you to beat the greatest players in the world from the comfort of your own home by making them believe you have played together and you won. Taking a Lesson illustrates the rudiments of the game with swing, stance and various grips from no-hand and werewolf to hair grip and surrealist (for which you play with a fish, apparently). Clubs and Clubhouses provides all the reader need know about life and conversation at the 19th hole, featuring handy hints to impress the Secretary and the essential, all-purpose golf joke. Not only that but also a sneaky look at the club's toilets with Oscar Wilde's immortal graffiti: 'I have nothing to declare but my handicap.' The Pro Shop takes the reader through the best in club and ball purchases including satisfactory advice on hitting Nicholas Parsons, while A Spectator's Guide to Golf is a do's and dont's banter shouting lesson in dealing with famous players you may meet and the etiquette of putting such people off. Golf for Kids is a charming way to introduce the younger members of your family to the great game, via adventures with Noddy and Big Ears at Fort Augusta, The Three Bears, nursery rhymes and licensed endorsement from the Care Bears, Barbie, Mr Men, and a particularly worse for wear, bar-settled, My Little Pony. Chapter 11 looks at golfing memorabilia, unearthing Hitler's multi-club and the mystic Turin golfing pullover as wore, allegedly, by the Lord himself. Sexy golf puts the raunch in your stroke play with Freudian analysis of golfing romp dreams, golf-line phone numbers and golf-a-gram glam girl adverts. Golf and the Arts tackles the influence of dance, Van Gogh's A Difficult Lie by a Jar of Sunflowers, the golfing version of *The Importance of Being Earnest* and Halliwell's Golfing Cinema Yearbook. Religion and Golf set the game in context of theology, while Who's Who on the Golf Course is a comic interpretation of Tim's photograph collection. Golfing Fiction memorably relates Escape From Stalagluft 48, Rupert Brooke's immortal verse, 'Struck the church clock at 10 to three, and is my golf ball on the tee...', and Agatha Christie's golfing collection including The Sand Trap! and Death on the Ninth. Golfing Tips promotes everything from slow play to the use of stilts and finally, hole 18 compiles The Golfing Book of Records celebrating, in detail, the world's rudest caddie, the tallest tee ever employed, and even, the roundest ball ever used. As with *Cricket Box*, the jokes extend to the end, with golfing terms, associations, the correct name for holes, the golfing pyramid letter, emergency advice and a

recommended book list, including that sci-fi classic, Invasion of the Death Ray Zombie Golfer from Planet X. The Tim golfing caricature by Ireland and the stunning photo of our author hero with one of his heroes — a truly great golfer with Seve Ballesteros — allows the reader for once to judge a book by its cover. The cover's fab, the book's fab and the world awaits Tim Brooke-Taylor's Fishing Net and Tim Brooke-Taylor's Snooker Pocket.

Stanley Paul & Co Ltd 1988.

TIME TEAM

Hugely informative and entertaining Channel 4 archaeology series hosted by Tony Robinson, away from the historical turnip obsession of *Blackadder*. Over a series of live broadcasts, teams of enthused diggers struggled to discover the legacy and importance of a selected area. Furthering his naturalist–historical broadcaster career Bill Oddie was recruited for a special Bank Holiday trawl through the Cotswold, relating via three, short, weekend-spanning bulletins in 1997.

TITMUSS REGAINED

A political drama sequel to John Mortimer's celebrated *Paradise Postponed* told the tale of a thrusting young Thatcherite by the name of Leslie Titmus. A struggling MP who has recently secured the position of Secretary of State for Housing, Ecological Affairs and Planning, faces his constituent village community of Rapstone. The 'greed is good' Eighties were reflected in this biting, hilarious tale of power and developers versus heritage and environment. Bill Oddie was ideally cast in this battle as Hector Bolitho Jones.

Did You Know? *The screening coincided with Bill's first 'My Kind of Day' for Radio Times (14–20 September 1991).*

Leslie Titmuss MP DAVID THRELFALL Jennie Sidonia KRISTIN SCOTT-THOMAS Hector Bolitho Jones BILL ODDIE Ken Cracken PETER CAPALDI Dr Fred Simcox PAUL SHELLEY Sue Bramble JANE BOOKER Dot Curdle ROSEMARY LEACH Joyce Timberlain HOLLY de JONG Elsie Titmuss SYLVIA KAY Barty Pine JOHN GRILLO Lorna Boland KATHERINE STARK Greg Boland WILL TACEY Jessica Hopkins EMMA STEPHENSON Dame Felicity Capulet JUDY CAMPBELL Sir Willoughby Blane JAMES GROUT Virginia Beazley TRICIA GEORGE. Written by John Mortimer. Producer Jacqueline Davis. Director Martyn Friend. Tuesdays, 3, 10 and 17 September 1991, ITV.

TODAY'S THE DAY

Having hoped that the news could be made more fun, Martyn Lewis was true to his word when he began hosting this enjoyable, trivia-friendly, quiz programme based around the faces and events of previous years that were in the news that very day. A very special Christmas special, broadcast on Christmas Day 1996, achieved the notable, albeit rather unheralded, coup, of landing four celebrity players, two of which were ex-Goodies – Tim Brooke-Taylor and Bill Oddie. Partnered by sitcom mothers, Belinda Lang and Jean Boht, it was party hats and *I'm Gonna Wash That Man Right Out of My Hair* sing-a-longs all round at the BBC's Manchester Studios. Copious clips included Tim playing the loveable old bag opposite Marty Feldman and a joyous moment from *The Goodies: Dodonuts* with Bill, protecting his new found fame as a nature film-maker, denying any involvement with the sequence. In the wake of *Free as a Bird* and *The Beatles Anthology*, Bill dismissed any plans for a Goodies reunion – not at their age! – while Tim wistfully commented that 'I'm very proud of *The Goodies*'. Clearly, the old Goods proved popular for when, in 1998, *Today's the Day* launched its celebrity season, Tim and Bill were invited back to partner past winning couples. Good-humoured rivalry and past glory celebration was again the order of the day for these four special programmes from Monday 7–Thursday 10 September, with Bill rearranging a George Formby classic and giving a hasty burst of Lenin on a Lamp post and Tim finally romping home to victory three editions to one. On 15–22 February 1999, Tim Brooke-Taylor returned for a further six editions beating his celeb competition, *The Likely Lad*'s Bridget Forsyth, four games to two.

THE TOILET BOOK or 11 ½ minutes a day... and how not to waste them

Only in Britain could an entire book be published about the pros, cons, self-improving and confidence-boosting techniques of the smallest room in the house and only Mr and Mrs Bill Oddie could make the result so charmingly hilarious. Usefully constructed in two clear sections, firstly suggesting ingenious, life-enhancing things to occupy your toilet time at home, which can stretch to several months of your life, and secondly, pinpointing the hazardous, potential nightmare of toilet behaviour in a foreign, unfamiliar situation. Naturally, designed for a place in the toilet itself, the book is small, concise, hard-backed and easily wiped, and a suggestion is made to equip yourself with at least 25 copies for safety. This guide to total toilet fulfilment also helpfully closes with the life-saving page 97... a blank sheet (for emergency use only). Toilet awareness and the hindrances that non-preparation can bring are dealt with in detail, there's even a bird's eye view of toilet locations to help the spotter fully relax. The joy of toilet sport is revealed with number two players open to cricket wicket-keeping practice, the relative safety of a light ping pong ball rally with the surrounding walls, and, even toilet board games, a chess or monopoly move essential for the occupier to gain exit. Ventriloquism, the endearing doll Lotty Loo-Brush and a helpful comic script, could provide hours of fun, time can be taken out to improve your word power with handy phrases intended to display your new found knowledge, while origami via various toilet roll textures, could leave your toilet decorated in style. Note the apt reference to a life-size Elvis Presley model and, later, a couple of name checks for that lady Goodie-philes loved to hate, Mary Whitehouse. Memory improvement, tap-dancing and general playful business with wiggling ears and one eye-brow raising, are all clearly noted for toilet occupation, before an intricate plan of the ideal toilet is unveiled. It's clearly Oddie's dream, with, not only *The Toilet Book*, but recording equipment and a bird field guide, to hand! The chapters dealing with other people's toilets are wonderfully funny – good for concealing those toilet noises – with a guide to surviving bowel activity out of the familiar surroundings of your own home. The 'no lock' terror is brilliantly covered, providing good toilet etiquette, a useful list of door-securing hints and do and don't conversations for when you inadvertently interrupt somebody else. No paper, flushing problems – both no go and overflow – and cough/sneeze/children's toy-playing hints for disguising the expected bodily sounds, leads into post-toilet comfort, appearance and anti-leaking precautions. Finally, a diagram of the complete toilet goer makes sure all the major points are driven home and the end is rounded off with an everyman guide to lavatorial euphemisms – so relentlessly hilarious, it's like a *Carry On at Your Convenience* convention. A masterpiece, and invaluable for any self-respecting toilet goer... oh, come on, you must do!

Written by Bill Oddie and Laura Beaumount. Metheun London Ltd 1984.

TOMMY COOPER

Patchy half-hour sketch format for the great comedian which features small bursts of inspired manic magic alongside half-baked historical parody and some surprisingly high-profile guest stars, Michael Bentine, Arthur Lowe and even Vincent Price among them. Bill Oddie was credited with writing additional material.

Producer Bill Hitchcock. Director Bill Turner. Saturdays, 7 February–18 April 1970, ITV.

TOP OF THE POPS

Television's seminal chart programme, during their Seventies' pop stardom, the Goodies were regular guest performers. The group made five appearances in all, prancing around in sparkling flares, tossing mini black puddings into the audience and delighting in Gibbon dance movement for the masses. The trio were the personification of classic comic pop in the decade that taste forgot. *A Man's Best Friend Is His Duck* skipped past the censors, with Graeme's flat-capped lead performance, Tim's piano-foundering (complete with *Beastly Record* on the music stand) and Bill arriving late in white duck suit. *Black Pudding Bertha* saw the team donning huge Ecky Thump hats, while Emperor Rosko introduced the legendary *Funky Gibbon* studio rendition featuring the lads wearing those unforgettable 'G'-inscribed dungarees. Not only that, but do you remember Graeme sporting that single, huge, gibbon glove? Pan's People, the presenter and all the audience got into the gibbon craze and even Ecky Thump-style Goodies, joined by Cuddly Scamp from *Frankenfido* – with Tim proudly wearing a cuddly Gibbon toy on his hat – were intercut into the fun. Oddie as songwriter and lead singer thoroughly enjoyed the experience, wandering in for a bit of fun and self-consciously contrasting the 'proper' rockers whose life, home and family rested on them riding high in the charts. Graeme Garden seemed mildly embarrassed by most of the pop scene, while Tim Brooke-Taylor gleefully threw himself into the action. Eventually, Pan's Peoples choreographer, Flick Colby, was recruited to structure the Goodies performances for the show.

The Inbetweenies Thursday 28 November 1974, Father Christmas Do Not Touch Me Thursday 12 December 1974, Funky Gibbon Thursday 20 March 1975, Black Pudding Bertha Thursday 10 April 1975 and A Man's Best Friend Is His Duck Thursday 7 December 1978.

TOP TEN: COMEDY RECORDS

A celebration of the best in humorous vinyl. Tim Brooke-Taylor, Graeme Garden and Bill Oddie were interviewed on all *Funky Gibbon* and *Nappy Love*. Broadcast on 15 April 2000 on Channel 4. Michael Grade, Phil Jupitus and, yours truly, Robert Ross, contributed to the Goodies section.

TOTAL TRIVIA

Tim Brooke-Talyor wrote the forward for this collection of 2000 zany quiz questions.

Written by Martin Plimmer with Roger Millington, Joyce Robins and George Smith. Hennawood Publications 1985.

TRANDEM

Forget giant kittens, beanstalks, oversized *Magic Roundabout* characters or even Union flag waistcoats, the ultimate trademark for those glorious Goodies is their unique mode of transport – the three-seater trandem. Despite being a regular feature from the outset, it was only dubbed the trandem in Episode 12 of Series Two – *The Baddies*. Indeed, its first appearance was all a bit of a con. For Series One, a normal tandem was used, with a third seat stuck over the back wheel. By the start of Series Two, the familiar trandem was in place – with three seats, three sets of pedals and three Goodies. A product of the BBC's special effects department, the design failed to include a free wheel, so accidents and near misses during filming were common place. But from that first clamber aboard to the *Needed* theme, the bike and the Goodies were forever linked.

THE TRAVEL SHOW

Combining a 30-year-old love for birding and the pleasures of home holidays, Bill Oddie delighted in this eight-minute presentation on the Shetland Islands for ITV's 1992 *The Travel Show*. Settling for the capital, Sumburgh, driving around fish shops, celebrating the island's Viking history, strolling among rough and ready ponies, sampling the pub and live music-enriched night life, and indulging in a bit of bird activity at Lerwick, the most Northern point of Britain, this is was enthused, tempting plug.

TRIVIA TEST MATCH

A gentle, witty comedy game based round the finer points of cricket. Recorded from Windsor and Eton Cricket Club in Berkshire, the *I'm Sorry I Haven't a Clue* influence was heavy with the show's current producer and three of its players, including cricket nut Tim Brooke-Taylor.

Umpire BRIAN JOHNSON. Players TIM RICE, WILLIE RUSHTON, BILL TIDY, TIM BROOKE-TAYLOR. Producer Jon Magnusson. Tuesday 4 September 1991, Radio 4.

TUBBY AND FRIENDS

As part of the National Trust's Spring Outdoor Concert series, Bill Oddie narrated this endearing children's concert. Performed on Sunday 21 June 1998 at Polesden Lacey, Dorking in Surrey.

TV ZONE: Sci-Fi Comedy Special

The 33rd bumper special edition of *TV Zone*, published in

May 1999, was literally packed with Goodies material. Eighteen pages of it in fact. Having previously contributed a Goodies page to *Playback* magazine in 1997, writer Andrew Pixley presented the intelligent and affectionate overview of the series as well as a complete episode guide, while Jane Killick conducted a fascinating interview with the one and only Bill Oddie – *Goodie, GoodieYumYum*. Easily the most satisfying magazine piece on the team, it was slightly let down by the tail-ending comment still insisting on sticking *The Goodies* in the Seventies' nostalgic time-warp. However, for the dedicated fan it was a reassuringly and enjoyable assessment of the show.

12 + 1 or Thirteen

Another Orson Welles short film co-written by, co-directed and co-starring Tim Brooke-Taylor. Filmed in Italy, Tim played a slightly effeminate sort of chappie and delighted in re-writing a third of the script with the great Welles and directing his scenes with youthful pride. Tim remembers, 'Vittorio Da Sica was in it and Willie Rushton was my lover who killed himself, sadly in the arms of Sharon Tate, who was murdered by Manson before even the final dubbing was completed.'

20 ORIGINAL MONSTER HITS

A tape-only compilation of Rock's great and good featuring the single release version of the biggest Goodies hit, *The Funky Gibbon*, alongside Elton John doing the Beatles with a little bit of help from John Lennon and that hip dude Issac Hayes doing his *Shaft* thang. All that plus a cool, futuristic dinosaur cover design with a pink thunder lizard rroarrrring away with gusto…

THE TWENTY-FIRST CENTURY SHOW

A humorous look at the world in the year 2001 with a couple of writing Goodies and the series director giving the sketches comic clout. Bill Oddie remembers the origins of this fascinating show. 'It was an overt entry for Montreaux. In theory you weren't suppose to make special programmes for the contest. It had to be something which had already been broadcast but Lord Grade and ATV finally cheated and won by editing down 10 one-hour shows of Marty Feldman to a single 21-minute programme. So the BBC commissioned Graeme and I to write this futuristic variety show. It was

THE SPACE-SUITED ELEPHANT FROM *THE TWENTY-FIRST SHOW*

consciously written in a too clever by half style purely to please lots of foreigners with no sense of humour! We had this elaborate weightless circus on the moon which featured elephants dressed in space-suits floating off as they did their begging trick. It was very weird stuff, all done with models. We weren't in it at all. One of my favourite bits was a sex scene done with test-tubes, a touch of Woody Allan's *Sleeper* I suppose. The scene was shot like a blue movie with Andrew Ray pouring liquid into different containers.' Despite the impressive Goodies pedigree, support from Benny Hill cohort and guest Goodie baddie Henry McGee and a pre-Goodies *War Babies* Andrew Ray, this special presentation was never screened on BBC1. It was obviously a last-minute decision for a *Radio Times* listing was published for 12 April 1979. The show has been firmly kept in the vaults ever since.

With ANN HAMILTON, JUDY LOE. Produced and directed by Jim Franklin. Never screened.

TWICE A FORTNIGHT

Or, if you like, once a week… This was a pivotal television series on the road to both *Monty Python's Flying Circus* and *The Goodies*, using the talents of two figures from each fledgling group. Although a meeting of the Cambridge and Oxford figures still basking in the satire glory of Peter Cook's generation, this programme reassuringly moved away from that style of comedy and embraced a love for corny gags and surreal characterisations akin to radio's *I'm Sorry I'll Read That Again*. Indeed, much of the material used was reheated or restructured radio sketches and, thus, often explained why it failed fully to ignite on the small screen. The show's producer and director was Tony Palmer who perceived *TAF* as the major launch pad for Graeme Garden as focal point comedy star. The musical and comical contributions of Bill Oddie were also very much part of the package while Terry Jones and Michael Palin, suggested for inclusion by Graeme, wrote and performed silent pieces in a bizarre twisting of Jacques Tati convention. Cambridge Footlighters Jonathan Lynn and Tony Buffery helped flesh out the supporting cast. The major problem was constant disagreement between Palmer and Oddie. Both were passionate about music and, indeed, Palmer would revolutionise and reinvent pop documentary for television with his ground-breaking edition of *Omnibus* for BBC1, *All My Loving*, broadcast on 3 November 1969. Whereas Oddie wanted to promote his own musical pieces and retain an edge of comedy throughout the programmes, Palmer preferred to break up the sketches with innovative use of the greatest rock acts of the day. As opposed to reliance on Oddie's massive back catalogue of numbers, this ushered in contemporary, straight, rock, cool. As with *The Young Ones* 15 years later, *Twice a Fortnight* embraced the youth culture of the age to heighten and balance the comedy content. As such, it was a product of the BBC Music and Arts department and not Light Entertainment. A second problem was the studio audience policy. It was the BBC and Oddie's intention to recreate and encourage in the television studio, the similar lion's den gusto which *I'm Sorry I'll Read That Again* was currently suffering and/or enjoying on radio. Some of the performers and, particularly director Tony Palmer, were less than satisfied with this, with all the pop interludes and Garden material being recorded live in front of the over-enthused crowd. The inserts of Jones and Palin were filmed on location, and as a result, cut the atmosphere immediately. Furthermore, the invited audiences were offered copious amounts of free booze before recordings to swell their already loud and uncontrolled reaction. Often the sketches were completely drowned out by the noise and, in particular, the sound recording of Show Two is almost inaudible. Not only that, but a clear rivalry between the Cambridge Goodies and Oxford Pythons was

developing. Oddie admitted he wasn't a fan of the Jones and Palin pieces, believing them 'so what!' moments which needed more explanation than they were worth. Besides, he considered that they held up the rest of the show. Although on retrospect, these are mini masterpieces, the comedy did indeed creep up on the viewer and several times, notably for the Croquet film, Graeme Garden and Bill Oddie insisted on adding jokes before it was produced. However, all this negative background should not cloud the importance of *Twice a Fortnight*. Many of the Garden and Oddie filmed sequences investigated the speeded-up camera, jump cuts and dutch angle photography later employed on *The Goodies*. Indeed, one sketch, exposing the secret life of miniature policemen using Chihuahuas for police dogs and Alsatians for horses, clearly experimented with elements further used in *The Goodies: South Africa*. Oddie even praised the innovative work of Palmer's direction, instructing his hired band of midget actors to perform in reverse. Filmed backwards this would then be projected and broadcast in reverse to make it look correct. The effect was a distinctive, nightmarish quality. Equally, the entire scheduling of the programme pre-empted the likes of *Monty Python's Flying Circus* and *Rutland Weekend Television* in its corruption of television convention. The opening programme was dubbed *Match of the Day Part Two* due to its broadcast immediately after the footie fest and later programmes similarly tapped into the BBC programming line-up with *Peter West Lives*, *Even Before Alan Melville* and *Suddenly, It's Sooty*. The Python-esque obsession with a distinguished newsreader was pioneered here with respectability exuded by the veteran Ronald Fletcher.

Did You Know? *A compilation edition, The Best of Twice a Fortnight, with guests The Who and Kenny Lynch, was broadcast on 3 June 1968 as a proposed prelude to a planned second series. This failed to materialise, cross-fertilising into the full Goodies-strength comedy sketch series Broaden Your Mind. Frustratingly, the BBC archives hold none of the 10 episodes of Twice a Fortnight. The only material to survive is the Jones and Palin inserts held in the Terry Jones collection. However, off-air sound recordings for all the programmes are in existence.*

GRAEME GARDEN, TONY BUFFERY, TERRY JONES, JONATHAN LYNN, BILL ODDIE, MICHAEL PALIN, DILYS WATLING and the voice of them all RONALD FLETCHER. Written by Graeme Garden, Bill Oddie, Terry Jones and Michael Palin. Script editors Terry Jones and Michael Palin. Produced and directed by Tony Palmer. **Show One:** THE WHO. **Show Two:** THE SPINNERS, GERMAINE GREER. **Show Three:** SIMON DUPREE AND THE BIG SOUND. **Show Four:** ROSS HANNAMAN. **Show Five:** THE SPINNERS, THE MOODY BLUES. **Show Six:** THE SCAFFOLD, GERMAINE GREER. **Show Seven:** CREAM. **Show Eight:** CAT STEVENS. **Show Nine:** THE SMALL FACES. **Show Ten:** THE SPINNERS, THE WHO. Saturdays, 21 October–23 December 1967, BBC1.

U

UNDER THE MOON

Channel 4 television sports discussion show with Tim Brooke-Taylor as guest on 2 April 1998. Interviewed about Derby County, cricket, football, women's boxing and life as a Goodie, Tim happily threw himself into the live telephone debate, fielding questions from punters, fans and loonies alike. One caller asked whether, after theoretically scoring the winning goal for England, Tim would rather have sex with Bill Oddie or Graeme Garden – Tim chose Graeme as he is a doctor! A bloke who once caddied for the great comic golfer called in for a renewed relationship and a question aimed to the attractive blonde was initially offered to Tim! Ultimately, Tim failed to bag a basketball goal successfully and forfeited a £50 bet on the Grand National for his team mate!

UNFULFILLED PROJECTS

The story of the Goodies is peppered with fascinating, long-awaited projects which were often mooted but never completed. Monty Python had pioneered television comedy as a viable stage production and, latterly, *The Fast Show* and *Shooting Stars* have embraced the medium. Back in the Seventies, the Goodies were seriously planning a British stage tour, the major stumbling block proved to be the content. Highlights from the television series were practically impossible to recreate on stage and Bill Oddie suggested a concert tour promoting the group's hit singles rather than comic performance. This was certainly on the list but both Tim Brooke-Taylor and Graeme Garden favoured the idea of balancing music with sketches, but the nearest the team got to stage work was a four-number spot in the 1976 Amnesty concert *A Poke in the Eye (with a Sharp Stick)* and a pop gig stage experience for television in *The Goodies Almost Live*. A further stage proposal, towards the end of the Seventies, was for a Christmas show-cum-pantomime parody developing elements of *The Goodies and the Beanstalk* and tossing in codes, ingredients and conventions from every panto known to man. The result was to have been family entertainment with 'he's behind you', 'rub my lamp' and 'slip this slipper on missus' material mixed with traditional Goodies humour. Again,

these promising ideas were abandoned, although the basic premise resurfaced in the team's first ITV episode, *Snow White 2* in 1981 and Rod Hull managed to present the cross-fertilising panto on stage to great success in the late Eighties. A Royal seal of approval from Prince Charles may have been hastily whipped away for the *Scatty Safari* episode but the Goon nut and Goodies admirer was keen to work with the trio in a short, amateur 'home movie' production. Akin to his earlier Milligan-esque RAF picture and Goon photo sessions, Charles wrote the story line himself. The plot revealed the long line of recently knighted subjects suffering from cuts and slices after Her Majesty 'had a go' at them with the sword. Typically, Bill Oddie reworked the idea with a harder edge, getting towards a Sam Peckinpah-style with beheaded Sirs and the like. In the end, Palace advice saw this short subject left unmade. However, it was a feature film that proved the most tantalising unfulfilled Goodies idea. From the mid-Seventies, rumours and suggested stories for the film were bandied about, before the special effect strain on the British film industry put the film firmly on the back burner. The trials, tribulations and corrupt rejections the trio faced, more than influenced their 1977 publication, *The Making of the Goodies' Disaster Movie*. Tim Brooke-Taylor believes that the entire film project was a mere bribe from their publishers, although Garden and Oddie were certainly on for the idea. However, the project was completely dead in the water, although a screenplay had been half written, commissioned by Lord Grade's ATV. The plot-line, revealing how the Goodies first met, was a promising hook to hang the film on but Bill Oddie admits that 'we just couldn't make the script work.' Perhaps the most intriguing and viable Goodies project was the resurrected feature film idea seriously considered in 1979. Amazingly Steven Speilberg, who had seen classic Goodies episodes on the American channel PBS and the 1975 edition *Movies* on HBO, contacted the team with a view to construct a Goodies feature and enquired whether they were interested. The resounding shouts of 'YES!' could be heard from here to Cricklewood. Having cut his teeth on *Duel* and *Jaws*, Speilberg was looking for a way to satisfy his major love for comedy. Sadly, bad experience and very poor box office showings for his 1979 John Belushi war farce *1941* curtailed further plans for comedy films and he set to work on cute aliens and restructured dinosaurs. The missing link in the Goodies continued success, a film version would not only have cracked the American market but, naturally, kept the trio as an active force on British television via regular small screen showings. Philosophically, the team still revel in the idea that the great director had let even the notion of a Goodies film pass through his brain. That Speilberg had even thought the idea was possible seems more than enough. In the mid-Eighties Children's BBC bosses suggested that Oddie and Garden resurrect some old scripts for *The New Goodies*. Comprised of the Philip Schofield school of kiddie's presentation, the writers thought the idea ill-advised and far too expensive. Even a mooted BBC plan to include the trio as part of a special Millennium tribute to the history of television was floored by the group's reluctance. Tim considered a very brief comeback with memories of 'youthful creatures' suddenly reappearing as 'bald and fat' would ruin chances of a repeat season and a full-blown reunion. In February 2000, the BBC announced that no repeats or documentary would mark *The Goodies* 30th anniversary.

THE UNVANISHED TRUTH

While Bill Oddie was establishing *Saturday Banana*, Tim Brooke-Taylor and Graeme Garden filled in the time between *The Goodies* Series Seven and Eight with a six-week nation-wide tour of this stage production. Glad to take the opportunity of being simply hired actors and leaving the job of scripting and general hassle in the hands of others, the play proved popular enough to warrant a limited West End run in September 1978.

THE UPPER HAND

Standard ITV situation comedy starring Joe McGann as an ex-footballer turned housekeeper keeping his glamorous companions, Diana Weston and Honor Blackman, at bay. Based on the popular American show *Who's the Boss,* this show proved to be ITV's biggest comedy asset of the Nineties. In this episode, *Blind Date*, our hapless hero attempts to help his old pal, Trevor, but causes comic misunderstanding and friction between his girlfriend and his female boss. Way, way down the cast list, was a floundering Tim Brooke-Taylor, guest-starring with his usual mix of comic cool and nervous bluster.

Charlie Burrows JOE McGANN Caroline Wheatley DIANA WESTON Laura West HONOR BLACKMAN Joanna Burrows KELLIE BRIGHT Tom Wheatley WILLIAM PUTTOCK Trevor TIM BROOKE-TAYLOR. Written by Paul Robinson-Hunter. Producer Christopher Walker. Director Martin Shardlow. Tuesday 27 October 1992, ITV.

THE VALLEY EXPRESS

A *Comedy Playhouse* pilot that failed to get a commission for series development, it was written by *Braden's Week* producer John Lloyd and centred round the boring life at a local Welsh newspaper, *The Valley Express* of the title. Stan and Reg spice up the action by inventing exciting stories and flogging them to the big boys in Fleet Street. This conjures up all the predictable, problematic results, forewarned by Stan's shrewd wife, Jenny, played by future Liver Bird and District Nurse, Nerys Hughes. Graeme Garden cropped up in a supporting role as a television director a few months before playing a television presenter in *Doctor in the House: Docs on the Box*.

Stan DAVID BAXTER Reg RICHARD DAVIES Jenny NERYS HUGHES Pet Shop Owner JESSIE EVANS Television director GRAEME GARDEN. Written by John Lloyd. Producer James Gilbert. Monday 21 April 1969, BBC1.

VIDEO ARTS

John Cleese's ultra-successful training films production company was started in 1975 and used several acting and writing contributions from old Cambridge pals Tim Brooke-Taylor and Graeme Garden. Rejuvenating the market with a mixture of 'stating the bleedin' obvious' fact points and Python-esque full-on rants, these short films continue to be the most popular among companies. The Goodies' connected titles include: *Budgeting and Return on Investment*, written by Graeme Garden; *In Two Minds* and *The Meeting of Minds* which starred Tim Brooke-Taylor and *More Bloody Meetings* with Graeme Garden as the manic dentist. Graeme has written and directed many more titles. The majority of programmes were designed for business conferences only, although the wealth of comedy acting and writing talent displayed within the films made them perfect for mainstream exposure. Three BBC2 seasons were constructed with *In Two Minds* being screened as part of *The Selling Line* on 27 October 1975. Almost 20 years later in 1994, the company was still going strong and Graeme Garden was drafted in to write and direct almost 50 *Videos for Patients*, a series of medical films with John Cleese and Rob Buckman which tried to demystify medical conditions.

AN ORIGINAL GRAEME GARDEN CARTOON CAPTURING THE BACKSTAGE FUN OF THE STAGE PRODUCTION, *THE UNVANISHED TRUTH*

VIDEO RELEASES

The Goodies on video has a long and rather frustrating history. In a way, the trio were shot in the foot by their very success. As one of the BBC flagship programmes of the late Seventies, the series was naturally chosen, alongside that other mistreated classic *Dr Who*, to launch the BBC Video range. The team were asked which episodes they thought fitted the bill and came up with a list of three titles for the first release. Shockingly, the powers that be insisted on selecting just one episode, *The Goodies and the Beanstalk*, and even more shockingly, putting it out at the retrospectively outrageous price of £56. Now, not to say that that particular Goodies masterpiece wasn't worth that and also fully aware that in 1983 the price of videos was uniformly high, unsurprisingly, this title was not a huge seller. Few had video recorders anyway and even fewer wanted to pay nearly 60 quid for a 45-minute

programme. The first batch of BBC videos were deleted and gradually re-released as cheaper stock through the Eighties... all except *The Goodies*. For some corrupt, sinister reason a secret BBC file obviously dictated that Goodies videos did not sell and none was released, although ITV put the first four episodes of Series Nine out in 1984. The BBC refused to yield until a decade later. After years of comments and campaigns from fans and Goodies alike, and almost 10 years since the final sighting of *The Goodies* on terrestrial television, BBC Video invited the lads back to select two lots of three titles for release. Brooke-Taylor, Oddie and Garden were sent tapes of all the BBC episodes to plough through for a selection of the best titles. *The Beanstalk* and *Kitten Kong* headlined the attack, the trio posed on the old trandem outside Broadcasting House and did *The Gloria Hunniford Show* for publicity. Both tapes were granted a PG certificate and the staggered

THE CAST OF "THE UNVARNISHED TRUTH" ARE UPSTAGED BY THE TEARS OF MR BERNARD LEVIN

AN ORIGINAL GRAEME GARDEN CARTOON CAPTURING THE FUN OF THE OPENING NIGHT OF *THE UNVANISHED TRUTH*

release campaign – *The Beanstalk* was released on September 5, the *Kitten Kong* on September 19 – aimed to act as an opening of the floodgates. The Goodies identification chart from *The Goodies File* and the construction of the trandem from *The Goodies Book of Criminal Records*, were resurrected for the inner sleeves and a low-key publicity drive kicked in. But the major problem was the marketing. It was totally misguided, pushing *The Goodies* as an almost second-rate, forgotten relics from the Seventies nestled in between flared trousers and spangles. Indeed, the actual BBC press hand-out was headed with 'Dig out your flares and turn back the clock with the return of *The Goodies*'. Not only that, but contrary to every other BBC video initiative, there were no television repeats of *The Goodies*, to wet the appetite, interest new audiences and actually advertise the fact that the two tapes were, at last, out there. As a result, the titles failed to match predicted sales figures. Almost immediately, the two tapes were reissued on the BBC budget label, Right Price Comedy, and unceremoniously consigned to the bargain bucket. The promise of further releases and even a Christmas reunion special, were shelved. The fans are still awaiting the complete availability of all episodes.

THE VIEWING

Graeme Garden played Mr Guest in a 1987 staging of this play at the Greenwich Theatre.

WE HAVE WAYS OF MAKING YOU LAUGH

The first ever programme to be transmitted by LWT was a mixed-up but inventive format which embraced the cream of Oxbridge comedy under the traditional guidance of scriptwriter and host Frank Muir. The very young Jenny Hanley co-hosted with her usual wide-eyed charm, Humphrey Barclay gathered together fresh from the first series of *Do Not Adjust Your Set*, Eric Idle and Terry Gilliam, while guest appearances came from Tim Brooke-Taylor, Graeme Garden and Bill Oddie. Despite warm reaction from the audience, teething troubles with the new station, a technicians' strike and a confused blend (of middle of the road attitude meets sparks of surreal imagination), lead to the premature end of the series. Its importance in the development of the Python–Goodie mafia is a long forgotten but vital one.

Written and performed by TIM BROOKE-TAYLOR, GRAEME GARDEN, TERRY GILLIAM, DENNIS GREENE, JENNY HANLEY, ERIC IDLE, FRANK MUIR, BILL ODDIE. DICK VOSBURGH. Producer Humphrey Barclay. Director Bill Turner. 23 August–18 October 1968, ITV.

WEEKEND ILLUSTRATED

Australian television journal, the Saturday 7 February 1998 edition of which featured the article 'Oldie but Goodie' by Kerrie Murphy, featuring interview material from Tim Brooke-Taylor.

WHAT'S THE BLEEDING TIME?

Doctor Graeme Garden hosted this enjoyable four-part celebration of medical comedy. Presented with a quiet, bedside manner air of a consultant physician, Garden trawled through the classic archives digging up loads of Monty Python, notably *The Meaning of Life*'s birth sequence, *Hancock*, *Fawlty Towers*, *One Foot in the Grave*, *Carry On* and, naturally, the *Doctor* series.

Keep Taking the Tablets, Draw the Screens Nurse, Under the Knife, On the Psychiatrist's Couch. Producer Gillian Russell. Saturdays, 12 December 1998–9 January 1999, Radio 2.

WHERE ARE THEY NOW?

The anticipated Goodies reunion for Australian television featured the three comic greats interviewed in a London pub, the Churchill. Host Peter Luck didn't seem to know what was going on, the trio looked slightly uncomfortable and despite the coolness of the occasion, this was, after all, the Goodies back together again, seated round a Union flag-adorned table, the heart and soul in presentation was missing. Clips from *Radio Goodies*, *Saturday Night Grease* and a snatch of *Funky Gibbon* from *Top of the Pops*, set the mood, but the piece was whittled down to just five minutes of screen time. Still, it is more than invaluable, if only for Bill's brief lapse into *The Goodies Theme* and Graeme's proud comment that 'I think my character could have saved the world!' Bill revealed himself as huge fans of the other two, Tim praised Bill's music and 'the Spice Girls of the Seventies' seemed delighted to be together.

Friday 14 November 1997, Channel 7, Australia.

WHO WEEKLY'S 'WHERE ARE THEY NOW?' SPECIAL EDITION

Bill Oddie was interviewed in 1995.

WHOOPS APOCALYPSE

Based on the epic 1982 television comedy drama and adapted by the original script-writers, Marshall and Renwick, this was a 1987 feature film version casting Cambridge legends Peter Cook and Graeme Garden opposite alternatives Rik Mayall and Alexei Sayle. The everyday story of an island invasion in the middle of Cold War dilemmas, saw Graeme Garden contribute a couple of eye-catching cameo performances. From inside the battle zone his elderly, befuddled servant of Stuart Saunders slowly makes his staggering way to the telephone. Calling for help as the place collapses around him, a burst of *Land of Hope and Glory* transformed the scene to London and another slow, eccentric staggering Graeme Garden character desperate to answer the phone. Falling over, stalling and ultimately missing the call, the scene cuts to the war-torn Graeme surrounded by military attackers. And that's it! Hilarious, wordless, painfully funny business from a true master of the visual joke.

LORETTA SWIT, PETER COOK, MICHAEL RICHARDS, ALEXEI SAYLE, RIK MAYALL, IAN RICHARDSON, HERBERT LOM, RICHARD WILSON, JOHN SESSIONS and GRAEME GARDEN as Man who takes a long time to walk to the phone and a different man who takes a long time to walk to a different phone. Written by Andrew Marshall and David Renwick. Producer Brian Eastman. Director Tom Bussman. 1987.

WHOSE LINE IS IT ANYWAY?

That expert ad-libber, Graeme Garden, appeared in a first series episode of this ground-breaking Channel 4 improv comedy show in 1988. Struggling with plastic bendy circles in the Props round, hosting the mime it and see

Party round, camping his way through mission control business, performing JB Priestly's version of *Sleeping Beauty* and showing folk round a TV studio in the style of an American musical, Garden proved the old Sixties' satire boomers could still deliver the goods.

WIFE BEGINS AT FORTY

Frantic stage farce in which the late Derek Nimmo toured Bejin and the Middle East with in late 1993. From August through to October 1994 the production took in the Far East, Mexico City and Moscow, and starred Tim Brooke-Taylor in the central role as the poor chap who has just had a vasectomy. Patricia Brake and Patrick Cargill also starred.

WILLY WONKA & THE CHOCOLATE FACTORY

One of those timeless films from your childhood which capture an era and remain eternally enchanting at the same time. Brash, colourful direction from Mel Stuart and hummable tunes from Bricusse and Newley combine perfectly with Dahl's surrealistic edge of young nightmare. Despite the fact that the author disliked Gene Wilder's interpretation of the sainted Mr Wonka. Too fresh-faced perhaps, but there's no denying the alien-like insanity of Wilder. He creates a towering man of genius, forever diving within his own, self-ruling persona, lapsing into WC Fields mannerisms, injecting moments of terror with throwaway songs and strolling through his domain in felt top hat. His mock serious first entrance is totally bewitching, the break into beaming smile totally charming and his ability to knit together Dahl's off-kilter imagination totally winning. He is the perfect chocolate wizard. One can forgive the essential leaning towards America in casting and plot development for, filmed in England and sticking laudably to Dahl's vision, the film delights in a British cynicism which peppers the more mawkish moments with real bite. Sentimentality rears its sickly head at only odd occasions and nothing interrupts the flow of warm confectionery. Veteran character player Jack Albertson makes a lovable Grandpa Jo and Leonard Stone's fast-talking car salesman is an unforgettable ingredient, but it's really the British actors that enrich the supporting cast. Aubrey Woods as the benevolent sweet shop keeper, David Battley as the gloriously embittered schoolteacher, Peter Capell making his few moments count with a chilling rendition of William Allingham's *The Fairies*, and, best of all,

Roy Kinnear, giving his usual flustered bemusement and chucking in amazed asides for a string of cutting laughs. Pat Coombs, uncredited as Kinnear's wife, turns in a disinterested, Northern lass, while Tim Brooke-Taylor – the reason this classic film is included in this book, after all – brightens up 70 seconds with his performance as a clipped English computer bod. It's a sublime cameo, typically Dahl and given full comic weight by Tim's fledgling Goodie delivery. His cheery attempt to trick his whiz bang computer into revealing the whereabouts of the remaining Golden tickets is hilarious. Sheepishly reading out its 'I won't tell… that would be cheating!' response with the perfect amount of embarrassment. Well worth checking out.

Did You Know? *Tim Brooke-Taylor's sequence was, in fact, filmed on the last day of production. Having been approached for an audition as opposed to his usual film roles coming via writer Denis Norden, Tim worked on location, suitably enough, at the Nestle' headquarters. In the days when computers were relatively new and still usually the size of a small house, Tim fiddled with the machine for his scenes and was warned not to touch certain buttons in case he wiped out the company's files! Executives looked menacingly on and added extra terror to Tim's terror-stricken performance.*

Willy Wonka GENE WILDER Grandpa Joe JACK ALBERTSON Mr Salt ROY KINNEAR Veruca Salt JULIE DAWN COLE Mr Beauregarde LEONARD STONE Violet Beauregarde DENISE NICKERSON Mrs Teevee DODO DENNEY Mike Teevee PARIS THEMMEN Mrs Gloop URSULA REIT Augustus Gloop MICHAEL BOLLNER Mrs Bucket DIANA SOWLE Bill AUBREY WOODS Mr Turkentine DAVID BATTLEY Mr Slugworth GUNTER MEISNER The Tinker PETER CAPELL Mr Jopeck WERNER HEYKING Winkelmann PETER STUART and introducing PETER OSTRUM as Charlie. Uncredited: PAT COOMBS as Mrs Salt and TIM BROOKE-TAYLOR as the computer expert. Lyrics and music by Leslie Bricusse and Anthony Newley. Screenplay by Roald Dahl, based on his book *Charlie and the Chocolate Factory*. Produced by Stan Margulies and David L Wolper. Director Mel Stuart.

CORBETT WOODALL

The epitome of unflappable BBC presentation for *The Goodies*, Woodall earnestly read through the headlines in black dinner suit for a total of 11 episodes: *Snooze, Pollution, The Music Lovers, Kitten Kong, The Goodies and the Beanstalk, Clown Virus, Lighthouse Keeping Loonies, The End, Goodies Rule OK?, Hype Pressure* and *Goodies and Politics*, spanning the entire BBC run from 1970–80.

WOMAN'S DAY

Magazine interview with Bill Oddie from 1993.

WOMAN'S WEEKLY

In the issue published 22 March 1997, Bill Oddie was interviewed by Eithne Power about his life, work and bird-watching. Titled 'Kitchen Sink Drama' Bill remembered his flat share with director Stephen Frears and the post-University awfulness of Tim Brooke-Taylor's kitchen. Tim also contributed interview material to the publication.

THE WORLD OF THE GOODIES

This was the one and only Goodies record in my Dad's collection and, as such, it was a bit of black vinyl I played over and over again during my formative years. As such, I still know all the words and the first notes of *All Things Bright and Beautiful* can still send shivers down my spine. A direct re-issue of the team's first album, *The Goodies Sing Songs From The Goodies*, Decca's 'World of…' series covered every comic treasure from *The Goons* to Kenneth Williams via Benny Hill. *The Goodies* were hastily added to the list in 1975, immediately before the launch of *The New Goodies LP* and repeating the self-mocking sleeve notes from the original cover. Another photograph from David Wedgbury's original shot was adopted for the cover image, sans instruments this time. It featured the Goodies still on the trandem but peddling in the opposite direction!

Side One: All Things Bright and Beautiful, Ride My Pony, Stuff That Gibbon, Mummy I Don't Like My Meat, Show Me the Way. **Side Two:** Goodies Theme, Sparrow Song, Taking Me Back, Sunny Morning, Winter Sportsman, Spacehopper. All compositions by Bill Oddie except *All Things Bright* (Oddie, Antony, Jackman) and *Sparrow Song* (Garden). Produced by Miki Antony. For additional credits see *The Goodies Sing Songs From The Goodies*. ZAL 12586P Decca May 1975.

WOWFABGROOVY

A hip and happening nostalgic Radio 2 quiz game hosted by laid-back broadcasting dude, Johnnie Walker. For the first of a new series on 3 June 1997, Goodie and Rock God, Bill Oddie, was recruited to take part, breezing through the quips and memories with ease and a Simpsons t-shirt! Helen Lederer proved a useful comic foil as his partner, while Jeremy Hardy shamelessly struggled to recall the theme tune to *I'm Sorry I'll Read That Again* and needed major nudges to remember Bill as part of the team!

WRITE A PLAY

An enterprising and laudable policy by Rediffusion Television to encourage and discover fresh writing talent for television. Short plays of about 10 minutes each were performed by a band of professional actors and screened on ITV. Tim Brooke-Taylor was roped in as part of this rep company featuring in one half-hour programme promoting two scripted efforts.

Introduced by Clive Goodwin. *The Mind of Man* by Margaret Eldridge and Jacqueline Pragnell: Mr Hogarth TIM BROOKE-TAYLOR Miss Hunter BEATTY WALTERS Claude Scot-Eeavens AUBREY MORRIS TV Interviewer JOHN BLYTHE Miss Hodgkiss HAZEL HUGHES Policeman DUDLEY JONES *Poetic Justice* by D Mansell David: Gladys Thomas HAZEL HUGHES Henry Thomas DUDLEY JONES George AUBREY MORRIS Fred TIM BROOKE-TAYLOR Sally BEATTY WALTERS Jim JOHN BLYTHE. Script by Scot Finch. Settings John Pant. Producer Ronald Marriott. Director Viv Hughes. Tuesday 30 May 1967, ITV.

Y

YES MINISTER

One of the great BBC situation comedies and, tellingly, most politicians all-time favourite television programme. Painfully close to the corrupt world of cabinet leaks, white papers and back handers, the intellectual, observational writing of Anthony Jay and Jonathan Lynn sparkles with a delicious satirical edge, while the ensemble playing of Paul Eddington, Nigel Hawthorne and Derek Fowlds is a constant joy. The elevation of the right honourable Jim Hacker to the leader of his party brought on the equally hilarious, although slightly less naïve, *Yes, Prime Minister*, but this episode, *The Death List*, from Series Two of the original features a very brief but wonderfully enthused cameo from Graeme Garden. Lynn, of course, had been a contemporary of the Goodies at Cambridge. The episode's basic premise involved poor old Hacker discovering, to his abject horror, that he's been subjected to extensive bugging and, now, with heightened irony, his department is in control of the continued bugging of other senior politicians. In his usual blustering, figure of authority style, he turns on the Churchillian grandeur and sets the wheels in motion for a total dismantling of the secretive policy. Trouble is, his name is found on the death list of the latest political activist group, blanket police protection guards his every move, and suddenly, intelligent surveillance seems like the greatest of ideas. There's some classic u-turning with the journalistic contact, Hawthorne is allowed one flight of impenetrable English language tongue-twisting and Fowlds fidgets in the background in a model performance of uncertain obedience. Graeme's contribution is in a sequence lasting just a few minutes, but it's the comic height of the show and a brilliantly constructed piece of farcical comic tension. Eddington, never better than when trying to remain calm in the least calm of circumstances, puts on a brave, frightfully British, frightfully stiff upper-lipped attitude to his, possible, impending demise. Garden, as the chief officer in the attempt to protect the minister, storms into the scenario with an energetic catalogue of all the things that could go wrong. Maniacally searching for bombs before introductions, he spirals through death by shooting, poisoning, surprise and every other fiendish plot up angst-ridden activist's sleeve. Delighting in his experience, knowledge and complete control of his authority, Graeme's cameo is a masterclass.

Rt Hon James Hacker PAUL EDDINGTON Sir Humphrey Appleby NIGEL HAWTHORNE Bernard Wooley DEREK FOWLDS Commander Forest of the Special Branch GRAEME GARDEN Mrs Hacker DIANA HODDINOTT Walter Fowler of the Daily Express IVOR ROBERTS With COLIN McCORMACK, MICHAEL KEATING, JAY NEILL. Written by Anthony Jay and Jonathan Lynn. Producer Peter Whitmore. Monday 9 March 1981, BBC2.

YOU ARE AWFUL BUT WE LIKE YOU! SHOWBIZ COMEDY TITBITS OF THE 60S AND 70S

A mind-blowing double CD collection presenting 50 tracks from the likes of Frankie Howerd, Sid James, Benny Hill, Terry Scott, Jim Dale and Dick Emery. Tim is backing vocal on *The Rhubarb Tart Song* and the Goodies' version of *Wild Thing* was also included.

NEMCD 477 Sequel Records March 2000.

YOU MUST BE JOKING

A BBC retrospective clip fest tackling war, religion, politics and the like, in terms of classic comedy. Wallowing in Parliamentary popularity from *If I Ruled the World*, Graeme Garden hosted this hilarious politics edition, campaigning for government via choice comedy moments. Struggling to get down from his soap box, muttering promises through his megaphone, explaining the loony left, loony right and loony middle system of rule and celebrating JFK's glory days, he laments the fact that Seventies' babe Suzi Quatro refused a political career and wistfully reveals that the boys had to settle for Margaret Thatcher instead. Graeme's short, witty interludes proved perfect cement for the bucket-load of classic clips. *Yes, Prime Minister* was, naturally, prominent, with other classic moments coming from *The Two Ronnies*, *Harry Enfield and Chums*, *Not the Nine O'Clock News* and, heavens above, *The Goodies*, with the 1980 *Politics* episode represented by Brooke-Taylor's Thatcherism chat with style marketing man Garden and the working class Oddie.

Did You Know? Second in broadcast order, Garden's edition was inadvertently screened instead of the advertised show (Annabella Weir's look at comic religion). There was no apparent reason for the change and the accompanying comedy show, Blackadder II's religious Bishop of Bath and Wells episode, was some what incongruously screened with the untallying political comic compilation.

Hosted by GRAEME GARDEN. Written by David and Caroline Stafford. Producer Charlotte Winby. Director Neil Duggan. Monday 29 March 1999, BBC2.

YOU MUST BE THE HUSBAND

The ultimate misunderstood situation comedy. While wallowing in the clichéd Terry and Juneisms on the surface, this tackled deep and important issues along the way. At the root of the comedy was the upheaval in a 20-year marriage when cosy, predictability is shattered by the sudden fame of one partner. Here, Tim Brooke-Taylor's easy-going, bathroom fittings employee, sees his familiar lifestyle with his loving wife, crumble away. Finally, shot of the twins – an 18-year-old son and daughter we never see – the main man's life centres round work, home, witty banter with his postman and poor beer sufferance at his local. Tim – allowed a more forthright, with-it attitude to sex, thanks to a stunning wife (Diane Keen) and, on occasion, lapsing into memories of naughty times during the Sixties before life got in the way – still maintained that nervous, uneasy edge from *The Goodies* and *Me & My Girl*. There was even time for the occasional moment of brilliant comic self-indulgence – notably during the wicked Squire and innocent maid act in *Mummy's Brave Little Soldier* – and golf. As the show went on, Tim seems to be on the course more and more, and when asked who decides on the rules of the sport he blissfully mutters, 'God I suppose!' The first show warranted a *Radio Times* interview and the comedy revolved around encounters with fame, fortune and misunderstood temptation, thanks to the publishing success of his wife's first novel, a raunchy sex adventure. Into this scenario strolled two conflicting factors – the feminist, acidic literary agent, Miranda, continually trying to drag her new author away from the boring confines of life with Tim and coining the 'You must be the husband' introduction (his vampire-killing cross action became a running gag), and Tim's child-like, tedious, toilet-obsessed, Boss figure, Gerald, who misguides and misinforms his, ever-more, panicked employee. Tim's time was split between the office, the home and the pub – with his circle of depressed friends suffering at the hands of the landlord's awful beer. On top of all this, of course, there's the burning, paranoid question as to where, and with whom, his wife researched the published sex scenes – the opening episode's stand-out moment is Tim's two frantic questions: 'Who is he? And, who the hell is he!' Tim's shocked reaction at the books could get a laugh out of 'Oh! My God!' for eternity… and he did. At first glance this may appear to be a standard sitcom but search it out. It's more

than worth it for Tim's jumps into delicious surrealism – with a door-banging, Fred Flintstone scream of 'Wilma!' at the close of *West of Swansea* and US trip excitement bringing on an on-going touch of duck-walking Chuck Berry pleasure in *Route 66* before collapsing in a drunken heap behind the sitcom sofa. The second series tended to overplay Tim's sexual angst over the possibility of his wife's affair, although the fun reached a peak with Peter Jeffrey's smooth celebrity in Alice and Her Yorkshire Pudding. Originally, both writer and star were agreed that this should be a 20-plus, tightly constructed, pioneering season with each episode performed in real time, and thus, allowing the characters and comic situations to slow burn for added effectiveness. In the end, the BBC and the show's producer played safe and went for a limited six-week run which used stereotypical sitcom conventions and flamboyant support acting. Ironically, the close of the last episode – with a midnight golfing session and touching heart-to-heart between the couple – promises darker, more challenging comedy which was never to come. Tom Hammond was the first sitcom role that Tim played and actually liked. It's still a show Tim is very proud of and the 'just a sitcom' label is one he resents, 'When I hear people saying, 'Oh! it's a sitcom!', I say, 'Yeah! So is *Frasier*, so is *Hancock*, so is *Only Fools and Horses…*' It's still good stuff. There's a sofa in it because most people tend to have a sofa in their sitting room!'

Tom Hammond TIM BROOKE-TAYLOR Alice Hammond DIANE KEEN Miranda SHEILA STEAFEL Gerald GARFIELD MORGAN Pat BRIAN HALL Don MICHAEL STAINTON. Written by Colin Bostock-Smith. Produced and directed by John Kilby. Series Two directed by Richard Boden. **Series One:** The Postman Cometh, More Money Than Sense, Little Round Objects, Mummy's Brave Little Soldier, West of Swansea, Big George Is Back, Doctors – What Do They Know? Tuesdays, 8 September–20 October 1987. **Series Two:** Shanks and Zips and Other Problems, In Sickness and in Wealth, Alice and Her Yorkshire Pudding, The Glittering Pressies, A Bit Prickly in the Morning, Big Boys Don't Cry. Mondays, 29 February–4 April 1988, BBC1.

YOU MUST BE THE HUSBAND: the stage show

Stage presentation of the BBC television situation comedy written by the show's creator, Colin Bostock-Smith, and casting Tim opposite that likely lass, Brigit Forsyth. A tour of the UK was followed by performances in the Far and Middle East.

YOU NEVER HAD IT SO GOODIE

Something was stirring in the late Nineties. *Cult TV* magazine and *Television's Greatest Hits* basked in the light of Goodies' reunions and contemporary comic references to the terrific trio were slowly invading popular culture. Peter Kay's *Let's Get Quizzical* section in Channel 4's *Quiz*

Night embraced the lads as a cultural touchstone via every Seventies game show contestant looking like all of The Goodies rolled into one. Even Cliff Michelmore's Radio 2 *A Year to Remember: 1970* gave the boys a brief mention, albeit pinpointing them via Mary Whitehouse disgust rather than major comic influence. *TV Zone* included Kitten Kong's London rampage in its 100 Best TV moments of all time and *Loaded* gave the 25th Greatest Living Englishmen honour to The Goodies. Geri Halliwell's plagiarism of Tim's Union flag motif for her Ginger Spice persona kept the flag flying, although the ex-Goodie commented 'About 1% of the royalties would shut me up!' The team were featured on the CD-Rom *BBC: 75 Years*. Nick Park, Terry Prachett and Mike Myers were among those celebrity fans who credited *The Goodies* as inspiration. Harry Hill, having adopted *The Goodies* font for his own, invited folk dude Billy Bragg to perform *Funky Gibbon* on 20 June 1997. With the fragmentation of British television and the Beeb going digital, the old corporation set up a new line of cable channels designed to showcase their past glories. UK Arena was designed for art and music programmes, classic repeats and new review discussions. Its comedy scheduling was for fondly remembered cult favourites such as *The Fall and Rise of Reginald Perrin*, *It's Marty*, *Rutland Weekend Television* and *The Goodies*. The edited season, completely gleaned from Series Three and Four, was started with *An Evening with the Goodies* on 11 July 1998. This showcased a trio of classic episodes, *The New Office*, *Winter Olympics* and *The Chase*. The most eagerly awaited part of the programme was a specially commissioned mini-documentary featuring new interview footage with Tim Brooke-Taylor, Graeme Garden and Bill Oddie. *You Never Had It So Goodie*, grounded in early Sixties' satire rather than the Goodies Seventies' madcap, was to tell the familiar story from Cambridge pals to *Top of the Pops* legends, but strangely, despite advance publicity, the special was dropped from the opening night gala without a mention and still remains unscreened. In fact, due to reluctance from Brooke-Taylor and Garden, the programme was never made and pre-screening publicity relied, as it turned out, unsuccessfully, on the fact that the show was planned for production. Regardless, World Cup fever dug deeply into the six nights a week at 9pm time slot for *The Goodies* and before most people realised what they were missing, the series was dropped from the schedules. Subsequently, the familiar collection of Series Three and

Four programmes was repeated and repeated at various, unearthly hours, on UK Arena. Few tuned in.

THE YOUNG DR TAYLOR

The Memoirs of Dr Henry Shinglewood Taylor chronicled life at Guy's Hospital during the 19th Century, edited by Peter Hadley and read in three parts by Graeme Garden.

Producer Pamela Hone. Tuesdays, 7–21 February 1989, Radio 4.

YUM YUM! THE VERY BEST OF THE GOODIES

A long overdue CD release of classic Goodies numbers, this emerged quietly at a bargain price and without much fanfare. Ironically, the title's a bit misleading for the compilation makes use of just the two Goodies albums produced for Bradley's Records, *The New Goodies Album* and *The Goodies Greatest*. Thus, there are no tracks from *The Goodies Sing Songs From The Goodies* or *The Goodies Beasty Record*, which certainly contain many of Oddie's finest compositions. The seamless flow between *Please Let Us Play* and *Custard Pie* is interrupted by the annoying cheap CD trait of a track break of several seconds. However, it was a delightful surprise to at long last enjoy pristine quality Goodies' songs. A rare surge of pride was experienced when the dedicated fan ferreted out a copy of this little beauty in the rock and pop section somewhere between Genesis and Guns 'n' Roses. The cover design wallows in Seventies' iconography with Spangles sweet wrappers bearing song titles – a confectionery link that invades the CD itself – while Bill Oddie gives the entire project an official thumbs up with his amusing, slightly embittered, and deservedly, self-congratulatory sleeve notes. The endearing opening gambit of the first track is enough to send shivers of nostalgia down your spine and outstanding numbers, *The Inbetweenies*, *Cricklewood*, *Sick Man Blues* and *Black Pudding Bertha*, can be stuck on repeat and played into infinity.

Did You Know? *Among Bill Oddie's promotional appearances was a spot on Virgin Radio's Russ and Jono Show, during which the singing Goodie lapsed into a sing song along with the record of Funky Gibbon.*

The Goodies' Theme, Funky Gibbon, The Inbetweenies, Please Let Us Play, Custard Pie, Black Pudding Bertha, Cricklewood, Good Old Country Music, Nappy Love, Baby Samba, Wild Thing, Rock With a Policeman, The Cricklewood Shakedown, Panic, I'm a Teapot, Working the Line, Sick Man Blues, The Last Chance Dance, Father Christmas Do Not Touch Me, Make a Daft Noise for Christmas. All tracks produced by Miki Anthony and written by Bill Oddie (except Wild Thing, written by C Taylor). Compiled by Nick Morrell. MCCD 294 Music Collection International March 1997.

Z

THE ZODIAC GAME

Standard ITV game show which featured guest Bill Oddie on 3 February 1984 and Graeme Garden, one week later, on 10 February 1984.

Recommended Goodies Reading and Viewing

Books:

British Television: An Illustrated Guide edited by Tise Vahimagi, Oxford University Press, 1996
Cleese Encounters by Jonathan Margolis, Chapman Publishers Ltd, 1992
Cult TV The Comedies: The Ultimate Critical Guide by Jon E Lewis and Penny Stempel, Pavilion Books, 1998
From Fringe to Flying Circus by Roger Wilmut, Eyre Methuen 1980
The Guinness Book of Classic British TV by Paul Cornell, Martin Day and Keith Topping, Guinness, 1993
The Guinness Book of Sitcoms by Rod Taylor, Guinness, 1994
Monty Python: Complete and Utter Theory of the Grotesque edited by John O Thompson, BFI, 1982
Monty Python Encyclopedia by Robert Ross, B T Batsford, 1998
Radio Comedy 1938–1968 by Andy Foster and Steve Furst, Virgin, 1996
Radio Times Guide to TV Comedy by Mark Lewisohn, BBC Books, 1998
Slapstick! The Illustrated Story of Knockabout Comedy by Tony Staveacre, Angus & Robertson, 1987
TV Laughtermakers: The Story of TV Comedy by Anthony Davis, Boxtree and Independent Television Books, 1989

Videos:

Barney (BBCV 4272)
BBC Comedy Greats: Marty Feldman (BBCV 6803)
Comedy Classics of the 60's: includes extracts from It's Marty and Hark At Barker (Watershed Pictures)
Comedy Classics of the 80's: includes an extract from The Goodies: Football Crazy (Castle Vision. A Castle Communications PLC release, CVB 1056)
The Detectives: Undercover Operations, includes Twitchers. Celador/VCI VC6612.
The Goodies and the Beanstalk (BBC 7008)
The Goodies and the Beanstalk, with The End and Bunfight at the OK Tea-Rooms (BBCV 5370)
The Goodies: Kitten Kong, with Scatty Safari and Scoutrageous (BBCV 5391)
The Goodies: includes the ITV episodes Football Crazy, Robot, Bigfoot and Change Of Life (Video Collection VC 6008)
How to Irritate People (Castle Vision, CVI 1143)
It's Marty (BBCV 5360)
Kenny Everett: In the Best Possible Taste (BBCV 6592)
My Summer With Des (Carlton Home Entertainment 30370 50443)
One Foot In The Grave: Endgame (BBCV 6593)
The Plank (Carlton Home Entertainment RCC 3077)
The Secret Policeman's Early Bits (Columbia Tristar CVR 21432)
The Secret Policeman's Other Ball (Columbia Tristar CVR 16917)
The Secret Policeman's Third Ball: The Comedy (Virgin WD 271)
Whoops Apocalypse
Willy Wonka & the Chocolate Factory
Yes Minister: includes The Death List (BBCV 5863)

<http://www.thegoodies.oztek.com.au/>http://thegoodies

'Am I proud of The Goodies? You've written the book, you're asking me these questions, I'm working. What do you think?'
Graeme Garden, 28th December 1999.